THE PRINCETON REVIEW
STUDENT ADVANTAGE

GUIDE TO

L A W
SCHOOLS

1997 EDITION

Books in The Princeton Review Series

Cracking the ACT
Cracking the ACT with Sample Tests on CD-ROM
Cracking the CLEP (College-Level Examination Program)
Cracking the GED
Cracking the GMAT
Cracking the GMAT with Sample Tests on Computer Disk
Cracking the GRE
Cracking the GRE with Sample Tests on Computer Disk
Cracking the GRE Biology Subject Test
Cracking the GRE Literature in English
   Subject Test
Cracking the GRE Psychology Subject Test
Cracking the LSAT
Cracking the LSAT with Sample Tests on Computer Disk
Cracking the LSAT with Sample Tests on CD-ROM
Cracking the MAT (Miller Analogies Test)
Cracking the SAT and PSAT
Cracking the SAT and PSAT with Sample Tests on
   Computer Disk
Cracking the SAT and PSAT with Sample Tests on CD-ROM
Cracking the SAT II: Biology Subject Test
Cracking the SAT II: Chemistry Subject Test
Cracking the SAT II: English Subject Tests
Cracking the SAT II: French Subject Test
Cracking the SAT II: History Subject Tests
Cracking the SAT II: Math Subject Tests
Cracking the SAT II: Physics Subject Test
Cracking the SAT II: Spanish Subject Test
Cracking the TOEFL with Audiocassette
Flowers & Silver MCAT
Flowers Annotated MCAT
Flowers Annotated MCATs with Sample Tests on
   Computer Disk
Flowers Annotated MCATs with Sample Tests on CD-ROM

Culturescope Grade School Edition
Culturescope High School Edition
Culturescope College Edition

SAT Math Workout
SAT Verbal Workout

All U Can Eat
Don't Be a Chump!
How to Survive Without Your Parents' Money
Speak Now!
Trashproof Resumes

Biology Smart
Grammar Smart
Math Smart
Reading Smart
Study Smart
Word Smart: Building an Educated Vocabulary
Word Smart II: How to Build a More Educated Vocabulary
Word Smart Executive
Word Smart Genius
Writing Smart

Grammar Smart Junior
Math Smart Junior
Word Smart Junior
Writing Smart Junior

Business School Companion
College Companion
Law School Companion
Medical School Companion

Student Advantage Guide to College Admissions
Student Advantage Guide to the Best 310 Colleges
Student Advantage Guide to America's Top Internships
Student Advantage Guide to Business Schools
Student Advantage Guide to Law Schools
Student Advantage Guide to Medical Schools
Student Advantage Guide to Paying for College
Student Advantage Guide to Summer
Student Advantage Guide to Visiting College Campuses
Student Advantage Guide: Help Yourself
Student Advantage Guide: The Complete Book of
   Colleges
Student Advantage Guide: The Internship Bible
Student Advantage Guide to Graduate Schools:
   Engineering
Hillel Guide to Jewish Life on Campus
International Students' Guide to the United States
The Princeton Review Guide to Your Career

Also available on cassette from Living Language

Grammar Smart
Word Smart
Word Smart II

THE PRINCETON REVIEW

STUDENT ADVANTAGE

GUIDE TO

LAW SCHOOLS

1997 EDITION

BY IAN VAN TUYL

Random House, Inc.
New York 1996

http://www.randomhouse.com

Princeton Review Publishing, L.L.C.
2315 Broadway, 3rd Floor
New York, NY 10024
E-mail: info@review.com

ISBN: 0-679-77123-9

Manufactured in the United States of America on partially recycled paper.

9 8 7 6 5 4 3 2 1

CONTENTS

That's Professor *Socrates*
Page 22

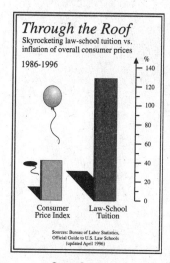

Start Saving
Page 86

BACKGROUND

Created out of thin air in the 1870s, law school as we know it is a uniquely
American institution that has changed relatively little in the last 120 years.

The content and the form of American legal education varies little from
law school to law school. Whether you attend Harvard or Hawaii, you
can expect to confront certain material in a certain fashion.

By far the most dramatic and important change in American legal
education in the last quarter century was a purely demographic one.
While most American law schools were almost exclusively white and
male only twenty-five years ago, law schools today virtually reflect society
at large.

If you had chosen to go to medical school, you wouldn't hear snide
remarks and derisive jokes from friends about doctors. Lawyer bashing
is probably as old as the law itself.

After half a decade of rapid growth in the volume of law school
applicants, the number of prospective students has begun to decline. But
don't count yourself in yet.

The criteria used by law schools in making admissions decisions are easy
enough to identify, but that doesn't make your job any simpler.
Maximizing your chances of getting into the school of your choice takes
work.

Some law schools will accept your application electonically. Find out how.

Although it has been changed frequently and significantly, the LSAT
remains probably the toughest and strangest standardized test you'll
ever take.

Financial considerations will almost certainly influence your choice of
law schools. Considering how expensive law school has become, your
debt may make other, larger choices for you.

THE LAW SCHOOLS

A Brief History of the American Law School

[The law student] soon finds that he has fallen into a pit. He is given no map, carefully charting and laying out all the byways and corners of the legal field, but is left, to a certain extent, to find his way by himself. His scramble out of difficulties, if successful, leaves him feeling that he has built up a knowledge of law for himself. The legal content of his mind is of a personal nature; he has made it himself.

—EXCERPT FROM A SELF-DESCRIPTION OF THE HARVARD LAW SCHOOL ON THE OCCASION OF ITS CENTENNIAL IN 1917.

It should come as no surprise that the comment above—with its romanticization of the struggle, its glorification of the survivor—was not made by a first-year law student. It is not so difficult to imagine that a student's view of the situation described might differ in content and tone and might include a few choice expletives; the self-satisfied social-Darwinist proclamations of the outside observer would surely be met with something less than enthusiasm from those still trapped inside "the pit." Eighty years later, the sink-or-swim ethic this statement conveys would sound familiar to virtually any law student, yet law school was not always this way. If today law school is a jungle where only the strong survive, then for most of its first one hundred years the American law school was a relative paradise. The change did not come until 1870, when the Harvard Law School hired a new dean, Christopher Columbus Langdell. A century's worth of ulcers among law students can be traced directly to this date.

The trappings generally associated with law school—the casebook, the rigorous examinations, the so-called Socratic

Method—seemed to spring fully formed from the mind of this one man at this one school. The current climate in American law schools may again be one of change, but Langdell's imprint is probably indelible. His innovations came to define legal education and have continued to do so for more than one hundred years. The American law school entered the modern era with Langdell's appointment, but its history began even earlier, in the years just after the American Revolution.

AN EARLY BOOM, AN EARLY BUST

In the early days of American independence, preparation for the practice of law took place in the lawyer's office, not in the classroom. While universities like William and Mary and the University of Virginia established professorships in the law, they did not have full-fledged law schools. By and large, the legal profession chose to train its own— usually through apprenticeships of four or five years. It was out of this system of professional training that the first real law school grew. In 1784, the Litchfield Law School was established in Litchfield, Connecticut, by two practicing attorneys renowned for their successful training of apprentices. Litchfield thrived while, on the whole, the academic branch of legal education met with little success. Even the fledgling school of law at Harvard, established in 1817, had an undistinguished track record in its early years. It was the proprietary (for-profit) schools like Litchfield that proliferated in an atmosphere in which the legal profession grew significantly in size, prestige, and influence.

Among the students who flocked to the lectures in Litchfield seeking entry into the bar—and into the highest circles of American social and political life—were 2 future vice presidents, 101 congressmen, 28 senators, 14 governors, and scores of state supreme court justices. The degree to which lawyers influenced, and even dominated, the public and private spheres in early America is not to be underestimated. Though a law degree remains to this day a ticket to social mobility, it was seen by some in the early nineteenth century as a ticket to virtual nobility.

Alexis de Tocqueville made his famous tour of the United States during this period and noted the extent to which

Though a law degree remains to this day a ticket to social mobility, it was seen by some in the early nineteenth century as a ticket to virtual nobility.

Andrew Jackson—no friend of lawyers

lawyers had risen to the highest ranks in politics in specific and society in general. Tocqueville said of the United States in the 1830s that "the aristocracy occupies the judicial bench and bar." In a country that lacked both a sovereign and an entrenched noble class, the rule of law was more complete and the law itself more malleable. These were the years, most notably, of the Marshall Supreme Court, which may have done more than the framers themselves to define the social role of the U.S. Constitution. Many agreed with Tocqueville, and not everyone was happy about it. Attacks on the "pervasive and pernicious" legal profession were heard more and more frequently, and when Andrew Jackson was elected in 1829, change was in the offing.

The era of Jacksonian democracy was a bleak one for the legal profession, which was swept up in the broader trend toward radical democratization of the professions. The prevailing philosophy was that restrictions on access to the bar were incompatible with the democratic ideal of equality. In the Jacksonian era, nearly every state relaxed or abolished its previously strict standards on bar admissions, and establishing a law practice became nearly as simple as—literally—hanging out one's shingle. In the absence of academic credential requirements for lawyers, law schools slipped into virtual obsolescence. When legendary Litchfield called it quits in 1833, the professional standards of the legal profession had reached an astonishing low point. The law school at Princeton closed after graduating only six students, and when not a single student enrolled for classes in its first year, the University of Alabama's law school closed its doors even before they even opened. Even a modern-day stalwart, the New York University law school, failed miserably. In its first incarnation, that school lasted only one year, from 1838 to 1839.

HARVARD AND OTHER WRETCHED REFUSE

Harvard was among the few law schools to survive the Jacksonian era. Far from immune, however, to the effects of disappearing professional standards, Harvard had to fight tooth and nail to survive in a consumer's market. In competing for its share of a rapidly shrinking pie, Harvard let academic standards fall by the wayside. Course requirements all but disappeared and the residency requirement was halved. Moreover, the law school lifted its requirement that entering students possess a college degree. By 1829, admissions criteria had slipped to such a degree that students who were denied admission to Harvard College could go directly into the law school. One of the men who was later to turn Harvard around, Professor James Barr Ames, offered a bleak description of the school during this period:

> [Harvard] had a faculty of three professors giving but ten lectures a week to one hundred and fifteen students of whom fifty-three percent had no college degree, a curriculum without any rational sequence of subjects, and an inadequate and decaying library.

Its willingness to survive by any means necessary is perhaps best illustrated by the fact that the Harvard Law School, whose academic rigors are today the stuff of legend and literature, quit administering examinations in all of its classes.

By hook or by crook, Harvard muddled through what proved to be the American law school's darkest days. By mid-century, the backlash against Jacksonian democracy was strong in the law and other professions. Supreme courts around the country joined the American Bar Association in calling for tougher standards in bar admissions to ensure the competence of members of the profession. As a natural consequence of this reimposition of strict professional standards, the law school began to regain its luster. Harvard had persevered longer than Jacksonianism and was in a position to claim preeminence in a dubious field.

It must be kept in mind, however, that the vast majority of men (for there were as yet no women lawyers) continued to prepare for law practice by apprenticing themselves to working attorneys. Those law schools that did exist were little more than trade schools that sought to mimic law-office instruction while consolidating it in a quasi-academic setting. The profession itself was by and large disdainful of these institutions. There were, however, a few success stories among law schools in the 1850s and 1860s. Columbia University was one such success, thanks to the efforts of one of the giants of legal education, Theodore

Dwight. Through his work at Hamilton College and, later, at Columbia, Dwight helped establish the viability and respectability of a course of law study emphasizing "principle before practice." His successes were not enough to provide any momentum to the law-school movement, however, and even Dwight's Columbia relegated law to a few courses in the undergraduate curriculum.

The very concept of higher education was undergoing drastic revision, as the country became caught up in a broader societal trend toward institutionalization. Before the 1870s, colleges had restricted themselves to classical programs of Latin, Greek, mathematics, and moral philosophy. It was not until around 1870 that the development of the modern university got under way. The latter part of the nineteenth century saw tremendous expansion among existing colleges and the founding of dozens of new land-grant colleges under the Morrill Act. Concurrently, these new or expanded institutions began to establish affiliations with law schools.

At Harvard, the appointment of Charles Eliot to the presidency of the college in 1869 signaled the end of the old order. Among the myriad subjects that Eliot deemed fit for study within the university was law, and though the law school at Harvard was still only an adjunct of Harvard college proper, the two would not remain separate for long. Relations were warming, albeit slowly, between law schools and the legal profession and between law schools and their parent institutions.

SOCRATES COMES TO CAMBRIDGE

> *The library is to us what the laboratory is to the chemist.*
>
> —CHRISTOPHER COLUMBUS LANGDELL, 1870

When Christopher Columbus Langdell took over as dean of the law school at Harvard in 1870, he entered an atmosphere of great uncertainty. An evolution was under way in legal education, but it remained to be seen toward what. Forces beyond the influence of one man guaranteed, perhaps, the resurgence of the American law school, but in

Through his work at Hamilton College and, later, at Columbia, Dwight helped establish the viability and respectability of a course of law study emphasizing "principle before practice."

guiding almost single-handedly the transformation of Harvard at such a crucial juncture, Dean Langdell placed his indelible stamp on an ascendant institution.

Langdell is famed for the introduction of the case method to the law-school curriculum and of the Socratic Method to classroom instruction. Whether Langdell was actually the first to use either is very much in question. At the very least, however, his determined, systematic application of the new method and style was responsible for their success. Before Langdell, American law schools resembled undergraduate institutions in their reliance on lengthy treatises and lectures as, respectively, the material and means of instruction. Whether the traditional classroom format was to blame remains in question, but by the time of Langdell's appointment, the failure of the American law school was manifest. The few law schools still operating by 1870 were plagued by financial hardship. Langdell's innovations revitalized and revolutionized legal education, both philosophically and economically.

Dean Langdell was also a professor, and it was in his own Contracts course that he introduced these new approaches. He eschewed the textbook, replacing it with a simple compilation of written decisions from cases involving contract disputes. He abandoned the lecture in favor of an instructional format modeled on the Socratic dialogue. Langdell's students would read their cases and then come to class to be bombarded with an endless stream of questions. Their own responses to those questions were the only answers they would hear. By forcing them to follow, even duplicate the reasoning behind a decision, Langdell hoped that students would gain an understanding of the law that no mere laundry list of judicial findings could provide.

Harvard president Charles Eliot had been among the first to call for a complete overhaul of the old system of legal education. He criticized the effectiveness of lectures and derided the traditional approach, saying that it was not "a virile system," and that it "treat[ed] the student not as a man, but as a school boy reciting his lines." (The 1870s, it seems, were a time when men were men and wished to leave no doubt about it.) More to the point, Eliot compared attempts to teach the law by traditional means to "pump-

Christopher Columbus Langdell—
"Call me Socrates."
Courtesy Harvard University Archives

ing water through a sieve." It was when this pedagogic dissatisfaction with the state of legal education met the reigning nineteenth-century philosophy of "scientism" that the Harvard system was born.

A central assumption of the case method was that the law could be taught as a science. Langdell considered his approach self-contained, consistent and value-free. Rather than teach by rote the "black-letter law" (strict, codified law), Langdell sought to guide students along a path of independent discovery. Where no black-letter law existed and precedent seemed the sole basis of the law, Langdell would have his students struggle to comprehend the hidden "principles" upon which precedents are based. Champions of the case method often couched their rhetoric in the terms of natural science, asserting that the study of the law was a search for scientific reality. One early champion of the case method, Columbia's William Keener, offered a simple summary of this philosophy:

> *Under this system the student is taught to look upon law as a science consisting of a body of principles to be found in the adjudged cases, the cases being to him what the specimen is to the mineralogist.*

The so-called social sciences that many study in college today were born in this same atmosphere of yearning for empirical legitimacy.

The philosophical presumptions of the case method's first advocates have been periodically revised, rejected and revisited in the last 120 years, but one thing about the method was apparent almost instantly: its efficiency. Like Henry Ford's production line, Langdell's system was entirely novel but quickly became familiar, and like so many inspired innovations, it had the quality of seeming almost obvious in retrospect. Students now carried the burden of virtually teaching themselves. The material of the law was in their hands in the form of the casebook. The only assistance they received in making sense of it was from a single cajoling instructor who would provide them not with answers, but with questions.

In the Socratic Method, Harvard had found the solution for the law school's financial woes.

In the Socratic Method, Harvard had found not only the answer to president Eliot's intellectual complaint, but also the solution for the law school's financial woes. One professor could now easily and conscientiously service more than one hundred students at a time. It may seem that a question-and-answer format would require, if anything, a smaller classroom, but its advocates would argue that the Socratic Method requires only that a dialogue take place, not that all participate. While intellectual arguments for their adoption abounded, the case method and the Socratic Method may well not have taken hold so quickly and so decisively were it not for their economy. Langdell's methods spread extremely rapidly, and the law schools that adopted them thrived.

It should be noted, however, that there existed some opposition to Langdell's innovations. The greatest threat to Langdell's success may have been the reaction of the first students who came to the Harvard Law School (HLS) early in his tenure. Though respected as a great legal mind, Langdell was no charmer, and both he and his case method were immensely unpopular with students. More important, perhaps, was the fact that Langdell gave tests. Hard ones. Langdell's first pupils surely hadn't bargained for the rigor the new dean imposed. When one went to law school in the mid-1800s one hardly expected tests. In the face of this new rigor, enrollment suffered, and there were rumors that Langdell would be dismissed. The hiring of the more popular James Barr Ames as an assistant professor in 1873 helped save Langdell's hide.

THOSE WHO CAN DO, THOSE WHO COULD (BUT JUST DON'T WANT TO) TEACH

What qualifies a person to teach law, is not experience in the work of a lawyer's office, not experience with men, not experience in the trial or argument of cases, not experience, in short, in using law, but experience in learning law.

—C. C. LANGDELL, ON THE HIRING OF JAMES BARR AMES, 1873

Life in L

In his book One L, *Scott Turow recounts the story of his first year at Harvard Law School. In his first week, he was taken on a tour of the campus by his friend David, a third-year student:*

When we reached Langdell, he stood on the steps and lifted his hand toward the columns and the famous names of the law cut into the granite border beneath the roof.

"This is Langdell Hall," he said, "the biggest building on the law-school campus. It contains four large classrooms and, on the upper floors, the Harvard Law School library, the largest law-school library in the world.

"The building is named for the late Christopher Columbus Langdell, who was the dean of Harvard Law School in the late nineteenth century. Dean Langdell is best known as the inventor of the Socratic Method."

David lowered his hand and looked sincerely at the building.

"May he rot in hell," David said.

Quite apart from being popular, Professor Ames (later Dean Ames) was a figure of great practical and symbolic importance in the history of HLS and American legal education in general. His hiring and his success with the case method were two important factors in the divorce of the American law school from the American legal profession, a schism that persists to this day.

Ames was the first of a new breed of law professors, a breed that still dominates legal education in the United States. Ames was not a lawyer. He had been an outstanding law student, and he had shown great promise as a teacher, but Ames had never practiced law. Though today this is the norm, it raised eyebrows during a time when at least a brief stint in the legal profession was an unofficial prerequisite to teaching law. In staunchly defending the decision to hire Ames, Langdell articulated his philosophy that academic legal instruction was a skill unto itself, that it was something wholly separate from the legal profession. The case method went hand in hand with this notion, for it emphasized the law as an abstraction. No mere apprenticeship to a practicing lawyer, it was held, could ensure adequate intellectual preparation for a legal career. Harvard was emphatically declaring the birth of a new kind of law school, one that produced "legal thinkers" and proudly ceded to the profession itself the job of training them in the practical aspects of the law.

Initially, the legal establishment was far from convinced that Harvard's new system endowed its graduates with sufficient and satisfactory practical legal skills. As late as 1891, the American Bar Association's Committee on Legal Education assailed the Harvard system even as more and more schools were adopting it. The committee was explicit in its criticism of the case method in its official report:

> *The student should not be so trained as to think he is to be a mere hired gladiator.... The result of this elaborate study of actual disputes, and ignoring of the settled doctrines that have grown out of past ones, is a class of graduates admirably calculated to argue any side of any controversy, or to make briefs for those who do so, but quite unable to advise a client when he is safe from litigation.*

Within several years, however, pro-Harvard forces were in control at the ABA and the success of the Harvard method was assured. Indeed, Eliot himself was moved to comment that "if there be a more successful school in our country or in the world for any profession, I can only say that I do not know where it is."

When the Harvard method succeeded, the modern law school was born. By the end of the nineteenth century, the innovations that Christopher Langdell had introduced were the norm in nearly every school in the country.

The American legal profession had entered its second boom era, an era that some would argue has yet to pass. During the last half of the nineteenth century, the number of lawyers in the United States increased almost sixfold. Hand in hand with the steady growth of the legal profession came the dramatic renaissance of legal education. Shortly before the outbreak of the Civil War, there were only twenty-one law schools operating in the entire country. The success of the Harvard method in the postwar era fueled law school expansion. By 1916 there were 140 law schools, not many fewer than the 176 that operate today, with the approval of the ABA. The subsequent sixty years saw steady growth in the legal field, and by 1970 the U.S. lawyer population was almost three times greater than it was in 1910. The number of lawyers practicing in the United States continues to grow, from 355,242 in 1970 to almost 800,000 in 1990. Much of this increase was due to the entry of large numbers of women and minorities into the profession. There is some indication that the sharp increase in law school applicants that was seen in the 1980s and early '90s has begun to wane. Still, the legal profession remains attractive to many: In 1995, more than 78,000 men and women applied to three years of what even the best students consider very hard work.

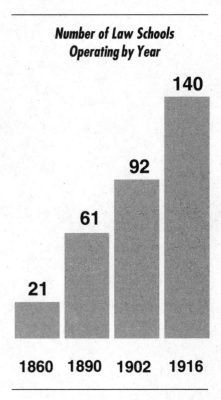

Number of Law Schools Operating by Year

Year	Number
1860	21
1890	61
1902	92
1916	140

THE LAW SCHOOL CURRICULUM

THE CONTENT

First year they scare you to death, second year they work you to death, and third year they bore you to death.

– OLD LAW-SCHOOL ADAGE

1L: THE SALAD DAYS

Remember those amazing courses listed in your college catalog? History 157: Psychopathy and the Presidency—The Nixon Years; or English 125: The Zen of Holden Caulfield. Now, remember what you took freshman year? Poli. Sci. 2, English 1A, and Geology 10: Rocks and You. Law school will be a little like that. You might want to become an environmental lawyer, or maybe you wish to practice family law. Perhaps a fire burns in your heart for Uruguayan shipping law, or you harbor a single-minded obsession with suburban noise statutes. Whatever the case, you may be expecting law school to be a veritable intellectual smorgasbord from which you will fill your mind with all varieties of legal exotica. Think again, or at the very least, put your expectations on hold.

If you already have an idea what areas of law might interest you, you would certainly do well to study carefully the course offerings of the schools you are considering. In many important respects, however, your first-year experience will depend very little on the particular school you attend. Along with a certain instructional style—the Socratic Method and the casebook—a fairly uniform course of study in the first year has traditionally defined the law-school experience. While neither the form nor the content of instruction is a constant among U.S. law schools, you can expect your first year to follow a relatively predictable course.

The first-year curriculum in the law school you attend will almost certainly be composed of a combination of the following courses:

Torts: From the Middle French for "injury," torts are wrongful acts, excluding breaches of contract, that are actionable under civil law. Students of torts might not be surprised to hear that the Latin root of the word means "twisted." Torts can range from the predictable to the bizarre, from Dog Bites Man to Man Bites Dog and everything in between. The study of torts is the study of civil-court cases with the goal of understanding the changeable legal rationale behind decisions pertaining to the extent of, and limits on, the civil liability of one party for harm done to another.

Contracts: Fairly self-explanatory, it seems. Sign on the dotted line and—presto!—you've got a contract. Well, not exactly. (See, generally, "The Devil and Daniel Webster.") Contractual relationships are a far sight more varied and complicated than that, as two semesters of your Contracts course will teach you. Again through the study of past court cases, you will follow the largely unwritten law governing the system of conditions and obligations a contract represents, as well as the legal remedies available when contracts are breached.

Civil Procedure: If Contracts and Torts teach you what lawyers do in civil court, then Civil Procedure teaches you how they do it. "Civ. Pro.," as it is generally referred to, is the study of the often dizzyingly complex rules that govern not only who can sue whom, but also how, when and where they can do it. This is not merely a study of legal protocol, for issues of process have a significant indirect effect on the substance of the law. To understand the importance of this subject, consider not only the complexities of trial procedure, but also the fact that such a small proportion of cases ever goes to trial. Rules of Civil Procedure govern the conduct of both the courtroom trial and the steps that might precede it: discovery, pleading, pre-trial motions, etc.

Property: Like so much U.S. law, the laws governing the purchase, possession, and sale of property in the United States often date back hundreds of years to the English common law. Hence the old saying that "possession is nine-tenths of the law." The broad rights of property ownership are a defining element of the society in which we live. You may never own a piece of land, but your life will inevitably and constantly be affected by the laws of property. Not that weeks and weeks spent dwelling on the difference between "real" and "personal" property are going to be very inspiring, but anyone interested in achieving an understanding of broader policy issues will appreciate the significance of this material. Many property courses will emphasize, to varying degrees, economic analysis of property law, particularly as more and more law professors of the Law and Economics school (originally associated with the University of Chicago) take their places on law school faculties.

Criminal Law: Wherein you learn that the answer to the question "What is a Crime?" is no less fuzzy than the answer to the question "What is a Sin?" Even if you become a criminal prosecutor or defender, you will probably never prosecute or defend someone charged with the crimes you will be exposed to here. Can a man who shoots the dead body of someone he believes to be alive be charged with attempted murder? What if someone else was forcing him to do so at gunpoint? What if they were both on drugs? What if they both had really rough childhoods? Find out next year. Nowhere will the Socratic dialogue be taken to such extremes as in your Crim. class, and criminal-law professors are notorious for their ridiculously convoluted exam questions.

Constitutional Law: Often a second-year requirement or even an elective now, Constitutional Law is still a part of the first-year program at many schools. As close to a history class as you will take in your first year, Con. Law will fill in the blanks between such *Jeopardy!* standards as Marbury, Plessy, Brown, and Roe. Most courses will emphasize issues of government structure (e.g., federalism and separation of powers) and individual rights (e.g., personal liberties, freedom of expression, property protection). Nearly every law school now offers advanced Con.

Um, Could You Repeat the Question?

Lest you decide that law school is too practical, too grounded in reality for you, consider the following example of an exam question from a criminal law course at New York University Law School.

Answer each of the following questions in terms of applicable New York law. In each case, you are expected to indicate crimes committed and any defenses thereto.

1. Louis, Juan, and Sam decide to have forcible sexual intercourse with the mysterious Elvira, who, unbeknownst to them, is in fact Juan's wife, whom he abandoned years ago. Louis drives Juan and Sam to Elvira's apartment. Juan and Sam enter the apartment through a back window and encounter Elvira, who recognizes Juan but who, in the dark, is not recognized (as Juan's wife) by either Juan or Sam. Juan and Elvira consummate sexually. For Elvira, this is a passionate and consensual reaffirmation of their marriage; for Juan, the experience is one of forcible intercourse. The terrified Commander, Elvira's father, believing himself to be protecting his daughter from forcible intercourse, fires a gun and kills Sam. Discuss the liability of Louis and Juan.

2. Immediately after the events in question 1, the Commander fires again at Juan, killing an innocent bystander. Finally, the Commander challenges Juan to a duel of honor in which each will play Russian roulette seriatim; after several turns, the Commander fires the gun at his own head, bruising himself slightly. He is, however, so humiliated by his "defeat" that he kills himself. Elvira, enraged at her father's death and coming to her senses about the true nature of Juan's intentions in having intercourse with her, fires at Juan, hitting her father's body by mistake. Elvira vows to Juan that she will pursue him forever, and follows Juan out of the house. She fires the gun again, killing a neighbor. Juan flees to his car, where he finds Louis in the midst of an LSD hallucination in which he is playing the role of Leporello in Mozart's opera **Don Giovanni.** *Louis's hallucination was induced by taking a capsule labeled "aspirin" that Juan had left in the car, a capsule which Louis believed to be aspirin when he took it. Juan, terrified that the bloodthirsty Elvira is in hot pursuit, orders Louis to drive away at 100 m.p.h. in a 30 m.p.h. zone. (Elvira, in fact, has collapsed.) Louis drives off at the speed commanded, all the time thinking he is singing on the stage of the Metropolitan Opera. The car careens out of control and reaches a point where it will hit a stone wall (which would kill Juan and Louis) unless Louis swerves into a nearby crowd (which would cushion the crash and save Juan's and Louis's lives). Louis, regaining consciousness, at first refuses to hit the crowd, but does so when Juan threatens to molest his underage sister and torture his parents to death (both are credible threats). Ten people are killed; Juan and Louis survive. Discuss the liability of Juan, Louis and Elvira.*

Law courses that focus on special areas like Civil Rights or Affirmative Action.

Legal Methods: One of the few twentieth-century improvements on the traditional first-year curriculum that has taken hold nearly everywhere, this course travels under various aliases, such as Legal Research and Writing or Elements of the Law. In recent years, increased recognition of the importance of legal writing skills has led over half of the U.S. law schools to require or offer a writing course after the first year. This will surely be your smallest class and possibly your only refuge from the Socratic Method. Methods courses are often taught by junior faculty or even by second- or third-year students, and are designed to help the first-year student acquire fundamental skills in legal research, analysis and writing. The Methods course may be the least frightening a 1L (a first-year law student) faces, but it can easily consume an enormous amount of time. This is a common lament, particularly at schools where very few credits are awarded for the Methods course.

So, a typical first-year law student's schedule might look like this:

Fall	Spring
Torts	Property
Contracts	Legal Writing
Civil Procedure	Civil Procedure
Legal Methods	(Probably Constitutional or Criminal Law, possibly an elective course)

In addition to these course requirements, many law schools require 1Ls to participate in a moot-court exercise. As part of this exercise, students—sometimes working in pairs or even small groups—must prepare briefs and oral arguments for a mock trial (usually appellate). This requirement is often tied in with the Methods course so that those briefs and oral arguments will be well researched—and graded.

BEYOND 1-HELL: FIGHTING THE MALAISE

After you survive your first year and recover some semblance of the free will you surrendered upon arrival at law school, you will have near-total freedom to choose your course of study. Though this sounds marvelous, critics of the law-school curriculum have called the second and third years of law school unfocused and even useless. One academic observer characterized the last two years of law school as "...disintegrate[d], consisting of a melange of hodge-podge." An informal survey of recent law graduates you may know would probably reveal the widely held opinion that, by third year, law school often degenerates into an exercise in clock-watching. The third year does, however, afford law students the opportunity to take more niche law courses, including environmental, family, or tax law.

SKILLS TRAINING AND CLINICAL LEGAL EDUCATION

The most significant curricular development in American legal education in the last thirty years is an ironic one. Though the modern law school came into being when certain legal scholars deemed academic training alone sufficient preparation for the practice of law, the latest so-called innovation in legal education is very much a return to the old way, to an emphasis on practical experience as a beneficial component in the training of future lawyers. Hands-on training in the practical skills of lawyering now travels under the name "Clinical Legal Education."

Clinics work in various ways, and the term encompasses a broad range of meanings. Generally, a clinical course is one that focuses on the development of practical lawyering skills rather than on the development of lawyerly thinking or on the communication of a body of legal knowledge. In some cases, the word "clinic" means exactly what an outsider would take it to mean: a working law office that serves actual human beings. In these clinics, second- and third-year law students counsel real clients under the supervision of a staff attorney. (A very limited number of law schools allow first-year students to participate in legal clinics.) In those states that grant upper-level law students a limited right to represent clients in court, student participants in a law school's clinic might actually follow cases through to their resolution in court. At some schools, there is a single on-site clinic, which operates something like a general law practice, dealing with cases ranging from petty crime to landlord-tenant disputes. At those schools that have dedicated the most resources to their clinical programs, numerous specialized clinics deal with narrowly defined areas of law like employment discrimination or on particular subjects like AIDS. Relatively speaking, however, the opportunities to participate in such live-action programs are limited. Because clinical legal education is so much more expensive than traditional classroom instruction, few law schools can accommodate more than a small percentage of their students in their clinical programs.

More widely available are external clinical placements and simulated clinical courses. In a clinical externship, a student might work with a real firm or public agency several hours a week and meet with a faculty adviser only occasionally. Students who participate in such programs are unpaid, and placements are generally chosen quite carefully to ensure that students stay students rather than becoming mere slaves.

In simulated clinical courses, students might perform all of the duties that a student in a live-action clinic would, but the clients would be imaginary, and their work might be recorded on video for later review with a clinical instructor.

SPECIALIZATION

A great number of schools now officially sanction special programs of study akin to undergraduate majors. At certain schools, you may receive your J.D. with an official emphasis in, say, taxation. The argument in favor of offering such opportunities is easily understood. As in medicine, specialization has become a watchword in the legal profession. General practitioners in the law are becoming less and less common, so it appears to make sense to let future lawyers begin to specialize while still in school. In some cases, however, "special programs" seem to do nothing more than add a few words to your diploma. But a good number of schools take specialization quite seriously, offering active guidance and near-immersion in a particular field of study after a traditional first year. It has been said that this is the trend of the future, particularly for those smaller or newer schools whose graduates cannot simply get by on their school's established reputation of excellence.

A majority of law schools still do not offer formal programs of specialized study. By no means, however, should you regard such a school as resistant to specialization. It is simply that most schools prefer to keep specialization informal.

JOINT DEGREE PROGRAMS

In addition to offering specialized areas of study, many law schools have instituted formal dual-degree programs. These schools, nearly all of which are directly affiliated with a parent institution, offer students the opportunity to pursue a J.D. while also working toward a master's degree. Although the J.D./M.B.A. combination is the most popular joint-degree sought, many universities offer a J.D. program combined with masters' degrees in public policy, public administration, and social work, among others. Amidst an increasingly competitive legal market, dual degrees may make some students more marketable for certain positions come job time. Dual degree programs, however, should not be entered into lightly; they are indeed a lot of work.

THE FORM—LEARNING TO CRAWL

Much of what you have heard about a law student's first year is probably true: It is more about intellectual survival than intellectual feasting. Just as the gung-ho army recruit wooed by promises of specialized training must survive boot camp before she storms her first beach, so too must the bright-eyed law student endure the homogenizing effects of that first, sleepless law school year before she files her first Supreme Court brief. It is said that you have to learn to walk before you can run. It is often ignored that before all that, you must learn how to crawl.

The first semester of law school has the well-deserved reputation of being among the great challenges to the intellect and the stamina that one may ever face. It is not merely the material itself and the amount of it that explain the challenge. Though complex and difficult, the subject

The particular, private terror that is shared by roughly forty thousand 1Ls every year stems as much from the style of law school as from its substance.

matter in first-year law-school courses is probably no more inherently difficult than what is taught in other graduate or professional schools. The particular, private terror that is shared by roughly forty thousand 1Ls every year stems as much from the style of law school as from its substance.

You have almost surely heard the stories of law professors who possess the ability to turn otherwise capable, confident, intelligent adults into frightened, quivering half-wits. If you have neither read nor seen *The Paper Chase*, perhaps you should do so before going any further with your law-school plans. While few survivors could honestly report having suffered the indignities perpetrated by the legendary Professor Kingsfield, they could no doubt name an instructor who represented for them, accurately or not, evil incarnate. Such reputations are not always wholly deserved, for it is typical of human nature to find a subject at whom to direct general feelings of resentment born of tremendous anxiety. One thing is certain: High stress and anxiety levels among law students—particularly 1Ls—are ubiquitous and real. This is the result of more than the burdensome workload. The two greatest enemies of the law student's mental well-being are a system of examination and grading that hopelessly frustrates those who require positive feedback and instant gratification, and a method of instruction that unapologetically punishes those who would learn passively.

Before Dean Langdell of the Harvard Law School in 1870, only subject matter differentiated the law-school classroom from any other on campus. Law students read thick textbooks and law professors gave lectures. Had you gone to law school 150 years ago, the system you honed to perfection in college—read the books, write the paper, attend a class or two along the way—would have stood you in good stead. Nothing you did in college has directly prepared you, however, for the case method and its dreaded spokesman, Socrates.

THE CASE METHOD

Look at it simply in the light of human nature.
Does not a man remember a concrete instance
more vividly than a general principle?

—OLIVER WENDELL HOLMES, 1886

In the majority of your law-school courses, and probably in all of your first-year courses, the only texts used will be casebooks—collections of written judicial decisions in actual court cases. The case method of instruction is one that eschews explanation and encourages exploration. In a course that relies entirely on the casebook, you will never come across a printed list of "laws." Indeed, you will learn that in many areas of law there is no such thing as a static set of rules, but only a constantly evolving system of principles. It is expected that a student will come to understand the law—in all of its ambiguity—through a critical examination of a series of cases that were decided according to such principles. You will often feel utterly lost, groping for answers to unarticulated questions. This is not merely normal, it is intended.

In practical terms, the case method works like this:

For every class meeting (including your very first), you will be assigned a number of cases to read. The cases you read are the written judicial opinions rendered in court cases that were decided at the appellate level. (The reason for reading cases from courts of appeals or supreme courts is that such cases turn on issues of law, not of fact. If you are charged, tried, and convicted of murder and wish to appeal your case, you do not simply get a whole new trial at a higher level. You must argue that your conviction was improper, not that it was inaccurate.) Your casebook will contain neither instructions nor explanations. Your assignments simply will be to read the cases and be in a position to answer questions based on them. There will be no written homework assignments, just cases, cases, and more cases.

You will write, for your own benefit, briefs of the cases you are assigned. Briefs are your attempts to summarize the issues and laws around which a particular case revolves and to make sense of the court's findings in terms of similar cases. Over the course of a semester, you will try to integrate the content of your case-briefs and your notes from in-class lectures, discussions, or dialogues into some kind of cohesive whole.

THE SOCRATIC METHOD

The actual problem...is not what to teach, but how to teach.... [A] lecturer pumps laboriously into sieves. The water may be wholesome but it runs through.

—Charles Eliot, president of Harvard College, in defense of the Socratic Method, c. 1870

As unfamiliar as the case method will be to most entering law students, it is the way in which it is presented that is the real source of anxiety. Simply put, Socratic instruction

Here, professor, drink this!
The Death of Socrates, *1787, Jacques-Louis David*

Courtesy The Metropolitan Museum of Art

entails directed questioning and limited lecturing. There are law professors who are alleged to have gone an entire semester without uttering a declarative statement. Though the Socratic Method has passed out of vogue in the last decade, it remains a common style of instruction in law schools around the country. The case method already places a dizzying burden of comprehension on the student, but when combined with the Socratic Method, it leaves many feeling helpless.

Generally, a student is invited by the Socratic professor to attempt a cogent summary of a case assigned for that day's class. Regardless of the accuracy and thoroughness of the student's initial response, he or she is then grilled on details overlooked or issues unresolved. A professor will often manipulate the facts of the actual case at hand into a hypothetical case that may or may not have demanded a different decision by the court. At its best, this approach forces a reasonably well-prepared student to go beyond the immediately apparent issues in a given case to consider its broader implications. The dialogue between the effective Socratic instructor and his victim-of-the-moment will also force non-participating students to question their underlying assumptions of the case under discussion. At its worst, the Socratic Method subjects an unprepared student to ruthless scrutiny and fosters an unhealthy adversarial relationship between an instructor and his students. At its best, it hones the law student's critical reasoning skills and prepares her to litigate before tough judges.

Professor Socrates?

The Socratic Method has been the bane of more than a few law students' existence in the last 120 years, but it has been said that Socrates the man has gotten a bad rap for the crimes of latter-day imitators. Having been forced to drink poison once already for his words, Socrates, who never wrote a casebook, might have suffered enough already. Perhaps not. Two thousand years before a law student first cursed the teaching method that goes by his name, Socrates was frustrating his students in a way that might sound familiar to any law student.

Socrates: And now Phaedrus, having agreed upon the premises we may decide about the conclusion.

Phaedrus: What conclusion?....I wish that you would repeat what was said.

Socrates: Consider: is the holy loved by the gods because it is holy? Or is it holy because it is loved by the gods?

Euthypro: I do not know what you mean, Socrates.

Socrates: ...and now dear Phaedrus, I shall pause for an instant to ask whether you do not think me, as I appear to myself, inspired?

Phaedrus: Yes, Socrates, you seem to have a very unusual flow of words.

— Plato, from Phaedrus and Euthyphro

The Doors Open Up

It goes without saying that for most of its history, the American legal profession has been the almost exclusive domain of white men. This is true, of course, of nearly every prestigious, lucrative profession in the United States. The obvious irony is that the profession at the forefront of the legal battles over institutional desegregation began to practice what it preached no sooner than did most other professions. Nonwhite men and women of all ethnicities did not gain entry to the legal profession in significant numbers until the 1970s.

The American Bar Association does not keep statistics on the racial or ethnic makeup of its membership. However, the U.S. law school represents a venue in which both the past and the future faces of the legal profession can be glimpsed. Those faces scarcely resemble each other. Complex cultural changes and pro-active efforts by law schools to remedy the underrepresentation of women and minorities in the law have gone a long way toward ensuring the eventual diversity of the American bar. Today, law-school student bodies roughly resemble the U.S. population as a whole. It is only recently, however, that they have come to do so.

According to the American Bar Association's Committee on Legal Education, 94.1 percent of the roughly 95,000 law students in the United States in 1972 were white. The last twenty years have seen a 43 percent increase in overall law-school enrollment, but this jump pales in comparison to the gains made by nonwhites. After 1972, and especially after 1978, nonwhites began entering law school in large and ever-increasing numbers. By the 1995–1996 school year, the law-student population was only about 80 percent white. In twenty-four years, the representation of historically excluded minority groups had more than tripled, from 5.9 percent to 18.2 percent.

This overall increase in minority representation was not distributed evenly among the various minority subgroups.

In 1995, as in 1972, African Americans were the largest minority group among law students. Their total numbers grew by 336 percent in this period. Their share of the total law-school population, however, grew by only about 56 percent, from just under 4 percent of all law students in 1972 to slightly more than 7 percent in 1995. The most dramatic increase in representation of any single minority subgroup was among Asian Americans. Between 1972 and 1995, the proportion of Asian Americans among U.S. law students grew from only one half of one percent to over 5 percent. This 1,000 percent increase (!) seems all the more dramatic when one considers that nearly all the growth came after 1982. Hispanic Americans, too, gained ground dramatically in the seventies and nineties; their proportional increase was almost 600 percent. Native Americans were not far behind with an increase of 265 percent. The necessary flip side to these numbers, of course, is the decrease in representation of whites among law students. A modest shrinkage of 10 percent in the dominant group made possible all of the growth among nonwhites.

This opening of the doors to the legal profession did not come about by accident, but rather through active efforts by the law schools. These efforts have usually taken the form of vigorous minority-recruitment programs and affirmative-action admissions policies. Few people object to or question the value of the relative diversity of today's law students, but let slip the phrase "affirmative action" and you'll hear some opinions.

Such was the case when the University of California Board of Regents announced plans in 1995 to end the use of racial and gender preferences in admitting students and in hiring and contracting workers. (The UC regents' position on hiring and contracting was largely symbolic as state and federal laws take precedence. There are, however, no state or federal laws mandating affirmative action in university admissions.) Although some voiced praise for the regents' plans, protests erupted throughout the state. At UCLA, 31 students were arrested after refusing to disperse in a major Los Angeles intersection.

These demonstrations failed to alter the sentiment of the regents, whose final vote in February 1996 put an end to affirmative-action admissions policies in the UC system,

At Georgetown University Law Center in 1991, a series of events occurred that served to dispel any illusion of comfortable consensus on the classic "hot-button" issue: affirmative action.

In April of that year, a Georgetown law student named Timothy Maguire wrote an article entitled "Admissions Apartheid" for the law-school newspaper. At the time he wrote the article, Mr. Maguire held a work-study position in the Georgetown law school's admissions office, and in this capacity he was privy to information in the confidential records of incoming students. As Mr. Maguire later allowed, he was hired simply to file these records, but he chose to do something more.

In the course of handling student files, Maguire—who is white—"noticed" that the LSAT scores and undergraduate GPAs of Georgetown's white students were higher than those of their black counterparts. His article reported these findings, and although the facts presented in the piece were undeniably accurate, the reaction to Maguire's argument nearly got him kicked out of the law school in his final year. Before you side with the apparent victim in this story, however, you may want to hear more, for while the attacks on Mr. Maguire may have been overzealous, they were hardly unprovoked.

In an article that was admittedly "mean-spirited," Maguire reported the following results of his covert analysis of Georgetown Law Center applicants:

	Whites	Blacks
Average LSAT	43	36
Average GPA	3.7	3.2

Exalting the principle of meritocracy, Maguire decried this apparent two-tier admissions system as a kind of "apartheid" whose intended beneficiaries, minority applicants, were in fact its ultimate victims. The logic of this argument was that, by virtue of their lower numerical qualifications, African-American students were in over their heads and would have to struggle harder than whites to survive law school. Maguire argued that these "less qualified" applicants should be denied admission to such a competitive law school as Georgetown. They would be better served, he reasoned, by attending less demanding law schools in which they could more easily compete for grades and academic honors. Mr. Maguire has defended this particular view by appealing to the work of the black conservative ideologue Thomas Sowell, who, Maguire says, has "shown" that affirmative-action policies are at best ineffectual and at worst counterproductive.

Maguire's hard-line meritocratic stance, it should be noted, also extended to women. In a defense of his article, he noted that the desire of the Georgetown Law Center to admit men and women in nearly equal proportions had the same sort of ill effects as did the affirmative action policies he criticized. Maguire argued that since Georgetown received fewer applications from women than from men, its efforts to achieve parity between the sexes led to lower admissions standards for women. It was this fact, Maguire said, that accounted for the under-representation of women among Georgetown's elite graduates. Mr. Maguire's evidence for this claim was that, in his year, only one third of all cum laude graduates from Georgetown were women.

For those who have followed the popular topic of "political correctness" on America's campuses, the rest of the Maguire plot will sound familiar. Angry students denounced Maguire and the entire editorial staff of the paper for what could charitably be called their "insensitivity" in printing the story, which, it was repeatedly pointed out, was based on confidential information. Students were not alone in their outrage. Dean Judith Areen joined the protest, circulating a letter to all Georgetown law students criticizing the piece as a "misleading mix of opinion and data." A dizzying series of attacks and counterattacks followed within the student body, the faculty, and the administration, and in the D.C. press, which followed the story closely.

Had Mr. Maguire presented his findings for what they were (complex and potentially misleading), he might have avoided the wrath he incurred by including the data in what he called an "exposé... of a major institutional problem." Perhaps the *presumptuousness of his claiming to speak in the interests of his black classmates invited the rabid reaction that followed the appearance of his article.*

Calls for Mr. Maguire's dismissal focused first on the impropriety of his printing of confidential information and second on the inflammatory nature of its presentation. Maguire's defense, which was a short-lived cause célèbre among certain right-wing Washingtonians, was to cast himself as the victim of rampant political intolerance in the guise of "political correctness." After initially having faced difficulty in obtaining legal representation, Maguire was successfully defended by a pair of D.C. Law School professors, Robert Catz and Thomas Mack. Amid protest, Maguire was graduated from the Georgetown University Law Center on schedule.

one of the largest state university systems in the country. The vote called for new, non-racially based admissions policies to be instituted beginning with the fall 1997 semester for graduate students and the spring 1998 semester for undergraduates.

The UC regents are not alone in scrutinizing affirmative action policies in educational institutions. Since the UC vote, other schools have announced plans to investigate admissions policies and the use of racial quotas. What all this means to a prospective law student—or any prospective student, for that matter—is not clear. Other universities may, however, follow the lead of the UC system. Groups which have been ensured representation in legal education through affirmative-action admissions policies and aggressive minority-recruitment programs may see their participation wane.

Affirmative-action admissions policies have been a contentious issue for decades. If you can't imagine why, the case of the former Georgetown law student Timothy Maguire illustrates what has become the crux of the argument. Maguire's case involved two often intertwined issues: affirmative action and political correctness. These two issues have often been conflated—as in the Maguire case—by those who perceive a tyranny of the political left at work in the ivory tower of academia.

In the wake of the appearance of "Admissions Apartheid," some of Mr. Maguire's most vocal opponents may have hurt their own case by attempting to silence him by mere force rather than by force of argument. Because his views were thought by many to be politically incorrect, Maguire says, his detractors refused to decide on its merits the case he presented against affirmative action. Indeed, no matter one's political leanings or one's gut reaction to the content of Mr. Maguire's argument, anyone who takes seriously the importance of public debate and free speech must be a little disturbed by the reaction to Mr. Maguire's piece. There was at least some merit to his charges of censorship and his complaint that his detractors refused to confront him on the issues he tried to raise.

Still, Mr. Maguire's attempts to cast himself in the role of the victim seem a bit disingenuous. Anyone as concerned with fairness and racial justice as he claimed to be could, with a little foresight, have avoided the ill consequences brought about by the strident tone and confrontational title of the offending article. Rather than provoking a substantive debate, as Maguire says he wished to do, the piece simply provoked.

None of this is to dismiss the substantive issues Maguire raised. It is simply that these issues deserve more serious treatment than they were given by Mr. Maguire. Far from being the "exposé" he considered it, Maguire's "Admissions Apartheid" was little more than a confrontational—and superficial—rehashing of old issues. What he might have discovered with a little research is that the disparity between the LSAT scores of whites and blacks—as between those of whites and every other minority group—is a long-standing fact that has confounded and troubled responsible observers for some time.

AFFIRMATIVE ACTION

If one is to discuss affirmative action responsibly, one must first understand it. It has been common, in the years since affirmative-action policies were first adopted, for disappointed job applicants, college applicants, and law-school applicants alike to focus their frustration on the perceived injustice of a policy that seems to fly in the face of the meritocratic ideal. The affirmative action debate, however, is not one without political implications. It was widely cited that California governor Pete Wilson exerted considerable pressure on the UC Board of Regents, making the debate a highly politicized one. Racially based policies—whether they involve hiring practices or educational admissions—have long occupied a place in partisan politics and will likely continue to do so for a long time.

As the case of Mr. Maguire illustrates, students also take part in the debate and are among those who are resentful of affirmative action policies. In a 1992 interview on National Public Radio, NYU law professor Derrick Bell, who is black, discussed the far subtler form that such resentment can take. He related the comments of students he encountered at Stanford Law School while he was on leave from his position at Harvard.

> *Students would say to me, "They must have a really great affirmative action program [at Harvard]," and I'd ask them, "What makes you say that?" They'd reply, "Well, I got in here but I didn't get into Harvard."*

Professor Bell rightly laughs at the conclusion of these students that they failed to get into an extremely competitive law school because of some less-qualified minority-group member. One begins to understand how dubious such a conclusion is when one considers that the overall acceptance rate at Harvard is around 5 percent.

Feel free to point out to anyone tempted to seek a scapegoat for his or her own misfortune that their blame-fixing is not supported by statistical evidence. The success rate (the percentage of all applicants in a racial/ethnic subgroup who go on to enroll in law school in a given year) of white law school applicants has indeed declined over time—from 64.3 percent in 1986 to 45.1 percent in 1992. But the success rate of minority applicants has also declined, from 47.3 percent to 41.1 percent in the same period. It seems that the disappointment has been spread around rather evenly. But this hardly constitutes a full response to the critics of affirmative action, whose fundamental objection involves not the ratios but the supposedly lower qualifications of successful minority applicants.

The problem with an assertion or even an implication that successful minority applicants to law school are less qualified than others stems from the word "qualified" itself. Generally, the only evidence used to support such claims is evidence of LSAT scores and undergraduate GPAs, which are the only ostensibly objective standards by which law-school applicants are judged. But consider the opinion of U.S. Supreme Court on the matter:

Diversity in the Law Schools: Almost...

Comparative diversity of law-school graduates, college graduates
and Americans in general.
1992

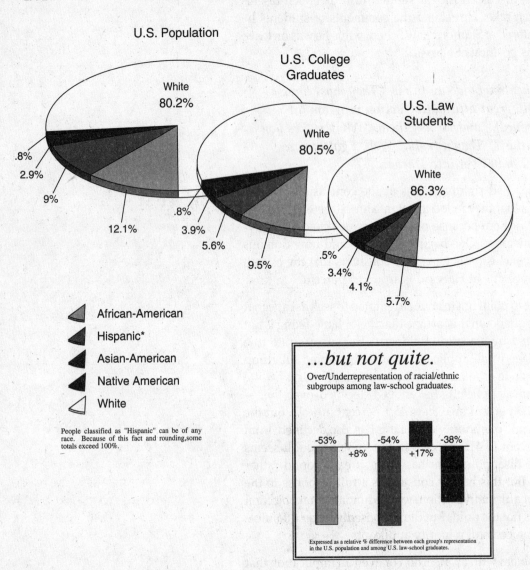

U.S. Population

U.S. College
Graduates

U.S. Law
Students

White
80.2%

White
80.5%

White
86.3%

.8%

2.9%

9%

12.1%

.8%

3.9%

5.6%

9.5%

.5%

3.4%

4.1%

5.7%

- ◢ African-American
- ◢ Hispanic*
- ◢ Asian-American
- ◢ Native American
- ◁ White

People classified as "Hispanic" can be of any
race. Because of this fact and rounding, some
totals exceed 100%.

...but not quite.

Over/Underrepresentation of racial/ethnic
subgroups among law-school graduates.

-53%   +8%   -54%   +17%   -38%

Expressed as a relative % difference between each group's representation
in the U.S. population and among U.S. law-school graduates.

Sources: U.S. Census, Journal of Education Statistics and ABA Review of Legal Education in the United States, 1992

*Insofar as the LSAT tests reflect the dimen-
sions and orientation of the Organization Man
they do a disservice to minorities. I personally*

know that admissions tests were once used to eliminate Jews. How many other minorities they claim I do not know. My reaction is that the presence of an LSAT test is sufficient warrant for a school to put racial minorities into a separate class in order better to probe their capacities and potentials.

—JUSTICE WILLIAM O. DOUGLAS IN *DE FUNIS V. ODEGAARD*

It is now part of the mandate of the American law schools that they treat minority applicants exactly as Justice Douglas recommended. The American Bar Association's accreditation standards require not only that a school provide equal opportunity "regardless of race, color, religion, national origin, sex or physical handicap," but also that a school show "special concern...consistent with [high academic] standards" for minority applicants.

Indeed, it seems pointless to address an argument like Timothy Maguire's on its own terms. It is ridiculously myopic to base a sweeping argument against affirmative action on the evidence of college grades and LSAT scores alone. If Mr. Maguire is prepared to call blacks less qualified to study law at an elite institution by virtue of their grades and test scores, he must also be prepared to say the same for every other group of nonmale, nonwhite students. By his calculus, the highest circles of the legal profession would remain the province of white men alone. When one considers how profoundly the law affects our lives, one begins to understand that a more morally defensible argument can be made for seeing to it that we are all entitled to a role in the law's management. After roughly twenty-five years of ongoing diversification, the profession as a whole still has a long way to go before it reflects the diversity of the overall U.S. workforce.

Until the legal profession is demonstrably representative of all the people on whose lives it has a daily impact, equal justice will be just an ideal.

Legal Foundation for Affirmative Action Admissions Policies

Bakke v. University of California (1977)

Arguably the most important and certainly the most highly publicized court case in the history of the legal battles over affirmative action, Bakke stemmed from an affirmative-action admissions policy at the medical school of the University of California at Davis. The policy established numerical admissions quotas based on race. Alan P. Bakke, a white applicant who had been denied admission to the medical school at Davis, charged that the university's policy amounted to "reverse discrimination." The Supreme Court agreed with a lower court's decision that, since race was the sole factor in the university's decision not to admit him, Mr. Bakke had suffered unduly. The court ordered that Mr. Bakke be admitted to the university's medical school. More important, however, the Supreme Court refused to use the case to declare all affirmative action illegal. Far from threatening the future of affirmative action, Bakke effectively legalized those race-based admissions preferences that stopped short of racial quotas.

In the wake of this landmark case, colleges and graduate schools around the country adopted affirmative-action policies of varying strength, all of them designed to bring about increased, if not equal, representation of minorities in American universities. In the law schools—and, therefore, in the legal profession—truly proportional representation for historically excluded minority groups remains a goal, not a reality. Activist admissions policies instituted in the wake of Bakke, however, have made the realization of that goal a very real possibility.

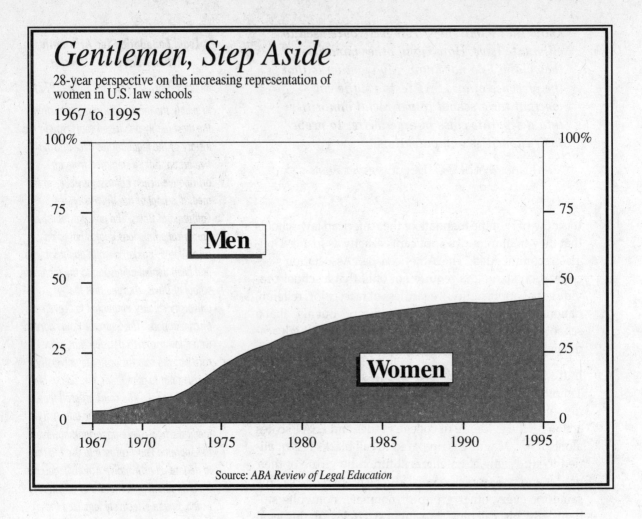

Gentlemen, Step Aside

28-year perspective on the increasing representation of
women in U.S. law schools

1967 to 1995

Source: *ABA Review of Legal Education*

WOMEN ENTER THE BOYS' CLUB

*The natural and proper timidity and delicacy
which belongs to the female sex evidently
unfits it for many of the occupations of civil
life. . . . The paramount destiny and mission of
women are to fulfill the benign offices of wife
and mother.*

—JUSTICE JOSEPH BRADLEY, DENYING ACCESS TO
    FEDERAL COURTS BY LAWYER MYRA BRADWELL,
    1869

Nobody but a few men will be surprised to hear that
women were kept out of the legal profession by something
other than their "natural timidity and delicacy." Invisible

roadblocks, semiorganized resistance, and plain old sexism barred women from high-level participation in the field in meaningful numbers until very recently. Times have changed quickly. Just as dramatic—though probably just as incomplete—as the ethnic and racial integration of the American legal profession in the last twenty years has been the transformation of the profession from a nearly all-male field into one in which women have begun to take a more significant place. While the ranks of the profession as a whole are still dominated by men, American law schools are infusing the boys' club with more and more women every year. Better late than never, perhaps, but it sure took a while.

Reliable historical statistics on the total number and percentage of women lawyers in the United States are difficult to come by, but law-school enrollment provides an obvious, useful barometer. In this venue, the progress of women has been dramatic. As recently as 1972, only 9.4 percent of all law students were women, this at a time when women made up 43.4 percent of all college graduates. In the years that followed, overall interest in law school skyrocketed, with much of the increase attributable to the relatively sudden entrance of women on the admissions landscape. Despite fluctuations in total enrollment during the period, women gained ground in the law schools in every single year between 1972 and 1990.

As a percentage of all law students, women have held steady at around 42 percent in the last three years. Today, only 14 law schools out of 178 have a student body that is at least half women, but the overall law-student population may yet achieve parity between the sexes as more and more women college graduates consider the law as a career option.

Notwithstanding the trend toward equality between the sexes in U.S. law schools, the legal profession has a long way to go before it can be called a level playing field. Despite twenty years of steady increase in the number of women leaving law school and entering practice, women lawyers still represent less than 20 percent of the total lawyer population. Further, it is estimated that women hold less than 10 percent of all partnerships in U.S. law firms, a disproportionately low number. It would be diffi-

First Females

First Admitted to the Bar (Illinois)
Arabella Mansfield
1869

First to try a case in court (Missouri)
Lemma Bankalloo
1870

First to receive a law degree (Union College, later to become Northwestern University)
Ada Kepley
1870

First to appear as lawyer in U.S. Federal Court
Belva Lockwood
1879

First women admitted to Harvard Law School (13 in first class)
1950

First Associate Justice of the U.S. Supreme Court
Sandra Day O'Connor
1981

First Attorney General of the United States
Janet Reno
1993

First woman elected to head the ABA
Roberta Cooper Ramo
1995

The first women to blaze the trail into the legal profession were, not surprisingly, in the feminist vanguard of the late 1800s. Despite the success of these early pioneers in breaking the sex barrier, significant participation by women in the legal profession was still another hundred years away.

cult to prove, however, the existence of a glass ceiling preventing the free advancement of women to the highest levels of the profession. Established male lawyers could point out that until enough women have practiced long enough, the upper echelon of the profession will remain overwhelmingly male. Whatever its origin, one hopes that the disparity that exists between the sexes today diminishes as more women enter law school and the legal profession.

LAWYER, DEFEND THYSELF

> Woe unto you, lawyers! for ye have taken away the key of knowledge.
> *Bible, Luke 11:52*

> What's black and white and brown and looks good on a lawyer? A doberman.
> *Mordechai Richler*

"Because New Jersey got first choice."

"Because there are some things you just can't get a rat to do."

*"There are skid marks in front of the skunk."**

If by now you can't supply the lawyer joke for each of the above punch lines, then you've either been living under a rock or you just haven't told anyone that you're considering law school. If the latter case applies to you, just wait. You'll hear plenty of it from friends and family soon enough. If the former case applies, then you may want to consider what you're up against.

The phenomenon of "lawyer bashing" is quite familiar to most, whether in the form of derisive jokes, oily movie villains, or righteous speech-making by a former president and vice president of the United States. Why is it that a once proud and honored profession has come to suffer such disdain, such mocking stereotypes? One doesn't hear dentist jokes or insurance-agent jokes. Why and when did lawyers get such a bad rap? Why should you care? Because before you've even started law school, you may find your-

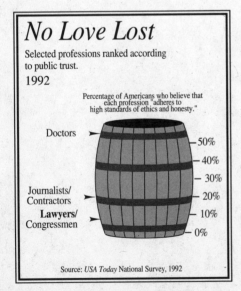

No Love Lost

Selected professions ranked according to public trust.
1992

Percentage of Americans who believe that each profession "adheres to high standards of ethics and honesty."

Doctors

Journalists/
Contractors
Lawyers/
Congressmen

- 50%
- 40%
- 30%
- 20%
- 10%
- 0%

Source: *USA Today* National Survey, 1992

*The jokes for each of the punch lines above are:

*"Why does Washington, D.C., have all the lawyers and New Jersey have all the toxic waste dumps?"

*"Why are they starting to use lawyers instead of rats in scientific lab experiments?"

*"How do you tell a dead skunk in the road from a dead lawyer?"

self on a barstool or around the dinner table arguing your first case—as defense counsel in World v. Lawyers, a case that has been dragging through the court of public opinion now for centuries.

BASH, BABY, BASH

The first thing we do, let's kill all the lawyers.

—SHAKESPEARE, *HENRY IV PART II*, IV. I.

Long before Shakespeare wrote his famous line about killing all the lawyers, the public had a love-hate relationship with the legal profession; even before the word "shyster" entered the popular vocabulary, negative stereotypes of attorneys were well known. At the very least, throughout centuries of lawyer-mocking, positive images of attorneys existed alongside the negative ones.

In the United States, advocates such as Clarence Darrow enjoyed something like rock-star status in the days when the lawyer–as–Robin Hood was still a viable image. Well into the twentieth century, lawyers continued to attract good press. During the Civil Rights Era it was difficult to ignore or deny the moral superiority of a Thurgood Marshall battling real-life racism before the Supreme Court, or of an Atticus Finch fighting fictional battles in a small Alabama courthouse in *To Kill a Mockingbird*. As long as the part was being played by the likes of Gregory Peck or Spencer Tracy (see: film versions of *To Kill a Mockingbird* and *Inherit the Wind*), the lawyer in the role of David fighting mighty Goliath was not too hard to sell.

Times have changed. When the famous Bible story is alluded to today in reference to lawyers, the roles are reversed. It's now the Philistine who wears the suit and carries the briefcase, while the helpless citizen carries the tiny sling. In the hierarchy of public esteem, it seems, lawyers are in closest company with journalists and used-car salesmen—somewhere above incumbent politicians and somewhere below root-canal specialists. According to a *USA Today* poll, in fact, lawyers rank second only to congressmen in terms of public mistrust.

He saw a lawyer killing a viper
On a dunghill hard by his own stable;
And the devil smiled, for it put him in mind
Of Cain and his brother Abel.

Samuel Taylor Coleridge,
"The Devil's Thoughts"

I think we may class lawyer in the natural history of monsters.

John Keats

Why is there always a secret singing
When a lawyer cashes in?
Why does a hearse horse snicker
Hauling a lawyer away?

Carl Sandburg,
"The Lawyers Know Too Much"

An incompetent attorney can delay a trial for months or years. A competent attorney can delay one even longer.

Evelle Younger

Recent, highly publicized trials have caused a surge of not only lawyer bashing but an outcry from the public—and from some within the legal community—regarding the state of the American legal system. Two trials in particular—those of O.J. Simpson and the Menendez brothers—both captivated and enraged the American public.

The trial of O.J. Simpson for the murders of his ex-wife, Nicole, and her friend Ron Goldman, was one of the most closely followed criminal proceedings in our nation's history. Dubbed the "Trial of Century," the jury's "not guilty" verdict left many disillusioned with our justice system. Regardless of O.J. Simpson's guilt or innocence, the proceedings did raise several important concerns. To many, Simpson's acquittal proved that wealthy defendants can literally buy their freedom. It was widely noted that Simpson's "Dream Team" defense, consisting of such heavy hitters as F. Lee Bailey and Alan Dershowitz, cost the defendant millions. Without his financial resources, it was argued, Simpson would have easily been convicted of the double murders in the face of what some thought to be inescapable forensic evidence. Many others cited Simpson's celebrity status and its possible influence on the jury and proceedings.

O.J. Simpson peers over the shoulder of one of his many trusty defenders, Robert Shapiro.

Reuters/Corbis-Bettman

One thing is certainly true of the nearly eight-month-long O.J. Simpson trial: the American public couldn't get enough of it. Televised live by CNN, these proceedings were the most highly publicized and highly criticized in our nation's history. What, if any, long-lasting impact the Trial of the Century will have on our legal system or on legal education is unclear. Several law professors, however, are making use of the case and the issues it raised, particularly those involving the handling of evidence. In an article published shortly after the verdict was delivered ("Trial & Error: Focus Shifts to a Justice System and Its Flaws," 10/8/95), the Los Angeles Times reported that one Georgetown University professor developed and taught an all-Simpson legal evidence course in the 1996 spring term. (The course was so popular, it was reported, that more than 100 students had to be turned away.) Other law schools, the paper reported, have also brought the Simpson case into the classroom. The Georgetown professor Paul Rothstein was quoted as saying: "[The Simpson trial has] been the world's biggest publicity binge for the law and the courts and lawyers... O.J. will be on trial in law schools for many years to come."

The ABA is working to mitigate any negative impact the trial had on the image of attorneys and the legal system. In an ABA Journal special report ("Verdict on Simpson," 11/95), it was reported that ABA President Roberta Cooper Ramo plans to work with the public to address concerns raised by the trial, such as the use of cameras in the courtroom, the commercialization of trails, and jury sequestration.

Those disillusioned by the Simpson trial and similar high-publicity cases seem to focus on the legal system as a whole. But previous attacks have been more pointed and far more politically motivated. Former president George Bush and his then vice president Dan Quayle declared open season on lawyers in the summer of 1991 at the annual American Bar Association convention. Before a room full of attorneys, Quayle, a featured speaker, delivered a speech that was stingingly critical of legal practitioners. Fulfilling his role as chairman of the now defunct President's Council on Competitiveness, Dan Quayle (not J. Danforth Quayle, Esq., Indiana University Law School '73) asked such inflammatory questions as, "Does America really need 70 percent of the world's attorneys?" (We'll deal with questions like these in the next few pages.)

President Bush jumped in on the lawyer-bashing action when a few sharp jabs directed at attorneys were written into his 1992 acceptance speech at the Republican National Convention. (See next page.)

TOO MANY LAWYERS? DEPENDS WHOM YOU ASK

Serious issues get lost in the finger-pointing game and rhetoric of lawyer bashing. Widespread agreement exists, for instance, that elements of the legal system need serious reform, or at the very least reevaluation. There are, to be sure, radically different points of view within this consensus, but very few who engage in the debate over the state of the system would argue that the debate itself is unnecessary. Yet it is amusing to read and hear how both sides of the debate skirt the complicated issue of how to fix a system clearly in need of repair. Consider the mutual

Bashing Back

Despite the apparent popularity of the rhetoric, lawyer bashing isn't always successful. In addition to losing reelection, Bush's Council on Competitiveness was disbanded just two weeks into the Clinton presidency. One should hesitate, however, before reading too much into the fact that the Bushes vacated the White House for the only all-lawyer First Couple in American history. Graduates of America's elite law schools remain ensconced in the halls of power in the nation's capital, but the fallout from the antilawyer rhetoric of Dan Quayle and the '92 Bush campaign has been felt in Illinois, at the headquarters of the American Bar Association. In January 1993, the ABA hired its first-ever full-time image consultant. His stated mission is to give the public "an accurate picture of what the ABA stands for" and to "show people that there's a face behind all those lawyers." If the ABA, an organization $4.3 million in the red for 1993, can see fit to shell out $170,000 per annum for image-burnishing, it seems lawyer bashing is no joke.

(See David Margolick's 1/29/92 At The Bar column in The New York Times.)

ANATOMY OF A BASHING

As a future lawyer, you should probably be aware that your chosen profession was considered despicable enough by one former president's campaign staff to be singled out for denigration before a nationwide television audience. While skillful lawyer bashing is a proven crowd-pleaser, President Bush's acceptance speech at the 1992 Republican National Convention proved to be too little too late. While this event may be long over, Bush's bashing represents all-too-current sentiments. Mr. Bush's attack was in many ways a textbook bashing, but it did have its weak points. A brief critique follows.

The use of "our" towns and "our" neighborhoods neatly introduces the Us vs. Them theme. (Never mind that lawyers happen to live in those neighborhoods too.) "Running wild" is a bit alarmist and heavy-handed, but no doubt an effective attention-getter.

Just in case you weren't sure whose side Norman Rockwell would be on, lawyers here are shown to be so un-American as to threaten our very national pastime. "Moms and Pops" sounds a little forced, but it may play in Peoria.

It is rather difficult to take this bit of posturing very seriously. Not that G.B. isn't muy macho but chances are

that he would be more at home tackling those evil lawyers on the golf course than in the boxing ring. Perhaps "We tee off tonight" would have sounded a bit too cozy, though.

G.B. seems to flirt dangerously here with the complexity of the issue of rampant litigiousness by

> And I see something else happening in our towns and neighborhoods. Sharp lawyers are running wild. Doctors are afraid to practice medicine. And some moms and pops won't even coach Little League anymore. We must sue each other less and care for each other more. I am fighting to reform our legal system, to put an end to crazy lawsuits. And if that means climbing into the ring with the trial lawyers, well, let me just say, Round One starts tonight.
>
> After all, my opponent's campaign is being backed by practically every trial lawyer who ever wore a tasseled loafer. He's not in the ring with them, he's in the tank.

pointing out that it is "we" who do the suing, not the lawyers themselves. Masterfully, however, G.B. avoids a sociological quagmire by objectifying the problem as "crazy lawsuits" and thereby sidestepping the issue of crazy us. A risky move, but deftly executed.

1. What in heaven's name does this mean? Is it an accurate generalization regarding lawyers' footwear?

If so, doesn't it perhaps undermine the Us. vs. Them position by betraying a degree of familiarity with lawyers that many listeners might not share?

2. If this is a purely aesthetic criticism of tassels, or, more hopefully, of loafers in general, with those atrocious glasses is G.B. really one to talk?

3. Does G.B. realize that some lawyers are women?

4. Is this meant to foster some sort of class resentment? If so, doesn't proto-preppy George Herbert Walker Bush seriously risk shooting himself in his (no doubt well-shod) foot?

This reference is quite ponderous. Possibly a G.B. ad lib.

This surprisingly subtle allusion to sharks is very much in keeping with a time-honored tradition: grouping lawyers with various un-cuddly predatory beasts or scavengers. Nicely done.

fixation of the pro- and anti-lawyer camps on the simple question: "Are there simply too many lawyers in the United States?" Even serious-minded critics and defenders of the legal system allow their debates to devolve into a battle of contradictory statistics. It is frustratingly difficult to know whose statistics to believe. Does the United States have too many lawyers? The answer may be that it doesn't matter, that perception is more important than reality. In any case, the battle for perception rages.

In the halls of academia, some have sought to prove scientifically, once and for all, that there is such a thing as an overabundance of lawyers and that the United States is a country that suffers from this condition. One of the most enthusiastically received examples of such an effort was a study published in 1989 by a finance professor at the University of Texas at Austin named Peter Magee. If Pulitzers were awarded for clever titles, the 1989 report would have won hands down for its contentious "The Invisible Foot and the Waste of Nations: Lawyers as Negative Externalities." (Just in case the title leaves any question in your mind as to Magee's views, the book version of the original eleven-page essay was slightly modified to read, after the colon, "Lawyers vs. the U.S. Economy") The title is a brilliant play on Adam Smith's *Wealth of Nations*, the free-market bible that introduced anatomy to the vocabulary of economics in the form of the "invisible hand," the unseen guiding force of a market economy. In Magee's construction, lawyers represent the disembodied hand's antithesesis; they are the clubfoot that drags the economy down. Clever imagery aside, "Invisible Foot" was a serious attempt to reveal the ill effects of America's burgeoning lawyer population.

Magee's work eschews moral and ethical arguments and focuses on empirical economic data, and so it is not surprising that his work has been embraced by the likes of William F. Buckley and others on the political right wing. The argument itself is based on a premise that is far from original: that lawyers are not economic producers but economic redistributors. If one accepts this proposition absolutely, common sense would dictate that, since the market needs only so many middlemen (or middlewomen), an overabundance of lawyers saps the economy of strength.

This is, of course, the type of argument that has been made around dinner tables for years, but Magee is the first to claim to have proof. His findings are expressed simply in the form of a graph comparing rate of economic growth to the number of lawyers relative to all white-collar workers (see below).

Magee's argument has captivated those predisposed to lawyer bashing. At last, it seems, incontrovertible evidence substantiates their criticism of the legal profession. Moreover, Magee's argument has attractive qualities quite apart from its politics: It is simple and even has a certain el-

The Magee Curve

*"The principal intellectual foundation for the lawyers-as-parasites view."**

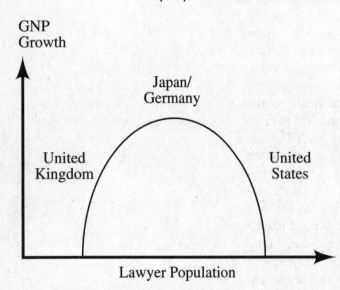

According to University of Texas finance professor Peter Magee, the widely held belief that the United States suffers from an overabundance of lawyers is scientifically verifiable. A transnational comparison of economic performance and lawyer populations enabled Magee to arrive at this conclusion. Though he initially believed that any increase in a country's lawyer population hindered economic development, Magee now holds that it is the proportion of lawyers relative to all white-collar workers that is of greatest importance to a nation's ecomomy.

By Magee's reckoning, a lawyer/white-collar disproportion on either extreme holds an economy back: In a country that has too few lawyers, certain necessary functions (e.g., "making property rights clearer, protecting individuals from harm-doers and facilitating transactions") go unperformed; in a country with too many lawyers, like the United States, one will find "predatory redistributive conflict, excessive litigation and the diversion of talent out of productive activity." Such an economy suffers accordingly. Somewhere on the parabola between the two extremes must exist an optimal number of lawyers, Magee argues. Not surprisingly, economic powerhouses Germany and Japan stand neatly in the region of this optimal point, and the United States falls significantly to the right (40 percent too far to the right, for instance, in 1983).

Magee's work has captured the attention of many critics of the legal profession, adding new fuel to the debate over the effects of a large, unregulated lawyer population.

* Charles Epp and Marc Galanter, "Let's Not Kill All the Lawyers," Wall Street Journal, 7/9/92

egance. Admirable as that may be, anyone who reads the papers has good reason to take simple, elegant arguments with a grain of salt when those arguments come from the mouth of an economist. Magee's simplistic formulation relies on only three variables: lawyers, white-collar workers, and GNP growth. Further, there is good reason to believe that his data is, if not simply wrong, very questionable. New and glamorous predictors of economic performance are regularly offered by eager economists—often those with a political ax to grind—only to fail in the face of a frustratingly complex and variable world. Magee's lovely curve is no exception.

The Neo-Magee Curve*

A decidedly messier reality.

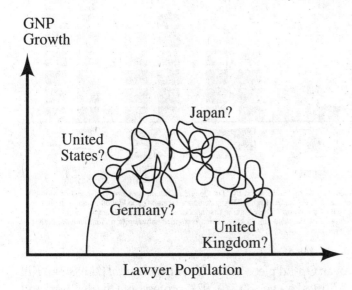

GNP Growth

Japan?

United States?

Germany?

United Kingdom?

Lawyer Population

The world, sadly, doesn't always cooperate with neat theories. Magee's parabola is attractive, but is it fair to make the assumptions that lead him to it? Certainly if a modern ecomomy had no lawyers, it would grind to a halt, and if an ecomomy were composed only of lawyers, there would be no economy at all. The tough part is figuring out what happens in between these extremes. Magee posits a smooth curve with a single peak using only one factor: lawyers.

As Ray August and others have pointed out, however, Magee's data may be seriously flawed. The beauty and accuracy of his model requires, for instance, that Japan have something less than one-tenth the number of lawyers it may actually have. Does Germany have forty thousand lawyers, or four times that number? With the answer to that simple question very much in doubt, Magee's argument loses some of its force.

The shakiness of Magee's compelling theory may become clearer if one recalls a nearly identical model that appeared in the early 1980s in a different context: the "Laffer curve," the intellectual foundation of Reaganomics. Substitute "taxes" for "lawyers" and "government revenue" for "GNP growth" in Magee's argument and you have the justification for supply-side economics, eighties style. Thirteen years and several trillion dollars of national debt later, Laffer's suggestion that government revenues could be maximized by reducing taxes seems quite a laugher indeed. Keep this in mind before you decide to do your part for the economy by killing a lawyer. Magee would not be the first eager economist to trot out a simple, elegant predictor of economic performance only to end up frustrated by a hopelessly complex and variable world.

* with apologies to Martin Gardner, who saw early on that the emperor had no clothes. (See: "The Laffer Curve and Other Laughs in Current Economics," Scientific American, 12/81.)

"Does America really need 70 percent of the world's lawyers?"

– Dan Quayle

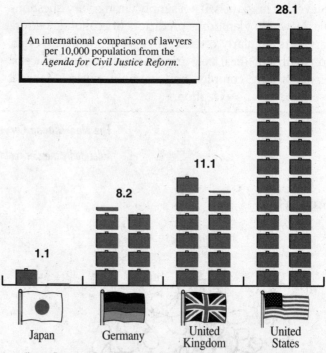

An international comparison of lawyers per 10,000 population from the *Agenda for Civil Justice Reform*.

28.1

11.1

8.2

1.1

Japan   Germany   United Kingdom   United States

According to figures released by Dan Quayle's Council on Competitiveness in a report published to coincide with his ABA appearance (see text), the United States is the lawyer capital of the world. These figures first appeared in the Council's tract *Agenda for Civil Justice Reform*, and they have since provided ammunition for lawyer bashers everywhere.

A lawyer is one skilled in the circumvention of the law.

Ambrose Bierce

It is the trade of lawyers to question everything, yield nothing, and to talk by the hour.

Thomas Jefferson

Lawyers are people whose profession it is to disguise matters.

Thomas More

In an Op-Ed piece in *The Wall Street Journal* ("Let's Not Kill All the Lawyers," 7/9/92), professors Charles Epp and Marc Galanter of the University of Wisconsin point out the fatal flaw in Magee's work. In an unrelated piece in the *ABA Journal* ("Mythical Kingdom of Lawyers," 9/92), law professor Raymond August effectively does the same. The data presented in these two pieces should, at least, serve to refocus the debate. Galanter and Epp fault Mr. Magee for his creative statistical manipulation of international lawyer data. August does not address Magee directly, but his work goes farther than Epp and Galanter's in that it challenges the very validity of comparing international lawyer populations—the basis of Mr. Magee's work. Refuting the

"Does America really <u>have</u> 70 percent of the world's lawyers?"

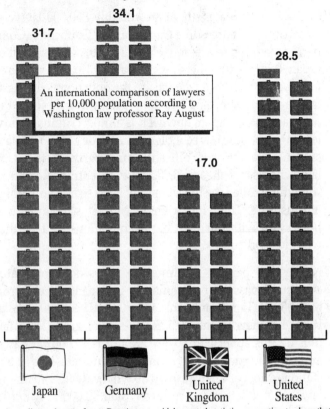

An international comparison of lawyers per 10,000 population according to Washington law professor Ray August

31.7 — Japan
34.1 — Germany
17.0 — United Kingdom
28.5 — United States

According to law professor Ray August, widely quoted statistics purporting to show that the United States is home to a majority of the world's lawyers are simply wrong. Using what he says is a more universally applicable definition of the term "lawyer," he comes up with the figures above, which stand in stark contrast to those of Dan Quayle's Council on Competitiveness.

contention that the United States was home to a grossly disproportionate number of the world's lawyers, August performed his own statistical analysis and concluded that as of 1987, the United States actually had only 9.4 percent of the world's 9.3 million lawyers and that percentage is decreasing daily.

Ray August has challenged a truth that many take to be axiomatic: that America is the most lawyer-rich environment on earth. It would be very surprising if you have never heard someone quote in an authoritative tone statistics concerning the relative size of the lawyer populations in the United States and in Japan: "There are three billion lawyers in the United States and only (fill in your own very

Lawyers are those whose interests and abilities lie in perverting, confounding and eluding the law.

Jonathan Swift

Lawyers are the only persons in whom ignorance of the law is not punished.

Jeremy Bentham

low number) in Japan. And people wonder why our economy blows!" Mr. August's work should debunk this popular myth.

In the United States, there are roughly 850,000 lawyers. According to sources like Dan Quayle's Council on Competitiveness, there are only about 13,000 lawyers in all of Japan. It is true that there are only about 13,000 *bengoshi* in Japan, and that these *bengoshi* are the only people licensed to perform certain legal functions. To say that these are the only lawyers in Japan, however, is almost criminally misleading. Japanese law schools graduate roughly 35,000 law students every year, significantly more per capita than U.S. law schools. Of these, 30,000 take an entrance exam to something called the JRTI, the Judicial Research and Training Institute. The temptation, of course, is to equate the JRTI exam with our own bar examinations. In fact, that would be ridiculous.

Nearly 100 percent of American law-school graduates eventually pass a bar examination. Of Japan's annual crop of 30,000 JRTI applicants, only 475 pass and become *bengoshi*. What happens to the 29,525 law-school grads who fall outside this super-elite? They are not taken out at dawn and shot, nor do they say, "oh well," and take jobs at gas stations. Most of them go on to do what we call "practicing law." In 1987, there were fewer than 13,000 *bengoshi* in Japan, but there were upward of 387,000 law school graduates performing legal work. The Sony Corporation employs 150 such people in its legal department. According to Dan Quayle, these aren't lawyers. Well, they certainly aren't potatoes.

Ray August calls such non-*bengoshi* law-school graduates "law providers," a more accurate and internationally consistent definition than "lawyer." An international comparison of "law provider" populations yields results very different from the glamorous and quotable numbers reported by the antilawyer camp. To conclude that Japan has only 13,000 lawyers on the basis of a head count of *bengoshi* would be like counting all the players in the NBA and declaring that only 324 Americans played basketball. Critics of the American legal system should do their homework more thoroughly and rely less on simplistic and erroneous arguments concerning the supposed "lawyer infestation" in the United States.

A Lawyer is one whose opinion is worth nothing unless paid for.
English proverb

A lawyer with his briefcase can steal more than a hundred men with guns.
Mario Puzo,
The Godfather

If law school is so hard to get through... how come there are so many lawyers?
Calvin Trillin

Critics of the American legal system should do their homework more thoroughly and rely less on simplistic and erroneous arguments concerning the supposed "lawyer infestation" in the United States.

MAKING SENSE OF THE SENSELESS

The battles just described are pitched in the ether of macroeconomics and yield little reward for the individual who hopes to understand something beyond what he or she stands to gain personally by entering the legal profession. Similarly, the "negative image" of lawyers in popular culture is not the most useful of decision-making criteria; sarcastic barbs may be difficult to take at times, but nobody considering law as a career should accept at face value uninformed assertions that lawyers are the root of all evil. To deny the need for lawyers in a society such as ours would be to ignore economic and social realities that render individuals free but powerless. Yet to dismiss out of hand the legal profession's detractors would be to deny that the law can be and often is used not to empower the individual but to protect the interests of established powers. What does this all lead to? Should we regard lawyers as a "necessary evil" or as a "problematic good"? The former may be pithier, but the latter is probably nearer to the truth.

One of the most eloquent and forceful arguments a prospective law student could hear on the topic was made by former Harvard president Derek Bok in an article in Harvard magazine called "A Flawed System":

> *Unlike medicine, few young people decide to be lawyers early in life. Instead, law schools have traditionally been the refuge of able, ambitious college seniors who cannot think of anything else they want to do. . . .The net result of [this trend] is a massive diversion of exceptional talent into pursuits that often add little to the growth of the economy, the pursuit of culture, or the enhancement of the human spirit. . . . [T]he supply of exceptional people is limited. Yet far too many of these rare individuals are becoming lawyers at a time when the country cries out for more talented business executives, more enlightened public servants, more inventive engineers, more able high-school principals and teachers.*

Nous savons tours ici que le droit est la plus puissante des écoles de l'imagination. Jamais poète n'a interprété la nature aussi librement pu'un juriste la réalité.
(All of us here know there's no better way of exercising the imagination than the study of law. No poet ever interpreted nature as freely as a lawyer interprets the truth.)

Jean Giraudoux,
La Guerre de Troie N'aura Pas Lieu

Lawyers, I suppose, were children once.
Charles Lamb

The supply of exceptional people is limited. Yet far too many of these rare individuals are becoming lawyers. . . .
Derek Bok

Bok seems to agree with Magee on some level, but we should keep in mind that Bok was employed by the same university that produced the Socratic Method and is today one of the country's premier law schools. Unlike Magee, Bok, however, focuses on the loss of so many "exceptional people" to the legal profession. Although Bok's thesis is an interesting one, it, like Magee's, seems somewhat flawed in its suppositions. Many would contend that lawyers can—and do—"add...to the growth of the economy, the pursuit of culture, [and] the enhancement of the human spirit." Bok may believe lawyers to be a "necessary evil," but in doing so gives little credit the lawyers who contribute to society both personally and professionally. At the very least, his statement is food for thought.

RECENT APPLICANT TRENDS

In the United States, the vast majority of those who matriculate in law school go on to graduate, and nearly all law school graduates eventually pass the bar examination. The hard part is getting into law school in the first place.

Some of the difficulties that you and others may face in gaining admission to the law schools of your choice next year are the result of dramatic demographic changes in higher education. Fifteen years ago, most observers would have predicted that law school admissions in the early 1990s would be relatively uncompetitive. They would have been wrong. Despite assertions to the contrary, the late 1980s saw the most dramatic and unexpected increase in applications to law school in history.

Many experts in the area of legal education have noted, however, that the trend of the late 1990s may prove to be one of downsizing. After the national law school applicant pool peaked at 94,000 in 1991, the number of applicants has steadily declined, according to the Law School Admissions Council. By 1995, the number of individuals applying to law schools dipped 17 percent to 78,200. In response, many law schools have announced plans to intentionally "downsize" their entering law classes in an effort to avoid a dip in the quality of admittees. The effect of this downsizing on admissions standards would probably mean little for prospective students, particularly those with solid credentials. The downsizing, publicly announced by only a handful of schools, would more than likely only maintain numerical averages of previous years. If the applicant pool continues to decline, however, more law schools are likely to make this move.

THE EARLY 1980S: A CRISIS LOOMS

In the early eighties, many believed that law schools would face a drastic decline in applicants due to a shrinking potential law-school applicant population. To make a long story short, nothing of the sort ever happened. Despite the baby bust, the number of applicants to law school has increased dramatically, while the number of first-year spots open to those applicants has remained nearly steady.

There are surely numerous reasons for this: the increasing proportion of all people attending college; the steadily climbing number of women interested in law school; the dramatic increase in minority applicants. All of these factors merit recognition, yet they alone do not account for this eruption of applications.

In 1980, the potential law-school applicant population in the United States (defined here as those between the ages of 21 and 25) was around 21.6 million, the all-time high figure for this age group. Colleges and law schools alike could foresee the changes the coming years would bring. The math was not too difficult. In 1980, members of the age group in question had been born between 1955 and 1959, the peak years of the baby boom. By 1990, the 21-to-25-year-old group would be made up entirely of the first of the post-baby boomers—kids born between 1965 and 1969—who would number only 18.9 million. Considering that there are spots for only about forty thousand new law students each year, 18.9 million may sound like a sufficiently large pool from which to choose, but this was not the point. This 12.5 percent decline in population, it was assumed, would be reflected in the applicant pool. One might wonder why this mattered. After all, if law schools were turning away nearly as many applicants as they were accepting, it would not be difficult to maintain full enrollment even if applications dropped by more than 12 percent. The fear of those who predicted a crisis was not, however, that classes could not be filled, but rather that the quality of the student bodies at law schools would suffer.

The logic went something like this: If the potential applicant population shrinks, so will the actual applicant pool. If the applicant pool shrinks, so will the number of "highly qualified" applicants (applicants with high GPAs and LSAT scores). If the number of elite applicants shrinks, all schools will be forced to relax their admissions standards. Why was this so worrisome? One thing is certain: Fears of lower standards in law school admissions were not motivated by the high standards of the legal profession itself. Every law-school graduate would still have to pass a rigorous bar examination, and it was never suggested that bar-admissions criteria be relaxed. It would seem, then, that the worst-case scenario, should the law-school applicant pool shrink, would be that fewer people would be admitted to the bar. In fact, the worst-case scenario was much worse than that for those schools that already accepted many applicants with less than stellar LSAT scores and grade-point averages. For marginal schools, the prospect of declining admissions standards was not in and of itself the source of concern. The real concern was that declining admissions standards could threaten such schools' very existence.

Law School Disappointments

Number of first-year law school seats available vs. overall demand for those spots.

1965-1995

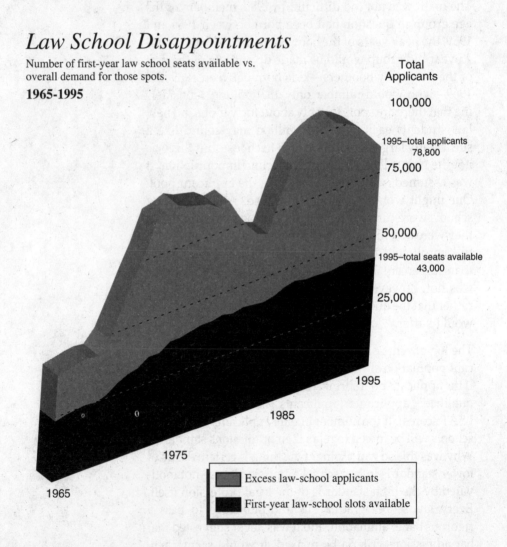

Total Applicants

100,000

1995–total applicants 78,800

75,000

50,000

1995–total seats available 43,000

25,000

1995

1985

1975

1965

■ Excess law-school applicants

■ First-year law-school slots available

Sources: Law Services, ABA Review of Legal Education 1995

The American Bar Association's standards for law-school approval require that schools admit only those applicants who have "reasonable chances of success." This was not the case in the United States some fifty years ago, and it is still not the case in many other countries where law schools have virtually open admissions policies but graduate only a fraction of those students initially admitted. The radically democratic survival-of-the-fittest approach taken in such countries is looked down upon by the ABA's legal-education committee. The governing body of the American legal profession chooses instead to set what is possibly the highest hurdle for would-be lawyers at the very beginning of the race. In the United States, the vast majority of those who matriculate in law school go on to graduate, and nearly all law-school graduates eventually pass the bar examination. The hard part is getting into law school in the first place.

Regardless of any financial pressure to do so, a law school may not accept candidates whom the ABA deems "demonstrably unqualified." The ABA further states that a steady decline in the GPAs and LSAT scores of admittees shall be taken to indicate that a school is not in compliance with this requirement. This of course puts enormous pressure on a law school to keep its numbers high. This policy fueled concern over the supposedly impending admissions crisis in the early eighties. The administration and faculty of a law school whose students fell on the lower end of the LSAT and GPA curve had every reason to fear what would happen if law schools higher up on the admissions food chain started consuming their prospects. The "weak" schools, it was reasoned, would not survive if the strong schools were forced to lower their numerical standards.

THE CURRENT BOOM: A CRISIS AVERTED

To make a long story short, fears of impending doom and plummeting applicant numbers proved utterly unfounded. The late 1980s saw the most dramatic increase in law-school applications in history. There are, in fact, eight more law schools today than there were in 1980, and far from falling, admissions standards have risen across the board.

If you are acquainted with more than a few people who have applied to law school in the last five years, you probably have a sense of just how competitive the admissions game has become. Nearly everyone can offer anecdotal evidence that it has only gotten more difficult in recent years to gain admission to the top law schools. This subjective judgment is borne out by statistics: As the number of applicants to law schools skyrocketed in the late 80s and early '90s, the number of seats in America's law schools did not. As a result, law schools turned away tens of thousands of applicants.

The number of aspiring attorneys has fluctuated considerably over time, not just in the last few years. For most of the years prior to about 1965, relatively few people who applied to law school were turned away. In 1965, for instance, it is estimated that there were only about 27,000 applicants to law school vying for about 20,000 slots. In absolute terms: 7,000 disappointments, 35 percent of the total applicant pool. Beginning in about 1968, however, applications began to stream into law-school admissions offices at an unprecedented rate. The number of applicants increased from about 45,000 in 1968 to nearly 75,000 in 1972: a 67 percent increase. The number of spots in first-year law school classes expanded in the same period at a rate of only 50 percent. By 1975, as many law-school applicants were being turned away as were being accepted.

Many observers have pointed to the Civil Rights Movement, the war in Vietnam, and the Free Speech Movement as factors that sent young people flocking to law school in unheard-of numbers in the late sixties and early seventies. As important as such events might have been in lending an ideological charge to the aspirations of many members of this first law-school stampede, it is likely that the surge in applications owed more to reproduction than to revolution. Beginning around 1968, the baby boomers started graduating from college. Combine the emergence of the largest generation in U.S. history with at least two major sociological trends—the increased access of all socioeconomic groups to higher education and the entry of women and people of color into previously inaccessible areas of the economy—and a dramatic increase in law-school applicants was inevitable.

Just as inevitable as the boom in applications during the Vietnam Era was the bust in the post–Watergate period. After reaching a peak of about 100,000 in 1975, law-school applications began a steady slide during the late seventies and early eighties. In 1984, only 65,000 people applied to law school. The correlation between this decrease and dwindling law-school-age population was nearly perfect.

Taking twenty-three as roughly the average age of law-school applicants, the chart at right indicates how neatly the applicant curve rose and fell with the generation curve throughout the period of the first law-school boom and the subsequent contraction. Had the correlation continued, the annual number of law-school applicants would have been only about 60,000 in 1991. In actuality, it was 99,327. The generation curve and the applicant curve parted company dramatically after 1985. Why?

In the late summer of 1985, *L.A. Law* premiered on NBC. That fall, law-school applications volume jumped almost 15 percent.

Could the recent decline in law-school applicants be attributed to the fact that this popular show can now only be seen in reruns? The reason behind the recent dip in law-school applications may not be known, but a few factors have been cited, most notably the increasingly competitive legal job market. An *ABA Journal* article ("Cutting Classes," 12/95), reported some grim findings from a survey by the National Association for Law Placement. The survey concluded that only 69.6 percent of the class of 1994 had full-time legal jobs six months after graduation, compared to 84.5 percent in 1985. In addition, according to a *Los Angeles Times* article ("Trial & Error: Focus Shift to a Justice System and Its Flaws," 10/8/95), the median starting salary for lawyers declined $3,000 between 1992 and 1994. Prospective students should be aware that the legal job market follows the overall economy in many respects, and although the job placement and starting salaries are presently on the downside, history tells us that they will certainly rebound. And although the application volume may not again reach the point it did in 1991, law schools will continue to have to turn away thousands of prospective students each year.

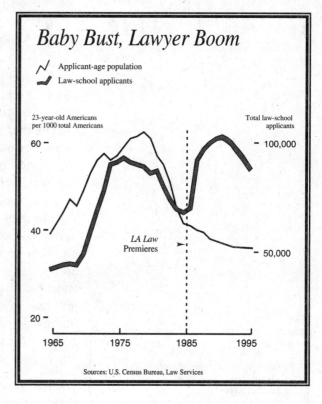

Baby Bust, Lawyer Boom

Applicant-age population
Law-school applicants

23-year-old Americans per 1000 total Americans

Total law-school applicants

LA Law Premieres

Sources: U.S. Census Bureau, Law Services

THE ADMISSIONS PROCESS

The first fact you must confront concerning your desire to go to law school is that you are not alone. Next year close to 130,000 people will be serious enough about law school to sit for the LSAT, and perhaps 90,000 of them will do well enough or maintain an interest level high enough to go ahead and apply to at least one law school. The fact is, however, that only about half of these people will end up in law school the following year. The harshest possible view of the situation is this: If you are just beginning to pursue law school, the odds are against your getting there. The more hopeful—and more realistic—view is that if you are serious, and if you are willing to put in a good deal of effort before getting any payoff, your chances of getting into law school are good. It's a good thing, too, since seriousness, assiduousness, and a willingness to delay gratification will be required if you want to survive law school once you get there.

When it comes to the actual application process, take this simple advice: Start early. All too many applicants sabotage their own efforts through last-minute sloppiness. Consider the sheer amount of time the law-school admissions process will demand: The LSAT alone can easily consume eighty or more hours of prep time, and a single application form might take upward of forty hours if you take great care with the essay questions. And indeed great care should be taken every step of the way if you are to maximize your chances of admission to the law school of your choice.

THE APPLICATION

Filling out a law-school application form is a fairly painless affair. Few of the questions that appear on these forms require much thought. Where did you go to college? When did you take the LSAT? Have you ever been convicted of a

Not Getting any Easier

Declining acceptance rates of applicants to a basket of top U.S. law schools.

1985 vs. 1991

Applicants with GPAs between 3.5 and 3.75 and LSAT scores between the 81st and 90th percentiles.

All applicants

Schools included: U. of California (Berkeley, Hastings, UCLA); Cornell:Emory; George Washington; Minnesota; NYU; Penn; U. Texas; and Wisconsin.

Source: Official Guide to U.S. Law Schools

felony or misdemeanor? Generally the sort of thing you should be able to answer off the top of your head. Every now and then, however, the drudgery is interrupted with something sneaky like "List your extra-curricular activities in order of importance," followed by two or three blank lines. It might be quietly tucked in right between "Have you ever served in the military?" and "What are your parents' professions?" in such a way that you are made to wonder if it is even considered an important question. There is something devious about the nonchalance with which a law-school application form asks you for truly personal information. Even the essay question is sometimes called "optional." The tone of the few questions that seem designed to elicit information relating to your individuality is often perfunctory. If you actually took at face value the apparent unimportance of such questions, the dossier you presented to an admissions committee would consist of little else but your college grades and your score on the LSAT. Is this really what they want?

"BEYOND THE NUMBERS"

Aside from LSAT scores and GPAs, what do law schools care about in deciding who's in and who's out? This is the eternal question. On the one hand, we should disabuse you cynics of the notion that they care about nothing else. On the other hand, those who harbor fantasies that a stunning application can overcome truly substandard scores and grades should realize that such hopes are unrealistic. It appears that, within limits, most law-school admissions committees attempt to balance their emphasis on cold, hard numbers with a good-faith effort to understand the minds of the thousands of applicants they assess. It may well be true that the law-school admissions process relies too heavily on such impersonal criteria as the LSAT, but admissions committees do give thoughtful consideration to what sort of human beings they admit.

This is particularly true at law schools that do not suffer from a lack of numerically qualified applicants. A "top ten" law school that receives ten or fifteen applications for every spot in its first-year class has no choice but to "look beyond the numbers," as admissions folks are fond of saying. Such a school will almost surely have to turn away hundreds of applicants with near-perfect LSAT scores and college grades, and those applicants who make the initial cut will be subjected to real scrutiny.

On the other end of the scale, those schools whose students are not generally among the numerical elite are just as concerned, in their own way, with "human criteria" as are those schools with an excess of high-scoring applicants. Given the vast annual surplus of applicants to law schools (see pages 54–55), all law schools are in a position to be selective. The fact is that many very capable people have relatively unimpressive GPAs and LSAT scores. The importance of the application is greatly magnified for these people, who must demonstrate their probable success in law school in other ways.

There can be little doubt that factors other than grades and test scores matter in the law-school admissions process. To what degree they matter, however, is the more important issue. Unfortunately, there can be no consistent, authoritative answer to the pragmatic question of just how much your so-called noncognitive qualifications (everything but your LSAT and GPA) help your chances of admission. In putting together your application, you should certainly regard such noncognitive factors as vitally important. For purposes of estimating your actual chances of admission to a particular school, however, it would be unrealistic to expect that your strength in such areas will get you in regardless of your grades and your LSAT score. If your grades and your LSAT score put you solidly in the running for acceptance to the school of your choice, strong nonnumerical qualifications may virtually guarantee your admission. Those same qualifications, however, will rarely be enough to make up for numbers that fall well short of a particular law school's median.

LETTERS OF RECOMMENDATION

The law schools to which you apply will require two or three letters of recommendation in support of your application. Some schools will allow you to submit as many letters as you like, while others make it clear that any more than the minimum number of letters of recommendation is unwelcome. If you've ever applied to a private school then you've gone through this before, so you know what recommendation forms usually look like. Unlike the evaluation forms for some colleges and graduate programs, however, law-school recommendation forms tend toward absolute minimalism.

All but a few recommendation forms for law-school applications ask a single, open-ended question like "What information about this applicant is relevant that is not to be found in other sources?" The generic quality of the forms from various law schools is a blessing and a curse. On the one hand, it makes it possible for your recommenders to write a single letter that will suffice for all the applications you submit. This convenience will make everyone's life much easier. On the other hand, if a free-form recommendation is to make a positive impression on an admissions committee, it must convey real knowledge of the applicant. Think carefully before choosing whom to ask to do this favor for you.

The application materials from most schools usually suggest that your letters come, whenever possible, from people in an academic setting. Some schools, however, make explicit their desire that the letters come from a professional setting if you have been out of school for a number of years. Whatever the case, your letters of recommendation should come from people who know you well enough to offer a truly informed assessment of your abilities.

An effective law-school application will present to the admissions committee a cohesive picture—not a pastiche.

If you want to maximize the contribution of your letters of recommendation to your overall application, provide your recommenders with a copy of your personal statement. The best recommendations fit neatly with the picture you present of yourself in your own essay, even when they make no specific reference to the issues it addresses. An effective law-school application will present to the admissions committee a cohesive picture—not a pastiche. The better a recommender understands the experiences that have brought you to your decision to attend law school, the better his or her recommendation will contribute to an integrated, cohesive application. (Make your mother proud: Write thank-you notes to your recommenders promptly.)

Keeping these general points in mind, you should consider some things peculiar to academic and professional recommendations:

ACADEMIC RECOMMENDATIONS

Most applicants will (and should) try to submit recommendations from current or former professors. The academic environment in law school is extremely rigorous. Admissions committees will be looking for assurance that you will be able not just to survive, but to excel. They consider strong recommendations from college professors a valuable corroboration of your ability to succeed in law school. While a perfunctory, lukewarm recommendation is unlikely to damage your overall application, it will obviously do nothing to bolster it.

First, choose at least one professor from your major field. An enthusiastic endorsement from such a professor will be taken as a sign that your choice of academic specialty was more than random. Second—and we hope that this goes without saying—your recommenders should probably be professors who do not immediately associate your name with the letter "C."

Most important, if it is at all possible, ask for recommendation letters from professors who already know you by name. Professors are quite talented at writing recommendations for students they barely know. Most consider it part of their job to do this. Even seemingly unapproachable academic titans will usually be happy to dash off a quick letter for a mere student. It is also true, however, that these same obliging professors are masters of a sort of opaque prose style that screams to an admissions officer, "I really have no idea what to say about this kid who is, in fact, a near-total stranger to me!" Although an admissions committee will not dismiss out of hand such a recommendation, they will be unlikely to consider it very seriously.

One thing in particular interests the people who will evaluate your recommendations: specifics. If a professor can make specific reference to a particular project you completed, or at least make substantive reference to your work in a particular course, the recommendation will be strengthened considerably. You should consider it your responsibility to enable your professors to do this for you. You might, for example, make available a paper you wrote for them of which you are particularly proud. Unless your professors are well-enough acquainted with you to be able to offer a very personal assessment of your potential, they will greatly appreciate a tangible reminder of your abilities on which to base their recommendation.

PROFESSIONAL RECOMMENDATIONS

If you have been out of school for some time, you will very likely be asking for recommendations not from professors, but from employers. The only problem with an application that is supported only by professional recommendations is that it renders your college grades the only indicator of your academic potential in law school. If, like most law-school applicants, you are just a few years out of college, try to submit one academic recommendation, even if it means taking time to track down an old professor and reminding him or her of your existence. Many applicants, however, have been out of school so long that securing academic recommendations is almost impossible. If you find yourself in this situation, you should give quite a bit of thought to the question of whom to ask for recommendations.

The most important general criterion on which to base that decision is the obvious one: degree of familiarity. Most law-school application materials say that a recommender should be "sufficiently familiar with the applicant to offer a careful, reasonable evaluation." In other words, recommendations should come from those who have had the opportunity to observe you over a significant period of time. The best sort of person to ask would be someone who can offer a sense not just of your ability, but of your professional development. Particularly if your professional experience is not directly related to the law—and even if it is—any recommendation from an employer should focus on accomplishments that bespeak overall competence and the ability to grow and learn. Like good academic recommendations, the most effective professional recommendations will not be limited to abstract assessments; the most effective recommendations will discuss your overall merit within the context of an ability or accomplishment of which you are particularly proud. Obviously, a copy of your personal statement will also be invaluable to the people writing in support of your application.

Like good academic recommendations, the most effective professional recommendations will not be limited to abstract assessments

THE PERSONAL STATEMENT

You will be asked quite a few questions on your application forms, but the simplest question may prove the most difficult to answer: Who are you, and why do you want to go to law school? This question, in one form or another, appears on virtually every law-school application form and often represents your only opportunity to string more than two sentences together. Aside from your numerical credentials, it is probably the most important part of your law-school application.

The personal statement is also the only element of your application over which you have total control, a fact that is both encouraging and scary. Writing about yourself often proves to be surprisingly difficult. Doing your lifetime of experiences justice in less than a thousand words is impossible. The opportunity to present yourself can easily turn into a burden if you start to think that a two-page statement must contain your entire genetic blueprint. Your goal should be much more modest.

Although some law schools set no limit on the length of the personal statement, you should not take their bait. You can be certain that your statement will be read in its entirety, but admissions officers are human, and their massive workload at admissions time has an understandable impact on their attention spans. You should limit yourself to two or, at most, three, typed, double-spaced pages. Does this make your job any easier? Not really. In fact, practical constraints on the length of your essay demand a high degree of efficiency and precision. Your essay needs to convey what kind of thinking, feeling human being you are. A two-page limit allows for absolutely no fat.

THE GOAL OF THE ESSAY

The primary goal of your personal statement stems from one potentially depressing fact: You will be competing against thousands of well-qualified applicants for admission to the law school of your choice. Rather than simply be discouraged, you should let your knowledge of this guide your work: Your primary task in writing your application will be to separate yourself from the crowd. Particularly if you are applying directly from college or if you have been out of school for a very short time, you must do your best to see that the admissions committee cannot categorize you too broadly. Admissions committees will see innumerable applications from bright twenty-two-year-olds with good grades. Your essay presents an opportunity to put those grades in context, to define and differentiate yourself.

THE CONTENT OF YOUR ESSAY

Like any good writing, your law-school application should tend toward clarity, conciseness, and candor. The first two of these qualities, clarity and conciseness, are usually the products of good methodology. Repeated critical revision by yourself and others is the surest way to trim and tune your prose. The third quality, candor, is the product of proper motivation. Honesty cannot be added in after the fact; your writing must be candid from the outset.

In writing your personal statement, you should pay particularly close attention to methodology and motivation. Admissions committees will read your essay two ways: as a product of your handiwork and as a product of your mind. Do not underestimate the importance of either perspective. A well-crafted essay will impress any admissions officer, but if it does not illuminate, it will not be remembered. Conversely, a thoughtful essay that offers true insight will stand out unmistakably, but if it is not readable, it will not receive serious consideration.

THINGS TO AVOID (OR AT LEAST THINK CAREFULLY ABOUT BEFORE) INCLUDING IN YOUR ESSAY:

"My LSAT score isn't great, but I'm just not a good test taker."

Before you say this, consider that law school is a test-rich environment. In fact, grades in most law-school courses are determined by a single exam at the semester's end. This claim does little to convince an admissions committee of your ability to succeed in law school once accepted. Consider also that a low LSAT score is one of those things that speaks for itself—all too eloquently. It doesn't need you to speak for it too. The attitude of most law-school admissions departments is that while the LSAT may be imperfect, it is equally imperfect for all applicants. That is to say that, apart from extraordinary (even if truthful) claims of things like serious illness on test day, few explanations for poor performance on the LSAT will mean much to the people who read your application. About the only situation in which a discussion of your LSAT score in your essay could possibly help you is if you have one score that is significantly better than another. If you did much better in your second sitting than in your first, or vice versa, a brief explanation doesn't hurt. Even in this scenario, however, your explanation may mean little to the committee, which may have its own hard-and-fast rules for the interpretation of multiple LSAT scores. Some schools may take a straight average, while others may give more weight to the first score or to the higher one.

The obvious and preferable alternative to an explicit discussion of such a weakness would be to focus on what you are good at. If you really are bad at standardized tests, you must be better at something else, or you wouldn't have gotten as far as you have. If you think you are a marvelous researcher, say so. If you are a wonderful writer, show it. Let your essay implicitly draw attention away from your weak points by focusing on your strengths. There is no way to convince an admissions committee that they should overlook your LSAT score. You may, however, present compelling arguments for making them look beyond it.

"My college grades weren't that high, but..."

This is a bit more complicated than the previous issue. Law school admissions committees do seem willing to listen to an applicant's interpretation of his or her college performance, but only within limits. Keep in mind that law schools require official transcripts for a reason. Members of the admissions committee will be aware of your academic credentials before they ever get to your essay. Make no mistake: If your grades are unimpressive, you should offer the admissions committee something else by which to judge your abilities. Again, the best argument for looking past your college grades is evidence of achievement in another area, whether in your LSAT score, your extracurricular activities, or your career accomplishments.

"I've always wanted to be a lawyer."

Many people seem to feel the need to point out that they really, really want to become attorneys. You will do yourself a great service by avoiding such throwaway lines, which do nothing for your essay but water it down. Do not convince yourself in a moment of desperation that claiming to have known that the law was your calling since age six will somehow move your application to the top of the pile. The admissions committee is not interested in how much you want to practice law, but it is interested in why.

The exact nature of the motivations you espouse in your personal statement may be less important than the way in which you discuss them. Nothing is as impressive to the reader of a personal statement as the ring of truth.

"I want to become a lawyer to fight injustice."

Though there surely exist some for whom this statement rings true, most people's motivations for attending law school are not so purely altruistic. Any need you may feel to profess only high-minded motives for attending law school is probably misguided. Law school admissions committees certainly do not regard the legal profession as a Saints vs. Sinners proposition, and neither should you.

Consider these facts: More than 60 percent of all law-school graduates in 1991 took jobs in private law firms while only 2 percent took public-interest jobs. Among the nearly one million practicing lawyers in the United States, there are relatively few who actually earn a living defending the indigent, saving the wetlands, or protecting our civil rights. Law schools are well aware of this, and they take the lofty goals professed by many applicants with a grain of salt. But while law school admissions committees know that the vast majority of working lawyers do little to "fight injustice" actively, they also know that these same lawyers are not slick, dishonest ambulance chasers.

If a Thurgood Marshall comes along only once a decade, a Roy Cohn comes along even less often. Do not be afraid of appearing morally moderate. If the truth of the matter is that you most want the virtual guarantee of a relatively good job that a law degree ensures, be forthright. If you can in good conscience say that you are committed to a career in the public interest, show the committee something tangible on your application and in your essay that will allow them to see your statements as more than mere assertions. If you cannot truthfully commit to a career spent Fighting the Good Fight, but you are willing to at least do your part, say so. Your essay might include a thoughtful discussion of your commitment to being a responsible, ethical professional while still being able to pay the rent. You should also realize, as the admissions committee will, that people often change their direction while in law school. The exact nature of the motivations you espouse may be less important than the way in which you discuss them. Nothing is as impressive to the reader of a personal statement as the ring of truth.

"My GPA of 3.5 from a respected university and my strong LSAT score of 165..."

It is almost always unnecessary to recapitulate your numbers in your personal essay, no matter how impressive or unimpressive they may be. For better or for worse, most law-school admissions committees group applications by grades and LSAT scores before getting to the essays. Though all schools claim not to have any cut off scores, many initially sort the hundreds or thousands of applications they receive into groups like "great chance," "some chance," and "virtually no chance." A school that does something like this will already know what they're looking for from your essay. That is to say that they already know what sort of consideration your grades and scores have earned you. The last thing the admissions committee needs to read is a laundry list of all your vital statistics.

If you know that your grades and LSAT score are strong points in your application, and if you feel it's necessary to remind the jury of this fact, be humble and subtle; don't actually mention the numbers. If you know that your grades and test scores are working against you, remember that the admissions committee knows this too. Be positive about something else; you've already got two strikes against you.

There is, however, a notable exception to this rule. If your cumulative college grade-point average hides something important, you should point this out. For instance, if one particularly bad semester or course dragged your GPA down, and if you can argue plausibly that those low grades should be viewed as anomalies, do so. If your GPA for courses in your major field is significantly higher than your overall average, you might allude to this fact. Even better, if your grade-point average masks an upward trend in your performance, make sure to call attention to your improvement. Admissions committees love this.

GRADUATE SCHOOL RECORDS

If you have attended graduate school in another discipline, you should make your records available to the law schools to which you apply. Your grades in graduate school will not be included in the calculation of your GPA (the LSDAS reports only the UGPA, the Undergraduate Grade Point Average), but will be taken into account separately by an admissions committee if you make them available. Reporting grad-school grades would be to your advantage, particularly if they are better than your college grades. Admissions committees are likely to take this as a sign of maturation.

WORK EXPERIENCE—IN COLLEGE

Most law-school applications will ask you to list any part-time jobs you held while you were in college and how many hours per week you worked. This should come as good news to those who had to (or chose to) work their way through college. A great number of law schools make it clear that they take your work commitments as a college student into consideration when evaluating your UGPA.

WORK EXPERIENCE—REAL LIFE

One of the great all-time catchphrases in law-school admissions brochures is "significant professional accomplishments." So many schools boast of their students pre–law school career achievements that one wonders where so many 23-year-olds found their killer jobs. In most cases this catchphrase might mean simply "held down a steady job for a couple of years," but you can be sure that the student bodies at the super-elite law schools are populated with some mighty impressive young men and women.

All law-school applications will ask you about your work experience out of college. They will give you three or four lines on which to list such experience. Some schools will invite you to submit a résumé. If you have a very good one, this is a marvelous idea. In any case, your only opportunity to discuss your experience meaningfully is in your personal statement. What sort of job you've had is not as important as you might think. What interests the admissions committee is what you have made of that job, and what it has made of you.

Whatever your job was or is, you would do well to offer credible evidence for your competence. Mentioning in your personal statement your job advancement or any increase in your responsibility is a very good idea. Your ability to present your professional experience in a fashion that lends context to your decision to attend law school, however, may be what matters most. This does not mean that you need to offer a geometric proof of how your experience in the workplace has led you inexorably to a career in the law. You need only explain truthfully how this experience influenced you and how its effects fit into your thinking about law school.

COMMUNITY INVOLVEMENT

An overwhelming majority of law schools single out community involvement as one of several specific noncognitive factors that are influential in making admissions decisions. Law schools would like to admit applicants who show a long-standing commitment to something other than their own advancement. It is certainly understandable that law schools would wish to determine the level of such commitment before admitting an applicant, particularly since so few law students go on to practice public interest law. Be forewarned, however, that nothing is so obviously bogus as an insincere statement of a commitment to public-interest issues. Admissions committees are well aware that very few people take the time out of their lives to become involved significantly in their communities.

Law School Admissions Goes Electronic

Law school admission is finally moving onto the "information superhighway." Here are a couple of ways to use your computer to best effect.

LOOKING FOR LAW SCHOOLS ON-LINE

First off, we at The Princeton Review have put up a lot of information about law schools and law school admissions through our on-line services on the Internet, America Online, and the Microsoft Network.

The Internet (and particularly, the World Wide Web) is the most informative of all on-line sources, because the law schools themselves have posted information there. You can connect to the 'net through an Internet service provider or through commercial services such as America Online, CompuServe, or Prodigy (if you've never played with the Internet, you'll find these last three companies the easiest way). Once you're on the Internet, you can reach the schools directly (we've listed each law school's address at the bottom right of its entry.)

Note that the Internet and the Web change every day—content is added or deleted, and sites change their look and feel regularly. Addresses (known as URLs) change; some sites disappear completely. All of the URLs that we have provided here were accurate and functioning at the time of publication, but the best way to find schools is through our own World Wide Web site. (For those without a speedy PC, we have a text-only Gopher server, too.) We've set up a search engine, and posted some of the information in this book, so you can access virtually every college and university Web site by just clicking. We've also posted useful (we hope) career and internship advice, information about all of our books and software, an extensive phone list of useful numbers, and hotlinks to our favorite educational sites on the Internet.

Our board on America Online offers more information, and a very different look and feel. One of the most popular features of these boards is our Student Message areas, where you can create your own topic folders and post questions for other students and for our own on-line admissions and testing experts. We also schedule live on-line forums where you can get answers in real time to your questions about admission, testing, and just about anything else to do with law school direct from our experts and special guests. We have recently launched our newest on-line board on the Microsoft Network.

To reach The Princeton Review at any of these sites, or to eMail us, use the following addresses:

- eMail: info@review.com

- World Wide Web: http://www.review.com

- America Online: keyword "student"

- Gopher: bloggs.review.com

- Microsoft Network: eMail us for the address

APPLYING TO LAW SCHOOL VIA ELECTRONIC APPLICATION

Once you've gathered all the information that you need about the schools and have decided where to apply, you may not need to leave your computer keyboard. Just a handful of years ago, electronic applications were never going to happen. Today, law schools are scrambling to make electronic versions of their applications available. The law schools that currently accept electronic applications are identified in our write-ups by the icon you see at left.

We've come across an excellent package of electronic applications. Law Multi-App is available for Windows and allows you to fill out your applications on screen, print, and submit them directly to the admissions offices.

In addition to printing out perfect duplicates of the regular applications, Law Multi-App has a clever data entry mechanism that allows you to fill out common application information only once. Law Multi-App is $45 for a package of fifty law schools (a 10% discount from its normal price; you must mention this book to get that discount), plus shipping. To order, call them at 800/515-2927 or 610/544-7197, e-mail them at mcs@ot.com, fax them at 610/544-9877, or write them at MCS, 740 South Chester Road, Suite F, Swarthmore, PA 19081.

A final note of advice: even if you fill out the application electronically, you should still contact the admissions office for an application packet. This is the only way that you can be sure to have all the information and materials that you need to put together the strongest candidacy possible. Despite the increasing on-line presence of law schools and the convenience of the electronic medium, "snail mail" remains an integral part of the process.

THE LAW SCHOOL ADMISSIONS TEST

When it was first devised, the Law School Admissions Test was intended to do the obvious: to offer law-school admissions committees an objective measure of an applicant's aptitude for studying law. "Measuring aptitude" with a No. 2 pencil in three and a half hours is, of course, a bit like trying to nail jelly to a wall. As its shortcomings became more apparent, the LSAT evolved and its mandate was revised. Today the LSAT administrators are careful to claim only that the test, when used in combination with other criteria—like college grades—is a useful predictor of a student's performance in the first year of law school. They do not claim that it can tell how good a lawyer you will be. They claim only that it can predict what sort of grades you might get in first-year Torts.

First administered in 1947 to 6,882 aspiring law students, nearly all of them white and male, the LSAT today is given to about 130,000 people a year, almost half of them women. In the years since it was introduced, the content and format of the LSAT have changed numerous times. Most lawyers now in practice would recognize little in today's LSAT. In its current incarnation, the Law School Admissions Test is a four-hour, three-subject, brain-scorching torture session. And for better or for worse, this half-day exam may do more to decide where and whether you go to law school than anything else.

THE CONTENT

If you expect this test to offer you some insight into the skills used and work done by attorneys, adjust your expectations. In fact, the LSAT may do nothing more than dredge up unhappy memories of junior high school algebra or geometry assignments that made you frustrated enough to scream, "When will I ever have to use this stuff?!" On the other hand, if you are the type who relishes a puzzle or who can't resist joining a good argument, you may be in for a treat.

LOGICAL REASONING, OR "ARGUMENTS"

This section of the test is the one many find the least objectionable. Every question in this section refers to a short passage of about one hundred words. The passages deal with every imaginable subject in the universe, from fossilized bees to left-handedness among the elderly. The questions ask you to respond in some way to an argument posed in the passage. You may be asked, for example, to identify a statement that weakens or strengthens the argument, or that represents a reasonable inference that can be drawn from the argument. Other, stranger questions will ask you to assess the cause of a disagreement between two speakers in a dialogue or to identify two arguments that share a similar kind of reasoning. The LSAT now has two 35-minute sections of arguments, each of which usually contains between 24 and 26 questions that refer to between 21 and 23 arguments.

ANALYTICAL REASONING, OR "GAMES"

This section is generally the most despised on the LSAT and, perhaps, on all standardized tests. In the analytical reasoning section, you will be forced to grapple with four separate sets of conditions, or "games." Anywhere from five to seven questions follow each game. On the basis of a set of clues provided (e.g., "A cannot sit next to B" or "If B sits next to A, then C cannot speak Finnish"), you will answer questions about the possible arrangements, qualities, etc., of the elements discussed. According to the LSAT, these games "simulate the kinds of detailed analyses of relationships that a law student must perform in solving legal problems." On the surface, at least, it is difficult to see how this could be true for a game that asks you to arrange poodles in pens or to determine what kind of fish to serve a dinner guest.

READING COMPREHENSION

Reviled by generations of standardized-test takers, this exercise in attention-span management should already be familiar to you. On the LSAT, you will confront four passages, each roughly 450 words long and each followed by six to eight questions. You can be sure that the subject matter of these passages will be less than thrilling. You may struggle as much with staying involved and awake as with answering the questions. As a saving grace, the variety of topics is wide (anything from political economy to invertebrate biology), so there is always the proverbial snowball's chance in hell that you will find a passage to your liking.

WRITING SAMPLE, OR "NAP TIME"

This thirty-minute addendum to your already long test-taking day is meant to provide law schools with a means to assess your ability to organize your thoughts and write skillfully. Yeah, right. If you think that Harvard is going to read 10,000 handwritten versions of an essay on whether Rita the Reporter should take the Small Job in the Big City or the Big Job in the Small City, you are greatly overestimating the size and patience of its staff. Admissions committees will already have in hand at least one substantial piece of your work (your Personal Statement) and are unlikely to turn to your LSAT writing sample when scrutinizing your application. Chances are that this section was added to answer the test's critics. Many people have criticized the LSAT for focusing too narrowly on a set of skills that are at best only somewhat analogous to the skills an attorney applies in her work. Of course, this does not mean that you should skip it, merely that you should not sweat about it.

THE LSAT SCORE

The 120 to 180 scale on which the LSAT is scored is the third scale to be used in the test's history. From its inception in 1947 until the early eighties, the LSAT employed the 200 to 800 scale familiar to everyone who has taken the SAT. On the LSAT, however, scores like 553 and 709 were possible, which meant that there was a total of 601 possible scores. Since there were only slightly more than 100 questions on the exam, the apparent precision of the three-digit scores was misleading. Admissions committees could not tell any meaningful difference between, say, a 613 and a 620, since only one correct answer may have separated those two scores. So the LSAT was recalibrated to a scale that ranged from 10 to 48, for a total of 39 possible scores on about a 100-

question test. This scale lasted until June 1991, when the current scale was introduced along with a slightly revised test format.

The change to the 120 to 180 scale was much more than cosmetic and was necessitated by at least two developments. First, the June 1991 test was given in a new format. The range of subject matter on the test remained the same, but the relative weight assigned to each type of question was altered. From 1988 to 1991, the test had consisted of three sections of equal duration (45 minutes), with one section of each question type. The new test consisted of four 35-minute sections, two of them Analytical Reasoning ("Arguments") and one each of Reading Comprehension and Logical Reasoning ("Games"). Yes, the change was less than radical, but the fact that the shift to an increased emphasis on the Arguments section was made at all indicates its significance in the eyes of the powers-that-be. The LSAT then faced the problem of reporting in an unconfusing fashion the scores of people who had taken very different tests. (Since LSAT scores remain valid for five years, people who would be applying to law school between 1991 and 1995 could have taken substantially different tests.) Naturally, the LSAT had to change its scoring scale to avoid confusion between scores earned on the old and new formats.

FIGHTING INFLATION

The second reason for the scoring change was surely the more significant. In fact, it probably motivated the change in the first place. To put it bluntly, in the years leading up to 1991, too many people were doing well on the LSAT. By 1991, a score of 40 on the LSAT corresponded to about the 85th percentile of all test takers. That is to say, 15 percent of the country was scoring 40 or higher. The problem with this was that from 40 to 48 there were only nine possible scores to be shared by roughly 19,000 "elite" test-takers. Furthermore, a "perfect" score of 48 corresponded to the 99.5th percentile, indicating that roughly 650 test-takers received such a score.

Why was this a problem? Put yourself in the shoes of an admissions officer at an Ivy League law school that enrolls roughly 185 new students each year. Most of the applica-

The LSAT Curve Steepens

A comparison of the old LSAT scoring distribution
with the new anti-score inflation curve

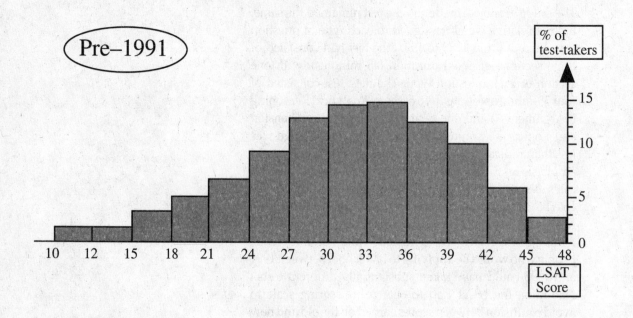

Pre–1991

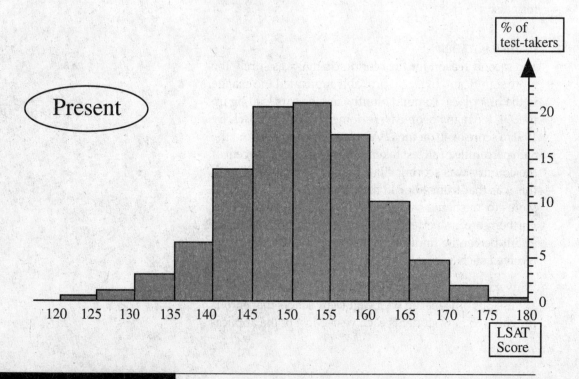

Present

tions you see will be from people who scored in the top 15 percent on the LSAT, and you must reject many of them. Obviously, it would be helpful to you if you could compare conscientiously one LSAT score to another within this top 15 percent. If there are only nine possible scores in this range, you will have great difficulty doing so.

Now put yourself in the shoes of the person in charge at LSAT headquarters. You have a product to sell, or, rather, a monopoly to preserve. You certainly don't want your most powerful customers to become dissatisfied with the service you provide. After all, you've got kids to feed. The twenty thousand humans that you have classified as elite could fill half of all the seats available each year in U.S. law schools, yet you offer your customers only nine scoring units with which to differentiate among these twenty thousand. To compound this, you call "perfect" roughly 650 test takers, nearly enough people to fill the entire first-year classes at Harvard and Yale. You've got a problem.

When the LSAT and law schools faced this situation in 1991, their solution was not simply to create twenty-two more possible scores by switching from the 10 to 48 to the 120 to 180 scale. They also changed the curve significantly to fight the "score inflation" of recent years in order to allow admissions officers at the top law schools to differentiate more easily among the great number of high-scoring applicants they assess. On the new scale, a score of 160 falls at or about the 85th percentile and a score of 140 at or about the 15th.

In one fell swoop, the LSAT's score inflation problem was solved. As you can see on the next page, the old curve was far shallower, with far more people scoring at either extreme than do so under the new format. On the current scale, the middle of the curve is packed tight, and very few people score at the extremes. Perhaps more important, there are now twenty-one scoring slots for the top 15 percent of the country (from 160 to 180), more than twice what there were under the 10 to 48 scale. Furthermore, a perfect score of 180 in the current format corresponds to a percentile of 99.9+, into which perhaps a few dozen test takers will fall annually. In 1991, perfect LSAT scorers could have filled Harvard's first-year class; now they would have a hard time fielding a softball team.

LSAT Score Conversion Scale

This conversion scale is based on the reported percentile equivalencies for versions of the LSAT given between 1988 and 1991. The exact percentile of a given score will vary with each test form, but only slightly. For purposes of estimating your chances of admission to a particular law school, such and approximation is more than close enough.

Do not think, however, that these changes are relevant only to those who score near the top of the curve. An understanding of the LSAT curve is important to all people taking the test, not just to the lucky few who fall in the top 15 percent. If, like most people who take this test, you have grown accustomed to relative academic success and have very good reason to believe in your own intelligence and capabilities, you may well be disappointed by your first LSAT score. As you can see, the vast majority of test takers (roughly 70 percent) will score between 140 and 160. Statistically speaking, the chances are very good that you would fall somewhere in this range if you were to take an LSAT today. The natural human tendency might be to regard such a performance as hopelessly mediocre. But it ain't necessarily so.

Imagine, for instance, that you got a 155 your first time out. Aesthetically, this may not be a very satisfying score. It may look to you just like a 150—the middle of the curve and approximately the national average. You would do yourself a disservice, however, to react so negatively. A 155 corresponds roughly to the 67th percentile, a far sight better than the 50th. Say you were to take the test again and get a 158. An increase of three points is not generally the sort of improvement that inspires elation, yet on the LSAT, this jump from 155 to 158 would represent an increase of roughly 10 percentile points. In other words, to achieve this gain would be to put behind you a very important 10 percent of the country, to leapfrog roughly ten thousand fellow test-takers and eventual law-school applicants.

For your own sanity, it is important to realize that most people will score in the 140 to 160 range and that every point difference in this range is very significant. If you want a better idea of what your score means (or will mean), the chart on the left shows the approximate percentile rank of all the scores from 120 to 180.

ADMISSIONS INDEXING: THE MAGIC CALCULUS OF HUMAN POTENTIAL

You might reasonably wonder why the LSAT is scored on a scale from 120 to 180. Why not simply 1–100, or 17–93? Although the choice of scale might seem to be a random one, there is always some method to the madness of those who devise the LSAT. The probable reason for the choice of a scale from 120 to 180 is its mathematical compatibility with a totally different value. Here's what we mean:

Write down your cumulative college grade-point average. (If you do not know it exactly, or if your school did not use the four-point scale, estimate or calculate it using the chart on the right):

After you take your three-digit GPA, multiply it by 20, add 100, and round off the decimal, you should see something that looks familiar. You now have a number on the same scale as the LSAT that can be added directly to your LSAT score to create a handy admissions index. For instance, if you have an LSAT score of 155 and an undergraduate GPA of 3.40, your admissions index would be 323 out of a possible 360.

Admissions committees at the law schools to which you apply will do something very much like this when they process your application. In actuality, each school will crunch its numbers in an idiosyncratic way. Law Services will calculate a suggested formula for each law school based on the past correlation between entering students' GPAs and LSAT scores and their first year's grades in law school. Different schools adhere to different indexing formulas, formulas that accord different weight to an applicant's LSAT score and undergraduate GPA. The particular fashion in which a law school creates its index should not be a matter of great concern to you, however, since it is only relative differences among applicants that matter, and every student will be subjected to exactly the same formula.

For purposes of estimating your chances of admission to a certain law school you can use the formula suggested above, which gives your GPA and your LSAT score equal weight. It is by no means unlikely that the schools you apply to will use exactly the same method. Refer to the school-by-school listings in this book to get an idea where you stand in relation to most students accepted by a particular school.

UGPA Calculation

Use this chart to calculate your undergraduate GPA on the scale used by the LSDAS. Your UGPA must include grades earned at any and all undergraduate institutions you've attended. No grades earned in graduate school may be included.

GRADE			Cumulative Units	4.0 Scale	Grade Points
A+	1+	98-100	×	4.33 =	
A	1	93-97	×	4.00 =	
A-	1-	90-92	×	3.67 =	
AB			×	3.50 =	
B+	2+	87-89	×	3.33 =	
B	2	83-86	×	3.00 =	
B-	2-	80-82	×	2.67 =	
BC			×	2.50 =	
C-	3+	77-79	×	2.33 =	
C	3	73-76	×	2.00 =	
C-	3-	70-72	×	1.67 =	
CD			×	1.50 =	
D+	4+	67-69	×	1.33 =	
D	4	63-66	×	1.00 =	
D-	4-	60-62	×	0.67 =	
DE, DF			×	0.50 =	
EF	5	<60	×	0.00 =	

Total =   Total =

Total Grade Points   Total Units   =   .

UGPA

Your result should be a number between 0 and 4 rounded off to two decimal places. You can use this value to calculate your Admissions Index, the combination of your UGPA and LSAT score that the school-by-school section of this book will use to indicate a school's relative selectivity in admissions.

THE LSAT: AN EQUAL OPPORTUNITY NIGHTMARE?

The way to find out whether a boy [sic] has the makings of a competent lawyer is to see what he can do in a first year of law studies.

—JOHN HENRY WIGMORE, *JURISTIC PSYCHOPOLYMETROLOGY—OR HOW TO FIND OUT WHETHER A BOY HAS THE MAKINGS OF A LAWYER,* 1929

No one understands the LSAT's limitations better than the LSAT itself. Law Services takes great pains to point out the imperfection of the test as a true barometer of academic potential. The disclaimer that is generally offered by the LSAT is that an applicant's score should not be used alone either to grant or to deny admission. It warns specifically of the dangers of setting absolute cutoff points in assessing applications. Several years ago, the LSAT downgraded itself from a predictor of law-school success to a predictor of first-year law-school success. This seemingly modest change put the defenders of the LSAT on much firmer ground, statistically if not morally.

From a coldly pragmatic point of view, the question of the LSAT's fairness is irrelevant, since you have no choice but to take it. But if you do not perform up to your own expectations on this exam you may take some solace in the fact that the LSAT is far from perfect. A low LSAT score is no more an indication of inadequacy than a high LSAT score is of genius.

HOW TO PREPARE

When we were in high school, we all heard the stories about the friend of a friend who overcame a woeful lack of preparation and sleep to ace the SAT, usually while tripping on acid. An informal survey of SAT survivors from coast to coast reveals that whoever this guy was, he sure told a lot of people of his exploits. It probably wouldn't have taken much reflection to see the story for the myth that it was, yet most of us passed it along, usually with the addition of a few flourishes ("He finished in twenty minutes," "He drew the starship Enterprise with the bubbles on his answer sheet.") Somehow, the belief that somebody somewhere had made a mockery of the system gave us all hope. Of course, most of us didn't take the story seriously enough to follow the hero's training regimen, except for the part about no sleep.

Perhaps you will also remember the relief you felt when the SAT was over and you could console yourself with the thought that you would never have to subject yourself to such torture again. Ah, youth. It has now been four, fourteen, maybe even forty, years since you last scoured your room for a No. 2 pencil in preparation for an ETS exam, and you're about to do it all over again.

In retrospect, of course, the SAT probably did little or nothing to significantly affect your future. Most people were accepted or rejected by colleges on the basis of much more than a test score. The truly depressing thing about the LSAT is that this time you'd be much closer to the truth to think that the results will determine your future. The LSAT is a major—perhaps even the major—determining factor for some applicants at every law school, and the law school you attend will have a great effect on at least the early stages of your law career. That said, it must also be pointed out that the surest way to psych yourself out on the LSAT is to think too much about its importance. There's a fine line between respecting the test's importance and fearing it, but it's a line you have to draw.

In any event, not to prepare at all for the LSAT would be a great mistake. Even those who will ultimately score very high on this strange exam will not do their best the first time around. At the very least, you should purchase copies of several LSATs (called Prep Tests) through Law Services and work through them in their entirety while timing yourself. Statistics released by the administrators of the LSAT indicate that this is the method of choice for the highest scorers. That statistic, however, is misleading, since it is the high-scoring type who is most likely to eschew more organized preparation in the first place. The most expensive, but probably the best, option for those who find the test vexing at first is to take a private preparation course. Courses like those offered by The Princeton Review force students to immerse themselves in the exam in a way that many would find difficult to do on their own.

MONEY MATTERS

[You'll get] a base salary of eighty thousand the first year, plus bonuses. Eighty-five the second year, plus bonuses. A low-interest mortgage so you can buy a house. Two country club memberships. And a new BMW. You pick the color of course. . . . All of our partners are millionaires by the age of forty-five.

—*The Firm*, John Grisham

In John Grisham's first million-seller, *The Firm*, a Harvard Law School graduate receives a job offer he can't refuse. The young Wall Street–bound protagonist lets pots of money and perks galore lure him to Memphis, Tennessee, where he learns in a rather dramatic way the lesson that most Wall Street–bound attorneys eventually learn: Expense accounts notwithstanding, there is no such thing as a free lunch.

You would probably be lying if you claimed that even in your most private moments you never, ever, thought about how much money you could make as a lawyer. On the other hand, you would be despicable if you claimed never to think of anything else. You probably reside somewhere on the motivational spectrum between unmitigated greed and uncompromising altruism, right along with the rest of us. However large the dollar signs in your eyes are, you should be aware of two things: Becoming a lawyer costs a great deal of time and money, and being a lawyer carries some not-so-hidden costs.

Simply stated, lawyers are extremely well paid. They are, on average, better compensated than any other professionals in the United States, including doctors. Prospective law students should know, however, that the average starting salary of attorneys has taken a downward turn, declining by $3,000 between 1992 and 1994. There is extreme varia-

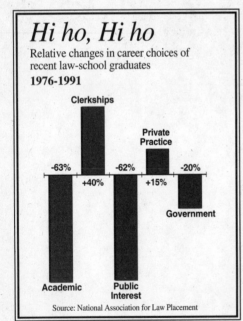

Hi ho, Hi ho

Relative changes in career choices of recent law-school graduates
1976-1991

Source: National Association for Law Placement

tion in the salaries lawyers earn, but a law degree represents one of very few surefire guarantees of a reasonably high standard of living. The highest-paid young lawyers can earn upward of eighty thousand dollars in their first year out of school. For every lifestyle bonus that a lawyer's comfortable salary can provide, however, there is an associated sacrifice. Six-figure salaries are not all that await Wall Street's young lions; young associates in large, big-city law firms earn their keep, often with many years of seventy-hour work weeks. It is hoped that you have taken these matters into consideration before deciding on a career in the law.

For the time being, however, you are probably less concerned with the long-term lifestyle costs associated with being an attorney than with something much more immediate: the opportunity costs. Before you ever collect a paycheck as an attorney, after all, you will have to expend enormous resources.

A student entering law school in 1993 can expect her total bill for three years of law school to range anywhere from $30,000 at a public institution in an area with a relatively low cost of living to upward of $100,000 at some private schools. Add to this three years of lost earnings, and you are looking at what may prove to be the largest investment you will ever make that doesn't come with a roof. The decision as to whether the law degree is worth this much is entirely subjective, so we will spare you the obvious rhetoric about investing in your future and concentrate instead on the nuts and bolts.

HOW TO PAY FOR LAW SCHOOL: THE $64,000 (OR MORE) QUESTION

At the outset of this section, it should be stressed that this is an issue that cannot be treated exhaustively in a few pages. We will at the very least, however, try to sketch the various subissues that fall under this heading. There are those for whom financing a legal education is not the primary concern. If you are not one of these lucky few, you will want to follow up on the information that follows with your own particular needs in mind. Wherever possible, we will refer you to another information source that may assist you in this effort.

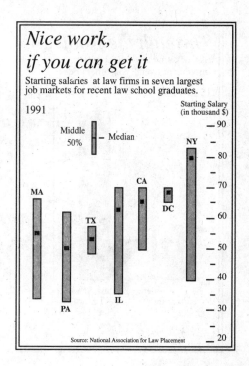

Nice work, if you can get it

Starting salaries at law firms in seven largest job markets for recent law school graduates.

1991

Source: National Association for Law Placement

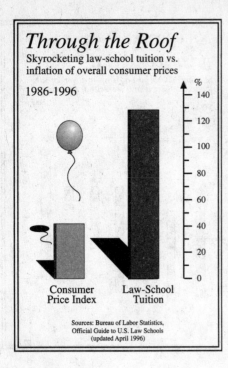

Through the Roof
Skyrocketing law-school tuition vs.
inflation of overall consumer prices

1986-1996

%
— 140
— 120
— 100
— 80
— 60
— 40
— 20
— 0

Consumer Price Index   Law-School Tuition

Sources: Bureau of Labor Statistics,
Official Guide to U.S. Law Schools
(updated April 1996)

There are really three interrelated questions that you must answer:

1. How much will law school cost you?

2. How will you pay the bill?
    and since the answer to question 2 will generally be through loans—

3. How will you pay it back?

None of these questions has a simple answer.

FIRST THINGS FIRST: HOW MUCH?

How much law school will cost you is a factor of more than just the tuition a school charges. Not all schools have equal financial resources to offer students in need of assistance. Furthermore, the amount of aid that a particular student will be offered by two schools will vary according to the policies of the schools in question. The result is that a degree from a seemingly inexpensive school can prove more costly than a degree from a school that charges a higher tuition fee.

FEDERAL FINANCIAL AID: THE FAMILY CONTRIBUTION

It is very difficult to make more than a rough estimate of what it will cost you to attend a particular law school. Indeed, until you receive a financial-aid statement from a law school to which you have been admitted, it may be impossible to know with any accuracy what your final bill might be. To determine your eligibility for the most common sources of aid (e.g., the Stafford Loan), law schools will apply what is called the Congressional Methodology. In a nutshell, this set of criteria set forth by the federal government uses your statement of income, assets, and financial liabilities to determine what is called your Family Contribution. This is the amount of money that a law school will expect you (and, if applicable, your spouse) to contribute to the financing of your legal education. Since it does not include the Parental Contribution (PC), however, the Family Contribution (FC) is sort of a misnomer for many applicants coming directly out of college and for all applicants to certain schools.

Many people consider these schools to be the top ten in the nation. As subjective as that judgment may be, one thing is certain: These schools have taken more advantage than most of the current sellers' market. Demand for spots in these ten schools continues to increase despite skyrocketing tuition.

SCHOOL	1986	1996	% INCREASE
Yale University	$9,900	$21,100	113%
Harvard University	$9,400	$21,700	131%
University of Chicago	$10,200	$20,499	101%
Stanford University	$10,006	$21,204	112%
Columbia University	$10,800	$23,818	121%
University of Michigan (out of state)	$8,590	$22,020	156%
New York University	$10,200	$22,144	117%
University of Virginia (out of state)	$5,814	$19,178	230%
Duke University	$9,393	$22,300	137%
University of Pennsylvania	$10,280	$20,664	101%
Average	$9,458	$21,463	127%

Total increase over the same period in the Consumer Price Index: only 41%

PARENTAL CONTRIBUTION

If you have never applied for financial aid in the past and are operating under the assumption that, as a tax-paying grown-up x number of years out of school, you will be recognized as the self-supporting adult that you are, well, you've got some growing up to do. Veterans of financial-aid battles past will not be surprised to hear that financial-aid offices have a difficult time recognizing when apron strings have legitimately been cut. Some schools will consider your parents' income in determining your eligibility for financial aid, regardless of your age or tax status. Policies vary widely, so be sure to ask the schools you consider exactly what their policies are regarding financial independence for the purposes of financial aid.

Only federal financial-aid standards for independence are simple and consistent. You will be considered independent for purposes of federal aid (e.g., Perkins or Stafford loan programs) if you will not be claimed by a parent or legal guardian on an income-tax return for the award year or if you are any ONE of the following:

- 24 or older by December 31 of the year in which an academic year begins (called the award year)

- an orphan or ward of the court

- a U.S. armed forces veteran

You are also automatically considered independent for federal financial aid if you have legal dependents of your own, other than your spouse. Again, these standards apply only to federal financial aid (Stafford and Perkins loans).

IF YOU HAVE TO ASK...

The basic point we are trying to make is that the real cost to you of attending law school depends on more than just the tuition charged by the school you choose to attend. Sooner or later, however, you do have to peek at the price tag. Get ready, it's not pretty.

A sampling of ten elite law schools tells the story (see inset). It's always inspiring to see the law of supply and demand at work, except when you're the one demanding and somebody else has his hands on the supply. Nowhere, perhaps, are free-market forces more readily observable than in the fees charged by America's institutions of higher education. The average increase in tuition at these schools between 1986 and 1992 was 75 percent, a rate of increase two and a half times as high as inflation in the same period. Unfortunately for the bargain hunter, no schools increased their fees more than the top public schools did. The nonresident fees at what are generally regarded as the top two public law schools in the United States, Michigan and Virginia, now approach the tuition charged in the Ivy League.

These numbers should do more than just make you angry that you didn't go to law school ten years ago. They should also alert you to the fact that the law-school tuition fees you see printed here and elsewhere are not just subject to change, but will definitely go higher. The schools listed above have increased their fees by an average of over 10 percent per year over a ten-year period in which inflation averaged only 4.1 percent. It is quite possible, of course, that prices will not continue to rise as sharply as they have in recent years. Unfortunately, it is no less likely that the salaries earned by recent law school graduates will fail to keep up.

SOURCES OF AID

Anyone who has ever considered applying to a private school has probably encountered the nearly universal financial-aid-office maxim that no student who is accepted to a school will be denied the opportunity to attend that school due to financial constraints. You will hear the same thing from law schools. Of course, anyone who has actually attended a private school on the financial-aid plan has further discovered that this noble principle of equal access does not generally translate to cash handouts. In the case of law school, too, there is no such thing as a free lunch. The bill will ultimately be yours, and it may be very large, but you will find no shortage of folks willing to cover the tab for now. Don't let it go to your head. You see, law students are very good credit risks.

The particular terms of your own financial-aid package are likely to be complex, and as a result, are impossible to predict with certainty. To be sure, the common denominator for nearly everyone is debt with a capital "D," but not all debt, as you shall see, is created equal.

The most common sources of financial aid to law students are several loan programs, which we will describe briefly. Not all schools have access to all of these funds, and some schools offer additional sources of aid not listed here. To get a general idea of the availability of aid at a given school, check its catalog. If you are serious about attending a particular school, you will, of course, need to contact its financial-aid office directly for reliable information on just how much aid you may stand to receive.

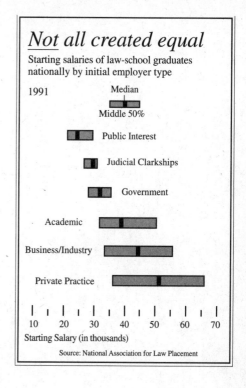

Not all created equal

Starting salaries of law-school graduates nationally by initial employer type

Starting Salary (in thousands)

Source: National Association for Law Placement

THE PERKINS LOAN

This need-based, federally funded loan is about as close as it gets to free money for law students. It is awarded by an individual school on the basis of the Federal Methodology for need assessment described earlier.

- Rate: 5 percent

- Amount: $5,000 per year cumulative $30,000 maximum, including any residual undergraduate Perkins debt

- Term: Ten years maximum after repayment begins

- Standard Deferment: Interest begins to accrue upon beginning repayment.

- Grace Period: Granted upon application, nine months post-graduation

- Minimum Payment: $30–40/month

- Sources: You will apply for the Perkins directly with the school you choose to attend. Perkins funds are limited everywhere and nonexistent in some places. Each individual school has control over the size and number of the Perkins loans it awards.

OTHER LOAN PROGRAMS

Currently, the Stafford, Supplemental Loan, and Law Access Loan programs are the source of most law students' loans, but the program is being phased out in favor of the William D. Ford Federal Direct Loan program, which will eliminate banks entirely from the lending process. Beginning in 1995, the Stafford was merged with the Supplemental Student Loan, and the details of the new loan's terms closely resemble the previous terms of the combined loans. Due to all of these changes, each school may have its own lending process, but you can expect to find these basic parameters.

THE STAFFORD LOAN

The Stafford Loan is more widely available than the Perkins. Stafford Loans are either subsidized or unsubsidized. A subsidized loan is awarded on the basis of financial need. The federal government pays interest on the loan until you begin repayment. An unsubsidized loan is not awarded on the basis of need. You'll be charged interest from the time the loan is disbursed until it is paid in full. You can receive a subsidized loan and an unsubsidized loan for the same enrollment period. The amount available is greater than under the Perkins program, but the interest rate is nearly twice as high. Before Ronald Reagan got to it, the Stafford was the Guaranteed Student Loan (GSL), and almost anybody could get one. But a lot of people decided not to pay it back, *60 Minutes* did an exposé, and the rest is history. The loan is now made by an outside lender (like your regular bank), but it is guaranteed by an independent agency and insured by the federal government.

- Rates: New Loans—variable interest rate with a 9% cap. (If you already carry Stafford or GSL debt at 7, 8, or 9 percent, any additional Stafford loan will be made at that rate.)

- Additional Fees: They stick it to you here on the Stafford. The lender may charge an "origination fee" of up to 5 percent and an "Insurance Premium" of up to 3 percent. These amounts are deducted automatically from the amount you receive but not from the amount you owe.

- Amount Available: Maximum $18,500 per year; maximum subsidized $8,500 per year. Cumulative maximum (including any residual Stafford or GSL debt): $138,500 (no more than $65,500 of this amount may be in subsidized loans).

- Standard Deferment: Interest starts to accrue upon beginning repayment for subsidized loans and on disbursement for unsubsidized loans

- Term: ten years maximum after repayment of principal begins

- Grace Period: By application, generally six months postgraduation

- Minimum Payment: $50/month

- Sources: You can apply for the Stafford loan through a bank, a credit union, or possibly through the school you attend, but the easiest way to apply is through the Access Group (next page).

THE SUPPLEMENTAL STUDENT LOAN (SLS)

Quite a bit closer to the real world, the SLS is guaranteed by the feds but issued by a private lender at a variable rate. Eligibility for the SLS, which is often used by students to cover the estimated Parental Contribution (PC) discussed earlier, is not based on need. In almost every respect, however, its terms are significantly less favorable than those of either the Perkins or the Stafford.

- Rate: 52-week T-Bill rate on June 1st plus 3.25 percent, capped at 12 percent. (In 1991, the rate was 11.49 percent.)

- Additional Fees: No origination fee, but a possible insurance fee of up to 3 percent to be deducted from the loan's proceeds but (of course) not from the amount owed

- Amount Available: Maximum $4,000 per year. Cumulative $20,000 maximum (including any residual undergraduate SLS debt)

- Term: Ten years postgraduation maximum

- Standard Deferment: Interest begins to accrue with the origination of the loan. Furthermore, only payments on the principal can be deferred until after graduation. This means that you may have to make payments while still in school. An exception to this rule is SLS loans taken through the Access Group, which in some cases will allow interest payments to be postponed until repayment of the principal begins. In any case, interest continues to accrue.

- Grace Period: None, though recipients of the SLS through Law Access may apply for a six-month grace period.

- Minimum Payment: $50/ month

- Sources: Banks, savings and loans, credit unions, Law Access.

THE LAW ACCESS LOAN (LAL)

The Law Access Loan is administered by the Access Group, the largest provider of private law school loans in the country, offering graduate and professional student loan financing to those in all disciplines. The LAL itself is very similar to the SLS; it is not need-based and its rate varies with the Treasury Bill rate. Applicants for the LAL are expected, however, to have clean credit histories and to apply for the Stafford and SLS first. Conveniently, LAL applicants can apply for the Stafford and the SLS through the Access Group itself, which can supply you with a handy packet containing all three applications.

- Rate: Varies quarterly. Ninety-one-day T-Bill rate plus 3.25 percent with no cap. The average rate has recently hovered around 11 percent.

- Additional Fees: Deducted from the proceeds of the loan are a guaranty fee of 11 percent [!] (7 percent at disbursement and an additional 4 percent upon repayment). These fees do not affect the amount owed.

- Amount: Maximum $120,000 for most schools.

- Term: Twenty years maximum

- Standard Deferment: Interest begins to accrue with the loan's origination, and payments on it can be deferred only under "limited circumstances."

- Grace Period: Principal repayment begins nine months after graduation.

- Minimum Payment: $50/ month

- Source: The Access Group

In addition to these major sources of loan funds, there are any number of commercial lenders that have student-loan programs, though the terms of the loans they offer will almost surely be less attractive than those of the loans described above. Also, some individual schools have loan programs specifically for their students. Such information will be made available to you when you apply for aid through a school's financial-aid office.

PAYBACK TIME

If, after all is said and done, you leave law school unsure whether you will pursue a legal career, the first loan-payment stubs just might rekindle the old flame. Five-figure debt has a way of making decisions for you and making any paycheck look mighty nice. One hopes, however, that a law-school graduate's career choice will be based on more personal concerns than debt repayment.

It is common these days to hear people inside and outside of law school bemoan the effects of high student debt on career choices, but no reliable data have as yet been gathered in support of the widely held belief that the rising cost of law school explains why fewer and fewer law- school graduates are choosing careers in the public interest. Of course, others have offered an explanation in the form of sweeping indictments of a generation they say is motivated more by greed than by ideology. Possibly nothing is more dubious or tiresome than this sort of generalization. It would be foolish or disingenuous to explain a sociologically complex trend in terms of any one factor, be it avarice or indebtedness, but the trend surely exists.

THE LAW SCHOOLS

BY REGION

With 178 approved schools in the country and only a relative handful of them enjoying broad name recognition, you might find it helpful to see how many law schools there actually are in your part of the country. On the following pages you will find a listing of all 170 ABA-approved U.S. law schools profiled in this book, arranged by geographic region. This handy reference should make it easy to come up with a tentative list of law schools for further consideration.

The geographic regions as we have drawn them correspond roughly with those of the United States Census Bureau. As we have designated them, those regions are:

The Mid-Atlantic: New Jersey, New York, and Pennsylvania

The South Atlantic: Delaware, The District of Columbia, Florida, Georgia, Maryland, North Carolina, South Carolina, Virginia, and West Virginia

The South: Alabama, Kentucky, Mississippi, Tennessee, Arkansas, Louisiana, Oklahoma and Texas

The Pacific Coast: Hawaii, Washington, Oregon, and California.

The Heartland: Iowa, Kansas, Minnesota, Missouri, Nebraska, North Dakota, South Dakota, Wyoming, Montana, Idaho, Colorado, Utah, New Mexico and Arizona

The Midwest: Illinois, Indiana, Michigan,
                Ohio, and Wisconsin

New England: Connecticut, Maine, Massachu-
                setts, New Hampshire, and
                Vermont

THE MID-ATLANTIC

The Mid-Atlantic region is one of the most law-school–rich in the nation. New Jersey, New York and Pennsylvania are home to twenty-six law schools all told, many of them among the most highly respected in the country. Columbia, NYU, Cornell and Penn, for instance, are perennial members of everybody's top twenty. The region is also home to several excellent public law schools, including both Rutgers schools and the State University of New York at Buffalo, as well as the nation's leading producer of public-interest lawyers—the City University of New York School of Law at Queens College. Overall, the Mid-Atlantic region is the second-largest producer of law graduates, yet demand for young lawyers in this region significantly outstrips supply. (This is particularly true in New Jersey, where there are nearly twice as many jobs as graduates.) Fully 85 percent of all the Mid Atlantic's 7,500 graduates remain in the region, and nearly 2,500 others move in. This is hardly surprising, of course, when one considers that the region is home to the capital of the American legal profession: New York. Indeed, the legal community of New York City alone accounts for nearly 10 percent of all the law jobs in the nation and nearly half of all jobs in this region.

New York   CUNY School of Law at Queens
                      College
                  SUNY at Buffalo
                  Brooklyn Law School
                  Columbia University
                  Cornell University
                  Fordham University
                  Hofstra University
                  New York Law School
                  New York University
                  Pace University
                  St. John's University

Syracuse University
Touro College
Union University, Albany Law
    School
Yeshiva University, Benjamin
    N. Cardozo School of Law

New Jersey   Rutgers University
                  Camden Rutgers University
                  Newark Seton Hall University

Pennsylvania   University of Pittsburgh
                  Temple University
                  Dickinson School of Law
                  Duquesne University
                  University of Pennsylvania
                  Villanova University
                  Widener University

THE SOUTH ATLANTIC

The states of the South Atlantic are packed with excellent law schools. Several of the region's twenty-nine schools are among the most highly respected in the nation; the law schools at Georgetown, the University of Virginia, Duke University and the University of North Carolina, for instance, are perennial members of everybody's top twenty, and those at George Washington and Emory aren't very far behind. Happily for the bargain hunter, neither quality nor value drops off much the farther one goes down the list of the region's schools. The law schools at George Mason, William and Mary, the University of Georgia, and the University of Florida are all among the finest public schools in the nation. All told, the South Atlantic law schools produce fully one fifth of all U.S. lawyers, and the region's legal communities employ a nearly identical proportion. The South Atlantic's largest job market, Washington, D.C., is the second-largest in the nation, accounting for more than 6 percent of all jobs nationally. The volume and prestige of these jobs means that the nation's capital imports highly qualified grads from all over the country, many of them from the top schools in nearby North Carolina and Virginia, states that produce far more law grads than they employ.

Maryland	University of Baltimore
	University of Maryland
Delaware	Widener University
District of Columbia	American University
	Catholic University
	George Washington University
	Georgetown University
	Howard University
Virginia	William and Mary
	George Mason University
	University of Virginia
	University of Richmond
	Washington and Lee University
West Virginia	West Virginia University
North Carolina	University of North Carolina
	North Carolina Central
	Campbell University
	Duke University
	Wake Forest University
South Carolina	University of South Carolina
Georgia	University of Georgia
	Georgia State University
	Emory University
	Mercer University
Florida	University of Florida
	Florida State University
	University of Miami
	Nova University
	Stetson University

THE SOUTH

Outside of Texas, the South as we have aligned it is a region that is sparsely populated with law schools. Happily for the bargain hunter, however, the majority of the region's law schools are public institutions, many of them among the least expensive in the nation. One of these public schools, the University of Texas School of Law, is also a perennial member of everybody's top twenty, as is Tennessee's Vanderbilt University Law School. These two schools, along with SMU and Tulane, are the most highly regarded schools in a region dominated by regional schools. The public and private law schools in Alabama, Arkansas, Kentucky and Mississippi draw the vast majority of their students from within their home states. Due to relatively limited job opportunities, however, a significant proportion of law grads from those states seek employment elsewhere. Indeed, Texas is the only state in this region that employs more recent law grads than it produces. More than one quarter of the law jobs in this region are to be found in Texas, the nation's fifth-largest and second-highest-paying legal job market.

Louisiana	Louisiana State University
	Southern University
	Loyola University, New Orleans
	Tulane University
Texas	University of Houston
	University of Texas
	Texas Southern University
	Texas Tech
	Baylor University
	Southern Methodist University
	St. Mary's University
	South Texas College of Law
Mississippi	University of Mississippi
	Mississippi College
Alabama	University of Alabama
	Samford University, Cumberland School of Law
Tennessee	Memphis State University
	University of Tennessee
	Vanderbilt University
Oklahoma	University of Oklahoma
	Oklahoma City University
	University of Tulsa
Kentucky	University of Kentucky
	University of Louisville
	Northern Kentucky University

| Arkansas | University of Arkansas, Little Rock |
| | University of Arkansas, Fayetteville |

THE PACIFIC COAST

The Pacific Coast is more densely packed with fantastic law schools than perhaps any other region in the country. The West's most highly esteemed schools—Stanford, Berkeley, Hastings, UCLA, and USC—are to be found in California, but quality and value are to be found throughout the region. The University of Washington School of Law, like the four schools in the University of California system, is one of the most highly regarded public law schools in the nation. The law schools at Lewis and Clark, the University of Oregon, and the University of Hawaii are also highly popular and well-respected institutions. Many of these schools draw thousands of applications from non-Westerners, relatively few of whom (fewer than 15 percent) elect to leave the region after completing their degrees. The reason for this is simple: the twenty-four law schools in this region do not produce as many law grads as the Western legal communities can consume. California alone accounts for roughly 11 percent of all U.S. law jobs, thanks largely to Los Angeles and San Francisco, respectively the fourth- and eighth-largest job markets in the nation. The high salaries commanded by recent law grads in these markets also make California the highest-paying state in the nation for young attorneys.

California	University of California, Berkeley
	University of California, Davis
	University of California, Hastings
	University of California, Los Angeles
	California Western
	Loyola Marymount University
	Pepperdine University
	Southwestern University
	University of San Diego
	University of San Francisco

	Santa Clara University
	University of Southern California
	University of the Pacific, McGeorge School of Law
	Stanford University
	Whittier College
	Golden Gate University
Oregon	University of Oregon
	Lewis and Clark College
	Willamette University
Washington	University of Washington
	Gonzaga University
	University of Puget Sound
Hawaii	University of Hawaii

THE HEARTLAND

It may be ridiculous to group such states as Arizona and Minnesota in the same region, but these thirteen states between the Pacific and the Mississippi share at least one characteristic: they are all relatively sparsely populated—with law schools as with people. Whatever the Heartland may lack in volume, however, it more than makes up for in quality and value; Residents of this region do not go wanting for lack of opportunity to pursue a legal education in a fine, inexpensive institution. Two of the public law schools in this region—those at the University of Iowa and the University of Minnesota—are perennial members of most top-twenty-five lists, and many of the others aren't far behind. The law schools of the University of Utah, the University of Colorado, and the University of Arizona, for instance, are easily among the finest public law schools in the country. Only slightly higher up the price scale, there is the BYU law school, the most highly respected private law school in the region after Missouri's Washington University School of Law. Though this region is home to sizable legal job markets in Denver, Minneapolis and Pheonix, the Heartland accounts for only 10 percent of all jobs for recent law-school graduates. This imbalance is greatest in Iowa and Utah, both of which produce nearly twice as many law grads as they employ.

North Dakota	University of North Dakota
South Dakota	University of South Dakota
Iowa	University of Iowa Drake University
Kansas	University of Kansas Washburn University
Minnesota	University of Minnesota Hamline University William Mitchell College of Law
Missouri	University of Missouri, Columbia University of Missouri , Kansas City Saint Louis University Washington University
Wyoming	University of Wyoming
Montana	University of Montana
Nebraska	University of Nebraska Creighton University
Idaho	University of Idaho
Colorado	University of Colorado University of Denver
Utah	University of Utah Brigham Young University
Arizona	University of Arizona Arizona State University
New Mexico	University of New Mexico

THE MIDWEST

The top-twenty law schools at the University of Chicago, the University of Michigan, Northwestern and Notre Dame are the most highly prestigious in a region that produces more than 6,000 young lawyers annually. Well behind these giants in terms of national prestige, but highly respected in and around the Midwest, is a group of schools whose quality and value represent a great resource to residents of this region. Indiana University, Bloomington; the University of Illinois; Ohio State University; the University of Cincinatti; and the University of Wisconsin are all among the finest public law schools in the nation. There is, however, a downside to the ready accessibility of a quality legal education in most of these states: The volume of law grads churned out by the twenty law schools in Indiana, Michigan, Ohio, and Wisconsin comfortably exceeds demand for young attorneys in the legal communities of those four states. Illinois does its part to absorb much of this excess, but a healthy proportion of all graduates of midwestern law schools begin their careers outside the region. Though Chicago is the country's third-largest job market for recent law school graduates, even its big shoulders can support only so many lawyers.

Illinois	University of Illinois
	Northern Illinois University
	Southern Illinois University
	University of Chicago
	DePaul University
	Illinois Institute of Technology, Chicago-Kent College of Law
	John Marshall School of Law
	Loyola University
	Northwestern University
Ohio	University of Akron
	University of Cincinnati
	Cleveland-Marshall School of Law
	Ohio State University
	University of Toledo
	Capital University
	Case Western Reserve University
	University of Dayton
	Ohio Northern University
Wisconsin	University of Wisconsin
	Marquette University
Michigan	University of Michigan
	Wayne State University

University of Detroit, Mercy
School of Law
Detroit College of Law
Thomas M. Cooley Law School

Indiana   Indiana University,
Bloomington
Indiana University, Indianapolis
University of Notre Dame
Valparaiso University

NEW ENGLAND

Though not the dominant region in legal education that it is in undergraduate education, New England is home to several of the best law schools in the nation, including the twin titans Harvard and Yale. It is also home to some of the largest schools in the nation; the average enrollment of the six schools in and around Boston is nearly 1,300. (By comparison, the national average is slightly more than 700.) The sheer volume of law students in these schools accounts for the fact that of all regions in the United States, New England is the most over-supplied with law-school graduates. Many future lawyers earn their degrees in New England, but fewer spend their careers here. The ratio of law graduates to legal jobs here is roughly 6 to 5, and only 65% of all graduates remain in New England. Of those who do, one in three works in Boston, the nation's sixth-largest legal job market. As large as many of New England's law schools are, few are inexpensive. In a region dominated by private institutions, there are fewer options for the bargain hunter than anywhere in the rest of the country. The law schools at the Universities of Maine and Connecticut are the only public law schools in the region, and both have very limited enrollments.

Connecticut   University of Connecticut
Bridgeport School of Law at
Quinnipiac College
Yale University
New England School of Law
Suffolk University

Maine   University of Maine

New Hampshire	Franklin Pierce Law Center
Massachusetts	Boston College
	Boston University
	Harvard University
	New England School of Law
	Suffolk University
	Northeastern University
	Western New England College
Vermont	Vermont Law School

Highs and Lows:
The Law Schools Ranked by Category

On the following pages, you will find a number of lists of law schools ranked according to various qualities. It must be noted, however, that none of these lists purports to rank the law schools by their overall quality. Nor should any combination of the categories we've chosen here be construed as representing the raw ingredients for such a ranking. We have made no attempt to gauge the "prestige" of these schools, and we wonder whether we could accurately do so even if we tried. What we have done, however, is present a number of lists using information from two very large databases—one of factual information gathered from various sources (e.g., the American Bar Association) and another of subjective information gathered in our survey of more than eleven thousand current law students at the 170 law schools profiled in this book. On the basis of the information from these two sources, we have put together a number of "top ten" lists and, where meaningful and appropriate, corresponding "bottom ten" lists.

ADMISSIONS INDEX

At least in terms of numerical admissions standards, these are the twenty toughest law schools in the country to get into. To calculate this, we combined the average undergraduate GPA and the average LSAT score of entering students into a single index. Our top-twenty list is heavily populated by the traditional powerhouses of American legal education. It should come as no surprise to hear that Yale and Harvard students possess the highest numerical credentials of all U.S. law students. In fact, this list very closely resembles most traditional "top 20" lists.

Applicants to any of these schools had better have their numbers somewhere near the stratosphere, for though grades and LSAT scores are not the only factors that law schools consider when assessing applicants, the importance of numerical credentials in the admissions process should not be underestimated. Simply stated, a great GPA and LSAT score may not be enough to get you into a school like Yale, but a mediocre GPA and an unimpressive LSAT score will almost surely keep you out.

Top Twenty

1. Yale University
2. Harvard University
3. Stanford University
4. University of Chicago
5. New York University
6. Columbia University
7. University of California, Berkeley
8. Duke University
9. University of Michigan
10. University of Pennsylvania
11. University of Virginia
12. Cornell University
13. Georgetown University
14. Vanderbilt University
15. University of Minnesota
16. Washington and Lee University
17. Northwestern University
18. University of California, Los Angeles
19. University of Washington
20. Boston College

DEMAND INDEX

If you are hoping to gain admission to one of these twenty law schools, prepare to fight tooth and nail. In an effort to convey the popularity of certain law schools with applicants, we have calculated the "Demand Index" of the twenty most in-demand law schools in the country. This value is an indicator of more than simply the number of applicants to each school. It also takes into account the rate at which admitted applicants accept offers of admission to a given law school. Fellow geeks, follow along: We have taken the number enrolled divided by the number accepted and divided the resulting number by the percent accepted of those who applied to arrive at our demand index.

$$\frac{\dfrac{\#\ enrolled}{\#\ accepted}}{\dfrac{\#\ accepted}{\#\ applied}} = demand\ index$$

Atop the list—no surprise here—is the Yale University Law School. Yale receives almost 4,000 applications for fewer than 200 spots in its first-year class. More than 50 percent of admitted applicants chose to attend Yale–a remarkably high proportion. Some very surprising appearances are made on the list by such young law schools as Georgia State and City University of New York, two schools that are relatively unknown on a national basis but are enormously popular with residents of Georgia and New York. The trait that these schools tellingly share with thirteen of the other top twenty is that they are inexpensive public institutions. Like bargain hunters fighting to get their hands on a great deal, law-school applicants flood the nation's top public schools with applications, and a very high proportion of those who gain admission choose to enroll.

Top Twenty

1. Yale University
2. Harvard University
3. Campbell University
4. North Carolina Central University
5. Stanford University
6. University of New Mexico
7. University of Hawaii, Manoa
8. City University of New York
9. Columbia University
10. Georgia State University
11. Arizona State University
12. University of Alabama
13. Northern Kentucky University
14. University of North Carolina
15. University of South Carolina
16. University of Minnesota
17. University of Georgia
18. University of Oklahoma
19. University of Virginia
20. University of Tennessee

QUALITY OF LIFE

Some may subscribe to the popular myth that law school is, by definition, a kind of hell. It appears, however, that even hell has its relatively nice neighborhoods. In our survey of more than twenty thousand current law students, clear differences emerged regarding what we have chosen to call the "Quality of Life" enjoyed by students at the 170 American law schools we surveyed.

To arrive at our quality-of-life index, we factored in students' responses to questions concerning three aspects of their law-school experience: the degree of competitiveness among students, the "sense of community" among students, and the quality of relations between students and faculty. As you can easily see, the quality of the education available to students at a given law school has nothing to do with their quality of life.

A few years ago, when Harvard also ranked last in this category for the second time, the Dean of the Harvard Law School was moved to say that our survey instrument must be "seriously flawed." This criticism is fair only in part. Yes, our survey is decidedly unscientific, and our calling this index a measure of the quality of overall life at a law school is, perhaps, presumptuous. But the fact remains that our unscientific survey method is equally unscientific for all of the law schools we profile. Harvard students had the same opportunity as all others to voice their degree of satisfaction with their law school. Furthermore, we have updated numbers on all of the schools for this year's edition and we resurveyed 70 schools as well. The result: Harvard came out last for the fourth year in a row.

Top Ten

1. Washburn University
2. Brigham Young University
3. William and Mary
4. University of Wyoming
5. University of Maine
6. Washington and Lee University
7. Baylor University
8. Western New England College
9. Ohio Northern University
10. University of California, Davis

Bottom Ten

161. Rutgers University, Newark
162. University of Akron
163. New York Law School
164. State University of New York at Buffalo
165. University of Tennessee
166. Columbia University
167. University of Maryland
168. Ohio State University
169. University of California, Berkeley
170. Harvard University

COMPETITIVENESS

Anyone who is at all familiar with the popular literature on life in law school (See: *The Paper Chase* or *One L*) knows that cutthroat competitiveness characterizes relations among struggling first-year students. At least that's how legend would have it. Whether such a perception was ever accurate is difficult to say, but the perception remains. There is a popular myth among law students, for instance, concerning the hyper-competitive student—always at "some other school, like Harvard"—who will, in order to render his classmates unprepared for class or an exam, remove pages containing key cases from every volume of the *Federal Reporter*. Suffice it to say that students in every discipline, like humans in general, perform some necessary psychological function by trafficking in such myths, which often have little basis in fact.

That said, it is quite clear that competition is a fact of life in law school. To some students at some schools, grades take on an importance that they never did in college. Coveted spots on a school's law-review staff are awarded solely on the basis of class rank, and jobs with the most prestigious private law firms and government agencies are tough to come by for those who have not distinguished themselves in this arena. Add to this the way in which grades are determined in most law-school classes—on the basis of a single exam at semester's end—and you have a volatile mixture. Those who give in to stress easily should have no problem finding the motivation to do so while in law school, but those who seek to avoid such stress do have their options. We asked students in our survey to characterize the degree of competitiveness among students at their schools, and we got strikingly different results. Atop our list among schools where competitiveness was described as "high" to "extreme" is the law school at Southwestern University. Near the polar opposite was Northeastern University.

THE BEST TEACHING FACULTIES

Nobody who has been to college should be surprised to hear that the quality of instruction varies widely from law school to law school and, indeed, from professor to professor within a given law school. Like most institutions of higher education, law schools are not immune to the publish-or-perish ethic, and most law-school faculty rankings are based narrowly on those faculties' scholarly output (read: number of law review articles published). It is, of course, impossible to quantify something as intangible as quality of teaching, but we took a stab simply by asking students how they would rate their faculty in this regard.

Top Ten

1. Boston University
2. University of Chicago
3. University of Virginia
4. Vanderbilt University
5. William and Mary
6. Cornell University
7. Washington and Lee University
8. Western New England College
9. University of Notre Dame
10. University of Texas

Top Ten

1. Southern Illinois University
2. Brigham Young University
3. University of Richmond
4. Southern Methodist University
5. University of Connecticut
6. University of Idaho
7. Yale University
8. New York Law School
9. New York University
10. Northwestern University

Bottom Ten

161. Loyola University, New Orleans
162. Capital University Law School
163. Western New England College
164. University of San Francisco
165. University of Houston
166. University of Akron
167. New England School of Law
168. Albany Law School of Union University
169. Gonzaga University
170. William Mitchell College of Law

MOST FAVORABLE STUDENT/FACULTY RATIOS

When the Socratic Method reigned supreme as the dominant teaching method, relatively high student-faculty ratios were the norm in most law schools. By and large, first-year classes at most law schools still follow the old format, with one professor holding forth before up to one hundred students. The introduction of alternate teaching methods (i.e., seminars and lectures) and, more important, the increasing emphasis of many schools on clinical education, have changed matters considerably. In a hands-on legal clinic, one instructor cannot adequately serve more than a handful of students, so it is not surprising to see that several of the law schools on our list—Yale and NYU, for instance—are schools that boast particularly large clinical programs.

Note: This list is derived from figures reported by the schools themselves. The rankings reflect the relative size of teaching faculty (full-time and part-time) only. They do not include administrators and staff.

MINORITY REPRESENTATION AMONG STUDENTS

Just twenty-five years ago, the list of law schools with minority enrollments exceeding 30 percent would have been mighty short: Howard, North Carolina Central, Southern, and Texas Southern. Those historically black institutions were once the only significant sources of nonwhite lawyers in the nation, and they still occupy four of the top five slots on our list. Over the course of the last twenty-five years, however, the rest of the country has gone a long way toward closing the gap. Today, nearly all of the nation's elite law schools boast minority enrollments that surpass the national average of 18 percent, and two of the top ten on our list—Stanford and Berkeley—are among the most highly respected schools in the country. Though they do not rank among the top ten, such elite schools as Yale and Harvard also boast minority populations that comfortably exceed the national average. These facts should shatter the ridiculous notion that diversity and excellence are mutually exclusive goals in higher education.

Top Ten

1. Howard University
2. Texas Southern University
3. University of Hawaii, Manoa
4. Southern University
5. North Carolina Central University
6. University of New Mexico
7. University of Washington
8. Loyola Marymount University
9. Stanford University
10. University of California, Berkeley

Bottom Ten

161. Creighton University
162. University of Montana
163. University of Louisville
164. Texas Tech University
165. Louisiana State University
166. University of Wyoming
167. Widener University
168. University of North Dakota
169. University of South Dakota
170. Campbell University

Top Ten

1. Texas Southern University
2. Howard University
3. North Carolina Central University
4. Southern University
5. University of San Francisco
6. William Mitchell College of Law
7. City University of New York
8. Golden Gate University
9. University of California
10. Whittier College

Bottom Ten

161. West Virginia University
162. Villanova University
163. University of Missouri, Columbia
164. Quinnipiac College
165. Northwestern University
166. Lewis and Clark College
167. Creighton University
168. Case Western Reserve University
169. University of Michigan
170. University of South Dakoa

GREATEST MINORITY REPRESENTATION AMONG FACULTY

The highly publicized case of New York University's Derrick Bell, one of the nation's most prominent law professors, brought to the general public's attention the controversial issue of ethnic diversity among law school faculty. Professor Bell, an African American, was formerly a member of the Harvard Law School faculty, where he was one of only five nonwhites among sixty-seven full-time professors. When HLS students formally protested the law school's failure to grant tenure to a black woman professor (she would have been the first), Professor Bell took a leave of absence in a show of support for the protesters. Two years later, the Harvard Corporation chose to call Professor Bell's bluff, ruling that Bell could not extend his leave of absence any longer. Noting that the law school had not taken significant steps in the interim to rectify the situation that prompted his departure, Bell chose to remain at NYU. Confrontation had not prompted Harvard to take action. Today, its faculty remains disproportionately white and male, though it does not rank among the bottom ten in this category. That dubious distinction belongs to a number of schools in states with very small minority populations (e.g. West Virginia and South Dakota) and to others located in areas with large minority populations (e.g, Michigan). On the other end of the scale, four historically black universities top the list of those with ethnically diverse faculties.

PROPORTION OF WOMEN STUDENTS

Women did not begin entering law school in significant numbers until the 1970s, and equal representation remains only an ideal at most U.S. law schools despite the dramatic increase in women applicants in the last decade. Nationally, women make up a bit more than 42 percent of all law students, but a sizable number of schools stray far from the average in both directions. On the top of the scale, a handful of schools actually enroll more women than men, and one, the Northeastern University School of Law, has almost reversed the national average. Fully 66 percent of Northeastern's nearly 600 J.D. students are women, and the law schools at Loyola, Chicago, and Howard University are not far behind. On the opposite end of the scale, a number of law schools fall well behind the national average. To be fair, the student bodies at the schools near the bottom of this list do tend to reflect the makeup of those schools' applicant pools. Until women begin to apply to these schools in greater numbers, they will remain underrepresented on these campuses.

Top Ten

1. Northeastern University
2. Howard University
3. Loyola University, Chicago
4. City University of New York
5. Stetson University
6. Suffolk University
7. University of New Mexico
8. American University
9. North Carolina Central University
10. University of North Dakota

Bottom Ten

161. Vanderbilt University
162. Touro College
163. Texas Tech University
164. Samford University
165. Mississippi College
166. Franklin Pierce Law Center
167. University of Kentucky
168. Ohio Northern University
169. Thomas M. Cooley Law School
170. Brigham Young University

HIGHEST PROPORTION OF FEMALE FACULTY

Although women now make up more than 40 percent of the law student population in the United States, such relative balance has yet to be achieved among law professors. Nationally, only 25 percent of all full- and part-time law teaching faculty members are women. In large part, of course, the tenure system creates a time-lag between female law school enrollment and female faculty representation. Equal representation for women will surely come, it could be argued, but until members of the overwhelmingly male old guard retire, women wishing to enter legal academia must bide their time. However valid that argument may be, a number of law schools have managed to hasten the inevitable. The clinic-oriented law school at the City University of New York, for instance, actually employs more women than men on its teaching faculty.

PUBLIC INTEREST PLACEMENT

It is certainly no coincidence that four of the ten law schools on this list are public schools. In 1991, the average starting salary for recent law grads in public-interest positions was only $25,000 per year—less than half of the average starting salary of first-year associates in private law firms. And while a big-firm lawyer five years out of school might make well over $100,000 per year, most public-interest lawyers do not enjoy the same kind of salary growth. Of course, this salary differential alone does not explain why only 2 percent of all law-school graduates begin their careers practicing law in the public interest. Indeed, more than 10 percent of current law students express a desire to do this kind of work despite its relatively low pay. Unfortunately, a sad economic reality faces nearly all would-be public-interest lawyers, and especially those who attend private law schools; because of skyrocketing tuition rates, the debt incurred by many graduates of private law schools forces them to seek more lucrative employment. Many of the nation's private law schools are beginning to establish loan-forgiveness programs intended to allow their graduates to pursue low-paying public-interest jobs. In the meantime, it is fortunate that inexpensive options exist.

Top Ten

1. Northern Illinois University
2. Northeastern University
3. Hamline University
4. Nova Southeastern University
5. City University of New York
6. Golden Gate University
7. Detroit College of Law at Michigan State University
8. University of Akron
9. University of Wyoming
10. Lewis and Clark College

Top Ten

1. *Yale University*
2. *Seton Hall University*
3. *University of North Dakota*
4. *Rutgers University, Camden*
5. *University of Baltimore*
6. *Stanford University*
7. *Dickinson School Of Law*
8. *Louisiana State University*
9. *Northeastern University*
10. *University of South Dakota*

CLERKSHIP PLACEMENT

Nationwide, roughly 12 percent of all law-school graduates begin their careers as judicial clerks, the worker ants of the judicial system. Most of those who serve clerkships do so as a prelude to a career in private practice, while some do so before entering a career in academia. Whatever the case, these one- or two-year positions typically go to graduates who excelled in law school. Law-school grades are an important factor in many employers' hiring decisions, but grades are especially important for those who seek to land a judicial clerkship. These research and writing jobs demand many of the same sorts of skills as law-school coursework does. Furthermore, the most prestigious positions tend to go to those who attended one of the nation's elite schools, so the proportion of a school's graduates who land clerkships is often a function of that school's prestige. Such is the case with the number one and number six schools on this list. It is also true, however, that judges tend to hire graduates of their own alma maters. Because of this fact, one can also roughly gauge the strength of the regional connections of a law school by the rate at which it sends its graduates into these positions. Consider the example of the number two school on this list, Seton Hall. That 39 percent of Seton Hall grads serve judicial clerkships is some indication of the degree to which the school's alumni dominate the bench and bar of New Jersey. In the case of Yale and Stanford, their places on this list clearly reflect the prestige of the degrees they confer. First-year clerks from these schools are likely to serve not local alumni but judges at the highest levels of state and federal judiciaries.

PRIVATE PRACTICE

The proportion of recent law-school graduates entering private practice has risen steadily in this last decade, reaching a peak of about 70 percent in 1991. Not coincidentally, law-school tuition was up sharply in the same period. While the employment patterns of most individual schools conform closely to the national average, a few stand out on either extreme. The schools on this list send a disproportionately high percentage of their graduates to work in private practice. Interestingly, four of these schools are very inexpensive public institutions, a fact that calls into question the assumption that high debt burden alone can explain this trend.

Top Ten

1. Loyola Marymount University
2. University of Southern California
3. University of California, Berkeley
4. University of California, Los Angeles
5. Baylor University
6. Pace University
7. New York University
8. University of Louisville
9. Columbia University
10. University of Houston

HOW TO USE THIS BOOK

Each of the law schools listed in this book has its own two-page spread, with two sidebars containing general, mostly factual, information; text with a general overview of the school; and a paragraph specifically on admissions. The information used in compiling the profiles in this book comes from several different sources, including student surveys, questionnaires filled out by the schools, and the American Bar Association's *Review of Legal Education in the United States*. In gathering information on each of the schools, we have surveyed more than twenty-five thousand law students over the past several years. We asked them dozens of questions on such matters as the quality of their relations with faculty and the quality of their schools' facilities. We also sent the entries to the administration for their comments. We have done our best to provide a balanced picture of each school. Do keep in mind, however, that while we do our best to choose only representative quotes, one student may express herself more strongly than another and the words are her opinion, not those of every student at the school. Use the information presented in this book as a guide to your own further exploration.

Material in the sidebars covers the following:

Type of School
Whether the school is public or private.

Environment
Whether the campus is located in a metropolis (big urban environment), city (smaller urban environment), suburb, or town.

Scholastic Calendar
How the school breaks up its academic year (i.e., semesters, trimesters).

Schedule
Whether the school offers full-time or part-time schedules.

Enrollment of Institution
Total number of students in the institution, including the law school.

Enrollment of Law School
Total number of students in the law school.

Percentage Male/Female, Percentage Out-of-state, Percentage Part-time, Percentage Minorities, Percentage International (Number of Countries Represented), Average Age at Entry
Demographic breakdown of last year's entering class.

Applicants Also Look At
Other schools applicants consider.

Survey Says...Hits and Misses
Strengths and weaknesses of the school as reflected by our student surveys.

Employment Profile
General demographics from the administration regarding the percentage of students employed immediately after graduation, the percentage employed within six months, the average starting salary, and the percentage breakdown by fields.

Student/Faculty Ratio, Percentage Female Faculty, Percentage Minority Faculty, and Hours of Study Per Day
The faculty makeup of a school and how much work that faculty piles on.

Financial Facts
The first set of numbers covers how much it will cost you to get the degree—tuition, books, living expenses. The second set of numbers tells you how students pay the first set of numbers—percentage of students receiving loans and assistantships, and number of students receiving scholarships, how much they're getting, and how much they'll have to pay off after graduation.

Admissions

How many applicants a school receives and what those applicants look like. This section includes the percentage of applicants accepted, the percentage of acceptees attending, the average LSAT score, and the average undergraduate GPA (UGPA). We also tell you the application fee for the 1995-96 school year, whether or not the school has an early decision program, the regular application deadline, when regular notification occurs, and possible admission deferment.

The Gourman Ranking

This is a numerical score from 2 to 5 that assesses the strengths and shortcomings of each school. It is compiled using material from educators and administrators at the schools themselves. These individuals are permitted to evaluate only their own programs. In addition, the Gourman Rankings draw on many external resources which are a matter of record. Finally, the Gourman Report is fortunate to have among its contributors a number of individuals, associations, and agencies whose business it is to make correct projections of the success graduates from given schools will enjoy in the real world. Using all these factors, Gourman Rankings rate schools and assign them a number that sums up their strengths and shortcomings in a nutshell.

SCHOOL
PROFILES

UNIVERSITY OF AKRON 💾
School of Law

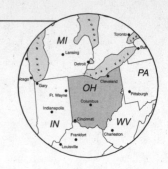

OVERVIEW

Type of school	public
Environment	city
Scholastic calendar	semester
Schedule	Full-time or part-time

STUDENTS

Enrollment of institution	26,000
Enrollment of law school	635
% male/female	61/39
% out-of-state	15
% part-time	28
% minorities	8
% international (# countries represented)	1 (NR)
Average age at entry	26

APPLICANTS ALSO LOOK AT

Case Western Reserve University
Cleveland State University
Ohio State University
University of Dayton
Duquesne University

SURVEY SAYS...

HITS
Socratic method
Diverse faculty
Left-leaning politics

MISSES
Quality of teaching
Intellectual challenge
Studying

EMPLOYMENT PROFILE

% grads employed immediately	50
% grads employed within six months	96
Average starting salary	$36,522
% grads employed by field:	
Private practice	49
Business/industry	18
Government	15
Judicial clerkships	8
Public service	7
Academic	2
Military	7

The University of Akron School of Law's hometown, the former "Rubber Capital of the World," now prefers to be called the world's leader in "polymer research." Technological issues aside, one quite understands why. The University of Akron itself is a well-funded research and teaching institution with particular strength in materials science and engineering. Students at the Akron law school, however, tend to busy themselves not with plastics and polymers but with more familiar, if less malleable, subjects like torts and contracts that are the mainstay of the law school's solid, traditional curriculum.

Akron does, however, supplement its straightforward J.D. program with a number of clinical programs and skills courses, among which the trial advocacy program draws many participants. In addition to its own considerable resources, the law school puts at students' disposal the vast resources of the broader university, through which they can pursue various joint-degree programs (e.g., J.D./M.B.A, J.D./master's in taxation or public administration). Like so many public law schools, Akron experienced an increase in applications during the late eighties that far outpaced the overall increase in law-school applications nationwide. In 1986, the law school admitted 63 percent of the candidates it evaluated. Since then, however, applications have almost tripled, and Akron now admits a much less generous percentage of those who apply. Though this clearly indicates that the numerical qualifications of the law school's students have risen, admissions standards at Akron remain moderate.

Students at Akron paint a picture of a law school that does little more than meet their basic needs. Their most consistent complaint concerned the unevenness of teaching abilities among the law school's faculty. Some, however, dissented from the majority opinion on this matter. "The school's greatest strength," said one 3L, "is the faculty's commitment to teaching and to maintaining contact with students." Few shared that specific opinion, but many Akron students did praise their faculty's academic abilities. As one put it, "Our professors are very knowledgeable and, most importantly, very approachable. I could have transferred to a so-called elite law school after my first year, but I believe that I

Lauri S. File, Director of Admissions and Financial Assistance
Akron, OH 44325-2901
Tel: (330) 972-7331   Fax: (303) 258-2343
eMail: lawadmissions@uakron.edu
Internet: http://www.uakron.edu/law/index.html

University of Akron

couldn't receive a higher quality legal education anyplace else—Ivy Leagues included." Several Akron students praised the school's emphasis on legal writing. Akron students also were notably charitable toward their placement staff. As one 3L about to enter a difficult job market said: "The alumni and staff are very supportive of recent graduates, which is good, because nobody else out there is."

Many students' criticisms of Akron centered on its lack of a national name. Said one 3L, "Probably the school's greatest problem is the lack of an effective public relations program." Others complained loudly about the facilities, despite recent renovations. On the academic front, even those students who offered praise for Akron's existing skills courses expressed their desire to see even "more access to courses imparting practical knowledge." Others criticized the law school administration for not supporting more extracurricular activities and student organizations. Of course to be fair, the responsibility for what one student called a "blah" atmosphere on campus may rest as much on the students themselves: "We are subdued, down-to-earth and realistic. We simply expect to get a degree, get a job and get on with our lives."

ADMISSIONS

Overall selectivity at the University of Akron School of Law is moderate, and numerical standards are relatively low, but a dramatic rise in total applications volume over the last several years has made the admissions process at this inexpensive public law school more competitive. The average GPA and LSAT scores of entering students are less than stellar, and candidates with above average numerical credentials are virtually guaranteed admission, thanks in part to an extremely generous overall acceptance rate.

ACADEMICS

Student/faculty ratio	26:1
% female faculty	40
% minority faculty	15
Hours of study per day	3.36

FINANCIAL FACTS

In-state tuition	$6,785
Out-of-state tuition	$11,633
Part-time tuition per credit	NR
Estimated books/expenses/fees	NR
On-campus living expenses	NR
Off-campus living expenses	$3,860
% first-year students receiving aid	59
% all students receiving aid	77
% aid that is merit-based	85
% all students receiving grants/scholarships	21
% all students receiving loans	67
% all students receiving assistantships	2
Average award package	$2,000
Average graduation debt	$35,000

ADMISSIONS

# applications received	1,621
% applicants accepted	44
% acceptees attending	33
Average LSAT	153
Average undergrad GPA	3.12
Application Fee	$35
No early decision program	
Regular application deadline	NR
Regular notification	rolling
Admission deferment	one year
Gourman Report Rating	**2.89**

UNIVERSITY OF ALABAMA ▣
School of Law

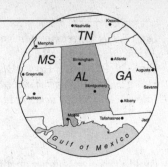

Located in the midsize college town of Tuscaloosa, the University of Alabama School of Law has served the state for almost 125 years, and while it has few pretensions to national status, Alabama's law school enjoys a very solid regional reputation. Alabama should not be tagged a local law school, however, if that description is meant to cast doubt on the breadth and quality of its offerings. This modern, well-staffed law school offers a J.D. program that is strong within traditional bounds and is administered by an able and relatively large faculty. As part of a major public university with some of the best research resources in the Southeast, it offers its students access to services uncommon at schools of its size.

Alabama's self-described goal is to live up to the concept of a "Law Center," an institution fully integrated with and involved in the surrounding community. Its efforts to meet that goal are aided by the fact that the overwhelming majority of its students are Alabama residents and that most of them remain within the state after completing their degrees. (It should be noted that the University of Alabama lags behind many of the nation's law schools in terms of the racial and gender diversity of its student body. More than anything, however, this fact reflects a broader problem facing many universities in the Gulf Coast states, most of which have not gone as far as Alabama has in opening themselves up to historically excluded minorities.) Admissions standards at Alabama are competitive, and those who are admitted possess solid mid- to high-range numerical credentials.

Students at Alabama say the law school satisfies them only up to a point. Though most of those we heard from expressed a fairly high degree of satisfaction with the quality of their training at the law school, many lamented Alabama's old-school emphasis on the Socratic Method and other trappings of the traditional curriculum. When asked to name the school's greatest strengths, however, few had difficulty responding: "Our faculty are all outstanding in their fields and bring a great deal of expertise to the classroom," wrote one. "They are, generally, very friendly with the students and very accessible." Though such sentiments

Betty McGinley, Admissions Coordinator
Box 870382, Tuscaloosa, AL 35487-0382
Tel: (205) 348-5440

were expressed by Alabama students with less frequency and enthusiasm than students elsewhere, they were still quite noticeable. Moreover, one point on which nearly all agreed was on the quality of relations among students themselves: "One of the greatest attributes of the University of Alabama," said one, "is the sense of community that you feel here. Most people don't notice your race, sex or economic status—they simply see a fellow law student and know what you're going through. It's comforting to know there are people here who understand you and that you can count on them for support and guidance."

Such compassion is especially important at a school like Alabama, where academic intensity often breeds unhealthy competitiveness. One 1L put it simply: "The quality of students and the level of competitiveness here far exceeded my expectations." Another 1L wrote that "the legal community itself is competitive and cutthroat, and these traits are ingrained in law school." Speaking for students at many of the nation's law schools, she continued: "Shouldn't the environment in law school focus more on learning than on rank?" Indeed, many here agreed that "the format is too traditional, overly rigid and authoritarian." Criticism was also heard concerning the perceived narrowness of the school's curriculum. "I'd like to see less of a focus on business courses and more on theoretical courses," went one fairly typical remark. On balance, however, even the most critical of the students we heard from were unable to say that the school's shortcomings completely outweighed its strengths, particularly considering its incredible affordability.

ADMISSIONS

The University of Alabama School of Law is one of the most selective in the entire Southeast. Indeed, Alabama ranks among the top 20 percent of all law schools nationally in terms of its numerical admissions standards. Since 1986, the average LSAT score of incoming students has leapt fifteen percentile points while the average GPA has inched up to a very respectable 3.4. Applications volume has risen steadily at this bargain law school to the point where slightly fewer than one in three applicants gains admission. Candidates whose numbers fall below Alabama's average face an uphill climb.

ACADEMICS

Student/faculty ratio	17:1
% female faculty	21
% minority faculty	7
Hours of study per day	3.00

FINANCIAL FACTS

In-state tuition	$3,578
Out-of-state tuition	$7,712
Part-time tuition per credit	NR
Estimated books/expenses/fees	NR
On-campus living expenses	NR
Off-campus living expenses	NR
% first-year students receiving aid	65
% all students receiving aid	65
% aid that is merit-based	67
% all students receiving grants/scholarships	66
% all students receiving loans	74
% all students receiving assistantships	7
Average award package	$4,743
Average graduation debt	$29,015

ADMISSIONS

# applications received	930
% applicants accepted	31
% acceptees attending	65
Average LSAT	156
Average undergrad GPA	3.40
Application Fee	$25
No early decision program	
Regular application deadline	March 1
Regular notification	rolling
Admission may be deferred?	No
Gourman Report Rating	**3.24**

AMERICAN UNIVERSITY
Washington College of Law

No city is more densely packed with both lawyers and law students than Washington, D.C., which boasts one lawyer for about every 12 residents (the national average is one lawyer for every 350), and six law schools with an average enrollment of more than 1,000. Even with 1,167 students in its day and evening divisions, American University's Washington College of Law is only the third largest law school in its home city. And although it places third in most other rankings behind Georgetown and George Washington law schools, this has more to do with the crowded law school neighborhood than with the quality of the school. American's reputation rests on the solidity of its traditional academic program and on the scope of its clinical programs. The latter were recently cited by a national magazine as among the top five programs in the U.S. Law students at American also have great opportunities for a wide array of externships in the D.C. area.

One aspect of the Washington College of Law that sets it apart from its D.C. rivals is its commitment to women. Celebrating its hundredth anniversary in 1996, the WCL was founded by two women who wished to ensure the inclusion of those who had historically been outside the mainstream of the legal profession. Today women make up nearly half the student body and the university offers a feminist law journal and associations. WCL students overall appear to be a tolerant and non-competitive group. "The best thing about WCL is the cooperative atmosphere among students," said a 1L. This congeniality may have worked its way down from the faculty who is, according to the school, dedicated to developing caring and responsible people as much as successful lawyers. In fact, many students we heard from cited what they termed a more "humane" approach to teaching as one of the university's main strengths. American "fosters a positive learning environment by encouraging teamwork and not competition," said one 2L. A 3L appreciated the school's "continuing commitment to public interest law, community activism, and humanizing legal experiences." American University also offers four joint-degree programs, a distinct advantage for students interested in cross-disciplinary studies.

4801 Massachusetts Avenue, NW
Washington, DC 20016
Tel: (202) 274-4004   Fax: (202) 274-4005

Law students at American are generally pleased with their professors and curriculum. Students we spoke with called the "open door policy" most faculty members maintain very helpful. "Professors treat students fairly and are willing to do whatever they can to assist with schoolwork, employment, and even just surviving law school," said a 1L. The Washington College of Law's legal clinics were also frequently praised by students, although several mentioned that there were not enough spots available. (Approximately 25 to 30 percent of all third year students participate in clinics.)

On the downside, several students we spoke with would like to see a more diverse faculty at the law school. One student called for "more women professors in non-clinical classes;" and another called for "more black professors." It is true that American's approximate 8 percent minority composition among the faculty is on the low side.

Since our last visit to the WCL, the construction of new, technologically advanced and state-of-the-art building has been completed. This multi-million dollar project came none too soon, as students were becoming very frustrated with the poor facilities. In fact, nearly every student we surveyed mentioned the new law school and how badly it is needed. Just as we were going to press, we received an enthusiastic letter from a 2L, who told us, "I can assure you that our new building is simply one of the best facilities of higher learning anywhere...[It] provides more than ample resources."

ADMISSIONS

American University College of Law's solid numerical standards place it among the sixty most selective law schools in the country. With more than 13 applications filed for every spot in its entering class of about 370, this is hardly surprising. Statistically, an applicant with an undergraduate GPA between 3.00 and 3.25 and an LSAT score between 155 and 159 stands a 14 percent chance of getting in.

ACADEMICS

Student/faculty ratio	18:1
% female faculty	32
% minority faculty	8
Hours of study per day	3.68

FINANCIAL FACTS

Tuition	$18,444
Part-time tuition per credit	$684
Estimated books/expenses/fees	$1,068
On-campus living expenses	NR
Off-campus living expenses	NR
% first-year students receiving aid	84
% all students receiving aid	NR
% aid that is merit-based	2
% all students receiving grants/scholarships	NR
% all students receiving loans	73
% all students receiving assistantships	NR
Average award package	$29,666
Average graduation debt	$66,000

ADMISSIONS

# applications received	5,100
% applicants accepted	33
% acceptees attending	22
Average LSAT	158
Average undergrad GPA	3.32
Application Fee	$55
Priority application deadline	NR
Priority notification	NR
Regular application deadline	March 1
Regular notification	rolling
Admission deferment	NR
Gourman Report Rating	**3.84**

ARIZONA STATE UNIVERSITY
College of Law

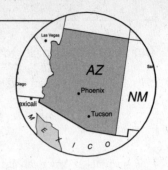

Few parts of the country saw the kind of growth in the last decade that Arizona did, and few parts of Arizona saw more growth than Phoenix, now the nation's ninth-largest city. More to the point, on the strength of an economy that is growing and diversifying nearly as quickly as its population, Phoenix—like Arizona generally—has become a major consumer of legal services, catapulting it into the top 20 job markets for recent law school graduates.

This surely goes a long way toward explaining the phenomenal success of the city's relatively young law school, Arizona State University School of Law. (Tempe, the actual site of the ASU campus, is a suburb of Phoenix.) Founded in 1966, ASU took no time to achieve local prominence, and national recognition as a top public law school wasn't far behind. Still, the law school remains primarily a regional institution, drawing the vast majority of its students from inside the state and sending a similar proportion of its graduates to work within Arizona. When one considers ASU's strong academic program, its incredibly low tuition and its location in a city where "winter" must be put in quotes, one understands why few Arizona residents feel a need to look elsewhere for their legal education and why few ASU grads feel compelled to look elsewhere for work. Thanks to an enormous increase in applications volume in the late eighties and early nineties, ASU admissions have become highly competitive. The law school's diverse student body possesses strong numerical credentials.

On the whole, students enrolled at ASU are highly satisfied with the fundamental quality of their program and with the extent to which it is preparing them for entry into the profession. The college has a multi-faceted clinical program—an in-house live client clinic, a public defender clinic, and a prosecutor clinic. ASU also offers a variety of practical skills courses—practice court, alternative dispute resolution, mediation, arbitration, and negotiation. They are also starting a lawyering theory and practice course this year. According to the administration, the school's "Indian Legal Program...has been cited as a model at a national level. We have many Native American law students and provide a number of curricular offerings in that area."

When asked to name the strengths of their school, many students cited "the faculty, the clinics and the location near the state and federal courts." ASU's location drew strong words of praise not only for its proximity to legal institutions that provide its students with significant co-curricular opportunities, but also for its overall pleasantness. "The campus atmosphere is wonderful here," was one typical remark, "and the student body is really diverse, which makes for interesting discussions in and out of class." Others agreed: "ASU law students are intelligent and serious about their studies. For the most part they bear little resemblance to the [insult deleted] types who populate the undergrad campus." "The faculty is available for questions and to help, and all staff members are helpful and responsive to individual students' needs."

ADMISSIONS

The admissions process at Arizona State is highly competitive. In part because of its strong program and in part because of its low tuition, the law school is inundated with applications from candidates with strong numerical credentials. (The average LSAT score of ASU students is slightly above the 80th percentile.) Numbers count heavily in the selection process. Factoring in both its low acceptance rate and the rate at which admitted applicants accept offers from the law school, Arizona State is in the top 30 percent of all law schools nationally in terms of overall demand for spots in its relatively small first-year class.

ACADEMICS

Student/faculty ratio	17:1
% female faculty	28
% minority faculty	16
Hours of study per day	3.83

FINANCIAL FACTS

In-state tuition	$3,940
Out-of-state tuition	$10,308
Part-time tuition per credit	NR
Estimated books/expenses/fees	NR
On-campus living expenses	NR
Off-campus living expenses	NR
% first-year students receiving aid	80
% all students receiving aid	82
% aid that is merit-based	NR
% all students receiving grants/scholarships	28
% all students receiving loans	82
% all students receiving assistantships	NR
Average award package	$10,755
Average graduation debt	$23,000

ADMISSIONS

# applications received	2,087
% applicants accepted	18
% acceptees attending	39
Average LSAT	157
Average undergrad GPA	3.36
Application Fee	$35
Priority application deadline	NR
Priority notification	NR
Regular application deadline	March 1
Regular notification	January-April
Admission deferment	NR
Gourman Report Rating	**3.30**

UNIVERSITY OF ARIZONA
College of Law

OVERVIEW

Type of school	public
Environment	metropolis
Scholastic calendar	semester
Schedule	Full time only

STUDENTS

Enrollment of institution	21,511
Enrollment of law school	482
% male/female	55/45
% out-of-state	21
% part-time	NR
% minorities	27
% international (# countries represented)	NR (NR)
Average age at entry	26

APPLICANTS ALSO LOOK AT

Arizona State University
U. of California, Los Angeles
University of San Diego
U. of California, Berkeley
U. of California, Davis

SURVEY SAYS...

HITS
Serving humankind
Faculty representation

MISSES
Socratic method
Legal writing

EMPLOYMENT PROFILE

% grads employed immediately	NR
% grads employed within six months	NR
Average starting salary	NR
% grads employed by field:	
Private practice	42
Business/industry	14
Government	17
Judicial clerkships	14
Public service	7
Academic	6
Military	5

Law students know a bargain when they see one, and they clearly see one in the University of Arizona College of Law, one of only two law schools in the state. Retirees have long flocked to the high Arizona desert for its clean air and year-round sunny climate, but it takes a bit more than the promise of a great suntan to provoke the dramatic increase in applications that Arizona, like so many public law schools, saw in the early 90s. It takes a strong academic program, a high success rate for graduates and a small price tag, all of which Arizona has. The university itself is a premier research and teaching facility, a rising academic star through which the law school offers a wide array of joint-degree programs. Arizona's law curriculum, administered by a large, highly respected faculty, is strong in all traditional areas. Many of Arizona's offerings unmistakably reflect the law school's setting. In addition to the kind of government placements that are available to students at almost any law school, Arizona offers internship programs with the governments of the Navaho, Pascua Yaqui, and Tohono O'odham tribes. The University of Arizona turns out a small, well-prepared group of graduates who have little difficulty finding employment in a state that needs more lawyers than it produces. And, perhaps most important, even the nonresident tuition here is on the low end of the scale for law schools of this caliber. Arizona also stands out for the true ethnic and racial diversity of its student body.

Arizona's J.D. program is highly demanding, and students acknowledge the high degree of competitiveness that keeps everyone from being numbed by the year-round stunningly beautiful weather. As nearly all the students we heard from pointed out, however, the law school sees to it that incoming Arizona students make a smooth transition as they adjust to the academic rigor. This is achieved by separating the entering class into small groups of and keeping those students together in all of their first-year courses. Arizona students attest to the success of this program in keeping them from being lost in the shuffle during their demanding first year. As one 3L reported, "The small sections during first year, first semester were extraordinarily helpful in integrating into law school." This integration is made yet easier by a faculty that most students seem to regard as "dedicated and accessible."

Naturally, Arizona students have their share of gripes about their chosen school. A large number, for instance, complained about inconsistency in the quality of classroom instruction, and few had kind words for the school's facilities. However, as we go to print, the school is beginning a major building program which will add several new seminar rooms and refurbish all existing classrooms and seminar rooms by the end of 1996. More fundamental criticisms tended to center on the limited availability of practical skills courses and the limited array of courses available on a regular basis. "Don't advertise aggressively the environmental and international programs when they barely exist," wrote one particularly disappointed 2L. To present the other side, the school said that they have made progress in international law, recently adding an additional faculty member to the program. Even though the law school's student body is incredibly diverse relative to the rest of the nation (as is its faculty), quite a few students called for even greater representation of historically excluded minorities. Still, most Arizona students seem satisfied with their overall experience at the law school, all agree that the price is right, and as one student put it, "Where else can you eat lunch outside in January?"

ADMISSIONS

The University of Arizona has become one of the most highly selective law schools in the country. The size of its first-year class (around 150) allows the admissions committee to admit only about one in five of the 1,800 candidates it considers annually. With their very solid undergraduate grade-point averages and a median LSAT score at the 89th percentile, Arizona students possess numerical credentials that rank them among the top 25 percent nationally. Compounding the already low acceptance rate is the fact that a very high percentage of those admitted (around 40 percent) actually choose to enroll at the law school. Arizona is, quite simply, in great demand.

ACADEMICS

Student/faculty ratio	18:1
% female faculty	21
% minority faculty	8
Hours of study per day	3.62

FINANCIAL FACTS

In-state tuition	$3,894
Out-of-state tuition	$9,500
Part-time tuition per credit	NR
Estimated books/expenses/fees	NR
On-campus living expenses	NR
Off-campus living expenses	NR
% first-year students receiving aid	NR
% all students receiving aid	NR
% aid that is merit-based	NR
% all students receiving grants/scholarships	NR
% all students receiving loans	NR
% all students receiving assistantships	NR
Average award package	NR
Average graduation debt	NR

ADMISSIONS

# applications received	1,800
% applicants accepted	22
% acceptees attending	38
Average LSAT	162
Average undergrad GPA	3.40
Application Fee	$35
Priority application deadline	NR
Priority notification	NR
Regular application deadline	March 1
Regular notification	NR
Admission deferment	NR
Gourman Report Rating	**3.33**

UNIVERSITY OF ARKANSAS AT FAYETTEVILLE 💾
School of Law

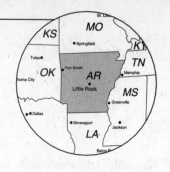

The University of Arkansas School of Law at Fayetteville, which has served its home state creditably for more than 70 years, holds the distinction of having been the first private-sector employer of President Clinton. (Although neither attended this, the older of Arkansas's two state law schools, both Bill and Hillary Rodham Clinton taught here briefly in the mid-seventies.) According to the law of averages, this small public law school won't employ another future president for another thousand years or so, but it will produce more than a few well-prepared attorneys in the meantime.

Arkansas at Fayetteville draws the vast majority of its students from within the state, and it puts them through a traditional, rigorous course of study that is particularly demanding in the first year, when students are required to take five full courses and a legal research class. After the first year, students are required to take a course in constitutional law, one in professional responsibility, and a writing course. Other than these courses, students are free to choose their program. The elective curriculum includes four client-based clinics, including the Federal Practice clinic, and a number of other professional skills courses. Open to J.D. students upon approval are the numerous courses offered through the law school's highly regarded graduate program in agricultural law. This program speaks to Arkansas's responsiveness to the imperatives of its home state, which has a substantial agricultural industry, most notably in poultry, and, according to the school's bulletin, ranks at or near the top in production of broilers, catfish, cattle, and calves. Of course, more Arkansas students feel the effects of this civic commitment in the extremely low tuition charged by the law school, which ranks among the least expensive in the nation.

This last fact certainly figures heavily in the assessments Arkansas students offer of their chosen school. The vast majority of those we heard from expressed a solid amount of fundamental satisfaction with their experience at the law school, and nearly all offered unsolicited praise for its very modest price tag. "Considering its cost vs. learning ratio," said one 1L, "U of A, Fayetteville, is a hard choice for anyone to overlook when considering law

James Miller, Associate Dean for Students
Leflar Law Center, Fayetteville, AR 72701-1201
Tel: (501) 575-3102
Internet: http://www.law.uark.edu/

school." On a purely substantive level, most of the students we heard from offered words of praise for the quality of the law school's academic programs, and especially for its recently revamped research and writing program, which most students called "excellent," "one of the best in the country," and other compliments to that effect.

Many students offered complaints about the bureaucracy of the broader university. "Most of the serious problems I see here are in the administration of the university itself," wrote one 2L. "It's a good feeling, however, to know that the law school is one of its few successful programs." As the conclusion of this last remark would seem to indicate, even those Arkansas students who see the most room for improvement in their chosen school seem to appreciate the quality of the school as it is.

ADMISSIONS

Like many state schools, the University of Arkansas, Fayetteville School of Law is constrained to admit a certain proportion of its students solely on the basis of their numerical credentials. At Arkansas, a complicated formula is used to arrive at an index score for each applicant. On the basis of this formula, the law school admits more than half of its class without considering other factors. What this means to you is that if your own numbers exceed the relatively modest average you see printed here, you can be virtually assured of gaining admission. Take note, however: numerical standards are on the rise here, and may not remain at this level for long.

ACADEMICS

Student/faculty ratio	12:1
% female faculty	29
% minority faculty	11
Hours of study per day	3.57

FINANCIAL FACTS

In-state tuition	$3,264
Out-of-state tuition	$7,296
Part-time tuition per credit	NR
Estimated books/expenses/fees	$1,231
On-campus living expenses	NR
Off-campus living expenses	NR
% first-year students receiving aid	27
% all students receiving aid	NR
% aid that is merit-based	50
% all students receiving grants/scholarships	24
% all students receiving loans	63
% all students receiving assistantships	NR
Average award package	$2,257
Average graduation debt	NR

ADMISSIONS

# applications received	824
% applicants accepted	41
% acceptees attending	41
Average LSAT	153
Average undergrad GPA	3.19
Application Fee	NR
No early decision program	
Regular application deadline	April 1
Regular notification	rolling
Admission may be deferred?	no
Gourman Report Rating	**2.86**

UNIVERSITY OF ARKANSAS AT LITTLE ROCK 🖫

School of Law

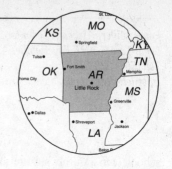

OVERVIEW

Type of school	public
Environment	city
Scholastic calendar	semester
Schedule	Full-time or part-time

STUDENTS

Enrollment of institution	5,416
Enrollment of law school	407
% male/female	55/45
% out-of-state	20
% part-time	35
% minorities	15
% international (# countries represented)	NR (NR)
Average age at entry	27

APPLICANTS ALSO LOOK AT

U. of Arkansas, Fayetteville
Vanderbilt University
Mercer University
Southern Methodist University
University of Georgia

SURVEY SAYS...

HITS
Great facilities
Research resources
Serving humankind

MISSES
Students feel poorly prepared
Clinical experience
Not enough courses

EMPLOYMENT PROFILE

% grads employed immediately	59
% grads employed within six months	97
Average starting salary	$35,000
% grads employed by field:	
Private practice	49
Business/industry	29
Government	11
Judicial clerkships	6
Public service	3
Academic	3
Military	0

Thanks to a certain former governor and his wife, the capital of Arkansas today enjoys a cachet previously unimaginable, and lawyers and Little Rock now go hand in hand in the minds of millions of Americans. Although the law school that comes to mind is Yale, perhaps in time it will be the University of Arkansas at Little Rock School of Law. For now, however, the law school remains primarily a local institution, and most of its graduates choose to work within the state. A young school in its current incarnation, Arkansas-Little Rock has grown since 1965 from a part-time division of its companion school in Fayetteville into an independent entity offering its own day and evening programs to well over four hundred students, the vast majority of them Arkansas residents. The law school recently experienced a comfortable expansion, thanks to its recent move into new, significantly larger quarters adjacent MacArthur Park near downtown Little Rock.

The curriculum at Arkansas, Little Rock, is relatively rigid, with a greater than average number of required courses. Its traditional classroom offerings are supplemented by several clinical programs in which enrollment is extremely limited. UALR is notable for its upperclass requirement of a trial advocacy course; the addition of this trial-skills requirement is part of the law school's continuing effort to increase its emphasis on practice skills. The volume of applications to the law school is relatively low, and the overall acceptance rate is quite high, although it has declined significantly in recent years. More than half of each entering class is admitted solely on the basis of a numerical index, so a moderately high GPA and LSAT score virtually assure admission.

Given the fact that they occupied the law school's new building relatively recently, it was not surprising that most of the students we heard from at Arkansas-Little Rock went out of their way to lavish praise on their new home. "The recent move to our new building has given us really excellent facilities," was one typical remark. "Our location in central Little Rock now gives us even greater opportunities for clerking." Judging from their other remarks, however, it is clear that the high morale here stems from more than just a change of scenery. Asked to name their school's

Jean Probasco, Director of Admissions/Registrar
1201 McAlmont, Little Rock, AR 72202-5142
Tel: (501) 324-9439

greatest strengths, nearly all cited the "beauty of the new facility and the superb, relaxed setting," but most went further: "The location is great, and the atmosphere is unpretentious and practical," said one 3L, "and the students, faculty and Dean are all quite pleasant." Many others echoed this last sentiment. "Faculty-student relations are very good," reported one 3L. "I cannot name a professor who I would hesitate to approach." And though few were quite as enthusiastic as this student, most seem to agree in spirit with his ringing endorsement: "The library is awesome, its director stellar, the Dean is great. All this under one fantastic New Roof at the most affordable price in the country—a real bargain."

All of which is not to say that students here do not see real room for improvement in some areas. Their criticisms were extremely consistent, focusing for the most part on the limitations of the curriculum itself. Though nearly all attest to a high degree of satisfaction with the quality of their program, most expressed their frustration with its inflexibility, and particularly with the inaccessibility of the law school's clinical programs such as the Legal Clinic, which is limited to eighteen students per semester. "They really should teach clinical skills to all" opined one student.

ADMISSIONS

UALR's numbers-driven admissions process allows the applicant to calculate her chances of admission much more accurately than she could for most other law schools. The average incoming Arkansas student has a respectable undergraduate GPA of 3.12 and moderately low LSAT score at about the 55th percentile. Since the law school's overall acceptance rate is relatively high, any applicant whose UGPA and LSAT exceed the Arkansas average probably stands a better than 50/50 chance of getting in—far better odds than at most law schools in the country.

ACADEMICS

Student/faculty ratio	16:1
% female faculty	34
% minority faculty	19
Hours of study per day	3.89

FINANCIAL FACTS

In-state tuition	$1,632
Out-of-state tuition	$3,696
Part-time tuition per credit	$1,496
Estimated books/expenses/fees	$496
On-campus living expenses	NR
Off-campus living expenses	NR
% first-year students receiving aid	NR
% all students receiving aid	NR
% aid that is merit-based	5
% all students receiving grants/scholarships	9
% all students receiving loans	55
% all students receiving assistantships	2
Average award package	$4,397
Average graduation debt	NR

ADMISSIONS

# applications received	576
% applicants accepted	45
% acceptees attending	48
Average LSAT	153
Average undergrad GPA	3.10
Application Fee	$40
No early decision program	
Regular application deadline	April 1
Regular notification	rolling
Admission may be deferred?	no
Gourman Report Rating	2.47

UNIVERSITY OF BALTIMORE 🖫
School of Law

OVERVIEW

Type of school	public
Environment	metropolis
Scholastic calendar	NR
Schedule	Full-time or part-time

STUDENTS

Enrollment of institution	NR
Enrollment of law school	1,066
% male/female	52/48
% out-of-state	20
% part-time	41
% minorities	13
% international (# countries represented)	NR (NR)
Average age at entry	27

APPLICANTS ALSO LOOK AT

University of Maryland
American University
Catholic University of America
George Mason University
Villanova University

SURVEY SAYS...

HITS
Legal writing
Center for International and Comparative Law
Practical lawyering skills

MISSES
Intellectual challenge
Sense of community
Not enough courses

EMPLOYMENT PROFILE

% grads employed immediately	70
% grads employed within six months	85
Average starting salary	$36,759
% grads employed by field:	
Private practice	48
Business/industry	2
Government	16
Judicial clerkships	32
Military	1

The city of Baltimore is home to two public law schools in the University of Maryland system. The younger and less well-known of the two is the University of Baltimore School of Law, founded in 1925. But whatever UB gives away to the neighboring University of Maryland School of Law in terms of reputation it more than makes up for in sheer size; with more than 1,000 J.D. students, approximately one quarter of them in the part-time evening division, this is one of the largest law schools in the nation.

The obvious benefits any large school provides are not lacking at the University of Baltimore. Like its companion school, Baltimore has dedicated significant resources to its clinical programs. In fact, this is one of very few law schools in the country to have what amounts to a clinical requirement. All students must satisfy an advocacy requirement through participation in the law school's several clinics, enrollment in an advanced advocacy course or competition as part of one of the law school's eleven inter-scholastic advocacy teams. UB has also developed a new curriculum, in which most students choose one of 12 areas of concentration on which to focus.

Notably, few of the students we heard from had any complaints about the quality of the school's existing programs, and most saw fit to offer unsolicited praise for the degree of practical preparation it has given them. "This school's emphasis is on teaching the practical skills needed to become a highly successful attorney," reported a 1L. "The program here focuses on the basics," said another, "and our bar-passage rate is excellent." Others offered broader endorsements. As one 2L wrote, "The curriculum adds just enough theory and academia to challenge the mind and expand understanding beyond the practical requirements." One 3L offered this ringing overall endorsement: "The top government and political figures in Maryland attended the University of Baltimore; I like being a part of the next generation of the state's leaders." And though few of the Baltimore students we heard from were quite that enthusiastic, nearly all appear to appreciate the value of their solid legal education. "For the price, it can't be beat if you plan to practice in the Mid-Atlantic region."

Claire Valentine, Assistant Director of Admissions
1420 North Charles Street, Baltimore, MD 21201-5779
Tel: (410) 837-4459   Fax: (410) 837-4450
eMail: lwadmiss@ubmail.ubalt.edu
Internet: http://www.ubalt.edu/www/law

University of Baltimore

Still, even the most highly satisfied Baltimore students had little difficulty naming areas in which their school could improve. Many students were dissatisfied with the quality and frequency of their interaction with faculty. "Although the education I am receiving is excellent," wrote one 3L who spoke for many, "the administration here is poor to say the least." Since we surveyed, however, an Assistant Dean for Student Affairs was added to the staff to provide a wide range of counseling and academic advising services for students, as well as hosting a series of open meetings with the Dean each semester to improve communication between students and the administration. Many here complained of a relatively high degree of competitiveness among students and relatively little diversity. Overall, however, even the most critical students managed to be even-handed: "The school could use serious improvement, but it should stop trying to compete with University of Maryland. Baltimore is a strong school that should be proud of the program it offers."

ADMISSIONS

In terms of the numerical standards to which it holds applicants, the University of Baltimore School of Law ranks in the bottom third of all U.S. law schools, but its bargain-basement tuition draws an applicant pool that is large enough to make the overall admissions process quite competitive. Nearly eight applicants vie annually for each spot in Baltimore's entering class of about 300. Those whose credentials fall short face very long odds.

ACADEMICS

Student/faculty ratio	22:1
% female faculty	32
% minority faculty	10
Hours of study per day	3.51

FINANCIAL FACTS

In-state tuition	$7,166
Out-of-state tuition	$12,788
Part-time tuition per credit	$296
Estimated books/expenses/fees	$1,600
On-campus living expenses	NR
Off-campus living expenses	$9,000
% first-year students receiving aid	NR
% all students receiving aid	60
% aid that is merit-based	NR
% all students receiving grants/scholarships	80
% all students receiving loans	90
% all students receiving assistantships	NR
Average award package	$3,800
Average graduation debt	$31,300

ADMISSIONS

# applications received	2,294
% applicants accepted	36
% acceptees attending	36
Average LSAT	153
Average undergrad GPA	3.13
Application Fee	$35
No early decision program	
Regular application deadline	April 5
Regular notification	rolling
Admission may be deferred?	No

Gourman Report Rating	**2.58**

BAYLOR UNIVERSITY 💾
School of Law

As a rule, Texas's eight law schools, which together enroll nearly 7,000 students, are a bit larger than average. The exception that proves the rule sits smack-dab in the middle of the Lone Star State: the Baylor University School of Law, Texas's oldest law school. The only concession this small, inexpensive private law school makes to the bigger-is-better ethos is its outsize reputation for training great lawyers. Located in the central Texas town of Waco, the Baylor law school has been in nearly continuous operation since 1857 on the campus of this midsize university, affiliated with the Texas Baptist Convention. Baylor's unassailable regional reputation owes much to the success of its graduates, a disproportionate number of whom hold or have held positions of power in the state's legal and political institutions. But the law school has seen to it that even its less prominent graduates distinguish themselves by the quality of their training. Baylor's J.D. curriculum, which is geared as much to practical as to intellectual training, includes far more required courses than does the traditional law school. Among these is a rare third-year requirement for which Baylor is well known, the Practice Court course. The broadbased advocacy training that this course provides has helped Baylor grads to continue to succeed in an increasingly competitive job market. Baylor operates on a quarter system, admitting students in Fall, Spring and Summer. Admissions are highly selective and numerical standards high.

Students come to Baylor for the excellent litigation training the school is known for, and in true Texas hyperbolic style, boast that their practical law preparation is unbeatable: "The program here is without a doubt the best trial preparation in the country; other law schools don't even come close to preparing their students for the practice of law, they prepare their students for malpractice," said one proud 2L. Baylor students offered gratitude for the small class size. They greatly admired their "firm but fair" professors and said that the faculty open-door policy cuts the edge off the intense competition and makes the rigorous course load bearable. One happy student said, "The faculty comprise some of the best attorneys in Texas who teach out of a desire to teach!"

Becky Beck, Admissions Director
P.O. Box 97288, Waco, TX 76798-7288
Tel: (817) 755-1911
eMail: law_support@baylor.edu
Internet: http//www.baylor.edu/baylor/department/grad/law/
welcome.htm/

Baylor University

Through gritted teeth, students expressed understanding of and appreciation for the intense workload that prefigures the now standard interminable office hours most will endure in private practice. However, they wholeheartedly denounced the administration's grade deflation policy. One 1L explained it's not "just 'grade deflation' but 'grade depression!'...This system has resulted in high prestige for some students and for Baylor, but low self-esteem and job opportunities for others."

According to one student, "The small student body of approximately 400 permits a close-knit family atmosphere." However, students commented on the lack of diversity at Baylor. As one student told us, "Diversity at this law school is practically non-existent, and therefore, the levels of tolerance are low for people who aren't white males (Protestant of course!)" Many complained this southern conservative school needs to "focus on attracting a diverse student body with a broader array of experiences, political, and social ideas, and goals!"

Applicants to Baylor should remember this 2L's comments: "If you want to have fun in law school and slide through third year, don't come to Baylor. They will work you like no other. But be assured that you will have a top rate education."

ADMISSIONS

Unlike most law schools, Baylor welcomes new students three times during the course of the year, in September, January, and June. If you hope to be among the roughly 180 people annually who take seats in one of these entering classes, be prepared to fight. The numerical credentials of Baylor students are astoundingly high. Their stellar GPAs and average LSAT score above the 90th percentile rank them among the most highly qualified student bodies in the nation. Taking into account both the low overall acceptance rate and the percentage of admitted applicants who accept offers to attend the law school, Baylor ranks among the 50 most in-demand schools in the country.

ACADEMICS

Student/faculty ratio	19:1
% female faculty	33
% minority faculty	9
Hours of study per day	5.12

FINANCIAL FACTS

Tuition	$10,023
Part-time tuition per credit	NR
Estimated books/expenses/fees	NR
On-campus living expenses	NR
Off-campus living expenses	NR
% first-year students receiving aid	100
% all students receiving aid	100
% aid that is merit-based	52
% all students receiving grants/scholarships	64
% all students receiving loans	75
% all students receiving assistantships	2
Average award package	$3,211
Average graduation debt	$35,335

ADMISSIONS

# applications received	746
% applicants accepted	34
% acceptees attending	22
Average LSAT	160
Average undergrad GPA	3.48
Application Fee	$40
Priority application deadline	NR
Priority notification	NR
Regular application deadline	March 1, Nov. 1
Regular notification	rolling
Admission may be deferred?	No
Gourman Report Rating	**3.31**

BOSTON COLLEGE
Law School

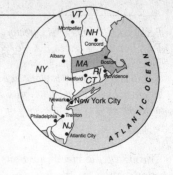

Boston is not only America's number-one college town, but also the nation's top law-school town. Every year close to 30,000 applications are filed by applicants seeking to fill one of the 2,000 first-year slots in Boston's six law schools. More than five thousand of those applications are addressed to the Boston College Law School, located on the city's outskirts in semi-urban Newton. After its neighbor in Cambridge (the one that starts with "H"), BC is probably the most esteemed school in the entire region. And the law school at Boston College, founded in 1929, has established a reputation for excellence that extends well beyond New England.

This reputation was built on the strength of the law school's faculty and the traditional curriculum they administer, a curriculum that is continually revised to keep up with the evolving profession. Advanced course offerings are many and varied, as are the clinical programs in which a large proportion of BC law students participate. With the resources of both the college and the city's legal community (the nation's fifth largest) close at hand, students here do not want for either learning or employment opportunities. Boston College law grads, slightly more than half of whom remain in New England, find very good work, and they find it very easily. Not surprisingly, given the law program's strength and the sheer volume of applicants, admissions standards are quite high; entering BC students have numerical credentials that rank among the nation's highest.

As hard as they worked to gain admission to the law school, students at BC do not let up once classes begin. Reports are that the motivation level of students is high, but that competition among them is mercifully moderate. As one 2L said, "Our profs are easily accessible, and the atmosphere here is the furthest thing from cutthroat." Indeed, collegiality seems to be the rule. "The people are BC's greatest strength," went one typical assessment. "This is a very friendly place, and it is never hard to find a helping hand when needed." This sentiment is almost universally held. In fact, the quality of life that Boston College students say they enjoy placed them far above students at a majority of the schools we surveyed. While BC students are not without their criticisms of their chosen school, they overwhelmingly attest to a general sense of well-being. We heard many comments that agreed that "there's no better friendlier, more supportive place to go."

On the downside, according to many students we interviewed, the general goodwill that characterizes relations within the BC community is offset somewhat by the law school's facilities and by certain curricular limitations. On the former issue, most agreed that "our physical plant is a big drawback," however, the recently completed new library should reverse many of these negative perceptions. On the latter issue, more than a few students complained about the limited number of spaces available in certain popular courses, and many called for expansion of the law school's clinical programs. "There are real problems with course scheduling and with the overall selection of courses," said one student who spoke for many. Several students who professed an interest in public interest law agreed with the student who said that "there should be better career resources and placement assistance for people who are not interested in large law firms." As one 3L put it: "There is too much emphasis on big firms as the career option."

Even those students who were the most openly critical of aspects of their experience at Boston College seemed to agree, however, that they could be much worse off. Their feelings were summed up by this statement from a BC 3L: "It's a great place to be—if you have to be in law school."

ADMISSIONS

While it is true that many applicants to the nation's five or six super-elite schools consider Boston College a "safety," it is hardly a safe bet that even well-qualified applicants will gain admission. If you hope to gain a spot in BC's entering class of almost 300, you'll have to earn it. Applications volume at the law school is extraordinarily high, and the qualifications of those applying are impressive. Those who are admitted and go on to enroll at BC possess very strong numerical credentials, including an average LSAT score above the 90th percentile. These credentials are stronger, in fact, than those of students at 85 percent of the nation's fully accredited law schools.

ACADEMICS	
Student/faculty ratio	16:1
% female faculty	56
% minority faculty	12
Hours of study per day	3.30

FINANCIAL FACTS	
Tuition	$21,230
Part-time tuition per credit	NR
Estimated books/expenses/fees	$6,740
On-campus living expenses	NR
Off-campus living expenses	NR
% first-year students receiving aid	75
% all students receiving aid	75
% aid that is merit-based	NR
% all students receiving grants/scholarships	32
% all students receiving loans	76
% all students receiving assistantships	NR
Average award package	$29,000
Average graduation debt	$60,500

ADMISSIONS	
# applications received	5,460
% applicants accepted	22
% acceptees attending	24
Average LSAT	163
Average undergrad GPA	3.47
Application Fee	$50
Priority application deadline	NR
Priority notification	NR
Regular application deadline	March 1
Regular notification	rolling
Admission deferment	NR
Gourman Report Rating	**4.29**

BOSTON UNIVERSITY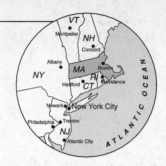
School of Law

Established in 1872, Boston University School of Law, a large and highly esteemed private law school enrolls almost 1,100 students on the urban campus of its well-respected parent institution. BU's extremely well-qualified law students pursue a course of study that is an interesting mix of innovation and tradition. The former is evident in the diversity and breadth of BU's curriculum. Unlike many schools of its size and long-standing reputation Boston University has not resisted the trend toward practical-skills training at the J.D. level. The law school's clinical program is large and multifaceted, and few schools have made a greater commitment to emphasizing legal writing skills. BUSL students rave about the First Year Research and Writing Seminar for its great instruction and small class size (there are fewer than twenty in each session). Said one, "The writing program here is outstanding!" Of the upperclass students, 47 percent are staff members of one of the school's seven journals. BUSL draws many driven students with its concentrations in six different areas of the law and dual degrees in six disciplines, not to mention the overseas programs in three countries. BUSL retains a strong grasp on the traditional through the medium of the Socratic Method.

Students thankfully report that BU has abandoned one long-standing tradition: the cut throat competition about students complained so vehemently in our earlier surveys. The much happier students we heard from recently told us that "the mythology of BU as a hyper-competitive, dog-eat-dog place is finally giving way to the more accurate description: BUSL is a community of hardworking, contentious, high-spirited, but largely good-hearted people. I'm proud to be here." Many students were pleasantly surprised to find human beings rather than cannibals as their peers, but the majority still rates the competition as "high" or "extremely high." One student explains this productive competition: "Because so many of the students come from top undergraduate institutions, the level of intellect at BUSL is very high. On some level this may push all of us to work harder and achieve more." Another positive change, still in process, is the university's efforts to improve the physical facilities. According to one student, "The university has approved plans to expand our

Kristine Marzolf, Director
765 Commonwealth Avenue, Boston, MA 02215
Tel: (617) 353-3100   Fax: (617) 353-2547
eMail: bulawadm@bu.edu

school to take over the undergrad library next door." As for the education itself, students at BU are overwhelmingly satisfied. As one very representative second year put it, BU's best asset is "the quality of the teaching—the faculty is outstanding, both in terms of credentials and in the way they care about their students and how well they are teaching. The school also offers a wide range of experience and training in both theoretical and practical areas. The clinical courses are great!" And another told us, "The writing program is excellent!" Students also raved about the Health Law, International Law, and Intellectual Property Law programs, plus the variety of classes, location and student diversity.

The main complaint many students expressed was with the BUSL facilities: "The building is very ugly; heating and cooling is inconsistent." However, this student put things in perspective: "The building is the brunt of many negative comments, but seriously, this is not a major component nor detractor from the excellent education." The school is trying to remedy the situation with three new student lounges and a new auditorium. We heard other complaints about the Career Placement Office: "Career Placement needs a major overhaul!" Several student felt that placement efforts were aimed at the top 15 to 20 percent of the class. However, some savvy students placed blame on the true monster: a bad job market. One student told us that people only complain at BUSL because they worry about status, but most come to realize they were lucky to attend: "A lot of people come here because they didn't get into their first choice. By the time they leave, though , they realize this is a great school." Confirms this student, a BUSL education "really translates into employable skills, yet preserves the philosophical knowledge and perspective which gives work meaning over the long term."

ADMISSIONS

Though competition among enrolled students at the Boston University School of Law reportedly runs much higher than at neighboring Boston College, the admissions process at BU is (ever so slightly) less selective. Still, the numerical credentials of students here rank them in the top quarter of all law students nationally, and with more than 4,500 applications filed annually, the BU admissions committee must choose carefully. Mercifully, however, almost five candidates are admitted for every spot in the law school's entering class of roughly 330.

ACADEMICS

Student/faculty ratio	17:1
% female faculty	32
% minority faculty	9
Hours of study per day	4.09

FINANCIAL FACTS

Tuition	$20,570
Part-time tuition per credit	NR
Estimated books/expenses/fees	$1,734
On-campus living expenses	NR
Off-campus living expenses	NR
% first-year students receiving aid	85
% all students receiving aid	85
% aid that is merit-based	20
% all students receiving grants/scholarships	38
% all students receiving loans	85
% all students receiving assistantships	NR
Average award package	$9,200
Average graduation debt	NR

ADMISSIONS

# applications received	4,671
% applicants accepted	36
% acceptees attending	21
Average LSAT	160
Average undergrad GPA	3.33
Application Fee	$50
No early decision program	
Regular application deadline	March 1
Regular notification	rolling
Admission deferment	one year
Gourman Report Rating	4.48

BRIGHAM YOUNG UNIVERSITY 🖫

J. Reuben Clark Law School

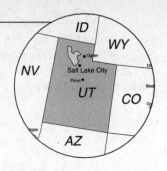

Brigham Young University, founded over 100 years ago, is the largest privately-owned, church-related university in the U.S. And since the J. Reuben Clark Law School was established in 1973, it has steadily gained a solid reputation for academic excellence. That reputation now extends well beyond the Mountain West, a region heavily populated by graduates of BYU's rigorous, traditional J.D. program.

Although few have failed to take notice of BYU's many successes, admissions standards at the law school have not risen appreciably in recent years. This has as much to do with the fact that standards were very high to begin with as it does with the fact that the applications volume has not increased significantly despite the law school's growing reputation. BYU is attractive to prospective law students for several reasons. But it is clear that the university is not for everyone. Though the law school encourages attendance by members of all faiths, the influence of the Church of Jesus Christ of Latter-Day Saints is inescapable. BYU, for instance, is the only law school with a dress code (no sleeveless shirts or skirts above the knee) and a total ban on alcohol, tobacco and caffeine. Of course, at least one effect of the school's Mormon affiliation is universally appealing: its extremely low tuition. Because of heavy church subsidies, the tuition at BYU is, by a fairly wide margin, the lowest of any private law school in the nation.

Aside from a small minority, current law students at BYU seem quite happy with their education and surroundings. Nearly 90 percent of students rated both the quality of teaching and facilities at BYU as excellent or very good. "The professors are top notch and available for students' questions and to give advice." said one student. Other students also showed great pride in BYU: "The profs are great. They care about the students, and it shows." A major addition being made to the law library will expand the university's electronic access to legal materials. Students are looking forward to completion of construction, set for December 1996, and see the new facilities as a sign of the university's dedication to legal education.

Lola K. Wilcock, Admissions Officer
340 JRCB, Provo, UT 84602
Tel: (801) 378-4277
eMail: rused@lawgate.byu.edu

Terms like "friendly," "helpful" and "moral" are often used by law students to describe the atmosphere at BYU. Although a few find the competition among students disturbing, many more have been encouraged at the level of cooperation. "Students are very willing to help each other, share notes, outlines, etc.," said one. A native East coast student agreed: "I was initially caught off guard when people were so friendly and helpful at the school...The honesty and decency of the people here make the law school a better experience."

If the school's resources are lacking in one area, said students, it is career counseling and job placement. Although the university has made some recent improvements, several students voiced dissatisfaction with the Career Services Office. One student noted, "Career Services appears to be doing more than was done in the past, but it still needs improvement." Even those who praised the university on every front noted that the student body is not diverse. "[The university] needs more female and minority students," said one student. "I would enjoy more diverse views from the faculty," said one. (Although BYU's law school faculty is one of the most ethnically diverse in the nation, it ranks the lowest in percentage of female members.) It must be noted, however, that even the relative discontents among the students we heard from had something good to say about BYU (close to great skiing and mountain climbing), and most expressed a high overall degree of satisfaction with their law school.

ADMISSIONS

The admissions process at Brigham Young University's J. Reuben Clark Law School is both kind and brutal. Because of its relatively small applicant pool, BYU's overall acceptance rate is moderate. Numerical admissions standards, however, are very high. In fact, with an average LSAT score at the 89th percentile and a very high average GPA, the student body at BYU ranks, by our calculations, among the 20 most qualified in the entire nation.

ACADEMICS

Student/faculty ratio	9:1
% female faculty	12
% minority faculty	12
Hours of study per day	4.74

FINANCIAL FACTS

Tuition	$4,760
Part-time tuition per credit	NR
Estimated books/expenses/fees	NR
On-campus living expenses	NR
Off-campus living expenses	NR
% first-year students receiving aid	84
% all students receiving aid	90
% aid that is merit-based	33
% all students receiving grants/scholarships	42
% all students receiving loans	82
% all students receiving assistantships	NR
Average award package	$10,500
Average graduation debt	$23,000

ADMISSIONS

# applications received	718
% applicants accepted	33
% acceptees attending	59
Average LSAT	160
Average undergrad GPA	3.60
Application Fee	$30
No early decision program	
Regular application deadline	February 15
Regular notification	rolling
Admission deferment	one year
Gourman Report Rating	**3.63**

BROOKLYN LAW SCHOOL 💾

OVERVIEW

Type of school	private
Environment	metropolis
Scholastic calendar	NR
Schedule	Full-time or part-time

STUDENTS

Enrollment of institution	NR
Enrollment of law school	1,451
% male/female	57/43
% out-of-state	15
% part-time	32
% minorities	15
% international (# countries represented)	2 (18)
Average age at entry	24

APPLICANTS ALSO LOOK AT

Fordham University
New York University
Yeshiva University
New York Law School
Hofstra University

SURVEY SAYS...

HITS
Clinical experience
Sleeping

MISSES
Research resources
Sense of community
Studying

EMPLOYMENT PROFILE

% grads employed immediately	NR
% grads employed within six months	84
Average starting salary	NR
% grads employed by field:	
Private practice	58
Business/industry	17
Government	14
Judicial clerkships	4
Public service	1
Academic	6
Military	4

Separated from bustling Manhattan by the narrow East River, Brooklyn Law School sits in one of the most historic and scenic neighborhoods in all of New York's five boroughs. The law school, located in Brooklyn Heights, just blocks from the federal and state courts, opened its doors in 1901. Since that time the school has grown from a student body of 18 to one of nearly 1,500, nearly a third of whom are in the part-time division. The school's solid regional reputation allows many graduates to obtain positions at nearby law firms and government offices. Many Brooklyn grads owe thanks to the network of over 13,000 alumni, most of whom live and practice around New York City, for their help in keeping the school's job placement rate relatively high. Having a strong regional reputation doesn't limit the geographic representation of the student body, however; over the past several years, an increasing number of students have come from across the United States and around the world, according to statistics from the admissions office.

What truly distinguishes the Brooklyn Law School curriculum from others is its diverse in-house and external clinical programs, which take full advantage of the law school's close proximity to several important offices: the U.S. District Court, the State Supreme and Family Courts, the City Civil and Criminal Courts, the offices of the U.S. Attorney, the King's County D.A. and the Legal Aid Society. Students at Brooklyn Law School appreciate the opportunities and the hands-on experience the school's excellent location provides. "The clinical programs at Brooklyn are excellent. They give students the opportunity to gain good practical legal experience, which employers look for," said one 3L.

In the classroom, Brooklyn's courses are what another 3L called "extremely practical with respect to passing the bar." This doesn't mean that the curriculum is just a three-year bar prep course; the school offers far more than that. Once a Brooklyn student navigates the standard first-year curriculum of torts and legal process, he can chart his own course of the next two years, choosing from the school's nearly 150 elective offerings. "The school offers a wide variety of courses, particularly in the area of intellectual

Henry W. Haverstick III, Dean of Admissions and
Financial Aid
250 Joralemon Street, Brooklyn, NY 11201
Tel: (718) 780-7906
Internet: http://www2.brooklaw.edu

Brooklyn Law School

property," said one 3L. Students spoke highly of the faculty at Brooklyn law school and the level of interaction between students and professors. When it came to the make-up of the faculty, however, several students called for more ethnic diversity. Although Brooklyn is quite gender balanced with women comprising 41 percent of the faculty, ethnic minorities account for only about 9 percent of the faculty. One student went so far as to call the school's "commitment to diversity a complete sham." The same student added: "It's a very good school if you're from white middle-class suburbia."

In the age of overlapping professions, a growing number of Brooklyn Law School students are pursuing other advanced degrees in addition to a J.D. The school co-sponsors, with other leading universities, joint-degree programs leading toward a J.D. degree with a master's degree in business administration, law and political science, library and information science, city and regional planning, public administration, and urban planning. In addition, students can satisfy interests in international law at the school's Center for the Study of International Business Law, established in 1987. The center offers more than twenty courses and seminars on international law and publishes its own journal.

Although responses to our survey were limited, by and large students at Brooklyn seem relatively content with the most fundamental aspects of their law school experience. Many praised the school's broad curriculum and clinical programs. However, one common complaint was the lack of a social community at Brooklyn. The school has historically been and continues to be a commuter school. On balance, though, most Brooklyn students were positive about the present and optimistic about the future, both for themselves and for their school.

ADMISSIONS

Although a few better-known schools in Manhattan are far more selective than Brooklyn, a prospective student's numerical standards have to be fairly solid to gain admittance. Before you count yourself a shoe-in consider that in 1995, the average incoming Brooklyn Law School student had an undergraduate GPA of 3.31 and an LSAT score at about the 80th percentile. Applicants whose numerical credentials exceed these numbers are highly likely to gain admittance to Brooklyn.

ACADEMICS

Student/faculty ratio	20:1
% female faculty	41
% minority faculty	9
Hours of study per day	3.13

FINANCIAL FACTS

Tuition	$17,600
Part-time tuition per credit	NR
Estimated books/expenses/fees	NR
On-campus living expenses	NR
Off-campus living expenses	NR
% first-year students receiving aid	NR
% all students receiving aid	NR
% aid that is merit-based	NR
% all students receiving grants/scholarships	NR
% all students receiving loans	NR
% all students receiving assistantships	NR
Average award package	NR
Average graduation debt	NR

ADMISSIONS

# applications received	2,678
% applicants accepted	37
% acceptees attending	27
Average LSAT	157
Average undergrad GPA	3.32
Application Fee	$50
No early decision program	
Regular application deadline	NR
Regular notification	rolling
Admission deferment	one year
Gourman Report Rating	3.62

CALIFORNIA WESTERN
School of Law

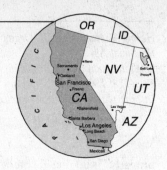

They may not realize it, but when Easterners imagine California, they are imagining San Diego. This fast-growing metropolis, the sixth largest in the United States, is blessed with the kind of climate that makes a mockery of winter and turns many casual visitors into lifetime residents. With 325 annual days of sunshine and 70 miles of brilliant beaches, San Diego County promises quality of life writ large, a fact that one of the city's two law schools, the California Western School of Law, sees fit to point out at the very beginning of its admissions materials.

Indeed, this midsize private law school understands quite well the power of its location, which surely helps explain why it draws such a great proportion of its students from outside California. From within the state and without, competition is tough for the more than 200 seats in Cal Western's first-year class. Those students who do succeed in gaining admission pursue a fairly straightforward J.D. program on the law school's downtown San Diego campus, a program that has been supplemented recently with special offerings in the growing fields of biotechnology law and telecommunications law. Like most law schools that lack weighty and long-standing reputations, however, Cal Western has seen to it that its students gain practical lawyering experience before graduation, experience that will prove invaluable when seeking employment. Between Cal Western's extensive clinical internship program and its classroom trial-advocacy program, a great majority of its students gain such experience.

As for their experience while at the law school, most Cal Western students express a fairly high degree of satisfaction with many fundamental aspects of their chosen school. By all accounts, for instance, the quality of the relations among students and between faculty and students is quite high. Asked to name their law school's greatest strengths, most Cal Western students cite its "good educational environment," "student camaraderie," and the "availability of faculty to students." "The faculty are very helpful," reported one 2L, "and have not forgotten what it is like to be a law student." As for their program itself, most of those we heard from were most enthusiastic about Cal Western's practical focus, in particular its trial advocacy program. "I've never learned more or been more challenged to expand my skills than on the moot trial team," said one 2L. "The practical, 'black-letter' approach to most classes helps with bar preparation," wrote another.

Most students at Cal Western have little difficulty pointing out areas in which the law school could stand to improve. Few students, for instance, had anything charitable to say about the law school's physical plant. In most cases, their criticism focused not on the quality of Cal Western's facilities but, rather, on the lack of facilities. "I would love to have access to all the facilities that a law school affiliated with an undergraduate campus has," said one. Less charitably, one out-of-state student complained that "the law school does not make prospective students who cannot afford to visit the law school aware of the fact that there is no campus whatsoever." Indeed, many students complained that their immediate physical surroundings worked against any sense of community among students, though the recent addition of a new administrative building should do much to mitigate these complaints.

All in all, Cal Western students seem unenthusiastic about some aspects of their experience at the law school, though nearly all seem to agree that they feel well prepared to enter the profession. This general assessment from one satisfied 3L nicely summed up the sentiments of many: "Cal Western is near enough to the beach, but with a seriousness and practicality that should create effective attorneys."

ADMISSIONS

The allure of the San Diego area is strong enough to draw roughly 3,000 applications annually to the California Western School of Law. But while only about 250 first-year students enroll annually, this midsize private law school sends acceptance letters to a relatively large group in order to fill this class. The result is that Cal Western ranks somewhere on the lower end of the midrange of all law schools in terms of overall selectivity. An applicant with an undergraduate GPA over 3.0 and an LSAT score above 155, for instance, should be virtually certain of gaining admission.

ACADEMICS

Student/faculty ratio	20:1
% female faculty	45
% minority faculty	17
Hours of study per day	4.05

FINANCIAL FACTS

Tuition	$19,100
Part-time tuition per credit	NR
Estimated books/expenses/fees	$720
On-campus living expenses	NR
Off-campus living expenses	NR
% first-year students receiving aid	75
% all students receiving aid	85
% aid that is merit-based	NR
% all students receiving grants/scholarships	NR
% all students receiving loans	85
% all students receiving assistantships	NR
Average award package	$21,000
Average graduation debt	$78,000

ADMISSIONS

# applications received	2,608
% applicants accepted	53
% acceptees attending	23
Average LSAT	152
Average undergrad GPA	3.09
Application Fee	$45
Priority application deadline	NR
Priority notification	NR
Regular application deadline	April 1
Regular notification	NR
Admission deferment	NR
Gourman Report Rating	**3.05**

UNIVERSITY OF CALIFORNIA, BERKELEY ⌷

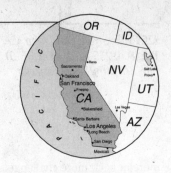

Boalt Hall School of Law

OVERVIEW

Type of school	public
Environment	metropolis
Scholastic calendar	semester
Schedule	Full time only

STUDENTS

Enrollment of institution	21,138
Enrollment of law school	770
% male/female	50/50
% out-of-state	25
% part-time	NR
% minorities	37
% international (# countries represented)	NR (NR)
Average age at entry	25

APPLICANTS ALSO LOOK AT

U. of California, Los Angeles
Stanford University
Harvard University
Yale University
New York University

SURVEY SAYS...

HITS
Prestige
Sleeping
Library staff

MISSES
Lack of diversity among faculty
Faculty-student relations
Practical lawyering skills

EMPLOYMENT PROFILE

% grads employed immediately	76
% grads employed within six months	94
Average starting salary	$59,531
% grads employed by field:	
Private practice	75
Business/industry	4
Government	7
Judicial clerkships	11
Public service	1
Academic	2
Military	2

The University of California's flagship campus is located in a town that Pat Buchanan and his ilk still enjoy referring to as "The People's Republic of Berkeley." But as apt a moniker as that might be for a city that celebrates indigenous Peoples' Day instead of Columbus Day and virtually refuses to enforce marijuana laws, the broad-based leftist activism of Cal students is mostly the stuff of nostalgia, fond or bitter depending on one's political leanings. These days, politics takes a distant backseat to academics as the focus of Berkeley's faculty, administration, and student body. The university is consistently ranked as the strongest overall graduate institution in the country, thanks in part to the strength of its hugely respected law school, Boalt Hall. The alma mater of former Chief Justice Earl Warren and longtime comics-page star Joanie Caucus of *Doonesbury*, Boalt is generally regarded as one of the nation's top 10 law schools and as probably the best bargain in American legal education.

The curriculum here is staunchly traditional in the first year; the Socratic Method is alive and well. In their second and third years, however, Boalt Hall students have a wide range of courses from which to choose. In recent years, programs of informal but organized concentration have been added at the J.D. level, and the law school's program in Jurisprudence and Social Policy is one of the country's finest interdisciplinary legal-studies programs. Upon completing their degrees, roughly 75 percent of Boalt students choose to remain in California, where they have their choice of top jobs. Berkeley's stellar reputation and very down-to-earth price combine to produce a torrent of applications every year. In recent years, the law school has admitted around 10 percent of all applicants. Said a 1L: "The whole first year hazing experience is very minimal here. They let you have a life and the Bay Area is a great place to have one."

The unique Boalt attributes that draw the lucky, talented and driven people who are admitted, in addition to those mentioned above, are the school's excellent reputation; its profusion of journals; proximity to Silicon Valley; the fantastic Intellectual Property law, Immigration, International and Environmental law programs; and perhaps most importantly, the enriching diversity of Boalt's "brilliant" students. One 2L spoke for many

Edward Tom, Director of Admissions and Financial Aid
220 Boalt Hall, Berkeley, CA 94720-7200
Tel: (510) 642-2274   Fax: (510) 643-6222
Internet: http://www.law.berkeley.edu

University of California, Berkeley

when she counted her blessings: "Great student body. I hope it will get to stay so diverse given the recent U.C. Regents' decision [to no longer consider race, gender, or ethnicity in applications]."

"I really like that it's a public school because I think the institution and the people are more concerned with their communities," one student said. As for their scholastic community, Boalt students would make certain changes if they could. A great majority wish the faculty would initiate diversification efforts, as one first-year told us, the "Faculty is too conservative, too white male dominated and too many 1L classes are taught by visiting professors." Some students wished course offerings were more numerous and broader as well.

However, the most frequent and insistent negative comment we heard will soon be obsolete according to this student who chimed in: "My bashing the facilities may be inapplicable soon because the building is currently undergoing renovation and expansion."

In general, most students would agree with this man: "Boalt is terrific. It exceeded all my expectations."

ADMISSIONS

The student body at the Boalt Hall School of Law is one of the most qualified in the nation, so if you are considering sending an application to Berkeley, take this simple advice: Apply to a backup school as well. This is straight up one of the four or five hardest schools in the country to get into, even for those with extraordinarily high numerical credentials. Demand for spots in Boalt's entering class of about 270 is so great that even an applicant with a GPA around 3.6 and an LSAT score at the 98th percentile stands a better chance of being rejected than of getting in.

ACADEMICS

Student/faculty ratio	16:1
% female faculty	27
% minority faculty	15
Hours of study per day	3.10

FINANCIAL FACTS

In-state tuition	$10,800
Out-of-state tuition	$19,194
Part-time tuition per credit	NR
Estimated books/expenses/fees	NR
On-campus living expenses	NR
Off-campus living expenses	NR
% first-year students receiving aid	85
% all students receiving aid	80
% aid that is merit-based	5
% all students receiving grants/scholarships	80
% all students receiving loans	76
% all students receiving assistantships	6
Average award package	$3,000
Average graduation debt	$24,000

ADMISSIONS

# applications received	4,798
% applicants accepted	17
% acceptees attending	31
Average LSAT	166
Average undergrad GPA	3.63
Application Fee	$40
No early decision program	
Regular application deadline	February 1
Regular notification	rolling
Admission deferment	one year
Gourman Report Rating	**4.89**

UNIVERSITY OF CALIFORNIA, DAVIS

School of Law

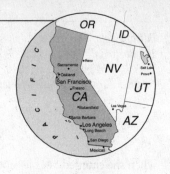

OVERVIEW

Type of school	public
Environment	suburban
Scholastic calendar	quarter
Schedule	Full time only

STUDENTS

Enrollment of institution	17,596
Enrollment of law school	467
% male/female	51/49
% out-of-state	9
% part-time	NR
% minorities	34
% international (# countries represented)	NR (8)
Average age at entry	25

APPLICANTS ALSO LOOK AT

U. of California, Berkeley
University of California, Hastings College of Law
U. of California, Los Angeles
University of Southern California
Santa Clara University

SURVEY SAYS...

HITS
Sense of community
Faculty-student relations
Left-leaning politics

MISSES
Lack of diversity among faculty
Not enough courses
Socratic method

EMPLOYMENT PROFILE

% grads employed immediately	46
% grads employed within six months	83
Average starting salary	$47,100
% grads employed by field:	
Private practice	57
Business/industry	7
Government	26
Judicial clerkships	15
Public service	4
Academic	2
Military	4

The youngest of California's four outstanding public law schools, the School of Law at the University of California, Davis, has a solid regional reputation for excellence and a stubborn case of sibling rivalry. The law school's excellent academic program and super-low tuition are no secret to residents of northern California, but to the consternation of many of its students, Davis doesn't command the national name recognition of its larger and older companion schools in the UC system. It is easy to lose perspective, however, if one is laboring in the shadows of two of the nation's best and best-known law schools; a law school could do much worse than to chase the coattails of Berkeley and UCLA.

There can be no doubt that Davis is widely regarded as one of the finest public law schools in the nation-approximately 3,000 applicants for under 150 first-year spots can't be wrong. Applications volume at Davis increased 133 percent between 1986 and 1991, with most of this demand coming from residents of California, for whom a legal education here is an extraordinary bargain. Davis charges virtually the same tuition as the other UC schools, but the cost of living in this Central Valley college town of 50,000 is very low. (Not that Davis students are universally enamored of their community, but more on that later.) Unsurprisingly, given the extreme selectivity of the admissions process, those candidates who are admitted possess numerical credentials as strong as those of students at virtually any school in the country.

Students here are also fairly happy with where they've landed. "It's a small, great environment here," said a 1L. "The professors are accessible and the students are friendly." "The atmosphere is friendly and competitive but not go-for-the-throat," wrote another. "They're also quite high on ethics. They want to put good lawyers in the workplace, NOT legal robots." Davis students are nearly unanimous in their praise of this civilized atmosphere. "We all say 'Thank God we're not at law school,'" reported one. "People here are extremely bright and competitive—but they're also friendly and balanced." Another student offered an explanation: "There is definitely peer pressure to be nice here. Overly competitive students learn early on to behave themselves or be ostracized." Happily, since our last survey, when students cried

Sharon Pinkney, Director of Admission
King Hall, Davis, CA 95616-5201
Tel: (916) 752-6477
Internet: http://kinghall.ucdavis.edu

out for a new dean to push the school into "greatness," Dean Wolk took office and has added vigor, direction, and most importantly, faculty, including five full-time faculty, of which four are women, one a Latino, and one an Asian-American.

But students at Davis do have their gripes. One of the more common substantive complaints was that the law school offers a disappointingly narrow selection of courses. Many students seem unhappy with this unfortunate flip side to the benefits of attending a small law school. Slightly angrier complaints were heard regarding the law school's career office. The comments we heard ranged from "sucks" to "awful."

But the most consistently negative reviews from Davis students were reserved for their school's hometown. "Well, the town of Davis is a wasteland," explained one student. Another suggested that the school be moved to southern California. "The rain and fog here are awful, and the heat in the fall makes the whole town smell like cow poop." While most students voiced opinions like "Not enough bars in Davis," at least one saw the hidden benefit of his semi-rural surroundings: "Davis is such a boring town you can't help but study."

ADMISSIONS

Demand for spots in Davis's small first-year class is still extremely high. It may be less selective than Berkeley and UCLA, the crown jewels in the University of California system, but considering how high the standards of those other schools are, that isn't saying much. Admissions at Davis are extremely competitive. With its very strong academic reputation and its super-low tuition, Davis draws a flood of applications from highly qualified candidates. Of the roughly 2,900 candidates it considers annually, the law school admits only one in four.

ACADEMICS

Student/faculty ratio	17:1
% female faculty	35
% minority faculty	14
Hours of study per day	3.79

FINANCIAL FACTS

In-state tuition	$8,726
Out-of-state tuition	$8,391
Part-time tuition per credit	NR
Estimated books/expenses/fees	$11,640
On-campus living expenses	NR
Off-campus living expenses	$6,623
% first-year students receiving aid	100
% all students receiving aid	100
% aid that is merit-based	NR
% all students receiving grants/scholarships	64
% all students receiving loans	79
% all students receiving assistantships	NR
Average award package	$3,498
Average graduation debt	$28,000

ADMISSIONS

# applications received	2,922
% applicants accepted	24
% acceptees attending	19
Average LSAT	161
Average undergrad GPA	3.43
Application Fee	$40
No early decision program	
Regular application deadline	February 1
Regular notification	rolling
Admission may be deferred?	no
Gourman Report Rating	**4.43**

UNIVERSITY OF CALIFORNIA, LOS ANGELES

School of Law

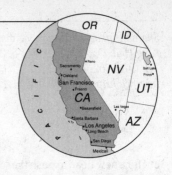

OVERVIEW

Type of school	public
Environment	metropolis
Scholastic calendar	NR
Schedule	Full time only

STUDENTS

Enrollment of institution	NR
Enrollment of law school	924
% male/female	50/50
% out-of-state	24
% part-time	NR
% minorities	13
% international (# countries represented)	NR (30)
Average age at entry	24

APPLICANTS ALSO LOOK AT

U. of California, Berkeley
U. of California, Hastings College of Law
Stanford University
Georgetown University
U. of California, Davis

SURVEY SAYS...

HITS
Clinical experience
Serving humankind
Faculty-student relations

MISSES
Research resources
Socratic method
Studying

EMPLOYMENT PROFILE

% grads employed immediately	66
% grads employed within six months	94
Average starting salary	$70,000
% grads employed by field:	
Private practice	75
Business/industry	3
Government	10
Judicial clerkships	8
Public service	3
Academic	1
Military	3

No list of the nation's top law schools will fail to include the School of Law at the University of California at Los Angeles. Inevitably, however, these lists rank UCLA somewhere behind its older companion school at Berkeley. If, in fact, there are any objectively verifiable reasons for this, you would be hard-pressed to find them. And if lists measured subjective factors such as pure popularity with other applicants and enrolled students, the balance might well tip the other way.

There are very good reasons for the fact the UCLA ranks behind only the massive law schools at Harvard, Georgetown, and George Washington in terms of applications volume. Among them are the sheer strength of the law school's J.D. program and the size and quality of the faculty that administers it. The traditional curriculum is supplemented by one of the largest and best-equipped clinical programs in the country, and the law school's overall student-faculty ratio is the most favorable of any of the UC schools. Combine these qualities with UCLA's incredibly low tuition and you get to the heart of the matter: value. No appreciably better bargain is to be found among the country's 175 fully-accredited law schools.

In addition to all the enthusiastic comments we heard regarding the school's great location and climate, students at UCLA are quite content with their atmosphere of the school itself. Perhaps it can be attributed to the abundance of sun and fun to be had in Los Angeles, but this is, by all accounts, a laid-back and social group of students. In fact, survey respondents praised their fellow students and the supportive and non-competitive atmosphere at UCLA most highly. "The people here are extremely open and helpful. Everyone smiles and pitches in to work together. There is no cutthroat competition," said a 1L. Another student, a 3L, offered: "I have been very impressed with the quality of students here. I think that most students at UCLA get into higher ranked schools but choose to come to UCLA because of the quality of student life here." And a 2L went so far as to make this bold statement in naming the student body as the school's greatest strength: "The quality, depth, and diversity of these highly qualified students make even the professors blush with

Michael Rappaport, Dean of Admissions
Los Angeles, CA 90095-1476
Tel: (310) 825-4041
eMail: admit@law.ucla.edu
Internet: http://www.law.ucla.edu

envy." It is true that the student body at UCLA is well diversified; 40 percent of it is made up of traditionally underrepresented ethnic groups, a fact that many students we spoke with appreciated. While students applaud the diversity of UCLA's student body, they fault the lack of it among the faculty, composed of only a little over 10 percent minority groups.

Students are happy to report that a new grading system has replaced the strict curve the school used to adhere to, which many students referred to as "unfair." The new system, reported one student, has made UCLA "a kinder, gentler law school." Prospective students will also be happy to hear that their loudest complaints—about the poor, out-of-date facilities—have been heard, and the facilities are being renovated. And it is happening none too soon, said students, one of whom described the current state of the library as "unconscionable."

It is not surprising that when it comes time to find employment, the majority of UCLA students remain in L.A., the nation's fourth-largest and second-highest-paying legal job market. As a rule, they have no difficulty finding great jobs there and elsewhere.

ADMISSIONS

As large as its student body is, the University of California at Los Angeles still must turn away more than three quarters of those who apply. Although not as selective as the law school at Berkeley, the average numerical credentials at this "first-tier" law school are very strong: a median LSAT of 163 and an undergraduate GPA of just over 3.50. An applicant with a GPA between 3.25 and 3.50 and an LSAT score between 155 and 159 stands only a 6 percent chance of getting in.

ACADEMICS

Student/faculty ratio	17:1
% female faculty	36
% minority faculty	13
Hours of study per day	3.59

FINANCIAL FACTS

In-state tuition	$10,782
Out-of-state tuition	$19,176
Part-time tuition per credit	NR
Estimated books/expenses/fees	NR
On-campus living expenses	NR
Off-campus living expenses	NR
% first-year students receiving aid	53
% all students receiving aid	99
% aid that is merit-based	3
% all students receiving grants/scholarships	60
% all students receiving loans	80
% all students receiving assistantships	15
Average award package	$5,510
Average graduation debt	$45,000

ADMISSIONS

# applications received	4,553
% applicants accepted	21
% acceptees attending	27
Average LSAT	162
Average undergrad GPA	3.57
Application Fee	$40
No early decision program	
Regular application deadline	January 15
Regular notification	January15-May
Admission may be deferred?	No
Gourman Report Rating	**4.75**

UNIVERSITY OF CALIFORNIA 🖫
Hastings College of Law

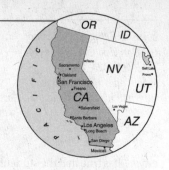

OVERVIEW

Type of school	public
Environment	NR
Scholastic calendar	NR
Schedule	Full time only

STUDENTS

Enrollment of institution	NR
Enrollment of law school	1,209
% male/female	51/49
% out-of-state	9
% part-time	NR
% minorities	31
% international (# countries represented)	NR (4)
Average age at entry	27

APPLICANTS ALSO LOOK AT

Boston College
Boston University
George Washington University
Georgetown University
University of Southern California

SURVEY SAYS...

HITS
Broad range of courses
Quality of teaching

MISSES
Sense of community
Facilities not great
Studying

EMPLOYMENT PROFILE

% grads employed immediately	43
% grads employed within six months	81
Average starting salary	$66,000
% grads employed by field:	
Private practice	60
Business/industry	12
Government	13
Judicial clerkships	8
Public service	3
Academic	3
Military	3

The University of California's Hastings College of the Law is the oldest law school in the University of California system and the one that supplies the most lawyers to its home state. Since its founding in 1878, Hastings has enjoyed a strong reputation within the state and certainly in the school's immediate setting, the San Francisco Bay Area. Over 14,000 Hastings alumni serve the legal community as lawyers, judges, and elected officials—80 percent of whom live and work in California.

It is not surprising that the vast majority of Hastings grads continue to go to work within the state, and a substantial proportion remain in San Francisco—arguably the legal capital of the West Coast—where the law school's connections to the legal community are strongest. The law school is located adjacent to the Civic Center, on the edges of a neighborhood called the Tenderloin, an area as negatively urban as San Francisco gets (which isn't bad compared to, say, New York or Los Angeles). Although Hastings students are quick to point out how undesirable their immediate neighborhood can be, they are happy to be located within one of the nation's most beautiful and diverse cities.

When asked to discuss areas in which their school could improve, an overwhelming number of students cited the school's tough grading curve, which, according to one respondent to our survey, leaves the vast majority of students in the 'C' range. However, the administration told us that regulations regarding the curve have changed, and, as of this writing, "require that 75 percent of the students receive a B-." "Thanks to our strict grading curve, we work harder and get less credit for it," lamented a 2L. "The administration implicitly encourages the competitive atmosphere in the use of the curve, class rank, and the low-weighted GPA that puts Hastings students at a disadvantage."

Hastings students we spoke to reported a poor sense of community at the school, possibly due in part to the intense competition. As a 1L noted, "the students here are the most unfriendly, cutthroat bunch around!" It should be noted, however, that a few students disagreed with the characterization of Hastings as a competitive school. One such student, a 1L, told us: "Hastings

Peter C. Storandt, Director of Admissions
200 McAllister Street, San Francisco, CA 94102
Tel: (415) 565-4623
Internet: http://www.uchastings.edu/

gets bad rap for being competitive. I'm a first-year here, and have not experienced this at all—in fact, we're all very supportive and helpful to each other so far."

Another frequent comment we heard from Hastings law students was that their school was having an identity crisis. "At times it seems Hastings isn't sure what type of school it wants to be—the next Harvard or a more clinical, practice-oriented school, "said a 1L. Another student put it this way: "Hastings is two, possibly three schools...There's the corporate crazy school dedicated to big firms, then there's the public interest school..." Asking students which school they want only clouds the matter. For instance, many students said Hastings needs to add "more clinical opportunities." Then a group of students agreed with the one who said: "Hastings has a fabulous clinical program." On the subject of the corporate versus the public interest focus, we heard these conflicting comments: "[There are] too many public interest lawyers. We need more conservative support." (1L); "Hastings has many excellent programs for students interested in public interest and public sector work." (2L); "Hastings seems to only pay attention to the 'corporate track.' There is not that much attention paid to other forms of lawyering." (2L). The disagreement over the school's mission—and how well it's meeting that mission—is probably largely due to the school's size and to its "amazingly diverse" student body (although Hastings students also disagree on the issue of diversity in the student body).

One the bright side, Hastings students are nearly all in agreement in regard to the quality of their instruction and their faculty, as summed up by this 2L: "The faculty at Hastings is second to none. Not only are they leaders in their respective fields, but they are extremely accessible as well." Overall, many students at the Hastings College of Law are upbeat about the fundamental strength of their school's prime location and solid reputation.

ADMISSIONS

The University of California's Hastings College of Law was not spared in the massive surge in applications volume during the last decade. Last year nearly 5,300 applicants vied to be among the entering class of 420 students. Those who were admitted possessed extremely impressive numerical credentials. With an average GPA of 3.38 and a median LSAT score of 162, the student body is more highly qualified than the student bodies at about 80 percent of the country's 178 ABA-accredited law schools.

ACADEMICS

Student/faculty ratio	22:1
% female faculty	28
% minority faculty	30
Hours of study per day	3.68

FINANCIAL FACTS

In-state tuition	$7,488
Out-of-state tuition	$8,392
Part-time tuition per credit	NR
Estimated books/expenses/fees	$10,978
On-campus living expenses	NR
Off-campus living expenses	$9,828
% first-year students receiving aid	97
% all students receiving aid	97
% aid that is merit-based	2
% all students receiving grants/scholarships	65
% all students receiving loans	80
% all students receiving assistantships	NR
Average award package	$3,190
Average graduation debt	$40,553

ADMISSIONS

# applications received	5,281
% applicants accepted	28
% acceptees attending	27
Average LSAT	162
Average undergrad GPA	3.38
Application Fee	$40
No early decision program	
Regular application deadline	February 15
Regular notification	rolling
Admission may be deferred?	no
Gourman Report Rating	**4.62**

CAMPBELL UNIVERSITY
Norman Adrian Wiggins School of Law

OVERVIEW

Type of school	private
Environment	rural
Scholastic calendar	semester
Schedule	Full time only

STUDENTS

Enrollment of institution	2,160
Enrollment of law school	318
% male/female	58/42
% out-of-state	25
% part-time	NR
% minorities	3
% international (# countries represented)	1 (NR)
Average age at entry	25

APPLICANTS ALSO LOOK AT

University of North Carolina
Wake Forest University
University of Richmond
North Carolina Central U.
University of South Carolina

SURVEY SAYS...

HITS
Socratic method
Practical lawyering skills
Students feel well-prepared

MISSES
Lack of diversity among faculty
Gender bias
Library staff

EMPLOYMENT PROFILE

% grads employed immediately	NR
% grads employed within six months	NR
Average starting salary	NR
% grads employed by field:	
Private practice	68
Business/industry	9
Government	6
Judicial clerkships	13
Public service	2
Academic	2
Military	0

The youngest of North Carolina's five law schools, Campbell University's Norman Adrian Wiggins School of Law is a Southern Baptist institution established in 1976 in semi-rural Buies Creek, thirty miles from the greater Raleigh area. With only a few hundred students, it is one of the smallest fully accredited private law schools in the country, and though its name is little recognized outside its immediate region, Campbell is certainly noteworthy—not for having a world-famous faculty or a world-class library, but, rather, for the very tangible evidence of its commitment to a simple goal: training good lawyers.

In a state well stocked with solidly established traditional law schools, Campbell probably had little choice but to distinguish itself from the norm somehow. It chose to do so by instituting what is surely legal education's most complete and rigorous required course of study in trial advocacy. Over the course of Campbell's four-semester litigation program, every student will receive extensive simulated training before trying two actual cases through to the appellate level. Of course, the maintenance of this innovative program has its downside. This kind of practical training cannot be accomplished in large classes, so the law school must dedicate enormous financial and faculty resources to its trial-advocacy programs. As a result, Campbell's traditional classroom curriculum is limited in breadth. The J.D. program is heavy in required courses, and students are allowed few electives.

Despite expected frustration over the lack of elective courses, most Campbell students expressed satisfaction with the school's chosen path and the practical knowledge the Trial Advocacy Program imparts. Upon graduation, Campbell students know they will possess an enviable confidence when they enter a courtroom. As one student said, they will be "off and running. The school is recognized for the strength of the trial lawyers it produces." Another student framed his praise even more strongly: "Campbell's greatest strength is that it is a leader, not a follower, in its approach to the teaching of law. Its conservative core curriculum, once thought to be backwards and outdated, is now being regarded as the way to produce practicing attorneys for the

Box 158, Buies Creek, NC 27506
Tel: (910) 893-1750

real world, as evidenced by the school's 100 percent bar passage rate in 1993 and 94."

Many survey respondents noted and appreciated the important sense of inclusion the faculty provides its small student body thanks to the "individual attention students receive" and the "dedication of faculty." However, some women enrolled at Campbell complained that condescension directed specifically at minority and female students sometimes hampers their efforts to succeed. This may not come as such a surprise when one considers that Campbell employs no minority faculty members and only one full-time female professor.

Although Campbell students adamantly voiced pride in their legal education, they just as loudly demanded better recognition from the less understanding world at large. Campbell law students agreed with this 2L's sage words: "With age, the name will improve itself; this is an excellent school." Many students blamed that ever-static target, the placement office, for lack of recognition for the school, but a few simply told us, and thence the world, to wake up to the fact that "Campbell is highly regarded by students, practicing attorneys, and the general public as the best law school in N.C. The most common example of this today is the high number of Duke, Carolina and Wake law school grads who say that if they were to do it all over again, they would go to Campbell."

ADMISSIONS

Very small and relatively unknown outside the immediate region, the law school at Campbell University selects its students from a relatively small pool of applicants. This fact has one obvious consequence: Numerical admissions standards are fairly low—lower, in fact, than numerical standards at about 60 percent of all U.S. law schools. Less obvious, however, is another advantage. Applications volume is low enough that Campbell can do something that is virtually unheard of among law schools: grant interviews to almost half of the candidates it considers. As a result, applicants to Campbell can be assured of getting the fullest consideration.

ACADEMICS	
Student/faculty ratio	20:1
% female faculty	17
% minority faculty	7
Hours of study per day	3.98

FINANCIAL FACTS	
Tuition	$12,400
Part-time tuition per credit	NR
Estimated books/expenses/fees	NR
On-campus living expenses	NR
Off-campus living expenses	NR
% first-year students receiving aid	NR
% all students receiving aid	NR
% aid that is merit-based	NR
% all students receiving grants/scholarships	NR
% all students receiving loans	NR
% all students receiving assistantships	NR
Average award package	NR
Average graduation debt	NR

ADMISSIONS	
# applications received	1,000
% applicants accepted	16
% acceptees attending	70
Average LSAT	157
Average undergrad GPA	3.10
Application Fee	$40
Priority application deadline	NR
Priority notification	NR
Regular application deadline	May 1
Regular notification	NR
Admission may be deferred?	No
Gourman Report Rating	**2.16**

CAPITAL UNIVERSITY LAW SCHOOL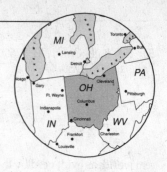

OVERVIEW

Type of school	private
Environment	metropolis
Scholastic calendar	semester
Schedule	Full-time or part-time

STUDENTS

Enrollment of institution	4,071
Enrollment of law school	812
% male/female	58/42
% out-of-state	30
% part-time	41
% minorities	9
% international (# countries represented)	NR (3)
Average age at entry	25

APPLICANTS ALSO LOOK AT

Ohio State University
University of Cincinnati
University of Dayton
University of Akron
Ohio Northern University

SURVEY SAYS...

HITS
Diverse faculty
Broad range of courses
Socratic method

MISSES
Facilities not great
Inadequate study space

EMPLOYMENT PROFILE

% grads employed immediately	NR
% grads employed within six months	89
Average starting salary	$40,000
% grads employed by field:	
Private practice	46
Business/industry	22
Government	15
Judicial clerkships	5
Public service	8
Academic	4
Military	4

The progenitor of the line of law schools that led eventually to the Capital University Law School was founded in 1903 under the auspices of the YMCA, an organization that was practically single-handedly responsible for making legal education available to the working classes in the early part of the century. Through the various incarnations that preceded its affiliation with its Lutheran parent institution in 1966, and up to the present day, the law school at Capital University has continued its tradition of putting accessibility first. Today, Capital enrolls almost 800 students, nearly half of them in its evening division, the second largest in the state.

Students follow a largely traditional course of study that is supplemented by a variety of highly regarded clinical and externship programs that take advantage of the school's downtown location. Though enrollment in these programs is limited, their variety is not. Among the most interesting is Capital's innovative "Night Prosecutors Program," which allows students to mediate, under attorney supervision, complaints brought by area residents against other residents. The university also supports the Center for Dispute Resolution, which produced a significant international "first" when it helped train personnel for and institute non-litigious methods of resolution at a national level in Jamaica. Capital also offers joint degrees in taxation and business.

The university's part-time and evening programs keep the majority of students we spoke with happy. Many of these future lawyers said that if it were not for Capital's evening course offerings, they would not be able to attend law school at all. "The school's night program makes an effort to accommodate folks who work 40 hours a week," said a 1L. Another student, a 2L, said that Capital is truly a "working persons' law school." Even students who are not enrolled in the part-time or evening divisions are appreciative of its effect on the quality of life at Capital. As one such student noted: "Capital's part-time program reflects a diversity of students. They bring a variety of employment and educational backgrounds and real-life experiences to each class." It should be noted that although it has attracted a quite diverse

Linda Mihely, Director of Admissions and Financial Aid
665 South High Street, Columbus, OH 43215
Tel: (614) 445-8836

Capital University Law School

student body in terms of age and profession, Capital has been less successful in diversifying the school's ethnic or racial composition, though they continue their efforts to do so. Since 1991 the percentage of minority students has increased; the 1995 entering class included 12 percent minority students. While Capital's minority population remains one of the smallest in the state, the law school has made a commitment to increasing that percentage.

Among Capital's strengths reported by students is the school's focus on practical lawyering skills. "The practical 'real law' approach is a definite advantage," said one 2L. Another student was thankful that professors "provide useful information so that little time is spent on theory." The school's focus may explain its traditionally high bar passage rate. Reviews of the faculty were mixed, however. We heard several comments like these: "The professors are brilliant," (1L); "The faculty is very knowledgeable and open to students," (1L). But these sentiments were countered with statements like this one from a 2L: "The quality of teaching varies a great deal. There are some very good professors, but also one or two that really have contributed little to my education."

If there is one thing that this group of law students is not in disagreement over, it's the school's "cramped," "terrible," and "out-of-date" facilities. As one student noted, the school is "lacking in technological advantages." Others cited the inadequate study areas and lack of computers. Keep in mind, though, that a new building will be completed in 1997. Given this news, many students see Capital's future as bright.

ADMISSIONS

Though no longer the least selective of Ohio's nine law schools, Capital still considers the entire application, putting less emphasis on the LSAT and GPA than other schools. Capital is considerably more expensive than Ohio's state law schools, but is the least expensive of Ohio's private law schools, which may help explain its less selective status. Still, this private school chooses its first-year class of about 260 students from a good-sized applicant pool, many of whom seek admission to the school's comprehensive evening and part-time divisions. Six out of ten candidates for admission to Capital are unsuccessful, despite the law school's relatively low numerical standards.

ACADEMICS

Student/faculty ratio	25:1
% female faculty	29
% minority faculty	12
Hours of study per day	3.85

FINANCIAL FACTS

Tuition	$13,416
Part-time tuition per credit	$497
Estimated books/expenses/fees	NR
On-campus living expenses	NR
Off-campus living expenses	NR
% first-year students receiving aid	80
% all students receiving aid	80
% aid that is merit-based	30
% all students receiving grants/scholarships	23
% all students receiving loans	72
% all students receiving assistantships	5
Average award package	$25,000
Average graduation debt	$43,000

ADMISSIONS

# applications received	1,107
% applicants accepted	60
% acceptees attending	41
Average LSAT	152
Average undergrad GPA	3.10
Application Fee	$35
No early decision program	
Regular application deadline	May 1
Regular notification	rolling
Admission deferment	one year
Gourman Report Rating	**2.78**

CASE WESTERN RESERVE UNIVERSITY
School of Law

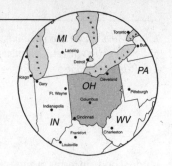

Although it has long commanded respect within its region as an important major research institution, Case Western Reserve University has not always enjoyed such recognition nationally. Until recently, the same held true for the Case Western law school, but with dramatic changes in recent years, its reputation has grown to extend beyond the state of Ohio. In 1986, Case drew the vast majority of its applicants from the immediately surrounding region, accepting almost 70 percent of them. Judging from the current competitiveness of its admissions process and the markedly increased geographic diversity of its student body, Case Western's law school has since gone national: it now denies admission to more than half of all applicants, and its students come in significant numbers from nearly every state in the union.

Why the apparent rush to Cleveland? Well, Paris on Lake Erie it's not, but neither is it a rusting urban wasteland. With two million people in the metropolitan area, Cleveland supports a sizable and successful legal community, to which Case Western annually adds a large group of capable law-school graduates. Ten years ago, if you asked a random sample of people living more than 500 miles from Cleveland what "Case Western Reserve" was, many would have guessed it was a savings and loan. Ask the same question today, and more than a few will be able to tell you it's a law school on the rise. The curriculum is strong in all the traditional areas, and the law school has, in recent years, added significantly to its clinical and skills offerings. Although these programs are limited in size (see below), they are admirable in scope.

The current students we heard from had nothing but praise for the law school's special programs, but many lamented their limited availability. "Case entices students with its 'hands-on' courses taught by well-known faculty members," complained one 3L, "but the sad truth is that only a few lucky students get into these courses." He was far from alone in voicing such frustration. "The administration needs to pay more attention to the needs of its students," went one typical remark, "specifically by increasing the availability of practical skills programs." Frustration runs high among Case Western students on this matter.

11075 East Boulevard, Cleveland, OH 44106
Tel: (216) 368-3600
eMail: lawadmissions@po.cwru.edu
Internet: lawwww.cwru.edu

Case Western Reserve
University

Students were almost invariably positive, however, about the quality of their academic preparation at the law school. Nearly every criticism of any aspect of their experience at Case was prefaced with a favorable remark about the "outstanding" faculty, with a significant number of students even naming names. Case Western students seem to feel sincere admiration and even affection for this "highly approachable, highly qualified" group of instructors. "They are all excellent at teaching," noted one surprised second-year.

Most students, however, had nothing kind to say about Case Western's career-placement office, which several called "inadequate." Some students went even further: "Career Services is the worst aspect of this school." Opinion was mixed when it came to the overall quality of life at the law school, but for every student who called the sense of community poor and the degree of competitiveness too high, there were two who praised the school's "great, supportive atmosphere." Like almost anything, it appears, an education at this respected private law school is what you make it.

ADMISSIONS

The admissions landscape at the Case Western Reserve University School of Law changed radically during the late 1980s. Not only did overall applications volume increase by 70 percent, but the numerical qualifications of those applying to the law school also increased significantly. With a solid average GPA and an average LSAT score at the 84th percentile, the credentials of current Case students are stronger than students at about two-thirds of fully accredited U.S. law schools. And if one believes in the law of supply and demand, the steadily increasing percentage of admitted candidates who accept offers to attend Case Western is a sure sign of this school's rising prestige.

ACADEMICS

Student/faculty ratio	15:1
% female faculty	26
% minority faculty	3
Hours of study per day	4.05

FINANCIAL FACTS

Tuition	$16,680
Part-time tuition per credit	NR
Estimated books/expenses/fees	$760
On-campus living expenses	NR
Off-campus living expenses	NR
% first-year students receiving aid	NR
% all students receiving aid	NR
% aid that is merit-based	NR
% all students receiving grants/scholarships	32
% all students receiving loans	73
% all students receiving assistantships	NR
Average award package	$9,000
Average graduation debt	$45,000

ADMISSIONS

# applications received	1,655
% applicants accepted	52
% acceptees attending	25
Average LSAT	158
Average undergrad GPA	3.36
Application Fee	$40
No early decision program	
Regular application deadline	April 1
Regular notification	NR
Admission deferment	one year
Gourman Report Rating	3.74

CATHOLIC UNIVERSITY OF AMERICA 🖬

Columbus School of Law

The Catholic University of America, Columbus School of Law, which will celebrate its 100th anniversary this year, is the product of the 1954 merger of Catholic University's School of Law with the law school of Columbus University in Washington D.C., an institution created three decades earlier by the Knights of Columbus. This large, well-equipped private law school is located within 10 minutes of downtown Washington D.C., and with the Supreme Court, the Capitol, and roughly 6,000 other law students within the city limits, the District of Columbia may well be a law student's heaven on earth. As its name would imply, Catholic University is surely more concerned than other schools with that other heaven, but students of all faiths are encouraged to apply and attend, and do so.

Both tradition and innovation are evident in Catholic's curriculum, and the law school allows a student to balance them as he or she sees fit. Particularly for students who take advantage of the city's vast resources, Catholic offers the possibility of fine legal education that combines academic and practical training. Students praised the school's emphasis on practical legal skills. "Catholic's lawyering skills program ensures that you will have the opportunity to be fully competent at your first summer job," offered a 1L. J.D. candidates at Catholic can now pursue official certificate programs of specialization in comparative and international law, communications law, and the law and public policy. In addition, the law school offers a broad and varied concentration of securities and corporate law courses. Outside the classroom, nearly infinite opportunities exist for students to become independently involved with the workings of federal government. Few students pass their three years at the law school without serving some kind of externship, be it with a government agency, federal court, or one of the thousands of private advocacy groups located in the capital. Several of the clinics, such as the advocacy for victims of gun violence clinic, focus on the serious issues facing the city.

Students are most enthusiastic about the intangible sense of "atmosphere" and "community" Catholic offers. As one 2L put it: "The environment at the school is great—very friendly." Another

George P. Braxton III, Director of Admissions
Cardinal Station, Washington, DC 20064
Tel: (202) 319-5151
Internet: http://www.law.cua.edu/

2L, who noted that she is "not even Catholic—or even Christian," said that she "strongly feels a part of this law school's community." And professors received praise from Catholic students as well. "The professors are caring and nurturing. They don't beat up on you," said a 1L. Professor accessibility contributes to the supportive atmosphere. In addition, reported students, there is a very low level of competition, probably due to the university's Pass/No Pass grading option for first-year students. Students were particularly vocal about Catholic's facilities, praising the new law building that was completed in 1994. "The new building and facilities are fabulous," said one student. Another upbeat 2L offered: "I think CUA law is one of D.C.'s best kept secrets. Our new building's moot court rooms, classrooms, and library are state-of-the-art."

Although overwhelmingly positive about their choice of law schools overall, most students we heard from voiced some criticism. One of the most common complaints we heard was that courses were "lacking in diversity," and that scheduling was "inflexible." And of course, as is the case with many private law schools today, students voiced concerns over rising tuition. However, students at Catholic are in agreement over the school's major strengths, including all the clinical, externship, and job opportunities its D.C. location provides. "The school helps you network in Washington, and," said one 2L, "Networking is everything in this town."

ADMISSIONS

Although often overshadowed by neighboring law schools like Georgetown and George Washington, The Catholic University Columbus School of Law has maintained a relative selectivity in composing its entering classes. After rising for the past few years due to increased admissions, Catholic's numerical admissions averages have leveled off. Although certainly solid, Catholic's standards remain moderate when compared to the better-known schools in Washington. Today, with roughly 2,700 applicants from which to choose, Catholic admits only about 42 percent of all candidates, putting together a well-qualified entering class of approximately 310 students. The average numerical credentials of students at Catholic University (average undergraduate GPA of 3.20 and LSAT score of 156) are stronger than the credentials of students at more than half of all fully accredited law schools in the country.

ACADEMICS

Student/faculty ratio	21:1
% female faculty	36
% minority faculty	13
Hours of study per day	3.88

FINANCIAL FACTS

Tuition	$20,874
Part-time tuition per credit	$751
Estimated books/expenses/fees	NR
On-campus living expenses	NR
Off-campus living expenses	NR
% first-year students receiving aid	75
% all students receiving aid	77
% aid that is merit-based	37
% all students receiving grants/scholarships	33
% all students receiving loans	77
% all students receiving assistantships	4
Average award package	$3,113
Average graduation debt	$66,807

ADMISSIONS

# applications received	2,735
% applicants accepted	42
% acceptees attending	26
Average LSAT	156
Average undergrad GPA	3.17
Application Fee	$55
No early decision program	
Regular application deadline	March 1
Regular notification	rolling
Admission deferment	one year
Gourman Report Rating	3.89

UNIVERSITY OF CHICAGO
Law School

OVERVIEW

Type of school	private
Environment	metropolis
Scholastic calendar	quarter
Schedule	Full time only

STUDENTS

Enrollment of institution	3,431
Enrollment of law school	528
% male/female	62/38
% out-of-state	85
% part-time	NR
% minorities	21
% international (# countries represented)	4 (NR)
Average age at entry	24

APPLICANTS ALSO LOOK AT

Yale University
Harvard University
University of Michigan
Stanford University
Columbia University

SURVEY SAYS...

HITS
Faculty representation
Quality of teaching
Socratic method

MISSES
Competition

EMPLOYMENT PROFILE

% grads employed immediately	NR
% grads employed within six months	NR
Average starting salary	NR
% grads employed by field:	
Private practice	67
Judicial clerkships	22
Military	2

No law school holds its students to more exacting standards or sets forth a course of study that is more rigorous or interdisciplinary than The Law School (always capitalized) at the University of Chicago. Since its founding in 1902, Chicago has taught law within the context of the social sciences, and the faculty has always included highly accomplished scholars from fields once considered outside the law, most notably economics. You'll get a good job when you finish, as well. The Law School's reputation is outstanding, and its graduates enjoy full and lucrative employment. A law degree from the University of Chicago gives a graduate virtual carte blanche in the legal profession.

Students at Chicago speak with one voice about many aspects of their program. They unanimously laud the excellent and accessible faculty. Faculty members, according to one student, "take time to talk to, mentor and critique students outside of class." Another commented, "There is an open door policy at all times." Survey respondents said their academic work is intense but intellectually stimulating; "If this is intense," said one, "I love it." The Socratic method, which has been phased out at many schools, is alive and well at Chicago, and the vast majority of students said they like it that way. Several students commented on the "harsh" curve which separates the weak from the strong, but said it lets up somewhat after the first year. Unlike students at many other law schools, Chicago students' praise for their teachers extends to the legal research and writing program, which several singled out for special mention. The only academic drawback cited by respondents was a relative lack of practical skills and clinical training. In all fairness, we must mention that Chicago's legal aid clinic involves more than 90 students each year, and the school offers several other opportunities for practical lawyering, including the Women's Clemency Project and the Immigration and Refugee Law Society.

The major source of disagreement among our respondents was Chicago's political climate. Chicago is known as a conservative school because it was the birthplace of the Law and Economics approach, which applies economic analysis to legal problems and tends to promote legal approaches that rely on the market rather than on government intervention. A sizable number of Chicago's current faculty members are Law and Economics adherents. Some students find this orientation oppressive; one stated that much of the faculty is "closed-minded" and "ultra-conservative." Others, however, acknowledged the strong Law and Economics influence, but said that Chicago is remarkably tolerant of all viewpoints. A 1L stated, "The faculty make this a community of intellectual discourse between the left and the right." He went on to say, "I am an openly gay man and expected to confront the orthodoxy when I came here, only to find that both my classmates and professors reaffirm my identity, criticize the market and challenge us to develop a legal intellect which will be responsible for change."

Students also disagree about Chicago's treatment of women and minorities. Chicago students ranked the school low for faculty diversity, and were all over the map on whether women and minorities are treated fairly. Others opined that Chicago's image, which is hampering efforts to recruit more women and minority faculty, is undeserved. Since the school hired a new Dean of Student Affairs in 1995 partly "to ensure that the environment is supportive to women," we expect our next surveys to be far more positive regarding Chicago's treatment of women.

Overall, students are happy to be at Chicago, though they admitted their time there is not always easy. As one said, "First year at U of C is one of the most miserable experiences you'll ever have that you wouldn't trade for anything."

ADMISSIONS

With Chicago, one can dispense quickly with the question that preoccupies most law-school applicants: "What are my chances of getting in?" Slim. Like its counterparts in the traditional "top five," the University of Chicago admits only a few hundred of its thousands of applicants. Indeed, it chooses more carefully than most: Chicago is the only elite law school that offers interviews to a substantial number of candidates as a matter of course. Although this would seem to offer hope to those whose numerical credentials do not make a strong case for admission, don't be fooled. Not only are numerical admissions standards extraordinarily high, applications volume is incredible heavy. The Law School is one of the most difficult schools to gain admission to in the country.

ACADEMICS

Student/faculty ratio	19:1
% female faculty	17
% minority faculty	13
Hours of study per day	3.80

FINANCIAL FACTS

Tuition	$20,499
Part-time tuition per credit	NR
Estimated books/expenses/fees	NR
On-campus living expenses	NR
Off-campus living expenses	NR
% first-year students receiving aid	NR
% all students receiving aid	NR
% aid that is merit-based	NR
% all students receiving grants/scholarships	NR
% all students receiving loans	NR
% all students receiving assistantships	NR
Average award package	NR
Average graduation debt	NR

ADMISSIONS

# applications received	3,367
% applicants accepted	17
% acceptees attending	30
Average LSAT	170
Average undergrad GPA	3.65
Application Fee	$45
Priority application deadline	NR
Priority notification	NR
Regular application deadline	NR
Regular notification	NR
Admission deferment	NR
Gourman Report Rating	**4.90**

UNIVERSITY OF CINCINNATI
College of Law

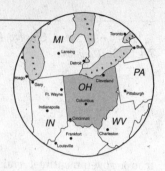

The College of Law at the University of Cincinnati, which bills itself as the fourth-oldest continuously operating law school in the United States, offers a solid, traditional legal education to a small, dedicated, and extremely able student body. UC draws the vast majority of its students from within Ohio, thanks to an extremely low in-state tuition. It regional reputation is more than solid. In a metropolitan region of almost 2 million people that is home to such corporate biggies as Procter and Gambel, a solid local name is not inconsiderable. Nor should it be taken as a sign of provinciality. Among the notable resources accessible to Cincinnati students are the programs of the Urban Morgan Institute for Human Rights, a major international research center dedicated to the area of law from which it takes its name.

Fully one half of all Cincinnati graduates choose to remain in the greater Cincinnati area, but the school's catalog is quick to point out that UC law grads are widely distributed geographically. Indeed, a law degree from the University of Cincinnati can travel. When one considers, however, the fact that Cincinnati apparently boasts "more four and five-star restaurants than anywhere in the country except San Francisco," the low tuition and the Ohio River Valley start to sound pretty nice. In 1988, Cincinnati accepted nearly 50 percent of tall the candidates it considered. Today, the law school draws its small first year class from a greatly enlarged and more highly qualified pool of applicants, accepting a far higher percentage of top students.

Current students we heard from overwhelmingly agreed that UC has earned its solid regional reputation for producing fine lawyers and for providing such a positive atmosphere in which to become an honored member of the legal community. One student exclaimed, "Having been accepted to 9 other law schools, I certainly had my pick; but if I had it to do all over again I would choose U of Cincinnati College of Law without a second thought. As soon as I walked through the doors I knew it was the best place to be. The faculty is incredible as well as accessible; the student body is incredibly intelligent as well as supportive, and the facilities are magnificent." Other students echoed her praise for the faculty, their peers, the quality of the facilities (sometimes

Al Watson, Assistant Dean and Director of Admission and Financial Aid
P.O. Box 210040, Cincinnati, OH 45221-0040
Tel: (513) 556-6805
eMail: admissions@law.uc.edu
Internet: http://www.law.uc.edu

tempered by the phrase "for a school of its size"), and added cheers for the International Human Rights program, and the low stress level all these factors combine to create. As one student noted, "The University of Cincinnati is an oasis of free thinking amongst an overly conservative population."

Although nearly all agreed that their minds are creatively challenged, many called for a few more specific arenas in which to exercise, such as more intensive legal writing and research courses and a greater variety of practical and clinical offerings. One woman explained the problem in simple terms: "Too much theory, too little know how." These complaints may only be a function of the school's small size, but its connection to such a large university causes problems as well, and "in terms of financial aid and other administrative issues, it is often difficult and time consuming to get anything accomplished." And although UC has an outsize tri-state reputation, students registered their common hopes that the greater national legal community would take notice of this fantastic breeding ground of law professionals. One student's experience speaks for that of many: "U.C. Law school is a hidden gem, a well kept secret! I have worked with students from Penn, Michigan, Vanderbilt, Emory, Indiana, and Wake Forest and felt at least as well prepared to practice as I perceived them to be. I came here because of the location and low tuition. I will leave impressed by my educational experience, instructors, and fellow students."

ADMISSIONS

Considering it is one of the best public law schools in its region, it is hardly surprising that competition for spots in the University of Cincinnati School of Law's very small first-year class is heated. Applications volume is moderate in absolute terms, but limits on the size of the entering class allows Cincinnati to admit only about one in every four of the more than 1,200 candidates it considers annually. Those who are admitted possess very strong numerical credentials. In fact, with its very solid average GPA and its average LSAT at the 89th percentile, the student body at Cincinnati is among the 40 most qualified in the entire country.

ACADEMICS

Student/faculty ratio	16:1
% female faculty	32
% minority faculty	8
Hours of study per day	4.07

FINANCIAL FACTS

In-state tuition	$6,897
Out-of-state tuition	$13,404
Part-time tuition per credit	NR
Estimated books/expenses/fees	NR
On-campus living expenses	NR
Off-campus living expenses	NR
% first-year students receiving aid	70
% all students receiving aid	90
% aid that is merit-based	10
% all students receiving grants/scholarships	65
% all students receiving loans	70
% all students receiving assistantships	NR
Average award package	NR
Average graduation debt	NR

ADMISSIONS

# applications received	1,202
% applicants accepted	28
% acceptees attending	35
Average LSAT	160
Average undergrad GPA	3.47
Application Fee	$35
No early decision program	
Regular application deadline	April 1
Regular notification	rolling
Admission deferment	one year
Gourman Report Rating	**3.28**

CITY UNIVERSITY OF NEW YORK
School of Law at Queens College

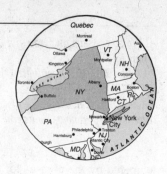

Superlatives are unavoidable when discussing the City University of New York School of Law at Queens College, without question the most genuinely innovative school in the country. From the day it opened in 1983, this very young, small public law school has charted its own course, questioning every premise of the traditional law school curriculum as it set a unique agenda that could actually make the world a better place. CUNY's motto, "Law in the Service of Human Needs," does not alone tell the story. All law schools exalt the ethical principles of public service, but many do nothing more than pay lip service. CUNY law school, the conscience of American legal education, makes even those schools that do back their words with action look like little more than corporate-lawyer factories. One simple statistic tells all. Nationally, only a very small percentage of all recent law school graduates choose to practice law in the public interest. At CUNY, nearly half of graduates do so. At no point in their three years at the law school do CUNY students simply plow through appellate-court cases and regurgitate abstract principles. Classroom courses emphasize legal theory as it tangibly affects human relations. The law school's nationally recognized clinical programs are designed to involve all students in those relations throughout their training. CUNY's mission to keep its students involved in the society they will one day serve is greatly aided by the degree to which the law school's faculty and student body resemble that society. Diversity is no empty phrase here, where over half (!) of all full-time professors are women and nearly a third of all students are members of historically underrepresented minority groups.

To judge from the results of our survey, those CUNY students who most embrace the ideals espoused by the school itself are the happiest here. Conversely, those whose interests might be better served at a more traditionally-oriented law school are the unhappiest. For instance, many here applauded their chosen school for its "focus on creating thinking lawyers and not just robots who can pass the bar," but others lamented the "lack of emphasis on the basic courses such as those needed to pass the bar." Suffice it to say that this is a unique school whose educational and, yes, political biases cannot and should not be ignored by any prospective student. Many here frequently use terms like "diversity" and "multiculturalism" in praising their school; if these buzzwords raise your anti-PC hackles, you might want to consider these remarks from several kindred spirits and look elsewhere: "As a white male I often feel like I am being asked to pay for the crimes of my ancestors"; "Diversity seems only to include those already left of center"; "Even Civil Procedure is politicized here!"

But for the student who knows what she's getting herself into, CUNY appears to satisfy in nearly every important respect. "The variety and quality of the clinical programs here is amazing," wrote one typical 3L. "I cannot possibly imagine another school that could do a better job of preparing me for the kind of law that I want to practice." Many others praised their school not only for the substance of its program but also for its style. As a 1L wrote, "The non-competitive atmosphere fostered here is one of the greatest assets this school has...I've learned a great deal more from collaborating with my colleagues than I would have from competing with them." This evenhanded assessment from a CUNY 2L summed up the sentiments of many others: "This school has its weak points (e.g., limited traditional course selection and uneven teaching), but there's no other place like it as far as I know, and the kind of lawyers they produce here are the kind of lawyers the world could use."

ADMISSIONS

To report simply that the numerical credentials of the average CUNY law student are lower than those of the average student at all but six of the law schools in this book would be dangerously misleading. The admissions process at CUNY, Queens is as different from the norm as the school's curriculum is. Consider this: When one factors in both relative applicant volume and the rate at which admitted students choose to enroll, this innovative school ranks among the 20 most selective in the nation. Indeed, CUNY admits nearly the same proportion of its applicants as do the national powerhouses NYU and Columbia. Hopeful candidates for admission here had better have more than just numbers; the admissions committee will be looking very carefully for other hopeful signs.

ACADEMICS

Student/faculty ratio	12:1
% female faculty	59
% minority faculty	35
Hours of study per day	4.33

FINANCIAL FACTS

In-state tuition	$4,700
Out-of-state tuition	$7,774
Part-time tuition per credit	NR
Estimated books/expenses/fees	NR
On-campus living expenses	NR
Off-campus living expenses	NR
% first-year students receiving aid	NR
% all students receiving aid	NR
% aid that is merit-based	NR
% all students receiving grants/scholarships	NR
% all students receiving loans	NR
% all students receiving assistantships	NR
Average award package	NR
Average graduation debt	NR

ADMISSIONS

# applications received	1,800
% applicants accepted	18
% acceptees attending	48
Average LSAT	150
Average undergrad GPA	3.00
Application Fee	NR
Priority application deadline	NR
Priority notification	NR
Regular application deadline	NR
Regular notification	NR
Admission deferment	NR
Gourman Report Rating	**2.10**

CLEVELAND STATE UNIVERSITY
Cleveland-Marshall College of Law

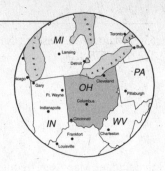

In a state that is heavily stocked with law schools and law students, the Cleveland-Marshall College of Law is the largest of all. Descended from two private schools (Cleveland and Marshall) founded in the early part of the century, this public law school became affiliated with the state university in 1969. Both the Cleveland State law school and the university itself are vital resources for this major urban center, which is otherwise lacking in opportunities for inexpensive higher education. Cleveland-Marshall has established itself as the most convenient and affordable option in the area for would-be lawyers for whom financial and/or scheduling constraints preclude full-time study at a private institution. Its low tuition (remarkably lower at the resident rate than the tuition charged by its better-known neighbor, Case Western Reserve) and its evening J.D. program attract a career-minded, older-than-average group of students, the vast majority of whom come from within Ohio. Upon completing their degrees, the majority also remain in or around the city of Cleveland, one of the highest-paying legal job markets in the Midwest.

Cleveland-Marshall offers a straightforward, traditional J.D. curriculum that is supplemented by a modest number of clinical programs and an increasing number of practical-skills courses, particularly in the area of trial advocacy. Through the broader university, the law school offers a joint J.D./M.B.A. program and a joint J.D./M.P.A. degree in law and public policy. Applications volume is moderate considering the law school's size, and a bit more than a third of all candidates gain admission. Numerical admissions standards are moderate to low.

At least in comparison with most students we surveyed, those at Cleveland-Marshall were fairly stingy with praise for their law school. But there were some kind words to be heard, particularly for Cleveland-Marshall's skills curriculum: "The law school is practical, not theoretical," reported one student. "We learn the application of law in order to directly prepare for immediate local practice." That sentiment was echoed by one of the more enthusiastic respondents to our survey: "The faculty is knowledgeable, and we have great access to practical opportunities. There is also

1801 Euclid Avenue, Cleveland, OH 44115
Tel: (216) 687-2304   Fax: (216) 687-6881
eMail: law@csuohio.edu
Internet: http://www.law.csuohio.edu/

Cleveland State University

a strong commitment to students making career changes." Indeed, when it came to their sense of preparation for a career in the immediate geographical area, Cleveland-Marshall students sounded quite positive. One cited "the power and prestige of the alumni in the Cleveland area" as one of the law school's greatest strengths. Others agreed: "There's a strong alumni base for greater employment opportunities"; "Relations are very good between lawyers in the community and the school itself."

No Cleveland-Marshall student we heard from, however, had anything nice to say about the school's facilities. This kind of statement was among the most diplomatic of its type: "We need great improvement in our building and facilities—I mean the basics, such as furniture that is comfortable and in one piece." These sorts of objections were much more than aesthetic. Several students blamed their poor, overcrowded facilities for the missing sense of community within the law school. "I feel like Cleveland-Marshall is the best value around," explained one, "but our facilities really need to be improved." True to the opinion expressed by one student, "most faculty members truly care about their students' needs and desires," the administration has decided to grant the wish for upgraded facilities: a new library will open in 1997, freeing more space for classrooms and offices.

ADMISSIONS

Admissions at the Cleveland-Marshall College of Law are not terribly competitive in comparison with other law schools in the region. But the mission of this midsize public law school has always been more about inclusion than exclusion. Almost 2,000 prospective law students file applications every year, the majority of them several years older than the average law student. Roughly one half of those who apply will gain admission, and those who go on to enroll will have only moderate numerical credentials: a respectable undergraduate grade point average and an LSAT score at about the 63rd percentile.

ACADEMICS

Student/faculty ratio	12:1
% female faculty	32
% minority faculty	9
Hours of study per day	2.70

FINANCIAL FACTS

In-state tuition	$6,583
Out-of-state tuition	$13,125
Part-time tuition per credit	$252
Estimated books/expenses/fees	$3,390
On-campus living expenses	NR
Off-campus living expenses	NR
% first-year students receiving aid	75
% all students receiving aid	75
% aid that is merit-based	30
% all students receiving grants/scholarships	50
% all students receiving loans	75
% all students receiving assistantships	NR
Average award package	$16,000
Average graduation debt	$42,000

ADMISSIONS

# applications received	1,668
% applicants accepted	48
% acceptees attending	38
Average LSAT	151
Average undergrad GPA	3.18
Application Fee	$35
Priority application deadline	NR
Priority notification	NR
Regular application deadline	March 1
Regular notification	May 1
Admission deferment	NR
Gourman Report Rating	**2.80**

University of Colorado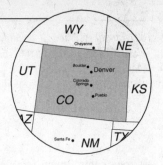
School of Law

Prospective law students are no doubt attracted to the University of Colorado School of Law primarily for its sheer academic strength. CU offers what is probably the strongest program of any law school within 500 miles (give or take), and it enjoys an extremely solid reputation for excellence, particularly in the West, still the source of most members of CU's small, well-qualified and admirably diverse student body. Because of its disproportionately large faculty—CU has one of the lower student-faculty ratios in the nation—Colorado's curriculum is extremely broad, with particular strength in the growing field of environmental law. This particular subspecialty is also the focus of Colorado's Natural Resources Law Center, one of the impressive array of clinical programs that supplement the law school's traditional classroom offerings. In fact, CU is one of the few schools in the country to have what amounts to a clinical graduation requirement. (This requirement can also be satisfied through a trial-advocacy program.)

But these considerable strengths may not be enough to explain the increasing popularity of this small public law school. Add in the fact that its Boulder, Colorado, campus is within spitting distance of what is undoubtedly the best hiking and skiing available to any U.S. law students, and you may explain the allure. Whether primarily for its solid academic reputation or for its location in one of the most physically appealing spots in the country, the University of Colorado School of Law draws applications from a rapidly increasing number of well-qualified aspiring lawyers.

Those who have made it through Colorado's increasingly selective admissions process and have gone on to enroll at the law school express a high degree of satisfaction with their decision. When asked to name the greatest strengths of their school, most CU students cited its manageable size and the "family atmosphere" that it fosters. "The small size makes for a connected student body," reported one 2L, "and for good rapport with professors and staff." "Professors know students by name outside of class," added another. "This makes for a supportive learning environment—cohesive and noncompetitive." Indeed,

Carol Nelson-Douglas, Director of Admissions
Fleming Law Building, Boulder, CO 80309-0403
Tel: (303) 492-7203   Fax: (303)492-1200
Internet: http://stripe.colorado.edu/~/awlib/lawscinf.htm

University of Colorado

the way Colorado students describe their school, it appears to be more like a mutual admiration society than a cauldron of cutthroat competitiveness. "My fellow students here are so impressive," said a 1L. "Students come here because they care about the environment, human rights, minority groups, and more," wrote another. Most of the CU students we heard from seem to agree that "people really care about what and how you are doing."

On the downside, a handful of those we heard from interpreted this same environment quite differently. Several older students expressed their feeling that Colorado was a place better suited to recent college graduates. "With lockers, gossip, etc.," explained one, "it's a bit too much like high school." Most of the criticism offered by CU students, however, focused on the law school's facilities. "They desperately need to improve both the holdings and the physical condition of the library," was one typical complaint. In response, the administration said, "We recognize that our facilities need improvement, but the library as a whole has utilized the criticism of years past to...implement solid improvements." They also said, "ABA review has shown that the holdings have been dramatically strengthened in the last five years."

For the most part, however, students at Colorado were more intent on praising their school than on criticizing it. This comment from one 1L neatly summed up the sentiments of many others: "Boulder is a great town to live in, and there happens to be a great law school here too." In addition to keeping its students quite happy, CU eventually graduates a small, highly employable group of lawyers. Anyone who has ever visited Boulder will understand why the state of Colorado keeps the majority of them there after graduation.

ADMISSIONS

The low price and high quality of the education available at the University of Colorado School of Law has not gone unnoticed by law-school applicants. Nor, probably, has the school's dream location. Demand for spots in Colorado's small entering class of about 170 is extraordinarily high. As if that weren't enough, numerical admissions standards alone rank this excellent law school among the 30 most selective in the country. The average entering student at Colorado boasts a solid undergraduate GPA and an LSAT score at the 93rd percentile.

ACADEMICS

Student/faculty ratio	14:1
% female faculty	21
% minority faculty	17
Hours of study per day	3.98

FINANCIAL FACTS

In-state tuition	$4,394
Out-of-state tuition	$14,630
Part-time tuition per credit	NR
Estimated books/expenses/fees	$3,933
On-campus living expenses	NR
Off-campus living expenses	NR
% first-year students receiving aid	100
% all students receiving aid	100
% aid that is merit-based	10
% all students receiving grants/scholarships	60
% all students receiving loans	79
% all students receiving assistantships	NR
Average award package	$14,500
Average graduation debt	$46,000

ADMISSIONS

# applications received	2,792
% applicants accepted	23
% acceptees attending	27
Average LSAT	161
Average undergrad GPA	3.46
Application Fee	$40
No early decision program	
Regular application deadline	February 15
Regular notification	rolling
Admission may be deferred?	No
Gourman Report Rating	3.50

COLUMBIA UNIVERSITY 🖫
School of Law

The reputation of the Columbia University School of Law as one of the undisputed leaders in legal education dates back to 1858, when the establishment of a law school on the campus of one of the country's oldest and finest universities lent much-needed credibility to the incipient movement toward academic preparation for the practice of law. Columbia rose to eminence in the field on the strength of its faculty, and particularly on the strength of the leadership of Theodore Dwight, one of the founding fathers of the American law school. Over the course of its first 138 years, this large, private law school on Manhattan's Upper West Side has employed some of the most respected legal scholars in the nation. The current faculty is as strong as they come. They may not be the most accessible bunch, but the quality and breadth of their scholarship is felt by every Columbia law student in the form of a curriculum that is exceedingly strong in all the traditional areas and particularly rich in fields, like Human Rights Law and Legal History, that receive little or no attention in most law schools. The vast resources of the law school, of the broader university, and, not least, of New York City itself have consistently drawn to Columbia a group of law students whose qualifications match those of students at any school.

While legend would have it that the law school is little more than a brutally competitive breeding ground for future corporate lawyers, and though the employment patterns of the law school's graduates do little to dispel that notion, Columbia is a far cry from the shark pool it is widely reputed to be. Students paint a picture of a law school that offers a tremendously rich academic experience but also has clear shortcomings. On the positive side, most students list Columbia's stellar faculty and the quality of the scholarship they demand from students. And, of course, they list Columbia's ability to land them top jobs. "This place is great (really great, awesome, the best) if you want to do corporate law," wrote one student who does. "The school's greatest strength is its reputation," wrote another. "Really, it gets you jobs." Just as important, most Columbia students we heard from had something like this to say: "There is a myth that CU is cutthroat, which I have found to be more or less false...People are helpful, concerned and supportive both academically and personally." That from a 1L in the middle of a notoriously rigorous first-year program. It should be noted that dissenting voices were also heard. From another 1L: "Students are snobby and the stress here can be unbearable."

When it comes to the faults of their school, Columbia students are forthcoming. Their loudest complaints concerned the overall quality of life within the law school. "With notable exceptions," said one LL.M. candidate, "faculty members are not accessible and do not put much effort into relations with students." Others disagreed, and noted that relations have been warming recently, with many students referring to professors as "friendly." By far the most common lament of Columbia students was summarized by one 3L: "Facilities suck." She refers not to Columbia's research facilities, which students unanimously praise, but, rather, to the law building itself. Prospective applicants, however, need not be deterred by past tales of woe, as a dramatic, $20 million renovation and expansion project is currently underway, aimed at improving the student experience at Columbia. A new building, and the vastly overhauled original building, thanks to the renovation of the library, up-to-the-nanosecond classroom computer capabilities, and a "new front door" (37-foot high atrium), will greet the lucky 1996 incoming class. The changes were driven by "the need for informal, social, study, and personal spaces," which hopefully will facilitate the faculty/student, student/student community, the lack of which current J.D. candidates decry.

Accordingly, even Columbia students' criticisms often conveyed a tone of optimism for the school's future, and many students offered unsolicited votes of confidence in their administration, and particularly in their new dean. "This is a dynamic place," was the judgment of one 3L. "Columbia is making a valiant effort to change with the times."

ADMISSIONS

The rumor mill would have it that the law school at Columbia is a bastion of cutthroat competitiveness. This reputation is very much overstated, and possibly wholly inaccurate. One area where ruthless competition certainly exists, however, is in the admissions process. Fewer than one in every six of the roughly 6,000 candidates Columbia considers annually will gain admission to the law school. Those who are admitted and actually go on to enroll possess numerical credentials that are higher than those of students at all but five of the nation's fully accredited law schools.

ACADEMICS	
Student/faculty ratio	16:1
% female faculty	27
% minority faculty	13
Hours of study per day	3.32

FINANCIAL FACTS	
Tuition	$23,818
Part-time tuition per credit	NR
Estimated books/expenses/fees	$1,842
On-campus living expenses	$9,410
Off-campus living expenses	$10,440
% first-year students receiving aid	31
% all students receiving aid	67
% aid that is merit-based	NR
% all students receiving grants/scholarships	29
% all students receiving loans	71
% all students receiving assistantships	9
Average award package	$9,524
Average graduation debt	$58,670

ADMISSIONS	
# applications received	5,761
% applicants accepted	15
% acceptees attending	36
Average LSAT	167
Average undergrad GPA	3.60
Application Fee	$65
Priority application deadline	December
Priority notification	late December
Regular application deadline	February 15
Regular notification	rolling
Admission deferment	one or two years
Gourman Report Rating	4.87

UNIVERSITY OF CONNECTICUT
School of Law

OVERVIEW

Type of school	public
Environment	metropolis
Scholastic calendar	NR
Schedule	full-time or part-time

STUDENTS

Enrollment of institution	NR
Enrollment of law school	641
% male/female	51/49
% out-of-state	34
% part-time	30
% minorities	17
% international (# countries represented)	NR (5)
Average age at entry	25

APPLICANTS ALSO LOOK AT

Boston College
Boston University
George Washington University
Fordham University
Georgetown University

SURVEY SAYS...

HITS
Serving humankind
Broad range of courses
Clinical experience

MISSES
Socratic Method

EMPLOYMENT PROFILE

% grads employed immediately	67
% grads employed within six months	88
Average starting salary	$56,500
% grads employed by field:	
Private practice	53
Business/industry	9
Government	14
Judicial clerkships	10
Academic	14
Military	1

New England, like the rest of the Northeast, is not lacking in fine law schools. A quality legal education is rarely more than an hour's drive away from any prospective law student living in the region, but inexpensive options are few and very far between. The University of Connecticut School of Law is one such option. Drawn as much by UConn's affordability as by its academic strengths and solid regional reputation, about 2,200 applicants vie annually to be among the roughly 200 day and evening students who enter one of the Northeast's most respected public law schools each year. Not surprisingly, the majority of students are Connecticut state residents who are happy to take advantage of the low in-state tuition. The law school also gives tuition breaks to students from Massachusetts, New Hampshire, Rhode Island, and Vermont. (They pay more than in-state students, but less than out-of-state students; $15,482 this year.) Most students are eligible to establish Connecticut residency for tuition purposes after one full year in Connecticut. With many of their contemporaries facing steep loan repayments, those attending the University of Connecticut School of Law are quick to mention the low in-state tuition as one of the school's greatest strengths.

UConn's traditional course offerings are broad for the school's size, a pleasant effect of the law school's employment of a relatively large faculty. UConn law school's student-faculty ratio is, in fact, one of the most favorable in the nation. The high caliber of teaching at UConn was strongly praised by students we heard from. With a few exceptions, the faculty was described as "highly accessible" and "engaging," and the atmosphere at the school was described as "friendly." A 1L, who is glad he chose UConn over the other schools to which he was accepted, said, "The supportive and collegial atmosphere is conducive to intellectual as well as social growth," and, "At UConn, students, faculty members, professionals, and administrative staff members collectively strive to enhance each student's law school experience."

Located apart from the semi-rural campus of its parent institution, this law school calls the city of Hartford—the nation's insurance capital—home. High on the list of the school's advantages is the "beautiful," spacious campus, which is listed on the

Ellen Rutt, Assistant Dean
55 Elizabeth Street, Hartford, CT 06105
Tel: (203) 241-4696
eMail: admit@brandeis.law.uconn.edu
Internet: http://www.uconn.law

National Register of Historic Sites. The student body applauded the school's new law library that opened in the Spring of 1996, as well as the library's support staff. The school's broad clinical programs rounded out the list of UConn's strengths. Connecticut's liberal student practice rules have facilitated the school's clinical and externship programs. The numerous legal clinics include a program dedicated to the legislative process and an array of external placements with the local judiciary.

Either UConn students do not like to complain or they are truly quite happy with their law school. Of the few criticisms waged against the school, complaints about the computers and the student lounge were most common, although little was added in terms of how these areas should improve. Lack of parking and disabled access were also mentioned as weaknesses. Several students we spoke with called for increased diversity. Although the sense of "cohesion" among UConn law students is probably due in large part to the relatively small size of the school and its favorable student faculty ratio, it may also speak of a homogeneity among its student body. These criticisms, however, were tempered by the overwhelmingly positive feedback we heard from students at the UConn School of Law.

ADMISSIONS

The strength of the University of Connecticut School of Law's regional reputation and its bargain status combine to make it an appealing and relatively selective law school. In fact, this "second-tier" law school ranks among the top 25 percent of all law schools in the nation both in terms of its numerical admissions standards and in terms of applicant demand for spots in its first-year class. The average incoming student at Connecticut has a very strong undergraduate GPA and an LSAT score at the 84th percentile and has had to overcome fairly stiff competition to get there. Two out of three students applying to this law school are unsuccessful.

ACADEMICS

Student/faculty ratio	10:1
% female faculty	27
% minority faculty	11
Hours of study per day	4.02

FINANCIAL FACTS

In-state tuition	$10,320
Out-of-state tuition	$21,766
Part-time tuition per credit	$360
Estimated books/expenses/fees	$1,042
On-campus living expenses	NR
Off-campus living expenses	$7,634
% first-year students receiving aid	96
% all students receiving aid	100
% aid that is merit-based	NR
% all students receiving grants/scholarships	24
% all students receiving loans	69
% all students receiving assistantships	16
Average award package	$7,974
Average graduation debt	$35,500

ADMISSIONS

# applications received	1,627
% applicants accepted	33
% acceptees attending	35
Average LSAT	159
Average undergrad GPA	3.29
Application Fee	$30
No early decision program	
Regular application deadline	March 1
Regular notification	rolling
Admission deferment	one year
Gourman Report Rating	**3.38**

CORNELL UNIVERSITY
Law School

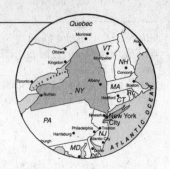

OVERVIEW

Type of school	private
Environment	suburban
Scholastic calendar	semester
Schedule	full time only

STUDENTS

Enrollment of institution	18,000
Enrollment of law school	569
% male/female	60/40
% out-of-state	75
% part-time	NR
% minorities	21
% international (# countries represented)	10 (18)
Average age at entry	24

APPLICANTS ALSO LOOK AT

Harvard University
Georgetown University
Columbia University
New York University
University of Pennsylvania

SURVEY SAYS...

HITS
Intellectual challenge
Studying
Quality of teaching

MISSES
Faculty-student relations

EMPLOYMENT PROFILE

% grads employed immediately	90
% grads employed within six months	95
Average starting salary	$70,000
% grads employed by field:	
Private practice	60
Business/industry	5
Government	10
Judicial clerkships	15
Public service	10
Military	1

With very good reason, Cornell Law School appears perennially on nearly everybody's list of the top law schools in the United States. With its stellar national reputation, its affiliation with an Ivy League university, and its strength in all the traditional areas—most notably International Law—Cornell attracts and will continue to attract thousands of highly qualified applicants every year. Only about one out of five applicants is accepted, and around 180 first-year students enroll each year. The intimacy that such a small student body engenders is notable among the nation's elite schools, and the physical beauty of the small-town environs at Cornell's upstate New York campus draw many students who could likely have their pick of urban law schools. Cornell has been mysteriously described as a "corporate" law school, a categorization that the school itself rightfully resists. The career choices of its graduates—and Cornell grads generally do have their choice of jobs—are no more skewed toward corporate law than at any top law school. And even if they were, it would not be the result of any bias in the school's curriculum. The Cornell Law School offers a program that is broad-based and flexible, and it boasts one of the country's better loan-forgiveness programs for graduates who choose to practice law in the public interest.

But even if the rate at which Cornell grads enter corporate practice is lower than it is for graduates of some comparable schools, the fact remains that the vast majority do choose this career path. Many of the students we surveyed lamented this fact: "The placement office is a pipeline to NYC—to go anywhere else you have to ignore classes for two months and spend all your time writing letters and calling firms"; "The placement office is improving, but if you aren't going for a big NYC law firm, think hard before coming to Cornell." For those who accept this orientation, Cornell appears to be an excellent choice. "As a traditional school emphasizing classroom training for law practice," wrote one 3L, "Cornell excels." Enthusiastically and almost unanimously, the students we heard from pointed to the teaching abilities of their highly respected faculty in explaining the quality of this program. Asked to name their school's greatest strengths, many responded as this 2L did: "The faculty, pure and simple.... They are great

Richard D. Geiger, Dean of Admissions
Myron Taylor Hall, Ithaca, NY 14853
Tel: (607) 255-5141
eMail: lawadmit@law.mail.cornell.edu
Internet: http://www.law.cornell.edu/admit/admit.htm

Cornell University

teachers with terrific knowledge and experience in their fields." Indeed, students here rated the quality of teaching they receive more highly than did students at nearly every law school in the country.

Cornell students' high praise for their faculty is all the more striking when one considers the paces that faculty puts them through. Consider this backhanded compliment from a 2L: "The faculty and curriculum here make Cornell graduates very attractive to employers, and they thoroughly prepare you for a life with little sleep or time outside the job you get." One less upbeat 1L put a slightly different spin on the same opinion: "The atmosphere here can often be the very stereotype of law school that students look to avoid when choosing a school—cold, sterile and alienating." Indeed, the academic atmosphere here is, by all reports, rigorous and competitive. "Realize if you come here," advised one 2L, "that everyone in your class was at the top of their college classes and everyone wants to be at the top here too." But most of the students we heard from seem to accept this state of affairs as a tolerable and necessary part of life at a school as esteemed as this one; few expressed any regrets at having chosen Cornell. And even though numerous complaints were heard concerning the misery of Ithaca winters, most even consider this a fair trade-off. As one 1L wrote, "If Cornell was in a major city, it would be ranked in the top five nationally, but it would lose what is best about it: the beauty and peace of Ithaca, and the friendly attitude that prevails here."

ADMISSIONS

It should come as no surprise to hear that this Ivy League law school—traditionally considered one of the 20 finest in the nation—is tremendously selective in filling its first-year class of about 200 students. In fact, the average numerical credentials of incoming Cornell students rank them, by our calculations, as one of the ten or so most qualified in the nation. Unfortunately for the highly qualified applicant, however, even very impressive numbers do not come close to guaranteeing one admission to Cornell. When estimating your own chances, consider that in 1993, only half of those applicants with undergraduate GPAs over 3.5 and LSAT scores above the 84th percentile were admitted.

ACADEMICS

Student/faculty ratio	14:1
% female faculty	26
% minority faculty	10
Hours of study per day	5.22

FINANCIAL FACTS

Tuition	$22,100
Part-time tuition per credit	NR
Estimated books/expenses/fees	NR
On-campus living expenses	NR
Off-campus living expenses	NR
% first-year students receiving aid	80
% all students receiving aid	82
% aid that is merit-based	NR
% all students receiving grants/scholarships	40
% all students receiving loans	80
% all students receiving assistantships	NR
Average award package	$7,000
Average graduation debt	NR

ADMISSIONS

# applications received	3,800
% applicants accepted	NR
% acceptees attending	5
Average LSAT	165
Average undergrad GPA	3.55
Application Fee	$65
No early decision program	
Regular application deadline	February 1
Regular notification	rolling
Admission deferment	two years
Gourman Report Rating	4.79

CREIGHTON UNIVERSITY
School of Law

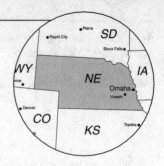

The larger of Nebraska's two law schools, the Creighton University School of Law is located in downtown Omaha, the state's largest business and population center and the largest metropolitan area in the immediate region. The 118-year-old Jesuit university is widely regarded as one of the finest private institutions in the Midwest. Its law school, founded in 1904, enjoys a solid regional reputation as a training ground for highly competent attorneys. The highest levels of the bench and bar of Nebraska and its neighboring states are heavily populated with Creighton graduates, whose successes are as responsible as anything else for the law school's standing.

With less than 500 students in its J.D. program and a combined full- and part-time teaching faculty of 45, Creighton has the resources to offer a broad curriculum. In terms of traditional course offerings, it clearly does so. The range of courses available to upper-level students is great, particularly within the broader category of commercial law. If the curriculum is lacking anywhere, it is in the area of clinical training. Creighton offers only one legal clinic, though it does sponsor numerous externships with the many government agencies and private law firms doing business in Omaha. The law school receives almost 1,000 applications annually, so competition to be among Creighton's entering class of about 150 students is fairly high. Numerical admissions standards, however, are moderate.

Students at Creighton are somewhat critical of many aspects of their experience at the law school, but on several fundamental quality-of-life issues, they express a high and uniform degree of satisfaction. Specifically, most of those we heard from praised the faculty and the general goodwill that characterizes interactions with them: "The faculty have an open-door policy—anytime for anything," explained one student. "They are wonderful, down-to-earth people." Others endorsed that position: "The faculty really seems to be interested in actually teaching; they don't just see it as a necessary evil that takes up time they could better spend writing law review articles." As for relations among students themselves: "The students have formed a very close-knit community. The atmosphere is very supportive and noncompetitive."

California Street, Omaha, NE 68178
Tel: (402) 280-2872   Fax: (402) 280-2244
eMail: adm.7@culaw.creighton.edu
Internet: http://www.creighton.edu/culaw/

When Creighton students turn their critical faculties on the law school that has helped to hone them, the majority of them find fault with two things: the limited availability of certain kinds of courses and their less-than-opulent physical plant. On the former count, quite a few students agreed that access to the law school's clinical program is far too limited. "They need to prepare all students to be lawyers," complained one 2L. "They need to offer hands-on experience to more than just the top one third of the class." A number of others expressed frustration with the scheduling of some fundamental courses, which always seem to conflict with one another. "Whoever does the calendar must be on drugs," opined a 2L. And although Creighton students have voiced complaints about their facilities in the past, recent interior refurbishments should please many critics.

It should also be noted that a good number of Creighton students we heard from had spent quite a few years out of college before attending law school, and that several of them pointed out how comfortable they felt in a student body that is a bit more mature than average. Whatever their age, and despite their criticisms, however, most students seem to agree that they chose wisely when they chose Creighton.

ADMISSIONS

Creighton resides in the lower end of the mid-range of all fully accredited U.S. law schools when it comes to the competitiveness of its admissions process. Still, its regional reputation is strong enough that, despite its much higher tuition, Creighton draws a larger applicant pool than, and is very nearly as selective as, Nebraska's fine public law school in Lincoln. In large part, this is due to the relatively higher percentage of non-Nebraskans who apply to and enroll at Creighton, whose reasonable tuition is competitive with the University of Nebraska's nonresident rate. Numerical standards are moderate: The average GPA of Creighton students is 3.21 and the average LSAT score is a 153—the 63rd percentile.

ACADEMICS

Student/faculty ratio	19:1
% female faculty	31
% minority faculty	3
Hours of study per day	3.33

FINANCIAL FACTS

Tuition	$14,216
Part-time tuition per credit	NR
Estimated books/expenses/fees	NR
On-campus living expenses	NR
Off-campus living expenses	NR
% first-year students receiving aid	NR
% all students receiving aid	NR
% aid that is merit-based	NR
% all students receiving grants/scholarships	NR
% all students receiving loans	NR
% all students receiving assistantships	NR
Average award package	NR
Average graduation debt	NR

ADMISSIONS

# applications received	1,000
% applicants accepted	50
% acceptees attending	35
Average LSAT	153
Average undergrad GPA	3.21
Application Fee	$40
Priority application deadline	NR
Priority notification	NR
Regular application deadline	May 1
Regular notification	NR
Admission deferment	NR
Gourman Report Rating	**3.09**

UNIVERSITY OF DAYTON 💾
School of Law

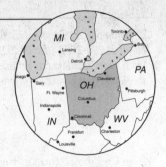

The University of Dayton School of Law is a small private law school on the campus of one of the largest Catholic universities in the Midwest. The city of Dayton is home to nearly one million people, the university to 10,000, the law school to fewer than 500, a sizable number of them Ohio natives. The course of study they follow includes a modest variety of traditional classroom offerings and several notable nontraditional offerings, including a required three-semester skills program ("Legal Profession") and an informal but organized program of specialization in law and technology. (The "Law and Tech" program focuses on computer-related law and on intellectual property law.) Although it is relatively small in absolute terms, the faculty that administers these programs is quite large for the law school's size. Dayton has undergone significant growth in the past decade, with the faculty size increasing by 50 percent. In the fall of 1997, they will dedicate a new $23 million facility, Keller Hall, which will integrate sophisticated technology in classrooms, the law library, and all student study areas, and nearly double the school's current space. For a private school, Dayton charges a reasonable tuition, and the cost of living in the surrounding area is low. Because of its relative affordability, Dayton draws a sizable group of applicants, and members of the student body possess solid midrange numerical credentials.

Part of Dayton's self-described mission is to train lawyers who are "sensitive to the impact of Judeo-Christian ethics on the law." That the law school sees fit to state this as an operating principle is surely not insignificant, but it would be a mistake to take this as a sign of religious zealotry. The impact of the school's affiliation with the Marianist order is benevolent and, aside from one course on Judeo-Christian Ethics and the Law, mostly intangible.

Dayton students are certainly not without their criticisms, but most of those we heard from expressed a fairly high—though hardly enthusiastic—degree of satisfaction with many aspects of their experience. When asked to name the greatest strengths of their chosen school, most cited the quality of Dayton's skills programs, the career placement services, and the overall pleasantness of the law school's academic environment. "The Legal

Charles Roboski, Assistant Dean, Director of Admission and Financial Aid
300 College Park, Dayton, OH 45469-1320
Tel: (513) 229-3555
eMail: lawinfo@odo.law.udayton.edu
Internet: http://www.udayton.edu

Professions program provides much practical experience for students," reported one, "and our professors are always accessible and willing to help when asked." Most others agreed: "Professors here encourage insightful discussion during class time and are respectful of divergent opinions," said one 3L, "and the kegs on Friday afternoons make for a relaxed, friendly atmosphere." And while many of the students we heard from voiced their frustration with Dayton's lack of a nationally recognized "name," many others went out of their way to express their appreciation for the solidity of its program and for their feelings of professional preparedness. "Dayton is an above average law school," began one such remark. "I worked the last two summers, and I was at least as competent as the students from other schools, and probably more competent in terms of practical skills." The student was possibly also more likely to pass the bar; Dayton has had the second-highest first-time bar passage rate in the state for 1993-1995.

In offering criticism of their law school, Dayton students are every bit as practical-minded as they are in praising it. In part, their negative comments focused directly on academic issues. "I have found the curriculum terribly narrow," wrote one 3L. Other negative comments concerned the lousy facilities, although some students pointed out that an upgrade is slated for 1997. Indeed, though the majority expressed satisfaction with the quality of the courses they have taken, many complained about the limited selection of courses from which they could choose. "This school needs more classrooms, more professors and a much broader offering of courses for every semester," said one 2L.

ADMISSIONS

After the state's big three law schools (Case Western, Cincinnati and Ohio State), the University of Dayton School of Law is the most selective of Ohio's nine schools. A moderately priced private school, Dayton competes quite well with the state's many public law schools for well-qualified prospective students. Dayton students, more than half of whom come from outside Ohio, possess solid numerical credentials that rank them smack-dab in the middle of all law students nationally. The law school's overall acceptance rate, however, is a bit lower than average, so even those applicants whose numbers approach Dayton's average are far from assured of gaining admission.

ACADEMICS	
Student/faculty ratio	19:1
% female faculty	37
% minority faculty	14
Hours of study per day	4.28

FINANCIAL FACTS	
In-state tuition	$16,900
Out-of-state tuition	$16,900
Part-time tuition per credit	NR
Estimated books/expenses/fees	$1,030
On-campus living expenses	$4,900
Off-campus living expenses	NR
% first-year students receiving aid	80
% all students receiving aid	75
% aid that is merit-based	25
% all students receiving grants/scholarships	25
% all students receiving loans	80
% all students receiving assistantships	NR
Average award package	$2,014
Average graduation debt	$55,000

ADMISSIONS	
# applications received	1,650
% applicants accepted	43
% acceptees attending	22
Average LSAT	153
Average undergrad GPA	3.33
Application Fee	$40
No early decision program	
Regular application deadline	May 1
Regular notification	rolling
Admission deferment	one year
Gourman Report Rating	2.62

UNIVERSITY OF DENVER
College of Law

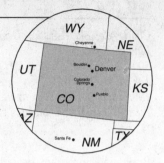

One mile above sea level, and head and shoulders above all law schools in the region in terms of size, the University of Denver College of Law is the only law school in Colorado's capital, a city that apparently "logs more annual hours of sunshine than San Diego or Miami." More relevant to the matters at hand, the city of Denver is the nation's twelfth-largest job market for recent law school graduates, and its thriving legal community has long depended on this highly regarded law school for more than a century as a major source of new blood. Denver has sought to differentiate itself from the masses of law schools with its Admissions required "Lawyering Process" first year course, where students work on client counselling, research, writing, and litigation skills in a simulated law firm setting. Denver also has a solid traditional J.D. curriculum with four semiformal specialization programs: the Natural Resources/Environmental Program, the Business Planning Program, the Lawyering Skills Program, and a program in international legal studies. These special programs, which do not lead to any official certification, were devised primarily to promote and exploit what the law school perceives to be its curricular strengths. In cooperation with its parent institution and with several other area universities, Denver offers programs leading to master's degrees in anthropology, business administration, international studies, psychology, social work, sociology, and urban planning, as well as the nation's only joint J.D./master's in mineral economics.

Judging from the results of our survey, this huge law school delivers, for better or for worse, just what one might expect of a huge law school. There is general agreement, for instance, concerning the huge variety in course offerings, flexibility of scheduling and vastness of resources offered by the DU law school. Students gave their chosen school high marks in all these categories. But they were also quick to point out what they perceive to be Denver's shortcomings, some of which are the seemingly inevitable side effects of the school's sheer size. "There is a pretty amazing selection of classes offered each semester," wrote one 2L. "So many, in fact, that I wish the program allowed for more electives than it does." "Besides having a wide variety of courses to choose from," added a 1L, "there is a lot of flexibility in course schedules, which will allow me to work during my 2nd and 3rd years." Many others offered their own such personal reasons for appreciating Denver's big-school amenities. "They are very open to nontraditional students here," said one 2L. "With a child-care facility on campus and a very positive atmosphere, DU has made law school bearable for myself and a good experience for my child." While that specific concern may not apply to all prospective students, it seems a good example of the accommodating atmosphere that many Denver students attest to. As one 3L wrote, "There are opportunities here to do almost anything if you are willing to seek them out."

That last remark suggests some problems that several of the students we heard from mentioned explicitly. "I can't say that the faculty and administration do much hand-holding," said one Denver 1L. "Like most established law schools," added a 3L, "DU rests on its laurels and is slow to change with the times." "Faculty here—as elsewhere—are chosen primarily for their legal reputation and not their educational prowess." Others echoed that sentiment, asserting that "only a minority of the faculty seems as concerned with teaching as they are with their own academic careers." On a similar theme, we heard numerous complaints about the law school's administration, not so much for specific failings as for its "unresponsiveness" and its production of "red tape." This evenhanded assessment from one 2L summed up student opinion here quite well: "There is a niche to be found here for almost anyone, and those who find theirs will be very happy. Those who do not, however, will find that it's not exactly paradise."

ADMISSIONS

The numerical standards to which it holds applicants fall slightly below the national average, but the University of Denver is in a position to be relatively selective thanks to the size of the applicant pool from which it draws its 350-member entering class. Overall, roughly three out of five candidates for admission are rejected. Statistically, an applicant to the University of Denver who has an undergraduate GPA between 3.00 and 3.25 and an LSAT score between 155 and 159, inclusive, stands only a 27 percent chance of getting in.

ACADEMICS

Student/faculty ratio	20:1
% female faculty	30
% minority faculty	15
Hours of study per day	4.13

FINANCIAL FACTS

Tuition	$17,732
Part-time tuition per credit	$10,380
Estimated books/expenses/fees	$1,490
On-campus living expenses	NR
Off-campus living expenses	NR
% first-year students receiving aid	75
% all students receiving aid	80
% aid that is merit-based	NR
% all students receiving grants/scholarships	23
% all students receiving loans	75
% all students receiving assistantships	NR
Average award package	NR
Average graduation debt	$45,000

ADMISSIONS

# applications received	2,688
% applicants accepted	40
% acceptees attending	30
Average LSAT	158
Average undergrad GPA	3.08
Application Fee	$45
No early decision program	
Regular application deadline	May 1
Regular notification	rolling
Admission deferment	NR
Gourman Report Rating	**3.85**

DePaul University
College of Law

For most of its years, the DePaul University College of Law enjoyed a large but limited role in this city of many law schools: to serve as the training ground for local residents—often ethnic and working class—who wished to enter the lower and middle reaches of the country's third-largest legal community. After years of creditable, quiet service in this role, and after producing thousands of fine lawyers and sending more than its share of graduates into positions of political power, this midsize Catholic law school has started to make some noise. In recent years, and with some success, DePaul has set about enhancing its reputation outside downtown Chicago's Loop. Statistics seem to point to the success of its efforts, and under its current leadership the law school is likely to attract more attention. There was a time when almost all of DePaul's students came from within Cook County. Recent classes are composed of a large percentage of nonresidents of Illinois. But since DePaul has continued to focus its attention on educating practicing Chicago attorneys, a more meaningful sign of its rising reputation is the ever-increasing proportion of its graduates who go to work in the city's largest and richest firms. Much of DePaul's success in this area stems from its long-respected skills-training programs, which continue to be the centerpiece in a varied curriculum that also includes one of the nation's most highly regarded programs in Health Law. Applications volume is up sharply in recent years, and the law school's entering classes possess increasingly stronger numerical credentials.

One thing that has not changed at DePaul is the focus of its students on their professional futures—specifically their professional futures in the city itself. "There are a lot of alumni in prominent legal positions in Chicago willing to help new grads," wrote one student, naming what he, like many others, considered his law school's greatest strength. One student among those praising the law school's connections to the Chicago legal community was, however, a bit more critical: "There are some excellent faculty here, but I sense that we are still riding somewhat on the reputation—built by its politically prominent alumni—that DePaul had about fifteen years ago."

25 East Jackson Boulevard, Chicago, IL 60604
Tel: (312) 362-6831   Fax: (312) 362-5448
eMail: lawinfo@wppost.depaul.edu

DePaul University

Indeed, DePaul students did not hesitate to point out their school's shortcomings. Students cited DePaul's location as what brought them to the school, but when it came to their immediate physical surroundings, they were not nearly so positive. Luckily for current applicants, De Paul's three-year renovation program will be entirely finished by the fall of 1996, so that much more accommodating and aesthetically pleasing library, classrooms, computer labs, and faculty and administrative offices will greet new students. Though most students expressed their satisfaction with the school's practical focus, some bemoaned what they perceive as DePaul's unintellectual atmosphere. Others, however, commented on the need for even more lawyering skills courses, especially legal writing.

Quite a few students also complained about the lack of diversity at the law school. "The most frustrating thing about DePaul," said one, "is that the student body is essentially homogeneous." Statistically speaking, she is correct. It is certainly not the least diverse law school in Chicago—that dubious distinction belongs to nearby John Marshall—but DePaul falls below the national average in terms of minority representation in its student body. If it is lacking in diversity, however, the DePaul faculty is certainly not too small. The law school boasts an excellent student-faculty ratio which contributes significantly to the overall sense of well-being among current DePaul students.

ADMISSIONS

In a town that is well-stocked with fine law schools, the DePaul University College of Law is far from the most selective, but admissions at this large, private law school are relatively competitive. Admissions standards have risen appreciably in the last six or seven years, and the average member of DePaul's entering class of almost 350 now possesses very respectable numerical credentials.

ACADEMICS

Student/faculty ratio	18:1
% female faculty	40
% minority faculty	10
Hours of study per day	3.88

FINANCIAL FACTS

Tuition	$17,500
Part-time tuition per credit	$11,300
Estimated books/expenses/fees	$710
On-campus living expenses	NR
Off-campus living expenses	NR
% first-year students receiving aid	NR
% all students receiving aid	NR
% aid that is merit-based	NR
% all students receiving grants/scholarships	NR
% all students receiving loans	NR
% all students receiving assistantships	NR
Average award package	NR
Average graduation debt	NR

ADMISSIONS

# applications received	2,688
% applicants accepted	48
% acceptees attending	29
Average LSAT	156
Average undergrad GPA	3.27
Application Fee	$40
Priority application deadline	NR
Priority notification	NR
Regular application deadline	April 1
Regular notification	March 1
Admission deferment	NR
Gourman Report Rating	**3.40**

DETROIT COLLEGE OF LAW AT MICHIGAN STATE UNIVERSITY

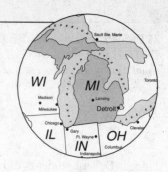

Established in 1891, the Detroit College of Law at Michigan State University is the oldest law school in the Motor City. Through all the changes the city has seen, this midsize private law school has remained a reliable source of well-trained lawyers. The bench and bar of Michigan are well populated by DCL/MSU alumni, many of whom occupy some of the most powerful positions of judicial authority. In its second century, the school is seeking to adapt itself to the changing face of the region's economy and to the changing face of the legal profession in general. To this end, beginning in fall 1996, the school will start offering classes in East Lansing, on the campus of Michigan State University, with which it will develop joint programs. DCL/MSU's new law school building, with a new library and state-of-the-art technology throughout the facility, will be completed in July, 1997.

The law school's efforts to remain competitive are evident in its curriculum. In response to the trend toward specialization in the profession, DCL/MSU has recently introduced two programs of formal concentration at the J.D. level. Students may elect to specialize in either taxation or international and comparative law. The law school is particularly strong in the latter category, but while "international law" may conjure up images of European capitals and a glamorous jet-set lifestyle, DCL/MSU's international focus is decidedly less exotic. The law school offers one of the nation's greatest variety of courses relating to the legal system of Canada, our country's biggest trading partner. DCL/MSU will soon be offering students the opportunity to participate in an electronic classroom for their Contracts I course, using laptop computers. It should be noted that virtually all specialization at DCL/MSU must occur in the third year of studies, since the relatively rigid curriculum leaves room for only two electives in the first and second years.

On the basis of the many comments we heard from students at the Detroit College of Law at MSU, the degree of a DCL/MSU student's satisfaction has to do mainly with how he or she feels about the demanding program. "They really pound the law into you," was one typical remark—delivered as a compliment—from one 2L. The most highly satisfied students generally sub-

N-210 North Business Complex, East Lansing, MI 48201
Tel: (517) 432-0222   Fax: (517) 432-0098
eMail: heatleya@pilot.msu.edu
Internet: http://www.dcl.edu

Detroit College of Law at
Michigan State
University

scribed to this evenhanded assessment from another 2L: "The quality of education here is extremely high. Some students do not like it, but professors make strict use of the Socratic Method and enforce rigid attendance requirements. Education by coercion—a method that DCL is very good at employing—may be unpleasant, but it is definitely effective." In fact, of the students we heard from, many share this belief. "The professors are outstanding," reported a 1L. "They challenge students every day, but they present the material in an easily understandable manner." "The professors are practical and demanding," agreed another, "so competition is inevitable, but I've experienced no alienation among students." On the negative side, for every student who praised the rigor of Detroit's J.D. program, there were two who found it far too traditional and rigid. When asked to name the specific strengths of their chosen school, many students sound a common note: "This school is thought of as a factory school that pumps out good litigators," said one participant in the law school's popular trial advocacy program. "That image may not be great, but from day one after graduation you are ready to litigate."

ADMISSIONS

Though numerical admission standards are not particularly high at either of Detroit's two private law schools, overall selectivity is much greater at the Detroit College of Law than at the larger, neighboring University of Detroit School of Law. Indeed, total applicant volume at Detroit College of Law has nearly doubled since 1986, when the law school admitted fully 75 percent of all the candidates it considered. Today, DCL turns away almost three out of four applicants in assembling its small first-year class. Still, the relatively low average GPA and LSAT scores of entering students virtually guarantee that applicants with moderately strong numerical credentials will gain admission.

ACADEMICS

Student/faculty ratio	21:1
% female faculty	39
% minority faculty	12
Hours of study per day	4.21

FINANCIAL FACTS

Tuition	$14,500
Part-time tuition per credit	NR
Estimated books/expenses/fees	NR
On-campus living expenses	NR
Off-campus living expenses	NR
% first-year students receiving aid	NR
% all students receiving aid	NR
% aid that is merit-based	NR
% all students receiving grants/scholarships	NR
% all students receiving loans	NR
% all students receiving assistantships	NR
Average award package	NR
Average graduation debt	NR

ADMISSIONS

# applications received	1,029
% applicants accepted	53
% acceptees attending	38
Average LSAT	151
Average undergrad GPA	2.95
Application Fee	$50
Priority application deadline	NR
Priority notification	NR
Regular application deadline	April 15
Regular notification	NR
Admission deferment	NR
Gourman Report Rating	**3.22**

UNIVERSITY OF DETROIT 💾
School of Law

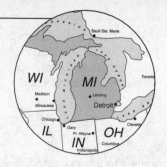

If, as David Letterman once said, Canada is "technically a nation," then the University of Detroit Mercy School of Law is, by the same logic, "technically" one of the most international in the country. Located in the heart of downtown Detroit, opposite the city's "Renaissance Center," this large Jesuit law school has served its home city for more than eighty years. It has also served—and continues to serve—the neighboring city of Windsor, Ontario, a five-minute trip away by bridge or tunnel. In conjunction with the University of Windsor Law School, the University of Detroit offers Canadian law students and lawyers interested in practicing in the United States the opportunity to earn their J.D.s. The two law schools also allow cross-registration on an elective course-by-course basis.

For those who stay on the American side of the river, Detroit offers a straightforward, traditional curriculum supplemented by a handful of special programs, including those of its Intellectual Property Law Institute and Health Law Center. The law school also operates a clinical program of modest size and sponsors various externships and judicial clerkships for upper-level students. By and large, however, Detroit students follow a course of study that stays well within traditional bounds. The bulk of course offerings falls under the general heading of business law, and the overwhelming majority of Detroit grads pursue careers in private practice in the immediate region.

Students at the University of Detroit Mercy Law School paint a picture of law school that has a ways to go before it can truly be said to satisfy. In fact, the Detroit students we heard from were among the most consistently negative of any we surveyed in compiling this book. When asked to name the greatest strengths of their school, however, most were able to manage a word or two of praise. The most positive reviews we heard concerned Detroit's clinical program, which one 3L called "the best part of my experience in law school." As another put it, "this school and law schools in general should place more of an emphasis on their clinics—they are an invaluable addition to anyone's legal education." Several of the students we heard from also had kind words for their classmates and themselves. "Students here all work

Dana Mortensen, Admissions Counselor
651 East Jefferson Avenue, Detroit, MI 48226
Tel: (313) 596-0200
eMail: udmlawao@udmercy.edu

together fairly well," wrote one. "I've never felt the presence of any really cutthroat types in my two years here," agreed another.

More typical of the remarks we heard from students at Detroit, however, was this one from a 1L: "If they did something about the facilities and were more responsive to student needs in general this would be a much more pleasant place to be." Similar sentiments were echoed many times over. "The administration fails entirely to listen to or be interested in what students want from the faculty and from the placement office," said one 2L. Whether the law school's administration actually has "failed entirely" to respond to student suggestions is, of course, impossible to say. But Detroit students certainly have some suggestions—from "improving our so-called 'placement' office" to "improving the quality of instruction." (You will note on the "Student Opinion" graph at right the uniformity of opinion among Detroit students concerning this last matter. Students here rated their faculty's teaching abilities lower than did students at most other law schools profiled in this book.) To be sure, many of the students we heard from expressed a fairly high degree of fundamental satisfaction with the law school, but the discontent conveyed in the remarks above appears to afflict a large proportion of the Detroit student body.

ADMISSIONS

Hopeful applicants to the University of Detroit Mercy School of Law will be glad to hear that this private law school ranks among the 25 least selective in the nation, thanks in large part to the relatively small applicant pool from which it selects. It should be noted that applicant volume here has risen appreciably in recent years, but the admissions process remains comparatively kind. Forty-seven percent of all candidates for admission are successful, and the numerical credentials of the average admitted applicant are modest: an undergraduate GPA of 3.15 and an LSAT score at the 50th percentile.

ACADEMICS

Student/faculty ratio	25:1
% female faculty	51
% minority faculty	8
Hours of study per day	3.49

FINANCIAL FACTS

Tuition	$14,400
Part-time tuition per credit	$10,350
Estimated books/expenses/fees	NR
On-campus living expenses	NR
Off-campus living expenses	NR
% first-year students receiving aid	NR
% all students receiving aid	99
% aid that is merit-based	5
% all students receiving grants/scholarships	61
% all students receiving loans	68
% all students receiving assistantships	NR
Average award package	$2,300
Average graduation debt	$50,000

ADMISSIONS

# applications received	1,021
% applicants accepted	47
% acceptees attending	43
Average LSAT	150
Average undergrad GPA	3.15
Application Fee	$50
No early decision program	
Regular application deadline	April 15
Regular notification	rolling
Admission deferment	one year
Gourman Report Rating	3.46

DICKINSON SCHOOL OF LAW 💾

The Dickinson School of Law, founded in 1834 and the smallest of seven law schools in its home state, bills itself as "one of the best buys in legal education." This is a rather audacious claim for a small private law school in central Pennsylvania, but one that is not entirely without merit. To be sure, as a private institution, Dickinson charges fees that are significantly higher than those of almost any public school, but its "best buy" claim has more to do with what you get than it does with what you pay. Dickinson's reasonable tuition buys the law student access to a fine, long-established law school that offers a broad academic and practical curriculum in a peaceful small-town setting. By any measure, this program has been quite successful in preparing its graduates for law practice. The large proportion of Dickinson grads who begin their careers in prestigious judicial clerkships is a sure sign of the esteem or, at the very least, the connections the law school enjoys. The school itself attributes much of this success to the fact that a large proportion of Dickinson's students gain direct practical experience during their second and third years by holding legal positions in nearby Harrisburg, the Pennsylvania state capital. Admissions at the law school are fairly selective, and the student body is very small,

Dickinson admits a small, well-qualified group and it pays them close attention once they enroll. It is not unusual for a small school like Dickinson to tout its ability to offer "personal attention" and an "intimate learning environment" as highly as it touts its academic strength. Often, however, the reviews of students at such schools reveal such promises to be overblown or even empty. If ever there was a school where such claims of small-school charms were firmly rooted in reality, it appears that Dickinson is that school. The remarks of Dickinson students make this clear. Consider the following typical examples, all from 1Ls: "There's no way to fail at this school if you desire to finish, because the faculty will help you whenever you ask, even on a weekend"; "Everyone is out to scratch everyone's backs...You can always count on someone to lend a helping hand"; "I chose Dickinson because I wanted to learn the law in the most friendly and least competitive atmosphere possible...I think I chose the right place!" This is only a small sample of the enthusiastic

Barbara W. Guillaume, Director, Admissions Services
150 South College Street, Carlisle, PA 17013
Tel: (800) 840-1122
eMail: admissions@dsl.edu
Internet: http://www.dsl.edu

Dickinson School of Law

comments we heard concerning the pleasantness of the academic environment at Dickinson. When students looked beyond such lifestyle issues in praising the school, their remarks often focused on Dickinson's trial advocacy program—one participant called it "simply awesome"—and on its solid regional reputation. "Dickinson grads are well prepared to excel in the legal profession," argued one. "The school's reputation in Pennsylvania is outstanding, as I have found out in several job interviews in the area."

It must be noted, of course, that not all Dickinson students find Dickinson's atmosphere quite so pleasing. "If one is looking for a small school, this is certainly it," began the mixed review of one 2L. "One can either choose to fit in with the mainstream—go out every Thursday night and drink—or be somewhat of an outcast." Indeed, several older students (more than five years out of college) we heard from called this "gossipy junior high-like" environment a bit stifling. "I wish they'd bring in a few more students with work experiences after college," wrote one. "Students here need to be more mature and accepting of one another's opinions." This less-than-tolerant comment from a 3L might give you reason to believe that remark: "It is evident that most faculty and students do not understand the real world, by view of their ridiculous liberal thoughts. If we had any conservative professors here they would quite aptly point out to students how incredibly stupid the ultra-liberal point of view really is."

ADMISSIONS

Overall, the admission process at the Dickinson School of Law is only slightly more competitive than average. Of course, these days, average is still quite competitive, so hopeful applicants to Dickinson had better get their act together. The numerical credentials of the incoming students at Dickinson are quite solid; their average GPA of 3.30 and average LSAT score at the 66th percentile rank them among the top 40 percent of all law students nationally. Applications volume at Dickinson was, however, down sharply in 1992 and again in 1993. As a result, more than three out of ten candidates for admission were successful—a relatively high proportion for a law school of this caliber.

ACADEMICS

Student/faculty ratio	17:1
% female faculty	29
% minority faculty	13
Hours of study per day	3.98

FINANCIAL FACTS

Tuition	$14,500
Part-time tuition per credit	NR
Estimated books/expenses/fees	$800
On-campus living expenses	NR
Off-campus living expenses	NR
% first-year students receiving aid	83
% all students receiving aid	84
% aid that is merit-based	33
% all students receiving grants/scholarships	26
% all students receiving loans	79
% all students receiving assistantships	6
Average award package	$3,100
Average graduation debt	$42,069

ADMISSIONS

# applications received	1,455
% applicants accepted	46
% acceptees attending	25
Average LSAT	155
Average undergrad GPA	3.30
Application Fee	$50
No early decision program	
Regular application deadline	March 15
Regular notification	rolling
Admission deferment	NR
Gourman Report Rating	3.27

DRAKE UNIVERSITY 💾
Law School

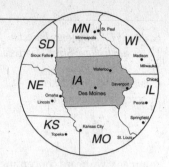

The Drake University Law School may be smaller and far less well known nationally than Iowa's powerhouse public law school in Iowa City, but the tradition of solid legal education at this midsize, private law school dates back almost as far. Drake, which became affiliated with its parent institution in 1887 and was accredited by the ABA in 1923 in the first round of that organization's law school approvals, is one of the oldest continuously operating law schools west of the Mississippi. Though its academic name is little recognized outside the Midwest, this professionally oriented law school's regional standing as a source of well-trained lawyers is quite solid.

For many years, Drake has recognized the importance of supplementing the traditional classroom education of its students with training in practical lawyering skills. Its clinical offerings are impressively broad for a law school of its size, thanks in large part to its location in Iowa's center of business and government, Des Moines. The legal community in this city of nearly 400,000 is large and diverse. Between it and the institutions of the state government, there are numerous opportunities for clerkships and externships. About 80 percent of students enroll for one or more clinical experiences. However, the law school does not depend entirely on the outside community to offer its students opportunities for professional training. On campus, Drake operates a well funded general legal aid clinic and two specialized programs: the Senior Citizens Legal Services Program, dedicated to the growing field of "elder law," and the Criminal Defense Program.

The appeal of these and other skills-oriented programs to students at Drake is great. Certain narrow but valid complaints notwithstanding, these students have a very high degree of overall satisfaction with their chosen school. Most important, the vast majority of those we heard from had nothing but praise for the most fundamental aspect of their law-school experience—its ability to prepare them for the practice of law. "Drake is a great 'nuts and bolts' law school," said one 2L. "I will be ready to walk out of here and step into a courtroom." His sentiments are shared by many, most of whom credit the practical focus of the school's

Susan Unkrich Guilford, Director of Admissions and Financial Aid
2507 University Avenue, Des Moines, IA 50311
Tel: (800) 44-DRAKE, ext. 2782 or (515) 271-2782
Internet: http://www.drake.edu

Drake University

traditional classroom instruction and the wealth of co-curricular opportunities available to them. As one student put it: "Drake offers numerous opportunities to apply what we learn—the clinical, internship, and clerkship offerings are great."

It should be noted, however, that while the law school's practical focus drew uniformly positive reviews, some felt it goes a bit too far. Though one student assured us that "attention is paid to forming critical thinking skills as well as good practical skills," several others expressed their desire that the traditional curriculum pay greater attention to theory. Less subjective, however, and more prevalent were the complaints from a great number of students concerning the lack of diversity in the Drake faculty, and the perception that "the administration doesn't seem to think this is an area of weakness." Other criticisms from Drake students focused on what they perceive as the law school's over-reliance on the Socratic Method of classroom instruction. Many pointed to this and to a fairly harsh grading system in explaining the relatively high degree of competition among students. These same students, however, called the sense of community strong.

As a final note, most seemed to agree that the atmosphere at Drake is rather conservative. Of course, feelings about this varied greatly. "Drake is no hotbed of political activity," explained one. "If you're a conservative Midwesterner, you'll love it." This is not to say that the atmosphere is intolerant or that the student body has uniform political beliefs, simply that the students are, as the Dean put it, "generally not given to being social activists." As another student who was slightly more enthusiastic about the situation said: "I like being in a 'normal' part of the country."

ADMISSIONS

In terms of admissions selectivity, the Drake University Law School ranks on the low end of the midrange of all fully accredited U.S. law schools. In part because of the presence of a hugely respected public law school in the state, only a moderate number of prospective law students file applications to this midsize private school. Drake admits about half of the roughly 1,200 candidates it considers annually, and those who are admitted and go on to enroll possess solid but hardly stunning numerical credentials. Applicants whose GPAs exceed Drake's average and whose LSAT scores are higher than about the 70th percentile are virtually guaranteed admission.

ACADEMICS

Student/faculty ratio	22:1
% female faculty	23
% minority faculty	9
Hours of study per day	4.20

FINANCIAL FACTS

Tuition	$15,550
Part-time tuition per credit	NR
Estimated books/expenses/fees	NR
On-campus living expenses	NR
Off-campus living expenses	NR
% first-year students receiving aid	NR
% all students receiving aid	NR
% aid that is merit-based	NR
% all students receiving grants/scholarships	47
% all students receiving loans	90
% all students receiving assistantships	NR
Average award package	NR
Average graduation debt	$47,500

ADMISSIONS

# applications received	1,202
% applicants accepted	48
% acceptees attending	25
Average LSAT	153
Average undergrad GPA	3.22
Application Fee	$35
No early decision program	
Regular application deadline	March 1
Regular notification	rolling
Admission deferment	one year

Gourman Report Rating	3.35

DUKE UNIVERSITY 💾
School of Law

OVERVIEW

Type of school	private
Environment	city
Scholastic calendar	semester
Schedule	Full time only

STUDENTS

Enrollment of institution	6,380
Enrollment of law school	593
% male/female	60/40
% out-of-state	88
% part-time	NR
% minorities	22
% international (# countries represented)	3 (12)
Average age at entry	23

APPLICANTS ALSO LOOK AT

Harvard University
Georgetown University
New York University
Columbia University
University of Virginia

SURVEY SAYS...

HITS
Inter-disciplinary options
Prestige
Serving humankind

MISSES
Clinical experience
Practical lawyering skills

EMPLOYMENT PROFILE

% grads employed immediately	90
% grads employed within six months	97
Average starting salary	$58,208
% grads employed by field:	
Private practice	69
Business/industry	3
Government	2
Judicial clerkships	21
Public service	1
Academic	2
Military	1

The Duke University School of Law is, quite simply, one of the finest and most selective schools in the country. Over 3,000 applicants vie annually for one of the coveted 200 or so slots in the first-year law class. In nearly all major respects—academic standards, campus life, location, and facilities—the Duke law school stands head and shoulders above most others in the U.S. It's no wonder that more than one student told us, "I love this place!" Although all responses weren't all quite that strong, the vast majority of law students we spoke with are very happy with their surroundings.

The law school's curriculum is broad within traditional boundaries, but relatively lacking in clinical programs, although a few students noted that the law school is focusing on improving this area. Duke's pro bono program, started in 1991, has since expanded and offers students the chance to test their skills in the real world. The law school also opened The Center on Law, Ethics, and National Security in September of 1993. The center sponsors courses, research, and conferences focusing on national security law topics. Many students, however, still see room for improvement. When asked to discuss the law school's weaknesses, many called for "more clinical offerings."

Like many law schools, Duke offers several concurrent-enrollment programs with various graduate departments of the broader university, but its level of commitment to inter-disciplinary study goes well beyond the norm. For one thing, the law school allows nearly all joint-degree candidates to begin their law study in the summer preceding their first year, allowing them to complete a J.D. and a master's in only three years. In part because of this arrangement, and in part because of the incredible strength of many of Duke's other graduate programs, more than 25 percent of Duke law students pursue joint-degrees. In addition to the dual-degree opportunities at the university, areas in which the law school is strong and has a great deal of depth in its curriculum include international and comparative law, corporate and commercial law, criminal law, constitutional law, and civil litigation.

Cynthia Rold, Assistant Dean for Admissions
Box 90393, Durham, NC 27708-0393
Tel: (919) 613-7200   Fax: (919) 613-7231
eMail: admissions@law.duke.edu
Internet: http://www.law.duke.edu

Duke University

From what current law students tell us, Duke is nowhere near as competitive as might be expected at a school with such high-caliber standards. In fact, students point to the unity and camaraderie that exists in the student body. "The atmosphere at Duke is not only non-competitive, but the students really try to help each other," said a 1L. The law school's "great professors" and "laid-back" atmosphere were frequently noted as boons of a Duke law school education. "The faculty and administration want us to succeed and to have fun and to work hard, and they help us (constantly) to do all of those," said one enthusiastic 2L. Another student agreed: "The students here root for each other on exams, support each other in class, and genuinely hope their classmates do well even when they themselves perform poorly." Part of the cohesiveness of this group of students may be due to Duke's small class size. "I know everyone in my class, and we have a blast" said one 2L, and added, "The work is hard, but we are all in it together. There is a sense of camaraderie here that I think must be extremely rare in law schools."

Duke University students have another thing going for them: a fantastic location. Along with nearby Chapel Hill and Raleigh, Durham is a point on the well-known Research Triangle, North Carolina's fastest-growing region. And if a booming economy isn't enough, the area boasts great weather and an exciting night life for young professionals and students. All in all, we heard almost nothing but positive remarks about Duke law school.

ADMISSIONS

If you have set your sights on this "top-ten" law school, your had better have some very impressive numbers. The numerical standards at Duke University School of Law are the seventh highest in the nation behind the likes of Yale, Harvard, and Stanford, and Columbia. If, however, your GPA approaches a 3.6 and your LSAT score is at or near the 98th percentile, you stand a slightly better chance of getting in here than at any of the aforementioned schools. This is due to Duke's relatively high overall rate of acceptance. But that may be no solace to the nearly 2,000 students who are rejected annually by Duke's highly selective admissions committee.

ACADEMICS

Student/faculty ratio	16:1
% female faculty	29
% minority faculty	12
Hours of study per day	3.44

FINANCIAL FACTS

Tuition	$22,300
Part-time tuition per credit	NR
Estimated books/expenses/fees	$1,590
On-campus living expenses	$6,300
Off-campus living expenses	$6,300
% first-year students receiving aid	NR
% all students receiving aid	NR
% aid that is merit-based	NR
% all students receiving grants/scholarships	71
% all students receiving loans	71
% all students receiving assistantships	NR
Average award package	NR
Average graduation debt	NR

ADMISSIONS

# applications received	3,014
% applicants accepted	29
% acceptees attending	22
Average LSAT	166
Average undergrad GPA	3.62
Application Fee	$65
Priority application deadline	November 1
Priority notification	December 15
Regular application deadline	April 30
Regular notification	rolling
Admission may be deferred?	No
Gourman Report Rating	**4.85**

DUQUESNE UNIVERSITY 💾
School of Law

Nearly one third of all the practicing lawyers in western Pennsylvania graduated from Duquesne (pronounced doo-KANE) University School of Law. If you want to attend a law school that has a strong sense of community, a provincial atmosphere and active alumni, then Duquesne may be for you. A 1L who likes the small, intimate nature of the law school explained: "If you want to go where everyone knows your name, this is the place." Duquesne University, a private, Catholic institution, established the School of Law in 1911. It has remained relatively small, with approximately 650 students, and relatively inexpensive, with its tuition ranking as one of the lowest for private U.S. law schools.

Duquesne School of Law is situated in downtown Pittsburgh, only blocks away from the city's courthouses. The schools attracts students and working professionals who are from the area and want to remain there. With nearly half of its students enrolled in the evening division, the law school has a stronghold on the fairly sizable market for legal education for older working professionals in western Pennsylvania. The average age of Duquesne day students is 24, while that of night students is 32. The close proximity to the Pittsburgh legal community, many of whose members are Duquesne alumni, allows students to network and make important contacts during their three years at the school. Several students noted that nearby alumni are a great resource when it's time to get an internship or job. Of course, the student who does not want to remain in the keystone state may be in a bit of a bind. "[The school needs] to keep in mind that not everyone who attends Duquesne wants to practice in Pittsburgh or even Pennsylvania," said one 3L. Perhaps this is the reason many students said the law school's career services office needs improvement. However, according to the administration, the school has a hard time persuading students to leave the area, though it schedules out-of-town interview trips.

The students at Duquesne are a tightly-knit group who reflect the university's traditional and conservative leanings. "There is a strong sense of community among students due, in large part, to the small size of the school," said one 3L. Another 1L agreed: "It's comfortable here, and you aren't just a number. People are very

Ronald J. Ricci, Dean of Admissions
900 Locust Street, Pittsburgh, PA 15282
Tel: (412) 396-6296
eMail: ricci@duq.z.cc.duq.edu

friendly and helpful..." However, with just under 10 percent of its student body comprised of minorities, Duquesne School of Law ranks as one of the least ethnically diverse schools in the Mid-Atlantic.

Since the new administration came into being at Duquesne in 1993, six skills courses have been added to the curriculum, and the school has dramatically expanded its externship program, with opportunities throughout western Pennsylvania and as far as Hawaii, Zimbabwe, and Ireland. Although the vast majority of students are content with their education at Duquesne, we did hear from several students who feel that course offerings need to be improved, particularly the writing program. One 1L said, "The writing program does is no way teach me how to write like a lawyer," and, "We are given assignments and told to do them with no directions how to do them." The administration has heard and agreed with student assessments and responded by creating four and a half new faculty positions for teaching legal writing and research in 1996. Responsiveness such as this might be one reason Duquesne students seem particularly pleased with the faculty and administration. "The faculty are very helpful," said one 3L, and "[the] faculty and dean are concerned about students' welfare." However, a small but vocal group of students spoke of a few less than stellar professors who seem to get by the administration. "We have a very few exceptionally poor professors," said one student, and added, "The administration seems deaf to the caterwauls of the students about these awful profs." But overall, students are content with their education and surroundings at Duquesne University School of Law.

ADMISSIONS

Admissions at Duquesne are fairly competitive with an acceptance rate of about one fourth. Only slightly less selective in its admissions process than the nearby public law school at the University of Pittsburgh, the Duquesne University School of Law maintains relatively high numerical standards. The strong grade point average of the typical admitted student combined with a respectable LSAT score places Duquesne's student body in the top 40 percent nationally in terms of numerical qualifications. These standards are particularly high in comparison with many other law schools that maintain large part-time divisions.

ACADEMICS

Student/faculty ratio	23:1
% female faculty	21
% minority faculty	20
Hours of study per day	3.62

FINANCIAL FACTS

Tuition	$12,215
Part-time tuition per credit	NR
Estimated books/expenses/fees	NR
On-campus living expenses	NR
Off-campus living expenses	NR
% first-year students receiving aid	40
% all students receiving aid	35
% aid that is merit-based	50
% all students receiving grants/scholarships	NR
% all students receiving loans	75
% all students receiving assistantships	NR
Average award package	NR
Average graduation debt	NR

ADMISSIONS

# applications received	NR
% applicants accepted	NR
% acceptees attending	NR
Average LSAT	156
Average undergrad GPA	3.25
Application Fee	$50
No early decision program	
Regular application deadline	April 1, May 1
Regular notification	rolling
Admission deferment	one year
Gourman Report Rating	**3.32**

EMORY UNIVERSITY
School of Law

To hear the admissions brochures of nearly every American law school tell it, there is not a city in this country that is neither "vibrant" nor "livable." Personal experience tells us that these terms are at times used so freely as to lose any sense of their original meanings. Some places, however, seem to embody the accepted definitions of these words. Atlanta, Georgia, is one. The city exudes confidence in its own future, as does the midsize private law school that calls Atlanta home. A fast-rising star in the firmament of U.S. law schools, the Emory University School of Law is no longer a very well-kept secret.

Emory has long enjoyed an unchallenged reputation as one of the finest law schools in the Southeast, but in recent years it has garnered praise from all quarters for its strong traditional curriculum and its model skills programs. Besides its broad and numerous academic course offerings and its various clinical programs, Emory runs an intensive two-week "trial training" workshop that is required of all students at the end of their second year. The success of this program has helped to boost Emory's reputation as a training ground for well-prepared young attorneys. Emory now attracts the vast majority of its very qualified students from outside the Southeast. A good many of these transplants choose to stay in Atlanta, a large and lucrative legal job market, after completing their degrees. Applications volume is very heavy, having nearly doubled over the last decade. Accordingly, the admissions process is extremely competitive, and numerical standards are high.

Just as high, it seems, are the standards to which Emory students hold their school. Although their fundamental satisfaction with their program and confidence in their futures is high, they criticize certain aspects of their experience at the law school. On the positive side, few students we heard from had anything but praise for Emory's outstanding faculty, opinions of which ran the gamut from "excellent" to "superb." Students also lauded the accessibility and diversity of the faculty. Most also offered unsolicited endorsements of the law school's innovative trial techniques program. "The litigation courses are very strong," went

Lynell A. Cadray, Assistant Dean for Admissions
Gambrell Hall, Atlanta, GA 30322-2770
Tel: (404) 727-6801
Internet: http://www.law.emory.edu

Emory University

one typical remark, "and the clinical programs in general offer fabulous experience in a broad range of legal fields."

But Emory students seem more eager to point out their law school's shortcomings than to belabor its obvious strengths. Most of their criticisms relate to the fairly high degree of competitiveness among students. This was a typical comment: "The quality of the student body is exceptionally high, and the faculty is solid, but the administration needs to work to alleviate the competitiveness and recognize the high quality of all its students and not just the upper tier." Most blame a strict and unforgiving grading curve for this competitiveness, and if the remarks we heard are any indication of the general mind-set of Emory students, grades are indeed the focus of much concern, particularly in regard to their effect on employment prospects. For example: "Great job opportunities if you are in the top 20 to 25 percent of class. More difficult if your grades are not up to par;" "Career services seems to cater only to the top 20 percent;" "Emory is not ranked among the top ten law schools, but job prospects for students who succeed academically are equivalent." It is understandable that some students would perceive some relative difficulty in landing good jobs when their most successful classmates get some of the best jobs in the nation, but top 10 percent of the class or no, Emory grads are among the most employable in the region.

ADMISSIONS

Thanks in part to its anointment by a major U.S. magazine as one of the country's "up-and-coming" law schools, the Emory University School of Law has become extremely popular with highly qualified applicants around the nation. In terms of the numerical standards to which it holds applicants, Emory is one of the forty most selective law schools in the nation. Statistically, an applicant with an undergraduate GPA between 3.00 and 3.25 and an LSAT score between about 155 and 159 stands only a 8 percent chance of getting in.

ACADEMICS

Student/faculty ratio	19:1
% female faculty	20
% minority faculty	5
Hours of study per day	4.00

FINANCIAL FACTS

Tuition	$20,600
Part-time tuition per credit	NR
Estimated books/expenses/fees	$1,080
On-campus living expenses	NR
Off-campus living expenses	NR
% first-year students receiving aid	70
% all students receiving aid	70
% aid that is merit-based	30
% all students receiving grants/scholarships	30
% all students receiving loans	76
% all students receiving assistantships	3
Average award package	NR
Average graduation debt	$58,917

ADMISSIONS

# applications received	3,251
% applicants accepted	31
% acceptees attending	24
Average LSAT	160
Average undergrad GPA	3.42
Application Fee	$50
No early decision program	
Regular application deadline	March 1
Regular notification	rolling
Admission deferment	one year
Gourman Report Rating	**3.90**

FLORIDA STATE UNIVERSITY
College of Law

OVERVIEW

Type of school	public
Environment	city
Scholastic calendar	semester
Schedule	Full time only

STUDENTS

Enrollment of institution	29,630
Enrollment of law school	627
% male/female	55/45
% out-of-state	21
% part-time	NR
% minorities	23
% international (# countries represented)	NR (2)
Average age at entry	25

APPLICANTS ALSO LOOK AT

University of Florida
Stetson University
University of Miami
University of Georgia
Mercer University

SURVEY SAYS...

HITS
Co-curricular offerings
Legal writing
Library staff

MISSES
Socratic method
Quality of teaching
Intellectual challenge

EMPLOYMENT PROFILE

% grads employed immediately	49
% grads employed within six months	81
Average starting salary	$42,067
% grads employed by field:	
Private practice	70
Business/industry	1
Government	17
Judicial clerkships	4
Public service	2
Academic	2
Military	1

Few states have experienced a higher rate of population growth in the last decade than Florida. In struggling to keep up with the demand for legal services placed on it by an ever-increasing populace, the Sunshine State's legal community has thrived, as have the state's six law schools, especially Florida State University College of Law. In its relatively short history, Florida State has matured from a tiny start-up operation into a midsize public law school that is widely regarded as one of the finest in the Southeast. The law school's curriculum is solid in all the traditional areas and is supplemented by a wide variety of clinical externship programs available through the legal and governmental institutions of Tallahassee, the state capital. The strength of Florida State's academic program stems in large part from its faculty, which is large and very well-qualified.

The same can certainly be said of the law school's applicant pool, which is immense and growing. Thanks in part to its incredibly low tuition, Florida State now processes almost three times as many applications annually as it did just eight years ago. The numerical credentials of entering students are solid and comparable with those of students at Florida's other top schools. In terms of both gender balance and ethnic diversity in the student body, however, Florida State certainly puts some other schools to shame. FSU is well ahead of almost every other school in the region.

Students at Florida State paint a picture of a fairly pleasant learning environment, and though they have their gripes, their overall level of satisfaction with their chosen school is high. Consider the typical comment of one 3L asked to assess her school's weaknesses: "There are too many opportunities here and not enough time to take advantage of them. Students need to be warned in their first year to plan ahead." Things could certainly be worse. Nearly every student we heard from, in fact, praised FSU's extensive co-curricular offerings, many of which exploit resources of the capital city. They also give mostly positive reviews to their faculty and to the school's overall atmosphere. "The young professors here are outstanding and are really interested in students as individuals," said one student. "The faculty

Marie Capshew, Director of Admissions
425 West Jefferson Street, Tallahassee, FL 32306-1034
Tel: (904) 644-3787   Fax: (904) 644-7284
eMail: admissions@law.fsu.edu
Internet: http://www.law.fsu.edu

Florida State University

are generally good, well-educated and understanding," agreed another, "and I particularly appreciated the strong emphasis on the writing program."

Needless to say, however, students here can see room for improvement. Although most students had kind words for their faculty generally, quite a few criticized its uneven quality. "Certain instructors are excellent and care both about teaching and their students," wrote one student, expressing a sentiment shared by many. "Some, however, need to retire or move on." And it wouldn't be a public school if there weren't numerous complaints about bureaucracy. Several reported that their school's share of bureaucratic nonsense is made even greater by the law school's physical separation from the administrative offices of the university's main campus.

Florida State students also gave voice to the requisite amount of concern for the difficult legal job market, and some bemoaned what they regard as the inadequacy of the law school's career services and alumni network. Still, most students expressing such concerns could see past this shortcoming. "I don't believe a large alumni base is all that makes a law school great," wrote one. "I'm completely satisfied with Florida State."

ADMISSIONS

Like so many other respected public law schools, Florida State experienced a dramatic increase in applications volume during the late 1980s. Between 1987 and 1993, the number of applicants to the law school more than doubled, and though FSU expanded its total enrollment during the same period, overall selectivity has climbed. Only one in four of the roughly 2,000 candidates considered annually will gain admission to the law school, and almost half of those admitted will actually choose to attend. Numerical standards are impressive: The average GPA of entering students is a solid 3.30, and the average LSAT score is 157, a score at the 80th percentile.

ACADEMICS	
Student/faculty ratio	17:1
% female faculty	25
% minority faculty	10
Hours of study per day	3.76

FINANCIAL FACTS	
In-state tuition	$3,732
Out-of-state tuition	$11,638
Part-time tuition per credit	NR
Estimated books/expenses/fees	NR
On-campus living expenses	NR
Off-campus living expenses	NR
% first-year students receiving aid	97
% all students receiving aid	98
% aid that is merit-based	10
% all students receiving grants/scholarships	21
% all students receiving loans	74
% all students receiving assistantships	NR
Average award package	NR
Average graduation debt	$55,500

ADMISSIONS	
# applications received	2,317
% applicants accepted	26
% acceptees attending	36
Average LSAT	157
Average undergrad GPA	3.30
Application Fee	$20
No early decision program	
Regular application deadline	February 15
Regular notification	rolling
Admission may be deferred?	No
Gourman Report Rating	**3.42**

UNIVERSITY OF FLORIDA

College of Law

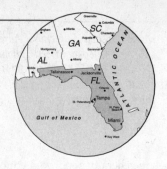

OVERVIEW

Type of school	public
Environment	city
Scholastic calendar	semester
Schedule	Full time only

STUDENTS

Enrollment of institution	34,000
Enrollment of law school	1,200
% male/female	58/42
% out-of-state	10
% part-time	NR
% minorities	22
% international (# countries represented)	2 (NR)
Average age at entry	25

APPLICANTS ALSO LOOK AT

Emory University
Florida State University
Georgetown University
Vanderbilt University
George Washington University

SURVEY SAYS...

HITS
Research resources
Prestige

MISSES
Faculty-student relations
Students feel poorly prepared
Clinical experience

EMPLOYMENT PROFILE

% grads employed immediately	50
% grads employed within six months	72
Average starting salary	$41,000
% grads employed by field:	
Private practice	53
Business/industry	5
Government	15
Judicial clerkships	7
Public service	0
Academic	2
Military	0

One of the Southeast's finest law schools, the University of Florida College of Law is the oldest in the state and, arguably, the best. Located on the Gainesville campus of one of the biggest universities in the country, this large, inexpensive public law school has served its home state since the beginning of the century. Importing an enormous number of law-school graduates, Florida may be as favorable a job market as exists these days, and its most respected source of home-grown lawyers is UF.

Florida's curriculum is traditional and modestly broad, and it includes a limited assortment of clinical programs and skills courses. The law school distinguishes itself less through any curricular innovations than through its overall academic solidity. The faculty is large and strong, the law library huge and well-staffed, the students serious and well-qualified. Add to that already impressive list of ingredients the super-low tuition, and you can see why applications volume at Florida has gone through the roof. The overwhelming majority of those who take advantage of the strong program at this bargain law school are native Floridians. A similar proportion of Florida grads remains in the state after completing their degrees. The law school enrolls around 400 new students each year, half in September and half in January. Numerical admissions standards are very high.

Equally high, it seems, are the standards to which Florida law students hold their chosen school. No student we heard from was totally negative in assessing his experience at the law school, but nearly all see real room for improvement. On the positive side, UF students voiced nearly unanimous praise for certain fundamentals, chief among them the law school's strong regional reputation, fine facilities (especially the library), and very low tuition. But Florida students also had kind words for their instructors and, not least, for themselves. Asked to name their law school's greatest strengths, most cited the "quality of students and faculty." As one 2L explained: "The one phrase that sums this place up is that no one phrase could sum this place up—very diverse individuals with diverse goals and attitudes, laid-back on the outside but on the whole very driven and ambitious."

J. Michael Patrick, Assistant Dean for Admissions
Box 117620, Gainesville, FL 32611
Tel: (352) 392-2087   Fax: (352) 392-8727

The assessment of this 3L, however, does seem to sum up the opinion of the majority of students we heard from: "Our tuition is very low, and because admissions are so competitive, the students here are possibly better than the school." Specifically, some UF students are dissatisfied with the limitations of their curriculum, which they consider far too narrow. "Due to a lack of funds," reported one 3L, "students suffer from over-crowded classes and poor choice of courses." "They really should provide for specialization in fields other than tax," said another. (Florida is generally considered one of the nation's leaders in tax law.) "I understand that resources are limited, but what is really bad is that the faculty and the deans and career placement encourage students only to go into corporate, commercial or tax law. They need to provide more opportunities for public interest, judicial clerkships and clinical programs."

These constructive criticisms, however, should not be taken as a sign of serious discontent among Florida students. Critical though they may be, few had difficulty reciting the law school's many strengths, and many went out of their way to say that they couldn't think of another school in the region that they would rather have attended.

ADMISSIONS

The University of Florida College of Law is one of the most selective in the Southeast and, indeed, in the nation. In the mysteriously derived national rankings of law schools that you have probably seen, this excellent law school generally resides somewhere in the "second tier." But try telling that to the country's most highly qualified law-school applicants in search of a great bargain. The average GPA and LSAT scores of incoming Florida students rank them among the top twenty-five in this book. This should come as no surprise given the remarkable value of this school's highly regarded J.D. program. Hopeful applicants to the U of F College of Law face a steep uphill climb.

ACADEMICS

Student/faculty ratio	14:1
% female faculty	34
% minority faculty	9
Hours of study per day	3.57

FINANCIAL FACTS

In-state tuition	$3,396
Out-of-state tuition	$10,776
Part-time tuition per credit	NR
Estimated books/expenses/fees	NR
On-campus living expenses	NR
Off-campus living expenses	NR
% first-year students receiving aid	100
% all students receiving aid	100
% aid that is merit-based	65
% all students receiving grants/scholarships	5
% all students receiving loans	63
% all students receiving assistantships	NR
Average award package	$7,235
Average graduation debt	$32,500

ADMISSIONS

# applications received	2,260
% applicants accepted	35
% acceptees attending	45
Average LSAT	158
Average undergrad GPA	3.50
Application Fee	$20
No early decision program	
Regular application deadline	February 1
Regular notification	rolling
Admission may be deferred?	No
Gourman Report Rating	3.78

FORDHAM UNIVERSITY 💾
School of Law

OVERVIEW

Type of school	private
Environment	metropolis
Scholastic calendar	semester
Schedule	Full-time or part-time

STUDENTS

Enrollment of institution	4,293
Enrollment of law school	1,479
% male/female	59/41
% out-of-state	33
% part-time	24
% minorities	26
% international (# countries represented)	NR (5)
Average age at entry	25

APPLICANTS ALSO LOOK AT

Emory University
Boston College
Brooklyn Law School
Boston University
George Washington University

SURVEY SAYS...

HITS
Broad range of courses
Prestige
Sleeping

MISSES
Library staff
Studying
Legal writing

EMPLOYMENT PROFILE

% grads employed immediately	NR
% grads employed within six months	92
Average starting salary	$60,848
% grads employed by field:	
Private practice	62
Business/industry	18
Government	16
Judicial clerkships	5
Public service	1
Military	1

If New York is the cultural capital of the United States, then Lincoln Center is the cultural capital of New York, by which logic the approximately 1,500 students of the adjacent Fordham University School of Law should be about the most sophisticated group of law students in the country. As it stands, the demanding J.D. program at this highly regarded nearly hundred-year-old law school requires that most students get their culture by osmosis, giving up champagne and evenings at the Met and sticking to coffee and long nights in the library. Although it may not approach NYU and Columbia in the slippery terms of prestige, Fordham is probably New York City's most highly regarded law school after these two, and in many quantifiable respects—the size and qualifications of its faculty, the breadth of its curriculum, the success of its graduates—it doesn't give away much to its powerhouse neighbors. An excellent law school by any objective measure, Fordham can surely lay claim to offering the most respected part-time J.D. program in the entire Northeast. Indeed, Fordham is a godsend to several hundred highly qualified working professionals who would otherwise be forced to step down a rung on the ladder of prestige in order to earn a law degree. Whether in the day or evening division, Fordham students follow a rigorous course of study that is strong in all the traditional areas and is supplemented by a wide variety of clinical programs, including the recently instituted disability law, tax and domestic violence clinics, most of which combine simulations with live client contact under faculty supervision. These programs, along with a mandatory moot court exercise and a significant writing requirement, are part of Fordham's growing emphasis on practical-skills training, professional ethics, and public service.

Students at Fordham paint a very consistent picture of their chosen school, both in terms of its strengths and weaknesses. One matter on which nearly all seem to agree is the quality of their preparation for the actual practice of law. "FLS has prepared me very well," wrote one. "I was a summer associate at a large Wall Street law firm, and I felt very well trained to compete with and even surpass students from the top Ivy League schools." Students raved about the quality of the faculty, who reportedly maintain an "open door" policy. Fordham's alumni network also was lauded for the role it plays in helping graduates land jobs in New York City. "One of the absolute best things about Fordham," wrote one 2L, "is its fanatically loyal alumni. They are very helpful and enthusiastic." While most of the comments we heard could hardly be called fanatically enthusiastic, they did, for the most part, convey a strong sense of well-being. "We have a dynamic young faculty and a Dean who lives, breathes, eats and sleeps Fordham," reported another 2L. "God is our Dean, how can we lose?"

All of which is not to say that Fordham students see no room for improvement in their school. Though most called the law school's New York City location a real strength, few expressed much love for their immediate surroundings. "This school has a truly horrible physical plant," went one all-too-typical comment from a Fordham 1L. "The library is hideous and the cafeteria abominable." The administration has heard these complaints and several renovations designed to improve study space in the library and triple the space devoted to clinical programs are scheduled for summer 1996. More generalized complaints were often heard from Fordham's night students. "As an evening student," wrote one, "I am a member of a discrete and insular minority, and have a substantially worse selection of classes." This fairly representative remark did, however, go on to conclude that "on the other hand, my fellow students are grown-ups, so it evens out." In spirit, most of the criticisms we heard matched this last one. Fordham students may wish for more, but also appreciate what they've got.

ADMISSIONS

After Columbia and NYU, whose students' numerical credentials are among the highest in the nation, the Fordham University School of Law is the most selective in the New York metropolitan area. In fact, the admissions process at Fordham is one of the forty most competitive in the entire country. The average incoming student here has a solid undergraduate GPA of 3.36 and an LSAT score above the 90th percentile. Applicants to Fordham whose numbers fall below these face an uphill climb. Consider this: In 1993 only 9 percent of all applicants with GPAs between 3.25 and 3.49 and LSAT scores between 155 and 159 were offered admission.

ACADEMICS

Student/faculty ratio	20:1
% female faculty	22
% minority faculty	8
Hours of study per day	3.39

FINANCIAL FACTS

Tuition	$20,499
Part-time tuition per credit	NR
Estimated books/expenses/fees	$675
On-campus living expenses	NR
Off-campus living expenses	NR
% first-year students receiving aid	47
% all students receiving aid	NR
% aid that is merit-based	5
% all students receiving grants/scholarships	47
% all students receiving loans	71
% all students receiving assistantships	NR
Average award package	NR
Average graduation debt	NR

ADMISSIONS

# applications received	5,237
% applicants accepted	28
% acceptees attending	30
Average LSAT	163
Average undergrad GPA	3.36
Application Fee	$60
No early decision program	
Regular application deadline	March 1
Regular notification	rolling
Admission may be deferred?	no
Gourman Report Rating	**4.47**

FRANKLIN PIERCE LAW CENTER 💾

If they ranked U.S. presidents according to the general public's ability to report a single fact about their administrations, Franklin Pierce would probably be in a twelve-way tie for last place with the likes of Millard Fillmore and Chester Arthur. History has, however, granted the nation's fourteenth president one significant consolation: a distinctive New England law school that bears his name. The Franklin Pierce Law Center, located in central Concord, the capital of New Hampshire, is one of the smallest private law schools in the country. The law school presents itself as an institution very much opposed to some of the negatives of traditional legal education: rigidity, impersonality and unhealthy competitiveness. Indeed, the curriculum is notably flexible. Beyond the first year, few requirements exist, and all students are encouraged to devise independent study projects that combine academic research with practical experience. Students at Franklin Pierce have the option of following one of several organized but informal programs of concentration, most notably in intellectual property law. This tiny law school has gained worldwide recognition as a leader in this growing field. The FPLC faculty, most of whom continue to practice in one fashion or another, is large enough to ensure a degree of personal attention to which most bigger law schools can only pay lip service. To be sure, there is a potentially negative flip side to each of these positive qualities. An emphasis on independent study, for instance, is all well and good, but also indicates the law school's tacit recognition of its own curricular limits. The mature, self-motivated law student, however, can thrive here. In fact, the average Franklin Pierce student is a good deal older than the national average and often has significant career experience prior to enrollment.

Students at Franklin Pierce appear, on the whole, to be a remarkably happy group. Although all were able to point to some areas in which their chosen school could stand to improve, their overall sense of well-being is impressive. Almost unanimously, they attest to the pleasantness of the atmosphere at the law school. As one 3L put it: "The size lends itself to a much more cooperative environment or communal spirit than you would traditionally expect from a law school." Most students give credit for this

Lisa Deane, Assistant Dean for Admissions
2 White Street, Concord, NH 03301
Tel: (603) 228-9217
eMail: admissions@fplc.edu
Internet: http://www.fplc.edu

Franklin Pierce Law Center

advantage to the school's administration and to a grading policy that precludes class ranking. "They definitely promote cooperation and respect rather than competition," reported one 3L. The positive remarks of students here did, however, go beyond such quality-of-life issues. Nearly all praised the quality and accessibility of FPLC's clinical programs, and enthusiastic endorsements of its Intellectual Property Program here was the norm. "The IP faculty are excellent," reported one participant. "This program allows graduates to leave the school with in-depth knowledge of the topic," said another, "which definitely puts them ahead of graduates from other schools."

On the downside, many of the Franklin Pierce students we heard from, including the 3L who offered that last comment, criticized the law school for dedicating educational and promotional resources to its highly respected Intellectual Property Program at the expense of its general program. "If I weren't interested in IP," wrote one such student, "I never would have come here." Furthermore, many of the same students who praised FPLC's "nontraditional" approach expressed their concern that it had gone, perhaps, a bit too far. "More of a 'black-letter' approach might be better," said one 3L. "They should remember that we do have to take the bar exam after three years," wrote another. On balance, however, most of the students we heard from considered these shortcomings to be minor, and expressed satisfaction with most aspects of their experience at Franklin Pierce.

ADMISSIONS

As noncompetitive and relaxed as the students at the Franklin Pierce Law Center are, the admissions process at this small private law school is even more so. In fact, the average incoming student at Franklin Pierce possesses numerical credentials lower than those of students at many of the law schools in this book. This is not to say, however, that admissions at Franklin Pierce are completely noncompetitive. Nearly two out of every three applicants to the law school are denied admission.

ACADEMICS	
Student/faculty ratio	24:1
% female faculty	27
% minority faculty	5
Hours of study per day	3.86

FINANCIAL FACTS	
Tuition	$14,955
Part-time tuition per credit	NR
Estimated books/expenses/fees	$525
On-campus living expenses	NR
Off-campus living expenses	NR
% first-year students receiving aid	83
% all students receiving aid	79
% aid that is merit-based	19
% all students receiving grants/scholarships	60
% all students receiving loans	80
% all students receiving assistantships	6
Average award package	$1,253
Average graduation debt	$56,568

ADMISSIONS	
# applications received	1,346
% applicants accepted	36
% acceptees attending	28
Average LSAT	155
Average undergrad GPA	2.92
Application Fee	$45
No early decision program	
Regular application deadline	April 1
Regular notification	rolling
Admission deferment	two years
Gourman Report Rating	2.60

GEORGE MASON UNIVERSITY
School of Law

OVERVIEW

Type of school	public
Environment	metropolis
Scholastic calendar	semester
Schedule	Full-time or part-time

STUDENTS

Enrollment of institution	9,508
Enrollment of law school	696
% male/female	63/37
% out-of-state	14
% part-time	45
% minorities	9
% international (# countries represented)	NR (2)
Average age at entry	28

APPLICANTS ALSO LOOK AT

University of Virginia
George Washington University
American University
Catholic University of America
College of William and Mary

SURVEY SAYS...

HITS
Intellectual challenge
Legal writing
Studying

MISSES
Clinical experience
Not enough courses
Facilities not great

EMPLOYMENT PROFILE

% grads employed immediately	NR
% grads employed within six months	84
Average starting salary	$51,324
% grads employed by field:	
Private practice	35
Business/industry	8
Government	30
Judicial clerkships	21
Military	3

Until very recently, the old guard of legal education in the United State clung defiantly to a promise that has now been called into question: that law schools should not engage in the business of specialized training. This was all well and good when the legal profession was still dominated by general practitioners, but those days are gone. Curricula within American law schools increasingly reflect the trend toward specialization within the legal profession, but most schools are only beginning to test the waters into which the George Mason University School of Law has already dived headfirst.

While most law schools have only dabbled with informal programs of specialization that merely suggest a particular combination of courses, George Mason has established five organized programs, or "tracks": Corporate and Securities Law, Financial Services and Real Estate Law, International Business Transactions, Litigation Law, and Patent Law. All were designed to provide George Mason graduates with levels of expertise that might otherwise take years of work experience to achieve. Students in these tracks follow a course of study that is almost entirely prescribed and so bears little resemblance to the traditional legal education offered in most U.S. law schools.

One does not drift through the George Mason School of Law. In addition to its specialization tracks, GMU operates a rigorous, highly regarded standard J.D. program. Even this program is unusual in one important respect: its inclusion of a two-semester, first-year requirement in Quantitative Methods, a course that gives GMU a truly unique flavor. The law school contends that all future lawyers must possess a grounding in the basic principles of economics, accounting, and statistics. GMU is a bastion of the conservative Law and Economics school of legal thought, so rigorous economic analyses are the stock-in-trade of many of the school's excellent faculty members.

Most students come from in-state for the bargain tuition rate, so they are well-aware of and, for the most part, drawn by the Law and Economics focus and staunchly conservative atmosphere. Most are extremely happy with just about everything they came looking for and found at GMU. One student proclaimed his pride

Wendy E. Payton, Assistant to the Director of Admissions
3401 North Fairfax Drive, Arlington, VA 22201-4498
Tel: (703) 993-8000
Internet: http://web.gmu.edu/departments/law/

George Mason University

of place in the strong tones we heard over and over: "I believe this is the strongest pillar in Virginia's triumvirate of great public law schools (UVA and William and Mary). Its innovative, strong writing program, metropolitan location, [and] low price probably make it one of the best law school bargains in the country." He answered those who complain about "comparatively more work and a lower grading scale than at other law schools" with this comment: "It's not supposed to be easy." Another listed very specifically why GMU appeals to him: "The faculty is mostly young and brilliant. The atmosphere is more accurately characterized as 'libertarian' than as 'conservative.' Minorities get no breaks here, and PC behavior gets no lip service. This school is absolutely colorblind. The quality of the education is the best in the D.C. area, and employers are beginning to notice. GMU places an inordinate number of graduates in judicial clerkships." And one 2L explained further: "The mandatory two-year Legal Research and Writing Program is a winner with employers—they are very impressed with GMUSL's emphasis on good writing skills."

A few changes would impress some students, however, like more clinical programs and perhaps a few more women faculty members. It should be noted that although many students agreed that diversity is lacking, this is one of the few schools where many students actually listed this as a positive characteristic. One change that should improve academic and nonacademic life is the planned expansion. As one person told us, "The faculties are the only area in need of real improvement and a new building will start construction in one month!"

ADMISSIONS

Judging by UGPA and LSAT score, GMU students rank in the top 20 percent nationally, with an average undergraduate GPA of 3.06 and an average LSAT score of 160, or the 84th percentile. Obviously the law school selects very highly qualified candidates, but there is more to selectivity than just that. If you consider both relative applications volume and the rate at which admitted students actually choose to attend the law school, George Mason ranks behind only Yale, Stanford, and Harvard in terms of popularity with prospective law students.

ACADEMICS	
Student/faculty ratio	21:1
% female faculty	11
% minority faculty	23
Hours of study per day	4.36

FINANCIAL FACTS	
In-state tuition	$7,084
Out-of-state tuition	$17,920
Part-time tuition per credit	NR
Estimated books/expenses/fees	NR
On-campus living expenses	NR
Off-campus living expenses	NR
% first-year students receiving aid	NR
% all students receiving aid	NR
% aid that is merit-based	7
% all students receiving grants/scholarships	7
% all students receiving loans	41
% all students receiving assistantships	NR
Average award package	NR
Average graduation debt	NR

ADMISSIONS	
# applications received	2,660
% applicants accepted	28
% acceptees attending	28
Average LSAT	160
Average undergrad GPA	3.06
Application Fee	$35
No early decision program	
Regular application deadline	March 1
Regular notification	NR
Admission deferment	one year
Gourman Report Rating	**2.73**

GEORGE WASHINGTON UNIVERSITY
Law School

OVERVIEW

Type of school	private
Environment	metropolis
Scholastic calendar	semester
Schedule	Full-time or part-time

STUDENTS

Enrollment of institution	19,670
Enrollment of law school	1,528
% male/female	56/44
% out-of-state	94
% part-time	14
% minorities	27
% international (# countries represented)	NR (5)
Average age at entry	24

APPLICANTS ALSO LOOK AT

Georgetown University
American University
Boston College
New York University
Boston University

SURVEY SAYS...

HITS
Broad range of courses
Prestige
Left-leaning politics

MISSES
Research resources
Facilities not great
Intellectual challenge

EMPLOYMENT PROFILE

% grads employed immediately	77
% grads employed within six months	91
Average starting salary	$55,077
% grads employed by field:	
Private practice	56
Business/industry	7
Government	13
Judicial clerkships	8
Public service	1
Academic	11
Military	3

Established in 1865, the George Washington University Law School is the oldest of the District of Columbia's six law schools, and only the District's highly esteemed behemoth, Georgetown, keeps it from being called the biggest and the best. But to discuss either George Washington's size or its hefty reputation only in terms of other law schools in the region is to understate matters; GWU is one of the largest and most widely respected law schools in the country. It is also a law school in great demand. In recent years, as many as 7,000 well-qualified applicants have vied to be among the roughly 460 entering students who enroll annually in the law school's day and evening divisions.

Surely, a huge law school in a very urban setting is not for everyone, but George Washington makes the most of both its size and its location in the nation's capital, the largest law-school laboratory in the world. The traditional classroom curriculum here is broad, with particular strength in Intellectual Property Law and International and Comparative Law, areas in which the law school also offers graduate law degrees. Unlike some schools that have great disparity in the breadth of course offerings in their full- and part-time divisions, GWU, by virtue of the size of its part-time and adjunct faculty, serves its over 200 J.D. evening students quite well. The academic strength of the law school is nicely augmented by an excellent clinical program that offers GWU students a rich variety of opportunities for hands-on lawyering experience.

Though students at George Washington have some serious complaints, none of these have to do with the school's location, student body, or teachers. GW students uniformly praise all three. "We have a great faculty, great location and, most importantly, great students," reported one. "They're not your typical competitive law students," she continued, "everyone gets along very well, helps each other out and has fun." Another praised her professors, whom she called "generally accessible and friendly" and the "laid-back attitude of students...People are competitive, but not cutthroat."

Despite this praise, however, something like a siege mentality seems also to be present here. The "Us vs. Them" theme was

720 20th Street, N.W., Washington, DC 20052
Tel: (202) 994-7230
eMail: jd@admit.nlc.gwu.edu
Internet: http://www.law.gwu.edu

George Washington University

remarkably consistent in the comments of GW students, with the student body and the faculty being "Us" and the administration being "Them." This evenhanded criticism of the law school's administration was the most generous of the many similar complaints we heard: "GW is a good law school but has a long way to go...It often fails to remember that it's here to serve students and not to run a business." Like many at private law schools, GW students complain about skyrocketing tuition, but their main concern is not the amount they pay, but, rather, what they get in return. When asked to name his law school's greatest strength, one student cynically identified GW's "ability to raise money through tuition that does not end up benefiting students." A 2L asked rhetorically, "Where the hell does the money go?....Charge us less to go here, or put our money to use in things in which we can see results!!" Since we surveyed, however, the school has reached an agreement with the university to receive a significantly increased portion of tuition revenue, and the library has undergone renovations that included new furnishings. Additionally, the student computer lab has all-new Pentium computers, and laptops are available for students to check out. We expect to see these changes reflected in our next survey.

Though George Washington students are clearly ambivalent about their school of choice, they also praise the education they receive and understand the advantages that their degrees will give them when it comes time to seek employment. One student summed up everything we heard, however, when she said this: "This school needs to care more about its students."

ADMISSIONS

At $55 a pop, the 6,471 applications that were filed by prospective George Washington students in 1995 filled the law school's coffers to the tune of $355,900. Of course, a sizable chunk of that kitty must be used to pay an admissions staff large enough to sort through the second-highest pile of applications in the country. When all is said and done, more than 4,000 people will be denied admission to GW, a great deal more than will even apply to most schools. Those who are admitted and go on to enroll possess tremendous numerical credentials. With an extremely high average GPA and an average LSAT score at the 90th percentile, the GW student body is in the top 20 nationally in terms of numerical qualifications.

ACADEMICS

Student/faculty ratio	18:1
% female faculty	27
% minority faculty	9
Hours of study per day	3.56

FINANCIAL FACTS

Tuition	$19,770
Part-time tuition per credit	$710
Estimated books/expenses/fees	$3,145
On-campus living expenses	NR
Off-campus living expenses	NR
% first-year students receiving aid	70
% all students receiving aid	85
% aid that is merit-based	NR
% all students receiving grants/scholarships	60
% all students receiving loans	85
% all students receiving assistantships	NR
Average award package	$8,000
Average graduation debt	$67,000

ADMISSIONS

# applications received	6,471
% applicants accepted	29
% acceptees attending	26
Average LSAT	161
Average undergrad GPA	3.42
Application Fee	$55
Priority application deadline	NR
Priority notification	NR
Regular application deadline	March 1
Regular notification	rolling
Admission deferment	NR
Gourman Report Rating	**4.39**

GEORGETOWN UNIVERSITY
Law Center

OVERVIEW

Type of school	private
Environment	metropolis
Scholastic calendar	semester
Schedule	Full-time or part-time

STUDENTS

Enrollment of institution	6,013
Enrollment of law school	2,032
% male/female	52/48
% out-of-state	NR
% part-time	25
% minorities	27
% international (# countries represented)	NR (NR)
Average age at entry	24

APPLICANTS ALSO LOOK AT

Harvard University
Columbia University
George Washington University
Yale University
New York University

SURVEY SAYS...

HITS
Broad range of courses
Research resources
Clinical experience

MISSES
Socratic method
Studying
Sense of community

EMPLOYMENT PROFILE

% grads employed immediately	NR
% grads employed within six months	NR
Average starting salary	NR
% grads employed by field:	
Private practice	57
Business/industry	6
Government	9
Judicial clerkships	13
Academic	13
Military	3

Set almost literally in the shadows of the U.S. Capitol and the Supreme Court, in the most lawyer-rich city on earth, the Georgetown University Law Center is the law school of Washington insiders past, present, and future. One cannot study law any closer to the halls of power than at this nearly one-hundred-year-old Jesuit institution, whose own halls are crowded with the largest student body of any American law school. Widely regarded as one of the 10 or 15 finest law schools in the country, and undoubtedly the most highly esteemed law school to offer a part-time J.D. program, Georgetown enrolls over 2,000 highly qualified students in its day and evening divisions.

Within the confines of the classroom, these students follow a course of study that is rich in academic possibilities. Georgetown's top-notch faculty administer a tremendously broad traditional curriculum that is particularly strong in areas like International Law and Public Interest Law. Georgetown's unique Public Interest Law Scholars Program provides a very small number of students with a rich array of academic and extra-academic support programs meant to facilitate their goal of practicing law in the public interest. With the recent addition of an optional "Plan B" first-year curriculum, a segment of Georgetown's class has the option of following a less traditional course of study emphasizing "the sources of law in history, philosophy, political theory and economics." The law school also operates what has been called the nation's finest and most comprehensive clinical program, the greatly varied offerings of which reflect and exploit Georgetown's proximity to the institutions of the federal government. If one is willing and able to brave the crowds, the opportunities here are almost limitless. This fact is clearly not lost on prospective law students, more of whom apply to Georgetown than to just about any other law school in the country. In terms of sheer popularity with applicants, Georgetown far exceeds even Harvard, with over 9,000 files processed annually.

Current Georgetown students have remarkably consistent feelings toward their chosen school. "Ambivalent" is the word that comes to mind. Although we heard almost uniformly positive reviews for things like Georgetown's excellent clinical program and cultural diversity, most of those we heard from were quicker to criticize than to praise. No single remark, perhaps, summed up the sentiments expressed by many as well as this one from a one 1L: "Each class, I've calculated, costs approximately the same as a Broadway show, and the audience is not much smaller. I'd get much more out of Georgetown if most of my classes didn't have so many damn people in them." Indeed, the students we heard from seem to appreciate the advantages such a large school offers—"vast and up-to-date research resources, widely varied course offerings"—but many were quick to point to the drawbacks—"lots of diversity and opportunities, but classes should be smaller so that people wouldn't be so intimidated to talk." In the eyes of some, such disadvantages are inconsequential when balanced against Georgetown's "excellent" facilities and other opportunities. "Everything's really big," wrote one such 2L, "and nothing is made very easy for you, but between the school itself and the city of D.C., there's enough here for any self-starter to do anything she pleases." And although a few students remarked on the competitiveness of the student body, most praised Georgetown's success in establishing a "sense of community" in a large school.

ADMISSIONS

Little more need be said about admissions at the Georgetown University Law Center than this: Nearly 10,000 prospective law students apply annually. From that fact, the rest follows obviously: The overwhelming majority of all candidates are denied admission, and those who are admitted possess incredibly strong numerical credentials. Sure, this gigantic law school must admit 2,000 applicants in order to fill its first-year class of more than 600, but those lucky 2,000 will have some serious numbers. In fact, by our calculation, the average undergraduate GPA and LSAT score of Georgetown students rank them as the twelfth most qualified in the nation.

ACADEMICS	
Student/faculty ratio	18:1
% female faculty	31
% minority faculty	11
Hours of study per day	3.54

FINANCIAL FACTS	
Tuition	$20,190
Part-time tuition per credit	NR
Estimated books/expenses/fees	NR
On-campus living expenses	NR
Off-campus living expenses	NR
% first-year students receiving aid	NR
% all students receiving aid	NR
% aid that is merit-based	NR
% all students receiving grants/scholarships	NR
% all students receiving loans	NR
% all students receiving assistantships	NR
Average award package	NR
Average graduation debt	NR

ADMISSIONS	
# applications received	9,528
% applicants accepted	21
% acceptees attending	31
Average LSAT	166
Average undergrad GPA	3.51
Application Fee	NR
Priority application deadline	NR
Priority notification	NR
Regular application deadline	Feb. 1, March 1
Regular notification	January-June
Admission deferment	NR
Gourman Report Rating	**4.69**

GEORGIA STATE UNIVERSITY 💾
College of Law

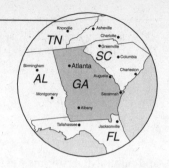

OVERVIEW

Type of school	public
Environment	metropolis
Scholastic calendar	quarter
Schedule	Full-time or part-time

STUDENTS

Enrollment of institution	7,664
Enrollment of law school	628
% male/female	52/48
% out-of-state	12
% part-time	43
% minorities	25
% international (# countries represented)	NR (5)
Average age at entry	29

APPLICANTS ALSO LOOK AT

University of Georgia
Emory University
Mercer University
University of South Carolina
Florida State University

SURVEY SAYS...

HITS
Diverse faculty
Legal writing
Intellectual challenge

MISSES
Sense of community
Library staff

EMPLOYMENT PROFILE

% grads employed immediately	NR
% grads employed within six months	97
Average starting salary	$45,480
% grads employed by field:	
Private practice	51
Business/industry	19
Government	12
Judicial clerkships	6
Military	1

Considering the short time the Georgia State College of Law has been in operation, it is very much in demand. Each year the school denies admission to over 80 percent of those who apply. Why does this midsize public law school in downtown Atlanta accept a smaller proportion of its applicants than do Cornell, Duke, and Georgetown? Consider this: In three years of law school at Georgia State, a Georgia resident will pay less in tuition than he or she would pay in one semester at any of those elite law schools.

More than 80 percent of GSU law school students are state residents, and an equal percentage of graduates stay and work in Atlanta after getting their degree. The school's location was high on students' lists of what attracted them to GSU. Atlanta, an up-and-coming city, is one of the country's fastest-growing and highest-paying legal job markets. Students certainly benefit from the school's connection to Atlanta firms and government offices. "I already have a very good job lined up for graduation in May which is directly related to being in downtown Atlanta because it afforded me the opportunity to work with great firms on a daily basis," said one 3L.

The school prepares students for the working world with a focus on practical lawyering skills through its curriculum and externship, trial-advocacy, and moot court programs. GSU's tax clinic has also garnered praise. When asked what the strengths of GSU law school are, one 2L said, "The practical skills that are taught and the opportunities to use these skills in the Atlanta legal community." Nearly 90 percent of law students rate the faculty as excellent or very good. One student said, "The faculty at GA State are great. They take a genuine interest in the students and the students' education." Although well over 75 percent of the students surveyed are satisfied with the school's legal writing program, a few students said it needed improvement.

GSU law school has an eclectic group of students who, despite their differences, get along well. "The diverse student body helps to enliven discussion and 'real-world' perspectives," said one 3L. Part of this diversity is due to the school's part-time program, which brings professionals and more mature students to the campus. One 2L said that the flexible program for night/part-

Cheryl Jester Jackson, Director of Admission
P.O. Box 4037, Atlanta, GA 30302-4037
Tel: (404) 651-2048
eMail: lawhld@gsusgi2.gsu.edu
Internet: http://www.gsu.edu/~lawadmn/gsulaw.html

Georgia State University

time students was one of the school's greatest strengths. "Although I'm full-time, it gives the school a better, more serious, diverse environment," said the same student. Indeed, Georgia State's student body is far and away the most diverse—in terms of both ethnicity and age—of any in the state, and its faculty is relatively balanced in terms of both gender and ethnicity. However, students did express concern about the lack of community at GSU. One student said the university could improve by "developing a campus atmosphere and sense of community."

Students had relatively few serious complaints about GSU College of Law. Although the parking situation was one of the most commonly reported concerns, if that's what students are most worried about, the school must be doing something right.

ADMISSIONS

Although the powers-that-be often dub this young institution as a "third-tier" law school, the far simpler calculation of supply and demand would yield Georgia State University College of Law a stellar rating. The school is, in fact, among the twenty most in-demand law schools in the entire nation. While its numerical admission standards still don't approach those of the traditional elite, consider the statistics for the 1995 class: There were 2,800 applications for 190 seats in the entering class; the average LSAT score was an impressive 159, and the median undergraduate GPA was 3.20.

ACADEMICS

Student/faculty ratio	15:1
% female faculty	41
% minority faculty	26
Hours of study per day	4.04

FINANCIAL FACTS

In-state tuition	$2,727
Out-of-state tuition	$7,719
Part-time tuition per credit	$1,558
Estimated books/expenses/fees	$3,770
On-campus living expenses	NR
Off-campus living expenses	NR
% first-year students receiving aid	NR
% all students receiving aid	NR
% aid that is merit-based	NR
% all students receiving grants/scholarships	4
% all students receiving loans	93
% all students receiving assistantships	9
Average award package	$2,403
Average graduation debt	NR

ADMISSIONS

# applications received	2,843
% applicants accepted	17
% acceptees attending	39
Average LSAT	157
Average undergrad GPA	3.10
Application Fee	$10
No early decision program	
Regular application deadline	March 1
Regular notification	rolling
Admission may be deferred?	no
Gourman Report Rating	2.12

UNIVERSITY OF GEORGIA
School of Law

OVERVIEW

Type of school	public
Environment	city
Scholastic calendar	quarter
Schedule	Full time only

STUDENTS

Enrollment of institution	30,000
Enrollment of law school	641
% male/female	57/43
% out-of-state	15
% part-time	NR
% minorities	14
% international (# countries represented)	NR (4)
Average age at entry	25

APPLICANTS ALSO LOOK AT

Emory University
Georgia State University
University of Virginia
Mercer University
Vanderbilt University

SURVEY SAYS...

HITS
Socratic method
Prestige
Research resources

MISSES
Practical lawyering skills
Faculty-student relations
Legal writing

EMPLOYMENT PROFILE

% grads employed immediately	70
% grads employed within six months	98
Average starting salary	NR
% grads employed by field:	
Private practice	70
Business/industry	6
Government	12
Judicial clerkships	11
Public service	2
Academic	3
Military	2

Even before the last decade's dramatic rise in law-school tuition, the prospective law student who was not independently wealthy had a lot of financial planning to do. Apart from the prominent public law schools in Michigan, Virginia, and California, the giants of American legal education have traditionally been expensive private institutions. The bargain hunter should be heartened, however, by the recent rise to prominence of a few inexpensive public law schools in other parts of the nation. With its rock-bottom tuition rates and top-notch faculty and facilities, the School of Law at the University of Georgia is one such school. Even for nonresidents, three years at the excellent law school in Athens ranks among the great bargains in legal education.

The Georgia J.D. program is traditional in the best sense. Requirements are few and offerings extensive, giving the student ample academic and co-curricular options from which to choose in plotting his or her own course of study. Among its special programs, the school of law is particularly proud of its perennially successful moot court teams and the programs offered through its Dean Rusk Center for International and Comparative Law, named for the former U.S. Secretary of State. Also at the law student's disposal are the extensive resources of UGA itself, a major research and teaching facility with 30,000 students. Admissions are highly selective, and admitted applicants have extremely strong numerical credentials. It should come as no surprise that Georgia grads have little difficulty finding very good jobs.

Dreams of future glory, however, cannot quite eradicate the stress of the present for some students, especially those on financial aid. Since UGA draws many bright students away from other schools with the lure of a low price and offers of financial aid, the unrealistic loan amounts authorized by the aid office (run by the university itself, not the law school, many students point out) created enormous problems in the past. More recently, however, the estimated cost of attendance has been greatly increased by the University's financial aid office and this problem should be remedied. Other problems we heard about via our survey included the dearth of practical skills and legal writing offerings, but the school has since opened a Civil Clinic and expanded offerings of advanced writing courses in response to these concerns. One student complained about the "horrendous grading curve." A particularly well-noted unfriendly aspect of the school has to do with UGA's perceived unwillingness to diversify its faculty and student body or incorporate the feminist courses many students cry for.

Regarding the student body, one person noted, "If Newt Gingrich were a student at GA, he'd surely be labeled a moderate, so overwhelmingly conservative is the student body here. At the same time, those of us who still believe in the rights of civil plaintiffs and criminal defendants are able to do so without interference. The right-wingers pity us, I think, but they pretty much let us be."

Despite problems, most students (especially those not dependent on aid) are happy at UGA. They delight in the excellent activities the school provides: "UGA has a diverse selection of student organizations, ranging from academic (The Law Practice and Technology Association) and service (Phi Alpha Delta) to social (Student Bar Association) organizations." Students also relish the outstanding International Law program and the local reputation: "If anyone wants to practice law in GA, they'd be foolish to not go here." According to one satisfied 2L: "We have the nicest faculty, administration, and support staff...Since all law schools are competitive, demanding, and most fall miserably short of their goal to prepare you to practice, wouldn't you rather be in a place where people smile, students have fun, and every day is not some hellacious experience? Oh yeah, the University of Georgia has a damn good law school."

ADMISSIONS

By all measurable standards, the University of Georgia School of Law is one of the most selective in the nation. Not only are the law school's numerical admissions standards higher than those of 85 percent of America's law schools, but applicant volume is so great that UGA admits a smaller proportion of its applicants than do many of the nation's so-called top-20 schools. Georgia's academic strength and bargain-basement tuition help explain the popularity of this excellent, inexpensive law school.

ACADEMICS

Student/faculty ratio	17:1
% female faculty	25
% minority faculty	5
Hours of study per day	3.67

FINANCIAL FACTS

In-state tuition	$2,736
Out-of-state tuition	$9,438
Part-time tuition per credit	NR
Estimated books/expenses/fees	$1,504
On-campus living expenses	NR
Off-campus living expenses	NR
% first-year students receiving aid	70
% all students receiving aid	70
% aid that is merit-based	10
% all students receiving grants/scholarships	20
% all students receiving loans	70
% all students receiving assistantships	NR
Average award package	$2,000
Average graduation debt	NR

ADMISSIONS

# applications received	2,315
% applicants accepted	22
% acceptees attending	42
Average LSAT	162
Average undergrad GPA	3.48
Application Fee	$30
No early decision program	
Regular application deadline	March 1
Regular notification	rolling
Admission deferment	case by case
Gourman Report Rating	**3.87**

GOLDEN GATE UNIVERSITY 💾
School of Law

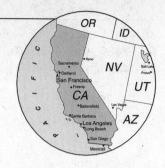

Students who want to be spend their three years of law school in one of the country's most beautiful and diverse cities have an opportunity to do so at Golden Gate University School of Law. Golden Gate has cashed in on the growing appeal of its location: the heart of downtown San Francisco. In fact, the San Francisco Bay Area has become so popular with law school applicants that the Golden Gate University School of Law could probably hold its classes in a bus station and still draw students in droves. In a region dominated by the world-class law schools of Berkeley, Stanford and the increasingly prestigious Hastings, several lesser-known law schools with moderate admissions standards, including Golden Gate, have long filled a niche by offering part-time and evening programs. Golden Gate makes a point of accommodating the schedule of the working law student, whether he or she is right out of college or has spent twenty years in the workplace. Its mid-year admissions option and flexible scheduling for even full-time students reflect Golden Gate's unusual commitment to making legal education accessible to working professionals.

Overall, Golden Gate students had only positive comments to make regarding their professors and the quality of their legal education. One thing is certainly true of the school's curriculum: it prepares students for the courtroom. Golden Gate, said students, is not a school for would-be professors; it's practical approach focuses on "real-world lawyering skills." The litigation program at Golden Gate is quite comprehensive. After completing the basic courses such as Trial Advocacy, Civil Litigation, and Lawyering Skills, students can choose from a wide array of advanced practical skills courses. Students praise these opportunities at Golden Gate as this 3L does: "The clinical and practical programs are excellent. I've been able to get a wide variety of legal experience and hone my research, writing, and advocacy skills." In addition, the faculty, who were often described as "unbelievable," and "always available," were ranked among the top twenty law school faculties in the nation in the April/May 1996 issue of *The National Jurist*. The same survey called Golden Gate the 11th best law school for women.

Where students gave glowing reports of their instructors, they had few kind words to say overall about the school's administra-

Cheryl Barnes, Admissions Coordinator
536 Mission Street, San Francisco, CA 94105
Tel: (415) 442-6630
eMail: lawadmit@ggu.edu
Internet: www.ggu.edu

tion. An uncharitable grading system was the main focus of a deep frustration that many GGU students feel. Griping about grading procedures is a favorite leisure-time activity of most law students, but in most cases students complain about mechanics: one semester, one exam, one grade. Students at Golden Gate, however, have far more serious and fundamental complaints about their school's grading system. Specifically, their complaint was that the law school has actively decided to deflate grades, thereby, students said, flunking about 20 to 25 percent of the first-year class. The administration said the actual figure is closer to 15 percent, and that it has modified the curve in response to student concerns. Those who don't flunk are shifted to the middle of the curve, not a pretty place to be around job-hunt time. Consider these statements: "While Golden Gate University strives to elevate its status by incorporating an unduly burdensome grade curve, those of us attending suffer the consequences"(2L); "The Dean and the administration are only concerned with one thing: the bar pass rate. As a result, the tyrannical grading system deflates not only grades but egos too" (2L); "Their grading curve (especially first year) is very tough and this was not disclosed to everyone." (1L). We heard from the admissions office, however, that the Associate Dean fully explains the curve to all first-year students at orientation, before classes begin. Students also spoke of a serious lack of communication between the administration and students on a wide variety of issues. "The school needs to improve its relationship with students. The administration doesn't listen to students once they are admitted." While concluding that many Golden Gate law students are generally relatively happy with their school, it is important to keep such statements in mind.

ADMISSIONS

Selectivity at Golden Gate has been on the rise in recent years as the volume of applications filed at the law school has inched up steadily. Now more than 2,500 students vie annually for spots in the law school's entering class of about 230. Because so many applicants of the Bay Area schools use Golden Gate as their "safety school," the law school must admit a relatively large portion of the candidates it considers in order to be sure of filling its class. Nearly one half of all applicants to the law school gain admission, and slightly fewer than a quarter of those admitted chose to enroll. Those who do tend to possess decent numerical credentials: a 3.02 undergraduate GPA and an LSAT score of 154.

ACADEMICS

Student/faculty ratio	20:1
% female faculty	37
% minority faculty	32
Hours of study per day	4.21

FINANCIAL FACTS

Tuition	$17,748
Part-time tuition per credit	$11,628
Estimated books/expenses/fees	$715
On-campus living expenses	NR
Off-campus living expenses	NR
% first-year students receiving aid	90
% all students receiving aid	95
% aid that is merit-based	8
% all students receiving grants/scholarships	23
% all students receiving loans	91
% all students receiving assistantships	3
Average award package	$6,500
Average graduation debt	$67,000

ADMISSIONS

# applications received	2,534
% applicants accepted	47
% acceptees attending	17
Average LSAT	154
Average undergrad GPA	3.02
Application Fee	$40
No early decision program	
Regular application deadline	April 15, June 1, Nov. 15
Regular notification	rolling
Admission deferment	one year
Gourman Report Rating	3.43

GONZAGA UNIVERSITY

School of Law

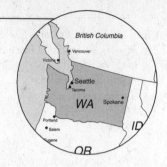

Named in honor of St. Aloysius Gonzaga, the patron saint of youth, Gonzaga University has been providing educational resources in eastern Washington state for over 100 years. This Jesuit institution opened its doors to law students in 1912 and has since built a solid regional reputation as a training ground for highly competent attorneys. Located in Spokane on the banks of the scenic Spokane River, the law school is near the city's law firms, courts, and government offices.

Gonzaga Law School takes its commitment to developing the best, most ethical attorneys it can very seriously. In fact, the school analyzed its own efforts in reaching these goals in 1992 when it asked faculty, students, alumni, and members of the bench and bar to evaluate the law school curriculum. According to the school's bulletin, the group found the curriculum to be strong in most areas of substantive law and gave the school's clinic and moot court programs outstanding ratings. Those questioned, however, felt that the school needed to create a more integrated approach that emphasized skills training throughout the process and reinforced professional and ethical issues. A new curriculum reflecting the school's strengths and the concerns of those questioned into consideration was introduced to all three law classes in 1996. By all accounts, students are content with the new Integrated Curriculum.

Students we spoke with couldn't say enough positive things about their instruction and the close, friendly relationship they share with many of their professors. Survey after survey referred to Gonzaga faculty as "supportive" and "dedicated." One 3L said, "The faculty and administration are accessible to the students and really care about students' education and well-being," and, "In areas of expertise, the faculty is very knowledgeable and competent." This well-liked faculty, along with a student body that is more cooperative than competitive, contribute to a "congenial" atmosphere. Several students also cited small class sizes as an area of strength. "I particularly enjoy the small classes because it gives you a chance to get to know your fellow students," said one 2L.

Sally Poutiatine, Admissions Administrator
P.O. Box 3528, Spokane, WA 99220
Tel: (509) 328-4220
Internet: http://www.law.gonzaga.edu

Does all of this sound too good to be true for all students at Gonzaga? From what some students said—even those who are very happy at the school—it may be. Many of them said that the university needs to focus on diversity, both racial and ethnic, among its student body and faculty. The school has a low percentage of minority students and one of the lowest percentages of minority faculty members nationwide. Some students indicated that the problem may stem more from conservative surroundings than from the school itself. "In many respects Spokane is a great town, but there is a pervasive feeling of intolerance towards minorities here," said a 1L. The same student added, "We have only three African American students in the entire law school. We are diminished by this, but I think I understand why they avoid this area of the country." Another third-year Gonzaga law student agreed and referred to "some racist incidents and attitudes" at the university. It should be noted that a few students said the university has recognized the need to diversify itself and is working toward improving race relations.

As of this writing, the administration is working hard to improve the law school's facilities. Nearly every student we spoke with said the school's physical plant desperately needed attention. Although the law library was the main focus, students also listed outdated computers, out-of-service restrooms, and crowded study areas among their grievances. However, Gonzaga is planning a $15-million law school building project tentatively scheduled to be completed in 1999.

ADMISSIONS

Despite steadily increasing applications volume over the past several years, the Gonzaga University School of Law remains one of the least selective in the country. That's good news for those whose numbers might otherwise prevent them from pursuing a legal education. The average incoming student at Gonzaga possesses numerical credentials lower than those of students at all but one of the law schools in the West, and lower than those of students at 75 percent of all the law schools in the country.

ACADEMICS

Student/faculty ratio	27:1
% female faculty	27
% minority faculty	9
Hours of study per day	4.05

FINANCIAL FACTS

Tuition	$17,050
Part-time tuition per credit	$550
Estimated books/expenses/fees	$1,000
On-campus living expenses	$16,850
Off-campus living expenses	NR
% first-year students receiving aid	NR
% all students receiving aid	81
% aid that is merit-based	NR
% all students receiving grants/scholarships	43
% all students receiving loans	90
% all students receiving assistantships	3
Average award package	$23,000
Average graduation debt	$65,000

ADMISSIONS

# applications received	1,735
% applicants accepted	57
% acceptees attending	23
Average LSAT	155
Average undergrad GPA	3.09
Application Fee	$40
No early decision program	
Regular application deadline	July 1
Regular notification	NR
Admission may be deferred?	no
Gourman Report Rating	**3.48**

HAMLINE UNIVERSITY 🖫
School of Law

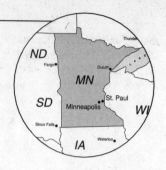

Since 1976, when Hamline University opened its School of Law, Minnesota's Twin Cities have supported three law schools. One, the University of Minnesota, has long enjoyed a reputation as one of America's finest, while the other two have established solid regional reputations. Like the William Mitchell College of Law across town, Hamline has discovered that working people—often with families and usually slightly older than average—represent a vast pool of qualified potential law students. Hamline is rare among day-program-only law schools in its efforts to accommodate these students. Needless to say, there are plenty of recent college graduates at Hamline, but the student body is remarkably diverse in terms of age. The average Hamline student is around 27 (significantly older than the national average of around 24) and often has professional and family commitments that require the sort of flexible scheduling that Hamline provides. The formal options of morning-only or afternoon-only reduced enrollment are what allow many of these "non-traditional" students to pursue a legal education in a university setting. Indeed, Hamline is more adamant than other law schools in insisting that its admissions process is driven by more than just numbers. Students' praise for the school's admissions staff bolsters this claim. Half of Hamline's students come from outside Minnesota, but many of them remain in the state after graduation.

Judging from their enthusiasm for their chosen school, however, Hamline students appear not to be in any particular hurry to graduate. Almost across the board, the students we heard from had little but praise for the quality of their program and, more often, for the quality of their relations with staff, faculty, and one another. "If there was a Midwest Ivy League," theorized one 2L, "HUSL would be a top member of that group." "Hamline is a young, dynamic, progressive educational community," added another. "The staff is remarkable, and the faculty genuinely care about helping students to excel in law school and in their future careers!!" One 2L reported that "morale among students is quite high," though another disagreed, claiming that "some students here have an unnecessary inferiority complex because they compare themselves to students at U. Minnesota." Overall, we heard none of the complaints of "lack of national reputation" from

Nancy A. Graf, Assistant Dean of Admissions
1536 Hewitt Avenue, St. Paul, MN 55104
Tel: (612) 641-2461
eMail: lawadm@seq.hamline.edu
Internet: http://www.hamline.edu

Hamline students that we so often heard from students at other non-elite schools. Quite the opposite. "There are some areas that need improvement here," reported one 3L evenhandedly, "but we are a young school and only getting better."

When asked to specify what areas at Hamline are in greatest need of improvement, many students cited the relative narrowness of the school's curriculum. "We need better access to clinical courses and traditional academic courses," wrote one 3L. Frequent complaints were heard made about Hamline's "aging and outdated" facilities. Though most noted that the school was set to undergo major expansion, consensus seemed to be that this is "long overdue." We also heard numerous remarks concerning "political correctness." "Hamline is quite liberal," said one 1L, "which is okay because I am too. I just don't like being pressured into a certain way of thinking. There is a sense of pressure from faculty and students that you are bad if you express conservative views, no matter how well reasoned."

Finally, if you are considering attending law school at Hamline, you may well also be considering the neighboring William Mitchell College of Law. If so, one Hamline 2L would have you add to your decision-making process a hitherto unconsidered criterion: "How about that HUSL hockey team? We beat Billy Mitchell 10 to 8 this year (1993)! "

ADMISSIONS

Regardless of whether numbers alone dominate the admissions process at the Hamline Law School, the numerical credentials of the average admitted student are respectable. The average undergraduate GPA is a relatively solid 3.12, and the average LSAT score is 154—at or about the 67th percentile. But Hamline admits students of diverse age and background and, hence, across a broad range of grade point averages and test scores.

ACADEMICS	
Student/faculty ratio	23:1
% female faculty	41
% minority faculty	6
Hours of study per day	4.22

FINANCIAL FACTS	
Tuition	$13,150
Part-time tuition per credit	NR
Estimated books/expenses/fees	NR
On-campus living expenses	NR
Off-campus living expenses	NR
% first-year students receiving aid	90
% all students receiving aid	90
% aid that is merit-based	8
% all students receiving grants/scholarships	14
% all students receiving loans	90
% all students receiving assistantships	NR
Average award package	$29,500
Average graduation debt	$60,000

ADMISSIONS	
# applications received	1,614
% applicants accepted	43
% acceptees attending	32
Average LSAT	154
Average undergrad GPA	3.12
Application Fee	$30
No early decision program	
Regular application deadline	May 15
Regular notification	rolling
Admission deferment	one year
Gourman Report Rating	2.76

HARVARD UNIVERSITY
Law School

Few observers of U.S. law schools would disagree that Harvard University Law School provides one of the best legal educations in the country. Harvard, in fact, has long served as the quintessential American law school as portrayed in the movie *The Paper Chase*: tough, cutthroat, and imperious. Today this image of Harvard law is only partially true. The school certainly boasts some of the best and brightest students and legal scholars in the country. But, for the most part, the days of cruel professors and browbeaten students are gone; you will now find a law school that is much more humane but no less demanding. The school has maintained its theoretical, rather than pragmatic, approach to the law. Harvard's mission to "impart the enduring principles of law, legal philosophy, and the historical development of legal institutions," is successfully met through the instruction of a first-rate faculty, which includes several famous legal personalities.

The power that a law degree from HLS grants is still unparalleled among U.S. schools. One 2L, when asked to name Harvard's strengths, put it this way: "PRESTIGE, PRESTIGE, PRESTIGE." It is true that Harvard grads, even those who coast through with average grades, are virtually assured of jobs upon graduation. This fact has not escaped students, who note that unlike their peers at other law schools, they do not have to worry too much about gaining employment. "HLS is a basically a job factory; regardless of expansion or contraction of the legal industry, there will always be jobs for HLS grads," said one confident 2L.

Students were quick to point out that a Harvard education puts them in touch with great people: the best professors and a dynamic, intellectual student body. "The strengths of Harvard Law School are its excellent faculty, who are on the cutting edge of research and practice in their fields, as well as its student body. I feel that I'm constantly learning from my fellow students...." said one 2L. The majority of students agreed that the level of competition among students at Harvard is not above the norm. However, many did criticize the law school's lack of community and the large class sizes. "Because of the large class sizes, I've had virtually no contact with my professors," said a 2L.

Contrary to what one might expect at a institution composed of such high-achievers, students claim that fun can be had at Harvard

1563 Massachusetts Avenue, Cambridge, MA 02138
Tel: (617) 495-3109
Internet: http://www.law.harvard.edu

Harvard University

Law School. In fact, several students we spoke with referred to their "active social lives," including Thursday night Bar Reviews at local pubs and other forms of relaxation. "I have found the student body much more diverse and more social than I expected. I'm actually able to go out drinking and dancing at many of Boston's great night spots at least once a week," said a 1L. However, some students noted that the school itself has little community space for its law students and that the recreational facilities, particularly the gym, are too limited.

Topping the list of student complaints was the Harvard Law School administration, often described as "inflexible" and "uncaring." One 3L, who referred to her time at HLS as "an incredibly alienating experience," said: "The administration is not the least bit interested in student concerns. Students arrive here first year full of interest and enthusiasm which usually gets sucked out of them by second year."

We heard sharply differing opinions regarding the school's support of publich interest law from students and the administration. Many students cited the administration's—and more pointedly, the dean's—lack of support for public interest law. "The administration is openly hostile to public-interest oriented students," said one 3L. Another suggested that the dean "tries periodically to cut the public interest career office and the clinical programs." We must say that the school's actions, including the creation of a public- interest professsorship, the purchase and renovation of the Legal Services Center teaching clinic, and the establishment of the Human Rights Journal, appear to strongly support public interest law.

Overall, Harvard is Harvard, a school which provides one of the most distinguished law degrees in the country.

ADMISSIONS

Last year nearly 6,800 prospective students competed to be among the 559 men and women admitted to the Harvard Law School's entering class, making this premier law school the second most selective in the country. However, most of those unlucky applicants could likely have their pick of most other law schools. With an overall acceptance rate of about 12 percent, it is inevitable that Harvard will reject thousands of very well qualified candidates. Those whose numbers fall even slightly short of stunning face long odds. But it never hurts to try.

ACADEMICS	
Student/faculty ratio	17:1
% female faculty	21
% minority faculty	22
Hours of study per day	3.50

FINANCIAL FACTS	
Tuition	$21,700
Part-time tuition per credit	NR
Estimated books/expenses/fees	$2,080
On-campus living expenses	NR
Off-campus living expenses	NR
% first-year students receiving aid	75
% all students receiving aid	75
% aid that is merit-based	NR
% all students receiving grants/scholarships	NR
% all students receiving loans	100
% all students receiving assistantships	NR
Average award package	$8,870
Average graduation debt	$62,814

ADMISSIONS	
# applications received	6,800
% applicants accepted	12
% acceptees attending	67
Average LSAT	NR
Average undergrad GPA	NR
Application Fee	$50
Priority application deadline	NR
Priority notification	NR
Regular application deadline	February 1
Regular notification	rolling
Admission deferment	two years

Gourman Report Rating	4.93

UNIVERSITY OF HAWAII, MANOA 💾

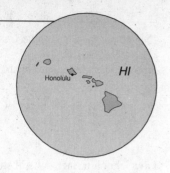

William S. Richardson School of Law

While many mainland Americans continue to view the fiftieth state as nothing more than a vacation destination, those who live and work in Hawaii know that their state's location means much more than great surfing and year-round sunshine. Far more than any state in the union, Hawaii feels the financial and cultural presence of Asia, the continent toward which America's economic and political focus is rapidly shifting as the twenty-first century approaches. Few institutions show a greater awareness of the future importance of the Pacific Rim to Hawaii and to the country as a whole than does the University of Hawaii, Manoa's William S. Richardson School of Law. Founded in 1973 on the largest of the state university's nine campuses, the law school began with only 56 students. And while UH could easily have secured its future by marketing itself to mainlanders as a law school/tropical resort, it has remained true to its mission: This public law school clearly reflects the people and the imperatives of its home state (70 percent of enrollees are residents). This is evident in the law school's student body and in its special offerings, which include the comprehensive Pacific-Asian Legal Studies (PALS) program and a formal certificate of specialization in environmental and natural resources law. Furthermore, the student body at Hawaii makes other law schools' claims of diversity seem laughable: Fully 70 percent of the students are members of what are elsewhere called minority groups. Applications volume at Hawaii is low in comparison to other law schools, but the size of its entering classes (around 80) necessitates a highly selective admissions process. State residents are given strong preferences in determining admissions.

To judge from the results of our survey, the few who do manage to gain admission to and enroll in the Richardson School of Law at UH seem quite pleased with their choice. They are well aware of certain shortcomings, but their criticisms are constructive and concern problems that stem mainly from the school's size. Still, most here seem to regard UH's smallness as a net positive. In the words of one Hawaii 1L, the environment at the law school is "very encouraging and supportive." "Cutthroat competition not in favor here," he said, "classes are small and personal, and you are given a lot of individual attention." "For a small regional school," added another, "Richardson has exceptionally bright and dedicated professors who are committed to teaching." They are equally committed, it seems, to making their students work. "Perhaps like many of the mainlanders who come here," wrote one Hawaii 3L, "I had it in the back of my mind that things would be sort of laid-back in the classroom. Instead, I found that most students here are very dedicated to meeting some fairly high standards." Indeed, many of those we heard from called the level of competition here quite high, but for every student who complained about the "brutal and depressing 'C' curve," there was another who praised UH for fostering a "competitive environment among very bright, qualified people."

While we have heard complaints about the Asian law curricula in the past, since then the school has hired a Chinese Law faculty and a Japanese Law faculty, and instituted a certificate program in Pacific Asian Legal Studies. The program is now a much better resource, according to the administration, which we expect will be reflected in our next surveys.

As for the negatives, most Hawaii students list the curricular limitations that result from the school's size. "Richardson could benefit from more clinics so that all interested students could participate in them," wrote one 3L, "and more professors would allow them to offer a broader variety of topics." "I am very pleased with the school overall," went another fairly typical remark, "but it needs more people, more funding, and more resources." Indeed, though they are well aware of what they would be trading away, most Hawaii students seem to regard growth as a necessary solution to many of the school's problems.

ADMISSIONS

As far off the beaten path as Hawaii is for most aspiring lawyers, it is not surprising that the University of Hawaii, Manoa, School of Law draws from a very small pool of applicants. What may surprise some, however, is the fact that from this small pool the law school is able to select one of the more highly qualified student bodies in the entire nation. Indeed, the numerical credentials of the average Hawaii student are better than those of students at 70 percent of American law schools.

ACADEMICS	
Student/faculty ratio	13:1
% female faculty	44
% minority faculty	22
Hours of study per day	4.23

FINANCIAL FACTS	
In-state tuition	$4,800
Out-of-state tuition	$12,744
Part-time tuition per credit	NR
Estimated books/expenses/fees	$1,018
On-campus living expenses	NR
Off-campus living expenses	NR
% first-year students receiving aid	NR
% all students receiving aid	NR
% aid that is merit-based	28
% all students receiving grants/scholarships	52
% all students receiving loans	38
% all students receiving assistantships	9
Average award package	$3,280
Average graduation debt	NR

ADMISSIONS	
# applications received	782
% applicants accepted	18
% acceptees attending	50
Average LSAT	157
Average undergrad GPA	3.43
Application Fee	$30
No early decision program	
Regular application deadline	March 1
Regular notification	April 1–15
Admission may be deferred?	no
Gourman Report Rating	**2.66**

HOFSTRA UNIVERSITY 🖫
School of Law

For over 20 years, heavily populated suburban Long Island has made do with only two law schools, one of them the midsize Hofstra University School of Law. Established in 1971 on the Hempstead campus of its 12,000-student parent university, Hofstra is a regionally respected law school that draws the vast majority of its students from and sends the vast majority of its graduates to the metropolitan New York area. Its traditional curriculum is solid and its faculty strong, and Hofstra graduates have historically had little difficulty securing good jobs. To better prepare its students for a tightening job market, however, Hofstra places great emphasis on practical-skills training, both in the classroom and in the community.

The law school administers a broad variety of special-subject workshops and externship programs, and it has long operated its own Neighborhood Law Office. Hofstra recently augmented its skills curriculum with a special three-credit "trial techniques" program held in January before the beginning of the spring semester. These and other programs in the law school's impressive array of simulated and live-action clinical courses involve a significant proportion of the Hofstra student body. The law school admits more than one in three applicants, but with a pool of more than 2,500 from which to choose, it holds candidates to high standards. The numerical credentials of admitted applicants are moderately strong.

For the most part, those who actually go on to enroll at the law school express overall satisfaction with their surroundings. Almost unanimously, in fact, Hofstra students praise their "often brilliant" faculty. As a 1L put it: "Our professors are intelligent, well-prepared, open and concerned about their students' academic and personal welfare." Most others agreed. "They have a nurturing attitude rather than trying to push out those who can't make it." Many also had words of praise for the practical focus of their curriculum, and particularly for its trial advocacy program. When asked to name their law school's greatest strength, quite a few cited its "growing reputation for producing great trial lawyers."

Amy Engle, Assistant Dean for Admissions
121 Hofstra University, Hempstead, NY 11550
Tel: (516) 463-5916
eMail: lawaee@vaxa.hofstra.edu
Internet: http://www.hofstra.edu

Hofstra students do, of course, have their gripes, but other than the small but vocal minority of students we heard from who called for more ethnic diversity in the law school's faculty, few had specific complaints. (Note: Only a tiny percentage of Hofstra's full-time teaching faculty are members of minority groups, far fewer than at most schools in the metropolitan area, and the entire nation.) By far the most prevalent concern of Hofstra students seems to be their future employment prospects. In many cases, this concern took the form of complaints about the limited number of slots on the school's single law journal. In most cases, however, it took the form of nonspecific criticism—even from 1Ls—of the law school's career placement office. Many also expressed their desire that the law school "improve its national reputation." Of course, things are not quite that simple. Given the lack of geographical diversity in the student body, Hofstra can't really aspire to the kind of standing that some of its neighboring schools enjoy. But when one considers the fact that practically all Hofstra graduates go to work in the New York area, one sees that concerns about the law school's perceived lack of "national" status are misplaced. New York is home to the single-largest legal job market in the world, and though the upper echelon of the city's legal community may still be the almost exclusive province of lawyers from "top-ten" schools, plenty of jobs await the graduates of strong regional schools like Hofstra.

ADMISSIONS

As highly selective as the 11 law schools in the metropolitan New York region are, it would be misleading to claim that admissions at Hofstra are much less competitive than at most of these schools. In the grand scheme of things, Hofstra is quite selective. With a solid average GPA and an average LSAT score at the 70th percentile, the numerical credentials of students in Hofstra's entering class of about 270 are stronger, in fact, than those of students at about 40 percent of the country's fully accredited law schools. These high numerical standards, however, are mitigated somewhat by a relatively generous overall acceptance rate.

ACADEMICS

Student/faculty ratio	21:1
% female faculty	29
% minority faculty	12
Hours of study per day	3.55

FINANCIAL FACTS

Tuition	$19,070
Part-time tuition per credit	NR
Estimated books/expenses/fees	$1,284
On-campus living expenses	NR
Off-campus living expenses	NR
% first-year students receiving aid	NR
% all students receiving aid	NR
% aid that is merit-based	34
% all students receiving grants/scholarships	39
% all students receiving loans	70
% all students receiving assistantships	7
Average award package	$3,846
Average graduation debt	NR

ADMISSIONS

# applications received	2,557
% applicants accepted	44
% acceptees attending	25
Average LSAT	157
Average undergrad GPA	3.30
Application Fee	$60
No early decision program	
Regular application deadline	April 15
Regular notification	rolling
Admission may be deferred?	no
Gourman Report Rating	**4.20**

UNIVERSITY OF HOUSTON 💾
Law Center

One of three mega-law schools in the nation's seventh-largest legal job market, the University of Houston Law Center is home to over 1,000 full- and part-time students. The law school's excellent faculty and high-caliber student body are both causes and effects of its long-established reputation as one of the finest law schools in the South. Its low public-school tuition is to thank for its standing as one of the better bargains anywhere.

The law school at Houston has succeeded in augmenting its overall strength by establishing several highly regarded special programs. In 1978, for example, it established its Health Law and Policy Institute in conjunction with the University of Texas Health Science Center. Since then, the law school has been recognized as a national leader in the growing field of health law, an area of specialization that is particularly appropriate in a city whose largest employer is the world's biggest medical complex. Besides including a wide array of health-law courses in its standard J.D. curriculum, Houston offers a master of laws (LL.M.) and two concurrent-degree programs in the field: a master's in public health and a Ph.D. in medical humanities, both through UT. The law school has also established special programs in international law and environmental liability law, as well as an Intellectual Property Law Institute. All of these subjects are areas of curricular strength at Houston.

Outside the classroom, Houston students can participate in several clinical programs, including the Family and Poverty Law Clinic and other clinical curricula dedicated to some of the fields of law discussed above. This broad-based strength has earned the law school increasing notice, not least from highly qualified applicants, who have driven Houston's numerical admissions standards significantly higher in recent years. As it stands, it is a law school in great demand.

Although they are vocally critical about particular aspects of their experience at the law school, those applicants who actually go on to become students at Houston are fundamentally satisfied with their chosen school. They find their curriculum solid and their faculty competent, and they exude a confidence about their professional futures, which a large percentage of graduates will

Leah Gross, Assistant Dean for Recruitment
4800 Calhoun, Houston, TX 77204-6371
Tel: (713) 743-1070
eMail: info@lawlib.uh.edu
Internet: http://www.law.uh.edu

spend in private practice. This confidence, in most cases, seems to have a basis in reality, since so many Houston students have gained practical experience in the field before earning their degrees. Asked to name their school's greatest strengths, many cite "its proximity to major law practices and its relationship with them." "I've been able to interact and network with many area lawyers," said one student only in her second year. "Our location in this major metropolitan area allows employment opportunities galore," reported another. "This law school is secretly striving to become a top-twenty school. It has the best reputation in town and growing." And, quite naturally, Houston students credit the low tuition they pay for a good part of their overall contentment. As one student asserted, Houston gives "the best bang for the buck." Future students will benefit from the recent extensive overhaul of and additions to the computer facilities and the much needed refurbishment to the library and grounds.

Houston students' criticisms ranged from the purely esthetic to the truly substantive. Since the vast majority commented on the "drab, lifeless appearance" of the physical plant, we can only assume that now that this problem has been addressed, they have nothing major to complain about. However, quite a few students who praised the quality of the Houston program expressed their frustration with the relatively limited selection of courses, which one student said "is not diverse enough during any given semester." These and other relatively minor criticisms aside, however, most Houston students are basically content.

ADMISSIONS

The University of Houston's respected J.D. program and its attractive tuition attract applications from the 2,650 prospective law students annually. The size and quality of this applicant pool allow the law school to choose its students quite carefully. Successful candidates for admission to Houston possess solid numerical credentials. Those who are admitted and actually go on to enroll have solid average UGPAs and LSAT scores.

ACADEMICS

Student/faculty ratio	26:1
% female faculty	17
% minority faculty	11
Hours of study per day	3.96

FINANCIAL FACTS

In-state tuition	$4,650
Out-of-state tuition	$9,300
Part-time tuition per credit	NR
Estimated books/expenses/fees	$1,338
On-campus living expenses	NR
Off-campus living expenses	NR
% first-year students receiving aid	NR
% all students receiving aid	100
% aid that is merit-based	15
% all students receiving grants/scholarships	NR
% all students receiving loans	NR
% all students receiving assistantships	NR
Average award package	NR
Average graduation debt	$35,000

ADMISSIONS

# applications received	2,650
% applicants accepted	28
% acceptees attending	36
Average LSAT	158
Average undergrad GPA	3.25
Application Fee	$50
Priority application deadline	NR
Priority notification	NR
Regular application deadline	February 1
Regular notification	May 1
Admission may be deferred?	No
Gourman Report Rating	**3.85**

HOWARD UNIVERSITY
School of Law

In 1869, in the wake of the Civil War, the Reconstruction-era Congress established Howard University in the District of Columbia. The university's mission was to provide the educational means by which the newly freed slaves could redeem their constitutional rights and claim the practical, social, and economic standing necessary to make those rights meaningful. But the collapse of Reconstruction ushered in the long and shameful era of Jim Crow, a time during which the emptiness of the Constitution's promises for African Americans was confirmed time and again by the U.S. Supreme Court. The Howard University School of Law fought and survived long enough to produce two lawyers who made a brighter future for all Americans possible: Charles Hamilton Houston and Thurgood Marshall of the NAACP, respectively the architect and builder of Brown v. Board of Education.

Due in large part to the efforts of these and thousands of other prominent graduates, Howard continues to thrive. The curriculum is straightforward and traditional, and while the law school's modest size means that course offerings are somewhat limited, it also gives Howard one of the more favorable student-faculty ratios in the nation. Every year, a small group of Howard grads leaves the Washington, D.C., law school to join one of the most active alumni networks in the country, a network that includes more than its fair share of the politically powerful. A historically black institution, Howard maintains a commitment to affirmative action in faculty hirings and student admissions that is stronger than that of any other law school. At Howard, where the overwhelming majority of the student body and full-time faculty members are African-, Hispanic-, or Asian-American, the term "minority" is definitely a misnomer. By a comfortable margin, this law school leads the nation in diversity. Howard's strong tradition, its relatively low tuition (for a private school), and its generous financial aid programs combine to draw a large pool of applicants every year. As a result, the admissions process here is highly competitive, but numerical considerations are not an all-important factor.

The employment pattern of Howard's graduates is also noteworthy. The rate at which Howard grads choose to begin their careers in private practice is well below the national average, and the proportion of Howard graduates who enter government positions is one of the highest. It is difficult to say which is more responsible for the fact that so many choose to work in the public sector: Howard's strong tradition of encouraging public service or the continuing difficulties that all minorities—along with women of all ethnicities—face in cracking the glass ceiling in private-sector institutions historically dominated by white men.

Students at Howard hold their chosen school to fairly high standards, as evidenced by their relative lack of enthusiasm for many aspects of their experience at the law school. They are very enthusiastic, however, about the quality of relations among the student body. Although several called the degree of competitiveness at the law school "excessive," nearly all called the sense of community "very strong." "My fellow students have made my education at Howard truly enjoyable," went one fairly typical remark from one 3L. On the downside, however, most of the students we heard from voiced dissatisfaction with Howard's physical facilities, and many expressed their desire that the law school "give [them] more training in practical skills." Despite this, the vast majority of Howard students appear to have a very high degree of confidence in their professional futures, as good a measure as any of a law school's ability to serve its students.

ADMISSIONS

Although the numerical credentials of the average member of the Howard University School of Law fall below the national average, admissions at Howard is no joke. Indeed, applications volume at this long-established law school is so great that Howard accepts a smaller proportion of its applicants than do some of the country's elite law schools.

ACADEMICS

Student/faculty ratio	16:1
% female faculty	32
% minority faculty	76
Hours of study per day	4.11

FINANCIAL FACTS

Tuition	$10,400
Part-time tuition per credit	NR
Estimated books/expenses/fees	NR
On-campus living expenses	NR
Off-campus living expenses	NR
% first-year students receiving aid	NR
% all students receiving aid	NR
% aid that is merit-based	NR
% all students receiving grants/scholarships	NR
% all students receiving loans	NR
% all students receiving assistantships	NR
Average award package	NR
Average graduation debt	NR

ADMISSIONS

# applications received	1,507
% applicants accepted	25
% acceptees attending	38
Average LSAT	152
Average undergrad GPA	3.04
Application Fee	$60
Priority application deadline	NR
Priority notification	NR
Regular application deadline	April 30
Regular notification	NR
Admission deferment	NR
Gourman Report Rating	**2.87**

UNIVERSITY OF IDAHO

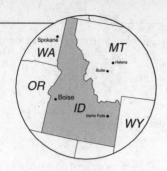

OVERVIEW

Type of school	public
Environment	town
Scholastic calendar	semester
Schedule	Full time only

STUDENTS

Enrollment of institution	7,398
Enrollment of law school	275
% male/female	57/43
% out-of-state	25
% part-time	NR
% minorities	10
% international (# countries represented)	NR ()
Average age at entry	25

APPLICANTS ALSO LOOK AT

Gonzaga University
University of Oregon
Brigham Young University
University of Washington
University of Utah

SURVEY SAYS...

HITS
Studying
Socratic method
Intellectual challenge

MISSES
Students feel poorly prepared
Quality of teaching
Legal writing

EMPLOYMENT PROFILE

% grads employed immediately	NR
% grads employed within six months	83
Average starting salary	$30,000
% grads employed by field:	
Private practice	40
Business/industry	5
Government	8
Judicial clerkships	22
Public service	2
Academic	11
Military	6

The other Moscow may have Red Square and cheaper vodka, but Moscow, Idaho, has its Russian counterpart beat on many other counts. The weather is nicer, for instance, and the currency is quite a bit more stable. They're about even in terms of potato availability, but this small town in the dry, northwestern Idaho panhandle definitely gets the nod when it comes to legal education, at least for those planning to take the bar exam in English. Moscow, USA, is, after all, home to Idaho's only law school, the University of Idaho College of Law, a small and inexpensive law school that has served its home state creditably since 1909.

The law school draws the overwhelming majority of its students from within Idaho or from nearby western Washington. (Spokane is only 80 miles to the Northwest and Washington State U. is 8 miles away.) The students in Idaho's J.D. program follow a course of study that is traditional and strictly prescribed, with relatively few elective courses even in the second and third years. This is, of course, the price that one often pays for attending a school that is small and friendly enough that all students know one another by name. The application process, however, has become significantly less friendly. Since more and more people have joined Idaho's applicant pool in recent years, the law school's acceptance rate has plummeted from 75 percent in 1986 to its current, less generous number.

Students at the University of Idaho paint a remarkably consistent picture of their surroundings. On the positive side, nearly every single student we heard from cited the same things in assessing the strengths of their chosen school: its manageable size and the quality of the human relations made possible by that size. "Our size is really a plus because of the easy access to professors and their willingness to help the students," said one whose sentiments were shared by many. "The law school's size and the individual attention we receive from faculty and staff are definitely its strong points."

Of course, as several pointed out, smallness also has its disadvantages, some more obvious than others. Strictly in terms of academic opportunities, a law school of this size is necessarily going to offer a relatively limited array of courses. This is a source of some frustration for Idaho students. "I wish the school could offer more courses besides those needed to pass the bar," wrote one 3L. "They really need to improve the diversity of the curriculum," agreed another. Less obvious is another difficulty that students at a small school face. "Our small size is also our greatest burden," said one student, explaining that "one cannot avoid participating in class, which is, of course, both good and bad." Such forced participation is intensified by the faculty's reported over-reliance on the much-despised Socratic Method of classroom instruction, a teaching style that contributes significantly to the high degree of stress and competitiveness that Idaho students report.

Despite their complaints about competitiveness and the limited selection of courses available, most Idaho students seem fairly content with their experience at the law school. As one student said: "Participation is expected and appreciated...I like the school as it is." It seems that most would endorse the assessment of the Idaho 1L who commented quite succinctly: "Good school, good opportunities, good location."

ADMISSIONS

Because Idaho's only law school draws the overwhelming majority of its students from a relatively small population base in eastern Washington and Idaho itself, applications volume is moderate. It has, however, more than doubled in the last eight years, making the overall admissions process fairly selective. Numerical admissions standards are only moderate, but the small size of the law school's entering class necessitates a careful screening process. Only about one third of the roughly 700 candidates Idaho considers annually will gain admission, and almost half of those who are admitted will actually choose to enroll.

ACADEMICS	
Student/faculty ratio	10:1
% female faculty	30
% minority faculty	4
Hours of study per day	5.23

FINANCIAL FACTS	
In-state tuition	$3,260
Out-of-state tuition	$8,640
Part-time tuition per credit	NR
Estimated books/expenses/fees	NR
On-campus living expenses	NR
Off-campus living expenses	NR
% first-year students receiving aid	NR
% all students receiving aid	NR
% aid that is merit-based	NR
% all students receiving grants/scholarships	NR
% all students receiving loans	NR
% all students receiving assistantships	NR
Average award package	NR
Average graduation debt	NR

ADMISSIONS	
# applications received	703
% applicants accepted	33
% acceptees attending	41
Average LSAT	155
Average undergrad GPA	3.22
Application Fee	$30
Priority application deadline	NR
Priority notification	NR
Regular application deadline	February 1
Regular notification	April 1
Admission may be deferred?	No
Gourman Report Rating	2.71

ILLINOIS INSTITUTE OF TECHNOLOGY 💾

Chicago-Kent College of Law

For much of its 108 years of existence Illinois Institute of Technology's Chicago-Kent College of Law was relatively unknown outside the region. Over the last decade, however, the second-oldest law school in Illinois has engineered a rise to well-deserved national prominence. It has done so by means of a campaign that other aspiring law schools would do well to emulate. The formula is deceptively simple: Build a first-rate faculty whose scholarship will burnish the law school's reputation within the academic community; foresee the importance of changes in technology by establishing a Center for Law and Computers and by building a new physical plant with a massive library and state-of-the-art facilities; exploit the strength of the parent institution by adding to the curriculum special programs in environmental and energy law and intellectual property law; and adapt to the changing demands of the job market by strengthening the trial advocacy program and instituting a rigorous three year course of study in legal research and writing.

All of the above changes and innovations within the school seem to have paid off. Students at Chicago-Kent highly praise them, especially the incorporation of technology into everyday life at the school, the hiring of excellent faculty members, and the tough LR&W program. Comments like these reflect the overwhelming sentiment of the student body: "The legal writing program has given me an edge in the job hunt due to my research experience and great writing samples that I have used." (3L); "The faculty is outstanding and has sincere interest in helping each student. Office doors are always open." (2L). While students elsewhere often complain about the scarcity and antiquity of their schools' computer facilities, comments like the one from this 1L are common at IIT: "The school's computer network is revolutionary, and the notebook computer project is the wave of the future." Students at Chicago-Kent also spoke highly of the school's clinical program that helps develop strong litigation skills, although several students remarked that there are too few slots available in the seven in-house and two out-of-house clinics. According to the administration, there are 85-90 slots available per semester and 40-45 slots in the summer for the in-house clinics, plus another 15-30 slots available throughout the year in the two external clinics.

Nancy Herman, Assistant Dean for Admissions
565 West Adams Street, Chicago, IL 60661
Tel: (312) 906-5020   Fax: (312) 906-5280
eMail: admitq@kentlaw.edu
Internet: http://www.kentlaw.edu

Illinois Institute of Technology

Chicago-Kent students did have some criticism about their school, however, but the source of much of it may be surprising. Many students we surveyed cited the school's strong desire to move up in the national rankings—at the cost, they say, of ignoring the woes of current students—as a source of major frustration. "I am worried that the school is more concerned with its public image rather than the students," said a 3L. Another more discontent 3L offered: "I think it's pathetic that the school worries so much about improving its image in the market but does nothing to keep from losing quality faculty or improving student relations." And a few students noted that although the majority of their professors were excellent, some didn't appear to be completely focused on their pupils. "Some teachers seem to be more interested in publishing because they show little interest in teaching," said one 3L. (Chicago-Kent faculty is, in fact, ranked in the top fifteen percent nationally in frequency of publication.) Tuition, a frequent source of law student dissatisfaction, did not go unmentioned either. "We need more straight answers from the administration—the tuition is out of control," said a 2L. Actually, according to the administration, Chicago-Kent has had the lowest percent increase in tuition in the Chicago area over 1994-1996. While many students praised IIT for its "growing reputation," image-building appears to have its price.

ADMISSIONS

After being dubbed an "up-and-coming" school by a leading U.S. magazine in the early 1990s, applications volume at the law school increased by an astonishing 25 percent. Numerical admissions standards consequently rose and have since leveled off at a quite respectable average. Still, admission standards at IIT's Chicago-Kent College of Law are somewhat more lax than those at the more elite regional law schools. But, as the school's applications pool rises as it has during the past several years, so does the school's selectivity. Approximately 2,500 prospective students vie annually for a place in the school's entering class of 400. Numerical admissions standards at the school would rank Chicago-Kent among the 85 most selective schools in the country if it were not for the law school's extremely generous overall acceptance rate of 40 percent.

ACADEMICS

Student/faculty ratio	17:1
% female faculty	37
% minority faculty	22
Hours of study per day	3.77

FINANCIAL FACTS

Tuition	$18,850
Part-time tuition per credit	NR
Estimated books/expenses/fees	$710
On-campus living expenses	NR
Off-campus living expenses	NR
% first-year students receiving aid	79
% all students receiving aid	64
% aid that is merit-based	NR
% all students receiving grants/scholarships	36
% all students receiving loans	64
% all students receiving assistantships	11
Average award package	$23,000
Average graduation debt	$73,000

ADMISSIONS

# applications received	2,550
% applicants accepted	NR
% acceptees attending	13
Average LSAT	156
Average undergrad GPA	3.20
Application Fee	$40
No early decision program	
Regular application deadline	April 1
Regular notification	rolling
Admission deferment	one year
Gourman Report Rating	**3.83**

UNIVERSITY OF ILLINOIS
College of Law

It is only appropriate that Illinois should be as heavily stocked as it is with excellent law schools. The state is, after all, the nation's third-largest legal job market for recent law-school graduates. Unlike some other states near the top of the list—New York and Massachusetts, most notably—Illinois is not completely dominated by private law schools. While its most highly regarded public school may lack the national name recognition of the state's top private schools (Northwestern and Chicago), the University of Illinois College of Law has long enjoyed a degree of esteem that places it among the country's finest law schools, public or private. And though Illinois's highly qualified students (a large percentage of whom are state residents) may be drawn to the law school by its very low tuition, they have given up very little academically by taking advantage of such a bargain. Competition for admission to the law school is fairly heated. Candidates lucky enough to gain admission possess very strong numerical credentials.

Illinois boasts a highly respected faculty (ranked first in terms of scholarly output) and a reputation for academic strength that simultaneously contributes to and derives from the strength of the broader university, one of the largest (40,000+ total students) and best equipped in the nation. Illinois law students can pursue joint degrees through any number of highly rated graduate departments. The law school itself offers a traditionally broad J.D. program that is virtually free of prescribed courses after the first year. In charting their own course of study in their second and third years, Illinois students can choose from, among others, courses in the law school's widely admired programs in trial advocacy and international law. The school has completely revamped their legal writing program in the past few years. According to the administration, "Students now are divided into mock law firms, and after learning research and writing skills and writing closed memoranda, they interview a mock client, prepare an office memo, write a memo in support of or opposition to summary judgment, and negotiate a settlement. They then prepare an appellate brief and argue the case before a panel of local attorneys."

Pamela B. Coleman, Director of Admissions
504 East Pennsylvania Avenue, Champaign, IL 61820
Tel: (217) 244-6415
eMail: dfalls@law.uiuc.edu
Internet: http://www.law.uiuc.edu//

University of Illinois

Those who actually go on to enroll at the University of Illinois express a fairly high degree of satisfaction with their chosen school, and though they surely have their gripes, most seem to appreciate the quality and, not least, the value of the education they are getting. The students we heard from seem particularly pleased with the people who, in large part, determine the quality of anyone's law school experience: their instructors and fellow students. "The school has really attracted a fine collection of individuals," was the opinion of one student whose assessment was quite typical: "excellent faculty, great school." You would be hard-pressed to find any law school whose students are unanimous in their praise for their professors, and Illinois is no exception. But inevitable complaints of uneven teaching abilities notwithstanding, most seem to share this feeling expressed by one 1L: "I came here for the faculty and I have not been disappointed." Most also agree that, as rigorous as their program is, competitiveness does not get the better of most students. "Students here aren't terribly competitive in the cutthroat sense," reported one 3L, "but everyone wants to perform well, so there is a moderate amount of competition."

A large proportion of students expressed real dissatisfaction with the law school's practical-skills programs and called for a greater emphasis on clinical training. Since we surveyed, however, the school has opened a new Civil Clinic in which 50 students will be able to participate every year. They also offer numerous courses in practical lawyering, including the popular trial advocacy course, taken by over half the student body. If all complaints are attended to as these were and earlier ones regarding facilities have been (Illinois completed massive renovations, including an addition to the law building, several years ago), then future students may well need to utilize all their research skills to find cause for criticism.

ADMISSIONS

Like all the nation's elite public law schools, the University of Illinois College of Law is fairly flooded with applications from highly qualified bargain hunters. Indeed, more than 10 applicants vie annually for each spot in the law school's entering class of about 200. Thankfully for the prospective Illinois student, the law school's overall acceptance rate is relatively generous.

ACADEMICS

Student/faculty ratio	22:1
% female faculty	25
% minority faculty	6
Hours of study per day	3.58

FINANCIAL FACTS

In-state tuition	$5,750
Out-of-state tuition	$15,343
Part-time tuition per credit	NR
Estimated books/expenses/fees	$1,740
On-campus living expenses	NR
Off-campus living expenses	NR
% first-year students receiving aid	NR
% all students receiving aid	NR
% aid that is merit-based	NR
% all students receiving grants/scholarships	17
% all students receiving loans	66
% all students receiving assistantships	4
Average award package	$7,908
Average graduation debt	$23,113

ADMISSIONS

# applications received	2,196
% applicants accepted	27
% acceptees attending	36
Average LSAT	160
Average undergrad GPA	3.41
Application Fee	$40
No early decision program	
Regular application deadline	March 15
Regular notification	NR
Admission deferment	NR
Gourman Report Rating	**4.33**

INDIANA UNIVERSITY, BLOOMINGTON 💾
School of Law

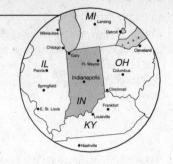

There is very little on the prospective law student's shopping list that the Indiana University, Bloomington School of Law lacks. Its curriculum is broad and up-to-date, its faculty is large, and its academic resources are vast. In an effort to better provide the practical-skills training more and more employers call for, IU recently added the Child Advocacy Clinic to its other clinical offerings—the Community Legal Clinic, Protective Order Project, Inmate Legal Assistance Clinic, and Federal Courts Clinic. Its tuition is low, and its location in the quintessential university town, set among the beautiful wooded hills of southern Indiana, is, by many people's standards, ideal. Founded more than 150 years ago on the campus of what is today one of the nation's largest universities, the inexpensive, midsize IU law school has long enjoyed a regional reputation for excellence. Over time, it has come to receive well-deserved recognition as one of the finest public law schools in the country.

Indiana law school's strengths are inseparable from those of the university itself. IU, with its highly esteemed graduate programs in business, English, medicine, music, psychology, and sociology, is an academic rising star, and its law school's interdisciplinary approach to legal education takes advantage of this. The IU Journal and program in global legal studies exist to facilitate law-related research in various disciplines, and concurrent enrollment between the law school and the schools of business administration, public affairs, and environmental sciences is common. Like most of the nation's top public law schools, Indiana has experienced a dramatic increase in applications volume in recent years. As a result the admissions process is quite competitive. IU students, the majority of whom are residents of Indiana or nearby states, possess strong numerical credentials.

Typical assessments of the law school's strengths by students went something like this: "Faculty are highly reputable, facilities are great and quality of fellow students is high"; "Good faculty/ student relationships, tremendous academic environment"; "Good, available, concerned faculty—a tremendous academic environment." Those comments from, respectively, a 3L and two

Frank Motley, Assistant Dean for Admissions
3rd Street and Indiana Avenue, Bloomington, IN 47405
Tel: (812) 855-4765
eMail: lawdean@indiana.edu
Internet: http://www.law/indiana.edu/

Indiana University, Bloomington

2Ls were echoed by many 1Ls in the midst of a very demanding first year program: "Some of the faculty are outstanding, and there is a very pleasant atmosphere at the school," wrote one.

Almost unanimously, Indiana students praised the scholarship of their professors and pointed out that some of them were also excellent instructors. We did hear, however, from a sizable group of students who were dissatisfied with the inconsistency of the faculty's teaching abilities. Nearly every complimentary statement regarding the faculty, in fact, began with the qualifier "some." The angrier comments on this matter—of which there were more than a few—were balanced by a greater number of candid, evenhanded assessments. "They really do need to improve the teaching," said one 3L. "The law school has some very good teachers but offsets that strength with some who are very sub-par." More widely scattered complaints came from conservative members of Indiana's politically diverse student body about the alleged liberal bias of the faculty: "The faculty is very nearly homogeneous in terms of political bent and outlook," said one. "It ranges only from centrist to far left," agreed another.

Finally, it must be mentioned that Indiana students speak clearly and with one voice when it comes to the quality of their facilities and the pleasantness of their surroundings. Few students from any other schools we surveyed were as unanimously enthusiastic on this count as were students at IU, whose overall sense of well-being seems quite strong.

ADMISSIONS

Considering the University of Indiana's widely acknowledged status as one of the finest public law schools in the country, it should not be surprising to hear that the qualifications of its students are higher than those of students at 135 of the nation's 175 fully accredited law schools. Almost 1,800 candidates vie annually for spots in the law school's entering class of about 200, and successful candidates possess strong numerical credentials: Their average GPA is a rock-solid 3.36 and their median LSAT score of 158 put them at the 80th percentile.

ACADEMICS

Student/faculty ratio	18:1
% female faculty	31
% minority faculty	4
Hours of study per day	3.79

FINANCIAL FACTS

In-state tuition	$4,926
Out-of-state tuition	$12,990
Part-time tuition per credit	NR
Estimated books/expenses/fees	NR
On-campus living expenses	NR
Off-campus living expenses	NR
% first-year students receiving aid	30
% all students receiving aid	83
% aid that is merit-based	9
% all students receiving grants/scholarships	34
% all students receiving loans	83
% all students receiving assistantships	10
Average award package	$3,400
Average graduation debt	$40,000

ADMISSIONS

# applications received	1,773
% applicants accepted	39
% acceptees attending	30
Average LSAT	158
Average undergrad GPA	3.36
Application Fee	$35
No early decision program	
Regular application deadline	rolling
Regular notification	rolling
Admission deferment	one year
Gourman Report Rating	**4.41**

Indiana University, Indianapolis 🖫

School of Law

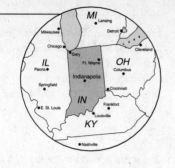

OVERVIEW

Type of school	public
Environment	NR
Scholastic calendar	NR
Schedule	Full-time or part-time

STUDENTS

Enrollment of institution	NR
Enrollment of law school	830
% male/female	52/48
% out-of-state	16
% part-time	30
% minorities	13
% international (# countries represented)	NR (7)
Average age at entry	27

APPLICANTS ALSO LOOK AT

Indiana University, Bloomington
Valparaiso University
University of Dayton
University of Louisville
University of Notre Dame

SURVEY SAYS...

HITS
Clinical experience
Faculty representation
Broad range of courses

MISSES
Library staff
Studying
Research resources

EMPLOYMENT PROFILE

% grads employed immediately	NR
% grads employed within six months	92
Average starting salary	$43,650
% grads employed by field:	
Private practice	53
Business/industry	22
Government	18
Judicial clerkships	6
Academic	1
Military	2

Indiana University School of Law students we surveyed displayed pride for their chosen school, like this happy future lawyer: "This school is the best value for the money of any school in the country," thanks to "The location, availability of local attorneys, and the accessibility of the faculty." One 2L praised the school's "clinical opportunities, practical skills emphasis and outstanding faculty closely tied to the development of the laws and policies of Indiana."

Located near downtown Indianapolis, the nation's twelfth-largest city and twentieth-largest legal-job market, IU School of Law is Indiana's largest law school in terms of overall enrollment. It attracts a student body that is quite a bit older than both the national average and the average at the state's other public law school on Indiana University's Bloomington campus. Tuition for state residents is quite low, and the higher rate for nonresidents (who face an uphill climb in achieving resident status) is quite reasonable. The law school receives only a moderate number of applications, so the overall acceptance rate is relatively high. Accepted students, however, tend to possess very strong numerical credentials.

At the disposal of IU-Indianapolis's students are the significant resources of both the broader university and the city itself. On campus, students can pursue joint degrees in business, public affairs, and health administration through IU's Schools of Business and Public and Environmental Affairs. Through its Center for Law and Health, the law school offers training in a field of growing national importance. Off campus, the institutions of the state capital are mere blocks away, affording IU-Indianapolis students ample opportunities for both research and employment. Those who came to IU-Indianapolis for the evening program or access to the state capital's jobs and externships were very satisfied with the opportunities this strongly regional school affords. Several praised the extensive clerkship possibilities. But don't make the mistake of thinking that IU-Indianapolis is entirely a regional school; one 3L told us the "Summer China program is excellent—and the school and Indianapolis law firms are developing significant ties and contacts within China." In the summer

Angela Espada, Assistant Dean for Admissions
735 West New York Street, Indianapolis, IN 46202
Tel: (317) 274-2459
eMail: amespada@indyvax.iupui.edu
Internet: http://www.iupui.edu/it/iuilaw/iuilaw.html

of 1997, the school will be beginning a foreign program in Lille, France.

Students were very happy with their excellent teaching staff. One 3L wrote in his questionnaire that IU-Indianapolis has that surprising combination, "Professors who are both highly respected in their field and are good teachers." Student opinion swung far and wide regarding faculty and student diversity; many called for increased minority hiring, while a few men complained that minority and/or female students siphon off some of the attention due the general student body. Some students complained about aspects of their legal education such as the outcome-based legal writing program.

Critical students mentioned that the entire facility, including the library, needs serious attention. One 3L summed up his problems with the school in one word, "Aesthetics." However, a new law school building is being planned as we write, and groundbreaking is expected in 1997. Future students, get your shovels ready.

Certainly many students are anxious over their futures and distressed by intense competition between students for grades and employment opportunities. However, if it's true, as numerous students declared, that IU-Indy has a "monopoly" on jobs in Indianapolis, then their anxiety should be for naught.

ADMISSIONS

Statistics for that era are hard to come by, but if admissions standards at the Indiana University School of Law, Indianapolis were as high in the early seventies as they are now, then Dan Quayle—the law school's most prominent alumnus—can't be nearly as dumb as his critics would like to believe. Indeed, the numerical credentials of the average IU-Indy student are higher than those of students at nearly 40 percent of all American law schools. Statistically, an applicant with an undergraduate GPA between 3.00 and 3.25 and an LSAT score between 150 and 154, inclusive, stands only a 13 percent chance of getting in.

ACADEMICS

Student/faculty ratio	17:1
% female faculty	28
% minority faculty	6
Hours of study per day	2.93

FINANCIAL FACTS

In-state tuition	$5,110
Out-of-state tuition	$13,020
Part-time tuition per credit	NR
Estimated books/expenses/fees	$580
On-campus living expenses	NR
Off-campus living expenses	NR
% first-year students receiving aid	NR
% all students receiving aid	NR
% aid that is merit-based	NR
% all students receiving grants/scholarships	40
% all students receiving loans	61
% all students receiving assistantships	NR
Average award package	$4,500
Average graduation debt	$44,000

ADMISSIONS

# applications received	1,206
% applicants accepted	39
% acceptees attending	53
Average LSAT	157
Average undergrad GPA	3.30
Application Fee	$35
No early decision program	
Regular application deadline	March 1
Regular notification	rolling
Admission deferment	one year
Gourman Report Rating	3.15

UNIVERSITY OF IOWA 🖫
College of Law

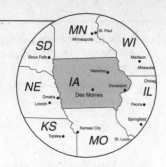

OVERVIEW

Type of school	public
Environment	suburban
Scholastic calendar	semester
Schedule	Full time only

STUDENTS

Enrollment of institution	25,778
Enrollment of law school	682
% male/female	58/42
% out-of-state	32
% part-time	NR
% minorities	21
% international (# countries represented)	5 (12)
Average age at entry	26

APPLICANTS ALSO LOOK AT

University of Minnesota
University of Michigan
University of Illinois
Northwestern University
University of Notre Dame

SURVEY SAYS...

HITS
Great facilities
Research resources
Legal writing

MISSES
Lack of paid clerkship opportunities
Strongest placement is regional
Cold winters

EMPLOYMENT PROFILE

% grads employed immediately	65
% grads employed within six months	95
Average starting salary	$44,000
% grads employed by field:	
Private practice	54
Business/industry	8
Government	11
Judicial clerkships	17
Public service	5
Academic	2
Military	6

Located on the Iowa City campus of its parent institution, one of the largest and best-funded state-supported universities in the nation, this inexpensive, midsize law school has long enjoyed a reputation for academic excellence that extends well beyond the borders of its home state. Indeed, while the University of Iowa College of Law draws the majority of its students from within the state, it boasts features that draw students from all over, and enrolled students at Iowa are an enormously well-qualified group. The course of study at the law school is notable for its overall strength and for its breadth. The relative size of Iowa's faculty makes possible the broad range of course offerings and lends the school, by all reports, an intimate academic atmosphere. (In fact, Iowa has one of the most favorable student-faculty ratios in the country.) The Iowa J.D. program is also notable for its emphasis on practical skill in general and legal writing in particular. The law school's clinic is relatively large and well-staffed, and its writing requirements are extensive.

Iowa students offer much praise for their chosen school, and one factor seems to outweigh all others in their assessments: value. Asked to name her school's greatest strengths, one student offered this unsurprising evaluation: "Tuition is low, rank is high." But while all of the country's leading public law schools (Iowa included) are relatively cheap, some appear to cut corners in areas that matter a great deal to law students. Complaints about substandard facilities, Byzantine bureaucracies and limited course offerings are not uncommon among students at some large state-supported schools. They are virtually nonexistent, however, among the law students we surveyed at the University of Iowa. "The facilities here (especially the Writing Resource Center) are all excellent," wrote one 1L. "Any cost/benefit analysis you might do weighs heavily in favor of the student." In most of the positive remarks we heard, the "tremendous, conscientious" Iowa faculty was singled out for praise. As another 1L wrote, "The professors here are great teachers as well as scholars...The atmosphere in classes is challenging and stimulating without being threatening and dehumanizing." "Our professors teach very well," added a typical 2L, "and they show a real concern for

Camille deJorna, Director of Admissions
Melrose at Byington Streets, Iowa City, IA 52242
Tel: (319) 335-9071   Fax: (319) 335-9019

individual students." In short, "You are not just a social security number here."

Indeed, the Iowa students we heard from gave their school very good marks on student-faculty relations and agreed that there was a strong sense of community among their fellow students. It should be noted, however, that they also ranked their school among the most competitive in the nation. Few complained loudly about this fact, though nearly all saw fit to mention it as a less-than-desirable side effect of Iowa's demanding academic program. When asked to specify how they would like to see that program improved, many students sounded a similar note. "I would like to see a greater emphasis placed on preparing students for the daily demands of law practice," wrote one 3L, "even if it means de-emphasizing the things we already do well, like scholarly writing and appellate advocacy." Many others agreed, citing the "absence of strong programs in Alternative Dispute Resolution, client counseling, etc.," and the perceived lack of opportunities to participate in the law school's existing clinical programs as Iowa's greatest academic deficiencies. That this sort of constructive criticism typified the "negative" remarks we heard from Iowa students speaks volumes. Even if, as one put it, "it floods in the summer and snows perpetually in the bitterly cold winter here," most Iowa students seem to share the sentiment of the 3L who wrote that she "would not trade my Iowa J.D. for one from Harvard or Yale (I really mean this)."

ADMISSIONS

As one of the nation's finest and least expensive law schools, the University of Iowa College of Law is selective. The numerical credentials of the Iowa student body rank it among the 50 most qualified in the entire nation.

ACADEMICS

Student/faculty ratio	14:1
% female faculty	26
% minority faculty	14
Hours of study per day	4.47

FINANCIAL FACTS

In-state tuition	$5,166
Out-of-state tuition	$14,020
Part-time tuition per credit	NR
Estimated books/expenses/fees	$1,428
On-campus living expenses	NR
Off-campus living expenses	NR
% first-year students receiving aid	100
% all students receiving aid	100
% aid that is merit-based	3
% all students receiving grants/scholarships	35
% all students receiving loans	74
% all students receiving assistantships	9
Average award package	$8,156
Average graduation debt	$32,652

ADMISSIONS

# applications received	1,564
% applicants accepted	31
% acceptees attending	45
Average LSAT	158
Average undergrad GPA	3.38
Application Fee	$20
No early decision program	
Regular application deadline	March 1
Regular notification	rolling
Admission deferment	one year
Gourman Report Rating	**4.50**

THE JOHN MARSHALL LAW SCHOOL

If Chicago is the "city of big shoulders," as Carl Sandburg once remarked, the shoulders of the John Marshall Law School are enormous. With more than 1,100 students, John Marshall weighs in as one of the largest law schools in the city of Chicago and the state of Illinois. Indeed, this law school, named for the estimable Chief Justice of the United States Supreme Court (1801-1835), is one of the biggest in the country, graduating close to 400 students (a substantial number of them Illinois natives) each year.

Through the operation of its centers for international law (with programs in China, the Czech Republic, and Ireland), real estate law, fair housing, trial advocacy, intellectual property law, and informatics (information and communications technologies) law, John Marshall endeavors to educate working lawyers in burgeoning legal sub-fields and to involve itself in the development of the law in these areas. Access to the resources of these centers is not limited to practicing attorneys. John Marshall students can take courses and participate in many special programs offered by the centers. Students may even choose an official degree concentration in informatics, intellectual property, advocacy and dispute resolution, business, estate planning, international law, and real estate.

Though John Marshall is one of a small number of law schools that allows for specialization at the J.D. level, the most of its students follows a more traditional course of study. The variety of courses from which these students have to choose is commensurate with the law school's size, and a vast array of co-curricular programs supplements the standard classroom fare, including extensive moot court competitions and externship programs. The school also operates a Fair Housing Clinic. John Marshall's solid program is well respected in the sizable legal community of Chicago, where thousands of the law school's graduates form an alumni network that represents an invaluable resource to current students preparing to enter the job market.

That market is, without a doubt, the focus of attention for most students at John Marshall, whose positive reviews of their chosen school tend to revolve around the direct effect their education will have on their professional futures. "This is a friendly, hard-working place that's well-connected for local clerkships and jobs in various legal fields," said one student. "The practical experience it gives is the law school's greatest strength," wrote another. "The program really concentrates on how to teach you to be a good lawyer in Chicago." The program he refers to is also, by most reports, quite rigorous. "The curriculum is very challenging," remarked a 1L, "and the teachers expect a lot from you, which helps us to think on our toes." Though perhaps not consciously, the wording of that last remark makes clever reference to the hypertraditional classroom style of many John Marshall instructors. As one student said: "Profs here work you hard and make you stand to recite answers in class, but they are largely good-natured and extremely competent."

It must be noted, however, that a significant proportion of the students we heard from expressed far less enthusiasm for their instructors. A 2L offered one of the milder remarks: "The professors need to set their egos aside and start pulling in the same direction." Many others had bigger complaints, deploring the "general attitude of faculty and staff towards students." "They could stop treating us as subhuman," wrote one student who was not the most extreme of the discontents we heard from. "We are paying them!" Many students expressed a fear that their school gets lost in the shadow of the smaller, more traditionally higher-rated schools. They worry about John Marshall's "inability to compete with the other law schools in the city of Chicago."

As unfortunate as it is that any student at John Marshall should be so negative about aspects of his law school experience, even the most disaffected expressed fundamental satisfaction with the training they receive. As one student who had her share of complaints put it, "They do crank out very practical lawyers with great writing, speaking, and trial skills."

ADMISSIONS

Although it is the least selective of the six law schools in Chicago, the John Marshall Law School is no sure thing for applicants whose numbers aren't decent. This is quite common at law schools that enroll a student body of diverse background and age. (The average age of incoming John Marshall students is 26.)

ACADEMICS

Student/faculty ratio	18:1
% female faculty	30
% minority faculty	7
Hours of study per day	4.15

FINANCIAL FACTS

Tuition	$16,950
Part-time tuition per credit	$565
Estimated books/expenses/fees	$470
On-campus living expenses	NR
Off-campus living expenses	NR
% first-year students receiving aid	70
% all students receiving aid	70
% aid that is merit-based	3
% all students receiving grants/scholarships	13
% all students receiving loans	67
% all students receiving assistantships	NR
Average award package	$17,380
Average graduation debt	$52,140

ADMISSIONS

# applications received	1,627
% applicants accepted	NR
% acceptees attending	19
Average LSAT	150
Average undergrad GPA	2.99
Application Fee	$50
Priority application deadline	October 1
Priority notification	NR
Regular application deadline	April 1
Regular notification	April 1
Admission deferment	1 semester
Gourman Report Rating	**3.08**

UNIVERSITY OF KANSAS 💾
School of Law

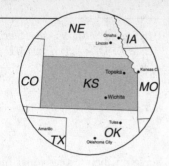

OVERVIEW

Type of school	public
Environment	suburban
Scholastic calendar	semester
Schedule	Full time only

STUDENTS

Enrollment of institution	28,000
Enrollment of law school	498
% male/female	60/40
% out-of-state	17
% part-time	NR
% minorities	13
% international (# countries represented)	NR (2)
Average age at entry	24

APPLICANTS ALSO LOOK AT

Washburn University
U. of Missouri, Columbia
U. of Missouri, Kansas City
University of Iowa
University of Colorado

SURVEY SAYS...

HITS
Intellectual challenge
Clinical experience

MISSES
Students feel poorly prepared
Faculty-student relations

EMPLOYMENT PROFILE

% grads employed immediately	76
% grads employed within six months	85
Average starting salary	$53,000
% grads employed by field:	
Private practice	60
Business/industry	12
Government	12
Judicial clerkships	9
Academic	7
Military	3

Among the advantages of residence in the Plains states is cheap and easy access to some of the nation's finest institutions of higher education. Kansas is no exception when it comes to the size and quality of its flagship public university. With 28,000 students and nearly 2,000 faculty members, the highly respected University of Kansas is one of the nation's largest comprehensive universities, and its midsize School of Law is one of the best in the region. The law school, which entered its second century in 1993, has long enjoyed a solid reputation in the professional and academic legal communities, a reputation that today derives in large part from the excellence of its 25-member faculty.

Current students had no problem defining those attributes that make KU such a good regional law school: the incredible price and their capable teachers. "Faculty! Faculty! Faculty!—the faculty is open and friendly and they make an effort to be available for students," cheered one 1L. Although many complained about the inconsistency of their teachers' abilities, most were extremely impressed by the quality of those teachers they liked.

The course of study that this faculty administers is notable not so much for any innovations as for its sheer strength within traditional bounds. The breadth of course offerings at Kansas is necessarily limited by the size of its faculty, and its clinical program, while broad in scope, is limited in size. Still, a wide range of joint-degree programs with various well-respected departments in the broader university's graduate division provides numerous opportunities for Kansas students to diversify their academic experiences.

Several students praised the tax and commercial law programs and the school's commitment to bestowing not only theoretical tools, but a strong ethical tradition. One 2L expressed gratitude that his pessimistic expectations of law school went unmet at Kansas: "The faculty expect you to behave like a professional...The faculty are not interested in intimidating or humiliating students...Ethical behavior is something you are expected to consider the moment you enter this program."

Diane Lindeman, Director of Admissions
15th and Burdick Drive, Lawrence, KS 66045
Tel: (913) 864-4378
eMail: lindeman@law.wpo.ukans.edu
Internet: http://www.lark.cc.ukans.edu/~kalaw/index.html

The happiest students we heard from were those particularly comfortable in a conservative Midwestern atmosphere. One current 1L gave his sound and simple reasons for feeling so content: "We are a healthy community, offering a Midwestern relaxed and yet urban environment with a good entertainment district, good shopping, and close proximity to Kansas City—America's best-kept secret."

Dissatisfaction was high among students approaching moving out of law school into the unfriendly legal market. As at many other schools, we heard a great deal of criticism focused on the career services department. One scared 3L told us, "The current placement director is only of help if you are in the top 25 percent of the class. That leaves the remaining 75 percent of us out in the cold." The resulting intense competition and its attendant chill on student relations sparked many students' ire. However, the career services director referred to retired in mid-1996, so student comments might be far different in our next survey.

Besides these standard gripes in the age of a downsized legal economy, there were also substantial (and some not so substantial) criticisms that the school may have more power to change, like increasing the number of practical skills courses and providing a smoking lounge. One uncommonly perturbed 3L told us. "Much of what I've learned in law school isn't practical. Nothing that I've learned in law school was helpful or even applicable to the clerking that I've done over the summer." We heard repeated cries to diversify hiring and enrollment. A 1L offered a simple three-pronged solution to make the school a more perfect place by bringing in "more computers, more clinical programs, more chicks." From his mouth to the Dean's ears.

ADMISSIONS

Like every excellent public law school, the University of Kansas School of Law is swamped with applications from highly qualified prospective law students. Okay, 803 applications isn't quite a swamp, but it's all relative. With a first-year class of only about 170, Kansas must deny admission to the majority of applicants. Indeed, its numerical admissions standards rank Kansas among the fifty most selective law schools in the nation.

ACADEMICS	
Student/faculty ratio	20:1
% female faculty	25
% minority faculty	12
Hours of study per day	3.74

FINANCIAL FACTS	
In-state tuition	$4,154
Out-of-state tuition	$10,819
Part-time tuition per credit	NR
Estimated books/expenses/fees	NR
On-campus living expenses	NR
Off-campus living expenses	NR
% first-year students receiving aid	74
% all students receiving aid	76
% aid that is merit-based	NR
% all students receiving grants/scholarships	34
% all students receiving loans	73
% all students receiving assistantships	7
Average award package	$8,500
Average graduation debt	$25,000

ADMISSIONS	
# applications received	803
% applicants accepted	43
% acceptees attending	48
Average LSAT	158
Average undergrad GPA	3.39
Application Fee	$40
No early decision program	
Regular application deadline	March 15
Regular notification	rolling
Admission may be deferred?	No
Gourman Report Rating	3.71

UNIVERSITY OF KENTUCKY 💾
College of Law

OVERVIEW

Type of school	public
Environment	city
Scholastic calendar	semester
Schedule	full time only

STUDENTS

Enrollment of institution	22,731
Enrollment of law school	435
% male/female	66/34
% out-of-state	14
% part-time	NR
% minorities	8
% international (# countries represented)	NR (2)
Average age at entry	25

APPLICANTS ALSO LOOK AT

University of Louisville
Vanderbilt University
Northern Kentucky University
University of Cincinnati
University of Tennessee

SURVEY SAYS...

HITS
Socratic Method

MISSES
Clinical experience
Practical lawyering skills
Legal writing

EMPLOYMENT PROFILE

% grads employed immediately	50
% grads employed within six months	92
Average starting salary	$32,000
% grads employed by field:	
Private practice	66
Business/industry	6
Government	10
Judicial clerkships	14
Public service	1
Academic	1
Military	6

Lexington, a charming city of 250,000 in the heart of the Bluegrass region of central Kentucky, is surrounded by some of the nation's most beautiful horse country and some of the world's most famous thoroughbred farms. At the city's center is one of the region's finest training facilities for two-legged creatures, the University of Kentucky College of Law. Established in 1908, this midsize public law school enjoys an unshakable reputation for excellence within Kentucky and the broader Ohio Valley area, where the vast majority of the law school's graduates choose to practice, and certainly thrive—the overall placement rate is higher than average and alumni hold such positions as Chief Justice of the State Supreme Court, Attorney General, and Secretary of State of Kentucky.

Kentucky students follow a traditional course of study, fully prescribed in the first year and almost completely elective in the second and third. The range of courses from which they may choose is fairly broad, but non-classroom offerings are somewhat limited. The law school sponsors various externship programs and extra-curricular such as VITA, the Volunteer Income Tax Assistance program, the *Kentucky Law Journal*, and the *Journal of Natural Resources and Environmental Law*: "a multi-disciplinary, refereed journal published twice a year by the University of Kentucky Mineral Law Center," which is itself a vital resource for students and attorneys regarding coal mining and other natural resource issues. The school is in the process of establishing the University of Kentucky Elder Law Clinic, a joint effort of the law school and UK's Sanders-Brown Center on Aging. Competition for spots in Kentucky's first-year class of about 160 has increased enormously since 1986: Applications volume has grown by more than 250 percent, and the overall acceptance rate has plummeted from 61 percent to under 30 percent.

Students we heard from at UK were not among the happiest groups we surveyed. While their new and very popular dean could very well improve the situation, students we heard from had quite a few complaints. They blamed their discontent on the sense of constriction they felt at UK, in their curriculum, the student body, and their professional options. They beseeched UK

Drusilla V. Bakert, Associate Dean
209 Law Building, Lexington, KY 40506-0048
Tel: (606) 257-1678
eMail: dbakert@pop.uky.edu
Internet: http://www.uky.edu/law/welcome.html

to "explore creative teaching methods!", increase "'real world' work experience" options, place "more emphasis on [the] writing program," and, "Expand the curriculum!", because "No classes are taught in emerging areas like computer law, law and technology or telecommunications law." Several students warned that if one is not devoted to tax law or legal accounting, UK can be what one called "snoozeville." One student pointed out that UK needs a "better curriculum which will encourage broad and diverse thinking and reasoning." It seems that such a curriculum might attract more female and minority applicants. One student said that the administration must improve the "admission and treatment of women students" to prove the school's commitment to its female students. For those who plan to attend, regardless of gender, they should be sure they love the bluegrass state, because, as one 3L told us, "Being a regional school, employment opportunities are largely limited to Kentucky."

That particular "limitation" is a world of opportunity for many. As one 2L said, the "job market in Lexington is excellent" for UK grads, and another student added, "UK College of Law is considered a major stepping stone for those who want to pursue a career in Kentucky politics." At the same time, the school's small size gives it a cozy air and "allows for close relationships between student and faculty." Many students vouched for the excellent education to be had at UK, soon to improve thanks to the Dean. One student proclaimed, "I have clerked with law students from Vanderbilt, Harvard, Duke, Indiana, Emory, and NYU, and I contend that UK prepares its students just as well or better than these 'highly rated' schools."

ADMISSIONS

The dramatic decline in the acceptance rate at the University of Kentucky College of Law between 1986 and 1992 raised the law school's numerical admission standards just as dramatically. Today, the average numerical credentials of the Kentucky student body rank it among the 60 best-qualified in the nation.

ACADEMICS

Student/faculty ratio	16:1
% female faculty	34
% minority faculty	12
Hours of study per day	3.60

FINANCIAL FACTS

In-state tuition	$4,440
Out-of-state tuition	$12,040
Part-time tuition per credit	NR
Estimated books/expenses/fees	$1,134
On-campus living expenses	NR
Off-campus living expenses	NR
% first-year students receiving aid	NR
% all students receiving aid	NR
% aid that is merit-based	NR
% all students receiving grants/scholarships	31
% all students receiving loans	69
% all students receiving assistantships	NR
Average award package	$2,474
Average graduation debt	$36,000

ADMISSIONS

# applications received	1,053
% applicants accepted	34
% acceptees attending	42
Average LSAT	159
Average undergrad GPA	3.23
Application Fee	$25
No early decision program	
Regular application deadline	March 1
Regular notification	rolling
Admission deferment	one year
Gourman Report Rating	**3.26**

LEWIS AND CLARK COLLEGE
Northwestern School of Law

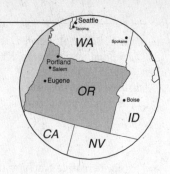

A longtime fixture in the legal community of the Pacific Northwest, the Northwestern School of Law at Lewis and Clark College has experienced a meteoric rise to national prominence in the last decade, thanks in large part to the strength of its program in environmental and natural resources law, for which it ranks at the very top. The law school offers an LL.M. program for graduate law students and a formal certificate of specialization in this popular and growing field for J.D. candidates.

The curriculum is not all that's growing around the Lewis and Clark campus. Though it is located only a few minutes from thriving downtown Portland, the law school is abutted by a 600-acre woodland park. Perhaps because of all the oxygen in the air, the atmosphere at Lewis and Clark is, by all reports, phenomenally congenial. Cutthroat competition among enrolled students here appears to be reserved for the softball field, but competition to be among these students has grown increasingly fierce as national awareness of and respect for Lewis and Clark have increased. Just how popular has this midsize private law school become? Consider this: Less than ten years ago, Lewis and Clark admitted fully 77 percent of all applicants. Sometime between then and now, things hit critical mass. Applications volume increased by 284 percent, more than any law school in the same period. Consequently, numerical admissions standards jumped, with the average LSAT score of entering students up an astonishing 23 percentage points.

Ask students at Lewis and Clark to name the greatest strengths of their chosen school, and you open a floodgate. Though certainly not without their criticisms, the students we heard from expressed a very high degree of satisfaction with their experience at the law school. And though many praised the substance of Lewis and Clark's academic program, their remarks often focused on the quality of the human relations among students, between students and faculty and, notably, among students, faculty, and administrators. "There's a very laid-back, family-type atmosphere here," reported a 1L. "Students are serious, but not overly competitive." "We have a uniquely wonderful faculty," added another, "they strongly support students." Another 1L offered this praise for the law school's administration: "Lewis and Clark has the great advantage of encouraging active student involvement and allowing students to initiate change within the school. This applies to the curriculum, extracurricular activities and school policies." Indeed, many of his fellow students agreed on whom to credit for the school's "humane environment and strong sense of community." "Care is given by faculty and administration," said one 3L, "to help each student succeed."

When asked to name areas in which the school could stand to improve, the various responses of Lewis and Clark students would mostly fit under the broader heading of diversity—ethnic, political, and curricular. "As a Portlander," commented one, "I was happy to see that the school draws students from all over the country. But the city and the school are still sort of white bread." Another warned more caustically: "If you're an ultra-left, crunchy granola Birkenstocker—stay away! I want a diverse campus at my law school!" Whether it pleases them or not, nearly all seem to agree with the facts of the situation as described by this 1L: "We are the 'environmental school' so you'd expect to attract a disproportionate amount of treehuggers." Rush Limbaugh devotees, be forewarned. Many students also offered more substantive criticisms of the Lewis and Clark program. "The environmental program is great," allowed one 2L, "but there simply aren't enough sections of popular classes, so scheduling can be a nightmare." On balance, however, few students here would quarrel with this overall assessment from this happy 1L: "Largely because of the great people and great faculty here, I've been very pleased with my decision to attend Lewis and Clark."

ADMISSIONS

The astonishing increase in applications volume at Lewis and Clark between 1986 and the present pushed numerical admissions standards at the law school into the stratosphere. As it stands today, the average numerical credentials of the Lewis and Clark student body rank it among the 60 most highly qualified in the entire nation. The law school admits few outside a relatively narrow range of grade point averages and test scores.

ACADEMICS

Student/faculty ratio	18:1
% female faculty	26
% minority faculty	3
Hours of study per day	4.15

FINANCIAL FACTS

Tuition	$14,740
Part-time tuition per credit	NR
Estimated books/expenses/fees	NR
On-campus living expenses	NR
Off-campus living expenses	NR
% first-year students receiving aid	NR
% all students receiving aid	NR
% aid that is merit-based	NR
% all students receiving grants/scholarships	NR
% all students receiving loans	NR
% all students receiving assistantships	NR
Average award package	NR
Average graduation debt	NR

ADMISSIONS

# applications received	2,470
% applicants accepted	37
% acceptees attending	25
Average LSAT	160
Average undergrad GPA	3.27
Application Fee	$45
Priority application deadline	NR
Priority notification	NR
Regular application deadline	March 15
Regular notification	NR
Admission deferment	NR
Gourman Report Rating	**3.17**

LOUISIANA STATE UNIVERSITY
Paul M. Hebert Law Center

The Louisiana State University Law Center is a midsize public law school in close proximity to the offices of the state government in Baton Rouge. Founded in 1906, the law school has been providing a solid, inexpensive legal education to Louisiana residents as long as any school in the state. Like all the state's law schools, LSU must cover both Louisiana's civil law and the common law of the other 49 states. Unlike some Louisiana schools, however, LSU does not deal with the divergent systems separately. Instead, the law school has configured most courses so that the subject matter they address is considered within both contexts. This approach has its advantages. Because the Roman Law doctrine of the Napoleonic Code of France and Las Siete Partidas of Spain form the cornerstone of Louisiana law and that of many other countries, such as Canada, Japan, Thailand, the Philippines, Turkey, and much of Europe and Latin America, LSU is somewhat justified in regarding its entire curriculum as a course of study in comparative law. Some added bonuses available thanks to this focus on international law are a summer study program at the University of Aix-Marseille III Law School at Aix-en Provence, France, and the master of Civil Law (M.C.L.) option.

LSU offers a unique and useful program even for the future lawyer who does not plan to practice in Louisiana. Be that as it may, most LSU students do choose to remain in the state after completing their degrees. Applications volume at LSU has risen significantly in recent years, but the overall selectivity of the admissions process remains moderate.

According to the admissions brochure, the faculty is a strong suit of LSU Law Center. Says the brochure: *"The Journal of Legal Education* recently reported that the LSU law faculty ranked second out of 68 schools of similar size in the quality of published works. When compared to the 169 law schools approved by the American Bar Association, the Law Center was listed as tenth in the nation. The quality of faculty writings, according to the Journal of Jurimetrics, has been displayed by consistent citation of LSU faculty work in reported cases throughout the country, in other journals and books, and by the ranking of the *Louisiana Law Review* as one of the top 15 law reviews in the United States."

LSU requires 97 hours of credit for graduation, "one of the highest and most demanding curriculums in the nation," according to their own publication, and class attendance and daily preparation are mandatory for every one of those credit hours. All second-year students not on Law Review are required to participate in a year-long moot court case. "Grade inflation is unknown at LSU." The solid work ethic the school instills will hopefully make the long hours most students look forward to in private practice seem luxurious.

Overall, LSU Law Center offers a singular, strong education that prepares students for law practice in Louisiana and beyond.

ADMISSIONS

Happily for the prospective student, the Louisiana State University Law Center ranks in the bottom half of all law schools in terms of the numerical admission standards to which it holds applicants. But despite the law school's very generous overall acceptance rate of 46 percent, those applicants whose numbers aren't quite in line with the averages you see at right are not likely to be offered admission to LSU.

ACADEMICS

Student/faculty ratio	20:1
% female faculty	16
% minority faculty	7
Hours of study per day	3.97

FINANCIAL FACTS

In-state tuition	$3,922
Out-of-state tuition	$8,542
Part-time tuition per credit	NR
Estimated books/expenses/fees	NR
On-campus living expenses	NR
Off-campus living expenses	NR
% first-year students receiving aid	NR
% all students receiving aid	NR
% aid that is merit-based	NR
% all students receiving grants/scholarships	NR
% all students receiving loans	NR
% all students receiving assistantships	NR
Average award package	NR
Average graduation debt	NR

ADMISSIONS

# applications received	1,188
% applicants accepted	46
% acceptees attending	51
Average LSAT	153
Average undergrad GPA	3.32
Application Fee	$25
Priority application deadline	NR
Priority notification	NR
Regular application deadline	February 1
Regular notification	NR
Admission deferment	NR
Gourman Report Rating	**3.39**

UNIVERSITY OF LOUISVILLE 💾
School of Law

Founded in 1846, the University of Louisville School of Law is Kentucky's oldest law school and the nation's fifth oldest in continuous operation. As one might expect, tradition is definitely a watchword at this school and in this city, which has a decidedly more southern atmosphere than its geographic location might lead one to believe. The school is particularly proud of the legacy it inherited from former Supreme Court Justice Louis D. Brandeis. The esteemed jurist gave the university his personal library and also left a legacy of public service. The University of Louisville was one of the first law schools in the nation—and the only one in Kentucky—to institute a 30-hour pro bono requirement for all students. In fact, the school's Samuel L. Greenbaum Public Service Program has served as a model for many other ABA-accredited law schools who are interested in increasing their service to their communities. Over 1,100 prospective students, a large number of whom come from within Kentucky, apply to this small public law school, located in the state's largest city.

The vast majority of students surveyed made positive comments about the faculty and the environment at the school. "The professors take the time to help students understand material. Students are encouraged and assisted in getting the most out of their education. Office doors are always open and programs are abundant," praised one 2L. Another student, a 1L, put it this way: "If you want a law school that has students and faculty who exemplify southern hospitality, come to Louisville."

The school's focus on public interest received the most admiration from students. "The public service program is wonderful; students help those who can't afford legal services and the students receive the benefit of practical experience and hopefully a commitment to helping others in their practice." When discussing the strengths of the school, a 1L, noted that the pro-bono requirement allows students "to interact with [the] community and change the impression of lawyers."

Although many students cited pro bono work as a great opportunity to get hands-on training, it is evidently not enough. When asked how their school could improve, many students called for more practical, clinical experience in and out of the classroom. To

Charlene Taylor or Glenda Jackson, Admissions personnel
2301 South Third Street, Louisville, KY 40291
Tel: (502) 852-6364
eMail: jltorb01@ulkyvm.louisville.edu
Internet: http://www.louisville.edu/groups/lawwww/

University of Louisville

be fair, we must mention the administration's comments that "in addition to the pro bono program, the school offers six credit-generating internship programs...[and] opportunities for students to participate in ten national professional skills competition programs (an unusually large number for a small public school)." As for courses themselves, one 2L suggested, "More teachers need to employ the Socratic Method. More assignments that focus on hands-on experiences could be used." Students also called for an increased number of classes in general as well as more areas of specialization. However, the school already offers 123 courses, which the administration pointed out as "an extraordinary number for a small public school."

The school did garner a few other complaints from those we surveyed. A few participants in the school's part-time program were particularly displeased with Louisville. One student said the school needs to realize that "night students work in the day time [and should make] competitions, meetings, and informational speakers available during times they can attend." Another student agreed: "Evening students are not offered the range of extracurricular functions the day students enjoy. Nearly all of the special functions occur during the day." When it came to ethnic and racial diversity, many students called for better representation of minorities, who currently compose just under 10 percent of the student body and just over 10 percent of the faculty. The school's reasonable tuition and commitment to the public interest, along with a bar passage rate above the general average in Kentucky, however, keep many law school students at Louisville quite happy.

ADMISSIONS

A solid regional reputation and a bargain basement tuition make the University of Louisville School of Law's admissions process fairly competitive. While the numerical credentials of the average Louisville student are equal to or slightly higher than the national average, the overall acceptance rate at the law school, particularly for out-of-state applicants, is relatively low at 37 percent. Happily for the prospective Louisville student, the law school does admit applicants across a range of grade point averages and test scores.

ACADEMICS

Student/faculty ratio	20:1
% female faculty	29
% minority faculty	11
Hours of study per day	3.69

FINANCIAL FACTS

In-state tuition	$4,470
Out-of-state tuition	$11,820
Part-time tuition per credit	$224
Estimated books/expenses/fees	NR
On-campus living expenses	NR
Off-campus living expenses	NR
% first-year students receiving aid	65
% all students receiving aid	70
% aid that is merit-based	NR
% all students receiving grants/scholarships	27
% all students receiving loans	66
% all students receiving assistantships	5
Average award package	$2,514
Average graduation debt	$24,000

ADMISSIONS

# applications received	1,174
% applicants accepted	37
% acceptees attending	40
Average LSAT	156
Average undergrad GPA	3.10
Application Fee	$30
No early decision program	
Regular application deadline	February 15
Regular notification	rolling
Admission deferment	one year
Gourman Report Rating	**3.29**

LOYOLA MARYMOUNT UNIVERSITY
Loyola Law School

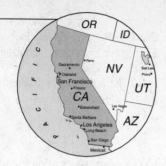

Loyola's recently completed expansion, designed by architect Frank O. Gehry, has radically transformed the previously nondescript downtown campus of California's largest law school into one of Los Angeles's many architecturally significant spaces. The new campus reflects Loyola's "energy and self confidence," according to the Dean, who calls the architecture "both provocative and congenial."

Loyola's admissions brochure describes a law school whose strong day and evening J.D. programs have earned it a well-deserved reputation in the L.A. legal community as a training ground for highly skilled practical attorneys. Loyola has always emphasized practical training: its traditional academic curriculum is supplemented by a number of well-run clinical programs and a highly-regarded trial advocacy program. The Externship Program, available to second- and third-year students, places them in judicial clerkships, public interest organizations, and government organizations. There is also an entertainment law practicum, which provides hands-on experience and has a required classroom component. While students appreciated the practical training, they had some critical comments for the legal research and writing courses, which they said should be integrated and improved. Effective for the 1997-98 academic year, these courses will be combined into one skills course.

All students matriculating after Fall 1994 must complete a mandatory public service requirement in order to graduate. Each student must contribute 40 hours of uncompensated supervised legal service to the disadvantaged in the community. The school hopes the experience will improve students' practical skills and impress upon them the need for lawyers to give back to society.

Overall, students are satisfied with the education they are getting at Loyola. Many respondents highlight their professors' practical knowledge. Said one, "Teachers know a lot about being a lawyer, as opposed to having only theoretical knowledge." Professors are not, commented another, "ivory tower academics." Professors are also very accessible and approachable. Loyola students believe they graduate ready to "hit the ground running." Many students praised the "sense of community" and "willingness to

919 South Albany Street, Los Angeles, CA 90015-0019
Tel: (213) 736-1180   Fax: (213) 736-6523
eMail: lawadmis@lmulaw.lmu.edu
Internet: http://www.law.lmu.edu

Loyola Marymount
University

help one another" although they said the competition was "intense." They called their classmates "wonderfully diverse."

On the negative side, some students criticize the administration as "unresponsive" and "obsessively image-conscious." According to one 3L, "The administration is openly mistrusted and maligned by students, and has earned at least part of its poor reputation." Specifically, a few say communication between students and the administration could be improved, and that student input should be heeded. Like law students nearly everywhere, Loyola students criticize the placement office, specifically the policy of charging firms to interview on campus and the focus on top-ranked students. In our last survey, students panned Loyola's facilities, especially the computer facilities and the library; however, since then, the school has improved its technological facilities, and now offers 45 general use terminals, 30 Lexis or Westlaw terminals, and laptops.

All in all, Loyola is home to a relatively happy and confident student body ("we're #3 in LA and rising"), which nonetheless sees real room for improvement. This evenhanded assessment of the school's strengths and weaknesses offered by a Loyola 3L sums things up: "Loyola is a school blessed with many intelligent and inspiring professors, and cursed with administrators more interested in architecture and alumni donations than in career services or alumni access to the school's resources."

ADMISSIONS

Applications volume is very heavy, and Loyola admits only about one-third of the roughly 3,400 who apply annually. Numerical admissions standards are high, having risen significantly in recent years as more qualified applicants have added Loyola to their lists.

ACADEMICS

Student/faculty ratio	23:1
% female faculty	42
% minority faculty	22
Hours of study per day	3.12

FINANCIAL FACTS

Tuition	$19,592
Part-time tuition per credit	NR
Estimated books/expenses/fees	$945
On-campus living expenses	NR
Off-campus living expenses	NR
% first-year students receiving aid	82
% all students receiving aid	81
% aid that is merit-based	NR
% all students receiving grants/scholarships	NR
% all students receiving loans	90
% all students receiving assistantships	NR
Average award package	$23,332
Average graduation debt	$60,000

ADMISSIONS

# applications received	3,454
% applicants accepted	32
% acceptees attending	39
Average LSAT	158
Average undergrad GPA	3.25
Application Fee	$50
Priority application deadline	NR
Priority notification	NR
Regular application deadline	Feb. 1, Apr. 17
Regular notification	rolling
Admission deferment	NR

Gourman Report Rating	**4.34**

LOYOLA UNIVERSITY, CHICAGO 🖫
School of Law

Founded in 1870 by Jesuit priests, Loyola is Chicago's oldest university. Just as its hometown has long since put away any inferiority complex stemming from its designation as America's Second City, the School of Law of the Loyola University, Chicago has no reason to doubt itself even if it is thought of as the city's "third" law school. A law school could certainly do worse than to occupy the third slot behind heavy hitters Northwestern and U. Chicago. And a law school could certainly do worse on its own terms than this fine midsize institution: Loyola, Chicago not only enjoys an extremely solid regional reputation, but it also appears to have one of the happier student bodies in the region. The program that Loyola's roughly 500 day and 250 evening students follow is quite comprehensive.

The breadth of its traditional classroom curriculum is enhanced by the programs of its Institute for Health Law, and its practical-skills offerings are extensive. Loyola, a nationally recognized leader in the growing field of health law, runs one of the nation's few graduate law programs in this field, and its J.D. students have access to a broad array of courses in this subject. Other special programs include: International Law, in which students can travel to London or Rome to study law for a brief period; and the CIVITAS Child Law Center, which prepares students "for professional careers in the service of children." The school runs two clinics: the Loyola University Community Law Center, which provides legal assitance to those who cannot afford private legal representation; and a Federal Tax Clinic. Loyola also takes great pride in its skills programs, particularly in its trial advocacy courses, which, along with the extensive variety of other clinical offerings, draws many students.

The strength of these programs appears to figure highly in students' overall satisfaction with their experience at Loyola. Asked to name their school's greatest strengths, many cited "the focus of the curriculum on the practical aspects of being a lawyer in addition to the theoretical underpinnings of the law." Indeed, few of the students we heard from expressed any doubts about the quality of their professional preparation. "Loyola is primarily a school for the Midwestern general practitioner or litigator," explained one 2L, "and a great one at that." As often as not, Loyola students explained their satisfaction with the school in terms of its atmosphere. "If you're looking for a place with a comfortable atmosphere in which everyone becomes friends as opposed to competitive enemies," wrote another 2L, "then Loyola is the place to be." Nearly all agreed on this matter. "The atmosphere is very friendly," said one 3L, "which makes coping with the pressures of law school much easier." Students gave as much credit for this state of affairs to their faculty and administration as to themselves. "The most prestigious professors here also enjoy teaching," wrote a 3L, "and they contribute to a strong sense of community by being available and interacting with students." "Loyola has a strong commitment to providing students full value for their tuition," she continued, "and to being responsive to their input. The student here is an integral part of an ambitious academic community."

Loyola recently added a new law library, with seating for 378 students, and 142 study carrels with the capability of connecting a laptop to the school's computer network. The Student Computer Center at the library offers a number of computer terminals and access to Lexis and Westlaw systems of legal research.

We heard some complaints about the inconsistency of teaching abilities among their faculty. "There are some excellent professors here," allowed one 3L, "but there are others who are very poor. Unfortunately, some of the poorer ones teach the required first-year bar courses." Several evening students also complained about the relative lack of flexibility in part-time scheduling and the perceived lack of attention given the evening division in general. Overall, however, even those students who were most critical on this and other matters expressed a clear sense of well-being and of satisfaction with their decision to attend Loyola.

ADMISSIONS

Any law school that receives more than 10 applications for every spot in its first-year class is going to disappoint more than a few well qualified applicants. Such is the case with the Loyola University, Chicago School of Law. Although the law school admits 35 percent of all applicants—a relatively generous acceptance rate for a school of this caliber—it holds those applicants to high numerical standards.

ACADEMICS

Student/faculty ratio	19:1
% female faculty	26
% minority faculty	11
Hours of study per day	3.34

FINANCIAL FACTS

Tuition	$17,628
Part-time tuition per credit	NR
Estimated books/expenses/fees	$980
On-campus living expenses	NR
Off-campus living expenses	$9,000
% first-year students receiving aid	NR
% all students receiving aid	NR
% aid that is merit-based	54
% all students receiving grants/scholarships	33
% all students receiving loans	77
% all students receiving assistantships	1
Average award package	$1,600
Average graduation debt	$47,500

ADMISSIONS

# applications received	2,553
% applicants accepted	35
% acceptees attending	26
Average LSAT	159
Average undergrad GPA	3.27
Application Fee	$45
No early decision program	
Regular application deadline	April 1
Regular notification	rolling
Admission deferment	one year
Gourman Report Rating	**3.49**

LOYOLA UNIVERSITY, NEW ORLEANS 🖫

School of Law

The Loyola University School of Law in New Orleans is just a few miles from the heart of the city's French Quarter. Indeed, Loyola is very much a Louisiana school and its curriculum reflects the state's unique history and blend of legal traditions. The law of every state but Louisiana is rooted in the English common law, a system in which the law is derived both from statutes and from judicial decisions or precedent. Louisiana's French and Spanish past has influenced its civil law system, in which law is explicitly codified. The two legal systems are very different, and to practice in Louisiana a lawyer must know both of them.

At Loyola, both common-law and civil-law programs are available in the day division, but only the civil law curriculum is taught in the night division. Students may elect either course of study or may set up a curriculum containing elements of both. However, those who must take both civil law and common law classes sometimes say they would like fewer required classes and more electives. Loyola offers joint degree programs in communications, religious studies, business administration, urban and regional planning, and public administration. Not surprisingly in light of the curriculum, nearly half of Loyola's students come from and practice in Louisiana.

Loyola is also different from many other law schools because it emphasizes the Jesuit tradition. According to the school, "While the Christian tradition is not wedded to any one philosophical, scientific, aesthetic or political ideology, it is not compatible with every point of view. The Christian view of reality is concerned ultimately with choice and action, and is premised on the concept of moral responsibility...[I]t is also deeply concerned with the promotion of service to others rather than self-aggrandizement." The Jesuit tradition also stresses intellectual rigor and individual excellence.

For the most part, Loyola students rate the faculty as satisfactory. As one student noted, "The Loyola faculty expects a lot of the students; they force us to think for ourselves instead of spoon-feeding us." Several respondents noted that many faculty members are very supportive and approachable, although one third-year says "teachers have asked me to come back later while they

K. Michelle Allison-Davis, Director of Admissions
7214 St. Charles Avenue, Box 901, New Orleans, LA 70118
Tel: (504) 861-5575

Loyola University, New Orleans

sat on the phone on a personal call." Our respondents generally liked their fellow students, who they characterize as moderately competitive. One 3L commented, "Students, for the most part, do not attempt to compete in a bad way...overall students here are kind, generous, truly interested and friendly." However, the most oft-cited criticism of the school was the low grade curve, which students said imposed a "C" average. "Getting a C at Loyola is like getting a B at Tulane," said one student. Those who called their classmates competitive sometimes attributed the atmosphere to the C curve.

While respondents praised the clinical experiences, which include the Gillis Poverty Law Center and the Public Law Center, they wish there were more such opportunities available for credit. Clinic participation is restricted to third-year students and space is limited.

The students who responded to our survey appreciated the local alumni network. Said one, "If you are interested in practicing in New Orleans, this is the place to be." The flip side of that local orientation is that Loyola does not have much of a reputation outside Louisiana. One student who criticized the "non-existent" common-law curriculum warned, "I would not recommend Loyola to students who will practice outside Louisiana." Job placement outside Louisiana has become more difficult in recent years, but Loyola has expanded the career services office and is doing more aggressive outreach to out-of-state firms.

As for the surroundings, New Orleans is given high marks by Loyola students: they like its climate and its social and cultural opportunities. Loyola's facilities do not fare as well: most students characterize them as "O.K." and several singled out the library and its "broken-down" copy machines (which have since been repaired, according to the school) as particularly needing improvement. But if you want to practice law in Louisiana, Loyola is a strong option.

ADMISSIONS

Loyola University Law School, New Orleans, can provide an opportunity for students who may not have stellar academic pasts, but aim for outstanding futures. The school's overall acceptance rate of 53 percent is none too generous, but it does not hold its students to particularly high numerical standards.

ACADEMICS

Student/faculty ratio	25:1
% female faculty	32
% minority faculty	19
Hours of study per day	4.31

FINANCIAL FACTS

Tuition	$17,515
Part-time tuition per credit	$11,865
Estimated books/expenses/fees	$945
On-campus living expenses	$5,420
Off-campus living expenses	$7,500
% first-year students receiving aid	82
% all students receiving aid	83
% aid that is merit-based	90
% all students receiving grants/scholarships	21
% all students receiving loans	80
% all students receiving assistantships	5
Average award package	$7,390
Average graduation debt	$37,000

ADMISSIONS

# applications received	1,869
% applicants accepted	53
% acceptees attending	29
Average LSAT	152
Average undergrad GPA	3.00
Application Fee	$20
No early decision program	
Regular application deadline	NR
Regular notification	rolling
Admission deferment	one year
Gourman Report Rating	**2.50**

UNIVERSITY OF MAINE
University of Maine School of Law

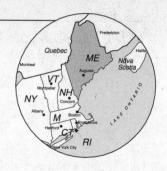

OVERVIEW

Type of school	public
Environment	city
Scholastic calendar	NR
Schedule	Full time only

STUDENTS

Enrollment of institution	NR
Enrollment of law school	277
% male/female	54/46
% out-of-state	39
% part-time	2
% minorities	7
% international (# countries represented)	1 (NR)
Average age at entry	29

APPLICANTS ALSO LOOK AT

Vermont Law School
Franklin Pierce Law Center
Boston College
Suffolk University
Western New England College

SURVEY SAYS...

HITS
Sense of community
Faculty-student relations
Intellectual challenge

MISSES
Not enough courses
Lack of diversity among faculty
Facilities not great

EMPLOYMENT PROFILE

% grads employed immediately	50
% grads employed within six months	80
Average starting salary	$35,000
% grads employed by field:	
Private practice	59
Business/industry	10
Government	10
Judicial clerkships	15
Public service	4
Academic	1
Military	2

If the images that come up when you think of Maine are spectacular scenery and small clean towns populated with friendly and honest people, then you could also be thinking of the University of Maine School of Law. Located in Portland, Maine's largest city, this public law school has all the small-town charm you might expect. Like many of its neighboring New England law schools, the University of Maine School of Law is relatively selective in whom it admits. However, there are several aspects of this law school that make it unique, most noticeably its size. With the total student body numbering 260, the University of Maine is one of the smallest of the 175 accredited law schools in the U.S. It is so small that the entire first-year class meets in one section. It is not uncommon for upper-level courses to have enrollments of fewer than 10 students, and many courses have enrollments of fewer than 30. The University of Maine also has the rare distinction of being the only law school in the entire state, a fact that sits well with students looking for local externships and employment in the state.

The University of Maine law school offers a fairly traditional curriculum combined with a rather limited clinical program open to third-year students. The school does offer a few distinctive programs, including the Ocean and Coastal Law Program, the Marine Law Institute, and exchange programs with two Canadian law schools.

Students at the University of Maine speak highly of the "friendly," and "open" social climate at the law school. The school's uncommonly small size allows for a sense of community that is found at few other institutions. A 1L who traveled quite a distance to attend the University of Maine said, "The small size has really helped me handle being so far from all I am familiar with." Another 1L enthusiastically agreed: "The atmosphere here is unbelievable. The administrators are out to help you in a friendly way," and, "The students are cooperative and diverse; you couldn't ask for a better place to go to school." Lack of competition among law students was praised by several respondents. One student, a 1L, noted that the school "encourages teamwork and resource sharing."

Barbara Gauditz, Assistant Dean
246 Deering Avenue, Portland, ME 04102
Tel: (207) 780-4341
Internet: http://www.usm.maine.edu/

University of Maine

University of Maine law students also reportedly share a close relationship with many of their professors. Small classes, individualized attention, and accessibility to professors were commonly listed as strengths of the school. "The small size allows you, if you choose, to get to know everyone, and there is instant access to any professor," said one 2L. Law students said the sense of community at the law school includes the town of Portland itself, particularly those employed in the legal community.

Of course the intimacy that such a small setting breeds can create a need for diversity. Indeed, a lack of diversity in the student body, faculty, and curriculum is at the top of students' lists of areas needing improvement. "There is no diversity here—no racial minority faculty, mostly white male faculty," said one 2L, and added, "[There is] no appreciation for the contributions nontraditional students make." There are, in fact, no minority faculty members at the University of Maine law school as of this writing.

Current students at the school agreed on the need for an improved physical plant. Some called for "improved facilities," or "more computers," while others were quite specific. Said this 1L: "Library: needs more study space; computer cluster is abominable; 1L lecture room is too cramped and uncomfortable; student lounge way too small..." But most of these comments were tempered with an appreciation of the school on the whole, like the same 1L, who, after criticizing the school's accommodations, said, "But it's worth the trade-off in reasonable tuition costs."

ADMISSIONS

If your dream is to attend law school in the state of Maine, this school is your only shot. In fact, the University of Maine School of Law is among the 50 most in-demand law schools in the country. Although the numerical standards are relatively moderate (a solid undergraduate GPA combined with an LSAT score at about the 75th percentile), the school is relatively selective. With an average applicant volume of 860, and an entering class of approximately 90, the admissions committee has to choose its incoming class carefully.

ACADEMICS

Student/faculty ratio	17:1
% female faculty	20
% minority faculty	0
Hours of study per day	4.35

FINANCIAL FACTS

In-state tuition	$7,920
Out-of-state tuition	$15,720
Part-time tuition per credit	NR
Estimated books/expenses/fees	$1,350
On-campus living expenses	NR
Off-campus living expenses	NR
% first-year students receiving aid	100
% all students receiving aid	100
% aid that is merit-based	NR
% all students receiving grants/scholarships	41
% all students receiving loans	81
% all students receiving assistantships	NR
Average award package	$2,961
Average graduation debt	$38,000

ADMISSIONS

# applications received	862
% applicants accepted	39
% acceptees attending	27
Average LSAT	155
Average undergrad GPA	3.24
Application Fee	$25
No early decision program	
Regular application deadline	February 15
Regular notification	rolling
Admission deferment	NR
Gourman Report Rating	2.54

MARQUETTE UNIVERSITY 🖪
Law School

In 1673, Fr. Pere Jacques Marquette, S.J., a renowned Jesuit explorer, and Louis Joliet, along with five companions, were the first Europeans to explore the Mississippi river. Little did Marquette know that nearly two hundred years later, in 1891, his name would adorn a new Jesuit college in the Great Lakes region. According to the Assistant Dean, Marquette University was named for him "in recognition of his spirit of exploration and discovery and his dedicated service to others."

Applications volume at the more than a century-old law school has nearly doubled over the last decade, and the qualifications of enrolled students have climbed accordingly. Selectivity appears to be on the rise, but Marquette still admits more than one third of the candidates it considers.

The fine traditional J.D. curriculum at this reasonably priced midsize Catholic law school is supplemented by a growing number of skills courses and by a handful of clinical programs, several of which offer students hands-on lawyering experience working with residents of Milwaukee's urban center. Marquette's other special offerings include joint-degree programs leading to a J.D./M.B.A. and a J.D./M.A. in political science. Marquette law students assert that their school's most appealing characteristics stem from its close ties to Milwaukee's courts and law community, providing graduates with a strong, practical legal education and likely venues to market their degrees.

Despite these positive attributes, the most common response to our survey was qualified praise. Most students expressed hope that the new Dean's changes, already in progress, will improve the amount and quality of attention the administration extends to students and raise teaching standards to those stellar heights favorite professors already reach. A 1L gave this mixed assessment of the process: "This school seems to be trying to attract a younger, newer breed of faculty with some success, but a gap has resulted; the old-line faculty are VERY traditional and Socratic, the young faculty are quite liberal."

Although some students expressed total satisfaction with certain aspects of their school, such as the DA and Public Defender

Geraldine A. Clausen, Assistant Dean for Admissions
1103 West Wisconsin Avenue, Milwaukee, WI 53201-1881
Tel: (414) 288-6767   Fax: (414) 288-5914
Internet: http://www.mu.edu/dept/law

Marquette University

clinics, the affiliation with the National Sports Law Institute, and the strong ethical tradition, one 3L spoke for many when he listed improvements he would like to see: "Upgrade facilities, improve career office, improve image in community, offer more courses, fire some professors, diversify student body, hire more liberal professors."

Those who offered more wholehearted praise followed the "relax and enjoy it" strain of thought, typified by this content 2L's remark: "Marquette is a great school. We know we aren't a Minnesota or Northwestern but we don't try to be. At Marquette you receive a practical education that prepares you to be an attorney right away." Another gave his philosophy, admirable in a field overpopulated by workaholics, "At Marquette I feel I am able to make law school my life by only making it part of my life. There are many opportunities to both further your education, and have a social life, like Bar Review every Thursday night (because Wisconsin doesn't have the bar exam—students review a different bar every Thursday)." A love for that ubiquitous Milwaukee product permeates and mellows the world of Marquette law school.

Even with a healthy sense of rivalry between Marquette students and those Midwestern giants named above, most recognize that Marquette's close ties to the city coupled with the enthusiasm of the new Dean truly brighten "the shine of the star of the north."

ADMISSIONS

The Marquette University School of Law ranks in about the middle of all U.S. law schools in terms of its numerical standards for admission. The average Marquette student has a solid undergraduate GPA and an LSAT score at roughly the 75th percentile nationally. The law school admits students across a fairly broad range of grade-point averages and test scores.

ACADEMICS

Student/faculty ratio	22:1
% female faculty	30
% minority faculty	8
Hours of study per day	3.47

FINANCIAL FACTS

Tuition	$17,310
Part-time tuition per credit	$630
Estimated books/expenses/fees	NR
On-campus living expenses	NR
Off-campus living expenses	NR
% first-year students receiving aid	85
% all students receiving aid	90
% aid that is merit-based	11
% all students receiving grants/scholarships	30
% all students receiving loans	85
% all students receiving assistantships	NR
Average award package	NR
Average graduation debt	$48,000

ADMISSIONS

# applications received	1,086
% applicants accepted	39
% acceptees attending	32
Average LSAT	156
Average undergrad GPA	3.07
Application Fee	$35
No early decision program	
Regular application deadline	April 1
Regular notification	rolling
Admission may be deferred?	No
Gourman Report Rating	4.31

UNIVERSITY OF MARYLAND ⊟
School of Law

If law schools were rated according to their proximity to beautiful baseball parks, the University of Maryland School of Law would win hands down. But even by more conventional criteria, this midsize public law school in the urban center of Baltimore looks quite good. Among the oldest institutions of legal education in the country, Maryland enjoys a long-established reputation as one of the finest public law schools on the East Coast. With its very low tuition and its extensive resources (which rival those of many larger, more expensive law schools) UM is one of the better buys in the region.

The law school's traditional curriculum, administered by a large, respected faculty, is strong and broad. Through innovations in its core curriculum and through its clinical program, widely regarded as one of the nation's best, UM has seen to it that none of its graduates enters the legal profession without some degree of practical experience. Maryland 1Ls cover the same core subjects as students at most other law schools, but the style of their first-year program is uncommon. In addition to a legal-methods requirement that is satisfied in conjunction with a substantive first-year course, Maryland students must elect either a "Legal Theory and Practice" class—effectively a clinical offering—which is also linked with a standard first-year course, or take a clinical offering in the second or third year.

Nearly all Maryland students cite UM's clinic and its low tuition first when expressing their overall satisfaction with the law school. A sense of camaraderie and goodwill is also evident in the comments of Maryland law students: "I'm very impressed with the diversity and quality of students—I don't mean just their intelligence. There are a lot of good people here—not the kind of people you'd think of as lawyers." Another student, a 3L, offered this candid assessment: "Maryland was a backup for me, and lo and behold the only school I got into! My expectations of a mediocre state school have been proven wrong—though only slowly, and after much effort to find a niche. When I served as a student attorney in the AIDS clinic, everything came together. Public-interest types must really make an effort to find support here, but once found, there is a rich experience to be had." The health care and environmental law programs are regularly ranked

James Forsyth, Assistant Dean
500 West Baltimore Street, Baltimore, MD 21201
Tel: (410) 706-3492
eMail: admissions@law.ab.umd.edu
Internet: http://www.ab.umd.edu

in the top ten. While the school's instruction in legal writing was criticized by those we surveyed, we'd like to add that the school has since revamped the program and hired a new Director, so our future surveys should reflect that fact.

The potential richness of the law school experience at Maryland derives in part from the school's excellent student-faculty ratio and its impressive diversity. Overall, though, the faculty was rated poorly compared to those of other schools in the region. While students expressed their displeasure with the teaching methods, some students did note that "the school is making great strides in hiring more student-friendly faculty." Several students called for an increase in diversity. "We need a more politically diverse student body, we need more conservatives," wrote one. "We look like America, we just don't think like America." Maryland students placed themselves among the most liberal law student bodies. However, the administration added that in the past few years, "a very active student-run Federalist society has helped create ideological balance."

Day and night students both expressed little love for their physical habitat. "We need land! And buildings!" shouted one. In response to complaints, we hear from the Dean that "a major addition and renovation...is planned for the near future." Others appeared more content with their surroundings, including one of many who expressed fondness for the Baltimore Oriole Park at Camden Yards: "No other law school offers such access to a great ballpark," he wrote, accurately. "This seems as logical a way to rank law schools as any I've seen."

ADMISSIONS

The University of Maryland School of Law's status as a true bargain among East Coast law schools is no secret among law-school applicants. At least, not anymore. Between 1986 and 1992, applications volume at the law school more than tripled, and though some of this increase was offset by a slight increase in enrollment, the result is this: Demand for spots in Maryland's entering class of about 260 is higher than demand for spots in more than 70 percent of the country's fully accredited law schools. Numerical standards are moderately high; the average U of M student has a solid undergraduate GPA and LSAT score.

ACADEMICS

Student/faculty ratio	16:1
% female faculty	32
% minority faculty	24
Hours of study per day	3.77

FINANCIAL FACTS

In-state tuition	$8,137
Out-of-state tuition	$14,872
Part-time tuition per credit	NR
Estimated books/expenses/fees	$1,500
On-campus living expenses	NR
Off-campus living expenses	NR
% first-year students receiving aid	75
% all students receiving aid	85
% aid that is merit-based	1
% all students receiving grants/scholarships	40
% all students receiving loans	68
% all students receiving assistantships	NR
Average award package	$3,178
Average graduation debt	$34,487

ADMISSIONS

# applications received	3,484
% applicants accepted	27
% acceptees attending	28
Average LSAT	156
Average undergrad GPA	3.25
Application Fee	$40
No early decision program	
Regular application deadline	May 1
Regular notification	rolling
Admission deferment	one year
Gourman Report Rating	3.77

UNIVERSITY OF MEMPHIS
Cecil C. Humphreys School of Law

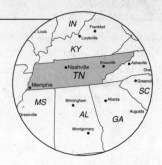

OVERVIEW

Type of school	public
Environment	NR
Scholastic calendar	NR
Schedule	Full-time or part-time

STUDENTS

Enrollment of institution	NR
Enrollment of law school	464
% male/female	59/41
% out-of-state	20
% part-time	6
% minorities	11
% international (# countries represented)	NR (NR)
Average age at entry	26

APPLICANTS ALSO LOOK AT

University of Tennessee
Vanderbilt University
University of Mississippi
Georgia State University
Samford University

SURVEY SAYS...

HITS
Socratic method
Library staff

MISSES
Lack of national name recognition
Legal writing

EMPLOYMENT PROFILE

% grads employed immediately	32
% grads employed within six months	82
Average starting salary	$38,426
% grads employed by field:	
Private practice	52
Business/industry	11
Government	11
Judicial clerkships	10
Public service	1
Academic	10
Military	3

At first blush, Memphis, Tennessee, seems an unlikely choice for the setting of John Grisham's popular novel, *The Firm*. But then, that was the whole point. Mr. Grisham set his tale of a law firm gone bad in Memphis precisely because you'd never expect to find such a quintessentially evil institution there. Drugs, murder, and mayhem are not much a part of actual law practice in this peaceful Mississippi River city of 1,000,000. Contracts, torts and income tax, on the other hand, are. It is only right, therefore, that these are the subjects that form the basis of the solidly traditional curriculum at the University of Memphis Cecil C. Humphreys School of Law, the youngest and smallest in the state of Tennessee.

In keeping with the national trend, the University of Memphis has begun to offer more practical-skills courses. Among these, the trial advocacy courses and moot court competitions draw the highest rate of participation and the most praise from students. It should be noted, however, that the J.D. program is extremely heavy with prescribed courses. With only one elective course in the first two years, the University of Memphis program leaves relatively little room for the student to chart his or her own course of study before the third year, when only one course is required. Since the law school enrolls less than 200 total students in its day and evening first-year classes, admissions are fairly selective. Around one third of all applicants are admitted, but numerical standards are quite moderate

When asked to name their school's greatest strengths, many students cite the practical emphasis of the University of Memphis's curriculum. "The structured, practical curriculum is great," wrote one 1L, "as you can see from our outstanding bar passage rate." Indeed, the perennial success of Memphis grads on the state bar exam is a source of some pride among students. "Most of our grads will make very fine, hard-working attorneys," argued a 1L, "because they aren't spoon-fed here; most have worked hard both inside the classroom and in the real world to get to where they are." Spoon-fed or not, most of the Memphis students we heard from had kind words for their faculty, whose "willingness to offer personal assistance anytime" complements their numbers nicely. (The University of Memphis has one of the more favorable student-faculty ratios in the country.) The feelings of many students were summed up neatly in this remark from a Memphis 1L: "We have great things to offer at this school, and it's time the world knew about it!"

Unfortunately, it is the second part of that statement which is echoed more frequently and forcefully than the first. Judging from their responses to our survey, students here are concerned to the point of preoccupation with what they perceive as the University of Memphis's lack of national name recognition. The positive side to their frustration, of course, is that most of those we heard from feel that their school is clearly good enough to merit greater recognition. As one 2L put it, "This is a very good school, but it needs its image to progress commensurately with its academic improvements." Still, not all agree that this law school is in a position to worry only about image-polishing. "They really need to have more elective class offerings," wrote one 3L who, like many others, considered the University of Memphis' program far too rigid. Students also heaped criticism on the law school's facilities, especially the "dirty" and "uncomfortable" building. Since we surveyed, however, the building has been renovated, and new carpeting and furniture have been added. More improvements are underway. On balance, most of the students we heard from, particularly those who wished to enter private practice in the immediate region, expressed a strong sense of satisfaction with their training at the University of Memphis.

ADMISSIONS

Strictly in terms of the numerical standards, the University of Memphis Humphreys School of Law ranks in the bottom third of all U.S. law schools. The school's bargain-basement tuition, however, draws a relatively large pool of applicants, and consequently the admissions process at Memphis State is no joke.

ACADEMICS

Student/faculty ratio	21:1
% female faculty	29
% minority faculty	5
Hours of study per day	3.82

FINANCIAL FACTS

In-state tuition	$3,514
Out-of-state tuition	$8,910
Part-time tuition per credit	$152
Estimated books/expenses/fees	NR
On-campus living expenses	NR
Off-campus living expenses	NR
% first-year students receiving aid	NR
% all students receiving aid	79
% aid that is merit-based	NR
% all students receiving grants/scholarships	NR
% all students receiving loans	NR
% all students receiving assistantships	NR
Average award package	NR
Average graduation debt	NR

ADMISSIONS

# applications received	1,213
% applicants accepted	37
% acceptees attending	41
Average LSAT	153
Average undergrad GPA	3.19
Application Fee	$15
Priority application deadline	NR
Priority notification	NR
Regular application deadline	February 15
Regular notification	NR
Admission deferment	NR
Gourman Report Rating	**2.63**

MERCER UNIVERSITY 🖫
Walter F. George School of Law

OVERVIEW

Type of school	private
Environment	city
Scholastic calendar	quarter
Schedule	Full time only

STUDENTS

Enrollment of institution	6,700
Enrollment of law school	408
% male/female	61/39
% out-of-state	45
% part-time	NR
% minorities	16
% international (# countries represented)	NR (1)
Average age at entry	26

APPLICANTS ALSO LOOK AT

University of Georgia
Georgia State University
Emory University
Florida State University
Wake Forest University

SURVEY SAYS...

HITS
Studying
Sense of community
Socratic method

MISSES
Clinical experience
Quality of teaching
Not enough courses

EMPLOYMENT PROFILE

% grads employed immediately	56
% grads employed within six months	98
Average starting salary	$35,166
% grads employed by field:	
Private practice	67
Business/industry	3
Government	11
Judicial clerkships	13
Public service	2
Military	0

There are law schools in the United States at which change occurs at a glacial pace, schools whose weighty reputations have the possibly ill side effect of stifling innovation. Mercer University's Walter F. George School of Law is not among them. Yes, one side of that equation means that Mercer's regional reputation has not traditionally received much recognition outside the Southeast, but if the faculty and administration of this small private law school have anything to say about it, that will soon change. (Indeed, Mercer's admissions standards are rising, and it now draws a significant number of its students from outside Georgia.) After receiving a sizable bequest in 1987, Mercer set about implementing its "Woodruff Plan," named for the generous donor and former chairman of the Coca-Cola Company. The plan mandated a reduction in overall enrollment (which was achieved) and a rededication to preparing Mercer law graduates for the realities of law practice. To this end, Mercer has revamped its curriculum to include "skills" workshops at the start of every year and has introduced a sixth-semester "pre-practice" program designed to combat the feeling of drift that envelops most 3Ls come springtime. Every year, Mercer University sends forth about 150 well-trained future lawyers from its campus in Macon, Georgia, known for its beautiful antebellum architecture and for being the town that gave the world Little Richard, Lena Horne, and the Allman Brothers. Mercer boasts very high passage rates to the Georgia bar; in some recent years it has even had the highest rate of all Georgia law schools. Mercer admits a respectably low percentage of applicants, and numerical standards are moderate.

Judging from our survey of students, Mercer delivers what one might expect from a very small law school located 80 miles from Atlanta, one of the nation's major legal communities. This can cut both ways. Mercer is not exempt from certain inherent disadvantages of any school in its situation; a small student body, for instance, means a small faculty (in absolute terms), which in turn limits the breadth of a school's course offerings. But a small school also has the potential to offer the prospective law student a comfortable, intimate learning environment that students at some schools can only hope for. The students we heard from seem to be well aware of both these advantages and disadvantages. This

Kathleen O'Neal, Director of Admissions
1021 Georgia Avenue, Macon, GA 31201
Tel: (912) 752-2605

Mercer University

remark from a 1L was quite typical of the positive reviews we heard: "Come here if you do not want to be pitted in battle against the faculty. Pleasant, personal relationships with professors are the rule here." "The professors here seem genuinely interested in their students," agreed one 3L, "and the practical curriculum is suited for people to jump right into practice." Many others echoed this last sentiment. "The new curriculum is great," wrote one 3L. "It focuses you at the start of the year and the sixth semester provides a helpful transition to practice." The result of this approach, according to another 3L, is Mercer's "great reputation for producing excellent Georgia lawyers."

But that last remark also contains a hint of something that seems to trouble many Mercer students: the essentially local nature of their school's "reputation." As one fairly typical 3L put it, "They need to do a better job of spreading Mercer's reputation outside of Georgia and Florida." Not surprisingly, the closer they were to graduation and the frightening prospect of finding a job, the more likely students were to express such anxiety. As another 3L wrote, "I'm worried that the big firms outside the region underestimate the quality of the program here."

ADMISSIONS

The Mercer University School of Law is situated in the lower-middle of all law schools nationally in terms of admissions selectivity. Today, the average Mercer student has a moderate undergraduate GPA of 3.23 and a solid LSAT score at about the 75th percentile, significantly higher than the average Mercer student of only six years ago. Prospective students should be aware that rising applicant volume and a reduction in total enrollment have made the admissions process at Mercer quite selective. The law school's overall acceptance rate is a none-too-generous 29 percent.

ACADEMICS

Student/faculty ratio	14:1
% female faculty	24
% minority faculty	6
Hours of study per day	4.51

FINANCIAL FACTS

Tuition	$17,429
Part-time tuition per credit	NR
Estimated books/expenses/fees	NR
On-campus living expenses	NR
Off-campus living expenses	NR
% first-year students receiving aid	100
% all students receiving aid	100
% aid that is merit-based	24
% all students receiving grants/scholarships	NR
% all students receiving loans	83
% all students receiving assistantships	NR
Average award package	$7,784
Average graduation debt	$53,308

ADMISSIONS

# applications received	1,413
% applicants accepted	29
% acceptees attending	30
Average LSAT	156
Average undergrad GPA	3.23
Application Fee	$45
No early decision program	
Regular application deadline	March 15
Regular notification	rolling
Admission deferment	one year
Gourman Report Rating	**2.94**

UNIVERSITY OF MIAMI
School of Law

On a national scale, the University of Miami is probably better known for its sports teams than for its degree programs, and many would be surprised to learn that it is one of the largest and best-funded research universities in the nation. It is also home to a well-equipped law school, the largest in Florida and possibly the finest anywhere in a subtropical setting. The University of Miami School of Law is located just a few miles south of Miami in the smallish community of Coral Gables, and its location surely has something to do with the fact that Miami draws more than half of its 3000-plus applicants from outside the state.

The University of Miami is a law school with solid academic credentials, though your average snowbound northeastern law student would wonder how Miami students muster the discipline to take full advantage of the curriculum. And there is plenty to take advantage of. The law school's broad traditional curriculum is supplemented by an increasing commitment to skills training and by special offerings like the Summer Public Interest Seminar Program. The vast resources of the broader university have begun to play a larger role within the law school as interdisciplinary research in areas like economics and the behavioral sciences has gained popularity within the field of law. Numerical admissions standards are moderately high, but entering classes are large enough that Miami still admits a relatively high percentage of all applicants.

Since our last survey, a new Dean has arrived and wrought important, much needed changes, improving the quality of life and education at Miami. The majority of respondents cheered the progress the new Dean has made toward realizing his Miami dreams. Two 2Ls explained why: "Since we brought in Dean Thompson from UCLA everything has changed. We have a brand new facility and a huge library with the most up to date technological advances. Dean Thompson also forced out all of the old, dry, Socratic professors and replaced them with younger, more interesting professors." "The Dean is absolutely committed to putting U. of Miami in the Top 20. With the current downsizing, this is going to increase median LSAT scores, GPAs and job placement numbers. We will be in the Top 20 very soon."

Therese Lambert, Director of Student Recruiting
P.O. Box 248087, Coral Gables, FL 33124
Tel: (305) 284-2523

University of Miami

A little work remains before that day comes, according to our survey. Those students who leveled criticisms against Miami used a harsh and bitter tone, surprisingly unmellowed by the relentlessly bright and cheerful sun. One unhappy 1L told us, "The professors orchestrate personal attacks upon the students...The writing program (tutorial) is in shambles." Another student said, "Information falls out of the sky...There's no efficient way for administrators and deans to communicate with the student body." Unfortunately, several people echoed this 2L's comment: "It is a very tense environment for minority students." Students called for the school to improve by eradicating the "unofficial" C-curve, diversifying hiring and enrollment, restructuring or jettisoning the legal writing program, increasing parking spaces, and most importantly, providing better help and guidance in that dreadful search for a means to pay back one's hefty student loans.

Though it may sound as if everything, and yet nothing, has improved, one 3L gave us some perspective on the jarring mood swings revealed in our responses when he remarked, "The school has made great strides since I first arrived here. The new dean is a godsend, and I believe, is well on the way to making this a very good law school. The aesthetics have improved tremendously! However, student/faculty relations are poor." With a little more work, perhaps all students will agree that "The only drawback is the tropical heat."

ADMISSIONS

Although the size of the entering class at the University of Miami School of Law requires the admissions committee to admit a large number of applicants, competition to be among those admitted is growing stronger. Between 1991 and 1992, total law school applications volume declined at the national level, but it was up five percent at Miami. Still, this expensive private law school offers admission to nearly half of the candidates it considers—a very generous acceptance rate for a school of its caliber.

ACADEMICS

Student/faculty ratio	16:1
% female faculty	24
% minority faculty	11
Hours of study per day	3.84

FINANCIAL FACTS

Tuition	$20,712
Part-time tuition per credit	NR
Estimated books/expenses/fees	$988
On-campus living expenses	$8,054
Off-campus living expenses	NR
% first-year students receiving aid	85
% all students receiving aid	85
% aid that is merit-based	9
% all students receiving grants/scholarships	17
% all students receiving loans	85
% all students receiving assistantships	5
Average award package	$12,905
Average graduation debt	$58,300

ADMISSIONS

# applications received	2,714
% applicants accepted	49
% acceptees attending	34
Average LSAT	154
Average undergrad GPA	3.20
Application Fee	$45
No early decision program	
Regular application deadline	July 31
Regular notification	rolling
Admission deferment	one year
Gourman Report Rating	3.35

UNIVERSITY OF MICHIGAN 💾
School of Law

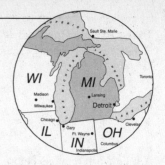

With its nonresident annual tuition rate exceeding $20,000 and its resident rate not far behind, the University of Michigan School of Law does not have the bargain attractions of your typical public law school, but never mind. By any yardstick—from the purely academic to the purely aesthetic—this large, old institution is widely acknowledged to be among a handful of law schools that can legitimately be called the best in the country.

In the classroom, Michigan's program is extremely flexible and terrifically strong. With virtually no requirements after the solidly traditional first year, and with a broad range of innovative courses from which to choose, Michigan students control their own academic fates. Outside the classroom setting, the law school's clinical programs are limited in neither capacity nor scope. Fully one–half of Michigan students participate in these programs, which include a clinic dedicated to AIDS and public health and another to women and the law. The Michigan faculty, which includes some of the country's top legal scholars, still favors the Socratic Method, and traditional case analysis forms the basis of many upper-division courses. Still, the law school is not without its structural innovations. One-quarter of each entering class is admitted to what the law school calls the "new section," in which the traditional disciplinary barriers within the first-year curriculum are eschewed in favor of a more integrated, less structured course of study. Michigan admits another quarter of its first-year class for study beginning in June. These summer admittees can use their head start to graduate early by attending summer sessions, to slow the pace of their legal education, or simply to prepare themselves for the Ann Arbor winter.

Not that winter could foster discontent among the highly qualified, satisfied students at Michigan. Though certainly not without their criticisms, the Michigan students we heard from expressed a very high degree of satisfaction not only with the quality of their program, but also with the overall quality of their experience at the law school. "The atmosphere created by the students, the community, the faculty, and even the facilities is excellent," wrote one 1L, "probably the best in the country." Though that last claim would be difficult to verify, prevailing opinion among Michigan

Dennis Shields, Assistant Dean
625 South State Street, Ann Arbor, MI 48109-1215
Tel: (313)-764-0537
eMail: ccureton@umich.edu
Internet: http://www.law.umich.edu/

students appears to be very consistent with the judgment of another 1L who said that "this is an easy place to love." Most give credit for this fact to their fellow students—"Students here are incredibly intelligent and, just as importantly, incredibly human"—and to their faculty—"Most members of the faculty are absolutely outstanding, both as scholars and as teachers."

When asked to name areas in which their school could stand to improve, many lamented the degree of competitiveness among students and the perceived inaccessibility of their "otherwise excellent" professors. For the most part, their substantive criticisms had little or nothing to do with the quality of any of the law school's existing programs. More often, their remarks concerned the future. "I want to work for a small public-interest firm, or for the Department of Justice," wrote one 2L, "but the debt required by this school forces students to go after the big firms and the big $$." Furthermore, many others complained that the school's placement office was of little help to those whose career plans fell outside the mainstream. "The placement office has limited ties to the legal community," reported one 3L. "Students are left mostly to their own initiative, particularly if they don't want to work in a large firm." Those Michigan students who do want such work, however, are as employable and as happy as any in the nation.

ADMISSIONS

Simply stated, the University of Michigan Law School is one of most selective law schools in the nation. How difficult is it to gain admission to this world-class school? Well, every year Michigan receives nearly 3,000 applications from prospective students with LSAT scores below 165—the 95th percentile. These luckless applicants stand a cumulative 26 percent chance of getting in. Bear this in mind when considering whether to write that application-fee check.

ACADEMICS	
Student/faculty ratio	25:1
% female faculty	18
% minority faculty	2
Hours of study per day	4.40

FINANCIAL FACTS	
In-state tuition	$15,820
Out-of-state tuition	$22,020
Part-time tuition per credit	NR
Estimated books/expenses/fees	NR
On-campus living expenses	NR
Off-campus living expenses	NR
% first-year students receiving aid	95
% all students receiving aid	95
% aid that is merit-based	24
% all students receiving grants/scholarships	32
% all students receiving loans	80
% all students receiving assistantships	NR
Average award package	$7,540
Average graduation debt	$36,000

ADMISSIONS	
# applications received	4,073
% applicants accepted	26
% acceptees attending	31
Average LSAT	167
Average undergrad GPA	3.56
Application Fee	$70
Priority application deadline	NR
Priority notification	NR
Regular application deadline	February 15
Regular notification	NR
Admission deferment	NR

Gourman Report Rating	**4.92**

UNIVERSITY OF MINNESOTA 💾
Law School

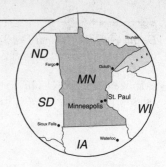

There are two ways in which one might interpret the fact that the University of Minnesota School of Law keeps its library, one of the largest in the nation, open twenty-four hours a day, seven days a week. On the one hand, it could be viewed as a sign of the law school's commitment to fostering scholarship by maintaining wonderfully accessible, top-notch facilities. On the other hand, it could be seen as a sign that the law school's students spend relatively little time anywhere else. Both interpretations, it seems, would be accurate. Minnesota is generally considered to be among the finest public law schools in the nation, and it has never chosen to rest on its laurels. Since 1913, for instance, Minnesota has recognized the importance of practical training as a supplement to the standard classroom curriculum in law schools. Its current clinical program, one of the largest in the country and in which 68 percent of students participate, has served as a model for other schools around the nation since its inception in 1968. Ninety percent of students participate in the clinics or practical skills courses. The school revamped its writing program in 1994 in response to student complaints; according to the administration, the new program has also been used as a model for other schools.

The law school's facilities, housed on the Minneapolis side of the university's twin-cities campus, are first-rate, and its faculty is very highly regarded. The greatly varied co-curricular activities available to students are far too numerous to mention, and the opportunities for interdisciplinary study through the many highly rated graduate departments of the broader university are tremendous. In terms of the substance of the legal education it provides, this top law school is as progressive as any of its peers. But be forewarned: The University of Minnesota is very much of the old school when it comes to style. The Socratic Method may elsewhere have been consigned to the ash heap of history, but it continues to thrive in Minnesota. The workload here is heavy, and competition among students is high. Still, one cannot argue with the results. Minnesota graduates tend to get very good jobs, and get them with relative ease.

Edward Kawczynski, Director of Admissions
229 19th Avenue, South, Minneapolis, MN 55455
Tel: (612) 625-5005
Internet: http://www.umn.edu/law/

University of Minnesota

And despite their criticism of aspects of their chosen school, Minnesota students seem to appreciate the advantages they have. "Our faculty and our facilities (especially the library) are excellent," said one 2L, "and the student body is strong and diverse." The law school's "reputation and location are excellent," wrote another, who, like many others, chose Minnesota for its perceived "prestige."

Their satisfaction with certain fundamentals notwithstanding, however, Minnesota students expressed frustration with some faculty members as well. "Some teachers are excellent," said one, "and all are open to talking with students one-on-one, but we need more teachers who focus on teaching and teaching well."

Minnesota has both a new placement director, and a new, expanded placement office. According to an associate dean, "the director is so popular the students invited her to an otherwise 'students only' graduation party." The school also has a new dean of students "who is immensely popular." Overall, Minnesota students are quite satisfied with their experience at the law school.

ADMISSIONS

As a result of the University of Minnesota Law School's huge reputation and its status as a relative bargain among Midwestern law schools, competition for spots in its entering class of about 270 is quite fierce. The overall acceptance rate is a very selective 25 percent, and the quality of the law school's average applicant pool of about 2,100 is very high. As a result, Minnesota's numerical admissions standards are among the highest in the country. In fact, the Minnesota student body is, by our calculations, one of the 20 most highly qualified in the nation.

ACADEMICS

Student/faculty ratio	18:1
% female faculty	34
% minority faculty	11
Hours of study per day	4.00

FINANCIAL FACTS

In-state tuition	$7,524
Out-of-state tuition	$13,420
Part-time tuition per credit	NR
Estimated books/expenses/fees	NR
On-campus living expenses	NR
Off-campus living expenses	NR
% first-year students receiving aid	85
% all students receiving aid	85
% aid that is merit-based	35
% all students receiving grants/scholarships	21
% all students receiving loans	85
% all students receiving assistantships	12
Average award package	$5,000
Average graduation debt	NR

ADMISSIONS

# applications received	2,120
% applicants accepted	25
% acceptees attending	49
Average LSAT	162
Average undergrad GPA	3.61
Application Fee	$30
No early decision program	
Regular application deadline	March 1
Regular notification	rolling
Admission may be deferred?	no
Gourman Report Rating	**4.64**

MISSISSIPPI COLLEGE 💾
School of Law

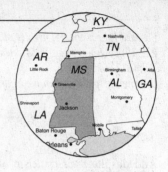

Founded in 1975 and accredited in 1980, the Mississippi College School of Law is a young, very small private law school operated by the Mississippi Baptist Convention. Mississippi College is forthright in stating that its goal is to build not another Harvard but "a strong, regional law school with a national focus." This effort is surely aided by the law school's location in downtown Jackson, the state capital. MC law students are only a short walk away from the federal courts and the offices of the state government. Mysteriously, however, especially considering that the law school does not operate any clinic of its own, MC puts a very strict limit on the number of academic credits that its students can earn through external placement in some of these government institutions. This archaic policy severely limits the options of students hoping to gain valuable practical experience prior to entering the profession.

The solidly traditional classroom curriculum at Mississippi College is administered by a well-liked faculty which includes several of the law school's own graduates. Beyond the standard requirements, Mississippi College students must complete a major research paper. This requirement is part of the school's effort to move toward a program that will produce competent graduates who are well equipped with practical lawyering skills. Numerical admissions standards at Mississippi College are relatively low, but the law school's tiny size necessitates a somewhat selective admissions process.

Students at Mississippi College are quick to find fault with many aspects of their chosen school. The extent of their criticisms varies widely, but most seem to agree at least on the areas most in need of improvement. But first the good news. MC students almost unanimously had kind words for their faculty, the people who, in large part, determine the quality of any student's law-school experience. "We have a really strong faculty that offers personal attention to students," went one typical remark. For many, this was the best effect of MC's small size. "The school's not very large," reported a 1L, "so there is a lot of faculty-student interaction." "At Mississippi College," said another, "students are adopted into a family.

Patricia H. Evans, Director of Admissions
151 East Griffith Street, Jackson, MS 39201
Tel: (601) 353-3907

This sincere and meaningful praise aside, however, most of the students we heard from had some specific complaints. Most negatively reviewed was the law school's apparently outdated physical plant. "They really need to improve the facilities," said one 2L, whose opinion was often more forcefully echoed. "The building is heinous," was the judgment of another student. A number of students focused their criticism of the facilities on security, which several considered "severely lacking." Since we surveyed, the law school has employed a full-time security service with a security guard on duty whenever the building is open, so our next surveys should reflect the improved conditions. On the academic front, most MC students seem to feel constrained by their school's relatively limited curriculum, and many complained that only those students in the top of their class had access to the law school's special programs. Furthermore, many students expressed great dissatisfaction with the lack of diversity in the law school's faculty and with the fairly high degree of competitiveness they said exists among students. To be fair, we must point out that perhaps the school has increased the diversity of the faculty since these comments were made, as the faculty is now 40 percent women and includes two African American members.

Needless to say, not all the students we heard from at Mississippi College were wholly negative about their law school. In fact, many of those who voiced the strongest criticism expressed their opinion that it is very much within the power of the law school's administration to correct the shortcomings that are at the root of its students' dissatisfaction.

ADMISSIONS

As the size of the law school's applicant pool has grown in recent years, admissions standards at the Mississippi College School of Law have risen appreciably. Between 1986 and 1993, applications volume grew by 80 percent, and the average LSAT score of entering students jumped by around 15 percentile points. But numerical standards at MC are still among the most lenient in the country, despite the steadily decreasing acceptance rate.

ACADEMICS

Student/faculty ratio	22:1
% female faculty	40
% minority faculty	11
Hours of study per day	4.01

FINANCIAL FACTS

Tuition	$12,000
Part-time tuition per credit	NR
Estimated books/expenses/fees	$1,100
On-campus living expenses	NR
Off-campus living expenses	NR
% first-year students receiving aid	80
% all students receiving aid	89
% aid that is merit-based	25
% all students receiving grants/scholarships	17
% all students receiving loans	89
% all students receiving assistantships	NR
Average award package	$7,200
Average graduation debt	$53,000

ADMISSIONS

# applications received	891
% applicants accepted	52
% acceptees attending	33
Average LSAT	152
Average undergrad GPA	3.10
Application Fee	$25
Priority application deadline	NR
Priority notification	NR
Regular application deadline	May 1
Regular notification	rolling
Admission may be deferred?	no
Gourman Report Rating	2.14

UNIVERSITY OF MISSISSIPPI
School of Law

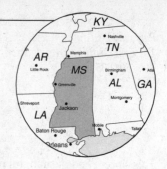

OVERVIEW

Type of school	public
Environment	town
Scholastic calendar	semester
Schedule	Full time only

STUDENTS

Enrollment of institution	7,263
Enrollment of law school	469
% male/female	61/39
% out-of-state	9
% part-time	1
% minorities	10
% international (# countries represented)	NR (NR)
Average age at entry	24

APPLICANTS ALSO LOOK AT

Samford University
University of Tennessee
The University of Memphis
University of Florida
Mississippi College

SURVEY SAYS...

HITS
Socratic method
Studying

MISSES
Students feel poorly prepared
Legal writing

EMPLOYMENT PROFILE

% grads employed immediately	NR
% grads employed within six months	NR
Average starting salary	NR
% grads employed by field:	
Private practice	55
Business/industry	9
Government	10
Judicial clerkships	9
Public service	7
Academic	10
Military	3

If you had only one day in which to experience the American South, you could do worse than to start in Oxford, Mississippi, the former home of William Faulkner and still the home of one of the finest law schools in the Southeast, the University of Mississippi School of Law. As evidenced by the namesake of the law school's main building—Lucius Quintus Cincinnatus Lamar—and the nickname by which even serious-minded scholars refer to the modern, comprehensive university of which it is a part—"Ole Miss"—this is a quintessentially southern institution. From its architecture to its curriculum, this law school—the fourth oldest state-supported law school in the country—is steeped in tradition, one that dates back over 120 years to its founding in the aftermath of the Civil War.

There is one aspect of the Ole Miss tradition, however, that the law school is working very hard to overcome: a shameful history of racial exclusion. The population of Mississippi includes a larger proportion of African Americans than does any other state in the union, but until very recently the state's flagship public university was almost completely white, and defiantly so. To its credit, the law school has made minority recruitment a high priority, and if the trend in recent years continues, the law school at Mississippi will soon be much closer to reflecting the population of the state it has served for so long.

Indeed, the law school's regional reputation, built on the quality of its extremely traditional curriculum, couldn't be stronger. Ole Miss is the alma mater of a sizable majority of Mississippi's lawyers, and this alumni network represents a significant resource for the law school's graduates when they enter the job market. This fact is certainly not lost on students at Ole Miss, who have nothing but praise for their chosen school when it comes to its ability to prepare them for practice within the state. And although most of those we heard from complained that an unforgiving grading curve fosters competitiveness among students, most did agree that the overall atmosphere at the law school is made livable by the "terrific relationships between professors and students." "The faculty is both interested and interesting," said one. "They seem strongly and genuinely interested in their students.

But the criticism of Mississippi students for certain aspects of their law school is every bit as heartfelt as their praise for others. Most of the negative reviews we heard concerned the general dissatisfaction with the lack of flexibility in the law school's highly prescribed curriculum. "We need more practice/clinical classes," said one 2L, "and more classes in general." Indeed, Mississippi students have relatively few courses from which to choose their electives and little access to clinical courses. As one student who criticized the rigidity of his program put it, "They need to quit relying on the 'ole' and bring in some 'new.'"

All in all, it seems that those Mississippi students who are most satisfied with their law school are those who are most satisfied with their geographical and cultural surroundings generally. To some, the "old South" atmosphere is a bit stifling. Said one such student, a non-Mississippian, "Unfortunately, the degree...is good for one ticket, valid only in the state of Mississippi and surrounding area." One even-handed 3L counseled that "if you are a Mississippi native this is the school for you. Oxford is a small, historical town that personifies the Old South and provides a positive and unique learning atmosphere." On the basis of the remarks we heard, this latter judgment is by far more indicative of the consensus among students at Ole Miss.

ADMISSIONS

In terms of the numerical standards to which it holds applicants, the University of Mississippi School of Law ranks as one of the sixty least selective law schools in the country. Still, all but the most highly qualified of hopeful applicants would be wrong to conclude that this long-established law school represents a sure bet. Applications volume at Ole Miss is quite heavy, and the overall acceptance rate is very low.

ACADEMICS

Student/faculty ratio	22:1
% female faculty	29
% minority faculty	14
Hours of study per day	4.05

FINANCIAL FACTS

In-state tuition	$3,096
Out-of-state tuition	$7,018
Part-time tuition per credit	NR
Estimated books/expenses/fees	NR
On-campus living expenses	NR
Off-campus living expenses	NR
% first-year students receiving aid	NR
% all students receiving aid	NR
% aid that is merit-based	NR
% all students receiving grants/scholarships	NR
% all students receiving loans	NR
% all students receiving assistantships	NR
Average award package	NR
Average graduation debt	NR

ADMISSIONS

# applications received	1,349
% applicants accepted	27
% acceptees attending	49
Average LSAT	151
Average undergrad GPA	3.30
Application Fee	$20
Priority application deadline	NR
Priority notification	NR
Regular application deadline	March 1
Regular notification	NR
Admission deferment	NR
Gourman Report Rating	**3.25**

UNIVERSITY OF MISSOURI, COLUMBIA 🖫

School of Law

OVERVIEW

Type of school	public
Environment	suburban
Scholastic calendar	semester
Schedule	Full-time or part-time

STUDENTS

Enrollment of institution	15,086
Enrollment of law school	434
% male/female	61/39
% out-of-state	15
% part-time	NR
% minorities	10
% international (# countries represented)	2 (6)
Average age at entry	25

APPLICANTS ALSO LOOK AT

U. of Missouri, Kansas City
Washington University
Saint Louis University
University of Illinois
University of Kansas

SURVEY SAYS...

HITS
Great facilities
Faculty-student relations
Sense of community

MISSES
Breadth of curriculum
Library staff
Studying

EMPLOYMENT PROFILE

% grads employed immediately	60
% grads employed within six months	95
Average starting salary	$33,000
% grads employed by field:	
Private practice	61
Business/industry	2
Government	13
Judicial clerkships	16
Public service	4
Academic	2
Military	4

Located in central Missouri, in one of the country's great college towns, the University of Missouri, Columbia School of Law has a long history as its home state's primary source of well-trained lawyers. Over the more than 150 years of its existence, its parent institution has grown into one of the nation's finest comprehensive research and teaching institutions. Since 1873, the School of Law has contributed to and benefited from the growth of this public university. Today, the UMC law school enjoys a reputation not only as a regional powerhouse (A huge percentage of the law school's students and alumni hail from and remain in Missouri) but also as one of the twenty or thirty finest state-supported law schools in the nation. As that fact would imply, it also ranks as one of the best bargains in legal education.

The course of study followed by UMC's 400 plus students is straightforward. All first-year and many second-year courses are prescribed, and most course offerings fall well within traditional bounds. The law school's curriculum is, however, rich in clinical offerings and supplemented by a variety of co-curricular programs. The law school takes particular pride in its highly regarded trial-practice program. UMC is also home to a Center for the Study of (Alternative) Dispute Resolution, dedicated to promoting and fostering research in that growing field. The integration of dispute-resolution problems into even first-year courses is surely responsible, in part, for what students here call "the practical emphasis in most courses." Still, the nearly eight candidates who vie annually for each spot in the UMC law school's first-year class are drawn not so much by innovation as by value and academic solidity.

Small, strong, and inexpensive, it is no surprise that the University of Missouri, Columbia School of Law is tremendously popular with law-school applicants. It is also quite popular with current students, who give the law school consistently high marks on most issues relating to the fundamental quality of their education. This is particularly true when it comes to the quality of teaching by the UMC faculty, which was rated very highly by the students we heard from. Most students also had kind words for the quality of their relations with faculty outside the classroom.

Sheryl Gregory, Admissions Advisor
103 Hulston Hall, Columbia, MO 65211
Tel: (314) 882-6042
eMail: gregory@law.missouri.edu
Internet: http://www.law.missouri.edu

University of Missouri, Columbia

"I've almost always felt like my professors were genuinely interested in my academic progress," wrote one 2L, "and they have always been available to help whenever I've needed it." This sentiment was echoed many times over. "There is a very strong communal feeling among faculty, staff and students," reported one 1L. "The learning environment here couldn't be better," said another.

There are aspects of their chosen school, however, that most UMC students feel could be quite a bit better. For all their praise of the quality of life at the law school, for instance, few expressed a great degree of satisfaction with the variety of their academic options. "I can't complain about the quality of most of the courses I've taken," wrote one fairly typical 3L, "but I do feel like my choices were often too limited." Another added that "the law school should make available greater opportunities for students to specialize in areas that are now lacking here, like international law." Students also felt that their library services and computer access to critical resources such as Lexis and Westlaw were less than competitive compared to other law schools and even compared to their own law school in the recent past. On balance, however, praise outweighed such criticism in the remarks we heard from UMC students. And while few students would probably go as far as the 2L who wrote that "Coming to Mizzou Law School is the best choice I've made in life so far," most appear to share the sense of satisfaction that such an enthusiastic statement conveys.

ADMISSIONS

Like all of the nation's better public law schools, the University of Missouri, Columbia School of Law draws a relatively large volume of applications by virtue not only of its quality but also its value. Consequently, Missouri is in a position to be selective in choosing members of its entering class of about 160. Still, the numerical standards to which the law school holds applicants are only slightly above the national average. Statistically, an applicant with an undergraduate GPA between 3.00 and 3.25 and an LSAT score between 150 and 154, inclusive, stands only a 2 percent chance of getting in.

ACADEMICS

Student/faculty ratio	15:1
% female faculty	28
% minority faculty	3
Hours of study per day	3.71

FINANCIAL FACTS

In-state tuition	$7,800
Out-of-state tuition	$15,600
Part-time tuition per credit	NR
Estimated books/expenses/fees	$1,470
On-campus living expenses	$6,000
Off-campus living expenses	$6,000
% first-year students receiving aid	70
% all students receiving aid	70
% aid that is merit-based	20
% all students receiving grants/scholarships	20
% all students receiving loans	70
% all students receiving assistantships	2
Average award package	NR
Average graduation debt	$33,000

ADMISSIONS

# applications received	890
% applicants accepted	40
% acceptees attending	40
Average LSAT	157
Average undergrad GPA	3.46
Application Fee	$40
No early decision program	
Regular application deadline	NR
Regular notification	rolling
Admission may be deferred?	no
Gourman Report Rating	**3.79**

UNIVERSITY OF MISSOURI, KANSAS CITY 💾

School of Law

OVERVIEW

Type of school	public
Environment	metropolis
Scholastic calendar	semester
Schedule	Full-time or part-time

STUDENTS

Enrollment of institution	9,931
Enrollment of law school	524
% male/female	57/43
% out-of-state	25
% part-time	6
% minorities	8
% international (# countries represented)	NR (4)
Average age at entry	27

APPLICANTS ALSO LOOK AT

University of Kansas
U. of Missouri, Columbia
Washburn University
Saint Louis University
University of Iowa

SURVEY SAYS...

HITS
Great facilities
Intellectual challenge
Socratic method

MISSES
Clinical experience
Competitive atmosphere
Sense of community

EMPLOYMENT PROFILE

% grads employed immediately	NR
% grads employed within six months	91
Average starting salary	$34,401
% grads employed by field:	
Private practice	57
Business/industry	13
Government	12
Judicial clerkships	16
Public service	2
Military	2

In one incarnation or another, the University of Missouri, Kansas City, School of Law has been the source of most of its region's lawyers for more than 100 years. Founded in 1895 as the Kansas City School of Law, it gained ABA accreditation in 1936 and affiliated with the University of Missouri in 1963. Located in a residential district of Kansas City, Missouri, the law school draws nearly all its students from within Missouri and from nearby counties in Kansas. The law school's low tuition and the reasonable cost of living in Kansas City combine to make a legal education here quite inexpensive. Nearly all UMKC students remain in the metropolitan region after completing their degrees. The curriculum is a traditional one supplemented by a handful of clinical programs. In an effort to foster a good environment for learning, the law school has increased the size of its faculty in recent years and has designed its law library in a novel fashion: Second- and third-year students have individual assigned spaces in office "suites" that are shared by faculty members. Entering classes at UMKC are relatively small, so admissions are somewhat selective. Since the law school uses a straight index to admit most of its students, however, applicants with solidly midrange numerical credentials are virtually guaranteed admission.

Those applicants who go on to enroll at UMKC express a moderate sense of fundamental satisfaction with their chosen school, though few were enthusiastic. In their responses to our survey, students here spent as much time in comparing UMKC to the better-known University of Missouri, Columbia, as they did in assessing their school on its own merits. One 2L voiced a common concern when he called on his school to "Improve [its] ties with the legal community in Missouri outside of Kansas City—our isolation makes us the forgotten stepchild of Missouri law schools." This concern with outsiders' perception of UMKC's reputation is understandable, but according to many of the students we heard from, that concern is misplaced. Asked to name their law school's greatest strengths, many UMKC students cited a much more immediate concern: its reputation in and around Kansas City, one of the Midwest's largest legal job markets. "Its location is one of UMKC's biggest advantages," explained one 3L. "Law firms in Kansas City know that this is a good school and they are eager to

Jean Klosterman, Director of Admissions and Student Services
5100 Rockhill Road, Kansas City, MO 64110-2499
Tel: (816) 235-1644
eMail: klosterj@smtpgate.umkc.edu
Internet: http://www.law.umkc.edu

**University of Missouri,
Kansas City**

hire from here." But what about life at the law school prior to graduation? The highest praise we heard from students was for their faculty and, notably, for the solidity of the academic program itself. "Our faculty are a relatively diverse and committed group," wrote one typical 2L. "The professors are, with notable exceptions, good teachers as well as scholars," added another, "and I feel like they do a good job of preparing us for the practical realities of practicing law."

When asked to name areas in which their school could stand to improve, few UMKC students offered specifics. Those who did often cited the relatively narrow selection of courses offered in any given semester. "The variety of courses here leaves something to be desired," went one such remark. "Beyond the basics there's not a whole lot to choose from." We did also hear quite a few negative reports concerning the degree of competitiveness among students here. "The curve is pretty tight and A's and high B's are hard to come by," reported one 2L. "As a result, there is a good deal of anxiety-producing stress, though few become really cutthroat." To most ears, though, that probably sounds like law school just about everywhere, and though UMKC students gave their school only mediocre marks for quality of life, their degree of satisfaction with their school is a bit higher than the national average in most every category. And few are unaware of its bargain status. "Dollar for dollar," wrote one typical 3L, "I'm more than satisfied with my decision to go here."

ADMISSIONS

Although significantly less well known than its companion school in Columbia, the University of Missouri, Kansas City, School of Law enjoys a regional reputation that is solid enough and charges a tuition that is low enough to draw a relatively large pool of well qualified applicants. Numerically, Missouri K.C. ranks in the middle of all U.S. law schools in terms of admissions selectivity, and has a very generous overall acceptance rate of 55 percent.

ACADEMICS

Student/faculty ratio	18:1
% female faculty	26
% minority faculty	7
Hours of study per day	3.99

FINANCIAL FACTS

In-state tuition	$8,272
Out-of-state tuition	$16,061
Part-time tuition per credit	NR
Estimated books/expenses/fees	$1,879
On-campus living expenses	NR
Off-campus living expenses	NR
% first-year students receiving aid	86
% all students receiving aid	77
% aid that is merit-based	9
% all students receiving grants/scholarships	15
% all students receiving loans	74
% all students receiving assistantships	12
Average award package	$3,130
Average graduation debt	NR

ADMISSIONS

# applications received	931
% applicants accepted	55
% acceptees attending	34
Average LSAT	154
Average undergrad GPA	3.12
Application Fee	$25
No early decision program	
Regular application deadline	NR
Regular notification	rolling
Admission may be deferred?	no
Gourman Report Rating	**3.37**

UNIVERSITY OF MONTANA 💾
School of Law

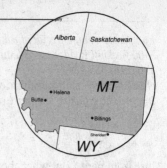

OVERVIEW

Type of school	public
Environment	city
Scholastic calendar	semester
Schedule	Full time only

STUDENTS

Enrollment of institution	11,000
Enrollment of law school	235
% male/female	60/40
% out-of-state	33
% part-time	NR
% minorities	6
% international (# countries represented)	2 (5)
Average age at entry	29

APPLICANTS ALSO LOOK AT

Lewis and Clark College
Gonzaga University
University of Colorado
University of Denver
University of Idaho

SURVEY SAYS...

HITS
Students feel well-prepared
Diverse faculty
Serving humankind

MISSES
Intellectual challenge
Not enough courses

EMPLOYMENT PROFILE

% grads employed immediately	NR
% grads employed within six months	87
Average starting salary	$28,000
% grads employed by field:	
Private practice	50
Government	18
Judicial clerkships	21
Academic	11

A river doesn't actually run through the campus of the University of Montana School of Law, but it comes pretty darn close. Missoula, the city of 50,000 plus that is home to the nearly 11,000-student university and its tiny student law school, sits on the western slope of the Rocky Mountains. It is surrounded by some of the world's most beautiful wilderness, a landscape known to many from the stories of Norman Maclean. Thanks to the 1992 Hollywood version of Mr. Maclean's best-known story, millions of Americans will forever imagine Montana as Eden with big trout and handsome, pious fly-fishermen. Not to spoil this idealized image, but accuracy demands the inclusion of a few hundred hardworking, library-bound law students.

Montana is one of the nation's most sparsely populated states, and its only law school is one of the nation's smallest and least expensive. Crowds are virtually unheard of here, on the streets or in the classroom. Montana's low student-faculty ratio and its creative curricular efforts to combine theory and practice serve its students well. The first-year curriculum is particularly broad and includes a heavier-than-average emphasis on the team-oriented problem-solving techniques that actually characterize the practice of law. Reflecting its setting, the law school offers a broad range of courses in natural resources law and even a clinical program in conjunction with the U.S. Forest Service. Montana receives about six applications for every spot in its tiny first-year class, but numerical admissions standards are moderate.

The words of praise that most students at the University of Montana used for their school are quite strong. Most seem to have come here with the goal of practicing law in the state of Montana. For those individuals, the law school was a known quantity before they came. As residents of the state, the majority of students at Montana couldn't help but know the solid reputation that their school enjoys throughout the region. Nor could they have been ignorant of the extent to which graduates of the law school dominate the Montana bench and bar. (The high percentage of Montana grads who serve judicial clerkships is clear evidence of this.) But perhaps they were pleasantly surprised by the relaxed collegiality that seems to characterize relations among

Christine Sopko, Admissions Officer
Missoula, MT 59812
Tel: (406) 243-2698
eMail: crs@selway.umt.edu
Internet: http://www.umt.edu/law/homepage.htm

students and between students and their instructors. "The school is small enough," said one Montana 1L, "that the dean actually knows the students and actually teaches classes." Many others praised the law school's "congenial" atmosphere and its "location, price, and laid-back method of teaching." As one 3L put it: "Montana's strengths are its good people and its humanitarian approach to the law."

As for the most fundamental aspect of their experience at the law school, their training to be lawyers, most Montana students were positive. "The school is geared to prepare you to practice in Montana," said one. We must add that the Associate Dean has pointed out that while the school, "certainly [is] geared to prepare students to practice law, but no more in Montana than in North Carolina." However, another student said, "Law professors make their own casebooks that incorporate Montana law into the curriculum, and it really prepares students for the bar (we have a very high pass rate in Montana)." Indeed, most praised the law school's practical emphasis, though a few who did so expressed their wish that the practice-oriented curriculum could be supplemented with a bit more theory and that more elective courses were available. But, for the most part, the complaints of Montana students were mild, and some were even backhanded compliments. Asked to say how the law school could improve, one student offered only this: "Pay teachers more."

ADMISSIONS

Although its overall admissions standards are moderately low, the University of Montana School of Law chooses quite carefully in putting together its entering class of about 75 students. Because it strictly limits nonresident enrollment to 33 percent of this total, the admissions process is significantly more selective for outsiders hoping to take advantage of the fine program at this inexpensive law school. Those who are admitted and enroll at Montana possess moderate numerical credentials, with a solid average undergraduate GPA and an average LSAT score at about the 74th percentile.

ACADEMICS

Student/faculty ratio	13:1
% female faculty	33
% minority faculty	7
Hours of study per day	3.91

FINANCIAL FACTS

In-state tuition	$5,091
Out-of-state tuition	$10,252
Part-time tuition per credit	NR
Estimated books/expenses/fees	NR
On-campus living expenses	NR
Off-campus living expenses	NR
% first-year students receiving aid	82
% all students receiving aid	86
% aid that is merit-based	3
% all students receiving grants/scholarships	42
% all students receiving loans	82
% all students receiving assistantships	7
Average award package	$1,392
Average graduation debt	$37,500

ADMISSIONS

# applications received	614
% applicants accepted	30
% acceptees attending	42
Average LSAT	157
Average undergrad GPA	3.20
Application Fee	$60
No early decision program	
Regular application deadline	March 15
Regular notification	rolling
Admission may be deferred?	no
Gourman Report Rating	**2.84**

UNIVERSITY OF NEBRASKA 💾
College of Law

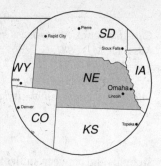

OVERVIEW

Type of school	public
Environment	city
Scholastic calendar	semester
Schedule	Full time only

STUDENTS

Enrollment of institution	24,000
Enrollment of law school	402
% male/female	60/40
% out-of-state	33
% part-time	NR
% minorities	9
% international (# countries represented)	NR (3)
Average age at entry	26

APPLICANTS ALSO LOOK AT

Creighton University
University of Iowa
University of Minnesota
University of Kansas
University of South Dakota

SURVEY SAYS...

HITS
Library staff
Diverse faculty
Great facilities

MISSES
Students feel poorly prepared

EMPLOYMENT PROFILE

% grads employed immediately	40
% grads employed within six months	92
Average starting salary	$33,000
% grads employed by field:	
Private practice	40
Business/industry	18
Government	26
Judicial clerkships	11
Public service	3
Academic	1
Military	3

It is indeed true that $80,000 starting salaries do not await most graduates of the College of Law at the University of Nebraska, Lincoln. Neither Lincoln nor Omaha, Nebraska's other major job market, is New York or Los Angeles. But this suits Nebraskans just fine. The obsession with salaries and rankings that preoccupies so many law students on both coasts are distant phenomena in Lincoln. While a share of its graduates do venture out to the major markets, the University of Nebraska College of Law is, in the best sense, a regional institution. U of N holds the franchise when it comes to supplying the state's lawyers: More than half of Nebraska's practicing attorneys are Nebraska Law graduates. Few law schools of its size can match the educational resources the Nebraska law school offers its students. In a part of the country where higher education is dominated by state-supported schools, the University of Nebraska is one of the finest. Numerous joint-degree programs are available to the university's law students, including a highly regarded course of study leading to a J.D./Ph.D. in psychology. As residents of the state, the majority of Nebraska students pay a tuition that is as low as that of practically any law school in the country.

Equally moderate is the praise that we heard from Nebraska law students for their school. Most of those we surveyed expressed satisfaction with the basic quality of their program, but few did so enthusiastically. This remark from one 2L was typical of those we heard: "Some of my classes have been great, and a few of my professors have been excellent, but certainly not all...Only when I consider how much students at some private schools pay for the same thing do I really appreciate UNL as much as I probably should." Indeed, such praise seems far less faint when one considers how many other law schools utterly fail to satisfy their students in fundamental areas in which Nebraska students seem to want for very little. As one 3L put it, "The facilities here are excellent, and there are enough talented and helpful members of the faculty and staff that you can, if you try, get just about anything you need here." Most seem to share this opinion, giving Nebraska very high marks for its research facilities and the Nebraska faculty better-than-average marks for their teaching abilities.

Glenda J. Pierce, Assistant Dean
P.O. Box 830902, Lincoln, NE 68583-0902
Tel: (402) 472-2161
eMail: lawadm@unlinfo.unl.edu
Internet: http://www.unl.edu.

University of Nebraska

That said, it must be noted that students here see room for serious improvement in several areas. There is general agreement among Nebraska law students—as there appears to be among law students almost everywhere—that their curriculum, however strong, fails to prepare them for the daily demands of law practice. As one 3L lamented, "There are no courses that teach billing practices or how to find a courthouse. Law schools in general are geared to produce research associates (for big firms), not individual lawyers." This complaint was quite common, especially among the relatively large number of Nebraska students who expressed a desire to become solo practitioners. At the same time, the administration said they have offered clinical education programs every semester for over 20 years. "In the civil clinic, our third-year students represent indigent clients in a wide variety of matters, and in our criminal clinic, our students conduct most of the misdemeanor prosecutions for Lancaster County." Perhaps the discrepancy between student and administrative opinions can be explained by student comments on lack of class selection.

Nebraska students also expressed dissatisfaction in several areas where many smaller law schools appear to fall short: career services and class selection. "They need to offer more classes on a regular basis," wrote one 2L, "rather than once a year or even less." "The selection of classes is too limited," agreed a 3L, "and you're basically on your own when it comes to career services." The latter opinion appears to be widely held, and cannot easily be dismissed. As for course selection, which is often a function of faculty size, Nebraska students may not realize how lucky they are. In comparison with many private schools of its size, the state-supported University of Nebraska College of Law has a favorable student-faculty ratio.

ADMISSIONS

In 1986, the University of Nebraska College of Law admitted nearly 70 percent of all applicants. Today, Nebraska is hardly among the most selective of law schools, but gone are the days when practically all one had to do to get into this fine public law school was have a pulse and file an application. The numerical credentials of the average Nebraska student are only slightly above the national average for current law students, and the law school's overall acceptance rate is still quite generous.

ACADEMICS

Student/faculty ratio	13:1
% female faculty	18
% minority faculty	11
Hours of study per day	3.88

FINANCIAL FACTS

In-state tuition	$3,402
Out-of-state tuition	$8,748
Part-time tuition per credit	NR
Estimated books/expenses/fees	$1,737
On-campus living expenses	NR
Off-campus living expenses	NR
% first-year students receiving aid	NR
% all students receiving aid	NR
% aid that is merit-based	44
% all students receiving grants/scholarships	53
% all students receiving loans	80
% all students receiving assistantships	NR
Average award package	NR
Average graduation debt	$20,000

ADMISSIONS

# applications received	777
% applicants accepted	49
% acceptees attending	35
Average LSAT	155
Average undergrad GPA	3.34
Application Fee	$25
No early decision program	
Regular application deadline	March 1
Regular notification	rolling
Admission deferment	one year
Gourman Report Rating	3.23

NEW ENGLAND SCHOOL OF LAW

OVERVIEW

Type of school	private
Environment	NR
Scholastic calendar	NR
Schedule	Full-time or part-time

STUDENTS

Enrollment of institution	NR
Enrollment of law school	1,097
% male/female	54/46
% out-of-state	47
% part-time	41
% minorities	13
% international (# countries represented)	2 (12)
Average age at entry	27

APPLICANTS ALSO LOOK AT

Suffolk University
Boston College
Northeastern University
New York Law School
Western New England College

SURVEY SAYS...

HITS
Practical lawyering skills
Clinical experience
Students feel well-prepared

MISSES
Studying

EMPLOYMENT PROFILE

% grads employed immediately	40
% grads employed within six months	66
Average starting salary	$36,282
% grads employed by field:	
Private practice	45
Business/industry	21
Government	21
Judicial clerkships	6
Public service	2
Academic	4
Military	4

The unique history of the New England School of Law began on Boston's Beacon Hill in 1908 when it was established as the Portia Law School. What is notable is not that this huge private law school began life under a different name, but that under that name it was an all-women's law school, the only such school in the country. Coeducational since 1938 and accredited by the ABA under its current name only since 1969, New England now enrolls over 1,100 full- and part-time students, more than half of them men, who study in a recently renovated building. In a city that is jam-packed with excellent law schools, New England is the most decidedly local of these schools. The proportion of Massachusetts natives in New England's student body is higher than in any of Boston's six other law schools. The law school's flexible scheduling options (full-time day, part-time evening, flex time) surely go a long way toward explaining this.

The New England curriculum is straightforward, with relatively few required courses after a traditional first-year course of study. In their second and third years, New England students have numerous opportunities to gain practical experience through the law school's wide-ranging clinical programs. Most of these programs take the form of external placements that run concurrently with a course in the law school dedicated to the subject matter of the externship. For instance, a New England student might work part time with the Department of Public Health while taking the law school's course in health and hospital law. Prospective New England students would probably be well advised to take advantage of such programs, if only to improve their resumes. In a tight legal job market in the region of the country most saturated with law students, a law degree from Boston's most recently accredited law school might not open every door.

This fact is certainly not lost on current students at New England. The only consistent "complaints" from students here about their chosen school concerned what they perceive as a lack of outside recognition of its many strengths. We heard dozens of remarks very much like these: "Our school is highly underrated. The recent bar results—a 90 percent pass rate—are an accurate sign of what we are capable of. Other schools may have a 'name' and

Pamela Jorgensen, Director of Admissions
154 Stuart Street, Boston, MA 02116
Tel: (617) 422-7210   Fax: (617) 422-7200
Internet: http://www.nesl.edu

New England School
of Law

'prestige,' but look at the facts, and don't be biased or prejudiced"; "One sees that NESL is extremely underrated when one takes into account factors like location (in Boston's theater district), costs (much lower than comparable schools), and its success with preparing students for the bar." Indeed, school pride seems to run as high here as at any law school we heard from. And while one student's judgment that "NESL is as good as or better than any school in the Northeast" seems to go a bit overboard, this assessment from a 3L is right on the mark: "A great proportion of students here believe in this school and are willing to work hard to make a 'name' for it in their professional lives."

Students here go well beyond mere cheerleading, however, and do not hesitate when asked to name their chosen school's greatest strengths. Most often cited were the teaching skills of the New England faculty. "The faculty get an A+," said a 1L. "They are so helpful." They do everything to make things easier and less stressful." Most students also praised the law school's clinical courses and its overall focus on practical skills. "There is great diversity in courses," wrote one, "all with an emphasis on producing practical lawyers who can help clients and not just spout legal theory." All in all, most students we heard from would surely agree with the opinion of one 3L who called the New England School of Law "the best-kept secret in the Boston area." "If you want professors dedicated to teaching you will be most satisfied with NESL."

ADMISSIONS

Although admissions standards at the New England School of Law have crept up slightly over the last five or six years, the numerical credentials of the average NESL student are still lower than those of students at nearly all other law schools in the Northeast. Rising demand from applicants, however, has kept New England's admissions process somewhat competitive. NESL denies admission to nearly 60 percent of the candidates

ACADEMICS

Student/faculty ratio	26:1
% female faculty	25
% minority faculty	25
Hours of study per day	3.74

FINANCIAL FACTS

Tuition	$12,500
Part-time tuition per credit	$505
Estimated books/expenses/fees	$650
On-campus living expenses	NR
Off-campus living expenses	NR
% first-year students receiving aid	78
% all students receiving aid	78
% aid that is merit-based	2
% all students receiving grants/scholarships	28
% all students receiving loans	76
% all students receiving assistantships	NR
Average award package	$2,400
Average graduation debt	$45,600

ADMISSIONS

# applications received	3,422
% applicants accepted	42
% acceptees attending	24
Average LSAT	150
Average undergrad GPA	2.92
Application Fee	$50
No early decision program	
Regular application deadline	March 15
Regular notification	rolling
Admission deferment	one year
Gourman Report Rating	**3.07**

UNIVERSITY OF NEW MEXICO
School of Law

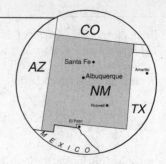

OVERVIEW

Type of school	public
Environment	metropolis
Scholastic calendar	semester
Schedule	Full time only

STUDENTS

Enrollment of institution	24,431
Enrollment of law school	335
% male/female	48/52
% out-of-state	9
% part-time	NR
% minorities	45
% international (# countries represented)	NR (NR)
Average age at entry	28

APPLICANTS ALSO LOOK AT

University of Arizona
Arizona State University
Texas Tech University
Lewis and Clark
University of Colorado

SURVEY SAYS...

HITS
Clinical experience
Diverse faculty
Faculty-student relations

MISSES
Socratic method
Studying
Library staff

EMPLOYMENT PROFILE

% grads employed immediately	NR
% grads employed within six months	NR
Average starting salary	$35,600
% grads employed by field:	
Private practice	66
Business/industry	3
Government	16
Judicial clerkships	12
Public service	0
Academic	3
Military	3

Many previously insulated law schools are only now awakening to the realities of the communities they exist to serve, but the University of New Mexico School of Law has been awake and making progress now for years. Small, innovative, inexpensive, and well-funded, New Mexico seems to fulfill the ideal of the dynamic public law school, reflecting both academically and demographically the state that supports it.

The law school's curriculum is strong in the traditional areas, but it stands out most for its regional (and general social) consciousness. The law school operates several respected research and training institutes, most notably the American Indian Law Center and the Transboundary Center, which is concerned with natural resource management on an international scale. New Mexico students can choose from a number of courses in these areas and can earn their J.D.'s with formal certificates of specialization in Natural Resources Law. The law school's commitment to practical-skills training is exceptionally strong; New Mexico is one of a handful of schools nationwide that requires significant clinical participation by all students. Most UNM students fulfill this requirement on campus at the school's well-staffed Law Practice Clinic.

The student body at New Mexico is strongly representative of the state it serves. The vast majority of students are state residents and almost half are members of traditionally underrepresented ethnic groups, giving UNM a level of student diversity unmatched by any public law school, "save the University of Hawaii." UNM's tiny class size insures an enormously favorable student-faculty ratio and extremely selective admissions process. The school admits less than 20 percent of all applicants, and gives strong preference to state residents. Overall, however, numerical admissions standards are rather moderate.

Decidedly immoderate is the enthusiasm current students express for their chosen school and the very particular attributes that draw them here. Students include among their many blessings the incredible location, the small size and corresponding "incredible closeness of the community and the amount of caring shown among faculty, staff, and students," the excellent Environmental Law and Indian Law programs, and, most of all, each other. One first year explained, "Fellow students help me 'see' things in new ways. The diversity of experience and background is astounding."

Students called the faculty inspiring; one called the professors "the greatest asset," adding, "They are accessible and always willing to help," Many students love sharing their teachers' commitment to changing the makeup of law practitioners to transform and humanize the law and the country it serves. A 1L told us: "There aren't 'too many' lawyers in society. Those people who have access to lawyers make up a small percentage, however. There are too many lawyers representing the interests of the upper classes/corporations of society. This must change." One 3L added that UNM is "a great law school for people who want to learn how to use the law to help people solve their problems." These students will certainly have the chance to do so, as their job-prospect confidence indicates, thanks to UNM's reputation and their excellent legal writing and practical lawyering training which makes them especially attractive to future employers.

Some UNM students did muster a few complaints, but these were generally tempered with (or canceled out by) general satisfaction. One 2L hesitantly asked for "more courses," but said "that would compromise its [the school's] size, which is ideal." Many students agreed that UNM needs "more money for library and computers" saying that the facilities were insufficient to meet student needs. A few students requested more business law, critical race relations, and feminist jurisprudence courses. The general level of contentment must surely be pretty high when the only thing an otherwise happy student requests is "more gothic architecture."

ADMISSIONS

If one looks only at the grade-point average and LSAT score of the average student at the University of New Mexico School of Law, one runs the risk of seriously underestimating the competitiveness of the law school's admissions process. Extremely high demand for spots in New Mexico's tiny entering class makes this fine, inexpensive law school one of the most selective in the nation. No applicants save those with stratospheric numerical credentials can be certain of gaining admission—New Mexico accepts and rejects applicants across a broad range of GPAs and test scores.

ACADEMICS

Student/faculty ratio	12:1
% female faculty	43
% minority faculty	25
Hours of study per day	3.61

FINANCIAL FACTS

In-state tuition	$3,952
Out-of-state tuition	$9,981
Part-time tuition per credit	NR
Estimated books/expenses/fees	NR
On-campus living expenses	NR
Off-campus living expenses	$13,252
% first-year students receiving aid	NR
% all students receiving aid	NR
% aid that is merit-based	NR
% all students receiving grants/scholarships	NR
% all students receiving loans	NR
% all students receiving assistantships	NR
Average award package	NR
Average graduation debt	NR

ADMISSIONS

# applications received	1,136
% applicants accepted	18
% acceptees attending	51
Average LSAT	155
Average undergrad GPA	3.24
Application Fee	$40
Priority application deadline	NR
Priority notification	NR
Regular application deadline	February 15
Regular notification	NR
Admission deferment	NR
Gourman Report Rating	**2.85**

NEW YORK LAW SCHOOL

OVERVIEW

Type of school	private
Environment	metropolis
Scholastic calendar	NR
Schedule	Full-time or part-time

STUDENTS

Enrollment of institution	NR
Enrollment of law school	1,374
% male/female	57/43
% out-of-state	28
% part-time	35
% minorities	23
% international (# countries represented)	8 (31)
Average age at entry	24

APPLICANTS ALSO LOOK AT

Brooklyn Law School
Saint John's University
Fordham University
Yeshiva University
Seton Hall University

SURVEY SAYS...

HITS
Location
Great facilities
Broad range of courses

MISSES
Intellectual challenge
Studying
Sense of community

EMPLOYMENT PROFILE

% grads employed immediately	NR
% grads employed within six months	89
Average starting salary	$60,000
% grads employed by field:	
Private practice	60
Business/industry	18
Government	13
Judicial clerkships	5
Public service	1
Academic	3
Military	2

For the price of a single subway token, and without changing trains, you could get yourself within about two blocks of all of Manhattan's five law schools. Near the end of the line for the downtown No. 1 Train—probably the most law-school-rich subway line in the world—sits one of the city's and country's oldest law schools, the New York Law School. Established in 1891 by former students and administrators from Columbia's young law school, New York Law has put in a century of solid service to the nation's largest legal community. Additionally, this private law school has, through its operation of one of the country's largest evening divisions, put in a century of service to the working men and women of New York City.

Today, New York Law has a total enrollment of almost 1,400, approximately one-third of them part-time students, most of whom are already working professionals. The course of study they follow at the law school represents a good mix of tradition and innovation. Through a variety of classroom courses in "Lawyering Skills," through one of the law school's several clinical programs, or through one of a number of opportunities for external placement, students at New York Law have ample opportunity to gain practical skills before entering the profession. However, some students are unhappy with the current legal writing program. One 3L had some visionary advice, told in the confident style of the New York Law School students we heard from: "All law schools should provide concentration programs so students will be prepared for a specialization. Also, the future of law is in mediation. This should be a required course."

Current NYLS students wish that people would pay attention to the fact that NYLS consistently turns out "successful business leaders and politicians." Their vocal ambition and self-esteem is admirable and absolutely necessary in a city chock-full of prestigious law schools. One student declared, "New York Law School is underrated and its students have the ability to compete with the surrounding likes of Columbia, NYU, Fordham, etc., intellectually, academically, and ethically. Let's get an update on those statistics, our ratings should be going up. NYLS is being treated unfairly, the curriculum and grading system are far more stringent than those schools formerly mentioned." In response to such outcries, the school has revised its grading system to be comparable to its New York brethren. Another student articulated the general perception, "It's better than its reputation." If the tide of national opinion could be turned by force of sheer will alone, Columbia and NYU would soon be considered merely second-rate New York law schools.

Many students expressed dissatisfaction with several areas more within the realm of their administration's ability to change, such as instituting longer library hours. Relations between students, between students and faculty, and between students and the president were also cited as impediments to the strong sense of community that most students said the school currently lacks. One student commented that the school must "improve representation of students to reflect diversity of the surrounding geographic area."

Most NYLS students who responded to our survey expressed typical worry over that precarious step out the law school door and the likelihood that a welcome mat into some friendly office or another would present itself, but they proclaimed adamant pride and enthusiastic confidence in their school.

ADMISSIONS

Although its numerical admissions standards are lower than those of many law schools in the New York region, a massive applicant pool allows the New York Law School to be somewhat selective. Still, New York Law represents by far the safest bet for law-school-bound Manhattanites. Statistically, an applicant with an undergraduate GPA between 3.00 and 3.25 and an LSAT score between about 155 and 159 stands a 95 percent chance of gaining admission. And to make the school even more friendly to applicants, the admissions office tells us that "every applicant is assigned to a specific counselor in Admissions."

ACADEMICS

Student/faculty ratio	11:1
% female faculty	33
% minority faculty	9
Hours of study per day	2.97

FINANCIAL FACTS

Tuition	$17,600
Part-time tuition per credit	NR
Estimated books/expenses/fees	NR
On-campus living expenses	NR
Off-campus living expenses	NR
% first-year students receiving aid	NR
% all students receiving aid	NR
% aid that is merit-based	12
% all students receiving grants/scholarships	38
% all students receiving loans	75
% all students receiving assistantships	NR
Average award package	$5,522
Average graduation debt	$47,000

ADMISSIONS

# applications received	4,642
% applicants accepted	46
% acceptees attending	23
Average LSAT	154
Average undergrad GPA	3.01
Application Fee	$50
Priority application deadline	NR
Priority notification	NR
Regular application deadline	April 1
Regular notification	rolling
Admission deferment	NR
Gourman Report Rating	3.36

NEW YORK UNIVERSITY ⌶

School of Law

OVERVIEW

Type of school	private
Environment	metropolis
Scholastic calendar	semester
Schedule	Full time only

STUDENTS

Enrollment of institution	13,464
Enrollment of law school	1,330
% male/female	54/46
% out-of-state	NR
% part-time	NR
% minorities	23
% international (# countries represented)	NR (13)
Average age at entry	NR

APPLICANTS ALSO LOOK AT

Columbia University
Harvard University
Georgetown University
Yale University
University of Pennsylvania

SURVEY SAYS...

HITS
Sleeping
Left-leaning politics
Prestige

MISSES
Socratic method
Studying

EMPLOYMENT PROFILE

% grads employed immediately	94
% grads employed within six months	97
Average starting salary	$69,000
% grads employed by field:	
Private practice	73
Business/industry	2
Government	4
Judicial clerkships	16
Public service	3
Academic	2
Military	3

If you were to set about ranking law schools, you would be forced to make some idiosyncratic, even arbitrary decisions as to what criteria to consider. Whatever formulas you chose to try out, however, three little letters would start to look mighty familiar at the top of your list: N-Y-U. Established more than 150 years ago just off Washington Square Park in the heart of Greenwich Village, the New York University School of Law is a leader among American law schools in nearly every category. Its students are enormously well qualified, its admirably gender-balanced faculty is world-class, and the ratio of the latter to the former is marvelously low. Its research resources are vast, and its facilities are state-of-the-art. Its traditional classroom curriculum is strong and terrifically broad, and its widely respected clinical programs are innovative and numerous. Upholding the NYU motto, "A private university in the public service," NYU is currently involved in programs offering unparalleled support for students who wish to pursue public interest law, expanding resources in scholarships and loan repayment. Though its tuition is one of the highest charged by any of the nation's 178 ABA approved law schools, its graduates are, on average, some of the most highly compensated in the nation. Beyond these manifold strengths, however, there is something equally important. NYU students are, by our reckoning, among the happiest of all the students at the nation's elite schools.

We could certainly go further, but perhaps that is best left to current NYU students, a highly qualified, remarkably self-assured bunch whose lavish praise for their chosen school speaks for itself. As one student reported: "This school has its attitude as its greatest asset." Indeed. From a 1L asked to assess her law school: "How do I love thee? Let me count the ways....With every part of the law school on your side, it's hard not to feel like you'll be a success." Students praise the "laid-back attitude" of their fellow students, a "diverse" and "community oriented" group. From one of the many students who lionized NYU's career placement staff: "NYU gets its students jobs...Placement takes it personally if you are not employed." From various others who declined to enumerate their beloved's many strengths: "I love NYU"; "Best school in the country"; "NYU=Godhead." When

Nan McNamara, Dean of Admissions
40 Washington Square South, New York, NY 10012
Tel: (212) 998-6060

New York University

asked to name their school's weaknesses, the majority of NYU students we heard from could muster little more than "There could perhaps be..." this or that. And several asserted that the only ways in which NYU could improve would be through the addition of "more copiers in the library," "hors d'oeuvres carts," and "back rubs for all."

In a more serious vein, some students at NYU do see real room for improvement. The law school's clinical programs for instance, whose quality students rightly praise, are criticized by many for their limited enrollment. "Clinics should be open to all who want them," argued one 2L. A number of students also voiced complaints like this one: "NYU has some of the top academics in the country teaching here, which gives us prestige but not necessarily good teaching." While most seem to consider this only a relative weakness, they nevertheless cry out for more "professors who put teaching before their own careers and publishing records."

In the end, it is hard to ignore the near unanimity of opinion and the preponderance of evidence supporting this conclusion from one NYU 2L: "If you are ridiculous enough to go to law school, this is the place to go. The quality of life is better than any other place, and the prestige and respect of going to this school goes a long way."

ADMISSIONS

Once classes begin, cutthroat competitiveness among NYU students is clearly considered unseemly, but they all had to scratch and claw their way in. NYU is universally regarded as a "top-ten" school, and the selectivity of its admissions process is very much in keeping with that status. Numerical admissions standards couldn't be much higher; the average credentials of entering NYU students place them, by our calculations, among the eight or nine most qualified student bodies in the nation. Numbers aren't everything when it comes to getting into a school like this, but they certainly play a major role.

ACADEMICS

Student/faculty ratio	11:1
% female faculty	37
% minority faculty	9
Hours of study per day	3.40

FINANCIAL FACTS

Tuition	$22,144
Part-time tuition per credit	NR
Estimated books/expenses/fees	NR
On-campus living expenses	NR
Off-campus living expenses	NR
% first-year students receiving aid	100
% all students receiving aid	100
% aid that is merit-based	5
% all students receiving grants/scholarships	28
% all students receiving loans	75
% all students receiving assistantships	20
Average award package	$9,101
Average graduation debt	$51,800

ADMISSIONS

# applications received	6,623
% applicants accepted	20
% acceptees attending	30
Average LSAT	168
Average undergrad GPA	3.65
Application Fee	$65
Priority application deadline	October 15
Priority notification	December 1
Regular application deadline	February 1
Regular notification	rolling
Admission deferment	one year
Gourman Report Rating	4.78

NORTH CAROLINA CENTRAL UNIVERSITY

School of Law

The cities of Raleigh, Durham, and Chapel Hill, North Carolina, form what has come to be known as the "Research Triangle," a burgeoning center for industrial and governmental research. The triangle also encompasses three law schools: the nationally prominent law schools at Duke and UNC and the North Carolina Central University School of Law. NC Central is the smallest of the three, and it is certainly the least well known. This public law school cannot compete, perhaps, with its larger, better-known neighbors in terms of prestige, but then it has never tried to. Instead, NC Central has dedicated itself to serving and reflecting the population of the state it serves, and it has succeeded admirably. Founded as the country's first public liberal-arts college for African Americans, NC Central joined the UNC system in 1972, and it now stands as a tremendously important complement to the system's flagship campus in Chapel Hill. The same is true of its law school, which enrolls over 90 percent North Carolina residents, 55 percent of them African Americans. (At Chapel Hill, these statistics are about 70 percent and 9 percent.) In terms of both its student body and its faculty, NC Central is very nearly the most racially diverse of the country's ABA-approved law schools.

The law school's J.D. curriculum is highly structured, with relatively few elective courses even in the third year, but co-curricular opportunities are ample and varied. NC Central also offers a limited clinical program and a joint-degree program with the School of Library and Information Sciences. Overall admissions are relatively selective because of the small size of entering classes, but numerical standards are fairly low.

The law school operates the only evening division available in any of North Carolina's five law schools. The evening students we heard from expressed a heartening combination of excitement, thrill and gratitude that this wonderful program exists and at such an affordable price, enabling working people "to pursue a life long dream, the best legal representation to clients."

We did hear some negative comments, of course, especially from day students, many of whom expressed dissatisfaction with limitations stemming from those characteristics that draw people to NCCU. Many claimed the night students receive better treatment. The low class size and tuition restrict NCCU's ability to provide all the physical comforts and extensive course offerings which many students said would make NCCU a more perfect place. Future NCCU students need not be unduly concerned, however, since, according to one student, "The school has undergone and will continue to undergo some much needed change under the leadership of Dean Luney. New life has been breathed into the school." What troubles students most, besides the perceived lack of effort on the part of Career Services, is the misperception on the part of other schools and employers in the area, who refuse to take proper account of NCCU. One student told us, with typically positive emphasis: "My only concern is traditional employers' limited way of thinking that only certain law schools produce exceptional attorneys...At the NCCU School of Law 'Excellence Without Excuse' is not just a motto, but a way of life."

ADMISSIONS

The admissions process at the North Carolina Central University School of Law is competitive despite the low numerical standards to which the law school holds its applicants. The numerical credentials of the average NC Central student are lower than those of students at most other law schools, but Central's small size necessitates a high degree of selectivity since the law school enrolls only about 100 new students annually.

ACADEMICS	
Student/faculty ratio	15:1
% female faculty	41
% minority faculty	59
Hours of study per day	4.18

FINANCIAL FACTS	
In-state tuition	$1,364
Out-of-state tuition	$9,470
Part-time tuition per credit	NR
Estimated books/expenses/fees	NR
On-campus living expenses	NR
Off-campus living expenses	NR
% first-year students receiving aid	NR
% all students receiving aid	NR
% aid that is merit-based	NR
% all students receiving grants/scholarships	NR
% all students receiving loans	NR
% all students receiving assistantships	NR
Average award package	NR
Average graduation debt	NR

ADMISSIONS	
# applications received	1,350
% applicants accepted	12
% acceptees attending	49
Average LSAT	149
Average undergrad GPA	3.00
Application Fee	$15
Priority application deadline	NR
Priority notification	NR
Regular application deadline	April 15
Regular notification	NR
Admission deferment	NR
Gourman Report Rating	2.17

UNIVERSITY OF NORTH CAROLINA 💾

School of Law

OVERVIEW

Type of school	public
Environment	suburban
Scholastic calendar	semester
Schedule	Full time only

STUDENTS

Enrollment of institution	13,702
Enrollment of law school	696
% male/female	57/43
% out-of-state	25
% part-time	NR
% minorities	18
% international (# countries represented)	NR (4)
Average age at entry	NR

APPLICANTS ALSO LOOK AT

Duke University
Wake Forest University
University of Virginia
Georgetown University
College of William and Mary

SURVEY SAYS...

HITS
Prestige
Serving humankind
Left-leaning politics

MISSES
Research resources
Practical lawyering skills
Students feel poorly prepared

EMPLOYMENT PROFILE

% grads employed immediately	NR
% grads employed within six months	90
Average starting salary	$40,000
% grads employed by field:	
Private practice	60
Business/industry	8
Government	12
Judicial clerkships	7
Public service	6
Academic	7
Military	2

The University of North Carolina School of Law, located on the campus of the nation's oldest state university, enjoys a long-established reputation as one of the twenty or so finest law schools in the country, public or private. For a combination of reasons, some more tangible than others, thousands of highly qualified applicants vie annually for one of the roughly 235 slots in North Carolina's first-year class. Some of this popularity is easily explained by the law school's obvious strengths. The law school's broad, traditional curriculum is administered by a large and esteemed faculty and is supplemented by numerous opportunities for interdisciplinary study in several of the university's widely respected graduate departments and by a modest variety of clinical programs. But two other factors certainly do a better job of explaining the flood of applications that UNC receives every year: value and location. The law school is a bargain if ever there was one. The non-resident tuition is practically the lowest in the country, and its resident tuition is, relatively speaking, negligible. North Carolina also has a trump card to play in the form of Chapel Hill, the archetypal college town that, to a great degree, both defines and is defined by the university. While a large percentage of Carolina students are state residents, the vast majority of applicants are not, and the admissions process at UNC, which is competitive for all, is extraordinarily selective for nonresidents. Across the board, admitted applicants have very strong numerical credentials.

Carolina students express a relatively strong sense of satisfaction with their chosen school, and when asked to name its greatest strengths, many offered laundry lists very much like this one from a satisfied 1L: "The town itself is great, the people are friendly and not overly competitive, the teachers tend to be approachable and to care about the students, there are plenty of social activities, and the school has a good reputation in the job market." To be sure, not all of the Carolina students we heard from offered such sweeping endorsements, but largely positive reviews were certainly the norm. "The school itself is well respected and deservedly so," wrote one 3L. "When you consider the pleasantly relaxed atmosphere of Chapel Hill and the cost-for-quality ratio, you can't do a whole lot better.

J. Elizabeth Furr, Assistant Dean for Admissions
Campus Box 3380, Chapel Hill, NC 27599-3380
Tel: (919) 962-5109   Fax: (919) 962-1170
eMail: law_admission@unc.edu
Internet: http://www.law.unc.edu

University of North
Carolina

When asked to name areas in which the school could stand to improve, most of the Carolina students we heard from complained about the limitations of their program and about the uneven quality of their faculty. On the former matter, the prevailing opinion seems to be that the law school pays far too little attention and dedicates far too few resources to its practical-skills programs. "They offer a clinical program here," explained one, "but due to limited number of spaces, they can't really encourage participation." "The older faculty in particular look upon the clinical program with some disdain," said another, "and until the new guard are in the majority here, Carolina will be very much behind the times in this respect." A similar theme was sounded with regard to the teaching abilities of Carolina faculty members. "They need to get rid of the deadwood faculty," argued one 3L bluntly, "and hold on to the younger faculty who are truly interested in teaching." Numerous other Carolina students also offered unsolicited remarks about the political atmosphere within the law school. "Conservatives are looked down on by many people (faculty and students) here." Many of these same students also warned prospective students from the Northeast and elsewhere that "the reputation of this school is incredibly strong within the state, but you've really got to do well here if you're shooting for a job in the big city."

ADMISSIONS

Like all the nation's elite public law schools, the University of North Carolina School of Law is extremely selective. The law school has the luxury of denying admission to hundreds of candidates whose numbers would get them into almost any law school in the country. Nonresident applicants be forewarned: You will face stiffer competition and be held to even higher standards.

ACADEMICS	
Student/faculty ratio	20:1
% female faculty	32
% minority faculty	10
Hours of study per day	3.39

FINANCIAL FACTS	
In-state tuition	$2,242
Out-of-state tuition	$12,396
Part-time tuition per credit	NR
Estimated books/expenses/fees	NR
On-campus living expenses	NR
Off-campus living expenses	NR
% first-year students receiving aid	NR
% all students receiving aid	NR
% aid that is merit-based	NR
% all students receiving grants/scholarships	NR
% all students receiving loans	NR
% all students receiving assistantships	NR
Average award package	NR
Average graduation debt	NR

ADMISSIONS	
# applications received	2,767
% applicants accepted	20
% acceptees attending	40
Average LSAT	162
Average undergrad GPA	3.50
Application Fee	$60
No early decision program	
Regular application deadline	February 1
Regular notification	rolling
Admission deferment	one year
Gourman Report Rating	4.46

UNIVERSITY OF NORTH DAKOTA
School of Law

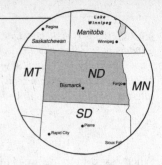

OVERVIEW

Type of school	public
Environment	suburban
Scholastic calendar	semester
Schedule	Full time only

STUDENTS

Enrollment of institution	8,123
Enrollment of law school	243
% male/female	49/51
% out-of-state	47
% part-time	NR
% minorities	4
% international (# countries represented)	NR (NR)
Average age at entry	26

APPLICANTS ALSO LOOK AT

University of Minnesota
Hamline University
William Mitchell College of Law
University of South Dakota
University of Idaho

SURVEY SAYS...

HITS
Faculty-student relations
Sense of community
Legal writing

MISSES
Not enough courses
Research resources
Library staff

EMPLOYMENT PROFILE

% grads employed immediately	NR
% grads employed within six months	NR
Average starting salary	NR
% grads employed by field:	
Private practice	36
Business/industry	7
Government	11
Judicial clerkships	34
Public service	0
Academic	12
Military	0

In the spirit of full disclosure, the bulletin of the University of North Dakota School of Law reports that the average temperature in Grand Forks, ND, for the month of January is 4 degrees Fahrenheit. Low temperatures during what is laconically termed the "cold period" tend to reach -25 degrees. Less-than-hardy prospective law students probably needn't read any further. Located in the fertile Red River Valley, in the northeastern part of sparsely populated North Dakota, this small, inexpensive public law school draws the majority of its students from within the state and from nearby Minnesota, a state with which North Dakota has a reciprocal residency agreement for purposes of tuition. Other states in the upper Midwest are also well represented. The curriculum at North Dakota is decidedly traditional, but clinical programs and skills courses are on the rise. Many of the course offerings reflect regional priorities: "Oil and Gas Law," and "Water Law." The Scandinavian roots of many of the state's residents are reflected not only in the law library (named for former dean Olaf Thormodsgard) but also in the school's exchange program with the University of Oslo in Norway. Those who wish to become part of the roughly eighty new students who bundle up each year and join the first-year class at North Dakota will want to know that fewer than half of all applicants are admitted. Numerical admissions standards, however, are moderate.

Maybe it's just that the chilly weather makes people huddle together for warmth, but the degree of closeness and camaraderie that current North Dakota law students attest to feeling for both their colleagues and their professors is striking. Though not without their criticisms, the students we surveyed expressed a solid sense of satisfaction with their chosen school, particularly when it came to quality-of-life issues. A sampling of the comments we heard follows: "There is very close faculty-student contact here. Professors are your friends and are very concerned with students' learning." "Our size allows you to get to know fellow students very well—there is a family atmosphere despite the inevitable degree of competition among students." "The faculty treat you more like a peer than like a lowly student. That makes for a comfortable classroom environment that stimulates lively discussion."

But for all of the good will which seems to stem from the advantages of North Dakota's size, few of the students we heard from failed to mention some of the disadvantages. "There are not enough professors here to offer the kind of class selection I would ideally like to have," wrote one 3L. "This is basically a meat-and-potatoes law school where you learn the basics to become a competent attorney," added a 2L. "If you want more specialized training, look to a larger school." Indeed, most seem to agree that UND does at least an adequate job of "stick[ing] to the basic general-law courses," but that it "lacks the sort of curricular diversity (not to mention ethnic diversity) that you might find in a larger, more cosmopolitan setting."

Such criticisms are probably inevitable from students at a school as small as this one. What is not inevitable, however, is the fact that, much to its credit, the University of North Dakota School of Law appears to be populated by satisfied customers. The following remark from a UND 2L was typical of most we heard: "North Dakota's lack of financial resources has led to its poor national 'rank' among law schools. But while the library is not gigantic, it is adequate. Although the faculty do not earn comparatively high salaries, they are for the most part talented, knowledgeable, and enthusiastic. They know and care about the students here, which is probably not the case at most larger schools. If you're looking for an inexpensive legal education in a small school with a family atmosphere, UND is ideal."

ADMISSIONS

With a first-year class as tiny as that of the University of North Dakota School of Law, any law school would have to be quite selective. With an applicant pool that is, in relative terms, as large as those of some "top-twenty" schools, North Dakota must be somewhat selective. Still, the numerical credentials of the average student here are lower than those of students at two thirds of all U.S. law schools.

ACADEMICS	
Student/faculty ratio	14:1
% female faculty	38
% minority faculty	5
Hours of study per day	3.64

FINANCIAL FACTS	
In-state tuition	$3,848
Out-of-state tuition	$8,074
Part-time tuition per credit	NR
Estimated books/expenses/fees	NR
On-campus living expenses	NR
Off-campus living expenses	NR
% first-year students receiving aid	NR
% all students receiving aid	NR
% aid that is merit-based	NR
% all students receiving grants/scholarships	NR
% all students receiving loans	NR
% all students receiving assistantships	NR
Average award package	NR
Average graduation debt	NR

ADMISSIONS	
# applications received	446
% applicants accepted	40
% acceptees attending	49
Average LSAT	151
Average undergrad GPA	3.31
Application Fee	NR
Priority application deadline	NR
Priority notification	NR
Regular application deadline	April 1
Regular notification	NR
Admission deferment	NR
Gourman Report Rating	**2.35**

NORTHEASTERN UNIVERSITY 💾
School of Law

As the job market for young attorneys has tightened in the 1990s, employers have come to place a high premium on practical experience in hiring recent law-school graduates. No longer can a fledgling attorney count on the willingness of legal employers to take on the responsibility and expense of training him or her in the skills of lawyering. In response to this situation, an ABA study recommended that law-school curricula be adjusted in an effort to bridge the gap between theory and practice; law schools responded by increasing the number and quality of their clinical programs and skills courses. While many institutions of legal education have been slow to take meaningful action, the Northeastern University School of Law has led the pack.

By virtue of its unique co-op program, this midsize Boston law school is the only school in the country that can truly promise the prospective student that he or she will not enter the legal profession as an unskilled bookworm. After a traditional first year of academic studies, Northeastern law students alternate every three months between classroom instruction and full-time work in the legal field. They finish school in the same amount of time as any full-time law student, but by foregoing summer breaks, they graduate with a J.D. and a full year of legal work experience on their resumes. All students are encouraged to take one of their co-op placements with a public-service organization, and most choose to do so. The law school administers a number of stipend programs designed to make such low-paying work possible for students demonstrably in need. Something like the Northeastern approach will almost surely be adopted by some other law schools in the not-too-distant future, but until then, this is the only such game in town.

Northeastern students picked their law school with its unique attributes in mind, so it is not surprising to hear how satisfied they are with their choice. "I feel much more prepared for my career having had [co-op] experience," said one student, "and my impression is that NU students have superior analytic and writing skills compared to other law students." School pride runs high here. One 2L actually said, "I cannot imagine going to law school anywhere else. I think about how fortunate I am every day."

Lorraine Physic, Director of Admissions
400 Huntington Avenue, Boston, MA 02115
Tel: (617) 373-2395
eMail: mmanware@slaw.neu.edu
Internet: http://www.slaw.neu.edu/public/new_def.htm

Northeastern University

Yet Northeastern students have their gripes. As overwhelmingly satisfied as they are with its co-op program, some wonder if the law school should make some concessions to tradition. "Teach me to write," begged one student, "force me to write more." Another expressed reservations about Northeastern's nontraditional grading system: "We have only written evaluations, which are often problematic when it comes to employment—employers often don't know how to 'fit' NU students with everyone else." The happiest students here seem to be those who wish to practice law in the public interest. "Incoming students should know that there is a strong public interest atmosphere here," advised one student, "and that there is an internal debate on whether to declare that the school officially has a mission to train P.I. lawyers." Not surprisingly, most students' political inclinations are decidedly liberal. One otherwise highly satisfied student remarked that "the atmosphere here is very P.C., and I find this somewhat stifling. If you are at all conservative, NUSL will be culture shock. Be forewarned." The placement office also came in for some criticism, with some remarking that it needed to make more of an effort to help students interested in working outside Boston.

Finally, enough students saw fit to mention the chilliness of their library that we thought we should at least mention this relatively minor shortcoming. "Always have a sweatshirt handy," suggested one Northeastern 2L, "because the temperature is suited for penguins all year round." She also added that "the library lacks soft couches for quick naps," a favorite activity of law students everywhere.

ADMISSIONS

As Northeastern's unique program has become more widely known, both the size and quality of the law school's applicant pool has increased. In terms of numerical admissions standards, NU is still considerably less selective than most of the nation's traditional "elite" schools, but a fairly high degree of overall admissions selectivity is necessitated by the sheer size of its applicant pool. Northeastern denies admission to roughly 2,000 well-qualified candidates annually. Successful candidates who actually go on to enroll at the law school possess very solid, but hardly stratospheric, numerical credentials. Their average undergraduate GPA and LSAT scores are strong.

ACADEMICS

Student/faculty ratio	20:1
% female faculty	39
% minority faculty	17
Hours of study per day	3.90

FINANCIAL FACTS

Tuition	$18,830
Part-time tuition per credit	NR
Estimated books/expenses/fees	NR
On-campus living expenses	NR
Off-campus living expenses	NR
% first-year students receiving aid	100
% all students receiving aid	100
% aid that is merit-based	23
% all students receiving grants/scholarships	49
% all students receiving loans	82
% all students receiving assistantships	14
Average award package	$5,066
Average graduation debt	$56,000

ADMISSIONS

# applications received	2,811
% applicants accepted	27
% acceptees attending	26
Average LSAT	157
Average undergrad GPA	3.29
Application Fee	$55
No early decision program	
Regular application deadline	March 1
Regular notification	rolling
Admission deferment	one year
Gourman Report Rating	**3.10**

NORTHERN ILLINOIS UNIVERSITY 💾
College of Law

OVERVIEW

Type of school	public
Environment	suburban
Scholastic calendar	semester
Schedule	Full time only

STUDENTS

Enrollment of institution	23,171
Enrollment of law school	300
% male/female	59/41
% out-of-state	20
% part-time	2
% minorities	20
% international (# countries represented)	NR (NR)
Average age at entry	27

APPLICANTS ALSO LOOK AT

The John Marshall Law School
Southern Illinois University
Loyola University, Chicago
University of Iowa
University of Illinois

SURVEY SAYS...

HITS
Diverse faculty
Sense of community
Library staff

MISSES
Clinical experience
Quality of teaching
Legal writing

EMPLOYMENT PROFILE

% grads employed immediately	36
% grads employed within six months	85
Average starting salary	$32,000
% grads employed by field:	
Private practice	51
Business/industry	11
Government	33
Judicial clerkships	5
Public service	0
Academic	1
Military	18

Statistically, the Northern Illinois University College of Law stands out among Illinois law schools in several respects. Founded in 1974, this public institution is the youngest, smallest, and one of the least-expensive of the state's nine law schools. This last statistic probably helps explain the most surprising and impressive fact of all: among the state's law schools, most of which are far better known, Northern Illinois ranks behind only the national powerhouses Northwestern and Chicago in terms of overall admissions selectivity. Of course, the small size of its entering class accounts in large part for the low acceptance rate at NIU, and this very young law school has a long way to go before it will compete with these schools for the same applicants. But considering the additional fact that the law school recently experienced a huge surge in applications volume, it seems clear that at least a certain segment of students is seeking out Northern Illinois. Located in DeKalb, a town of about 35,000 in the semi-rural area just outside Chicago's suburban sprawl, NIU is the only public law school in the northern part of the state. So it should not be surprising to hear that a significant proportion of the law school's students are residents of the surrounding area. NIU's J.D. program is largely traditional, with relatively few formal clinical offerings. But like all law schools whose reputations alone do not guarantee their graduates their jobs-of-choice, Northern Illinois is beefing up its assortment of "skills" courses.

Not surprisingly, reputation is something with which many students at Northern Illinois are very much concerned. The following assessment from one such student neatly sums up the general theme of most of the remarks we heard: "The most unfortunate thing about NIU is that it is a secret that is too well-kept. It's small and relatively new, so people don't know we're here, but it's a great school with a closely-knit, diverse student body." The morale of students here appears to be exceptionally strong, with most expressing a high degree of satisfaction with their chosen school. "The greatest strength of our law school is the intimate setting in which we work," went one typical comment. "The small student body creates a friendly 'neighborhood' atmosphere, and the diverse student body provides equally diverse classroom discussions." Most students credited both their faculty

Judith L. Malen, Director of Admissions & Financial Aid
De Kalb, IL 60115-2890
Tel: (815) 753-9485   Fax: (815) 753-4501
eMail: lawadm@niu.edu
Internet: http://www.niu.edu/claw/lawhome.html

and administration for contributing to the comfort of their academic environment. "Our professors are very personable and willing to assist students in any way possible," reported a 1L. "Our deans solicit feedback and attempt to make the school a more pleasant place to be." Several students remarked that NIU treats nontraditional students well—for example, a low cost preschool is available for students with children.

When asked to name areas in which their school could stand to improve, however, most students had little difficulty coming up with something. For the most part, their criticism focused on the limitations of NIU's relatively narrow curriculum. They called for "a greater number of courses generally and more skills courses specifically." The need for more instruction in legal writing was also mentioned by some students. Numerous complaints were also heard about the size and condition of the law school's library and the extent of its research facilities. Several of those who voiced such complaints did, however, recognize this drawback as "an obvious negative side-effect of attending a small, inexpensive public law school."

Indeed, even the most critical Northern Illinois students took pains to point out their fundamental satisfaction with their experience at the law school. "NIU has its shortcomings, and it needs a better reputation," said one, "but that will come with time." Or, as one 2L put it: "I suppose that the low tuition is probably to blame for the fact that the furniture is so sparse and uncomfortable, but basically this school has given me an education worth more than the tuition I paid."

ADMISSIONS

With spots for only about 100 new students in its first-year class, it is hardly surprising that the Northern Illinois University College of Law must deny admission to as many applicants as it does. Indeed, increasing demand has driven NIU's overall acceptance rate steadily lower in recent years, so prospective students can expect to face stiff competition. Still, the law school's numerical admissions standards remain in the low-to-moderate range.

ACADEMICS

Student/faculty ratio	15:1
% female faculty	29
% minority faculty	20
Hours of study per day	3.97

FINANCIAL FACTS

In-state tuition	$4,272
Out-of-state tuition	$8,544
Part-time tuition per credit	NR
Estimated books/expenses/fees	$2,570
On-campus living expenses	NR
Off-campus living expenses	NR
% first-year students receiving aid	69
% all students receiving aid	78
% aid that is merit-based	18
% all students receiving grants/scholarships	24
% all students receiving loans	42
% all students receiving assistantships	13
Average award package	$5,000
Average graduation debt	$20,000

ADMISSIONS

# applications received	1,295
% applicants accepted	27
% acceptees attending	27
Average LSAT	156
Average undergrad GPA	3.00
Application Fee	$35
No early decision program	
Regular application deadline	NR
Regular notification	rolling
Admission deferment	one year

Gourman Report Rating	**2.43**

NORTHERN KENTUCKY UNIVERSITY 🖫

Salmon P. Chase College of Law

OVERVIEW

Type of school	public
Environment	metropolis
Scholastic calendar	semester
Schedule	Full-time or part-time

STUDENTS

Enrollment of institution	7,084
Enrollment of law school	407
% male/female	60/40
% out-of-state	41
% part-time	44
% minorities	9
% international (# countries represented)	NR (1)
Average age at entry	28

APPLICANTS ALSO LOOK AT

University of Kentucky
University of Louisville
University of Cincinnati
University of Dayton
Ohio State University

SURVEY SAYS...

HITS
Sense of community
Socratic method
Diverse faculty

MISSES
Clinical experience
Studying

EMPLOYMENT PROFILE

% grads employed immediately	81
% grads employed within six months	90
Average starting salary	$43,000
% grads employed by field:	
Private practice	36
Business/industry	34
Government	13
Judicial clerkships	5
Public service	5
Academic	2
Military	2

The thousands of people whose mental maps of the United States are woefully incomplete will be confused to learn that the law school at Northern Kentucky University is located in a suburb of Cincinnati, Ohio. In fact, for most of its history, the Salmon P. Chase College of Law was actually in Ohio, moving across the river only in 1971 to merge with NKU in Highland Heights, Kentucky. Though they came together only twenty-five years ago, the Salmon P. Chase law school and NKU share a similar history. Northern Kentucky University evolved from a two-year community college spun off of the University of Kentucky to serve a segment of the state's population that previously lacked easy access to higher education. Chase began life as a night-school program of the Hamilton County (Ohio) YMCA in 1893. Before the turn of the century, the YMCA founded many such law schools to make legal education available to the vast majority of Americans who couldn't possibly afford to attend school by day. The WASP-dominated ABA resisted the YMCA's efforts, fearing an influx of "undesirable elements" into the bar.

Those days are gone, but schools like Salmon P. Chase, with its evening and part-time programs, low tuition, and relatively open admissions standards, continue to perform the vital service of preserving some semblance of egalitarianism in American legal education. Of course, those same ingredients can also pose certain disadvantages. Except at the biggest and most established public law schools, low tuition sometimes means inadequate funding. And flexible scheduling, while improving overall access, can also mean that resources get spread too thin. On the basis of comments made by current Chase students, it seems that their law school meets their needs, but is not entirely immune to such problems.

Most students we heard from, especially the night students, were grateful for the wonderful opportunity the school provides by being geared to both working and traditional students. As one student wrote, "Chase is unique. Half of the student body are evening students who work full time. The school is dedicated to its students and shows a real interest in each student's success."

Victoria Garry, Assistant Dean for Admissions
Nunn Drive, Highland Heights, KY 41099
Tel: (606) 572-6476

The word "nice" in relation to professors and the Dean was used far more frequently than one might expect from people in law school. More than one student remarked on the "good relations between professors and students." "Professors are very accessible and willing to help," said a 2L. Many students praised their teachers' abilities, echoing the 3L who said, "Professors...have a strong and genuine concern for their students." Although class size is kept low so teacher-student interaction works, nearly all respondents asked for more professors, as talented as the ones they so admire, to facilitate more classes at more convenient times for all students. As a 1L explained, NKU needs "more professors so once we get into second and third years we don't have to take so many night classes."

Many students said that additional practical skills courses, legal writing courses, clinical options and possibilities for specialization would vastly improve the education NKU offers. A few disheartened students went so far as to say that NKU could stand to upgrade in every area. Students we surveyed felt that a new building, away from the undergrads, would make the atmosphere more professional and serve as a declaration of commitment to the law students on the part of the Dean and the administration. However, simply continuing its commitment to provide an "excellent opportunity for non-funded students," not to mention both funded and non-funded working students, constitutes the main challenge NKU students hope their school will continue to meet.

ADMISSIONS

In terms of numerical admissions standards, the law school at Northern Kentucky is in the bottom of the midrange of all U.S. law schools, but the small size of its entering class necessitates a fairly high degree of overall selectivity. With about seven applicants for every spot in that class, the law school must deny admission to more than three out of four applicants. Successful candidates tend to possess moderate numerical credentials.

ACADEMICS

Student/faculty ratio	21:1
% female faculty	27
% minority faculty	5
Hours of study per day	3.21

FINANCIAL FACTS

In-state tuition	$4,700
Out-of-state tuition	$12,300
Part-time tuition per credit	NR
Estimated books/expenses/fees	$1,000
On-campus living expenses	$3,550
Off-campus living expenses	$5,400
% first-year students receiving aid	100
% all students receiving aid	100
% aid that is merit-based	NR
% all students receiving grants/scholarships	NR
% all students receiving loans	NR
% all students receiving assistantships	NR
Average award package	$4,939
Average graduation debt	NR

ADMISSIONS

# applications received	1,028
% applicants accepted	23
% acceptees attending	46
Average LSAT	155
Average undergrad GPA	3.19
Application Fee	$25
No early decision program	
Regular application deadline	May 15
Regular notification	rolling
Admission deferment	one year
Gourman Report Rating	2.24

NORTHWESTERN UNIVERSITY
School of Law

With a reputation for academic excellence and with roots that go back nearly as far as those of any law school in the nation, the Northwestern University School of Law is a charter member of the club of elite law schools. Though in the slippery terms of "prestige" it may be overshadowed by its neighbor in Hyde Park, the University of Chicago Law School, Northwestern is hugely respected on its own terms, both within and outside the large legal community in the city it calls home. Housed in beautiful facilities on a downtown Chicago campus (its parent institution is in nearby suburban Evanston), this law school is widely regarded as one of the top 20 in the nation. The curriculum at Northwestern is comprehensive, with a large and multifaceted clinical program adding a practical complement to the law school's richly diverse traditional course offerings. This curriculum is administered by a highly respected faculty whose relative size gives Northwestern one of the most favorable student-faculty ratios in the nation. Between the law school's own offerings and those of the university at large, the Northwestern J.D. student does not want for intellectual opportunities. As a supplement to its own offerings, the law school encourages concurrent enrollment in the university's outstanding graduate division. Not surprisingly, the joint degree most often pursued by Northwestern J.D. candidates is the master's of management (MM) through the Kellogg School of Management, widely regarded as one of the top five business schools in the country. Quite apart from being enormously well qualified, the Northwestern student body stands out for its admirable ethnic diversity—particularly in comparison with Chicago's five other law schools, several of which are woefully homogeneous.

Students at Northwestern express a very high level of fundamental satisfaction with their chosen school. The students we heard from conveyed an unmistakable sense of well-being that they trace primarily to the quality of their relations with one another. "For being such bright, highly driven future lawyers," wrote one 2L, "people here are very normal." And, apparently, friendly. "Northwestern is a rarity among top schools in terms of the strong sense of community and lack of competitiveness among students," said one 3L. Northwestern students also stood out for

357 E. Chicago Avenue, Chicago, IL 60611
Tel: (312) 503-8465   Fax: (312) 503-0178
eMail: nulawadm@harold.law.nwu.edu

Northwestern University

their enthusiasm for their immediate physical surroundings, which several called "incredible." "If you're having a bad day," explained one 2L, "the esthetics of the school and its great location can save you."

When asked to name areas in which their school could stand to improve, Northwestern students tended to offer constructive criticism of their program's substance, rarely questioning its quality but often lamenting its limits. "I'd like to see a greater variety of courses offered," wrote one, "particularly in less traditional areas not geared towards corporate practice." A similar note was sounded by many others who expressed their dissatisfaction with the dominant ideological orientation of their faculty. "I wish there were fewer professors of the Law and Economics school and more who would address less conservative viewpoints," went one fairly typical remark. Negative comments were also directed at the Northwestern faculty for their homogeneity. Notably, however, there was a total lack of rancor in even the most negative remarks we heard, and even those students who were most critical of their program took pains to equivocate. "I probably would have been dissatisfied with any law school," said one such student, "but Northwestern is probably better than most—I'd put it in the 2nd or 3rd circle of Hell, not the 8th or 9th."

ADMISSIONS

The Northwestern University School of Law is one of the most selective law schools in the nation. In terms of numerical admissions standards it may rank second in the city of Chicago, but in terms of sheer applicant demand, Northwestern outranks its neighbor in Hyde Park. (Twenty-one applicants vie annually for each spot in Northwestern's entering class of about 200, twice as many as do so at the University of Chicago.) In any case, Northwestern is in the top 20 nationally in both categories.

ACADEMICS

Student/faculty ratio	11:1
% female faculty	26
% minority faculty	3
Hours of study per day	3.70

FINANCIAL FACTS

Tuition	$21,316
Part-time tuition per credit	NR
Estimated books/expenses/fees	NR
On-campus living expenses	NR
Off-campus living expenses	NR
% first-year students receiving aid	NR
% all students receiving aid	76
% aid that is merit-based	NR
% all students receiving grants/scholarships	NR
% all students receiving loans	NR
% all students receiving assistantships	NR
Average award package	NR
Average graduation debt	NR

ADMISSIONS

# applications received	4,213
% applicants accepted	18
% acceptees attending	26
Average LSAT	NR
Average undergrad GPA	NR
Application Fee	$60
Priority application deadline	NR
Priority notification	NR
Regular application deadline	February 1
Regular notification	rolling
Admission deferment	NR
Gourman Report Rating	**4.73**

UNIVERSITY OF NOTRE DAME
Notre Dame Law School

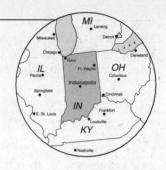

South Bend, Indiana, is more than just the center of the college-football universe. It is also the home of the nation's oldest and finest Catholic law school. On Saturdays in autumn, while men in gold helmets hit one another for the pleasure of millions of television viewers, the more than 500 hardworking students at the University of Notre Dame Law School hit the books. Theirs is a highly regarded law school that offers a demanding, staunchly traditional legal education to a small, well-qualified group of students. The curriculum here is highly prescribed, and class offerings hew very much to the traditional line, so those who seek innovation could be left wanting, although the school does have about a dozen clinical programs. Nevertheless, Notre Dame's sheer academic strength is undeniable, and variety can certainly be found by those who seek it.

Notre Dame's law students have always come from all parts of the country, and the law school's large, loyal and far-flung alumni network plays no small part in the success of its students in securing good jobs upon graduation. Only a very small percentage of all applicants are admitted to the law school, and successful candidates tend to possess very strong numerical credentials. More significant if one is to understand the unique "flavor" of this institution, however, is the fact that more than half of these students are Roman Catholics. Notre Dame is, by its own description, a humanistic institution that not only tolerates but also encourages the "manifestations of other faiths and commitment," but the school is emphatic about maintaining its own commitment to the preservation of its religious character. Indeed, the university's affiliation with the Catholic church has an unmistakable effect on the atmosphere within all of its classrooms—attendance at the law school's Sunday Mass is reportedly very high, and some classes begin with a recitation of the Lord's Prayer.

As one might expect, such an atmosphere is not going to please everyone, but to judge from the results of our survey, students at the Notre Dame Law School are among the most satisfied in the nation. Though most had praise for the nuts and bolts of their academic program, students here pointed mainly to intangibles

("Tradition, honor, values!" offered one 1L) in assessing Notre Dame's strengths. "I have obtained so many skills that will benefit my practice," wrote one 3L, "and at the same time I have enjoyed law school immensely, not so much because of what was taught as because of my colleagues—this is a spirited community of professionals unlike any in the country." The remarkable thing about the tone of the preceding comment is how typical it seemed when set against the comments of others: "This is a law school that abides by an honor code—a person's word is his bond!"; "If you are sick, people give you their notes, and if you struggle when called on in class, hands will shoot up to bail you out." "They educate the 'Whole Lawyer' here. Cheer, Cheer for old Notre Dame!" (all exclamation points in the original). Even the most committed cynic is eventually worn down in the face of such zeal.

Still, one does hear the occasional dissenting voice among Notre Dame law students. "If you are Catholic and conservative, this is a great place to be," wrote one 3L, "but if you happen not to fit the cookie-cutter image they expect here, life can be very tough." But even that remark came from a student who otherwise lavished praise on her chosen school, particularly on "Notre Dame's outstanding female faculty members—the best role models I've ever encountered." On a more substantive note, there is wide agreement among students here that Notre Dame's traditional curriculum can be limiting. One 2L summed up the opinions of many with this remark: "They don't offer you a lot to choose from here, but what they do offer you is awfully good."

ADMISSIONS

In every quantifiable respect, the Notre Dame Law School is one of the most selective in the nation. Not only does Notre Dame receive more than fifteen applications for every spot in its small entering class, but those it admits choose to attend the country's premier Catholic law school at a very high rate. All of this adds up to a very simple conclusion: Applicants whose numbers fall below the averages of a particular year's applicants are highly unlikely to be admitted while even those with credentials that exceed Notre Dame's average stand a less-than-even chance of admission. The administration asked us to point out that the "admissions office does consider each applicant's file individually, and special qualities may occasionally overcome lower numbers."

ACADEMICS

Student/faculty ratio	17:1
% female faculty	28
% minority faculty	9
Hours of study per day	3.81

FINANCIAL FACTS

Tuition	$19,400
Part-time tuition per credit	NR
Estimated books/expenses/fees	$4,100
On-campus living expenses	NR
Off-campus living expenses	NR
% first-year students receiving aid	77
% all students receiving aid	77
% aid that is merit-based	NR
% all students receiving grants/scholarships	34
% all students receiving loans	77
% all students receiving assistantships	NR
Average award package	$6,750
Average graduation debt	$35,000

ADMISSIONS

# applications received	2,481
% applicants accepted	22
% acceptees attending	30
Average LSAT	162
Average undergrad GPA	3.40
Application Fee	$45
Priority application deadline	NR
Priority notification	NR
Regular application deadline	March 1
Regular notification	rolling
Admission deferment	NR
Gourman Report Rating	**4.68**

NOVA SOUTHEASTERN UNIVERSITY 💾

Shepard Broad Law Center

Few think of the Socratic Method or constitutional law when the city of Fort Lauderdale, Florida is mentioned. More often, images of young, rowdy college students swarming to the city's beaches come to mind. But if you go to law school here, thoughts of Fort Lauderdale might have less to do with criminal behavior and more to do with Criminal Procedure as studied by the 900 or so diligent law students enrolled at the Nova Southeastern University Shepard Law Center. This private law school, not much over 20 years old, has been growing strong in recent years. Applications to the school have increased dramatically. In need of more space, the school opened a brand new law building in 1992. Beginning in 1996, the Shepard Law Center will also offer a part-time evening program limited to approximately 60 students.

The law school's administrators hope to see Nova's academic reputation keep up with its growing size and popularity. Toward that end, the straightforward, traditional curriculum is supplemented by an impressively wide array of trial-skills courses and clinical programs designed to offer students the practical experience necessary to compete in a tightening legal job market. Among the more interesting special opportunities available to students at Nova are the law school's King Disability Law Institute and the Center for the Study of Youth Policy. Students we surveyed said that they feel they receive sufficient practical experience, but many cited the narrowness of the Nova curriculum and indicated the need for more specialties. "It would be nice if the school offered more specialized courses," said one 2L. And a 1L called for "more clinical programs" and "more upper-level specialties." Possibly in answer to comments such as these, the law school recently initiated a four-semester Lawyering Skills and Values curriculum that allows students to select either business or litigation tracks. All third-year students will be able to enroll in one of six full-semester clinics: Business, Criminal Justice, Environmental, International, Public Service, or Children and Family.

Current students express a fairly high level of satisfaction with their decision to attend Nova law school. Nova's "close" atmosphere, "helpful" faculty, and small student/faculty ratio were

Valencia Price, Assistant Dean
3305 College Avenue, Fort Lauderdale, FL 33314
Tel: (954) 452-6117   Fax: (954) 452-6109
eMail: admiss@law-lib.law.nova.edu
Internet: http://www.law.nova.edu/nova/nova.htm

commonly listed as the strengths of the law school. "I particularly like the fact that the school is small," said one 3L. Another enthusiastic student said, "The faculty members are extraordinarily accessible and concerned about students, both academically and personally." Students frequently mentioned the "diverse" student body as one of the school's strengths. Nova Southeastern University law school does have a solid representation of minorities at just above 20 percent. But almost as frequently mentioned as one of the school's weaknesses was poor race relations.

Although a majority of the students are relatively content with the content of their law education, few are content with the cost. Many students remarked that the tuition at Nova Southeastern law school is far too expensive. A 1L who otherwise called Nova an "excellent" law school added: "However, the tuition is outrageous." For some Nova students, the dissatisfaction with the tuition is related to what the students perceive as a poor reputation and national ranking of the law school. "[The school is] too expensive for the lack of reputation Nova maintains locally and nationally," said a 1L, and added, "$18,000 for one year's tuition should entitle a student to a great deal more than a degree from a very unknown and unrecognized law school." A few students went so far as to suggest the school should "select fewer students" and "maybe raise the qualifications/requirements" of its applicants. Many other students, however, noted that the school's reputation in the Miami area and in-state is strong. And for those who enjoy sunshine and beaches, this may be an ideal location.

ADMISSIONS

Although the average numerical standards of those attending Nova Southeastern University's Shepard Broad Law Center are far from stellar, the sheer number of applications the school receives makes its admissions process quite competitive. Nova receives almost 1,500 applications from candidates with LSAT scores below about 150 and offers admission to only about 150 of them. A prospective student is only guaranteed admittance if his or her numerical credentials slightly exceed those listed. Because the law school is reducing the size of its first-year class, admissions is likely to become even more competitive.

ACADEMICS

Student/faculty ratio	23:1
% female faculty	45
% minority faculty	26
Hours of study per day	3.96

FINANCIAL FACTS

Tuition	$18,850
Part-time tuition per credit	NR
Estimated books/expenses/fees	NR
On-campus living expenses	NR
Off-campus living expenses	NR
% first-year students receiving aid	NR
% all students receiving aid	NR
% aid that is merit-based	NR
% all students receiving grants/scholarships	27
% all students receiving loans	85
% all students receiving assistantships	20
Average award package	$3,531
Average graduation debt	NR

ADMISSIONS

# applications received	2,463
% applicants accepted	37
% acceptees attending	32
Average LSAT	150
Average undergrad GPA	2.93
Application Fee	$45
No early decision program	
Regular application deadline	NR
Regular notification	March-April
Admission deferment	one year
Gourman Report Rating	2.55

OHIO NORTHERN UNIVERSITY 💾
Claude W. Pettit College of Law

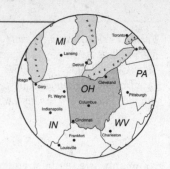

OVERVIEW

Type of school	private
Environment	town
Scholastic calendar	quarter
Schedule	Full time only

STUDENTS

Enrollment of institution	2,643
Enrollment of law school	353
% male/female	67/33
% out-of-state	70
% part-time	NR
% minorities	10
% international (# countries represented)	NR (2)
Average age at entry	22

APPLICANTS ALSO LOOK AT

Capital University
Ohio State University
University of Dayton
University of Toledo
Case Western Reserve University

SURVEY SAYS...

HITS
Studying
Socratic method
Faculty-student relations

MISSES
Library staff
Research resources
Intellectual challenge

EMPLOYMENT PROFILE

% grads employed immediately	NR
% grads employed within six months	79
Average starting salary	$31,000
% grads employed by field:	
Private practice	52
Business/industry	10
Government	18
Judicial clerkships	16
Academic	2
Military	0

Ohio Northern University's Claude W. Pettit College of Law is a small private law school in the northwestern Ohio town of Ada. Actually, Ada is not officially a town but a village, which makes Ohio Northern the only U.S. law school to be located in a village besides NYU, but that's different. While tiny Ada (Pop. 5,000) offers all the distractions of Mayberry, its cost of living is exceedingly low, and its quiet atmosphere is cited by ONU students as being particularly conducive to the intensive study of law.

Ohio Northern offers the nation's only program leading to joint degrees in law and pharmacy. These programs are overseen by the school's Pharmacy-Law Institute, which was established in 1990 as a center for research and education in this growing field dealing with, among other things, the "regulatory problems of pharmaceutical, bio-technological, and genetically engineered substances." Of course, this subject is not one in which most ONU students become involved. The general curriculum at Ohio Northern is a traditional one supplemented by several clinical programs, including one focusing on the problems of the local poor and elderly. ONU students, an immoderately large percentage of whom are men, come, to a large extent, from Ohio and Pennsylvania and possess midrange numerical credentials. Each entering class is very small, however, so the overall admissions process is somewhat selective.

Those applicants who actually go on to enroll at Ohio Northern paint a picture of a law school environment that is pleasant. Although most had little difficulty naming areas in which their chosen school could stand to improve, most praised its comfortable, congenial atmosphere. "Because there is such a small number of students here," said one, "the whole program is more personalized." Most ONU students expressed similar sentiments, with many giving credit for their satisfaction to the law school's faculty, whose "concern for the quality of education that their students receive seems very genuine." Most of those we heard from also praised the law school for its efforts to keep class sizes small and the overall student-faculty ratio low in order to preserve the closeness and sense of community that students currently enjoy. On the strictly curricular front, mixed reviews were

George Justice, Director of Law Admissions
525 South Main Street, Ada, OH 45810-1599
Tel: (419) 772-2211
Internet: http://www.law.onu.edu

Ohio Northern University

heard, though most students seem to agree on the quality of Ohio Northern's traditional classroom offerings and its limited clinical programs. And though not all listed it as a strength, most ONU students remarked on the school's location, which "lets students do nothing else but study."

On the negative side, most of the Ohio Northern students we heard from focused their criticism on what they regard as a strong but disappointingly limited curriculum. "I'd really like to see greater diversity of classes and to see the curriculum expanded into new fields of law," went one typical remark from a slightly dissatisfied 2L. Indeed, Ohio Northern's J.D. program is much heavier in prescribed courses than that of most schools, and the breadth of its course offerings leaves something to be desired. Specifically, many students believe the law school could stand to beef up its practical-skills programs. "We could really use a class in the practical writing aspects of civil practice," suggested one 2L, who voiced a concern held by many regarding their professional preparedness. As one student put it: "I wish more attention were paid to the day-to-day demands of being a lawyer."

Finally, students griped about the school's facilities, especially the computing facilities and the building. With respect to the latter, students report that an addition should be complete within the next 2-3 years, which may solve the problem.

ADMISSIONS

If one considers only its numerical standards, the Ohio Northern University College of Law appears not to be very selective. With 9 applicants for every spot in its very small entering class, however, applicant demand at Ohio Northern is higher than it is at many better-known schools. Consequently, ONU has the luxury of choosing its students very carefully.

ACADEMICS

Student/faculty ratio	15:1
% female faculty	21
% minority faculty	5
Hours of study per day	4.79

FINANCIAL FACTS

Tuition	$20,450
Part-time tuition per credit	NR
Estimated books/expenses/fees	$2,120
On-campus living expenses	$4,830
Off-campus living expenses	$5,100
% first-year students receiving aid	85
% all students receiving aid	82
% aid that is merit-based	35
% all students receiving grants/scholarships	40
% all students receiving loans	82
% all students receiving assistantships	15
Average award package	$7,141
Average graduation debt	NR

ADMISSIONS

# applications received	1,164
% applicants accepted	53
% acceptees attending	20
Average LSAT	151
Average undergrad GPA	2.83
Application Fee	$40
No early decision program	
Regular application deadline	NR
Regular notification	rolling
Admission deferment	one year
Gourman Report Rating	**2.67**

OHIO STATE UNIVERSITY
College of Law

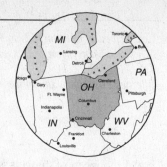

With very good reason, Ohio State University College of Law is widely regarded as the best law school in the state and, indeed, as one of the finest public law schools in the country. The university's 500,000-volume law library is the 14th largest in the United States, and the resources of the university (one of the biggest in the world) and of the state capital are vast, accessible, and first-rate. The school's broadly traditional curriculum is administered by a top-notch faculty. Particularly for residents of Ohio, who make up most of the student body, the school is one of the country's best bargains in legal education. The law school's reputation carries weight around the country, but the vast majority of Ohio State's graduates choose to remain in one of the state's three sizable and well-paying legal centers.

Ohio State students were unanimously positive about the newly renovated law building, which is now double its previous size and contains state-of-the-art teaching facilities, plus expanded space for student activities and organizations, not to mention faculty and staff offices. "Excellent new building!" was the familiar refrain. "Our new clinical facilities are most likely the best in the country," wrote one student, "and the library has no equal among law schools."

Many Ohio State students have expressed dissatisfaction with the law school's curriculum in the past, calling it far too traditional. "Our curriculum is not diverse, let alone cutting-edge," said one. Students wanted more sound practical training in addition to academic preparation. One student spoke for many when she said that she hoped that, in the future, the law school would "be more practical, instruct students much more fully on procedural matters and prepare them better for everyday encounters in practicing law." "Theory may be wonderful to some," she continued, "but it is not the real world." The administration seems to have taken heed of student comments, and the curriculum is being reworked. Classes in criminal law, legislation, and legal writing and analysis were added to the first-year course load in the 1995-96 school year, and additional courses for 2Ls and 3Ls are forthcoming. According to a 1L, "the faculty is attuned to

Karen Cutright, Associate Dean/Student Affairs
55 West 12th Avenue, Columbus, OH 43210-1391
Tel: (614) 292-2631   Fax: (614) 292-1383
Internet: http://www.acs.ohio-state.edu/units/law/index.htm

Ohio State University

student concerns and is committed to making further improvements."

We must emphasize that Ohio State does operate five clinics, offers joint degree programs with other colleges and departments, and runs the Center for Socio-Legal Studies which explores law "using tools and concepts developed in the social sciences," plus two journals, the newer of which, the Journal on Dispute Resolution, is anything but traditional. So in the past, it seems that students have gained practical experience through extracurricular activities.

We've heard about great improvements in the area of race relations, a troubled issue at Ohio State in the past. A 1L who wrote to us credited the change in part "to the efforts of Dean Gregory Williams," saying, "Dean Williams's life story-about growing up in a sort of cultural isolation, as a physically white-appearing African American may have provided him with some insight into bridging race-relations issues." The school has brought the percentage of faculty members of color up to 20 percent, and the new building provides plenty of communal space for students to interact comfortably, whether hanging out or participating in extracurricular organizations, with enough resources for all to share.

ADMISSIONS

The rush of law-school applicants to the nation's top public law schools in the late 1980s certainly didn't leave the excellent law school at Ohio State behind. Applications volume nearly doubled between '86 and '92, and, numerical admissions standards rose accordingly. As it now stands, the numerical credentials of the average entering OSU law student are stronger than those of students at 80 percent of the nation's fully accredited law schools. In comparison to other schools with such high standards, however, Ohio State is relatively generous in its overall acceptance rate.

ACADEMICS

Student/faculty ratio	20:1
% female faculty	31
% minority faculty	20
Hours of study per day	3.70

FINANCIAL FACTS

In-state tuition	$5,860
Out-of-state tuition	$13,890
Part-time tuition per credit	NR
Estimated books/expenses/fees	NR
On-campus living expenses	$12,800
Off-campus living expenses	NR
% first-year students receiving aid	85
% all students receiving aid	85
% aid that is merit-based	2
% all students receiving grants/scholarships	65
% all students receiving loans	85
% all students receiving assistantships	NR
Average award package	$1,500
Average graduation debt	$30,000

ADMISSIONS

# applications received	1,500
% applicants accepted	40
% acceptees attending	39
Average LSAT	159
Average undergrad GPA	3.48
Application Fee	$30
No early decision program	
Regular application deadline	March 15
Regular notification	rolling
Admission deferment	one year
Gourman Report Rating	**4.38**

OKLAHOMA CITY UNIVERSITY
School of Law

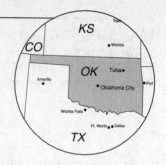

The Oklahoma City University School of Law, established in 1907, was the first school in the state to train future lawyers. Since that time Oklahoma has become home to two other law schools, and the Oklahoma City School of Law has grown to 640 students, a third of them in the evening division.

The Native American Legal Assistance Clinic, the only legal clinic the school operates, is quite notable. Through it, Oklahoma City law students provide free legal services to the area's large Native American population. The university's Native American Legal Resource Center, an institution within the School of Law, serves as a clearinghouse for scholars and attorneys practicing in the field.

Students at OCU follow a traditional J.D. curriculum, with an ever-increasing number of opportunities to increase their practical skills. All of the standard co-curricular activities, including law review and moot court, are to be found here, and in the past few years, the school has added several practical and clinical courses, including a criminal practice seminar. The school's Center for Alternative Dispute Resolution trains students to be mediators and provides them with opportunities to mediate disputes referred to the Center by state courts.

Students we spoke with told a familiar story: OCU provides a "good basic education," but is lacking in the depth of courses offered and flexibility in scheduling. "The greatest strength of OCU law is that a student gets the nuts and bolts of what it takes to be a practicing attorney," said one 2L. Indeed, many students told us they felt very confident of their practical lawyering skills and their preparedness upon graduation to enter the courtroom. But, the same student quoted above continued: "OCU law needs a broader curriculum with more courses that would enable students to specialize in a particular field." Since we surveyed, though, the school says the curriculum has expanded to include courses in intellectual property, and benefits and health care to complement their traditional strengths in commercial and business law. They also allow the possibility of emphases in certain areas. However, we must present a balanced picture, so we have to add that another student did sum up the school's weaknesses as a "lack of a meaningful clinical experience." OCU law students

Gary D. Mercer, Assistant Dean for Admissions
2501 North Blackwelder, Oklahoma City, OK 73106
Tel: (800) 633-7242
eMail: ladmissions@frodo.okcu.edu
Internet: http://www.okcu.edu/www/departments/law/law.html

Oklahoma City University

also feel slighted by the school's lack of a study abroad program, which, as a couple of students noted, are available at most other law schools. Students were critical of Oklahoma's Legal Research and Writing Program, which many said needed a major overhaul. The administration heard their complaints and has expanded the course to last the first three semesters with small class size, with more changes planned for the 1996-97 school year. If all goes well, comments such as, "[The] legal writing program [is] extremely poor with an 'ambush' method of instruction," should be a thing of the past.

Overall, students had only complimentary comments to make when it came to the faculty. Not only did they praise their professors' fine teaching abilities and sound knowledge of the law, but again and again students referred to the teaching staff as "approachable," "open," and "available." Students were also quite vocal about the school's new facilities that opened in 1994, a new law center and a new facility that houses the library, faculty offices, and offices of the university's law review. "The new facilities are great," said one student, and added, "They provide a wonderful environment to learn."

On the downside, many students cited a lack of ethnic diversity among the faculty and students. "I believe my academic career would be enhanced if I were exposed to a more minority students. They should recruit more," said a 1L.

For the most part, the law school administration is, as we quote the Dean of Admissions, "very concerned about the welfare of the students, and has even been willing to fight the faculty or university administration on a number of important issues," including improving student loan practices and investing substantial financial and human resources in the career services office. Overall, the majority of students surveyed felt like the 2L who said, "This is a school concerned with increasing their reputation outside of Oklahoma and becoming one of the best."

ADMISSIONS

Oklahoma City University School of Law's admissions standards are quite generous. Each year, 45 percent of applicants are granted admission. With an average LSAT score of 150 and undergraduate GPA of about 3.0, applicants with moderate credentials have a very good chance of being admitted. Those whose numbers exceed these averages are virtually assured of gaining admission.

ACADEMICS

Student/faculty ratio	21:1
% female faculty	29
% minority faculty	16
Hours of study per day	4.78

FINANCIAL FACTS

Tuition	$11,850
Part-time tuition per credit	$7,900
Estimated books/expenses/fees	$928
On-campus living expenses	NR
Off-campus living expenses	NR
% first-year students receiving aid	100
% all students receiving aid	100
% aid that is merit-based	5
% all students receiving grants/scholarships	23
% all students receiving loans	88
% all students receiving assistantships	NR
Average award package	$3,968
Average graduation debt	$42,042

ADMISSIONS

# applications received	1,367
% applicants accepted	45
% acceptees attending	37
Average LSAT	150
Average undergrad GPA	3.01
Application Fee	$35
No early decision program	
Regular application deadline	August 1
Regular notification	rolling
Admission deferment	one year

Gourman Report Rating	**2.69**

UNIVERSITY OF OKLAHOMA
College of Law

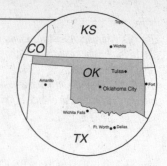

OVERVIEW

Type of school	public
Environment	metropolis
Scholastic calendar	semester
Schedule	Full time only

STUDENTS

Enrollment of institution	13,118
Enrollment of law school	661
% male/female	59/41
% out-of-state	15
% part-time	NR
% minorities	10
% international (# countries represented)	NR (NR)
Average age at entry	24

APPLICANTS ALSO LOOK AT

Oklahoma City University
University of Tulsa
University of Texas
Southern Methodist University
Baylor University

SURVEY SAYS...

HITS
Cut-throat competition
Serving humankind
Socratic method

MISSES
Students feel poorly prepared
Legal writing
Practical lawyering skills

EMPLOYMENT PROFILE

% grads employed immediately	NR
% grads employed within six months	NR
Average starting salary	NR
% grads employed by field:	
Private practice	58
Business/industry	17
Government	15
Judicial clerkships	1
Public service	4
Academic	5
Military	3

The most respected of Oklahoma's three law schools is also the least expensive: the University of Oklahoma College of Law, established in 1909 on the Norman campus of the state's excellent public university. As the only publicly funded law school in the state, Oklahoma boasts vast resources in comparison with other schools in the region. The overall value of the legal education the school provides draws a large portion of the students. Tuition at Oklahoma makes it what one current student called "an unbeatable deal."

The law school's excellent reputation rests on the strength of its solid, traditional J.D. curriculum. After a fully prescribed first year, Oklahoma students can choose from a relatively broad array of course offerings, including a greater-than-average selection of courses in energy law and criminal law and corrections. Upper-level students can also participate in Oklahoma's fairly extensive clinical programs, which include an in-house legal aid clinic and numerous externship opportunities. Several students critiqued the school's legal writing program, though. One such student, a 1L, made this observation: "The writing program seems very weak compared to other schools." And another 1L said: "Research and writing is a joke. They don't teach you anything." Oklahoma students also expressed a desire to have a wider course selection at the law school. We heard the following suggestions: "The school needs more specialization-environmental law and health law." (2L); "[We need] more international law courses." (1L).

Many students spoke highly of the faculty who, they reported, go out of their way to help students achieve their goals inside and outside the classroom. One student, who dubbed Oklahoma a "simply outstanding law school," said: "The faculty here are incredible. They are very effective in teaching students the important material, yet they are also warm and personable." And another student, a 2L, said: "The entire faculty has an open door policy to help students in our pursuit of a J.D."

When asked to name the school's weaknesses, Oklahoma students frequently mentioned the school's facilities, but also noted that the law school is planning a move to a new building located on the main campus in the near future. The school's lack of racial and ethnic diversity were also noted by the students surveyed. "More female and minority faculty and students are needed," said one 3L. Oklahoma students join with the majority of other student bodies who feel their school's job placement office is not sufficient. Students who plan to look for employment after they receive their degree may face an additional challenge due to their location. "[This is] a good school, but Oklahoma has a very bad economy. [It] would be best to take advantage of the low tuition and then move to a better job environment," said a 3L. Considering the low tuition and fine instruction, prospective students should keep the following statement from an upbeat 2L in mind: "After working with law students from such schools as NYU and UVA I know that those who apply themselves here are equipped to compete with students from the best law schools in the country."

ADMISSIONS

Although it is more selective than the state's other two law schools, the University of Oklahoma College of Law holds applicants to numerical standards that are slightly lower than the national average. The law school selects from a relatively small applicant pool, but still accepts only a third of all candidates who apply. Even though the law school receives a moderate number of applicants for its size, since Oklahoma law limits enrollment of nonresidents to only 10 to 15 percent of the roughly 690 students in the school, admissions are far more selective for non-Oklahomans.

ACADEMICS

Student/faculty ratio	23:1
% female faculty	22
% minority faculty	12
Hours of study per day	3.80

FINANCIAL FACTS

In-state tuition	$3,160
Out-of-state tuition	$9,198
Part-time tuition per credit	NR
Estimated books/expenses/fees	NR
On-campus living expenses	NR
Off-campus living expenses	NR
% first-year students receiving aid	NR
% all students receiving aid	NR
% aid that is merit-based	NR
% all students receiving grants/scholarships	NR
% all students receiving loans	NR
% all students receiving assistantships	NR
Average award package	NR
Average graduation debt	NR

ADMISSIONS

# applications received	1,153
% applicants accepted	31
% acceptees attending	59
Average LSAT	154
Average undergrad GPA	3.30
Application Fee	$25
Priority application deadline	NR
Priority notification	NR
Regular application deadline	March 15
Regular notification	rolling
Admission deferment	NR
Gourman Report Rating	3.41

UNIVERSITY OF OREGON
School of Law

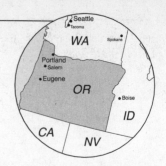

In one of the most beautiful parts of the country, on one of the loveliest college campuses in the West, you will find the highly respected—and popular—School of Law at the University of Oregon. Established in 1919, Oregon's only public law school is also its youngest, and probably its best. Oregon's curriculum is strong and broad, and while most law schools continue to resist offering areas of formal concentration at the J.D. level, U of O has embraced the trend toward specialization. Oregon now offers official "Statements of Completion" in a handful of subjects: environmental and natural resources law, ocean and coastal law, business law, criminal practice law, and estate planning. The law school's wide-ranging clinical programs afford a limited number of students the opportunity to supplement their academic training with hands-on experience in these and several other areas of law. The law school has a long established reputation for excellence in and around the Pacific Northwest, and if demand from highly qualified prospective law students is any indication, its reputation is well deserved. Since 1986, applications volume at Oregon has increased 160 percent and the average LSAT score of entering students has climbed by 15 percentile points. More than half of the law school's students now come from outside the state. People have begun to take notice, it seems, of Oregon's highly respected faculty, its strong, broad curriculum and its low tuition, all of which surely make it one of the better bargains anywhere—at least for state residents. (Residency requirements in Oregon are quite strict, and a large number of the law school's student body pay tuition at the nonresident rate.

Students at Oregon, residents and nonresidents alike, are largely in agreement when it comes to the strengths of their chosen school. Although criticism of several fundamental aspects of their program was widespread, the vast majority of the U of O students we heard from expressed a high level of satisfaction with the overall quality of their experience, and most notably with their relations with faculty and fellow students. "U of O is not your average law mill," asserted one 3L, "student groups are active and the student body as a whole is involved, committed and supportive." As one 3L commented, "You can find a conservative male student sitting comfortably next to a woman with a nose

Katherine Jernberg, Admissions Director
1221 University of Oregon, Eugene, OR 97403
Tel: (541) 346-3846 Fax: (541) 346-1564
eMail: admissions@law.uoregon.edu
Internet: http://www.law.uoregon.edu

ring in almost every class." Most echoed this sentiment, some even more enthusiastically. "My respect for the faculty here is exceeded only by the respect I have for my fellow students," wrote a 1L. "The academic program," she continued, "encourages us to maintain our idealism in the face of the oppressive cynicism which is often perpetuated by 'the system.' "This last remark likely referred to Oregon's strong record of encouraging public-interest work and in particular, environmental public-interest work. "The Enviro program, the Enviro clinic and the Enviro faculty are all excellent," reported one 3L. On the basis of the unanimously positive reviews we heard, it appears that such students have not been disappointed.

On the other hand, a large proportion of the students we heard from expressed a feeling that the law school has paid too little attention to other areas in its quest to build a highly respected environmental program. "The public-interest emphasis is great," wrote one, "but there is insufficient non-environmental public-interest instruction, and there is an insufficient number of spaces in all of the clinics." Another consistent area of criticism concerned the lack of diversity in Oregon's faculty. "The faculty is great," allowed a 2L, "but most profs are left-wing white males—we need more political, ethnic and gender diversity." The facilities were universally denounced, with two students describing the building as "butt-ugly." And just in case you've never been to Oregon, consider carefully both parts of this evenhanded overall assessment from one damp but happy law student: "Great school, but bring an umbrella."

ADMISSIONS

Like any excellent public law school, the University of Oregon School of Law has the luxury of choosing its students from a very large applicant pool. Even those applicants whose numbers slightly exceed Oregon's averages are in for a fight. A not-so-generous overall acceptance rate of 32 percent ensures that many highly qualified candidates will be turned away.

ACADEMICS

Student/faculty ratio	15:1
% female faculty	38
% minority faculty	13
Hours of study per day	3.82

FINANCIAL FACTS

In-state tuition	$9,053
Out-of-state tuition	$13,537
Part-time tuition per credit	NR
Estimated books/expenses/fees	NR
On-campus living expenses	NR
Off-campus living expenses	NR
% first-year students receiving aid	NR
% all students receiving aid	97
% aid that is merit-based	NR
% all students receiving grants/scholarships	77
% all students receiving loans	97
% all students receiving assistantships	3
Average award package	NR
Average graduation debt	NR

ADMISSIONS

# applications received	1,424
% applicants accepted	32
% acceptees attending	33
Average LSAT	158
Average undergrad GPA	3.39
Application Fee	$50
Priority application deadline	December 15
Priority notification	January 15
Regular application deadline	April 1
Regular notification	rolling
Admission may be deferred?	No
Gourman Report Rating	**3.67**

PACE UNIVERSITY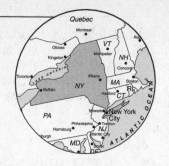
School of Law

Founded in 1978, the Pace University School of Law is one of the youngest law schools in the Northeast, but it has come far in its short history. Like most latecomers to legal education, Pace has not had the luxury of resting on tradition. But as tradition has been called into question lately, this midsize private law school has tried, with much success, to turn its youth to its advantage. Pace has begun to set about building a national reputation not by imitating the established giants but by helping to usher in change. The most tangible sign of this is, perhaps, the law school's embrace of the trend toward specialization at the J.D. level. Pace now offers certificates of specialization in three areas: health law and policy, international law, and environmental law. It is in this last area that the law school has drawn the most attention. By cannily choosing to dedicate substantial resources to such an up-and-coming field of study and practice, Pace fairly guaranteed the notice it has now received: Its curriculum in environmental law has been recognized as one of the most comprehensive in the nation. It also operates a clinical program dedicated to the subject and offers one of the country's few master of laws (LL.M.) and doctor of laws (S.J.D.) degrees in the field. While Pace has a way to go before it can hope to compete head-to-head with some of the region's powerhouse schools for the most highly qualified law-school applicants, standards are already high and rising. Admissions are quite selective (more so for the day division than for the evening division), and the average numerical credentials of entering students are now quite strong, having risen significantly in the last several years.

Students at Pace are remarkably consistent in their assessments of their chosen school—both in terms of its advantages and its drawbacks. Although nearly all express a fairly high degree of satisfaction with the uniqueness and overall quality of the law school's program, few could not point to areas in need of improvement. Not surprisingly, Pace students had strong words of praise for the school's specialization programs, especially the environmental program. "Pace is definitely an up-and-coming law school on the cutting edge of several expanding areas of law," went one fairly typical remark from a 3L. Another soon-to-be graduate agreed, noting that "I feel like the clinics here have

Angela M. D'Agostino, Director of Admissions
78 North Broadway, White Plains, NY 10603
Tel: (914) 422-4210
eMail: Ottinger@genesis.law.pace.edu
Internet: http://www.law.pace.edu

Pace University

prepared me very well in a practical way to pursue my area of interest—environmental law." Some students also had kind words for their faculty, particularly one more mature student who noted that "as an older student, it is a pleasure to be treated as an adult rather than an adolescent." Nearly all agreed that "the faculty is very involved with the student body and is very willing to interact with the students individually."

Specific and tangible criticisms were heard. For instance, although few had anything but praise for the quality of the law school's various clinical programs, a very large number of those we heard from lamented their limited enrollment. "The clinical programs here are quite good," wrote one 2L, "but they really need to find a way to accommodate more students." On balance, however, most here seem pleased with their surroundings and with their prospects. "More and more employers are becoming aware of Pace," claimed one student, "and I have found that Pace grads are looked upon with growing and well-deserved esteem."

ADMISSIONS

In its relatively short history, the Pace University School of Law has made significant progress toward achieving the goal of any rising law school: to attract students of the highest caliber possible. Since 1986, for instance, the average LSAT score of entering students has risen nearly twenty percentile points as applicant volume has grown by more than 50 percent. While Pace has a long way to go before it competes with the region's powerhouses for the most highly qualified students, its current admissions standards are anything but lenient. Purely in terms of numerical admissions criteria, Pace is in the top third of all U.S. law schools and rising steadily.

ACADEMICS
Student/faculty ratio	16:1
% female faculty	32
% minority faculty	8
Hours of study per day	4.05

FINANCIAL FACTS
Tuition	$19,394
Part-time tuition per credit	$13,670
Estimated books/expenses/fees	$950
On-campus living expenses	NR
Off-campus living expenses	NR
% first-year students receiving aid	100
% all students receiving aid	100
% aid that is merit-based	52
% all students receiving grants/scholarships	31
% all students receiving loans	74
% all students receiving assistantships	NR
Average award package	$4,095
Average graduation debt	$58,000

ADMISSIONS
# applications received	2,525
% applicants accepted	38
% acceptees attending	28
Average LSAT	152
Average undergrad GPA	3.20
Application Fee	$55
No early decision program	
Regular application deadline	March 15
Regular notification	rolling
Admission deferment	one year
Gourman Report Rating	2.40

UNIVERSITY OF THE PACIFIC ▢
McGeorge School of Law

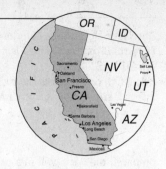

The capital of the nation's most populous state, California, supports a large population of lawyers but only one law school: the McGeorge School of Law. Its name may be unfamiliar to those on the East Coast, but this very large private law school is one of the major sources of new blood for the sizable legal communities of northern California. Affiliated since 1966 with the University of the Pacific, California's oldest private university, 70-year-old McGeorge continues to emphasize the strengths on which its long-established regional reputation for excellence was built.

McGeorge students we talked to offered almost unanimous praise for the quality of their program and for the extent to which it is preparing them for the demands of professional practice. As one 3L put it: "Practical training is emphasized at McGeorge instead of heady, yet impractical, legal theory." Often cited by students was the university's prime location, minutes from downtown courts and the state's legislative offices. Sacramento is no cultural mecca, but the law school community is, by all reports, quite pleasant, and McGeorge students can satisfy their wanderlust through enrollment in international summer programs in Salzburg, London, and Budapest. For those interested in international business law, a growing legal specialization in this region of the country, McGeorge offers a concentration that can include special study abroad programs and moot court competitions.

Earlier than most law schools, McGeorge began to supplement its traditional curriculum with training in the practical skills of lawyering. It was, in fact, the first law school in the country to build a sophisticated mock-trial courtroom fully equipped with audiovisual teaching aids. This facility continues to be the focus of McGeorge's highly regarded trial-advocacy program, which is one of the many clinical programs offered through the law school. In addition to maintaining a relatively large in-house legal clinic, McGeorge sponsors externships through dozens of state and local government agencies, from Social Services to Seismic Safety.

McGeorge students praised the rigorous curriculum that has given the school the second-highest bar-passage rate in the state. "The discipline that one must develop here in order to survive

Jane Kelso, Dean of Students
3200 Fifth Avenue, Sacramento, CA 95817
Tel: (916) 739-7089   Fax: (916) 739-7111

will later in our careers be a great strength, but right now it can be a pain," said a 2L. Most students, however, placed a great deal of blame on the university for instituting what is said to be an unfair and burdensome grading curve. Luckily for prospective students, however, a new grading scale has been adopted after study by a faculty/student committee which addressed students concerns about the "demoralizing" effect of the prior difficult grading policy and its possible effects on finding jobs after graduation.

In part due to this kind of attention to student's complaints, most McGeorge attendees are quite pleased with the quality of their education and the practical skills training it affords. And as one 3L put it: "It is a tough time here, but that makes us work harder...thus preparing us very well for legal practice in any area."

ADMISSIONS

Although it is true that the McGeorge School of Law is third from the bottom among California's 16 ABA-approved law schools in terms of numerical admissions standards, the long-established law school enjoys a regional reputation that is strong enough to draw a huge pool of applicants. The law school considers more than 2,000 applications annually, but the size of its entering class (around 450 total day and evening students) keeps overall admissions selectivity moderate.

ACADEMICS

Student/faculty ratio	23:1
% female faculty	30
% minority faculty	18
Hours of study per day	4.31

FINANCIAL FACTS

Tuition	$16,400
Part-time tuition per credit	NR
Estimated books/expenses/fees	$648
On-campus living expenses	$8,883
Off-campus living expenses	$8,883
% first-year students receiving aid	NR
% all students receiving aid	92
% aid that is merit-based	11
% all students receiving grants/scholarships	28
% all students receiving loans	92
% all students receiving assistantships	NR
Average award package	NR
Average graduation debt	$64,510

ADMISSIONS

# applications received	2,257
% applicants accepted	53
% acceptees attending	33
Average LSAT	156
Average undergrad GPA	3.01
Application Fee	$40
No early decision program	
Regular application deadline	May 1
Regular notification	rolling
Admission may be deferred?	No
Gourman Report Rating	4.37

UNIVERSITY OF PENNSYLVANIA 💾

Law School

OVERVIEW

Type of school	private
Environment	metropolis
Scholastic calendar	semester
Schedule	Full time only

STUDENTS

Enrollment of institution	22,469
Enrollment of law school	750
% male/female	58/42
% out-of-state	85
% part-time	NR
% minorities	25
% international (# countries represented)	2 (6)
Average age at entry	24

APPLICANTS ALSO LOOK AT

Harvard University
Georgetown University
New York University
Columbia University
Cornell University

SURVEY SAYS...

HITS
Sleeping
Prestige
Research resources

MISSES
Legal writing
Practical lawyering skills

EMPLOYMENT PROFILE

% grads employed immediately	88
% grads employed within six months	96
Average starting salary	$70,000
% grads employed by field:	
Private practice	68
Business/industry	4
Government	5
Judicial clerkships	18
Public service	4
Academic	1
Military	2

In continuous operation for over 140 years on the Philadelphia campus of its Ivy League parent institution, the University of Pennsylvania Law School is one of the acknowledged giants of legal education. Its reputation was built on the strength of its highly esteemed faculty and the strong traditional curriculum it administers. In the past decade, a changing of the guard within the law school's faculty created the conditions for significant changes in the Penn curriculum, changes that have done nothing but burnish the law school's already golden reputation and ensure the continuing success of its graduates in entering the highest reaches of the legal profession.

Among the curricular innovations at Penn are two elective courses in the first year. This seemingly modest allowance is almost unheard of in the elite law schools, and it contributes to an overall first-year experience at Penn that is, by all reports, dynamic, exciting and, perhaps most important, humane. Philadelphia itself is, of course, the City of Brotherly Love, and while it would be going just a bit too far to call Penn the Law School of Sisterly and Brotherly Love, collegiality among students seems to be the rule. In large part, this is due to a grading system that discourages cutthroat competition by precluding class ranks. Any obsessive competitiveness at Penn seems limited to the search for employment at the nation's top law firms, a search that begins almost on arrival. Given that the vast majority of Penn grads do go to work for these large, high-paying private firms, the law school's recent addition of a 70-hour public-service graduation requirement seems particularly appropriate and admirable.

On the whole, law students at Penn seem quite satisfied with their choice of school. They are well aware of the advantages their degrees will give them when entering the profession, and they are thankful for a learning environment that spares them the blood-thirsty competitiveness. "Penn's greatest strengths are its students and the congenial and friendly atmosphere that permeates the law school," said one student. Another student expressed a sentiment held by many: "Students strive to excel—but not at the expense of their classmates." Among the most enthusiastic respondents to our survey were several Penn students who had

Janice L. Austin, Assistant Dean of Admissions and Financial Aid
3400 Chestnut Street, Philadelphia, PA 19104-6204
Tel: (215) 898-7400   Fax: (215) 573-2025
eMail: adms@oyez.law.upenn.edu
Internet: http://www.law.upenn.edu

University of Pennsylvania

transferred from other law schools. One of them called her decision to transfer "the best decision I could have made," and another wrote that she "would not trade [her] Penn Law experience for anything."

Of course, you couldn't possibly assemble a group of individuals this bright and not expect to hear some criticisms. Many students also bemoaned what they consider the law school's overemphasis on corporate law, though they were split on its public-service requirement: some students, who violently oppose the requirement, said the school should "kill" it, while others praised it.

ADMISSIONS

If you hope to earn a spot in the University of Pennsylvania Law School's entering class of around 230, plan to face stiff competition. Relative to many other top schools, the overall acceptance rate at Penn is fairly generous. Of course, it probably doesn't seem so to the more than two out of three well qualified candidates who are denied admission. Those who do manage to squeeze through and go on to enroll possess numerical credentials higher than those of students at all but seven American law schools. Their stellar average undergraduate GPA is very near the highest reported, and their average LSAT score stands impressively at the 94th percentile.

ACADEMICS

Student/faculty ratio	17:1
% female faculty	25
% minority faculty	20
Hours of study per day	3.54

FINANCIAL FACTS

Tuition	$20,664
Part-time tuition per credit	NR
Estimated books/expenses/fees	$2,253
On-campus living expenses	NR
Off-campus living expenses	NR
% first-year students receiving aid	75
% all students receiving aid	NR
% aid that is merit-based	1
% all students receiving grants/scholarships	31
% all students receiving loans	69
% all students receiving assistantships	NR
Average award package	$8,171
Average graduation debt	$54,379

ADMISSIONS

# applications received	4,135
% applicants accepted	29
% acceptees attending	19
Average LSAT	166
Average undergrad GPA	3.60
Application Fee	$65
No early decision program	
Regular application deadline	February 15
Regular notification	beginning Jan. 1
Admission deferment	one to two years
Gourman Report Rating	**4.83**

PEPPERDINE UNIVERSITY 🖪
School of Law

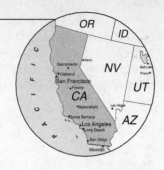

OVERVIEW

Type of school	private
Environment	city
Scholastic calendar	semester
Schedule	Full time only

STUDENTS

Enrollment of institution	2,661
Enrollment of law school	702
% male/female	52/48
% out-of-state	26
% part-time	NR
% minorities	24
% international (# countries represented)	1 (3)
Average age at entry	27

APPLICANTS ALSO LOOK AT

U. of California, Los Angeles
Loyola Marymount University
University of Southern California
University of San Diego
University of California

SURVEY SAYS...

HITS
Great facilities
Faculty-student relations

MISSES
Lack of diversity among faculty
Intellectual challenge
Studying

EMPLOYMENT PROFILE

% grads employed immediately	30
% grads employed within six months	70
Average starting salary	$55,000
% grads employed by field:	
Private practice	60
Business/industry	18
Government	14
Judicial clerkships	5
Academic	1

Just in case its address on the Pacific Coast Highway doesn't mean anything to you, the Pepperdine University School of Law includes in its promotional materials more full-color photographs of itself than perhaps any law school in the nation. One forgives narcissism, however, in the truly beautiful. From its perch atop Pepperdine's Malibu campus, this young law school commands a view of the Pacific Ocean that is stunning. Its incomparable physical surroundings alone explain much of the law school's appeal, and while Pepperdine would probably not deny this, it would quickly point out—accurately—that this appeal has been used as a means to an end. In its relatively short history, Pepperdine has never wanted for students, and it has firmly established itself as a respected source of successful attorneys. This reputation may carry relatively little weight outside southern California, but never mind. Pepperdine grads do quite nicely for themselves in nearby L.A., the nation's fourth-largest job market for recent law school graduates. The law school's J.D. program is solid in all the traditional areas, and its Institute for Dispute Resolution offers one of the country's most comprehensive programs in an area of law practice that most agree is the wave of the future. The roughly 3,000 applicants who vie annually for spots in Pepperdine's first-year class of about 250 are a qualified bunch. Admitted applicants, the great majority of whom are California residents, possess strong numerical credentials.

But the preceding description leaves out one piece of information that is vital to understanding the School of Law at Pepperdine University: founded in 1937 by George Pepperdine, the devoutly Christian owner of a chain of auto-parts stores, the university that bears his name, though officially nonsectarian, "maintains a relationship" with the Church of Christ. According to the Pepperdine students we surveyed, this relationship is reflected in the law school's conservative bent. Needless to say, views on this matter differ among Pepperdine students. From the left: "If you are politically liberal, the best thing about Pepperdine is the view, and the worst thing is the views [of most students and faculty]." "The hold the Church of Christ possesses over the students, faculty and administration is counterproductive and detrimental to the pursuit of knowledge and intellectual growth." From the

Jill Bardarson, Director of Admissions
24255 Pacific Coast Highway, Malibu, CA 90263
Tel: (310) 456-4631
eMail: soladmis@pepperdine.edu
Internet: http://law-www.pepperdine.edu

Pepperdine University

right: "I appreciate the emphasis on ethics as rooted in Christian principles and the absence of any conformist Political Correctness." "The emphasis on [Christian] values is important to me, especially since the legal profession is so criticized for not having any values or ethics." Whatever his or her own leanings, the prospective Pepperdine student will want to take into consideration the law school's affiliation and students' self-assessment of the political atmosphere on campus.

The Pepperdine students we surveyed evinced a strong sense of satisfaction with the school's academics. Asked to name Pepperdine's greatest strengths, many pointed to its emphasis on the practical and to the faculty's dedication to teaching. "There is a strong emphasis on legal research and writing and preparation for the bar exam," reported one 3L. And one 1L asserted that "faculty members are enthusiastic about teaching and are willing to work with students to help them improve...Instead of being a mere number you are treated like a King."

On the negative side, many of the Pepperdine students we heard from griped about the shortcomings of the law school's career placement office. "The career office does a very poor job of informing students of the various employment options," wrote one 3L, "and they are not very useful if you are interested in working somewhere besides California."

ADMISSIONS

The view from the hilltop campus of the Pepperdine University School of Law is indeed spectacular, but you face a steep climb in getting there. More than 12 applicants vie annually for each spot in Pepperdine's entering class, so the law school has the luxury of choosing its students very carefully. If you want to feel at all sure of your chances, make sure your numbers approach the respectable numerical credentials of the average Pepperdine student.

ACADEMICS	
Student/faculty ratio	20:1
% female faculty	16
% minority faculty	23
Hours of study per day	3.41

FINANCIAL FACTS	
Tuition	$20,900
Part-time tuition per credit	NR
Estimated books/expenses/fees	$725
On-campus living expenses	NR
Off-campus living expenses	NR
% first-year students receiving aid	100
% all students receiving aid	100
% aid that is merit-based	66
% all students receiving grants/scholarships	67
% all students receiving loans	81
% all students receiving assistantships	10
Average award package	$3,475
Average graduation debt	$67,000

ADMISSIONS	
# applications received	2,804
% applicants accepted	36
% acceptees attending	24
Average LSAT	158
Average undergrad GPA	3.20
Application Fee	$50
No early decision program	
Regular application deadline	March 1
Regular notification	rolling
Admission may be deferred?	no
Gourman Report Rating	3.68

UNIVERSITY OF PITTSBURGH 🖫

School of Law

OVERVIEW

Type of school	public
Environment	metropolis
Scholastic calendar	semester
Schedule	Full time only

STUDENTS

Enrollment of institution	12,933
Enrollment of law school	741
% male/female	64/36
% out-of-state	39
% part-time	2
% minorities	13
% international (# countries represented)	1 (7)
Average age at entry	24

APPLICANTS ALSO LOOK AT

Boston University
George Washington University
University of Maryland
Temple University

SURVEY SAYS...

HITS
Faculty representation
Prestige
Research resources

MISSES
Legal writing
Intellectual challenge
Practical lawyering skills

EMPLOYMENT PROFILE

% grads employed immediately	NR
% grads employed within six months	76
Average starting salary	$40,442
% grads employed by field:	
Private practice	63
Business/industry	10
Government	5
Judicial clerkships	15
Public service	1
Academic	3
Military	3

For 100 years, the University of Pittsburgh School of Law, a midsize public institution, has served this western Pennsylvania city and the corporate headquarters that make their homes here. The law school's numerous strengths are complemented by its reasonable tuition, which, although extremely high by public-school standards, is moderate when compared to other schools.

Pittsburgh's faculty has been rated among the finest in the country in terms of scholarly output, and the law school asserts that their strength in teaching is comparable. The faculty, described by students as "energetic," "approachable," and "bright," garnered high praise from students. The curriculum here is traditional in the best sense of the word: Requirements are few and options are many. The breadth of the law school's course offerings, which include an increasing number of courses in the growing field of health law, is great.

Overall, Pittsburgh students had positive comments to make regarding their law school. A 1L appreciated the "friendly, outgoing student body and generally relaxed atmosphere." Indeed, congeniality seems to be a strong aspect of Pittsburgh law school, where "students actually help one another" and "are more interested in working together than in working against one another."

Students do have some complaints, however. When asked to discuss areas of needed improvement in the school, many cited the lack of "practical skills development." As one 3L noted: "[The] school offers clinical experience, but does not necessarily encourage it." Other students criticized the school's facilities, singling out the computer lab.

Pittsburgh is one of the nation's top twenty legal job markets in terms of both volume and compensation and the highly regarded public law school at the University of Pittsburgh is the city's primary supplier of lawyers. Although corporate headquarters in the city employ some of the law school's graduates, students seem to have had some fairly consistent gripes about the school's career placement office for the past several years. One student said, "When I went in for a meeting, they didn't even ask what field of law I was interested in." A 2L suggested that the "career

Fredi G. Miller, Assistant Dean for Admissions and Financial Aid
3900 Forbes Avenue, Pittsburgh, PA 15260
Tel: (412) 648-1412
Internet: http://www@law.pitt.edu

University of Pittsburgh

planning office needs to develop, and should expand beyond the Pittsburgh area and offer more information." Other students complained of the career office's contribution to what they consider the school's overemphasis on corporate law. "Career placement is pathetic unless you wish to practice corporate law in Pennsylvania or D.C.," said a 3L. Another 3L added: "While Pitt is a great law school for persons who might want to practice corporate law, I would like to see expansion of the public interest and environmental law offerings."

Overall, however, students at the University of Pittsburgh School of Law appreciated their faculty, the school's relaxed atmosphere, and its relatively low tuition.

ADMISSIONS

If you'd like to attend law school at the University of Pittsburgh, you had better make sure that your numerical credentials are up to par. Although overall admission selectivity is relatively moderate due to the high volume of applications the school receives, the qualifications of entering students are solid: an impressive average LSAT score of 156 and a undergraduate GPA of about 3.24. These standards, are, in fact, higher than those of 60 percent of all American law schools.

ACADEMICS	
Student/faculty ratio	19:1
% female faculty	32
% minority faculty	16
Hours of study per day	3.79

FINANCIAL FACTS	
In-state tuition	$10,491
Out-of-state tuition	$16,241
Part-time tuition per credit	NR
Estimated books/expenses/fees	$792
On-campus living expenses	NR
Off-campus living expenses	NR
% first-year students receiving aid	25
% all students receiving aid	30
% aid that is merit-based	NR
% all students receiving grants/scholarships	30
% all students receiving loans	85
% all students receiving assistantships	NR
Average award package	$2,500
Average graduation debt	$45,000

ADMISSIONS	
# applications received	1,655
% applicants accepted	50
% acceptees attending	28
Average LSAT	156
Average undergrad GPA	3.24
Application Fee	$40
No early decision program	
Regular application deadline	March 1
Regular notification	rolling
Admission deferment	one year
Gourman Report Rating	**3.75**

QUINNIPIAC COLLEGE
School of Law

OVERVIEW

Type of school	private
Environment	city
Scholastic calendar	semester
Schedule	Full-time or part-time

STUDENTS

Enrollment of institution	3,772
Enrollment of law school	794
% male/female	64/36
% out-of-state	45
% part-time	31
% minorities	12
% international (# countries represented)	NR (NR)
Average age at entry	26

APPLICANTS ALSO LOOK AT

University of Connecticut
Pace University
Western New England College
Saint John's University
New England School of Law

SURVEY SAYS...

HITS
Diverse faculty
Faculty-student relations
Legal writing

MISSES
Sense of community
Library staff

EMPLOYMENT PROFILE

% grads employed immediately	NR
% grads employed within six months	88
Average starting salary	$35,000
% grads employed by field:	
Private practice	61
Business/industry	12
Government	13
Judicial clerkships	9
Military	0

Finding a decent apartment is hard enough when you have only yourself to please. Imagine trying to find a comfortable new dwelling on short notice for 29 professors, 700 law students and a 225,000-volume library. It boggles the mind, but that was the task that faced the former University of Bridgeport School of Law in early 1992 when its financially strapped parent institution began to unravel. While the ABA threatened to rescind the school's accreditation, the law schools administration cast about for new digs. It found them in March, 1992, and re-formed itself as the Quinnipiac College School of Law. Still, the law school's fight for survival is not over, and until the dust fully settles, to enroll at Quinnipiac is to take a calculated risk. So far, however, Quinnipiac's administrators have succeeded in making this huge transition as smooth as can be expected.

The new building, located in Hamden, Connecticut, sometimes referred to as the "Taj Mahal," affords a lovely view of Sleeping Giant Mountains from its perch directly across from Sleeping Giant Park. In addition to the move, some other exciting changes happened in 1995. New hires who formerly taught at such estimable seats of learning as Vanderbilt, the University of Chicago, and Oxford University joined Quinnipiac's faculty. The school is making a name for itself by sponsoring events such as a conference on Forensics attended by most of the defense experts from the O.J. Simpson trial.

Even with all the change, the school happily continues its traditions of sound programs in Health Care Law and Tax Care Law, and its commitment to public service. According to the Quinnipiac School of Law bulletin, "The School of Law's curriculum reflects the belief that complete legal training includes a full understanding of ethical issues and values and an appreciation of a lawyer's professional and social responsibilities." To this end, the school operates three clinics, the Tax Clinic, the Civil Clinic, and the new Appellate Clinic, which provide vital legal services to the population of greater New Haven.

Many students expressed appreciation for the help their professors provide to improve their personal, more immediate futures. One 2L informed us, "Our professors are always available and

John Noonan, Dean of Admissions
275 Mount Carmel Avenue, Hamden, CT 06518-1950
Tel: (203) 287-3333
Internet: http:/qcinet.quinnipiac.edu/q.html

Quinnipiac College

willing to provide help and answer questions outside the class-room." Many praised the Tax Clinic and the "stress on practical law," including Quinnipiac's extensive lawyering skills program. One said, "I would recommend Quinnipiac to anyone as a viable, nurturing school."

Thanks to all the recent changes, students we heard from are justifiably optimistic about the future of the school. We heard extensive gratitude for "the quality of the faculty and the effort of the administrators to improve the facilities and reputation of the school." The administration's efforts will surely go a long way to diminish students' greatest worry, the reputation, and increase name recognition. Another student spoke for many when she placed her praise in more guarded terms: "The school has great potential, and the faculty and administration seem willing to realize it." As a 1L told us, "The only direction this law school is going is up, especially with the devoted administration and motivated student body. Some predict the school will be among the top law schools in the nation within twenty years."

ADMISSIONS

The Bridgeport School of Law's much-publicized woes in 1992 did not fail to have an effect on the law school's admissions process. In the 1991 application year, Bridgeport received more than 3,300 applications for admission to its entering class of about 200. In 1993, it received fewer than 2,500. Furthermore, Bridgeport admitted almost 200 more students in order to fill its class. In other words, between '91 and '93 the acceptance rate here jumped from a low of 25 percent to the current, lenient rate of around 40 percent. Numerical standards, however, declined only slightly, and it is likely that Quinnipiac's overall admissions selectivity will once again increase as the law school settles in to its new home.

ACADEMICS

Student/faculty ratio	11:1
% female faculty	29
% minority faculty	3
Hours of study per day	4.14

FINANCIAL FACTS

Tuition	$17,560
Part-time tuition per credit	$732
Estimated books/expenses/fees	$2,375
On-campus living expenses	NR
Off-campus living expenses	NR
% first-year students receiving aid	85
% all students receiving aid	85
% aid that is merit-based	30
% all students receiving grants/scholarships	30
% all students receiving loans	80
% all students receiving assistantships	8
Average award package	$5,300
Average graduation debt	$67,000

ADMISSIONS

# applications received	2,408
% applicants accepted	41
% acceptees attending	25
Average LSAT	153
Average undergrad GPA	2.85
Application Fee	$40
No early decision program	
Regular application deadline	NR
Regular notification	rolling
Admission deferment	one year
Gourman Report Rating	2.22

UNIVERSITY OF RICHMOND
The T.C. Williams School of Law

The University of Richmond School of Law is a midsize private law school with a solid, long-established regional reputation. Its home state of Virginia has one of the biggest trade surpluses in law-school graduates of any state in the union. Every year, the state's six law schools turn out many more fledgling attorneys than its legal profession can absorb. At first blush, this fact does not bode well for the prospective Richmond law student. But several of Virginia's law schools are among the nation's elite, and a huge proportion of these schools' graduates leave the state for the job markets of New York and Washington, D.C. Richmond fills the resulting void by sending the vast majority of its grads to work within the state.

The law school is committed to seeing that they hit the ground running upon arrival. Richmond's required two-year course in "Lawyering Skills" follows an uncommon but increasingly popular format: Students are divided into small simulated law offices in which they perform all the tasks associated with servicing real legal clients. This approach is intended to expose the law student early on to the sort of work that he or she would otherwise have to learn on the job after graduation. Richmond was the first law school in the country to require its students to own a laptop computer upon entering the law school. The Richmond curriculum is also notable for its including environmental law in the required first-year curriculum. Admissions are selective, and admitted students possess strong numerical credentials.

Those who actually go on to enroll at Richmond paint a picture of a school that serves its students well and has an overall pleasant atmosphere. As one might expect, given the law school's stated emphasis on practical-skills training, a good number of students see this as Richmond's area of greatest strength. This assessment from a 1L sums up the feelings of many others: "In three years working in a law firm before starting school, I saw attorneys who had recently graduated from top institutions who were not able to react and act in the 'real world' of the legal profession. I feel like U of R is doing its part to correct this all-too-prevalent problem." Richmond students are also positive about the law school's facilities and the quality of their relations with faculty members.

University of Richmond, VA 23173
Tel: (804) 289-8189   Fax: (804) 287-6516
Internet: http://www.urich.edu/^law/

"You gotta love professors who whip up on you in class and then let you whip up on them in the racquetball court!" "Richmond is an all-around excellent value." (With an annual tuition of more than $15,000, it is rather remarkable that even a handful of students offered that same unsolicited judgment.) "Most students are intense but very well-guided," said another 1L. "Generally, we are a very happy but very busy bunch."

Though almost uniformly positive in the grand scheme of things, Richmond students did have their criticisms. Most critical comments focused on inadequate out-of-state career placement. Part of this is reflected in the two words that cropped up on nearly half our respondents' questionnaires: "national recognition." Recent activity aimed at redirecting the curriculum and philosophy of the school seem to have failed, according to some students. "U of R is trying to build an image as an 'innovator,'"explained one student who went on to assert that "it's not working, at least with the students. We didn't come here for such programs and I doubt students will do so in the future." Though few others were so cynical, many expressed their desire that the law school focus its attention on providing better fundamental services to its current students rather than on image-building. Paradoxically, some of these same students called on the administration to "market the qualifications of the law school outside Virginia." The vast majority of Richmond students seemed to understand, however, that it's pretty tough to have it both ways.

ADMISSIONS

In purely numerical terms, the law school at the University of Richmond is in the front half of the pack of American law schools, reflecting the extent to which admissions selectivity has increased nationwide. Seven or eight years ago, "moderate" admissions standards were truly moderate. Today, the term is relative. Consider, after all, the undeniable strength of the credentials of Richmond students. Their average undergraduate GPA and LSAT scores are solid.

ACADEMICS	
Student/faculty ratio	9:1
% female faculty	37
% minority faculty	13
Hours of study per day	4.49

FINANCIAL FACTS	
Tuition	$17,170
Part-time tuition per credit	NR
Estimated books/expenses/fees	NR
On-campus living expenses	$3,870
Off-campus living expenses	$5,715
% first-year students receiving aid	NR
% all students receiving aid	NR
% aid that is merit-based	25
% all students receiving grants/scholarships	75
% all students receiving loans	86
% all students receiving assistantships	NR
Average award package	$3,164
Average graduation debt	NR

ADMISSIONS	
# applications received	1,631
% applicants accepted	34
% acceptees attending	31
Average LSAT	159
Average undergrad GPA	3.02
Application Fee	$35
No early decision program	
Regular application deadline	January 15
Regular notification	May 1
Admission deferment	NR
Gourman Report Rating	2.64

RUTGERS UNIVERSITY, CAMDEN
School of Law at Camden

In 1950, the State University of New Jersey absorbed its second school of law, one that was and is, in many positive respects, identical to the older state law school in Newark. The Rutgers University School of Law, Camden, is a moderately large, inexpensive public law school with an esteemed faculty, a favorable student-faculty ratio, academically strong day and evening programs, and a solid regional reputation. Both attract a highly qualified group of students, primarily state residents, who are slightly older and significantly more diverse than the average. The most tangible difference between the two law schools stems from their geographic locations. In contrast to its New York-oriented companion school in Newark, Rutgers, Camden, is as much a part of Pennsylvania as it is of New Jersey. Located in the Delaware River Valley, the law school sends many of its graduates into the greater Philadelphia metropolitan area, the nation's fifth-largest legal job market.

Academic options at Rutgers are many. The law school's course offerings are quite extensive, and the programs of the broader university afford the law student ample opportunity for interdisciplinary study. (Joint J.D/master's degree programs are available through the departments of Urban Planning, Business Administration, and Political Science and students may petition the Dean to pursue other joint degrees. Like so many public law schools, Rutgers, Camden, has seen a significant increase in applications volume in recent years. While demand seems to have leveled off, the law school remains somewhat selective.

Students paint a picture of a law school that has much to offer, particularly considering its reasonable tuition. "The intellectual acumen of the faculty is high," said one 2L, expressing a sentiment that is held by many, "and they are tremendously accessible to students." As pleased as most Rutgers students seem to be with their instructors, they seem even more pleased with their fellow students. "The student body is composed of nice, friendly people," reported one typical 3L, "and even at the top of the class I've found my classmates to be supportive and non-competitive." Even the law school's 1Ls, entrenched in a rigorous first-year program, agree. "It is a school with a healthy, competitive, intellectual atmosphere," said one.

But few students found it difficult to point to their chosen school's shortcomings. A number of them made remarks that were strikingly similar to this one: "The school attracts capable and hard-working students, but it offers only adequate guidance and 'atmosphere.' "As for the perceived lack of guidance, many students focused their criticisms on the law school's placement office. "Career services has a reputation of catering only to the best students," went one fairly typical complaint. "If your grades are moderate, you're more or less shrugged off." Others concurred: "Too much attention is paid to the high-GPA, Law Review crowd." While our goal is to let students tell the story, to be fair, we must add that the administration claimed the comments regarding career services are no longer correct, so we expect our next survey to reflect that fact. As for the less tangible quality of "atmosphere," most students agreed that it was missing and called on the law school to sponsor more co-curricular programs.

Complaints about the uneven quality of teaching were almost always mild. As one who identified this as an area in need of improvement put it: "Newer, younger, better faculty have started to arrive. This trend should continue." All in all, most students felt a bit like this one: "If I end up getting a job, I'll feel RU-Camden served me well at a great price."

ADMISSIONS

Numerical admissions standards at Rutgers, Camden, crept up steadily during the late 1980s, as they did at most of the nation's public law schools. Though Rutgers saw a less dramatic increase than some, standards were quite high to begin with. As it now stands, the law school is quite selective, denying admission to seventy percent of all applicants and admitting a midsize class of students with strong credentials: solid undergraduate GPAs and good LSAT scores at or about the 75th percentile. Rutgers' status as a true bargain is not unknown to successful candidates for admission. Admitted applicants accept offers to attend the law school at a high rate.

ACADEMICS	
Student/faculty ratio	17:1
% female faculty	19
% minority faculty	10
Hours of study per day	3.33

FINANCIAL FACTS	
In-state tuition	$8,550
Out-of-state tuition	$12,305
Part-time tuition per credit	$313
Estimated books/expenses/fees	NR
On-campus living expenses	NR
Off-campus living expenses	NR
% first-year students receiving aid	75
% all students receiving aid	77
% aid that is merit-based	7
% all students receiving grants/scholarships	NR
% all students receiving loans	NR
% all students receiving assistantships	NR
Average award package	NR
Average graduation debt	NR

ADMISSIONS	
# applications received	2,084
% applicants accepted	39
% acceptees attending	39
Average LSAT	156
Average undergrad GPA	3.32
Application Fee	$40
Priority application deadline	NR
Priority notification	NR
Regular application deadline	March 1
Regular notification	NR
Admission deferment	NR
Gourman Report Rating	**3.69**

RUTGERS UNIVERSITY, NEWARK 💾

School of Law

The history of Newark, a hardworking northern New Jersey city has been, in large part, a history of immigrants and industry. Over time, the origin of the immigrants and the identity of the industries changed, but the city has known one constant: a fine public law school that was once the country's second largest. The Rutgers University School of Law, Newark, boasts an excellent faculty and a highly qualified group of law students who are, in terms of both ethnicity and gender, among the most diverse in the nation. The law school's large evening division and its active alternative admissions program for applicants from under-represented minority groups are evidence of its dedication to making a quality legal education accessible to all New Jersey residents, who make up the great majority of the student body. The resources at the disposal of Rutgers law students are considerable, from the numerous clinical programs run by the law school to the extensive academic offerings of the university itself, through which interdisciplinary work is encouraged. The applicant pool from which Rutgers draws its first-year students is large and growing, so selectivity is high. Admitted applicants possess strong numerical credentials.

They also possess keen critical faculties, judging from the results of our survey. The students we heard from did not hesitate to criticize their chosen school on any number of matters, from its "decaying" facilities to its "mediocre" career services office. Yet nearly all of their criticism was constructive and offered in a manner that did not hide their overall satisfaction with the most basic aspect of their law-school experience: their academic and practical preparation for the practice of law. "The facilities at Rutgers-Newark leave much to be desired," began one fairly typical assessment from a 3L. "The library shows signs of neglect and the building is awful," it continued, "but the program itself is very strong and the tuition is so low that I cannot regret my decision to come here." It appears that most here would agree with that last judgment. Despite seeing real room for improvement elsewhere, most Rutgers students heaped praise on their school for its commitment to maintaining a strong, broad and nontraditional curriculum while keeping tuition low, at least in comparison with other schools in the region. As one 2L put it,

Olga Hunczak, Director of Admissions
15 Washington Street, Newark, NJ 07102-3192
Tel: (201) 648-5557
eMail: rabrams@andromeda.rutgers.edu

"The clinical and public interest programs here are top-notch, particularly considering the low cost of an education." Indeed, many of the respondents to our survey used a similar cost-benefit analysis in assessing their overall feelings for their school. "There's a lot of things I would fix here if I could," wrote one such student, "but I don't think I'd have been willing to pay three times as much just to have a pretty campus."

Still, one cannot ignore the fact that many Rutgers students' complaints go deeper than the ugliness of their campus. Most see the condition of their physical plant as a serious drawback. "The students here are friendly, bright and fairly relaxed, but there is almost no school social life," said one 2L. The reason? "Our building sucks and Newark's worse." Some went even further. "Sometimes it seems that it's not just the building that's falling apart," said one 2L. "The great reputation this school once enjoyed is threatened by the failure to replace some of our better retiring professors with high-caliber younger ones." In fact, though most students here seem to agree that their faculty is nothing if not uneven, the majority expressed more optimism than is conveyed in that last remark. "Although the atmosphere and facilities at Rutgers-Newark are marginal, a new building is coming shortly, which should be a great improvement," went one fairly evenhanded assessment by one 3L, "[and] our new dean of placement and new Dean of the school have injected some much-needed energy into a largely uninterested faculty." If that trend continues, it seems that future students at Rutgers-Newark will agree even more strongly that "This is a flawed but excellent school, and you can't beat it for the price."

ADMISSIONS

With a strong academic reputation and a bargain-basement price tag, it should come as no surprise to hear that the Rutgers School of Law, Newark, draws its students from a huge applicant pool. In fact, with more than 10 applicants for every spot in its first-year class, Rutgers, Newark, is in a position to select its students extremely carefully.

ACADEMICS

Student/faculty ratio	21:1
% female faculty	25
% minority faculty	28
Hours of study per day	3.76

FINANCIAL FACTS

In-state tuition	$8,179
Out-of-state tuition	$11,790
Part-time tuition per credit	NR
Estimated books/expenses/fees	NR
On-campus living expenses	NR
Off-campus living expenses	NR
% first-year students receiving aid	NR
% all students receiving aid	NR
% aid that is merit-based	5
% all students receiving grants/scholarships	15
% all students receiving loans	67
% all students receiving assistantships	4
Average award package	$1,100
Average graduation debt	$49,755

ADMISSIONS

# applications received	2,835
% applicants accepted	22
% acceptees attending	38
Average LSAT	161
Average undergrad GPA	3.38
Application Fee	$40
No early decision program	
Regular application deadline	March 1
Regular notification	rolling
Admission deferment	one year
Gourman Report Rating	3.73

SAMFORD UNIVERSITY 💾
Cumberland School of Law

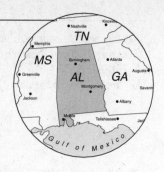

The Cumberland School of Law at Samford University is the larger of Alabama's two law schools and, depending on how you measure it, the older. Cumberland began life in 1847, but in Lebanon, Tennessee. The law school was not acquired by this private university in suburban Birmingham until 1961. Since it began its residency in Alabama, Cumberland has firmly established itself as a regionally respected institution, and it has built a widely recognized reputation for its practical-skills program. In fact, Cumberland claims to offer "the nation's finest program in trial advocacy." At least in terms of the law school's dedication to building its strength in that area, the rather audacious claim has some merit.

Although it offers no more courses in the field than many law schools, Cumberland dedicates tremendous human and financial resources to instilling strong advocacy skills in its students. The law school's emphasis on courtroom skills is evident in its sponsorship of eight different on-campus mock trial competitions. The victors in these hotly contested competitions have had great success at the national level, drawing much attention to Cumberland's strong suit. On the traditional side of the curriculum, Cumberland students follow a straightforward course of study that is heavy on requirements and relatively light on electives. Through the broader university itself, law students can also pursue concurrent degrees in education, business administration, public health, divinity, accountancy, environmental management, and public administration. Cumberland students, most of whom come from and stay in the Southeast, possess midrange numerical credentials.

Students at Cumberland have mixed feelings about their chosen school. They convey a strong sense of satisfaction with many aspects of their experience at the law school, but their criticism is stronger and more consistent than their praise. Not surprisingly, Cumberland students are more enthusiastic about the law school's clinics and trial-advocacy program than about anything else. When asked to name their school's greatest strengths, however, many went farther, offering praise for their "friendly and caring teachers" and for a curriculum that "allows students to graduate

Mitzi S. Davis, Assistant Dean for Admissions
800 Lakeshore Drive, Birmingham, AL 35229
Tel: (800) 888-7213
Internet: http://www.samford.edu

with broad-based knowledge in most major areas of law—particularly business-oriented law." (Cumberland's second- and third-year course requirements are almost all business-oriented: "Business Organizations"; "Estates and Trusts"; "Federal Tax"; "Commercial Transactions"; plus the happy exception "Professional Responsibility.") The law school also boasts a new $8.4 million library, finished in March 1995.

Far more of the students we heard from, however, were not pleased with the rigidity of Cumberland's J.D. program. In addition to calling on the law school to expand its skills curriculum by establishing a community legal clinic, most lamented the limited number of elective courses allowed and many offered unsolicited complaints about the limited selection of courses from which their few electives must be chosen. One 2L complained that "there is really no diversity in the curriculum," and a 3L said that "it would be nice if they'd simply offer the classes that are shown in the catalog." Also, while Cumberland students expressed little love for the school's support services, many students complained about the limited resources of their career placement office, and several reported that "the administration has a poor rapport with the students."

ADMISSIONS

In most quantifiable respects, the Cumberland School of Law at Samford University resides in the middle of the pack of all U.S. law schools in terms of admissions selectivity. Still, a large applicant pool allows the law school to select its students rather carefully, denying admission to more than half of all candidates it considers.

ACADEMICS

Student/faculty ratio	19:1
% female faculty	26
% minority faculty	12
Hours of study per day	4.02

FINANCIAL FACTS

Tuition	$16,480
Part-time tuition per credit	NR
Estimated books/expenses/fees	NR
On-campus living expenses	NR
Off-campus living expenses	NR
% first-year students receiving aid	99
% all students receiving aid	99
% aid that is merit-based	11
% all students receiving grants/scholarships	31
% all students receiving loans	77
% all students receiving assistantships	15
Average award package	$5,896
Average graduation debt	NR

ADMISSIONS

# applications received	1,220
% applicants accepted	45
% acceptees attending	40
Average LSAT	154
Average undergrad GPA	3.07
Application Fee	$40
No early decision program	
Regular application deadline	May 1
Regular notification	rolling
Admission may be deferred?	no

Gourman Report Rating	**2.70**

UNIVERSITY OF SAN DIEGO 💾
School of Law

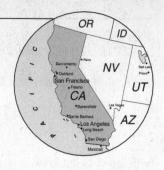

It is not difficult to understand why prospective law students would be attracted to the idea of studying in San Diego. Beautiful weather alone can, on occasion, go a long way toward relieving the stresses of law school. Indeed, the year-round sun and balmy temperatures of its home city must help explain the enormous popularity of the University of San Diego School of Law. During the early 1990s, the volume of applications filed at this large Catholic law school increased by more than 150 percent, and San Diego's overall acceptance rate was slashed in half. However, three years of sunshine is far from the only reason future lawyers come here.

Faculty vied with location as one of the greatest strengths of the school. Students praised their professors' willingness to help them understand material. We also heard many kind comments about the administration, a rare occurrence in the world of law schools. A 1L said that "professors as well as administrators sincerely care about our welfare and well-being." More than a few students called the administrative staff helpful, efficient, and friendly. One 2L said the "Dean of Students is always willing to help individual students." Another 2L proclaimed, "The records office staff is the best."

San Diego's J.D. program is rigorous and its students serious-minded. The course of study they follow at the law school is straightforward: a fully prescribed first year and then a few required courses in the next two. A 1L praised the atmosphere of "group effort and broad learning." The school has relatively extensive course offerings within traditional bounds. The San Diego curriculum is supplemented by a considerable array of skills programs. The size of the clinical programs is limited, but the school offers a wide variety of them. USD takes particular pride in its advocacy programs; participation in San Diego's numerous moot-court competitions is reportedly quite high.

While the school's tuition is on a par with other private law schools, it is far steeper than that of California's higher-ranking state law schools. One student, who appreciated the school's "excellent library" and described the faculty as "helpful and insightful," still called the school's tuition "almost oppressive."

Jo Ann Szymonik, Assistant Director of Admissions and Financial Aid
5998 Alcala Park, San Diego, CA 92110-2492
Tel: (619) 260-4528
eMail: jdinfo@acusd.edu
Internet: http://www.acusd.edu/~usdlaw/

University of San Diego

Another voiced concerns that students were not getting their money's worth.

Students did express a need for more computer training and a greater use of computers in their legal research than they are currently receiving at San Diego. "For the money we pay and the technology available today, this and other law schools are using teaching methods that must come directly from the Dark Ages," said a 1L.

Unfortunately most students we heard from were far quicker to criticize than to praise, and those who did make positive comments lacked enthusiasm in their delivery. This possibly speaks of an alienation that many students seemed to feel, despite the friendly administration. "There could be more ways for students to voice their opinions without feeling threatened," said a 1L. "Student input needs to be seriously considered as opposed to off-handedly disregarded," said a 2L.

The positives we heard from students tended to focus on the school's environment—the great weather and the school's relaxed social climate. One student who noted that San Diego "affords students with an abundance of extracurricular activities," formed his list as such: "sailing, golfing, jogging...and tennis..." Another student, a 1L made this observation:"[This is a] very caring environment—no shark tank here."

ADMISSIONS

It is testimony to the popularity of all of California's law schools that the University of San Diego School of Law ranks only eighth of the state's sixteen in admissions selectivity. In terms of numerical standards to which it holds its applicants, San Diego is one of the 70 most selective law schools in the country.

ACADEMICS

Student/faculty ratio	20:1
% female faculty	26
% minority faculty	12
Hours of study per day	3.32

FINANCIAL FACTS

Tuition	$18,940
Part-time tuition per credit	$640
Estimated books/expenses/fees	$800
On-campus living expenses	$7,177
Off-campus living expenses	$7,177
% first-year students receiving aid	76
% all students receiving aid	80
% aid that is merit-based	NR
% all students receiving grants/scholarships	21
% all students receiving loans	76
% all students receiving assistantships	NR
Average award package	NR
Average graduation debt	$55,000

ADMISSIONS

# applications received	3,320
% applicants accepted	35
% acceptees attending	26
Average LSAT	160
Average undergrad GPA	3.24
Application Fee	$35
Priority application deadline	February 1
Priority notification	NR
Regular application deadline	NR
Regular notification	rolling
Admission deferment	one year
Gourman Report Rating	**3.81**

UNIVERSITY OF SAN FRANCISCO 💾
School of Law

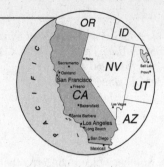

For more than 80 years, the University of San Francisco School of Law has been a major supplier of fledgling attorneys to one of the nation's largest legal communities. USF is a relatively large Jesuit institution, and its law school has a strong regional reputation. As one of the only two schools in San Francisco that offers a part-time J.D. program, USF has a relatively secure place as a prominent regional law school.

USF's active efforts to stay on top of the trend toward more practical-skills training seem to reflect its desire to protect its regional status. Like many schools that lack hefty national reputations, USF has responded more quickly than the elite law schools to recent changes in the legal profession. As the job market for law school graduates has tightened, employers have come to place a higher premium on the practical skills of law practice, and USF is quick to tout its commitment to preparing its students accordingly. In the classroom this means an increased reliance on the case method and practice courses that emphasize "lawyering" skills. Outside the classroom, this means a sizable and diverse collection of clinical and externship programs.

Students at USF gave high ratings to the school's legal writing and clinical programs, as well as the faculty. One student described the school's curriculum as designed "to create the best lawyers possible out of the caliber of students the school can attract." Students also noted the university's strong ties to the area's legal community and the help that affords after graduation. "[There are] great networking opportunities due to the fact that most judges and senior practitioners in San Francisco attended this university," said one 3L.

Although the majority of students surveyed spoke highly of the school's pragmatic approach to legal education, some students lamented the absence of theoretical instruction on campus. A 1L said, "I would prefer a less practical and more theoretical/critical-thinking approach." Another 1L said: "one is deluded if one believes that the level of discussion and intellectual instruction can even approach that found in one of the first-tier institutions."

Saralynn T. Macy, Director of Admissions
2130 Fulton Street, San Francisco, CA 94117-1080
Tel: (415) 666-6544

University of San Francisco

Many student comments focused on the political climate at USF. This school seems to draw students with different, although equally vocal, political ideas and assumptions of what the social climate at the school should be. Although the majority of students surveyed placed the school on the liberal side of the political spectrum, there are those at USF who find it too conservative and homogenous. One 3L said that USF espouses "a commitment to intellectual diversity and social justice which is simply not reflected in the course offerings, faculty, or administration. If you want to change the world—or even your law school—this is not the place to come." There were also students who felt the school was too liberal. When asked how USF could improve, a 3L made this suggestion: "Get some Republicans on the staff. [There are] too many liberals."

Students with both conservative and liberal leanings were in agreement on USF's facilities, which one student described as "tired." In particular many students reported that the school's library and computer lab are in need of attention. Despite these concerns, it appears that students at USF School of Law are content enough with their location and practical training to look positively on their educational experience.

ADMISSIONS

As the appeal of attending law school in the Bay Area has increased over the past several years, so has USF's applicant pool. The numerical standards of its students have increased accordingly, and USF now accepts only about one out of three candidates, the vast majority of whom are already Bay Area residents. In terms of numerical standards, USF ranks almost exactly in the middle of U.S. law schools. The class that entered in the 1995-96 term had a median LSAT score in the 73rd percentile and an average undergraduate GPA of a little over 3.2. For those whose averages exceed these figures, USF is very nearly a sure bet, but those whose numbers fall short face stiff competition.

ACADEMICS

Student/faculty ratio	26:1
% female faculty	29
% minority faculty	37
Hours of study per day	3.88

FINANCIAL FACTS

Tuition	$18,900
Part-time tuition per credit	NR
Estimated books/expenses/fees	$810
On-campus living expenses	NR
Off-campus living expenses	NR
% first-year students receiving aid	95
% all students receiving aid	99
% aid that is merit-based	NR
% all students receiving grants/scholarships	75
% all students receiving loans	75
% all students receiving assistantships	15
Average award package	$4,000
Average graduation debt	$50,000

ADMISSIONS

# applications received	3,497
% applicants accepted	29
% acceptees attending	21
Average LSAT	157
Average undergrad GPA	3.20
Application Fee	$40
No early decision program	
Regular application deadline	April 1
Regular notification	rolling
Admission may be deferred?	no
Gourman Report Rating	3.80

SANTA CLARA UNIVERSITY 🖫
School of Law

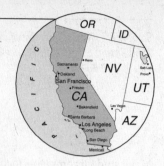

OVERVIEW

Type of school	private
Environment	metropolis
Scholastic calendar	quarter
Schedule	Full-time or part-time

STUDENTS

Enrollment of institution	3,977
Enrollment of law school	865
% male/female	50/50
% out-of-state	12
% part-time	24
% minorities	32
% international (# countries represented)	NR (NR)
Average age at entry	24

APPLICANTS ALSO LOOK AT

University of California
U. of California, Davis
U. of California, Berkeley
University of San Francisco
University of the Pacific

SURVEY SAYS...

HITS
Diverse faculty
Studying
Left-leaning politics

MISSES
Legal writing
Socratic method
Not enough courses

EMPLOYMENT PROFILE

% grads employed immediately	72
% grads employed within six months	93
Average starting salary	$51,000
% grads employed by field:	
Private practice	59
Business/industry	24
Government	7
Judicial clerkships	5
Public service	3
Academic	1
Military	3

After nearby Stanford and the two area law schools in the University of California system, the Santa Clara University School of Law is probably the most highly regarded law school in the greater Bay Area. Established more than 80 years ago in what is now the heart of the Silicon Valley—about an hour's drive south of San Francisco—this large private law school has long enjoyed a solid reputation in and around northern California. This region is the source of most of its well-qualified students and the destination of nearly all of its well-trained graduates. Santa Clara's J.D. curriculum is broad within traditional bounds and is supplemented by a relatively extensive clinical program, including an in-house clinic and a wide variety of externships with local courts and public agencies.

The law school also offers formal certificate of specialization in computer and high technology law, public interest law, and international law. Course offerings are richest, however, in the broader category of business and commercial law, and despite the curricular emphasis on public service, the overwhelming majority of Santa Clara grads begin their careers in private practice. A significant number of students pursue a joint J.D./M.B.A. through the university's regionally well-respected business school. Prospective students should note that the massive upsurge in law-school applications in the last decade has affected Santa Clara more than most private law schools. Since 1986, applications volume has more than doubled, and admissions standards have risen significantly. Members of Santa Clara's remarkably diverse entering classes now possess very solid numerical credentials.

They also appear to be satisfied with their chosen school. Although nearly all the students we heard from had their gripes, their overall sense of well-being was notable. "Santa Clara is a good school with very few low spots," said one 3L succinctly. "The academic atmosphere is generally very supportive," wrote another, "and though competition among students is strong, it is not so much so that learning is hindered." Indeed, Santa Clara students agreed almost unanimously that relations among students and between students and faculty are quite good. "The

Julia Yaffee, Assistant Dean of Admissions
500 El Camino Real, Santa Clara, CA 95053
Tel: (408) 554-4800   Fax: (408) 554-7897
Internet: http://www.scu.edu/SCU/Departments/Law

Santa Clara University

availability of profs and their willingness to meet with students and work one on one with them is one of this school's greatest strengths," reported one 1L. "The attitude encouraged by the administration," he added, "is one of community and not of competition."

When asked to name areas in which their school could stand to improve, many students noted that while the academic elite (top 10 percent) are professionally provided for, the remainder of the students "feel the future looks bleak for the rest of us." Most criticisms were never harsh and were often followed by reiterated praise. Many students, for instance, called on the school to improve its job placement services outside the immediate region, but as one such student allowed, "there is great community support when trying to find a job in the San Jose area." "Most lawyers down here," she explained, "are Santa Clara graduates." "I wish Santa Clara had more of a national reputation," wrote another, "but I'm glad it's a place where you can still feel human. I think that's something important to consider." Though many other students expressed similar sentiments concerning their school's lack of national stature, they seemed to have a sense of humor and perspective on this matter. One student noted that "we almost don't care that the school's reputation isn't quite what it deserves to be—it's truly a fantastic school."

ADMISSIONS

Rising applications volume in the last several years has driven numerical admission standards at the Santa Clara University School of Law ever higher. As it now stands, Santa Clara ranks fifty-eighth among all U.S. law schools in terms of its students' numerical credentials. Happily for the hopeful applicant, however, Santa Clara's overall acceptance rate isn't very low.

ACADEMICS

Student/faculty ratio	22:1
% female faculty	37
% minority faculty	20
Hours of study per day	4.25

FINANCIAL FACTS

Tuition	$19,130
Part-time tuition per credit	$666
Estimated books/expenses/fees	NR
On-campus living expenses	NR
Off-campus living expenses	NR
% first-year students receiving aid	77
% all students receiving aid	NR
% aid that is merit-based	NR
% all students receiving grants/scholarships	34
% all students receiving loans	72
% all students receiving assistantships	NR
Average award package	$22,447
Average graduation debt	$61,926

ADMISSIONS

# applications received	3,416
% applicants accepted	32
% acceptees attending	23
Average LSAT	157
Average undergrad GPA	3.26
Application Fee	$40
No early decision program	
Regular application deadline	March 1
Regular notification	rolling
Admission deferment	one year
Gourman Report Rating	3.72

SEATTLE UNIVERSITY

School of Law

OVERVIEW

Type of school	private
Environment	metropolis
Scholastic calendar	quarter
Schedule	Full-time or part-time

STUDENTS

Enrollment of institution	6,000
Enrollment of law school	800
% male/female	55/45
% out-of-state	34
% part-time	18
% minorities	22
% international (# countries represented)	1 (3)
Average age at entry	29

APPLICANTS ALSO LOOK AT

U. of California, Hastings College of Law
University of Colorado
Lewis and Clark College
Santa Clara University
University of Washington

SURVEY SAYS...

HITS
Legal writing
Socratic method
Library staff

MISSES
Lack of diversity among faculty
Facilities not great
Not enough courses

EMPLOYMENT PROFILE

% grads employed immediately	42
% grads employed within six months	90
Average starting salary	$40,000
% grads employed by field:	
Private practice	50
Business/industry	17
Government	21
Judicial clerkships	5
Public service	5
Academic	2
Military	5

Decades before the Pacific Northwest became fashionable in the 1980s, the area had become a magnet for immigrants-mostly Asian-whose settlement here did much to create the region's identity and the favorable conditions that have made it the destination of choice for tens of thousands of re-settlers from the Northeast and southern California. More than the cool weather and the great coffee, what has drawn people here is the economic promise of the Pacific Rim, the perennial Next Big Thing in international trade. The acknowledged American capital of the Pacific Rim, the Seattle-Tacoma region, is home to, among other things, the largest law school in the Northwest-Seattle University School of Law, formerly the University of Puget Sound School of Law.

A regionally prominent institution for several decades, the law school, like its home, has begun to draw many outsiders: Nearly half of Seattle's students now come from outside the state. On the strength of its solid academic program, its respected, teaching-oriented faculty, and, of course, its location, the law school has in recent years seen a sizable increase in application volume and a commensurate increase in the qualification of its student body. Seattle still admits more than a third of all applicants, but numerical standards are fairly high and rising. The law school offers both day and evening courses for all students, not just for those officially enrolled as part-time. Not surprisingly, given this flexibility, Seattle attracts a group of students that is slightly older than average.

Thanks to SU's spectacular geographic situation and convenient part-time option, the law school draws an incredibly wide range of individuals, each of whom bring very firm, very singular opinions about the world, each other, and their shared law school, most of which run in favor of the mix. One woman told us, "We have people far to each side of the issues which has made for some interesting debate," and another exclaimed, "Older students (self-actualized and mature) and younger faculty members are cool. Public Interest Student Organization rocks!" One student shared her approval of a specific variety of tolerance: "Faculty and students tend to be 'gay friendly,' including several gay and lesbian faculty."

Karen Dietz, Associate Director of Admission
950 Broadway Plaza, Tacoma, WA 98402
Tel: (206) 591-2252
eMail: lawadmis@seattleu.edu
Internet: http://www.law.seattleu.edu

Seattle University

Many lauded SU's commitment to practical education: The clinical programs, the Legal Writing Program, and the Public Interest Law Foundation all received significant praise. The classroom focus on the Socratic method, which some students deplored, complements practical extracurricular programs.

In our surveys, SU students called for more of the good things they already have: more clinical programs, more practical skills offerings, more diversity in hiring and enrolling, more public interest support, even better teachers, more amenities for nontraditional students (i.e., daycare facilities), and much more sensitivity towards students from diverse backgrounds.

Competition is keen at SU. Students complained about the "very tough mandatory grade curve for 1L classes, which is great to prevent grade inflation but difficult when you are compared with students at other schools with higher GPA." Inter- and intra-school rivalry create palpable anxiety, intensified by a slow grade posting system. One 2L explained the reason for all the fuss and fret: "Because this school is not 'nationally' recognized like some others, i.e., Harvard, Michigan, Boalt Hall, etc., the level of competition is extremely high among students, which is good because it raises the level of academic excellence, but bad because it limits the friendships you are able to develop."

As far as national name recognition goes, positive change has started and everyone expects it to continue, thanks to the upcoming move to Seattle. No one will miss the facilities now housed in a "renovated (five-story) department store complete with five noisy escalators in continual operation." Though the move will happen too late to change the school days of students we surveyed, most are confident that the likely boost in national name recognition can only help them as they navigate the world of legal employment.

ADMISSIONS

Seattle University School of Law considers almost 2,000 applications annually, which puts it in a position to select its students somewhat carefully. The size of the law school's entering class, however, requires the school to admit a relatively large proportion of all applicants.

ACADEMICS

Student/faculty ratio	22:1
% female faculty	37
% minority faculty	18
Hours of study per day	4.12

FINANCIAL FACTS

Tuition	$15,330
Part-time tuition per credit	$12,775
Estimated books/expenses/fees	$667
On-campus living expenses	NR
Off-campus living expenses	$6,204
% first-year students receiving aid	85
% all students receiving aid	88
% aid that is merit-based	33
% all students receiving grants/scholarships	37
% all students receiving loans	88
% all students receiving assistantships	NR
Average award package	$4,057
Average graduation debt	$42,000

ADMISSIONS

# applications received	1,609
% applicants accepted	46
% acceptees attending	39
Average LSAT	158
Average undergrad GPA	3.24
Application Fee	$50
No early decision program	
Regular application deadline	April 1
Regular notification	rolling
Admission may be deferred?	no
Gourman Report Rating	2.88

SETON HALL UNIVERSITY

School of Law

New Jersey's only private law school, the Seton Hall University School of Law is also its largest, with over 1,300 students enrolled in its day and evening divisions. Housed since 1991 in a modern office complex in downtown Newark, the law school is physically separate from its parent institution, one of the largest Catholic universities in the country. Nevertheless, Seton Hall points to its Christian heritage in explaining its commitment to community service. Seton Hall operates a large and exceptionally well funded clinical program that serves the dual purpose of providing much-needed legal services to Newark's citizens while also affording the law school's students the opportunity to gain practical lawyering experience.

Seton Hall's traditional curriculum is as broad as one would expect in a law school of its size, and co-curricular activities abound. Seton Hall's regional reputation is quite solid, particularly within the sizable legal communities of Newark and, more generally, New Jersey. Probably because of the law school's comparatively high tuition, applications volume at Seton Hall is lower than at the state's two public law schools. As a result, overall admissions selectivity is moderate. Admitted applicants, the vast majority of whom come from within New Jersey, tend to possess solidly midrange numerical credentials.

Seton Hall students are nothing if not comfortable in their surroundings, even in the most literal sense. The law school's virtually brand-new physical plant draws rave reviews from surveyed students, and it seems to have given the entire school a sense of modernity and confidence in its future. "The new facility is first-rate in every regard," wrote one. "Our research resources are top-notch, and the administration seems very responsive to students' needs." Seton Hall students are in a distinct minority nationally in their ability to discuss their administration without resorting to angry epithets. In fact, a great many offered unsolicited endorsements like this one: "The staff—especially the dean—really cares about the students." The cordial relations among staff, faculty, and students at the law school seem to contribute significantly to the overall level of satisfaction. On the strictly curricular side, reviews were solidly positive, with most students praising the

Sharon Hardy, Acting Director of Admissions
One Newark Center, Newark, NJ 07102
Tel: (201) 642-8747

Seton Hall University

law school's "practical approach, which emphasizes the skills necessary to become an able practitioner."

This is not to say that these students had no complaints about their program. Notably, however, nearly all of their criticisms were constructive suggestions, not angry denunciations. The area most often identified as the one in which the law school could stand to improve was the lack of geographical diversity in the student body. As one 3L said: "Seton Hall needs to make a commitment to attracting students from outside New Jersey." Others agreed, expressing their concern that the law school's reputation was too regionally limited. But one should hardly complain about a "limited" reputation like Seton Hall's. The extent to which the law school's alumni dominate the New Jersey bench and bar is evident in the employment patterns of its recent graduates, an unusually large number of whom begin their careers in judicial clerkships, nearly all of which are in the tri-state area.

ADMISSIONS

The numerical standards to which the Seton Hall University School of Law holds applicants are slightly lower than the average for all U.S. law schools, but relatively heavy applications volume keeps the admission process here somewhat competitive.

ACADEMICS	
Student/faculty ratio	21:1
% female faculty	39
% minority faculty	12
Hours of study per day	4.18

FINANCIAL FACTS	
Tuition	$17,214
Part-time tuition per credit	$12,604
Estimated books/expenses/fees	$642
On-campus living expenses	NR
Off-campus living expenses	NR
% first-year students receiving aid	62
% all students receiving aid	67
% aid that is merit-based	1
% all students receiving grants/scholarships	86
% all students receiving loans	85
% all students receiving assistantships	11
Average award package	NR
Average graduation debt	$51,000

ADMISSIONS	
# applications received	3,176
% applicants accepted	43
% acceptees attending	32
Average LSAT	153
Average undergrad GPA	3.10
Application Fee	$50
No early decision program	
Regular application deadline	April 1
Regular notification	NR
Admission deferment	one year
Gourman Report Rating	3.44

UNIVERSITY OF SOUTH CAROLINA 💾

School of Law

Whatever else it has to import, when it comes to lawyers South Carolina may be the most self-sufficient state in the nation. The state's single law school churns out graduates at a rate that is almost perfectly in sync with the demand of the state's legal profession for new blood. This arrangement is so neat that in the well over one hundred years since the University of South Carolina School of Law was established, its home state has had no need for another law school. The natural result of the law school's exclusive franchise on legal education is a bench and bar populated by men and women who needn't even return to campus to hold alumni reunions.

Located in the inland capital city of Columbia, South Carolina offers its nearly 800 students a strong traditional legal education and ready access to the resources of the state government. The curriculum is broad within traditional boundaries and is supplemented by an increasing number of clinical programs designed to provide students with practical experience in a variety of fields. Carolina's most obvious shortcoming is the relative lack of diversity in the student body, which is disproportionately white. Minority representation is, however, on the rise, and the law school has increased its efforts to serve the community that supports it by instituting a voluntary but highly organized pro bono program. Applications volume more than doubled between 1986 and 1991, and numerical admissions standards rose right along with it. Admitted students, a huge percentage of whom are South Carolina residents, possess very solid numerical credentials.

They also possess a fairly high degree of satisfaction with many aspects of their experience at South Carolina, though they speak clearly and almost unanimously when it comes to their school's shortcomings. On the positive side, most of those we heard from praised their faculty and the pleasant atmosphere that they help to foster. "Relationships between students and professors are excellent," went one typical remark. "This is a small, supportive school," went another, "with a beautiful campus and gorgeous weather." But South Carolina students reserve their strongest praise for something more pragmatic: "the networking [the law

John S. Benfield, Assistant Dean for Admissions
Columbia, SC 29208
Tel: (803) 777-6605

University of South Carolina

school] makes possible with practicing South Carolina attorneys." Indeed, students here express great appreciation for the professional contacts they will automatically have as SC alumni. As one 3L put it: "There are splendid opportunities here for meeting and developing relationships with members of the state bar, judiciary and legislature."

Still, few South Carolina students had any difficulty naming areas in which their chosen school could stand to improve. The most commonly voiced complaint concerned the relative lack of diversity in course offerings. A vocal minority of South Carolina students also offered comments like this one from a 3L: "Students here are a little to the right of Jesse Helms." Although for some this fact appears to represent a real negative, others feel quite differently. "From what I hear," reported one 1L, "this is one of the most conservative law schools in America. I like that."

Opinion among South Carolina students is not so mixed, however, when it comes to the overall quality of their program, its value, and its success in preparing them to enter the profession. Most of those we heard from expressed great confidence in their professional futures, and most would probably agree with this endorsement from one soon-to-be graduate: "This is a great law school, and the only one to go to if you want to practice in South Carolina."

ADMISSIONS

The numerical standards to which the University of South Carolina School of Law holds applicants are just about equal to the average for all U.S. law schools, but like all good public law schools, South Carolina chooses its students carefully from a relatively large applicant pool. Those whose numbers fall even a bit short of South Carolina's averages have only an outside shot at gaining admission.

ACADEMICS	
Student/faculty ratio	21:1
% female faculty	13
% minority faculty	6
Hours of study per day	3.77

FINANCIAL FACTS	
In-state tuition	$6,168
Out-of-state tuition	$12,224
Part-time tuition per credit	NR
Estimated books/expenses/fees	$4,008
On-campus living expenses	NR
Off-campus living expenses	NR
% first-year students receiving aid	NR
% all students receiving aid	NR
% aid that is merit-based	NR
% all students receiving grants/scholarships	NR
% all students receiving loans	NR
% all students receiving assistantships	NR
Average award package	NR
Average graduation debt	$35,000

ADMISSIONS	
# applications received	1,540
% applicants accepted	28
% acceptees attending	55
Average LSAT	157
Average undergrad GPA	3.18
Application Fee	$25
Priority application deadline	December
Priority notification	early February
Regular application deadline	February 15
Regular notification	rolling
Admission deferment	one year
Gourman Report Rating	2.92

UNIVERSITY OF SOUTH DAKOTA
School of Law

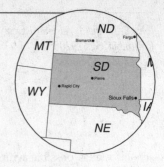

If you suffer from a fear of wide-open spaces, or if you treasure the anonymity of a crowd, cross the University of South Dakota School of Law off your list. Located on the Vermillion campus of its parent institution, on the vast and sparsely populated upper Midwest plains, this nearly one hundred-year-old public law school isn't just small, it's one of the smallest of the nation's 176 fully accredited law schools. With just a little over 200 total students in its J.D. program, and 15 full-time faculty members, South Dakota certainly offers the law student intimacy. But do not be misled. The breadth of the academic and co-curricular offerings at this full-service law school belies its diminutive size. The curriculum includes all the traditional subject areas, and law students have ample opportunity for interdisciplinary study through various graduate departments. Needless to say, a law school on this scale has its disadvantages, but they may be easily overlooked when that school charges as little as South Dakota does. With a tuition that is near the low end of the national scale and a local cost of living that is even lower, this is one law school that does little to add to the mountain of law-school debt in America.

To judge from their responses to our survey, students at the University of South Dakota School of Law are, on the whole, quite satisfied with their chosen school. Not surprisingly, most of their satisfaction seems to stem from the indirect benefits of attending such a small school. "There is no possibility of getting lost in the shuffle here," wrote one 1L, "since everybody knows you and most faculty and staff seem to be genuinely concerned with seeing you do well." Nearly all of those we heard from voiced similar sentiments, attesting to a fairly strong sense of community among students and between students and faculty. "Our small size obviously permits a lot of student-faculty interaction," said one 2L, "and the quality of most of our professors makes that a really great opportunity." Particularly when they weigh these factors in combination with the advantage of paying one of the lowest tuitions in the nation, South Dakota students feel they are missing little.

414 East Clark Street, Vermillion, SD 57069-2390
Tel: (605) 677-5443   Fax: (605) 677-5417
eMail: request@jurist.law.usd.edu
Internet: http://www.usd.edu/law/legal.html

University of South Dakota

But their criticisms show they are aware of what they have given up in choosing such a small school. In two areas in particular, students here see real room for improvement. One of those areas is, predictably, the variety of course offerings at the law school. Even though South Dakota's relatively large faculty makes possible a greater variety of offerings than one might expect at a school less than one-third the size of, say, Georgetown's first-year class, there are limitations. One 2L put it this way: "As long as you're interested in the nuts and bolts of a legal education you'll be fine here. The library is great and the professors are usually very good, but your academic horizons are limited."

But most here seem to feel that South Dakota looks pretty good on balance. One put it this way: "I came out to study here from Chicago, [where] most people think of South Dakota as not having much to offer educationally or in the job market. After studying here, I would strongly disagree. If one will work to avail himself of the opportunities here, this school has the same potential as any of the schools I've seen in Chicago."

ADMISSIONS

With only about 80 students, the first-year class at the University of South Dakota School of Law would barely fill a city bus. South Dakota's size puts the law school in a position to choose its students very carefully. The numerical standards to which South Dakota holds applicants are rather low. Statistically, an applicant with an undergraduate GPA between 3.00 and 3.25 and an LSAT score between about 150 and 154 has a 40 percent chance of getting in.

ACADEMICS

Student/faculty ratio	13:1
% female faculty	18
% minority faculty	1
Hours of study per day	4.55

FINANCIAL FACTS

In-state tuition	$7,008
Out-of-state tuition	$8,260
Part-time tuition per credit	NR
Estimated books/expenses/fees	NR
On-campus living expenses	NR
Off-campus living expenses	NR
% first-year students receiving aid	NR
% all students receiving aid	NR
% aid that is merit-based	NR
% all students receiving grants/scholarships	NR
% all students receiving loans	NR
% all students receiving assistantships	NR
Average award package	$2,139
Average graduation debt	NR

ADMISSIONS

# applications received	529
% applicants accepted	36
% acceptees attending	36
Average LSAT	154
Average undergrad GPA	3.37
Application Fee	$15
No early decision program	
Regular application deadline	March 1
Regular notification	NR
Admission may be deferred?	No
Gourman Report Rating	**2.48**

SOUTH TEXAS COLLEGE OF LAW 💾

True to the reputation of its home state, South Texas College of Law is nothing if not big. In fact, South Texas weighs in as one of the largest law schools in both Texas and the nation. Located in the middle of downtown Houston, America's fourth-largest city and seventh-largest job market for recent law-school graduates, South Texas is the model of a working-person's law school. Like many other schools, South Texas offers both full- and part-time enrollment, but this law school is nearly unique in the scheduling flexibility it allows all of its students. Rather than being separated into distinct evening and day divisions, as they are at most law schools, part-time and full-time students at South Texas choose their own schedules. Because the sheer size of the school's faculty and student body allows it to offer and fill classes at all hours of the day, students' options are numerous.

The effects of this accessibility are evident in the makeup of the student body: With a median age of about 30, South Texas law students, many of whom are embarking on second careers, are significantly older than the national average. The course of study they follow is straightforward and traditional, with very few required courses in the second and third years and a broad range of electives from which to choose. The law school also places significant emphasis on practical-skills training and prides itself in particular on its trial-advocacy program, which has helped build the law school's reputation as a respected source of strong litigators. Applications volume at South Texas is heavy, but a generous number of all candidates is admitted, and numerical admissions standards are moderate.

Far from moderate, however, is the degree of satisfaction that students at South Texas express for their chosen school. This mature, dedicated group of future lawyers is almost uniformly positive about all the fundamental aspects of their experience at the law school. "Members of the faculty are readily available to students," reported one. "The personal attention we are given and the friendly, noncompetitive atmosphere among students are the school's greatest strengths." "The classes are extremely challenging and fulfilling," said another, "and the friendships I've made here will be long-lasting." Even busy first-year stu-

Alicia K. Cramer, Director of Admissions
1303 San Jacinto Street, Houston, TX 77002-7000
Tel: (713) 646-1810
eMail: wmorrow@stcl.edu
Internet: http://www.stcl.edu

dents seem to agree that "there's not a lot of competition here—we have a strong sense of community."

Most of those we heard from also had specific praise for the practical focus of their program, and specifically for its litigation courses. "South Texas is no academic Ivory Tower," said one fairly typical student. "We have two appellate courts housed here permanently and we have what is arguably the strongest advocacy program in the country." Indeed, school pride runs high here, with more than a few students taking pains to point out the unheralded strengths of the law school: "This school deserves more respect than the rigid ratings systems give it. So what if our library isn't huge; the quality of our skills teaching is very high"; "This is a fine school; it's time [those who measure such things] realized it."

Complaints from these students were few and mild. Several criticized the condition of their library, but more pointed out that construction of a new one is being planned. Perhaps the most consistent complaints we heard involved the law school's heating and air-conditioning systems. But aside from concerns about climate control, and despite frustration with outside perception of their school, the vast majority of those Texas students expressed (relatively) little anxiety about their professional futures. This is probably not surprising, considering that most of them had several years of experience in the "real world" before entering law school.

ADMISSIONS

In terms of numerical standards for admission, the South Texas College of Law is less selective than three quarters of the law schools profiled in this book. Applications volume has risen significantly in recent years, however, keeping the admissions process here somewhat competitive.

ACADEMICS	
Student/faculty ratio	22:1
% female faculty	29
% minority faculty	5
Hours of study per day	3.84

FINANCIAL FACTS	
Tuition	$13,800
Part-time tuition per credit	NR
Estimated books/expenses/fees	$1,440
On-campus living expenses	NR
Off-campus living expenses	NR
% first-year students receiving aid	97
% all students receiving aid	99
% aid that is merit-based	2
% all students receiving grants/scholarships	67
% all students receiving loans	96
% all students receiving assistantships	5
Average award package	$17,351
Average graduation debt	$47,000

ADMISSIONS	
# applications received	2,224
% applicants accepted	41
% acceptees attending	36
Average LSAT	153
Average undergrad GPA	2.94
Application Fee	$40
No early decision program	
Regular application deadline	March 1
Regular notification	June 1
Admission may be deferred?	no
Gourman Report Rating	**2.27**

University of Southern California
Law School

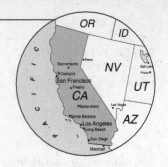

Undergraduates at crosstown rival UCLA enjoy teasing their counterparts at the University of Southern California. In conversation they cast aspersions on USC's undergrad admissions standards by referring to it as the University of Second Choice. At football games, they jangle their car keys mockingly in reference to USC's high tuition and perceived status as a "rich-kid" school. Quite apart from the fact that law students tend not to involve themselves in such undergraduate rivalries, students at the University of Southern California Law School receive no such ribbing from anyone, least of all their neighbors in Westwood. While tuition at USC is indeed near the top of the scale, so is the average salary its graduates command. And one thing is certain: USC Law is practically nobody's second choice. Between 1985 and 1992, the number of applicants seeking entry into USC's small first-year class nearly doubled. In any quantifiable way, USC is a standout, and the numerical credentials of its small student body place it among the most highly qualified anywhere.

Those who make it through USC's increasingly competitive admissions process and enroll at the law school express a high degree of satisfaction with their decision to do so. After "the weather," most cite the law school's equally pleasant academic environment as one of its greatest strengths. "USC has a great atmosphere and a very diverse population," remarked one 2L, "and once you're in they do everything they can to keep you in. The atmosphere is very non-competitive." Indeed, partly because of a strict grading curve that clumps two thirds of the class within five points of one another on a 25-point scale, USC students enjoy relations that are, by all reports, "friendly, with little or no unhealthy competition." "USC Law School feels at times like a pleasant oasis in the living hell that is law school." Students give credit for much of their satisfaction to the quality and size of their faculty. "Most are excellent teachers," reported one 1L, "and all are, for the most part, readily available to students." Another student noted that "not only does the Dean teach first-year torts every year, but he is very proud of doing so without the assistance of teaching assistants or graders."

William J. Hoye, Director of Admissions
University Park, Los Angeles, CA 90089-0071
Tel: (213) 740-7331
eMail: admissions@law.usc.edu
Internet: http://www.usc.edu/dept/law-lib/index.html

University of Southern California

When asked to name areas in which their chosen school could stand to improve, many called for greater "diversity of viewpoints" among faculty ("They should hire some [one?] conservative professor...All seem to share a mushy leftism.") and, more tangibly, for a lower price-tag. Right-wingers should not be daunted, however, as the "smaller Gingrich Gang is (annoyingly) vocal." As for the academic program itself, opinion ranged fairly widely among the USC students we heard from. While all praised the quality of their courses, quite a few called for greater variety. "They should really offer more classes each semester," went one fairly typical criticism. Specifically, several students expressed their frustration with what they perceive as an overemphasis on business-related courses in the USC curriculum. In fact, USC's course offerings are no more skewed toward the corporate than are the offerings at most comparable schools, but for one reason or another, USC grads enter private practice at a rate well above the national average and well above most elite schools.

ADMISSIONS

In keeping with its strong reputation, the University of Southern California Law School is one of the most selective law schools in the country. Not only are the numerical credentials of the average USC student very strong, but with more than 17 applicants for every spot, this excellent law school can pick and choose carefully. Fifty percent of admitted applicants have LSAT scores above 165—the 94th percentile.

ACADEMICS

Student/faculty ratio	15:1
% female faculty	31
% minority faculty	14
Hours of study per day	3.04

FINANCIAL FACTS

Tuition	$21,566
Part-time tuition per credit	NR
Estimated books/expenses/fees	$1,200
On-campus living expenses	NR
Off-campus living expenses	NR
% first-year students receiving aid	89
% all students receiving aid	85
% aid that is merit-based	NR
% all students receiving grants/scholarships	40
% all students receiving loans	70
% all students receiving assistantships	NR
Average award package	$9,080
Average graduation debt	$48,000

ADMISSIONS

# applications received	3,647
% applicants accepted	21
% acceptees attending	27
Average LSAT	163
Average undergrad GPA	3.40
Application Fee	$60
No early decision program	
Regular application deadline	February 1
Regular notification	March-April
Admission deferment	one year
Gourman Report Rating	4.44

SOUTHERN ILLINOIS UNIVERSITY 🖫
School of Law

Nearly the youngest, practically the smallest and, by a small margin, the cheapest of the nine law schools in its home state, Southern Illinois University School of Law has much to recommend it. Just over 20 years after it graduated its first class, this small public law school has established a solid regional reputation that continues to grow. Remarkably, SIU has achieved its standing while keeping its tuition in control and without growing beyond the intimate scale that distinguishes it from other area law schools. Indeed, this is a school where anonymity is impossible. With a total enrollment of just under 350 students and a full-time teaching staff of 32, SIU's student-faculty ratio is one of the lowest in the country, putting the university in a place to offer what it calls, "an exceptionally dynamic and personalized style of education."

As for the substance of that education, while a small faculty limits the number of courses available in any given semester, the range of courses offered at SIU is relatively broad, and the required curriculum includes a sizable dose of skills-oriented courses. Students frequently praised the strength of the school's pragmatic approach to legal education. "SIU's emphasis on practical skills such as advocacy, alternative dispute resolution, clinical experience, and writing make students more prepared for practice than other programs with a more focused legal approach," said a 1L. One area of the curriculum that drew criticism from students was the legal writing program, which was described by one student as "poorly instructed and lacking uniformity."

Southern Illinois has three clinical programs open to third-year students as of this writing. In addition, the parent university has great resources, affording the law school's students ample opportunity for interdisciplinary study. In addition to joint J.D./master's degree programs in business administration, public administration, and accountancy, SIU offers one of the country's few concurrent J.D./M.D. programs.

Students at SIU clearly explain the source of their fundamental satisfaction with the school. "SIU's small class size and the accessibility of the faculty make the academic environment extremely positive for learning the law," said a 1L. Indeed, when

Ed Dorsey, Assistant Dean for Admissions
Lesar Law Building, Carbondale, IL 62901-6804
Tel: (618) 453-8767
Internet: http://www.siu.edu/~lawsch/

asked to name the school's strengths, many students spoke of SIU's "strong community spirit." Several students also praised the school's policy of giving all law students keys to the library so that they have 24-hour access to research materials and study areas.

Among the list of complaints from students were many of the common woes of students attending small law schools, most notably a lack of course availability and clinical opportunities and a need for more diversity among the student body and faculty. "The classes here would be much more beneficial if the scheduling allowed us to take them," said one disgruntled 3L. And another 3L offered: "The clinical programs are great but need to be made available to more students." The location of the school—praised by the vast majority of the students who appreciate its beautiful surroundings—is also a cause for a major concern among students: few job opportunities. With a resident population of about 27,000 SIU's home of Carbondale provides few outlets for employing graduates. Although St. Louis and Chicago are within the region, students report that the university does not do enough to encourage on-campus recruiting.

ADMISSIONS

Although the number of places in SIU's entering classes has increased slightly over the past few years, there is still room for only about 140 first-year students. The school, one of the twelve smallest accredited law schools in the country, selects its newly-enrolled class from about 850 applications annually. Consequently, SIU admissions process is somewhat selective. The grades and test scores of the average Southern Illinois law student are a little below the national average, but applicants to this very inexpensive law school face stiff competition from fellow bargain-hunters.

ACADEMICS	
Student/faculty ratio	8:1
% female faculty	32
% minority faculty	17
Hours of study per day	4.05

FINANCIAL FACTS	
In-state tuition	$4,004
Out-of-state tuition	$12,012
Part-time tuition per credit	NR
Estimated books/expenses/fees	$1,322
On-campus living expenses	NR
Off-campus living expenses	NR
% first-year students receiving aid	93
% all students receiving aid	97
% aid that is merit-based	62
% all students receiving grants/scholarships	28
% all students receiving loans	76
% all students receiving assistantships	18
Average award package	$2,950
Average graduation debt	$35,000

ADMISSIONS	
# applications received	848
% applicants accepted	43
% acceptees attending	35
Average LSAT	153
Average undergrad GPA	3.11
Application Fee	$25
No early decision program	
Regular application deadline	NR
Regular notification	rolling
Admission deferment	one year
Gourman Report Rating	3.16

SOUTHERN METHODIST UNIVERSITY ⊟

School of Law

OVERVIEW

Type of school	private
Environment	metropolis
Scholastic calendar	semester
Schedule	Full-time or part-time

STUDENTS

Enrollment of institution	4,949
Enrollment of law school	822
% male/female	57/43
% out-of-state	27
% part-time	4
% minorities	18
% international (# countries represented)	4 (65)
Average age at entry	25

APPLICANTS ALSO LOOK AT

University of Texas
University of Houston
Baylor University
Texas Tech University
Tulane University

SURVEY SAYS...

HITS
Diverse faculty
Business and tax courses
Intellectual challenge

MISSES
Not enough courses
Library staff
Gender bias

EMPLOYMENT PROFILE

% grads employed immediately	NR
% grads employed within six months	NR
Average starting salary	$42,593
% grads employed by field:	
Private practice	71
Business/industry	13
Government	2
Judicial clerkships	11
Military	0

Southern Methodist University School of Law, self-described as "a tree-lined campus in the heart of one of the nation's most vibrant urban centers," has a solid reputation throughout the region, and particularly strong stature on a local level. A quick look at the school's bulletin provides you with glimpses of the lush and well-groomed 164-acre campus and the high urban skyline of Dallas. Students from all 50 states and more than 65 foreign countries come to Dallas every year to study at SMU. As the only accredited law school in the city, SMU is in a unique position to take advantage of the Dallas's thriving business community. Nearly 90 percent of SMU graduates remain in the Lone Star State after graduating. Many of them leave the school to work minutes away in downtown Dallas, one of the largest and highest-paying job markets in the country.

The school's program focuses on business law. For that reason, the atmosphere at the law school is more conservative and career-minded than at others. Nearly all students are in agreement that the school's business and tax courses are superb. Several students, however, would like to see the selection of courses broadened and scheduling made easier. "The law school should refocus its curriculum to include an emphasis on other areas and not focus so intensely on business/tax courses," said one 2L. When asked how SMU could improve, another student said, "[It could add] more curriculum in the areas of environmental law or other specialties." It should be noted that the university recently began a public service program in which all students must complete 30 hours of law-related public service to graduate.

When it came to the law school faculty, comments ranged from "great faculty [with] quality and interest in students," to "need better teachers" and "faculty does not have an interest in students." Whether these differences in opinion are the result of a few isolated cases or differing expectations, it is clear that a minority contingent of students do not regard the faculty as competent or accessible.

When asked to name SMU's greatest strength, many students cited the great diversity, particularly the ethnic diversity, among its students. One of the school's minority students who is rela-

Alison Cooper, Assistant Dean and Director of Admissions
P.O. Box 750116, Dallas, TX 75275-0116
Tel: (214) 768-2550
Internet: http://www.smu.edu/~law

tively happy with his education said, "As a minority student, it's good to know that SMU offers extracurricular activities and organizations..." and, "SMU is a shining example of a school that aims to increase minority participation in our legal system."

On the downside, students complained about the facilities, ranging from library hours to needed improvements in the physical plant. One 2L said, "The facilities are not good—rooms are drafty, [it's] hard to see the board, [there are] not enough electrical outlets for computer use and the chairs are uncomfortable." There also seems to be some disgruntlement in regards to tuition, or more accurately, the law school's share of SMU's revenue. One quite vocal 3L said, "Don't share my $18K in tuition with the undergrads!" Another student emphatically agreed: "[A] large amount of tuition goes to fund undergrad, so it is frustrating to pay [a] huge tuition."

Keeping in mind the relatively high price tag and conservative leanings of the school, SMU offers great opportunities to students interested in business law or those who want to be near a thriving business community. As one 1L put it: "If you want to suffer through law school, SMU offers a beautiful campus set in the middle of a fabulous town, to help ease the suffering."

ADMISSIONS

The relatively modest applicant pool to the Southern Methodist University School of Law helps maintain the school's relatively generous overall acceptance rate. Over 40 percent of all candidates are granted admission, but the numerical standards are solid.

ACADEMICS

Student/faculty ratio	10:1
% female faculty	27
% minority faculty	18
Hours of study per day	4.33

FINANCIAL FACTS

Tuition	$17,130
Part-time tuition per credit	NR
Estimated books/expenses/fees	$2,618
On-campus living expenses	NR
Off-campus living expenses	NR
% first-year students receiving aid	100
% all students receiving aid	100
% aid that is merit-based	NR
% all students receiving grants/scholarships	20
% all students receiving loans	NR
% all students receiving assistantships	NR
Average award package	$9,450
Average graduation debt	$60,000

ADMISSIONS

# applications received	2,082
% applicants accepted	42
% acceptees attending	29
Average LSAT	157
Average undergrad GPA	3.18
Application Fee	$45
Priority application deadline	December
Priority notification	end of January
Regular application deadline	February 15
Regular notification	end of April
Admission deferment	one year
Gourman Report Rating	**4.36**

SOUTHERN UNIVERSITY
Law Center

There was a time when law schools were semi-officially designated as either national or regional schools, depending on the make-up of their student bodies and the focus of their curricula. A regional school was one which drew its students predominantly from the immediately surrounding region and educated them in the law of that same region. The Southern University Law Center, which officially opened in 1947, is one law school that would probably embrace such a designation unapologetically. In terms of both its curriculum and the individuals who administer and follow it, Southern is truly a Louisiana school. Unlike other law schools in the state, for instance, Southern places primary curricular emphasis on Louisiana's civil law, hardly ignoring the common law for the rest of the nation, but definitely not attempting to give it equal time. This focus on the peculiar legal tradition of its home state is part of Southern's recognition of where the vast majority of its students come from and where the vast majority of its graduates go.

Southern runs three law clinics (Administrative, Criminal, and Juvenile), housed in spacious new quarters in the recently renovated Law Center building, which provide practical experience to those students certified by the Louisiana Supreme Court for such activity and which prepare students to meet the specific needs of their fellow Louisiana citizens. Thanks to Southern's central location in Baton Rouge, the capital of Louisiana, a large industrial center and the nation's fifth largest port, and its proximity to the Crescent City of New Orleans, just 85 miles away, students have access to all the professional and cultural amenities of the two most important cities in their state.

Southern's dedication to its region is most clearly evident in the faces of its faculty and students. In comparison with Louisiana's other law schools, Southern, the smallest and least expensive of the four, has a makeup that reflects the population of the state it serves. Southern enrolls more than three times as many African Americans as some of its larger neighbors. The faculty is nearly half female and more than half black.

A strong honor code lends an air of integrity and tradition to the school, which probably contributes an honorable air to a profession so often derided of late. Student associations include: Law Review, Moot Court Board, Student Bar Association, Student ABA, two law fraternities, Black Students Law Association, Women in Law, Sports and Entertainment Legal Association, Environmental Law Society, and the Advocates of Christ.

Southern students greatly appreciate the law school's commitment to teaching law "from a black perspective," their professors' caring attitudes and strong teaching skills, the clinical and oral advocacy training, and the excellent new facilities. One 3L, who has watched many changes take place, said Southern "should win the most improved school award." Another happy woman described her beloved law school: "Southern has a really nice facility, new classrooms, tons of computers, a good mix of ethnicities and genders, highly-qualified teachers, and a small college feel. It's located on the scenic Mississippi-atop the bluff-and is wooded with old, beautiful trees. The people are friendly, motivated, and smiley. Everyone here is determined to better themselves and those around them. Highly recommended."

When students complain, they have no fundamental qualms with Southern. Rather they request that the school extend itself even more towards prospective African-American students, especially those in need of funds, and hire more teachers from diverse backgrounds, expand the curriculum, and strengthen the bar exam preparation. Most revel in the "diversity, scholarship, and the opportunity for an open, free exchange of ideas" to be had at Southern.

ADMISSIONS

If one considers only numerical standards, the Southern University Law Center appears to be one of the least selective law schools in the country. Simply stated, this is a law school that cares relatively little about numbers. Southern actually admits a larger proportion of applicants with LSAT scores between 145 and 149 than above 160. All hopeful applicants had better present the Southern admissions committee with a comprehensive and impressive picture in their applications.

ACADEMICS	
Student/faculty ratio	12:1
% female faculty	35
% minority faculty	59
Hours of study per day	4.19

FINANCIAL FACTS	
In-state tuition	$3,088
Out-of-state tuition	$6,288
Part-time tuition per credit	NR
Estimated books/expenses/fees	NR
On-campus living expenses	NR
Off-campus living expenses	NR
% first-year students receiving aid	NR
% all students receiving aid	NR
% aid that is merit-based	NR
% all students receiving grants/scholarships	NR
% all students receiving loans	NR
% all students receiving assistantships	NR
Average award package	NR
Average graduation debt	NR

ADMISSIONS	
# applications received	250
% applicants accepted	80
% acceptees attending	63
Average LSAT	145
Average undergrad GPA	2.62
Application Fee	NR
Priority application deadline	NR
Priority notification	NR
Regular application deadline	March 1
Regular notification	January-May
Admission deferment	NR
Gourman Report Rating	**2.08**

SOUTHWESTERN UNIVERSITY
School of Law

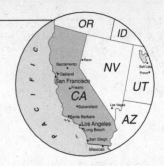

Founded in 1911 in downtown L.A., Southwestern University School of Law is one of the oldest law schools on the West Coast, with one of the newest state-of-the-art libraries as of fall 1996. In the years since its founding, law schools have proliferated in California, and Southwestern's reputation has long since been eclipsed by the state's many powerhouse schools. But to assess this law school in terms of such narrow and problematic qualities as "prestige" and "reputation" misses the point entirely. Southwestern is a law school that has always existed to serve its community and innovate, not merely to cultivate an image. A photo included in its promotional materials of a law-school class from the 1920s is particularly telling: At a time when the legal profession was almost exclusively the domain of white men, Southwestern was graduating women and African and Asian Americans in more than token numbers. Since then, most law schools have caught up in those departments, but Southwestern has moved on to new territory. Through its unique SCALE (Southwestern's Conceptual Approach to Legal Education) program, established in 1974 with the aid of a substantial federal grant, Southwestern offers an alternative course of study leading to the J.D. that differs radically in both substance and form from the traditional law school curriculum. SCALE not only accelerates the process to two calendar years, but it also eschews traditional curricular divisions like torts and contracts, instead of trying to teach the law "as an integrated whole." In practical terms, this means that SCALE students, after an initial semester that is not entirely revolutionary, spend most of their remaining time in law school working as part of a simulated law firm within the school or as actual legal externs in the L.A. legal community. In addition to this relatively radical alternative, the law school offers a traditional four-year evening program. The only law school to offer four different J.D. programs of study, Southwestern aims to make law school more accessible to a wide range of students. Not surprisingly, Southwestern students are significantly older than average, particularly those enrolled in SCALE or in the part-time division.

And those students enrolled in the SCALE program also appear to be among the happiest at Southwestern, judging from our survey of current students. The moderate overall degree of satisfaction Southwestern students feel about their curriculum stems mainly from the enthusiasm of the SCALE students for the flexibility and quality of their program. "This program has made it much more feasible for me as an older student to get a law degree," wrote one, "and I am quite pleased overall with the quality of the education I've received, though it hasn't been easy." It is the sentiment expressed at the end of that last remark, however, that one hears most often from Southwestern students. "The professors here are very supportive of students," commented another student, "but it is very tough academically." "If you graduate from here you have studied hard; you do not coast once you get in." While it is true that for many this fact was expressed in the form of complaints about the school's strict grading curve and significant attrition rate, more than a few others regard this survival-of-the-fittest atmosphere as a net positive. "The legal job market—especially in L.A. where there are six ABA schools—is extremely tight," explained one 2L, "so I appreciate that Southwestern maintains very high academic standards...Employers in the area appreciate it also." One fairly evenhanded assessment from a current 3L summed matters up this way: "It may be argued that Southwestern is very competitive...[but] we are prepared not only intellectually but mentally for the highly competitive world of law."

ADMISSIONS

Although nearly 3,000 prospective students apply annually, the numerical standards to which Southwestern University School of Law holds applicants rank it in the bottom third of all U.S. law schools in terms of admissions selectivity. This is because of the size of Southwestern's first-year class and the relatively low rate at which admitted applicants choose to attend the law school.

ACADEMICS

Student/faculty ratio	22:1
% female faculty	32
% minority faculty	16
Hours of study per day	3.93

FINANCIAL FACTS

Tuition	$19,020
Part-time tuition per credit	$634
Estimated books/expenses/fees	$720
On-campus living expenses	NR
Off-campus living expenses	NR
% first-year students receiving aid	NR
% all students receiving aid	83
% aid that is merit-based	NR
% all students receiving grants/scholarships	25
% all students receiving loans	80
% all students receiving assistantships	NR
Average award package	$2,911
Average graduation debt	NR

ADMISSIONS

# applications received	2,840
% applicants accepted	42
% acceptees attending	41
Average LSAT	153
Average undergrad GPA	3.10
Application Fee	$50
Priority application deadline	NR
Priority notification	NR
Regular application deadline	June 30
Regular notification	NR
Admission deferment	NR
Gourman Report Rating	**3.47**

ST. JOHN'S UNIVERSITY 💾

School of Law

A list of graduates of the St. John's University School of Law from the not-too-distant past reads like a New York Democratic party hall of fame: Governors Hugh Carey and Mario Cuomo, Congressman Charles Rangel, and the late U.S. Commerce Secretary Ronald Brown. St. John's alumni aren't limited to New York, however; they can also head to warmer climates, like alums California Governor George Deukmajian and former Virgin Islands Governor Alexander Farrelly. Along with many other prominent local, state, and federal judges, all took degrees from this large, practical-minded Catholic law school located in Jamaica, Queens. St. John's is home to nearly 1,200 students, most of them New York natives, and competition to be among them can be heated. As it has for more than 70 years, St. John's continues to play a significant role in New York's massive legal community, where its alumni are partners in many of the city's top corporate law firms. Today, St. John's graduates continue to secure their share of top-notch jobs. Both internal and external clinical programs and courses in lawyering skills have become a bigger part of the curriculum, which is evolving in order to give the school's graduates every advantage in the tightening job market by preparing them for the courtroom.

Students at St. John's express a moderate sense of satisfaction with their school, particularly in terms of the practical curriculum that has resulted in a high bar-passage rate among graduates. "The clinicals and the overall ability of St. John's to teach 'real-world' experience is worth its weight in gold," said one positive 3L. Noting that the school historically has produced strong litigators, another 3L offered this advice: "If you want to pass the bar and gain practical lawyering skills..., St. John's is the school for you." The strong alumni network in the New York City area as described above was also frequently mentioned as one of the school's strengths.

Students offered positive comments on the faculty and the overall atmosphere at the school: "Professors are always happy to take time to help students and are most knowledgeable in the areas they teach," said a 3L. The majority of St. John's students we surveyed focused their dissatisfaction on the school's administra-

Mary Conlon, Assistant Dean
8000 Utopia Parkway, Jamaica, NY 11439
Tel: (718) 990-6611

tion. Consider these statements: "The administration seems to go out of its way to make life more difficult for students and are very unapproachable." "Administration does not seem too interested in helping students get the electives they want, nor in assisting students with other comparative scholastic problems..." To be fair, we must say that deans can be seen without an appointment in order to, among other things, advise on elective selection, and they frequently attend meetings to answer student concerns and write articles for the school paper on student issues.

Those enrolled in St. John's evening division were even more ruffled by the school's reported disregard of their needs. "My impression of this school has declined since attending," said one such student, and added, "[Evening students] are ignored, disregarded, impaired, unconsidered." At the same time, St. John's Dean of Students keeps late hours specifically to see evening students. As one evening student remarked, students should come to St. John's knowing what the school is about: "This is not one of the most prestigious schools, nor does one attending it suppose it to be otherwise. Indeed, at least for the evening division, one attends St. John's primarily because of geographic convenience, existence of a night program, and general competence. That said, perhaps one should not expect so much."

ADMISSIONS

The strength of its regional reputation makes St. John's a perennially popular choice for law school applicants with numerical standards slightly lower than those necessary to gain admission to the area's top schools. Each year, St. John's turns away almost 2,000 applicants in selecting a class of about 300. Numerical admission standards are moderately high, as is the law school's tuition. Only about 10 percent of all applications are filed by candidates with LSAT scores above 159. Consequently, competition is stiff among all others.

ACADEMICS	
Student/faculty ratio	20:1
% female faculty	34
% minority faculty	15
Hours of study per day	3.76

FINANCIAL FACTS	
Tuition	$19,000
Part-time tuition per credit	NR
Estimated books/expenses/fees	NR
On-campus living expenses	NR
Off-campus living expenses	NR
% first-year students receiving aid	75
% all students receiving aid	75
% aid that is merit-based	NR
% all students receiving grants/scholarships	33
% all students receiving loans	75
% all students receiving assistantships	8
Average award package	$2,500
Average graduation debt	NR

ADMISSIONS	
# applications received	2,974
% applicants accepted	34
% acceptees attending	25
Average LSAT	156
Average undergrad GPA	3.00
Application Fee	$50
No early decision program	
Regular application deadline	March 1, Oct. 1
Regular notification	rolling
Admission deferment	NR
Gourman Report Rating	3.64

St. Louis University

School of Law

Among U.S. law schools, the Saint Louis School of Law scores in the middle of many quantifiable criteria. Its size is neither big nor small; its cost and its admissions standards are neither the highest nor the lowest. And this medium-sized city sits smack dab in the middle of the country. Yet this midsize, Midwestern law school actively sees to it that its midrange statistics do not add up to mediocrity.

One of the strongest features of SLU law school is its specialty programs. The School of Law is located on the grounds of Saint Louis University, a Catholic Jesuit institution, and makes the most of its affiliation with the main campus. The university has strongly influenced the law school's widely recognized leadership in the growing field of health-care law. A long-time leader in this area, the School of Law's health law program was recently ranked by a major U.S. magazine as one of the top five in the U.S. Saint Louis University School of Law also boasts one of the few employment law programs in the country. "Employment law is one of the fastest growing areas of law today," said one 2L, and, "SLU has one of the only employment law certificates in the country. [It's] a great program." The law school also offers areas of specialization in international and comparative law and professional skills. Many students we spoke with saw these opportunities to specialize, particularly in the health law program, as one of the law school's greatest strengths.

Students were quick to mention the "non-competitive," "unified," yet "diverse" atmosphere. "Students are willing to help each other out. [There is] no backstabbing," said one 2L. Another student, a 3L, agreed: "The student body is not that competitive; everybody works together so that every student can get the best possible legal education." At least one student, a 2L, feels that the lack of competition at the school stifles the exchange of ideas. "The non-confrontational posture possibly robs students of insight into the real legal world," he said. The law school community also seems to be open and encouraging to racial and ethnic diversity. SLU law school's percentage of minority students is slightly under 20 percent.

Valerie Lampe-McFarlane, Assistant Dean
3700 Lindell Boulevard, St. Louis, MO 63108
Tel: (314) 977-2800   Fax: (314) 977-3966
eMail: admissions@lawlib.slu.edu
Internet: http://www.lawlib.slu.edu/home.htm

St. Louis University

Our surveys indicated a high level of satisfaction with the overall quality of teaching and range of courses offered at the School of Law. "The faculty is very interested, and the Dean is progressive in thinking," offered a 1L. "[The] professors are willing to answer questions outside of class about anything, including career options and classes you should take," said one 2L. The school offers over 25 professional skills courses each year, including simulated courses such as Moot Court, live clinic courses, and externships. While some students had only good things to say about the administration and faculty, a few law students are not so content. Frequently mentioned as an area of needed improvement was the law school's legal writing and research program. A 1L said, "The legal research and writing department is terrible. [It is] poorly organized and [has] poor instructors." Another student noted that there is "no consistency between the professors in that department. Some are excellent; some teach poorly." Apparently the law school's legal writing/research program was restructured recently, and although a few students noted these changes as positive, many responses were not so upbeat. A couple of students also mentioned a need for more emphasis on the Socratic method in the classroom.

The law school's physical plant also received much criticism. Complaints mentioned "very outdated" and "crowded" facilities. However, these complaints should be a thing of the past when the new facility, scheduled to be completed in August 1997, increases the size of the current facility by 40 percent. These and other criticisms aside, the general sense of well-being among students at St. Louis University School of Law seems strong.

ADMISSIONS

Saint Louis University School of Law's numerical standards fall slightly below the average for all U.S. law schools. With a generous acceptance rate of over 40 percent, applicants have good reason to be hopeful. It should also be noted that the administration reports that, "Scholarship money is generous for students with outstanding credentials."

ACADEMICS	
Student/faculty ratio	24:1
% female faculty	20
% minority faculty	6
Hours of study per day	3.93

FINANCIAL FACTS	
Tuition	$17,120
Part-time tuition per credit	$12,787
Estimated books/expenses/fees	NR
On-campus living expenses	NR
Off-campus living expenses	$7,000
% first-year students receiving aid	85
% all students receiving aid	85
% aid that is merit-based	40
% all students receiving grants/scholarships	47
% all students receiving loans	76
% all students receiving assistantships	NR
Average award package	$3,800
Average graduation debt	NR

ADMISSIONS	
# applications received	1,361
% applicants accepted	44
% acceptees attending	43
Average LSAT	154
Average undergrad GPA	3.23
Application Fee	$40
No early decision program	
Regular application deadline	rolling
Regular notification	rolling
Admission deferment	one year

Gourman Report Rating	3.65

St. Mary's University
School of Law

San Antonio, Texas, America's tenth-largest city, is home to only one accredited law school, the 750-student Saint Mary's University School of Law. This midsize Catholic law school was founded in 1934 and has been operated since 1948 by members of the Marianist order. Overall costs of a legal education at St. Mary's are kept down by the increasingly low cost of living in the San Antonio area and by the law school's tuition, which is reasonable by private-school standards.

Long known for its solid, traditional curriculum, Saint Mary's law school describes itself as "a lawyer's law school." Many current law students we spoke with, however, feel that this mission is in jeopardy. The majority of students surveyed told us that they are content with the quality of teaching and the curriculum at Saint Mary's, but there are some who worry that a more "theoretical approach" is replacing the historically pragmatic slant at the school. "[There are] too many courses on human rights and race and not enough practical skills [courses]" said one 3L.

Some of the concern over the curriculum seems to focus on what a few students perceive as a "new agenda" from the law school's current Dean. When asked how the school could improve, one such student, a 2L, said: "[We have an] extremely liberal Dean, and she only hires professors with her beliefs regardless of their teaching ability." Another student referred to his professors who "turn Business Association classes into racial issues." Some of these students also cited the university's apparent drop in the percent of graduates who pass the state bar as proof of the change in focus at the school. "[The Dean's] perceived agenda of diversity at any cost is hurting the school's reputation. Look at the bar-passage rates," said one 2L. Whether these statements are isolated and more indicative of the political leanings of their authors, or whether they indicate a real shift in St. Mary's approach to providing a legal education, is not clear.

Where some students complained of a de-emphasis on traditional, practical lawyering skills at St. Mary's, others ask for a still broader curriculum and more opportunities to help make a change in the community. The majority of students are in agreement on the commitment of their professors, citing the popular "open door policy" and the sense of community at the law school. Many students described St. Mary's as a "friendly," and "diverse" school. "The atmosphere of the school is friendly, and I don't feel the intense competition among students that you hear about regarding other law schools," said one 2L.

The law school offers an interesting array of clinical programs, including immigration and human rights, community development, civil justice, and criminal justice. According to the administration, nearly one quarter of the senior class is enrolled in live-client clinics. Participants in the Immigration and Human Rights Clinic gain hands-on lawyering experience in areas of particular concern to the Texas-Mexico border region. Saint Mary's also operates a summer-study institute in Innsbruck, Austria, called the Institute on World Legal Problems, and conducts a summer study tour to Guatemala as part of its Institute on International Human Rights. In cooperation with other departments at St. Mary's University, the law school has also established seven joint-degree programs. The newest combines a Master of Arts in Justice Administration with a J.D.

When asked how the law school could improve, many students mentioned the library facilities and staff. "The law library needs to expand the resources available and improve the training of their staff," offered one 2L. Other students called for "longer library hours," an "expanded library," and "more Macintosh computers." The law school's career office was also the focus of several complaints. "The career services office is terrible and unable to place students in jobs," said a 2L. However, a school that offers a practical legal education at a relatively decent price can't be turned away from too quickly.

ADMISSIONS

The doors at St. Mary's School of Law are wide open. Although application volume is relatively heavy, St. Mary's admits 35 percent of all applicants in order to fill its entering class of about 250. As a result, numerical standards are moderate and candidates are admitted across a broad range of grade point averages and test scores.

ACADEMICS

Student/faculty ratio	19:1
% female faculty	26
% minority faculty	23
Hours of study per day	4.15

FINANCIAL FACTS

Tuition	$15,500
Part-time tuition per credit	NR
Estimated books/expenses/fees	$4,100
On-campus living expenses	NR
Off-campus living expenses	NR
% first-year students receiving aid	85
% all students receiving aid	85
% aid that is merit-based	NR
% all students receiving grants/scholarships	NR
% all students receiving loans	NR
% all students receiving assistantships	NR
Average award package	$18,500
Average graduation debt	$60,000

ADMISSIONS

# applications received	1,850
% applicants accepted	35
% acceptees attending	36
Average LSAT	152
Average undergrad GPA	2.95
Application Fee	$45
Priority application deadline	NR
Priority notification	November-May
Regular application deadline	March 3
Regular notification	May/June
Admission deferment	NR
Gourman Report Rating	2.52

STANFORD UNIVERSITY
School of Law

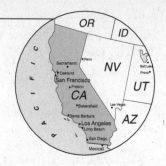

To call the Stanford University Law School the most highly esteemed law school west of the Mississippi is to risk understating the strength of its reputation. Along with the law schools at Harvard and Yale, Stanford forms a sort of holy trinity of American legal education. A generation ago, while California was still in the process of becoming the nation's most populous state, Stanford University was widely known as "the Harvard of the West." The days are long gone when Stanford, one of the world's preeminent universities, had to define itself on anything other than its own terms. The same can surely be said for its small, highly esteemed law school.

The curriculum at Stanford is traditional only in the freedom it affords the student to chart his or her own course of study. After completing their first semester in sunny Palo Alto, Stanford law students have virtually total control over the style and substance of their education. In their second and third years, Stanford students can cobble together their own programs or pursue studies in one of several informal but organized fields of concentration (e.g., "Business Law," "Comparative and International Law," and "Law and High Technology"). Stanford also actively encourages interdisciplinary and independent study. All students can earn up to 11 semester credits in relevant non-law fields, and it is not uncommon for third-year students to spend an entire semester engaged in a faculty-supervised independent research project. Only a tiny percentage of applicants to Stanford will gain admission, and those who do possess tremendously strong numerical credentials. In recent years, the law school has admitted and hired more and more women and minorities. Both Stanford's faculty and its student body are among the most ethnically diverse in the nation and among the most gender-balanced of the elite schools.

On the basis of what we heard from current students, it is also one of the more pleasant of the nation's top schools. Stanford's faculty and students are of absolutely the highest caliber, so intellectual challenge is a constant, but the atmosphere at the law school is, by most accounts, serious and scholarly without being unduly competitive. Competition does exist, but the general attitude of

Stanford students is that they have overcome their toughest obstacle in gaining admission to the law school. "The tough part about Stanford Law School is getting admitted," said one 3L. "Once you're in, it's a piece of cake." Perhaps, but as one 2L put it, "You can be lazy and simply get through if you wish to, but the students and the faculty are all incredibly sharp, and they definitely keep you on your toes." Most seem to agree on this last count. "My class is astonishingly diverse and exciting," reported a 1L. "Stanford offers an outstanding climate for learning." added another. Not surprisingly, the students we heard from expressed even more enthusiasm for the outdoor climate at Stanford; asked to name their law school's greatest strengths, these students cited the "weather" even more often than "reputation."

All of which is not to say that Stanford students do not see room for improvement in their school. More often than not, their criticisms concerned the apparent lack of emphasis on practical skills in the law school's curriculum. Although Stanford operates what is surely one of the finest clinical programs in the nation, many students we heard from said they would like to see the law school encourage participation more actively. Others were more adamant: "Practical skills—particularly legal research and writing—are ignored here," asserted one 3L. Quite a few others criticized Stanford's perceived focus on private practice. Stanford does indeed send a smaller proportion of its graduates into public-interest work than do some other top schools (e.g., Yale), but it is just about right in line with the national average in this respect.

ADMISSIONS

Good Luck. The Stanford University Law School, one of the four most selective in the nation, denies admission to more extremely well qualified applicants than even Yale. Most others stand a better chance of winning the lottery. As a group, 95 percent of the applicants with LSAT scores below 167—the 95th percentile—are rejected. The Stanford admissions office would probably encourage such applicants to apply anyway. After all, at $65 a head, these luckless souls bring in more than a quarter of a million dollars annually.

ACADEMICS

Student/faculty ratio	14:1
% female faculty	29
% minority faculty	13
Hours of study per day	2.87

FINANCIAL FACTS

Tuition	$22,350
Part-time tuition per credit	NR
Estimated books/expenses/fees	NR
On-campus living expenses	NR
Off-campus living expenses	NR
% first-year students receiving aid	NR
% all students receiving aid	NR
% aid that is merit-based	NR
% all students receiving grants/scholarships	NR
% all students receiving loans	NR
% all students receiving assistantships	NR
Average award package	NR
Average graduation debt	NR

ADMISSIONS

# applications received	4,298
% applicants accepted	10
% acceptees attending	40
Average LSAT	168
Average undergrad GPA	3.77
Application Fee	$65
Priority application deadline	NR
Priority notification	NR
Regular application deadline	February 15
Regular notification	NR
Admission deferment	NR
Gourman Report Rating	**4.88**

STATE UNIVERSITY OF NEW YORK AT BUFFALO ▯

School of Law

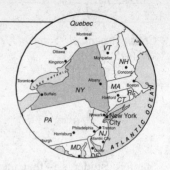

OVERVIEW

Type of school	public
Environment	metropolis
Scholastic calendar	semester
Schedule	Full time only

STUDENTS

Enrollment of institution	24,493
Enrollment of law school	765
% male/female	51/49
% out-of-state	8
% part-time	NR
% minorities	20
% international (# countries represented)	NR (11)
Average age at entry	26

APPLICANTS ALSO LOOK AT

Albany Law School
Syracuse University
American University
Cornell University
George Washington University

SURVEY SAYS...

HITS
Affordability
Practice-oriented curriculum
Friendly atmosphere

MISSES
parking
Not enough black letter law
Grading system

EMPLOYMENT PROFILE

% grads employed immediately	NR
% grads employed within six months	95
Average starting salary	$36,949
% grads employed by field:	
Private practice	59
Business/industry	14
Government	8
Judicial clerkships	5
Public service	5
Academic	9
Military	6

With more than 200 graduate and professional programs, the State University of New York at Buffalo is the largest and most comprehensive of the four SUNY schools. It is also home to what may be the finest public law school in the Northeast. For many, Buffalo itself conjures up images of cold medicine and ice storms, but the admissions materials assert that "Buffalo winters gain more fame than they deserve." Of course, as busy as the average student at this highly regarded law school is kept, the only thing that may matter to the prospective applicant is that the law library is heated. And chilly winters or no, there are three other seasons in this upstate New York city of nearly one million, and the surrounding region, home to Niagara falls and the Finger lakes, is wonderfully scenic. The strength of the University at Buffalo's traditional J.D. program is greatly enhanced by the vast resources of the university itself. Interdisciplinary work by all students is encouraged, and the law school maintains its Baldy Center for Law and Social Policy to serve "as a focal point for interdisciplinary research and teaching." The results of the law school's emphasis on the social ramifications of the law are quite clear: the University at Buffalo grads begin their careers in public-interest positions at a rate much higher than the national average. Tuition at this state school is, of course, very low for state residents, but even at the nonresident rate, fees here are appreciably lower than those charged by New York's least expensive private law school.

The remarkable value of the training they receive at the University at Buffalo is certainly not lost on students here, several of whom called the law school "easily the best for the money." According to the administration, "The value of the training they receive at University at Buffalo was further augmented when a new, practice-oriented curriculum was introduced in the fall of 1995. Students are very excited by this enriched program that exposes them from day one to the varied ways that lawyers actually work and, they believe, will give Buffalo grads a leg up in their future job searches." Most Buffalo students expressed a great degree of satisfaction with several important aspects of their experience at the law school. "The education they offer here is excellent," said one, "and I really appreciate the school's non-traditional emphasis on public interest. There is a great commu-

Kimberly DeWaal, Assistant Director of Admissions and
Financial Aid
John Lord O'Brian Hall, Buffalo, NY 14260-1100
Tel: (716) 645-2061   Fax: (716) 645-2064
eMail: DEWAAL@ms.mail.buffalo.edu
Internet: htttp://www.buffalo.edu

State University of New
York at Buffalo

nity atmosphere among students, sans intimidation and cut-throat competitiveness." The non-traditional grading system could be a contributor to the laid-back atmosphere. Indeed, Buffalo students rated their school very highly on several quality-of-life issues, and their satisfaction with the quality of their academic program is obvious. A remark from a 2L summed up the feelings of many: "This school is seriously capable of being one of the top 20 law schools in the country. The student body is very talented in many ways, and you can't beat the price tag."

We received quite a variety of comments on the faculty. Said one student, "The faculty attitude toward students needs to improve. They could stand to take a much more caring attitude." However, according to the administration, "There's been a dramatic turn-around with this new curriculum." It must be noted that many of the students who criticized faculty-student relations took pains to praise their faculty's scholarship—even "brilliance." Some students called professors "accessible," "approachable," and "friendly and capable," so the negative comments don't mean the faculty in general is uncaring. The administration said that "quality of the faculty...[was] never an issue," but that "student-faculty relations are steadily improving." Perhaps what students perceived as inaccessibility reflected less-than-stellar relations, not lack of teaching ability. Since 11 new faculty members have recently been hired, perhaps these difficulties have been ameliorated; we'll tell you what students say in our next survey. In the meantime, keep their comments of "excellence" in mind along with the less favorable remarks.

ADMISSIONS

With its solid academic reputation and its bargain-basement tuition, the University at Buffalo School of Law consistently attracts highly qualified applicants. In terms of its numerical standards, this is in fact one of the 70 most selective law schools in the nation. The University at Buffalo's overall acceptance rate, however, is quite generous for a law school of such high caliber. The administration reminds us that "numbers aren't the sole criterion. The admissions process is different from that at similar schools because of the unusual percentage of applications that receive active review from the Admissions Committee. In any given year, fewer than 20 percent will be admitted without committee review of the application."

ACADEMICS

Student/faculty ratio	17:1
% female faculty	37
% minority faculty	12
Hours of study per day	4.11

FINANCIAL FACTS

In-state tuition	$6,100
Out-of-state tuition	$10,750
Part-time tuition per credit	NR
Estimated books/expenses/fees	$1,395
On-campus living expenses	NR
Off-campus living expenses	NR
% first-year students receiving aid	10
% all students receiving aid	NR
% aid that is merit-based	5
% all students receiving grants/scholarships	15
% all students receiving loans	70
% all students receiving assistantships	NR
Average award package	$9,800
Average graduation debt	$34,144

ADMISSIONS

# applications received	1,339
% applicants accepted	49
% acceptees attending	40
Average LSAT	155
Average undergrad GPA	3.26
Application Fee	$50
No early decision program	
Regular application deadline	February 1
Regular notification	rolling
Admission deferment	one year
Gourman Report Rating	**4.32**

STETSON UNIVERSITY

College of Law

The Stetson University College of Law was Florida's first law school, and it continues to enjoy its strongest reputation in and around the state. Stetson's students, however, come from all parts of the country, and are drawn, no doubt, as much by factors climatic as matters academic. The Stetson law school is located in St. Petersburg, on Florida's west coast, a couple of hundred miles from the DeLand campus of Stetson University proper. The school's facilities, housed in a group of low-slung, pale stucco buildings arranged in the fashion of a medieval Spanish village, include a well-appointed student courtroom in which actual sessions of the Florida Court of Appeals are occasionally held.

Trial practice is, in fact, one of Stetson's strong suits. Stetson students interested in developing skills as trial lawyers are well served by classroom instruction in trial practice and by the ample opportunities outside the classroom to participate in simulated and live-action clinical programs. The law school is particularly proud of the results these programs produce; Stetson students turn in consistently strong performances in interscholastic moot court competitions. Stetson also operates a significant continuing legal education program, through which the law school remains actively involved with the legal profession outside the academy. Students may participate in some of these programs and also in some of the programs offered through Stetson's Center for Dispute Resolution. These specialized strengths and the law school's overall pleasant ambiance probably account for the great demand for spots in its entering class of about 225. Although numerical standards remain moderate, the heavy volume of applications and the high rate at which those offered admission actually choose to attend Stetson make it one of the most in-demand law schools in the country.

Judging from the comments of students, this high demand is not entirely unwarranted. Unlike students from nearly every law school we surveyed, a huge number of Stetson students actually offered unsolicited praise for the staff of the law school, and for its administration generally. When asked to name their school's greatest strengths, many echoed the feelings of one student who pointed to "the personal attention we receive from all staff, not

Kathy Hartman, Director of Admissions and Financial Aid
1401 61st Street South, St. Petersburg, FL 33707
Tel: (813) 562-7800   Fax: (813) 343-0136
eMail: info@hermes.law.stetson.edu
Internet: http://www.law.stetson.edu

Stetson University

just from the faculty." "The faculty and staff here are always available and accessible," wrote one 3L. "Most of our classes are small," she added, "and professors take the time to get to know individual students."

For the majority of Stetson students we heard from, those factors combine with the law school's fabulous location to create a fairly satisfying experience. But these same students pointed to more than a few areas in which their chosen school could stand to improve. Chief among them is the inconsistent quality of class-room instruction. Most students had kind words for certain members of their faculty, but, as one pointed out, "our teachers vary wildly from wonderful, caring professors to "I-don't-give-a damn, I've-got-tenure' types."

All in all, however, students at Stetson seem to be a fairly happy group. Though they find fault with certain aspects of their experience at the law school, their criticisms are not as strong as their praise for the school's "very accessible faculty," its "beautiful campus," and, perhaps just as important, "the sun."

ADMISSIONS

If you factor in both the relative volume of applications and the rate at which admitted students actually go on to enroll, you find that the upstart Stetson University School of Law is extremely popular with law-school applicants. Stetson receive more than 10 applications for every spot in its entering class of 225 and one quarter of those it admits choose to attend. And while numerical admissions standards at Stetson do not come close to those at the country's elite schools, few but the most highly qualified can consider this school a sure bet.

ACADEMICS

Student/faculty ratio	22:1
% female faculty	20
% minority faculty	17
Hours of study per day	3.82

FINANCIAL FACTS

Tuition	$18,175
Part-time tuition per credit	NR
Estimated books/expenses/fees	$1,085
On-campus living expenses	$5,850
Off-campus living expenses	$8,120
% first-year students receiving aid	96
% all students receiving aid	99
% aid that is merit-based	2
% all students receiving grants/scholarships	72
% all students receiving loans	90
% all students receiving assistantships	NR
Average award package	$3,200
Average graduation debt	$62,600

ADMISSIONS

# applications received	1,336
% applicants accepted	37
% acceptees attending	25
Average LSAT	154
Average undergrad GPA	3.19
Application Fee	$45
No early decision program	
Regular application deadline	NR
Regular notification	NR
Admission deferment	one semester
Gourman Report Rating	2.56

SUFFOLK UNIVERSITY 🖫
School of Law

Harvard may top all the other lists, but if Boston's law schools were ranked by weight, the undisputed number one would reign in the shadow of the gold-domed State House on historic Beacon Hill: the Suffolk University Law School. With well over 1,500 total full- and part-time students, Suffolk is the law school that put the mass in Massachusetts. Founded in 1906 and accredited by the ABA in 1953, Suffolk has over 12,000 living alumni spread throughout the country. Its evening division alone dwarfs many schools' entire student bodies, and while a big law school certainly isn't for everyone, it does have its advantages. The breadth of Suffolk's course offerings and the number and extent of its co-curricular programs are impressive. For over 60 years, the law school's traditional curriculum has been supplemented by clinical programs, which are now numerous and varied. Among them is the Clinica Legal, a program that is open to bilingual law students who wish to gain practical experience while serving members of Boston's Hispanic and Asian communities. Suffolk is a private school that charges a moderate tuition, and half of its students are Massachusetts residents. The most notable statistic regarding the student body, however, is its gender parity. Suffolk is one of only a handful of law schools at which men are (barely) in the minority. The law school grants admission to almost 1,000 applicants in order to fill its first-year class of about 500. Of course it receives well over 3,000 applications, so admissions are somewhat selective. The numerical qualifications of entering students are moderately high.

The overall level of satisfaction of currently enrolled students with their chosen school is even higher. Although they criticize some aspects of their school, Suffolk students are, on balance, quite positive about their experience at the law school. In particular, most of them praised the curricular focus of the Suffolk program, which, as one student put it, is "not tied to book law but to practical application, focusing on your practical skills in and out of courtroom." Many others agreed, and pointed to this focus when explaining their notable sense of confidence about their professional futures. "Suffolk offers a competitive edge to its graduates," asserted one soon-to-be graduate, "because its curriculum is heavily centered on programmatic skills, legal writing

Gail Ellis, Director of Admissions
41 Temple Street, Boston, MA 02114
Tel: (617) 573-8144
Internet: http://www.suffolk.edu/law

and clinical programs." "Lawyers who graduate from Suffolk are highly valued for their ability to apply knowledge immediately." Lawyers who graduate from Suffolk are also in good company. "One percent of all American lawyers are graduates of Suffolk Law," explained one student, "and the alumni connections and the school's regional reputation in the legal field are excellent." Students also seem thrilled about the relatively noncompetitive atmosphere at the law school. As a 1L said: "The school encourages teamwork, which in my estimation reduces stress and produces results in and out of class."

Few students had any difficulty, however, in naming areas in which their law school could stand to improve. For the most part, their complaints were related to Suffolk's size. Not surprisingly, a number of students complained that classes are too large, and many characterize their faculty and administration—particularly the placement office—as "too busy to help" the individual student. More widespread, however, is discontent with the heavily prescribed curriculum at Suffolk. Indeed, Suffolk students do not get to take significant advantage of the law school's extensive course offerings until their final year. "The number of required courses needs to be lowered," said one student who spoke for many. By and large, however, students here seem quite content.

ADMISSIONS

Despite its size, the Suffolk University Law School has no difficulty filling all the seats in its entering class of more than 500 students. In fact, this massive law school is moderately selective, admitting less than half of the 2,600 candidates it considers annually. Those who actually go on to enroll at Suffolk possess numerical credentials stronger than those of students at 60 percent of all U.S. law schools. Still, Suffolk does admit students across a relatively broad range of grade point averages and LSAT scores.

ACADEMICS

Student/faculty ratio	19:1
% female faculty	27
% minority faculty	7
Hours of study per day	4.12

FINANCIAL FACTS

Tuition	$17,740
Part-time tuition per credit	$13,306
Estimated books/expenses/fees	NR
On-campus living expenses	NR
Off-campus living expenses	NR
% first-year students receiving aid	100
% all students receiving aid	100
% aid that is merit-based	5
% all students receiving grants/scholarships	25
% all students receiving loans	74
% all students receiving assistantships	NR
Average award package	$4,000
Average graduation debt	$60,000

ADMISSIONS

# applications received	2,600
% applicants accepted	41
% acceptees attending	46
Average LSAT	155
Average undergrad GPA	3.20
Application Fee	$50
No early decision program	
Regular application deadline	March 1
Regular notification	rolling
Admission may be deferred?	No
Gourman Report Rating	3.12

SYRACUSE UNIVERSITY ⌷
College of Law

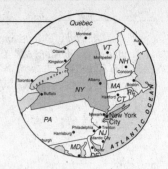

OVERVIEW

Type of school	private
Environment	city
Scholastic calendar	semester
Schedule	Full-time or part-time

STUDENTS

Enrollment of institution	14,600
Enrollment of law school	791
% male/female	58/42
% out-of-state	55
% part-time	NR
% minorities	23
% international (# countries represented)	2 (7)
Average age at entry	25

APPLICANTS ALSO LOOK AT

Hofstra University
Temple University
American University
Boston University
State University of New York at Albany

SURVEY SAYS...

HITS
Clinical experience
Prestige

MISSES
Sense of community
Facilities not great
Socratic method

EMPLOYMENT PROFILE

% grads employed immediately	NR
% grads employed within six months	81
Average starting salary	$42,400
% grads employed by field:	
Private practice	57
Business/industry	11
Government	15
Judicial clerkships	10
Public service	2
Academic	1
Military	2

Ask any student to comment on the Syracuse experience and the first thing you're likely to hear about is the weather. It's a popular topic of conversation among students, particularly those from warmer climates. The cold and snowy winters that Syracuse has long been known for, however, may be the perfect setting for law students in need of limited distractions. The Syracuse University College of Law, which celebrated its hundredth anniversary in 1995, provides a unique combination of tradition and innovation in its educational program.

The university offers a wide variety of clinical programs, co-curricular activities and opportunities for interdisciplinary work. Many of these programs fall under the school's new Applied Learning Program, which focuses on integrating legal theory with practice. Syracuse Law takes particular pride in its trial-advocacy program, which has been cited by the New York State Bar Association as the best trial skills law program in the state for eight of the past fifteen years. Formal dual-degree programs, offered through more than a dozen of the university's graduate departments, have also garnered praise from students. "Programs such as the joint J.D./M.B.A. with the Maxwell School afford J.D.'s an opportunity many other schools do not," said one 3L.

Overall, current Syracuse law students we talked to seemed satisfied with the education they receive. Approximately two-thirds indicated that they are happy with the quality of teaching and range of courses offered at the university. Many students praised the faculty, its dedication, and the diversity of its members. A 1L described the faculty as, "extremely accessible and willing to provide instruction outside the classroom." Another student emphatically agreed: "I would say the caring nature of the faculty is Syracuse's biggest strength." Where the majority of students lauded the faculty, a few remarked that getting a good professor can be a measure of luck. "Syracuse has both the best and worst professors I have ever had," said one 3L who added, "Every course seems to have a very strong professor and a very weak one teaching it. The problem is knowing who is who before you register for the class."

If there is one item Syracuse law students agree on, it is the university's need to expand physically. Many students cited the facilities as an area in need of improvement, and said that they feel cramped in crowded classrooms and study areas. The administration has heard the students' message on this point. Plans to expand the library and facilities are underway, and construction and renovation are expected to be completed by 1998.

We heard repeatedly from students that the administration is open to criticism and suggestions for change from the students. Many students we surveyed spoke highly of the school's new dean and his efforts to improve the law school. "[Syracuse Law School] has a dean who is very accessible, very dedicated to serving the law school community," said one 3L. Another student remarked: "Syracuse law has been working hard to improve its educational experience for its students. The new dean has taken a very proactive approach to his new students which is making a difference..." It should be noted that the dean has recently announced plans to intentionally downsize the school by about 50 students.

One complaint from Syracuse students, one common to law students nationwide, is the price of their education. Several students we spoke with indicated that Syracuse should focus more attention on financial aid. Since all indicators seem to point in the direction of change and innovation at the law school, perhaps this concern will soon be addressed as well.

ADMISSIONS

Among the 25 schools in the highly-competitive Mid-Atlantic region, Syracuse University College of Law is one of the least selective. The volume of applications at the law school is heavy, but 46 percent of all applicants are admitted, and numerical standards are moderate. Numbers may increase due to announced plans to limit admittance. The average numerical credentials for Syracuse students are moderate. According to the administration, "because they feel rigid use of cut-off LSAT scores and GPAs below which no candidate will be considered may deny qualified applicants a fair opportunity to gain admission to law school, Syracuse Law reviews all applications received for admission."

ACADEMICS

Student/faculty ratio	20:1
% female faculty	41
% minority faculty	20
Hours of study per day ·	3.99

FINANCIAL FACTS

Tuition	$19,660
Part-time tuition per credit	$860
Estimated books/expenses/fees	$2,003
On-campus living expenses	$8,397
Off-campus living expenses	$8,300
% first-year students receiving aid	85
% all students receiving aid	85
% aid that is merit-based	NR
% all students receiving grants/scholarships	36
% all students receiving loans	83
% all students receiving assistantships	11
Average award package	$5,200
Average graduation debt	$56,000

ADMISSIONS

# applications received	2,518
% applicants accepted	46
% acceptees attending	24
Average LSAT	152
Average undergrad GPA	3.25
Application Fee	$50
No early decision program	
Regular application deadline	April 1
Regular notification	rolling
Admission deferment	one year
Gourman Report Rating	3.82

TEMPLE UNIVERSITY
School of Law

The city of Philadelphia is home to the country's fifth-largest job market for recent law-school graduates and to one of the country's largest law schools, the Temple University School of Law. By a wide margin the largest law school in the state of Pennsylvania, this more than 100-year-old, state-supported law school on Philadelphia's north side enjoys a long-established reputation as a highly respected training ground for fine attorneys. The nearly 1,300 students in Temple's day and evening divisions follow a course of study that is remarkably balanced, as it has been for many years, between academic and practical preparation.

Though the law school does not allow for formal specialization at the J.D. level, it has recently designated several "areas of concentration" that students may pursue. The strongest of these are probably the programs in litigation, international law, business and tax law, and public interest law, which combine, to varying degrees, traditional classroom coursework with practical instruction through some of Temple's highly regarded clinical programs. The numerous clinical opportunities available to Temple students include programs focusing on such widely varying subjects as "Bankruptcy" and "Mothers with AIDS." Temple also offers international programs in Rome, Athens, Tel Aviv, and Tokyo. These special programs nicely augment the law school's overall strength, and Temple's reasonable tuition qualifies it as one of the region's better bargains in legal education. This standing is well known to the roughly 3,500 prospective students who vie annually for spots in Temple's entering class of around 350.

Those who go on to become part of that class are quite satisfied with fundamental aspects of their Temple experience. "The greatest strength of the law school is its emphasis on practical lawyering," said one. "Little time is spent on inane, arcane issues that will never appear in practice; the clinical education aspect is unmatched in breadth and scope, and this is one of the best places for trial advocacy!" Another 3L, who also praised the school's clinic, did have this criticism: "We should have more clinical access. I was only able to get one course in three years." In any case, most heartily endorse the law school's curriculum. "Turns out real world lawyers are not theoreticians," wrote one 3L, "and Temple has a knack for job practice over story telling or theory."

James G. Leipold, Director of Admissions
1719 North Broad Street, Philadelphia, PA 19122
Tel: (215) 204-5949
eMail: law@astro.ocis.temple.edu
Internet: http://www.temple.edu/departments/lawschool/

Temple University

The overwhelming majority of Temple students express much fondness for most of these (apparently) non-story-telling instructors: "Teacher-student relations are excellent," said one. "Teachers are truly there for the students." "The faculty," another agreed, "are very accessible, helpful and concerned about the students." All of this adds up to what one student called "a warm, loose, and fairly friendly environment to study law."

In response to student concerns about the physical environment, the building has been improved in a number of ways over the past few years, including additional lighting, a new moot court room, new mock trial practice rooms, new computer labs, and classrooms revamped to accommodate video and audio equipment. In addition to these improvements, a recently completed $10 million capital campaign will enable the school to restore two buildings: its first home, built 100 years ago, and a historic landmark building on the main campus. When the projects are finished, comments such as, "There are no student lounges or reading rooms, and the building itself looks and feels like a concrete bunker at the end of a mall," should be a thing of the past.

Few students expressed much fondness for the area immediately surrounding their school. When asked to name an area in which his law school might improve itself, one 2L replied that "that's the wrong question; it is the area the school is in that needs to be improved." One student, who probably should have done his homework before attending this urban school, warned prospective students: "If you want to attend Temple prepare yourself for the nightmare of North Philadelphia." While students may not appreciate the neighborhood, the administration called it "a vibrant urban neighborhood, a setting conducive to the study of real law for the real world."

ADMISSIONS

Although the numerical standards to which it holds applicants are slightly lower than the national average, the Temple University School of Law chooses its students from a relatively large applicant pool and is more than a little selective in doing so. This is thanks, no doubt, as much to the law school's reasonable tuition as to its solid regional reputation. Overall, seven out of ten candidates are denied admission to Temple.

ACADEMICS

Student/faculty ratio	23:1
% female faculty	25
% minority faculty	15
Hours of study per day	3.46

FINANCIAL FACTS

In-state tuition	$7,800
Out-of-state tuition	$14,314
Part-time tuition per credit	NR
Estimated books/expenses/fees	$985
On-campus living expenses	NR
Off-campus living expenses	NR
% first-year students receiving aid	NR
% all students receiving aid	71
% aid that is merit-based	23
% all students receiving grants/scholarships	55
% all students receiving loans	70
% all students receiving assistantships	1
Average award package	$1,712
Average graduation debt	NR

ADMISSIONS

# applications received	3,529
% applicants accepted	30
% acceptees attending	34
Average LSAT	155
Average undergrad GPA	3.16
Application Fee	$50
No early decision program	
Regular application deadline	March 1
Regular notification	rolling
Admission deferment	NR
Gourman Report Rating	3.88

UNIVERSITY OF TENNESSEE
College of Law

Even if it were fair to think of the University of Tennessee College of Law as Tennessee's "other" law school, there would be no shame in such a designation, considering that the state's top law school is the powerhouse Vanderbilt. But in terms of more than just national recognition, the two schools are further apart than their geographic locations imply. While Vanderbilt draws the overwhelming majority of its students from and sends a similar majority of its graduates to other states, at least in terms of where its graduates choose to practice, UT is truly a Tennessee school. Located near the foothills of the Smoky Mountains in Knoxville, this very inexpensive public law school has provided the bulk of Tennessee's lawyers for more than 100 years. The curriculum at Tennessee is strictly traditional in the first year, but includes several innovations thereafter. Upper-level students must complete three nontraditional requirements, in "Expository Writing," "Planning and Drafting" and "Interviewing, Counseling and Dispute Resolution." These requirements, however, can be fulfilled through various courses. The law school also operates a large legal clinic that is among the oldest in the nation. Those lucky UT students who happen to be state residents choose the school not just because it provides a solid J.D. program, but also because it provides great value. Even at the nonresident rate, three years' tuition at Tennessee adds up to little more than one year's tuition at mighty Vanderbilt. Applications volume at the law school is moderate, but the relatively small size of entering classes makes the admissions process fairly selective. Admitted applicants possess very solid numerical credentials.

To judge from the results of our survey of students, the academic program at the University of Tennessee College of Law succeeds marvelously in at least one fundamental respect: sharpening the critical faculties of those who follow it. The UT law students we heard from were not blind to their school's strong points, but neither were they reluctant to criticize. In nearly every category of student opinion, students here see real room for improvement. On the curricular front, most offered a complaint common among students at most small law schools: their course selection is too limited in any given semester. "The catalog here may list hundreds of courses," exaggerated one 2L, "but you have very few

Karen Britton, Director of Admissions and Financial Aid
1505 West Cumberland Avenue, Knoxville, TN 37996-1800
Tel: (615) 974-4241
eMail: lawadmit@libra.law.utk.edu
Internet: http://www.law.utk.edu/

electives to choose from in reality." But the fact that this limitation is partially balanced out by their unusually easy access to practical skills training was not lost on everyone. As one 3L put it, "The practical education offered here is a great plus—jobs are hard to come by now and we can use every advantage."

But the relatively optimistic tone of that last remark was usually missing in the expressions of anxiety we heard again and again from UT students about their job prospects. In fact, this understandable concern seemed to come out in much of their generalized criticism of their chosen school. Consider these comments: "UT may get you in at law firms in Tennessee, but if you don't want to practice here, you might be in trouble."; "The job market is dismal out there but UT seems to be doing nothing to build its national recognition." Well, this is a state school, and just how one would "build" a reputation on command is quite unclear. We also hear from the Dean that the career services director says the problem lies in getting UT graduates to leave the state, not in the lack of offers from out-of-state firms. It should be noted, however, that UT has set about improving the most glaring weakness students here see by building new facilities, the completion of which is scheduled for early 1997. One UT student who sees reason for hope in such steps offered this fairly evenhanded summation: "We've gotten a bad reputation because of our inadequate facilities, but UT offers a strong, practical education that prepares students for broad areas of legal work. When the new building is finished, this will once again be a top-notch state school. I'd recommend it to anyone."

ADMISSIONS

Like all highly regarded public law schools, the University of Tennessee College of Law attracts a relatively large pool of applicants from which it chooses its students very carefully. The numerical standards to which Tennessee holds applicants are only slightly higher than the national average, but the size of the law school's entering class limits the overall acceptance rate to a none-too-generous 28 percent.

ACADEMICS

Student/faculty ratio	17:1
% female faculty	24
% minority faculty	6
Hours of study per day	3.69

FINANCIAL FACTS

In-state tuition	$3,284
Out-of-state tuition	$8,678
Part-time tuition per credit	NR
Estimated books/expenses/fees	$1,254
On-campus living expenses	NR
Off-campus living expenses	NR
% first-year students receiving aid	100
% all students receiving aid	100
% aid that is merit-based	NR
% all students receiving grants/scholarships	20
% all students receiving loans	70
% all students receiving assistantships	NR
Average award package	NR
Average graduation debt	NR

ADMISSIONS

# applications received	1,141
% applicants accepted	28
% acceptees attending	52
Average LSAT	155
Average undergrad GPA	3.40
Application Fee	$15
No early decision program	
Regular application deadline	February 1
Regular notification	NR
Admission deferment	NR
Gourman Report Rating	2.95

TEXAS SOUTHERN UNIVERSITY
Thurgood Marshall School of Law

OVERVIEW

Type of school	public
Environment	metropolis
Scholastic calendar	semester
Schedule	Full time only

STUDENTS

Enrollment of institution	5,595
Enrollment of law school	541
% male/female	57/43
% out-of-state	NR
% part-time	NR
% minorities	77
% international (# countries represented)	NR (NR)
Average age at entry	NR

APPLICANTS ALSO LOOK AT

University of Houston
South Texas College of Law
Texas Tech University
University of Texas
Saint Mary's University

SURVEY SAYS...

HITS
Studying
Intellectual challenge

MISSES
Library staff
Quality of teaching
Research resources

EMPLOYMENT PROFILE

% grads employed immediately	NR
% grads employed within six months	NR
Average starting salary	NR
% grads employed by field:	
Private practice	62
Business/industry	8
Government	12
Judicial clerkships	5
Public service	1
Academic	12
Military	6

Originally established as the "Texas State University for Negroes" in 1947, the institution that was created under the provision of the state's separate-but-equal doctrine was renamed Texas Southern in 1951. Its school of law took the name of the late Justice Thurgood Marshall 25 years later. In its 50 years of service, the school continues the tradition of providing a sound legal education to all students. With over three–fourths of its student body and 85 percent of its faculty comprised of minorities, this midsize public law school is doing as much as any law school in the nation to diversify the legal profession.

Whatever their background, students at the Thurgood Marshall School of Law pursue a staunchly traditional, highly prescribed course of study. The law school's classroom curriculum is composed almost entirely of required courses in the first two years, and nearly all third-year electives fall under the broader heading of business. The school does operate a fairly broad clinical program that focuses on advancing the concept of equal justice under the law.

While far from being easy to get into or stay in, the law school does provide opportunities for many individuals to study law who would otherwise not be able to do so. Although the admissions committee relies on undergraduate GPA and LSAT scores, according to the school's promotional material it also "seeks to determine the applicant's level of motivation by reviewing personal experience indicating determination, patience, and perseverance." What is not included in the school's bulletin is the exceedingly high rate of attrition of 1L's at Thurgood Marshall School of Law, about 30 percent, say students. Students we spoke with repeatedly referred to the "grading curve" that "curves out" a sizable chunk of the first-year class. "My law school did a very poor job of communicating to its potential applicants the extremely high attrition rate among the first-year class," said a 1L, who added, "Had many of the students in the first-year class known of this high attrition rate, they most likely would not have attended law school here." Whether this substantial downsizing of the 1L class is a formal policy or the result of tough standards is not clear, but its effects on students, particularly 1L's, as explained by a 2L, is: "Because the attrition rate is so high, most 1L's spend too much time worrying if they will make it back," and, "Competition among 1L's is extremely fierce, which adds to the stress."

Many other students described the "cut-throat" atmosphere at Thurgood Marshall as one of the school's major drawbacks, and blame the administration and their instructors for it. "The faculty and the administration here at TSU promote a level of competition among students that could be likened to 'legal boot camp,'" said a 1L. The administration, particularly its financial aid arm, was widely criticized, dubbed as "offensive" and "unprofessional" by students.

Although some students referred to an "uncaring" and "unsupportive" faculty, many others had only positive comments to make. "Professors encourage and maintain professional and working relationships with students to develop lawyering skills. They devote personal time to numerous tutorials and extend their office hours to accommodate student schedules," said a 1L.

One thing is certain of Thurgood Marshall School of Law: it is a place of great diversity and opportunity. "While most other schools rely on LSAT and GPA scores as their main concern, TSU looks at the overall package which I think is great," said a 1L, and added, "My scores weren't the best but I know and always knew that I could succeed."

ADMISSIONS

As you would expect from a school named after the late Justice Thurgood Marshall, this law school's mission is to make legal education accessible to those who would elsewhere be excluded. The implications of that policy to the prospective student are fairly obvious: the admissions process at Thurgood Marshall is not driven by numbers.

ACADEMICS

Student/faculty ratio	17:1
% female faculty	20
% minority faculty	83
Hours of study per day	5.05

FINANCIAL FACTS

In-state tuition	$3,900
Out-of-state tuition	$8,200
Part-time tuition per credit	NR
Estimated books/expenses/fees	NR
On-campus living expenses	NR
Off-campus living expenses	NR
% first-year students receiving aid	NR
% all students receiving aid	NR
% aid that is merit-based	NR
% all students receiving grants/scholarships	NR
% all students receiving loans	NR
% all students receiving assistantships	NR
Average award package	NR
Average graduation debt	NR

ADMISSIONS

# applications received	1,460
% applicants accepted	37
% acceptees attending	49
Average LSAT	38
Average undergrad GPA	3.00
Application Fee	$40
Priority application deadline	NR
Priority notification	NR
Regular application deadline	NR
Regular notification	NR
Admission deferment	NR
Gourman Report Rating	**2.33**

TEXAS TECH UNIVERSITY
School of Law

Established in 1967 on the Lubbock campus of its nearly 30,000-student parent institution, the Texas Tech University School of Law is the youngest, westernmost law school of Texas's eight. In its relatively short history, however, this midsize law school has built a very solid regional reputation. Law firms in and around West Texas are well stocked with Tech alumni. This fact is hardly surprising given the highly prescribed, traditional nature of Tech's J.D. program; even a student's second year at the law school is dominated by required courses, most of which fall under the broad heading of business law. In short, Texas Tech has built a name for itself not on innovation but on the undeniable quality of its traditional program.

Although the law school does not operate an in-house legal clinic, it does sponsor a limited number of external placements and its traditional classroom curriculum is supplemented by a variety of simulated clinical courses on topics like trial advocacy. Participation in these skills programs and in Tech's extensive intra-school moot court competition is quite high.

Tech selects its well-qualified student body from a relatively large applicant pool, which is probably drawn as much by Tech's price as by its curricular strength. Three years at Tech's rate of resident tuition costs less than a single year at most private law schools.

The low tuition rate is surely the most crucial reason student satisfaction runs high at Texas Tech. Running neck and neck at second are the relatively small class size and faculty open-door policy, which combine to produce a friendly, supportive atmosphere. This satisfied 3L had some wise advice for prospective law students: "What most people don't realize is how emotionally challenging law school can be. That is why it is important to choose a school where the faculty and students have a good rapport between them. Students need to have a strong support system within the school so that the emotional burdens do not become too great." Another gave some important consumer advice for those shopping within the Texas legal education market: "If you're looking for an education in legal theory, go to UT; if you're looking for a practical legal education that teaches you how to litigate, then Tech is the place for you. You just can't get a better education for the money." Texas Tech's very high Texas bar passage rate, which many of our respondents requested we mention, seems proof of that. The excellent facilities, of which the library and computers received substantial praise, surely aid the student's success.

Since so many people attend Texas Tech for the "real world" education, it's no surprise that students universally approve of and enjoy the practical extracurricular activities, like the first-year Board of Barristers competition. Nearly all students requested "more skill courses with hands on training, better legal practice classes," and much more attention to legal writing. We also heard more than a few complaints about some of the teaching staff, although not all went as far as this sullen 3L: "The number of excellent teachers can be counted on one hand." Most students' comments ran closer to the opinion that "While there are larger and more prestigious law schools in Texas, I doubt seriously that I would be getting a better legal education at another school. The facilities are excellent and the city is a nice place to live."

ADMISSIONS

Although the numerical standards to which the Texas Tech University School of Law holds applicants are only slightly higher than the national average, this law school's regional reputation is strong enough and its price tag low enough to draw a large pool of applicants. Those whose numbers fall more than a little short of Tech's averages face long odds.

ACADEMICS

Student/faculty ratio	25:1
% female faculty	32
% minority faculty	7
Hours of study per day	3.59

FINANCIAL FACTS

In-state tuition	$4,130
Out-of-state tuition	NR
Part-time tuition per credit	NR
Estimated books/expenses/fees	NR
On-campus living expenses	NR
Off-campus living expenses	NR
% first-year students receiving aid	NR
% all students receiving aid	NR
% aid that is merit-based	NR
% all students receiving grants/scholarships	NR
% all students receiving loans	NR
% all students receiving assistantships	NR
Average award package	NR
Average graduation debt	NR

ADMISSIONS

# applications received	1,483
% applicants accepted	35
% acceptees attending	42
Average LSAT	156
Average undergrad GPA	3.38
Application Fee	NR
Priority application deadline	NR
Priority notification	NR
Regular application deadline	February 1
Regular notification	rolling
Admission deferment	NR
Gourman Report Rating	**3.18**

UNIVERSITY OF TEXAS
School of Law

OVERVIEW

Type of school	public
Environment	metropolis
Scholastic calendar	semester
Schedule	Full time only

STUDENTS

Enrollment of institution	30,100
Enrollment of law school	1,468
% male/female	58/42
% out-of-state	15
% part-time	NR
% minorities	25
% international (# countries represented)	NR (11)
Average age at entry	25

APPLICANTS ALSO LOOK AT

University of Houston
Harvard University
Southern Methodist University
University of Virginia
Georgetown University

SURVEY SAYS...

HITS
Research resources
Library staff

MISSES
Studying
Sense of community
Legal writing

EMPLOYMENT PROFILE

% grads employed immediately	73
% grads employed within six months	92
Average starting salary	$53,669
% grads employed by field:	
Private practice	69
Business/industry	1
Government	9
Judicial clerkships	10
Public service	1
Academic	11
Military	2

When it comes to law schools, size alone may not guarantee variety and strength, but whether quantity or quality is your thing, the University of Texas at Austin School of Law is sure to satisfy. With around 1,500 full-time students in its J.D. program, this public law school is one of the largest in the nation, and the biggest in a state well stocked with giants. With a respected faculty, top-notch facilities, a broad and comprehensive curriculum, and one of the most highly qualified student bodies anywhere, it is also widely acknowledged as one of the fifteen or twenty finest law schools in the nation. With a ridiculously low tuition, it is also probably the best bargain in American legal education. Not for nothing do approximately 4,000 applicants vie annually to be among Texas's entering class of about 520.

Those who are fortunate enough to gain admission follow a course of study that is strong in all the traditional academic areas and increasingly rich in skills programs. UT's various clinical offerings run the gamut from "Children's Rights" to "Capital Punishment," and the law school takes great pride in its highly regarded trial-advocacy program. Texas is also notable for its emphasis on legal writing—an impressive number of the law school's students are member's of UT's ten law journals. More than any of these numerous strengths, however, the law school touts the teaching abilities of its faculty. A rarity among law schools—"elite" or not—Texas takes quite seriously the importance of quality instruction when making faculty hires and changes, and the results of this commitment are quite clear.

When asked to assess the strengths of their chosen school, Texas students enthusiastically endorsed many aspects of their program, most notably the teaching abilities of their faculty, about which the students were incredibly enthusiastic. "Our faculty is absolutely second to none," said one Texas 1L. "They are high-level scholars who can also teach," he continued, "and for a school of this size, it is surprising how much attention you get as an individual. The faculty make a sincere attempt to help each student understand and succeed." Moreover, few students failed to mention their program's rigor. "You'll work quite hard here," reported one 2L, "and you'll find it rather competitive, but the

Shelli Soto, Director of Admissions
727 East 26th Street, Austin, TX 78705
Tel: (512) 471-3207
eMail: msharlot@mail.law.utexas.edu
Internet: http://www.law.utexas.edu

University of Texas

competition never gets too unhealthy, and it always feels like your fellow students support you." Predictably, UT students also trumpeted the virtues of their incredibly low overhead. "It's so inexpensive here," said one 2L, "that I'm almost embarrassed to talk about it with my friends at other law schools."

All of which is not to say that Texas students see no room for their school to improve. "As a traditional law school," began one fairly typical remark, "UT is a classic, but with its size and resources, it would be nice to see it be more innovative." Indeed, many of the students we heard from lamented the law school's relative lack of courses in specialized areas like environmental law and its focus on business and commercial law. They also wished the school emphasized practical skills more, especially legal writing, which is usually taught by third-year students. And, although such complaints are common among all law students, a large number of Texas students griped about the career placement office. Asked to list the areas in which Texas could stand to improve, one 2L wrote, "Career services, career services, career services, and, finally, career services." On balance, however, Texas students seem to be satisfied with their legal education—and the price is right.

ADMISSIONS

Although the entering class of the University of Texas School of Law is nearly as large as that of any U.S. law school, competition for those spots among applicants is fierce. Applications volume is heavy, and numerical standards are very high—in fact, the seventeenth-highest in the nation. All but the most highly qualified applicants must consider Texas a "reach" school.

ACADEMICS	
Student/faculty ratio	23:1
% female faculty	21
% minority faculty	10
Hours of study per day	3.31

FINANCIAL FACTS	
In-state tuition	$3,780
Out-of-state tuition	$9,800
Part-time tuition per credit	NR
Estimated books/expenses/fees	$2,710
On-campus living expenses	NR
Off-campus living expenses	NR
% first-year students receiving aid	70
% all students receiving aid	80
% aid that is merit-based	22
% all students receiving grants/scholarships	76
% all students receiving loans	80
% all students receiving assistantships	NR
Average award package	$1,500
Average graduation debt	$30,532

ADMISSIONS	
# applications received	4,131
% applicants accepted	26
% acceptees attending	48
Average LSAT	161
Average undergrad GPA	3.53
Application Fee	$65
Priority application deadline	NR
Priority notification	mid-January
Regular application deadline	February 1
Regular notification	rolling
Admission deferment	one year
Gourman Report Rating	4.76

THOMAS M. COOLEY LAW SCHOOL

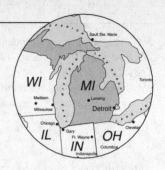

OVERVIEW

Type of school	private
Environment	city
Scholastic calendar	trimester
Schedule	Full-time or part-time

STUDENTS

Enrollment of institution	NR
Enrollment of law school	1,740
% male/female	68/32
% out-of-state	75
% part-time	97
% minorities	11
% international (# countries represented)	29 (8)
Average age at entry	26

APPLICANTS ALSO LOOK AT

Wayne State University
Whittier College
Nova University
The John Marshall Law School
University of Michigan

SURVEY SAYS...

HITS
Sense of community
Faculty-student relations
Clinical experience

MISSES
Studying
Cut throat competition
Socratic method

EMPLOYMENT PROFILE

% grads employed immediately	NR
% grads employed within six months	73
Average starting salary	$32,811
% grads employed by field:	
Private practice	57
Business/industry	17
Government	24
Public service	2
Academic	2
Military	0

Michigan's largest and youngest law school, the Thomas M. Cooley Law School, stands out for much more than its size and its relative youth. Established in 1973 and accredited by the ABA in 1978, Cooley pursues a mission that is similar enough to that of other law schools, but much of the form in which it does so is unique, or at least distinctive. Consider first that this law school has turned on its head the standard scheduling scheme: Nearly all of its students study year-round, part-time, and application must be made to study full time. For this reason, Cooley bills itself as the largest U.S. law school "for working people." (It is also notable for its Anglophile eccentricity: Cooley calls its autumn, spring and summer terms, respectively, Michaelmas, Hilary, and Trinity.)

As much as the law school dedicates itself to making legal education accessible to the working professional, it also actively rewards the dedication of the hardworking law student more than any other school. On the basis of their admissions index and their law school grades, Cooley students can qualify automatically for up to 100 percent tuition reimbursement in their second and third years. This aggressive attempt to attract highly qualified students to Cooley is, however, not the sum total of the law school's efforts to construct a true meritocracy. While the dominant admissions philosophy in legal education is that selectivity should be high and attrition near zero, Cooley has chosen to go the other way. Admissions to the law school are virtually open—new classes enter three time a year, and even applicants with a 2.0 and an LSAT score at the thirteenth percentile are "virtually guaranteed" admission. But be forewarned: matriculation at Cooley is no guarantee of graduation. Seventeen percent of entering students will be lost to academic failure. Depending on one's perspective—or actually, on one's grades—this innovation is either bold or brutal. In the same way, one can view the fact that around three-quarters of the courses in the law school's curriculum are required as a creative way to instill a sense of clear direction or as a heavy-handed way to limit creativity. What this all boils down to is this: The Thomas M. Cooley Law School is admirably unique, but it may not be for everyone.

So before enrolling, prospective students should be very sure they want the particularly rigorous, practical legal education Cooley provides and that their confidence can withstand the constant threat of Academic Probation and possible dismissal. If you are looking for a stepping stone to another school, look elsewhere; said one student, "Cooley—it's easy to get in but damn hard to graduate. We have the dreaded 'C' curve. If you come to Cooley, you might as well sign a three-year housing agreement because transferring out of here is next to impossible!!" Some students feel that the administration actively works against them: "I feel that the school keeps grades low to avoid paying academic scholarships to people. These GPAs will hurt us in the end when we are trying to seek employment. This does not benefit us or the school." Given such circumstances, competition between students is rather high and student morale is understandably lower than average.

Those who love a challenge thrive here. One 3L expressed appreciation for Cooley's "rigorous academic standards," saying, "Required courses give students firm background in business law and in practical lawyering skills." Some reveled in the school's punitive approach to learning: "They bust your ass so much that when you get out of here, you can challenge anyone." Most were grateful for the chance to enter that exclusive bastion, the legal profession; "Here, you don't have to be part of the cognitive elite with high grades and high scores on the LSAT to get in. They guarantee you a spot." Many emphasized Cooley's success: "I'll work harder here and get lower grades than other law students, but I feel I'll pass the bar more easily than those other students."

ADMISSIONS

Simply stated, the Thomas M. Cooley Law School has probably the most open admissions policies of any U.S. law school. The competition at Cooley is not to get in, but rather to earn a merit scholarship under the law school's unique financial-aid system. A certain UGPA and LSAT score, set by the school, qualifies Cooley students who earn honors in their first year for a tuition rebate on a sliding scale from 10 to 100 percent. If one is concerned simply with getting in, criteria are fairly low.

ACADEMICS

Student/faculty ratio	17:1
% female faculty	31
% minority faculty	7
Hours of study per day	4.93

FINANCIAL FACTS

Tuition	$13,950
Part-time tuition per credit	NR
Estimated books/expenses/fees	NR
On-campus living expenses	NR
Off-campus living expenses	NR
% first-year students receiving aid	NR
% all students receiving aid	80
% aid that is merit-based	NR
% all students receiving grants/scholarships	NR
% all students receiving loans	80
% all students receiving assistantships	NR
Average award package	NR
Average graduation debt	NR

ADMISSIONS

# applications received	2,200
% applicants accepted	82
% acceptees attending	42
Average LSAT	147
Average undergrad GPA	2.84
Application Fee	$100
Priority application deadline	NR
Priority notification	NR
Regular application deadline	rolling
Regular notification	rolling
Admission deferment	NR
Gourman Report Rating	**2.90**

University of Toledo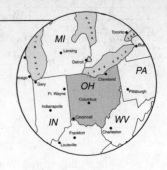
College of Law

OVERVIEW

Type of school	public
Environment	metropolis
Scholastic calendar	quarter
Schedule	Full-time or part-time

STUDENTS

Enrollment of institution	22,000
Enrollment of law school	672
% male/female	60/40
% out-of-state	35
% part-time	31
% minorities	11
% international (# countries represented)	NR (NR)
Average age at entry	26

APPLICANTS ALSO LOOK AT

Ohio State University
University of Akron
University of Dayton
University of Michigan
Capital University

SURVEY SAYS...

HITS
Faculty representation
Broad range of courses
Faculty-student relations

MISSES
Intellectual challenge
Studying
Gender bias

EMPLOYMENT PROFILE

% grads employed immediately	60
% grads employed within six months	70
Average starting salary	$35,000
% grads employed by field:	
Private practice	52
Business/industry	18
Government	11
Judicial clerkships	11
Public service	2
Academic	3
Military	2

Few states are as well stocked with law schools as Ohio is. More important to the cost-conscious law student, however, is the fact that Ohio is a state exceptionally rich in opportunities to pursue a legal education at an inexpensive public institution. Though rarely mentioned in the same breath as the nationally recognized public law schools in Columbus and Cincinnati, the University of Toledo College of Law is an inexpensive law school with a long tradition and a solid regional reputation.

Established shortly after the turn of the century, Toledo's only law school is located on the 25,000-student campus of its parent institution in a peaceful residential neighborhood. With over 600 total students in its day and evening divisions, the law school is large enough to offer a comprehensive program and small enough, by all reports, to offer a comfortable learning environment. Toledo's curriculum is relatively broad within traditional bounds. After their first year, most students follow a recommended course of study—the "standard program"—in the basic bar exam topics. The law school also operates a long-established clinical program of modest size and sponsors a wide variety of co-curricular programs. Administering all of this is a faculty of adequate size and, according to the law school's bulletin, more than adequate teaching abilities. Indeed, Toledo presents itself as a law school that is as much concerned with serving the individual student as with burnishing its own reputation.

Happily, this self-assessment appears to have at least some basis in reality. To judge from the results of our survey of students, the University of Toledo College of Law delivers a fairly satisfactory product to a group of appreciative customers. While most see room for improvement in several areas (e.g., financial aid and administrative matters generally), Toledo students gave their chosen school moderately good marks in nearly every category of student opinion printed here. Their highest praise was reserved for the Toledo faculty, not only for their scholarship but for their interest in teaching. "I have found that nearly all of my professors are usually available outside of class," wrote one satisfied 1L. "They're bright and motivated and care about their students." "The faculty are absolutely the greatest asset of UT," agreed another. "They could teach anywhere and we are lucky to have them here." Furthermore, the quality of student-faculty relations here appears to set a collegial tone that is not marred by any unhealthy competition among students. "As a rule," said one 2L, "there is no cutthroat competitiveness here...Students are willing to help each other out rather than trying to beat each other out."

But while nearly all of the Toledo students we heard from agreed that the campus atmosphere was "relaxed and easy-going," some expressed ambivalence on this matter. "It's definitely relaxed here," said one 2L, "but that's both good and bad." As another 2L put it, "I feel funny mentioning this, but I almost wish it were a bit more rigorous here, especially considering the difficult job market we face." Indeed, even some of the most satisfied Toledo students we heard from offered seemingly faint praise like this from one 3L: "University of Toledo College of Law as a label will not carry even an above-average law student much outside the Midwest after graduation...If you like Ohio, however, it is a great choice." This perceived lack of stature notwithstanding, the general good will that characterizes Toledo students' reviews of their school is notable. The results of our survey of other schools have taught us that Toledo could do a lot worse than to keep its students moderately content.

ADMISSIONS

With more than five applications filed for each spot in its first-year class, the University of Toledo College of Law is in a position to be somewhat selective, but a very generous overall acceptance rate makes this inexpensive law school a virtual sure thing for bargain-hunting applicants with moderately high numerical credentials. Those whose numbers fall below these values face less favorable but not insurmountable odds.

ACADEMICS

Student/faculty ratio	14:1
% female faculty	19
% minority faculty	12
Hours of study per day	3.26

FINANCIAL FACTS

In-state tuition	$6,167
Out-of-state tuition	$11,600
Part-time tuition per credit	NR
Estimated books/expenses/fees	$7,182
On-campus living expenses	NR
Off-campus living expenses	$4,559
% first-year students receiving aid	95
% all students receiving aid	87
% aid that is merit-based	25
% all students receiving grants/scholarships	38
% all students receiving loans	81
% all students receiving assistantships	NR
Average award package	$2,852
Average graduation debt	NR

ADMISSIONS

# applications received	760
% applicants accepted	53
% acceptees attending	36
Average LSAT	155
Average undergrad GPA	3.11
Application Fee	$30
No early decision program	
Regular application deadline	March 15
Regular notification	rolling
Admission deferment	NR
Gourman Report Rating	**2.49**

TOURO COLLEGE
Jacob D. Fuchsberg Law Center

The early 1980s saw a fairly sharp decline in law school applications, and it was widely believed that some of the country's less established law schools would be forced to close in response to this decreased demand. Yet in 1980, Touro College established its Jacob D. Fuchsberg Law Center in a region already saturated with law schools. Because of massive population growth in Long Island's Suffolk County, Touro survived during a tough time for legal education. As the only law school in this heavily populated suburban area to offer a part-time J.D. program, Touro filled a large void. Today Touro law school enrolls a total of about 800 students, approximately a third of them in its part-time and evening divisions. Touro's largely local and suburban student body is drawn from a sizable pool of applicants.

Touro University was established under Jewish auspices in 1970. The Law Center provides for the study of the Jewish legal experience through its Institute of Jewish Law. Other specialized programs offered at Touro law school include the Institute of Local and Suburban Law, the International Summer Law Internship Program, and a joint master's degree program in taxation through Long Island University. Students at the Law Center can take advantage of a wide range of legal clinics and externship programs. The Domestic Violence Externship Project and the Elderlaw Clinic are two examples of programs the school has instituted to meet the needs of surrounding communities.

Touro's admirably gender-balanced faculty administers a straightforward and traditional course of study with a wide variety of elective courses. Law students at Touro appear to be reasonably happy with this curriculum and their surroundings. Students we spoke with repeatedly cited the faculty and the close relationship it shares with students as a major strength of the school. One 2L said, "Law school professors at Touro inspire students and push each student individually to achieve their maximum potential," and "The professors take an interest in knowing the students' names and pushing until they click with each individual." Touro students also praised the efforts of their faculty and administration to make their education manageable. In fact, Touro is one of the first law schools in the country to offer discussion sessions led by third-year students. The Law Center's commitment to all students is also evident through its Legal Education Access Program (LEAP), a three–week summer program that introduces minority students to law school in a supportive and challenging way.

What concerns Touro students we spoke with most is the school's lackluster reputation. "I am disturbed by the reputation Touro has in comparison to other law schools...employers who are unfamiliar with the school, due to its age, are hesitant to employ graduates," said one 3L. Another student, a 2L, was somewhat more vocal: "I resent the classification of Touro as being one of the least selective law schools!... Our [bar] passage rate is 86 percent—not bad for a school with no 'quantifiable standards.'" Some students believe the Law Center, particularly its placement office, need to take a more active role in selling the school. "Somehow the school should convey the standard of excellence it expects from its students to prospective employers," offered one 2L. A 3L suggested: "The career placement office could work harder to assist students in breaking the barriers to employment in New York City."

However, students themselves may be the best promoters of the school. Touro law students remain proud and spirited. Several spoke of their belief that Touro will soon gain the recognition it deserves. As one 2L put it: "Students from Touro will be the movers and shakers of the legal community...[the school's] reputation will increase trifold in the near future."

ADMISSIONS

The Touro College-Jacob D. Fuchsberg Law Center's numerical standards make it one of the least selective law schools in the nation. Because this is still a young law school, numerical standards may rise as the law school's applicant pool continues to grow; but for now, Touro remains a virtual sure thing for all prospective law students with even modest credentials.

ACADEMICS

Student/faculty ratio	19:1
% female faculty	39
% minority faculty	8
Hours of study per day	4.16

FINANCIAL FACTS

Tuition	$15,940
Part-time tuition per credit	$12,740
Estimated books/expenses/fees	NR
On-campus living expenses	NR
Off-campus living expenses	NR
% first-year students receiving aid	NR
% all students receiving aid	NR
% aid that is merit-based	NR
% all students receiving grants/scholarships	NR
% all students receiving loans	NR
% all students receiving assistantships	NR
Average award package	NR
Average graduation debt	NR

ADMISSIONS

# applications received	2,028
% applicants accepted	43
% acceptees attending	34
Average LSAT	151
Average undergrad GPA	3.00
Application Fee	$45
Priority application deadline	NR
Priority notification	NR
Regular application deadline	May 1
Regular notification	rolling
Admission deferment	NR
Gourman Report Rating	**2.13**

TULANE UNIVERSITY

School of Law

Students at Tulane University Law School enjoy the best of both worlds. This private university, the twelfth oldest law school in the nation, is located in New Orleans, one of the most historic cities in the country, and is a short drive from the famous French Quarter. Tulane Law School is also bringing its graduates into the 21st century by becoming one of the most progressive and diverse law schools in the nation. The school recently opened a new state-of-the-art law library in its brand-new law building and has added hundreds of computer terminals. If Tulane's stunningly professional promotional materials are any indication, it won't be long before public perception catches up with the reputation that this law school feels it deserves.

In at least two notable respects, Tulane is top among the nation's law schools: its commitment to the public interest and to ethical, principled law practice in general (the law school operates several community law clinics and was the first law school to institute a pro bono graduation requirement) and its active recruitment and support of minorities in legal education. The school is also acknowledged as a leader in specialized fields: admiralty and maritime law, in which the law school offers the nation's only LL.M degree and a formal certificate of specialization; and environmental law, European legal practice, and sports law, in which Tulane also offers formal certificates of specialization.

Tulane combines a solid core curriculum with a very broad range of upper-level courses and electives. Even first-year students, who follow a strict schedule at every law school, including this one, feel Tulane gives them something extra. "As a 1L, I see the greatest strengths coming from the opportunities this school has—a 1L can work as a law clerk for the Tulane Legal Assistance Program," said one new student. When it came to the quality of teaching at the law school, students spoke highly of their "young, energetic" professors. "The faculty here is outstanding and generous with their time. All the professors I have had have been extremely helpful and knowledgeable," said a 2L. The only complaint waged against the faculty was a call for more women

Susan L. Krinsky, Associate Dean
6329 Freret Street, New Orleans, LA 70118
Tel: (504) 865-5930   Fax: (504) 865-6710
eMail: admissions@law.tulane.edu
Internet: http://www.law.tulane.edu

Tulane University

on staff. (Just under 30 percent of Tulane's 50-person full-time faculty are women.)

Whether they were talking about the new, technologically advanced facilities, the university's diverse trial advocacy and clinical programs, or their overall experience, this is a happy student body. "This school seems like it has something for everyone. I don't know of any other school that provides so many opportunities for its students," said one student.

With all of these positive statements in mind, consider the price of a legal education at Tulane: about $22,000 per year, excluding living expenses. These costs do not go unnoticed by students. When asked in what areas the law school could improve, students again and again cited Tulane's high tuition. Many students feel the tuition is particularly high when looking at the job market a Tulane graduate faces, particularly in markets outside the south. "[The] price is grossly disproportional to the job opportunities available," said one 3L. The school's career placement office also came under heavy fire from students surveyed. "The real problem here is that we receive this tremendous legal education, but the career placement office seems unable to effectively find jobs for most of the students," said one 1L. Another student, a 2L, said the school needs to market itself better: "More people need to know how good this institution is." Although its location may keep Eastern law firms from actively recruiting at Tulane, from all accounts students sound quite happy with New Orleans. As one student put it: "Where else does law school close for Mardi Gras?"

ADMISSIONS

Tulane's applicant pool has been on the rise in recent years, and today about 3,000 applicants vie to be among the 300 seats in the incoming class. Having its applicant pool more than double in the past several years, Tulane Law School is now much more selective than average in terms of both its acceptance rate and the numerical standards to which it holds its applicants. But do consider that 20 percent of the places in each class are reserved for "special admission students" whose predictors of success may be less objective than those of other applicants.

ACADEMICS	
Student/faculty ratio	20:1
% female faculty	24
% minority faculty	12
Hours of study per day	3.60

FINANCIAL FACTS	
Tuition	$22,076
Part-time tuition per credit	NR
Estimated books/expenses/fees	NR
On-campus living expenses	$6,920
Off-campus living expenses	NR
% first-year students receiving aid	NR
% all students receiving aid	NR
% aid that is merit-based	NR
% all students receiving grants/scholarships	36
% all students receiving loans	77
% all students receiving assistantships	NR
Average award package	$5,500
Average graduation debt	$60,850

ADMISSIONS	
# applications received	4,051
% applicants accepted	43
% acceptees attending	19
Average LSAT	158
Average undergrad GPA	3.24
Application Fee	$45
No early decision program	
Regular application deadline	August 10
Regular notification	rolling
Admission may be deferred?	no
Gourman Report Rating	4.42

UNIVERSITY OF TULSA
College of Law

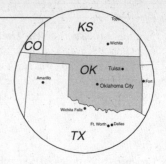

OVERVIEW

Type of school	private
Environment	metropolis
Scholastic calendar	semester
Schedule	Full-time or part-time

STUDENTS

Enrollment of institution	2,699
Enrollment of law school	628
% male/female	62/38
% out-of-state	64
% part-time	30
% minorities	12
% international (# countries represented)	NR (NR)
Average age at entry	27

APPLICANTS ALSO LOOK AT

Oklahoma City University
University of Oklahoma
Texas Tech University
Southern Methodist University
University of Houston

SURVEY SAYS...

HITS
Studying
Sense of community
Faculty-student relations

MISSES
Socratic method

EMPLOYMENT PROFILE

% grads employed immediately	53
% grads employed within six months	84
Average starting salary	$36,000
% grads employed by field:	
Private practice	55
Business/industry	22
Government	10
Judicial clerkships	3
Public service	0
Academic	10
Military	3

The University of Tulsa College of Law traces its roots back to 1923 when a group of attorneys founded the Tulsa Law School. In those early days the school was housed in the city's courthouse and classes were taught in the evening after the faculty, all practicing attorneys, had finished a long day of work. An equally dedicated and knowledgeable faculty administers classes today at this midsize private law school, located about three miles from downtown Tulsa, a city of 700,000. In its geography and climate—temperate and quite lush—Tulsa may not fit many outsiders' image of Oklahoma as hot, flat, and dry. In many important aspects, however, the TU law school is distinctly Oklahoman, and the majority of students (64 percent) come from Oklahoma and its neighboring states, though the remaining 36 percent of the student body represents almost all other states.

The course offerings at the University of Tulsa College of Law reflect the continuing regional importance of two subjects: oil and Native Americans. The campus is home to the National Energy/ Environmental Law and Policy Institute (NELPI) and to one of the nation's largest collections of materials relating to American Indian law and history. The significant resources of NELPI, a national center for energy policy research, are at the disposal of TU law students who choose to pursue a concentration in energy law and policy. Students at Tulsa may also earn a Certificate in American Indian law, an appropriate option in a city that is second only to the Navaho reservation in Native American population. The curriculum at TU isn't limited to regional concerns, though; students may also pursue certificates in dispute resolution; comparative and international law; public policy and regulation; and health law.

An overwhelming majority of students praised the faculty, describing them as "knowledgeable," and "down to earth." Students claimed that professors are there for them in every way, from classroom instruction and career guidance to just plain socializing. "One of the greatest strengths of TU is the faculty. Not only are they extremely versed in their respective fields, but they are also truly interested in teaching us how to be good lawyers," said a 1L. Apparently, their efforts pay off in the school's high

3120 East Fourth Place, Tulsa, OK 74104
Tel: (918) 631-2709
eMail: Law_VLS@Centum.UTulsa.edu
Internet: http://www.UTulsa.edu/

University of Tulsa

bar–passage rate. Another student emphatically agreed with the 1L just quoted: "The faculty is the most open and honest I have ever dealt with." Unlike students at many law schools who feel alienated by the administration, students at Tulsa spoke highly of their new Dean, who, they said, is working hard to make improvements.

Students at Tulsa University reported minor complaints about the poor facilities (particularly a lack of up-to-date computers), although they also said that renovations will be underway soon. The major criticism cited by many students at the school may not be so easily fixed: the polarized political atmosphere. One student, who certainly did not represent the majority of Tulsa students, put it like this: "TU is an extremely harsh environment for women and minorities, particularly those who do not buy into the Bible-belt conservatism so prevalent here. Liberal thinkers will not find this a comfortable place at all." Whether this comment reflects more the student's own political views than the views of many is not clear, but this 2L was not alone. Another student, a 1L, warned: "Tulsa is extremely conservative and extremely homogenous. If you find diversity frightening, you'll like TU." Students' comments regarding the school's racial and ethnic diversity—or what they often described as a lack thereof— were quite common. Given the school's low proportion of minority students and faculty, about 12 and 17 percent respectively, these complaints are not surprising. At the same time, the administration reminded us that "the law faculty was referred to as 'liberal' in last year's edition" of this book, and that they have a high percentage of women faculty. But all of this could be inconsequential if you are more concerned with the quality of your education—an area Tulsa students seem quite satisfied with—rather than a prospective school's political climate.

ADMISSIONS

Between 1991 and 1993, the University of Tulsa College of Law reported a nearly 80 percent surge in applications volume. This dramatic jump would seem to indicate that admissions selectivity will very soon be on the rise here. As it stands now, however, Tulsa holds its applicants to lower numerical standards than do 85 percent of the law schools profiled in this book.

ACADEMICS

Student/faculty ratio	17:1
% female faculty	25
% minority faculty	17
Hours of study per day	4.45

FINANCIAL FACTS

Tuition	$14,700
Part-time tuition per credit	$9,800
Estimated books/expenses/fees	$1,280
On-campus living expenses	NR
Off-campus living expenses	NR
% first-year students receiving aid	96
% all students receiving aid	97
% aid that is merit-based	25
% all students receiving grants/scholarships	26
% all students receiving loans	90
% all students receiving assistantships	6
Average award package	$5,000
Average graduation debt	$52,624

ADMISSIONS

# applications received	1,461
% applicants accepted	45
% acceptees attending	33
Average LSAT	153
Average undergrad GPA	2.84
Application Fee	$30
No early decision program	
Regular application deadline	February 1
Regular notification	rolling
Admission may be deferred?	No
Gourman Report Rating	3.21

ALBANY LAW SCHOOL OF UNION UNIVERSITY

Albany Law School, an autonomous part of Union University, has served the upstate New York region continuously since 1851. The law school is the fourth oldest in the country, and its graduates have been prominent figures in state and national politics. Today it is a midsize school with moderate admissions standards and a solid regional reputation. The overwhelming majority of its students remain in New York after graduation. The bulk of the Albany Law School's facilities are housed in an imposing Tudor Gothic main building, but the tree-filled campus also includes a recently constructed modern library notable for its open, airy design.

Located, appropriately enough, in beautiful Albany, the capital of New York State and the setting for the novels of William Kennedy, the law school draws heavily on the city's resources. The proximity of both the state legislature and the Court of Appeals, the state's highest court, make possible significant exposure to and participation in the workings of government by Albany law students. The school's Government Law Center encourages such participation through its sponsorship of symposia and other activities focusing on a broad range of issues relating to all branches and levels of government. These and numerous other co-curricular opportunities available to students at Albany are supplemented by an impressive range of clinical programs, including one of the country's few law-student clinics dedicated to AIDS law.

Albany students are a relatively happy group, satisfied with the fundamental academic quality of their chosen school. Above all, students here praise the general lack of unhealthy competitiveness. "The work is intense," said one, "but the atmosphere is comfortable and non-competitive." Most of those who expressed such sentiments also agreed on where to give due credit: "Our young faculty is excellent, reported one student, "and because of the small size of our classes, they offer us a great degree of personal attention." Others praised the general quality of life: "I am extremely pleased with my decision to come here. Albany Law School can actually be fun and painless."

Dawn M. Chamberlaine, Assistant Dean of Admissions and Financial Aid
80 New Scotland Avenue, Albany, NY 12208
Tel: (518) 445-2326
eMail: postmaster@mail.als.edu

Albany Law School of Union University

The complaint most commonly voiced by Albany students had nothing to do with their experience at the law school per se, but, rather, with their prospects for employment after graduation. It must be noted, however, that these frustrations were expressed without a hint of anger toward those in charge of job placement. "The career planning center is very helpful," went one typical comment, "but their resources and contacts seem to be extremely limited." The concern that "[Albany students] really need better downstate job recruitment and placement" was very widely held.

Of course some students expressed little desire to break out of their immediate surroundings. As one put it, "Albany is a great city, and don't let anyone tell you otherwise." On balance, Albany students seem to be a relatively satisfied group, particularly when it comes to such fundamentals as the quality of their law school's curriculum.

ADMISSIONS

In terms of its numerical admissions standards, the Albany Law School ranks almost exactly in the middle of all U.S. law schools. This and the fact that Albany selects its students from a large applicant pool would seem to indicate a relatively high degree of admissions selectivity, but the law school's very generous overall acceptance rate indicates otherwise.

ACADEMICS

Student/faculty ratio	26:1
% female faculty	42
% minority faculty	22
Hours of study per day	4.03

FINANCIAL FACTS

Tuition	$17,995
Part-time tuition per credit	$13,500
Estimated books/expenses/fees	$655
On-campus living expenses	$4,500
Off-campus living expenses	$5,820
% first-year students receiving aid	85
% all students receiving aid	87
% aid that is merit-based	12
% all students receiving grants/scholarships	43
% all students receiving loans	83
% all students receiving assistantships	4
Average award package	$5,600
Average graduation debt	$60,000

ADMISSIONS

# applications received	1,705
% applicants accepted	53
% acceptees attending	28
Average LSAT	153
Average undergrad GPA	3.12
Application Fee	$50
No early decision program	
Regular application deadline	March 15
Regular notification	rolling
Admission deferment	one year

Gourman Report Rating	**4.35**

UNIVERSITY OF UTAH
College of Law

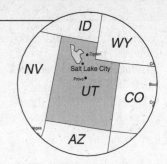

Located on the 25,000-student Salt Lake City campus of one of the most respected teaching and research universities in the nation, the tiny College of Law at the University of Utah ("The U" in local vernacular) is no less esteemed than its parent institution. Utah's only public law school enjoys a long-established reputation for excellence in the Mountain West, but the strength of its faculty and the qualifications of its students have also earned it recognition as one of the finest state-supported law schools in the nation. While dozens of schools offer programs of comparable or higher academic solidity, few do so on such an intimate scale and at such a moderate price. With fewer than 400 exceptionally well-qualified students in its J.D. and graduate law programs and a relatively large complement of full-time teaching faculty, Utah boasts a tremendously favorable student-faculty ratio, and with an incredibly low resident tuition rate, it can easily claim true bargain status.

The curriculum at Utah was revamped several years ago, in an effort to combat the drift that often characterizes the last two years of law school. Taking its imagery from architecture, Utah has organized its course offerings in three categories, corresponding with the three years of the J.D. program: Foundation courses, Cornerstone courses, and Capstone courses. As the terms would imply, the law school envisions its three years as integrated parts that build upon one another, from standard, case-method courses in the first year—"Foundation courses"—to small, specialized research seminars in the third—"Capstone" courses. Substantively, this reorganization may not mean much, but, at the very least, it has imposed some sense of direction.

On the whole, Utah students come across as some of the more contented in the nation. Though nearly all had words of praise for the substance of the program itself, the deep and fundamental satisfaction of most Utah students appears to derive as much from the relations with faculty and colleagues as from anything else. When asked to explain the reason for the quality of these relations, most point to the school's size. "Because each entering class has only about 130 students," wrote one 2L, "the level of student involvement in all areas is high and there is a strong collegial atmosphere between students and faculty." Nearly all of those we heard from expressed nearly identical sentiments. "We have a really good student-teacher ratio and our professors are excellent and approachable," said one, "and though students are very competitive, there are no cutthroat a**holes here." Faculty accessibility, of course, means little in and of itself. Utah students, however, gave the quality of their faculty's teaching an outstanding rating. "I chose to come to 'the U' from out of state, never having been to Utah," wrote one 3L, "and I have been very pleased with the quality of the education and the great variety of recreational experiences." (Indeed, recreational activities abound · in the surrounding Wasatch Mountains; the law school's bulletin begins and ends, in fact, not with photos of law students but photos of skiers.)

When asked to name areas in which the school could improve, few Utah students offered much criticism of the academic program itself. Those who did voiced the lament common among students at such small schools. "I'd like to see a broader range of courses offered and more opportunity for specialization," went one typical remark from a 2L. Others criticized the school's career placement office for its narrow geographical focus. "The law school does not work hard enough," claimed one, "at finding out-of-state placements." The school's minority percentage is roughly akin to the ethnic makeup of Utah, possibly explaining the numerous complaints concerning the law school's relative lack of ethnic diversity. As one 3L put it: "This is a great place to hang out with people just like you—assuming you're white and Mormon."

ADMISSIONS

As it does for all of the country's top public law schools, a combination of excellence and affordability puts the University of Utah College of Law in a position to be tremendously selective in its admissions process. Indeed, the rising numerical standards to which Utah holds applicants now rank it among the 25 most selective law schools in the nation.

ACADEMICS

Student/faculty ratio	13:1
% female faculty	35
% minority faculty	15
Hours of study per day	3.80

FINANCIAL FACTS

In-state tuition	$4,084
Out-of-state tuition	$9,682
Part-time tuition per credit	NR
Estimated books/expenses/fees	$1,450
On-campus living expenses	NR
Off-campus living expenses	NR
% first-year students receiving aid	80
% all students receiving aid	NR
% aid that is merit-based	10
% all students receiving grants/scholarships	50
% all students receiving loans	75
% all students receiving assistantships	NR
Average award package	$13,700
Average graduation debt	$30,000

ADMISSIONS

# applications received	920
% applicants accepted	32
% acceptees attending	43
Average LSAT	161
Average undergrad GPA	3.56
Application Fee	$50
Priority application deadline	NR
Priority notification	NR
Regular application deadline	February 1
Regular notification	rolling
Admission deferment	case by case
Gourman Report Rating	4.40

VALPARAISO UNIVERSITY 💾
School of Law

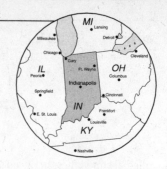

The Valparaiso (val-pa-RAY-zo) School of Law is the smallest of Indiana's four law schools and the only Lutheran-affiliated law school in the country. Located in the extreme northern part of Indiana, minutes away from Lake Michigan, Valparaiso draws a sizable proportion of its students from and sends a substantial number of its graduates to the major population centers of Illinois.

Like most small schools, Valparaiso has a curriculum that is only modestly broad. It is, however, remarkably balanced. In keeping with its stated goal of serving the student first and foremost, however, Valparaiso has decided that its relatively limited resources should not limit the range of experiences available to its students. Unlike many larger law schools, Valparaiso operates an in-house legal clinic that, while small, is an integral part of its stated effort to balance academic preparation for law practice with training in practical skills. The Valparaiso J.D. curriculum is traditional up to a point: First-year requirements are standard, and upper-year requirements are few. Those upper-year requirements that do exist, however, go beyond the standard Constitutional law and the universal professional responsibility courses to include a jurisprudence (or legal philosophy) course and, most notably, a pro-bono requirement, in place since 1989. This requirement is modest (only 20 hours), but admirable for its relative rarity. Applications volume at the law school is not particularly high, and a hefty percentage of all applicants are admitted annually. Accordingly, numerical admissions standards are moderate.

Students at Valparaiso are remarkably consistent in their assessments—positive and negative—of their chosen school. On the basis of the comments we heard, their criticisms, though serious, do not outweigh their praise. Asked to name the law school's greatest strengths, most pointed first to their faculty and to the quality of the traditional curriculum they administer. "Valparaiso is a very humane place in which to learn the law," said one 2L. "The first-year curriculum in particular is superbly taught by many of the school's best professors, most of whom are very warm and very accessible to their students." Most students also

Anne Levinson Penway, Director, Admissions and Student Relations
Wesemann Hall, Valparaiso, IN 46383
Tel: (219) 465-7829   Fax: (219) 465-7872
eMail: valpolaw@wesemann.law.valpo.edu
Internet: http://www.valpo.edu/law/

Valparaiso University

had kind words for their colleagues. "Students here manage to maintain an ability to smile and be friendly toward one another," reported one. "Academically it's very challenging," added another, "but the faculty and my fellow students have made the road to a law degree a little easier through their support and encouragement." Much more notably, Valparaiso students expressed widespread and sincere praise for their placement office, so often the object of scorn at other law schools. "The career services staff is excellent!!!" enthused one 2L, exclamation points and all. "They will do anything to help." Specifically, most who offered such praise commended the placement office for its success in finding them school-year externships.

On the other hand, few Valparaiso students had any difficulty naming areas in which the law school could stand to improve. By and large, their criticisms focused not on the quality of any of the school's programs but, rather, on their limited quantity and variety. "In my opinion," wrote one 3L, "class offerings are inadequate, and there are definitely not enough clinical opportunities." This precise sentiment was echoed many times over by the Valparaiso students we heard from: "We need the opportunity to gain more practical skills," said one. "The existing clinical programs are good, but they are far too difficult to get into." Other criticisms were similarly evenhanded: "Career placement personnel are generally quite good," said one 3L, "but they should try to improve their services in terms of the Chicago job market." On balance, the criticisms from Valparaiso students are hardly surprising given the law school's size. And though most wished for greater academic variety, it must be reiterated that few had anything negative to say about the school's existing offerings.

ADMISSIONS

In terms of the numerical standards to which it holds applicants, the Valparaiso University School of Law ranks slightly lower than average among all U.S. law schools. Hopeful applicants' prospects of gaining admission here are made even better, however, by Valparaiso's generous overall acceptance rate. Half of all candidates considered are offered admission.

ACADEMICS

Student/faculty ratio	21:1
% female faculty	28
% minority faculty	9
Hours of study per day	4.48

FINANCIAL FACTS

Tuition	$15,660
Part-time tuition per credit	$585
Estimated books/expenses/fees	NR
On-campus living expenses	NR
Off-campus living expenses	$13,950
% first-year students receiving aid	90
% all students receiving aid	80
% aid that is merit-based	NR
% all students receiving grants/scholarships	49
% all students receiving loans	81
% all students receiving assistantships	11
Average award package	NR
Average graduation debt	NR

ADMISSIONS

# applications received	945
% applicants accepted	50
% acceptees attending	34
Average LSAT	152
Average undergrad GPA	3.21
Application Fee	$30
No early decision program	
Regular application deadline	April 15
Regular notification	rolling
Admission deferment	one year
Gourman Report Rating	**3.60**

VANDERBILT UNIVERSITY 💾
School of Law

Ask the average American to name a major attraction in Nashville, the city synonymous with country music, and she will probably come up with the Grand Ole Opry. Ask the average American lawyer the same question, and he will almost certainly answer with the name of Tennessee's largest and most highly esteemed law school: the Vanderbilt University School of Law. This relatively small private law school has long enjoyed an outsized reputation. Located hundreds of miles from the closest major legal-job market, Vanderbilt is nonetheless recognized from coast to coast as one of the finest law schools in the nation. Its high admissions standards, the notable geographical diversity of its student body and the tremendous success of its graduates at landing good jobs make this fact perfectly clear.

Vanderbilt's reputation in the legal community derives in large part from its highly respected faculty, whose teaching abilities are touted by the law school as often as their scholarly achievements. Quite apart from its apparent quality, Vanderbilt's faculty is large enough to give the school a favorable student-teacher ratio.

The curriculum they administer is broadly traditional: Requirements are few, co-curricular activities many, and Vandy's diverse course offerings are richest in the broader area of business and commercial law. If curricular innovation is what you're looking for, you might look elsewhere. The curriculum here is relatively lacking in clinical programs and practical-skills courses. For sheer academic strength within a traditional mold, however, Vanderbilt cannot be overlooked.

Nor will the nation overlook Vandy, if current students have their say. Nearly all the students we heard from actually love going to law school, and some who chose Vandy over top ten schools gave us these raves: "Vanderbilt has moved beyond gauging itself against the ill-defined and 'moving target' standards of national rankings. Vandy is Vandy, and the identity, tradition of excellence and comfortable Nashville lifestyle is truly unique...not only in the South, but across the nation." "If you don't like law school at Vandy, you just don't like law school...I think our greatest strength is the collegial atmosphere here—people are incredibly bright, motivated (as at other law schools) but they're

Anne Brandt, Assistant Dean
21st Avenue South and Grand, Nashville, TN 37240
Tel: (615) 322-6452
eMail: sascott@law.vanderbilt.edu

Vanderbilt University

also friendly and positive. The same for the faculty—VERY approachable and accessible." Even the career placement office was heralded (although by no means universally). Many students praised the faculty and the excellent courses of "meat and potatoes law" served here.

On the non-scholastic front, Vandy helps bind the ties between students through sponsorship of certain social activities. As one 3L said (with some hyperbole, we imagine), "The weekly Blackacre parties often become drunken riots. I've seen people swinging on tree limbs and place kicking beer cans. Professors and administrators sometimes come. When they do, they seem to get into the spirit of things." He also told us that law students themselves devise getaways from the library: "Road-tripping is a common activity. Chicago, New Orleans, Memphis, and nearby SEC football games are frequent destinations."

Of course, despite the good time to be had, Vandy students have their share of gripes. One student, like others, was dissatisfied with "the clinic courses and the recruitment/placement office which focuses totally on corporate work. Vanderbilt is a lonely place for those interested in public interest work." Most students are happy with this direction, however. Our returned surveys contained a common cry for a broader range of classes, more diversity within the student body and faculty, lower tuition, and the eradication of the grading curve. The most common complaints followed this vein: "The law school building is a great example of a bad period in American architectural experimentation. It's a box," said one 3L. But a 1L put this aesthetic obsession into perspective: "People focus on the physical building because there is nothing else to complain about here."

ADMISSIONS

Though an overall acceptance rate of 24 percent is hardly generous, the Vanderbilt University School of Law admits more applicants relative to its size than do most of the nation's elite schools. More than three candidates are admitted for every spot in the law school's entering class of about 190. The good news—such as it is—for hopeful applicants stops there. In terms of the numerical standards to which it holds applicants, Vandy ranks thirteenth among the nation's law schools.

ACADEMICS	
Student/faculty ratio	18:1
% female faculty	22
% minority faculty	16
Hours of study per day	3.71

FINANCIAL FACTS	
Tuition	$19,750
Part-time tuition per credit	NR
Estimated books/expenses/fees	NR
On-campus living expenses	NR
Off-campus living expenses	NR
% first-year students receiving aid	80
% all students receiving aid	80
% aid that is merit-based	1
% all students receiving grants/scholarships	43
% all students receiving loans	80
% all students receiving assistantships	NR
Average award package	NR
Average graduation debt	NR

ADMISSIONS	
# applications received	2,528
% applicants accepted	24
% acceptees attending	30
Average LSAT	163
Average undergrad GPA	3.63
Application Fee	$50
No early decision program	
Regular application deadline	February 1
Regular notification	April 1
Admission deferment	two years
Gourman Report Rating	4.71

VERMONT LAW SCHOOL
Vermont Law School

Tucked away in Vermont's Green Mountains, in a village that looks as if it were designed by the Vermont Tourist and Visitors Bureau, sits the smallest and youngest private law school in New England and the only law school in the state of Vermont. In a region that reveres tradition, the upstart Vermont Law School has managed in just over 20 years to carve out a solid regional reputation and establish itself as one of the leaders in environmental-law education. In fact, for the sixth consecutive year, VLS's environmental law specialty was ranked one of the best in the country by a survey of law schools' environmental law faculties.

Vermont Law School's traditional core curriculum is supplemented with experiential programs such as its top-notch environmental law program. The school's Environmental Law Center, where students can pursue a joint Master of Studies in Environmental Law and Juris Doctor degrees or attend the school's summer session, open to both students and professionals, provides an interdisciplinary program of studies in environmental law and policy. Housed in its own building on the law school campus, the Center offers a broad array of courses on topics ranging from Global Impact of Energy Use to Water Resources.

The law school also offers several other notable innovative programs. In the General Practice Program, a limited number of students spend their second and third years working in a simulated law firm in addition to the library. Students may also participate in the Semester in Practice clinic, in which the classroom is abandoned for a semester of intensive field work. Students interested in government can take advantage of an internship in the Vermont General Assembly through the school's Legislation Clinic, or a fifteen-week stint in Washington, D.C., in the Environmental Semester in Washington Program.

All of these opportunities are not lost on students at Vermont, who cite the environmental law specialty and other progressive programs as the school's greatest strength. "The environmental law program is top-notch and the curriculum stresses other avenues for resolving disputes besides litigation," said a 1L. Another student, a 3L, said: "If you want to learn the mentality of

Chelsea Street, South Royalton, VT 05068
Tel: (800) 227-1395   Fax: (802) 763-7071
eMail: admiss@vermont.law.edu
Internet: www.vermontlaw.edu

Vermont Law School

the Washington environmentalists, this is the place." But, as this student also noted: "[Vermont's] strength is also its greatest weakness...the school is dominated by the Washington environmentalist mentality, and there is little room for anything else at this small school. "

Students used terms like "laid back" and "low-stress" to describe the atmosphere at the school. "The greatest strength of VLS has to be the community spirit, including the warmth, honesty, and accessibility of the faculty and administration," said one 2L. Perhaps this congeniality among students extends from the school's home, the small town of South Royalton, and the area's breathtaking scenery. But, as a couple of students noted, Vermont is not for everyone. "The quaintness of South Royalton could drive someone who grew up in a large city absolutely stir crazy..."said a 1L. Though the school's remote New England location might contribute to the lack of diversity among the student body and faculty, most students at Vermont have fallen in love with their physical surroundings, and an outdoorsy spirit pervades the school—hardly surprising given its environmental bent.

ADMISSIONS

In a short time, this young law school has become quite sought after, and by all indications Vermont Law School will continue to draw a large number of applicants who want to spend three years in Vermont's picturesque Green Mountains. About ten applicants now vie for each place in Vermont's entering class of 160 students, so overall selectivity is relatively high. Numerical admission standards, however, have remained moderate.

ACADEMICS

Student/faculty ratio	14:1
% female faculty	45
% minority faculty	7
Hours of study per day	4.20

FINANCIAL FACTS

Tuition	$17,950
Part-time tuition per credit	NR
Estimated books/expenses/fees	$855
On-campus living expenses	NR
Off-campus living expenses	$11,075
% first-year students receiving aid	85
% all students receiving aid	86
% aid that is merit-based	NR
% all students receiving grants/scholarships	80
% all students receiving loans	89
% all students receiving assistantships	NR
Average award package	$27,950
Average graduation debt	$66,000

ADMISSIONS

# applications received	1,669
% applicants accepted	51
% acceptees attending	19
Average LSAT	156
Average undergrad GPA	3.09
Application Fee	$60
No early decision program	
Regular application deadline	February 15
Regular notification	mid-April
Admission deferment	1 year
Gourman Report Rating	2.51

VILLANOVA UNIVERSITY
School of Law

The youngest and—by a slim margin—the smallest of the three fine law schools in the greater Philadelphia area, the Villanova University School of Law is a highly respected midsize, Catholic institution. Located in the decidedly non-urban Main Line suburb from which it takes its name, Villanova is only about a half-hour's train ride from downtown Philadelphia. It is there, in the nation's fifth-largest legal-job market, that the law school's reputation is strongest. This reputation was built, in part, on the strength of the law school's highly successful graduates. These former students form a large and powerful alumni network that benefits current Villanova students greatly when it comes time to seek employment. The strength of this network is evident in the employment patterns of Villanova grads, a fairly large number of whom begin their legal careers in prestigious judicial clerkships.

The Villanova J.D. program is broadly traditional and quite strong, particularly in areas like taxation and commercial law. The law school is quite proud of its trial-advocacy program, and has started a new clinic, the Information Law and Policy Clinic, in an effort to broaden practical skills courses. Applications volume at the law school is only moderately heavy, but admissions standards are quite high. Entering Villanova students, the majority of whom come from within Pennsylvania, possess strong numerical credentials.

Neither enthusiastically positive nor exceedingly negative about their experience at Villanova, students express a moderate but solid degree of satisfaction with most aspects of their chosen school. About their fellow students and faculty, for instance, Villanova students are nearly unanimously positive. "The students are all very closely knit," reported one, "and the faculty and administration are always there for you." "The people make Villanova a top-notch school." Most students we heard from seemed pleased with the law school's "very relaxed atmosphere" and with its very large, very able faculty. "The student body is very friendly and faculty members are always around for questions," said one 2L, who also listed "ample parking" among her law school's greatest strengths. And, most seem pleased with their general surroundings. "The school itself is excellent," said one 2L, "and Philadelphia is becoming an increasingly happening city."

But few Villanova students had any difficulty naming areas in which the law school could stand to improve. For the most part, their criticisms stemmed from what seems to be the overriding concern of most students here: their professional futures. Some of their most common complaints, for instance, concerned the perceived lack of support from the career-services office for those students not at the top of their class. Many students commented unfavorably about the physical plant, though not all as harshly as this dissatisfied student: "the facilities are like a Junior High." It should be noted however, that since our survey, Villanova completed major renovations on the library, adding networked computers and study centers, which should brighten such dim perceptions of the school's facilities. Students at all levels lamented Villanova's grading policy, which many consider unfairly deflated.

More tangibly, a significant proportion of Villanova students voiced dissatisfaction with the relative lack of practical-skills courses in the law school's curriculum. "I would really like to see more clinical programs and a greater emphasis on legal writing and research," wrote one student. "We need greater opportunities to hone and develop these invaluable lawyering skills." Aside from some of these understandable but probably overstated concerns about their employment prospects in a tightening legal job market, however, most students at Villanova expressed fundamental satisfaction with their academic preparation for the practice of law.

ADMISSIONS

In terms of its numerical admissions standards, the Villanova University School of Law ranks forty-sixth overall among U.S. law schools. The prospects of the hopeful applicant to Villanova are made only a little bit brighter by the law school's relatively generous overall acceptance rate.

ACADEMICS	
Student/faculty ratio	15:1
% female faculty	25
% minority faculty	3
Hours of study per day	3.83

FINANCIAL FACTS	
Tuition	$16,400
Part-time tuition per credit	NR
Estimated books/expenses/fees	NR
On-campus living expenses	NR
Off-campus living expenses	NR
% first-year students receiving aid	NR
% all students receiving aid	NR
% aid that is merit-based	NR
% all students receiving grants/scholarships	NR
% all students receiving loans	NR
% all students receiving assistantships	NR
Average award package	NR
Average graduation debt	NR

ADMISSIONS	
# applications received	1,440
% applicants accepted	50
% acceptees attending	33
Average LSAT	158
Average undergrad GPA	3.45
Application Fee	$75
Priority application deadline	NR
Priority notification	NR
Regular application deadline	January 31
Regular notification	rolling
Admission deferment	NR
Gourman Report Rating	3.70

UNIVERSITY OF VIRGINIA 💾
School of Law

From its architectural heart—the famous Thomas Jefferson-designed quadrangle—to its ethical backbone—a student-monitored honor code that is taken very seriously—the University of Virginia is steeped in tradition. So, to a great extent, is its highly respected School of Law. On the strength of its staunchly traditional curriculum, the UVA law school enjoys a reputation as one of the finest in the nation. On the strength of the students' enthusiasm for the quality of its academic environment, it also ranks highly in more subjective terms.

Academically, the J.D. program at Virginia is as strong as they come. After the first semester of their first year, students here have near-total control over their course of study, and with around 100 courses to choose from every semester, their options are many. Like many "first-tier" law schools, Virginia has remained focused on more theoretical aspects of the law. Amid rising criticism over the lack of practical experience, however, the school has begun offering limited clinical settings through its newly-established Principles and Practice Program. The quality of the school's historically non-pragmatic instruction, though, cannot be questioned. UVA's faculty is both highly-esteemed and well-liked, and the classroom atmosphere they foster is, by all accounts, friendly and productive. With a curve that puts 80 percent of students in the "B" range and only 10 percent at either extreme, Virginia students have little reason to compete in any unhealthy way.

The relative lack of competition creates a "laid-back" and "collegial" atmosphere that garnered rave reviews from students we surveyed. In fact, UVA is unique in the nearly unanimous level of complete satisfaction among its students. Even those who had specific gripes with the school said that they could not imagine studying elsewhere. "UVA is a law student's dream! Many will graduate saying their three years here was the best time of their lives," said one 3L, and added, "This truly is a place of cooperation and teamwork." Another student, a 1L, dubbed UVA "the most relaxed school in the nation."

The school's "softball and beer" image, however, is not the whole story, reported students. (The school does, however, support

Albert R. Turnbull, Associate Dean for Admissions and Placement
580 Massie Road, Charlottesville, VA 22903-1789
Tel: (804) 929-7351
Internet: http://www.virginia.edu/~law/home.html

University of Virginia

student relaxation through an active intramural softball league, and a free keg of beer is supplied every Thursday afternoon.) But do not be mistaken: UVA is a law school for serious students. "Yes, we play a lot of softball, and yes, we drink a lot of beer, but we also study a lot. It's really a work hard, play hard situation," said a 1L. Students provided equal praise for the faculty, who one student described as "an absolutely phenomenal cast of distinguished scholars."

Virginia students aren't without ideas for how their school could improve. Many cited the need for more clinical programs and said that because of high demand it is very difficult to gain admittance to the seven that presently exist. Even those who rated UVA's curriculum highly suggested that a more diverse selection of courses needs to be offered. "The law school needs to recognize a broader range of theories besides law and economics," said one 3L. One student, a 2L, who said UVA needs to realize that "corporate law is not the only kind there is," suggested that more environmental law courses and joint-degree programs be offered. Despite these comments, according to the administration, the school has a deservedly strong reputation for interdisciplinary work. There are 11 joint degree programs and many of the faculty have degrees in other disciplines.

Another complaint waged against UVA pertained the school's facilities which were described as "poor" and "crowded." Word has it, though, that a new building and computer lab are under construction and will have opened by August 1996. Overall, these faults did not weigh heavily in the analyses of most UVA students, whose extraordinary sense of well-being was summed up neatly by this remark from a 3L: "[UVA] is probably the only school where some students would sign up for a fourth year."

ADMISSIONS

UVA has recently been ranked by a national magazine as among the top ten most selective law schools in the country. In terms of both numerical standards and application volume, the hopeful applicant to Virginia faces the stiffest possible competition. About the only sure ticket into this world-class law school is to be a Virginia resident with more than stellar numerical credentials.

ACADEMICS	
Student/faculty ratio	19:1
% female faculty	20
% minority faculty	11
Hours of study per day	3.20

FINANCIAL FACTS	
In-state tuition	$12,030
Out-of-state tuition	$19,178
Part-time tuition per credit	NR
Estimated books/expenses/fees	NR
On-campus living expenses	NR
Off-campus living expenses	NR
% first-year students receiving aid	100
% all students receiving aid	100
% aid that is merit-based	NR
% all students receiving grants/scholarships	45
% all students receiving loans	67
% all students receiving assistantships	NR
Average award package	$6,300
Average graduation debt	NR

ADMISSIONS	
# applications received	4,101
% applicants accepted	22
% acceptees attending	41
Average LSAT	165
Average undergrad GPA	3.60
Application Fee	$40
No early decision program	
Regular application deadline	January 15
Regular notification	April 15
Admission deferment	NR
Gourman Report Rating	4.72

WAKE FOREST UNIVERSITY
School of Law

In its 99th year, 1993, Wake Forest University School of Law, a highly esteemed private law school in Winston-Salem, North Carolina, fulfilled its commitments to fully integrate the disciplines of law and management and to maintain technologically state-of-the-art facilities, when it opened the Worrell Professional Center for Law and Management, a new building it shares with Babcock, Wake Forest's graduate business school.

As one might expect, this effort also translated to a curricular focus on business and commercial law within the law school itself. Indeed, the Wake Forest curriculum is particularly rich in such offerings, and the majority of the school's graduates pursue careers in private practice. With fewer than 500 total students, the law school has an additional strength: one of the most favorable student-faculty ratios in the nation. Wake Forest may only be the third law school people think of when they think of North Carolina, but in a small state fairly bursting at the seams with fine law schools and able law students, this is nothing to sneeze at. This widely respected law school draws from a highly qualified, geographically diverse applicant pool, and its admissions standards are nearly as high and its acceptance rates nearly as low as those at North Carolina's better-known public law school in Chapel Hill.

Those who make it through Wake Forest's increasingly competitive admissions process and actually go on to enroll speak clearly and consistently when asked to name the greatest strengths of their chosen school. "The academic atmosphere is very friendly," said one 3L. "Classes are small," he continued, "the faculty seem to care about students and are primarily interested in teaching, and there is a good spirit of academic cooperation among students." These sentiments were voiced almost unanimously by other students we heard from. "Wake has its share of cutthroat students," reported one, "but the majority of us work together, play together and generally support one another...This has made these three years more enjoyable." One 1L offered this simple assessment: "I am very happy in law school, which I think says a lot about Wake Forest. Most of the students I know in other law schools are miserable." Not to say that students here had nothing

Melanie E. Nutt, Director of Admissions and Financial Aid
P.O. Box 7206, Winston-Salem, NC 27109
Tel: (910) 759-5437
eMail: admissions@law.wfu.edu
Internet: http://www.wfu.edu

Wake Forest University

more substantive to say about the law school, but lifestyle issues (e.g., "wide availability of afternoon kegs") dominated their remarks: "Wake Forest provides a great education in a down-to-earth, relaxed atmosphere without wasting energy attempting to be pretentious or overly uptight," wrote one contented 3L building to this punch line: "That is to say, without trying to be Duke."

When asked to name areas in which the law school could stand to improve, many Wake Forest students sounded a similar theme. "Wake Forest is a fine place if you want to stay in North Carolina," wrote a 1L who apparently doesn't, "but if you want to go anywhere else, then go anywhere else but here." Few were quite as negative as that, but many did offer similar remarks. Others complained about the school's placement office on two grounds. Said one critical 2L: "Placement is only useful for the top 30 percent of the class, and then only if you want to practice in a traditional corporate law firm." The latter of these two points was made with some frequency by the students we heard from. On balance, however, few seemed to consider these perceived shortcomings serious enough to detract from Wake Forest's overall strengths.

ADMISSIONS

As popular as the Wake Forest University School of Law is with its current students, it is even more popular with prospective students. Over 1,600 applicants vie annually to be among the roughly 160 students in Wake Forest's first-year class, so competition is fierce and selectivity high. In fact, Wake Forest ranks among the 50 most selective law schools in the nation in terms of the numerical standards to which it holds applicants.

ACADEMICS

Student/faculty ratio	16:1
% female faculty	28
% minority faculty	14
Hours of study per day	3.71

FINANCIAL FACTS

Tuition	$16,600
Part-time tuition per credit	NR
Estimated books/expenses/fees	NR
On-campus living expenses	NR
Off-campus living expenses	NR
% first-year students receiving aid	18
% all students receiving aid	20
% aid that is merit-based	20
% all students receiving grants/scholarships	20
% all students receiving loans	80
% all students receiving assistantships	15
Average award package	$8,600
Average graduation debt	$43,000

ADMISSIONS

# applications received	1,600
% applicants accepted	31
% acceptees attending	29
Average LSAT	160
Average undergrad GPA	3.28
Application Fee	$50
No early decision program	
Regular application deadline	March 15
Regular notification	rolling
Admission may be deferred?	no

Gourman Report Rating	3.14

WASHBURN UNIVERSITY
School of Law

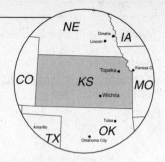

What is it about disastrous Kansas tornadoes that always seems to foster such a sense of renewal? Without even having to dodge flying monkeys or meet the great Oz, the Washburn University School of Law found out that there's no place like a new home after a tornado destroyed its old quarters in 1966. The law school's new building, completed in 1968 and expanded in 1991, comfortably houses Washburn's more than 400 J.D. students, 50 percent of whom also work next door in the school's legal clinic. This high degree of participation reflects Washburn's long-standing and ongoing commitment to legal education outside the traditional classroom setting.

Washburn grads come primarily from Kansas and nearby Missouri, and a healthy number of them choose careers in government. This is not surprising considering that the institutions and resources of the state capital play such a significant role in the education of students at Washburn. They have free and easy access, for instance, to the 200,000-volume library of the nearby Kansas State Supreme Court (on which, incidentally, Washburn grads hold the majority). Washburn is a municipal university, which is partially funded by the state. Nonresidents pay a bit more tuition than in-state residents. The low, low price and access to such great library and computer facilities, not to mention the clinic about which so many students raved, comprise the main draws for current Washburn students.

Many people attributed their decision to attend Washburn to what one termed the "family-like selfless attitude of both the faculty and the students." Most students praised the faculty's and administration's open-door policy. As one 2L put it, Washburn possesses an "excellent faculty. No matter how gruff or cantankerous a professor is in class, they are all very accessible after class." Or as another 2L said in an even more backhanded effort to praise, "The quality of education is incredible given the low ranking of the law school." Not only do the students love the professors and the Dean, who all apparently make every effort to deserve such devotion, they also love one another, at least those others who share the same political/social views. Indeed, one slightly left-out Washburn student rated the sense of community among students as remarkably high, but only if you happen to fit the conservative mold.

Reading through the student surveys, one feels a surreal sense that perhaps there are really two Washburns. Some students characterized Washburn's faculty as too diverse and stridently liberal, making life rough for themselves and fellow conservatives, and yet another said major improvement in "diversity of faculty and interpersonal communication between some students and faculty" is needed because "it is very easy to be considered invisible and inconsequential in some areas." One 2L shed some light on the confusion when he mused, "Who would have thought—two out lesbian law professors in Topeka, Kansas. The climate (political) is great at Washburn for liberals, so why so many conservative students?"

Some uniformity prevails in certain more tangible gripes, however. Although many students praised the existing clinic, the majority called for additional legal writing and practical skills courses. More than one person mentioned the need for better snow removal. And quite a few remarked upon the decrepit state of the library copiers. Not to disregard the importance of an abundant supply of quality copy machinery, but many students at less architecturally up-to-date schools dream of the day when the only problem they can find with their facilities is one so easily attended to. (Incidentally, the library copiers have been fixed since our survey.)

One thing most Washburn students shared with law students nearly everywhere is concern for their future. Although the career placement office, the usual butt of such anxiety, received extraordinarily positive remarks for their care and attention, many people expressed some doubt that they would indeed find that desired job upon graduation. However, with such meager loans to pay off, and strong state ties, one suspects their fears are overdeveloped, and their success is likely.

ADMISSIONS

According to the administration of the Washburn University School of Law, in terms of numerical admissions standards, they should be "somewhere in the middle third of the ABA-approved law schools," of which there are 178. Says the administration, "there are at least 58 schools that have both a lower uGPA and LSAT median than ours, at least 59 with a lower LSAT median, and at least 97 schools with a lower median uGPA."

ACADEMICS

Student/faculty ratio	16:1
% female faculty	33
% minority faculty	26
Hours of study per day	3.77

FINANCIAL FACTS

In-state tuition	$6,510
Out-of-state tuition	$9,750
Part-time tuition per credit	$217
Estimated books/expenses/fees	$740
On-campus living expenses	NR
Off-campus living expenses	NR
% first-year students receiving aid	40
% all students receiving aid	40
% aid that is merit-based	95
% all students receiving grants/scholarships	41
% all students receiving loans	86
% all students receiving assistantships	8
Average award package	$2,800
Average graduation debt	$30,000

ADMISSIONS

# applications received	991
% applicants accepted	44
% acceptees attending	34
Average LSAT	154
Average undergrad GPA	3.27
Application Fee	$30
Priority application deadline	NR
Priority notification	NR
Regular application deadline	March 15, Sep. 15
Regular notification	June 1, Dec. 1
Admission may be deferred?	No
Gourman Report Rating	3.20

WASHINGTON AND LEE UNIVERSITY 💾

School of Law

What distinguishes the Washington and Lee University School of Law from other respected, competitive law schools is not so much something it has—although it does seem to be the only U.S. law school with a prominent dead horse (Robert E. Lee's) buried beneath its campus—as something it lacks: crowds. Student-teacher ratios do not vary all that wildly from law school to law school, but the occasional school stands out on the favorable end of the scale. Washington and Lee is one such law school. Along with a student body that is among the smallest in the country, W&L has a full-time faculty that is as large as those of many schools twice its size. Such figures surely back up Washington and Lee's professed emphasis on quality teaching, but an 11-to-1 student–faculty ratio means relatively little in and of itself. Combine such a figure with something less quantifiable, however, like the accessibility of the faculty attested to by W&L students, and you can see why this law school has become such a hot property. Not only have applications to Washington and Lee doubled since 1986, but in a sure sign of rising prestige, the law school now accepts 20 percent fewer applicants to fill its already small first-year class. Those who are accepted possess very strong numerical credentials.

That high intellectual caliber (and small number) of peers, plus excellent, involved teaching professionals provide lucky W&L students with that anomalous experience, "a good time at LAW SCHOOL." Many of our survey respondents expressed the peace and contentment known only by the truly satisfied, thanks to the faculty's open-door policy. One first year told us, "You really can go and talk to any professor and they're glad to see you. They make an effort to know you outside the classroom." Partially thanks to the earnestly followed Honor Code, students take care of one another as well, creating a cooperative learning environment: "The atmosphere is NOT competitive. People constantly help each other out and actually offer outlines."

Another student praised the school's efforts to buttress Lexington's limited social scene (and entertain those who might not choose to "hunt, fish, hike or ride horses to relax") with slightly disturbing enthusiasm: "After a tough week, Friday kegs are a great way to

Susan Palmer, Assistant Dean
Lewis Hall, Lexington, VA 24450
Tel: (540) 463-8504
eMail: lawadm@wlu.edu
Internet: http://www.wlu.edu

unwind (without resorting to violence or mayhem!)" One be-
mused student added, "This is the only law school I know of that
sets up kegs of beer outside the front door every Friday at 5:00. It
does seem a little weird, though, that this school makes you buy
your own exam blue books, but gives away beer for free."
Actually, this particular Friday tradition is run and paid for by the
Student Bar Association, not the school. Luckily for those who
need to balance their early semester heavy drinking with an
intense pre-exam study schedule, the library is open 24 hours
a day.

The sense of "oneness" with each other that many students revel
in feels oppressive to some of those resistant to the prevailing
conservative, adamantly pro-business mindset. Consider this
friendly warning: "If you become too close to the other students,
you better be sure of your political views, because peer pressure
might swing you to the right. Hence, if you want to go to an
excellent law school with a close environment and if you already
are set in your beliefs, then come to W&L."

Students did have a few gripes. Although the business law
program received commendations all around, other areas need
help: "Washington and Lee is like a good restaurant that serves
only one thing. If you like it, you're O.K. If not, you're screwed."
Students also complained that the school should rely less on
visiting faculty, temper the harsh first-year grading curve, and
eradicate scheduling conflicts. Some students directed ire at the
placement office, that whipping post for prospective lawyers'
job-market angst. Despite these quibbles, most heartily recommended their school to prospective students.

ADMISSIONS

In every quantifiable respect, the Washington and Lee University
School of Law is one of the most selective in the nation. In fact, the
numerical standards to which this excellent and inexpensive law
school holds applicants rank it as the twenty-second most selective in the nation. A decidedly ungenerous overall acceptance
rate only compounds matters for the prospective Washington
and Lee student, who had better have very strong numerical
credentials to have a legitimate shot at gaining admission.

ACADEMICS

Student/faculty ratio	11:1
% female faculty	24
% minority faculty	6
Hours of study per day	4.31

FINANCIAL FACTS

Tuition	$16,130
Part-time tuition per credit	NR
Estimated books/expenses/fees	$721
On-campus living expenses	NR
Off-campus living expenses	NR
% first-year students receiving aid	NR
% all students receiving aid	100
% aid that is merit-based	NR
% all students receiving grants/scholarships	67
% all students receiving loans	90
% all students receiving assistantships	NR
Average award package	$5,500
Average graduation debt	$48,000

ADMISSIONS

# applications received	2,139
% applicants accepted	22
% acceptees attending	27
Average LSAT	163
Average undergrad GPA	3.57
Application Fee	$40
No early decision program	
Regular application deadline	February 1
Regular notification	rolling
Admission deferment	NR
Gourman Report Rating	2.93

WASHINGTON UNIVERSITY
School of Law

OVERVIEW

Type of school	private
Environment	metropolis
Scholastic calendar	semester
Schedule	Full-time only

STUDENTS

Enrollment of institution	10,000
Enrollment of law school	634
% male/female	62/38
% out-of-state	60
% part-time	NR
% minorities	14
% international (# countries represented)	NR (NR)
Average age at entry	24

APPLICANTS ALSO LOOK AT

American University
Boston University
George Washington University
Georgetown University
Tulane University

SURVEY SAYS...

HITS
Socratic method
Quality of teaching
Faculty representation

MISSES
Facilities not great
Research resources

EMPLOYMENT PROFILE

% grads employed immediately	60
% grads employed within six months	93
Average starting salary	$45,000
% grads employed by field:	
Private practice	51
Business/industry	5
Government	12
Judicial clerkships	11
Public service	3
Academic	18
Military	6

The 127-year-old Washington University School of Law is the oldest continuously operating private law school west of the Mississippi, located a bare seven miles west of the river in suburban St. Louis, just ten minutes from downtown. This mid-size private law school is solidly Midwestern. Washington University draws the majority of its students from and sends a majority of its graduates to the greater Midwest, where the law school's long-established reputation for excellence is best known. The overall strength of the Washington J.D. program comes in large part from the law school's highly respected (read: highly published) faculty. The law school offers numerous opportunities for interdisciplinary study through the many excellent departments of the broader university. Co-curricular activities abound, and participation is extremely high in the law school's Advocacy and Litigation Program.

While Washington students were not an overly verbose student body, nearly every student who listed the school's major strengths mentioned the faculty. "The faculty is amazing. They truly seem to enjoy teaching and are very available outside class," said a 1L. The school's proportion of female faculty, about 40 percent, is one of the ten highest among U.S. law schools. Another 1L called the professors "absolutely wonderful," saying: "They are on your side and really help you do well." In fact, the Washington U. faculty appears largely responsible for the fact that students here are so satisfied with the fundamental quality of their program.

The curriculum the faculty administers, which students also praised, is broad within traditional boundaries and is supplemented by a wealth of highly regarded clinical programs, including a D.C.-based Congressional Clinic, in which twenty-four third-year students participate annually. Unlike many law schools, Washington University offers clinical courses to students throughout their entire three-year curriculum. The Washington, D.C.-based clinic gives students the opportunity to work full-time for a member of Congress, a congressional committee, or an administrative agency, gaining insight into the national legislative process. Students mentioned other special programs that drew them to Washington U. as well, particularly the school's numer-

1 Brookings Drive, St. Louis, MO 63130
Tel: (314) 935-4525   Fax: (314) 935-6493
eMail: admiss@wulaw.wustl.edu
Internet: www.wulaw.wustl.edu

Washington University

ous joint-degree programs. With the school's parent institution, Washington University, students can, in conjunction with the J.D. program, work towards master's degrees in East Asian studies (Washington U. is one of only three universities in the nation to offer such a program), European studies, business administration, economics, engineering and policy (environmental), health administration, political science, and social work.

Current Washington students did report that there is room for improvement. Luckily, the area most often cited as needing attention, the law school facilities, will be replaced with a new building by the end of 1996. The law building was described as "weak," and an "eye sore," and several students mentioned a lack of up-to-date computers. All of these comments were tempered by students' enthusiasm for the new building. "The new building will be excellent," said one 3L. "[The school] will be much better when the new law building is completed," said another.

The only other major complaint waged by students was directed at the university's career placement office, which, it is claimed, does little to help students attain employment outside the St. Louis area. "For those wanting to practice law in the Midwest, Washington U. is ideal. Those from the coasts have much more to complain about," said one 3L.

Many Washington University students, however, feel like this 1L: "A new building, great faculty, and a community feeling— Washington U. is movin' up!"

ADMISSIONS

Prospective law students hoping to be among Washington University School of Law's entering class of approximately 200 should feel somewhat secure with the university's generous acceptance rate of over 50 percent. In terms of numerical standards, however, it is clear that only students with quite solid credentials are admitted.

ACADEMICS

Student/faculty ratio	14:1
% female faculty	40
% minority faculty	9
Hours of study per day	4.01

FINANCIAL FACTS

Tuition	$20,350
Part-time tuition per credit	NR
Estimated books/expenses/fees	$1,020
On-campus living expenses	NR
Off-campus living expenses	NR
% first-year students receiving aid	65
% all students receiving aid	NR
% aid that is merit-based	NR
% all students receiving grants/scholarships	50
% all students receiving loans	65
% all students receiving assistantships	NR
Average award package	$25,000
Average graduation debt	$50,000

ADMISSIONS

# applications received	1,770
% applicants accepted	53
% acceptees attending	21
Average LSAT	160
Average undergrad GPA	3.40
Application Fee	$50
Priority application deadline	NR
Priority notification	NR
Regular application deadline	March 1
Regular notification	April 15
Admission deferment	NR
Gourman Report Rating	4.30

UNIVERSITY OF WASHINGTON
School of Law

British Columbia
Vancouver
Victoria
Seattle
Tacoma
WA
Spokane
Portland
Salem
Eugene
OR
ID

OVERVIEW

Type of school	public
Environment	metropolis
Scholastic calendar	quarter
Schedule	Full-time only

STUDENTS

Enrollment of institution	20,448
Enrollment of law school	468
% male/female	56/44
% out-of-state	37
% part-time	NR
% minorities	40
% international (# countries represented)	NR (NR)
Average age at entry	24

APPLICANTS ALSO LOOK AT

U. of California, Berkeley
U. of California, Los Angeles
Seattle University
Stanford University
Georgetown University

SURVEY SAYS...

HITS
Library staff
Research resources
Intellectual challenge

MISSES
Socratic method
Not enough courses

EMPLOYMENT PROFILE

% grads employed immediately	NR
% grads employed within six months	NR
Average starting salary	NR
% grads employed by field:	
Private practice	53
Business/industry	5
Government	15
Judicial clerkships	12
Public service	1
Academic	14
Military	2

Many Americans seem not to have "discovered" Seattle, Washington, until the early 1990s. One wonders what took them so long. When the popular culture became infatuated with grunge rock and its attendant anti-fashion, it was simply waking up to a Seattle scene that indy-rock enthusiasts had been crowing about for years. And when a major U.S. magazine finally listed the city's law school in its "top 25," it was belatedly letting its readers in on a not-so-well-kept secret: that the University of Washington School of Law is one of the nation's finest law schools, public or private, and one of the country's great bargains in legal education.

Located just a few miles outside downtown Seattle, UW ("U-dub" to locals) is one of the largest and best public universities in the West, and its small law school has long enjoyed an unassailable regional reputation for excellence. The resources of the broader university are vast, and UW law students can pursue concurrent degrees in any of its ninety graduate departments. The law school itself is very well-funded, a fact that is evident most tangibly in the size and quality of its faculty. With more than 30 top-notch full-time professors and fewer than 500 students, Washington has one of the most favorable student-faculty ratios in the nation. The strength of UW's traditional curriculum, the cachet of its surroundings, and the attractiveness of its super-low tuition have combined to send applications volume through the roof. Numerical admissions standards are very high, and the law school's overall acceptance rate is understandably low.

Applicants who make it through this increasingly brutal admissions process and go on to enroll at UW appear to be incredibly satisfied with their decision to do so. Their praise is so effusive, in fact, and their criticism so mild that one wonders what they're putting in the "world's best coffee" up there. Specifically, students here heap praise on their faculty, their administration, and even themselves. "The professors, the administration and your fellow students care about you," reported one 1L. "They foster a strong sense of community and take a very humanitarian approach to law school." As a soon-to-be graduate put it: "If they accept you they expect you to graduate, and they provide the support services necessary to accomplish this." This rather typical comment from one ecstatic 2L didn't leave much out: "We have a diverse, interesting and bright group of students, a great faculty, an ambitious and progressive administration and a fabulous location...The academic rigor is extremely high, and it's a great bargain." As for this last fact, students at UW, like students at many of the country's great public schools, love to play "cheaper than thou." Here is one of the finer examples: "We get a great education for the cost of a few lattes per day."

When asked to name areas in which their beloved law school could stand to improve, UW students can muster negative comments only for the building itself, which one called "so ugly!" and several suggested be "demolished" outright. On a strictly academic front, however, quite a few students did call on the law school to increase its emphasis on practical-skills training, and to "make more clinic positions available, since space is currently limited and it is very hard to get into these classes." These widespread complaints notwithstanding, the criticisms of students here more often tended toward backhanded praise. Many students, for instance, echoed this lament: "UW would have more national recognition if more of its students would practice in other parts of the country." But as one student asked, "why would anyone want to leave Seattle anyway?"

ADMISSIONS

Though few people yet mention its name in the same breath as the elite public law schools in, say, California or Virginia, the University of Washington School of Law comes very close to equaling those giants in terms of admissions selectivity. Skyrocketing applicant demand has sent numerical standards through the roof here, to the point that those applicants whose numbers fall even a bit short of stellar might do better investing their application fees in lottery tickets.

ACADEMICS

Student/faculty ratio	12:1
% female faculty	31
% minority faculty	8
Hours of study per day	3.73

FINANCIAL FACTS

In-state tuition	$4,500
Out-of-state tuition	$11,500
Part-time tuition per credit	NR
Estimated books/expenses/fees	NR
On-campus living expenses	NR
Off-campus living expenses	NR
% first-year students receiving aid	NR
% all students receiving aid	NR
% aid that is merit-based	NR
% all students receiving grants/scholarships	NR
% all students receiving loans	NR
% all students receiving assistantships	NR
Average award package	NR
Average graduation debt	NR

ADMISSIONS

# applications received	2,550
% applicants accepted	21
% acceptees attending	34
Average LSAT	162
Average undergrad GPA	3.55
Application Fee	NR
Priority application deadline	NR
Priority notification	NR
Regular application deadline	January 15
Regular notification	April 1
Admission deferment	NR
Gourman Report Rating	**4.45**

WAYNE STATE UNIVERSITY
Law School

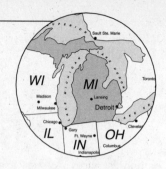

Residents of Michigan are as fortunate as any in the country when it comes to the availability of excellent, inexpensive institutions of higher education. When it comes to the availability of excellent, inexpensive law schools, however, their options are limited. For the lucky few, there is the University of Michigan Law School, a tremendously selective law school that enrolls a large proportion of nonresidents. Michiganians seeking a solid legal education at a bargain price have only one other option: Detroit's Wayne State University Law School, a law school with a very strong regional reputation and much lower admissions standards. Indeed, Wayne State is surely the finest law school in the state dedicated primarily to educating Michigan residents and producing Michigan lawyers. State residents make up almost all of Wayne State's well-qualified student body of 907, most of whom remain in the immediate region after completing their degrees.

The J.D. program at Wayne State is, by all reports, rigorous and comprehensive. After a traditional first-year curriculum that includes an especially intensive legal writing program, students chart their own courses of study, choosing from among the law school's varied and extensive classroom offerings and a sizable number of clinical programs. Special programs at Wayne State include those of its Intellectual Property Institute, dedicated to research and teaching in the growing area of law for which it is named.

Students at Wayne State express a moderate level of satisfaction with their chosen school. On certain matters (e.g., the "strength of the law school's connections to the Michigan legal community"), opinion among the students we heard from was unanimously positive. But the overall impression one gets is of a law school that meets students' needs without inspiring much in the way of enthusiasm. Still, many words of praise were heard from Wayne State students, particularly for the quality and accessibility of their faculty. "With a few exceptions," wrote one 2L, "professors here are excellent, and nearly all of them are open and accessible out of what seems to be genuine concern for their students' welfare." Most Wayne State students agreed that their faculty

468 Ferry Mall, Detroit, MI 48202
Tel: (313) 577-3937

deserves solid marks for their teaching abilities and their dedication to good relations with students.

Prevailing opinion on the general quality of life at the law school was summed up in this remark from one evenhanded 1L: "No one here is going to lead you by the hand, but if you are hard-working and competitive, you can get an excellent legal education." Many students shared this opinion: "Nobody is openly cutthroat," reported one 2L, "but the level of competitiveness among students is considerable." Others sounded similar themes in assessing the areas in which their school could stand to improve. "There really is no 'sense of community' among students here," wrote one 2L. "Okay, maybe among some students," she allowed, "but general camaraderie is missing." On the strictly academic front, many of the students we heard from focused on the curriculum's lack of practical focus. "It is unfortunate that a number of professors here feel duty-bound to adhere to a traditional curriculum," said one, "particularly since firms now want students who can practice law when they leave school." We also heard numerous complaints concerning what one student called "an inadequately equipped library staffed by some excellent librarians and a few who can't be bothered to assist the students." It must be noted, however, that even the most highly critical students at Wayne State often managed to see a silver lining. As one 2L put it, "The fact that this law school is so damn inexpensive often reminds me not to complain so much."

ADMISSIONS

Michigan's "other" public law school may not measure up to the world-class school in Ann Arbor in terms of admissions selectivity, but the admissions process at the Wayne State University Law School is, in the grand scheme of things, a bit more competitive than average. In terms of the numerical standards to which it holds applicants, in fact, Wayne State ranks 62nd among all U.S. law schools.

ACADEMICS

Student/faculty ratio	19:1
% female faculty	35
% minority faculty	6
Hours of study per day	3.19

FINANCIAL FACTS

In-state tuition	$6,050
Out-of-state tuition	$13,070
Part-time tuition per credit	NR
Estimated books/expenses/fees	NR
On-campus living expenses	NR
Off-campus living expenses	NR
% first-year students receiving aid	NR
% all students receiving aid	60
% aid that is merit-based	NR
% all students receiving grants/scholarships	NR
% all students receiving loans	60
% all students receiving assistantships	NR
Average award package	$19,000
Average graduation debt	$24,000

ADMISSIONS

# applications received	1,372
% applicants accepted	38
% acceptees attending	55
Average LSAT	156
Average undergrad GPA	3.32
Application Fee	$20
Priority application deadline	NR
Priority notification	NR
Regular application deadline	March 15
Regular notification	NR
Admission deferment	NR
Gourman Report Rating	**3.66**

West Virginia University □
College of Law

As the only law school in the state, the West Virginia University College of Law bears a heavy responsibility: It must import lawyers to meet the demand of its population for legal services. The school must also make itself as accessible as possible to all members of the state's populace, and it must provide its home state with lawyers competent to serve all segments of local society. On all counts, the law school succeeds, as it has for more than a century. Located at WVU's rural campus, just outside the northern West Virginia community of Morgantown, this very small public law school offers a solid, traditional J.D. program administered by a faculty that is large enough to ensure a relatively high degree of personal attention. And it charges very little to do it. At around $4,000, the annual tuition at West Virginia gives state residents little incentive to consider attending law school elsewhere. Nearly 90 percent of the law school's attendees are natives of West Virginia, and a similar—though slightly lower—proportion of them stay within the state after graduating.

Special programs at the law school include the standard array of clinical programs and co-curricular activities, including a trial-advocacy program of which the school is particularly proud. WVU is also the site of the Eastern Mineral Law Foundation, an institute dedicated to scholarship in an area of law that is of particular concern to this coal-producing state. Students extolled their school's commitment to public interest law and to the state's legal community. "Most classes emphasize West Virginia law, which is beneficial to those who intend on staying in the area," said a 1L. Although many students noted the school's commitment to the people of the state as impressive and inspiring, a few others feel the school needs to focus its attention elsewhere. "I think the law school must attempt to move itself to the national forefront of legal education rather than primarily serving the needs of this state," said a 1L.

However, students we surveyed often complained of the lack of clinical opportunities at the school as well as a generally "limited" curriculum. Some WVU students mentioned that the school needs to pay more attention to pragmatic instruction. One student, a 3L, gave us this list of needed improvements: "More

Janet L. Armistead, Assistant Dean
P.O. Box 6130, Morgantown, WV 26506
Tel: (304) 293-5304   Fax: (304) 293-6891
eMail: BARNETC@wvnvm.wwnet.edu

West Virginia University

clinical programs, class offerings for other subjects like sport and entertainment law, better professors that take a practical approach to teaching." A 3L suggested: "The law school needs to offer areas of concentration, so students can specialize in certain areas."

Students we spoke with at WVU are overall relatively pleased with their education and surroundings. They are quick to cite the affordable tuition as one the school's major strengths. "The best thing about WVU law school is the value. You get a good education at a great price," said one 2L, and added, "You may not be at Harvard, but you aren't paying anything close to Harvard prices."

The school also, reports students, maintains close ties to alumni, which comes in handy around job time. However, students who do not wish to reside in the state after graduation may have to do additional legwork in order to secure a job. Although a couple of students said the area needs "better restaurants," few complaints were heard on the geographic location of WVU. One vocal student who told us that WVU is "one of the finest schools in the country," also offered: "it's not the 'hillbilly-haven' everyone outside the state thinks it is."

The feelings of most WVU students were summed up well in this assessment of a 1L: "a student can get one of the most open, informative, and well-structured education in the country here. WVU is certainly one of the finest schools in the country." This public law school offers a great deal to future lawyers, particularly those who are from the state and want to practice there after graduation.

ADMISSIONS

Although the West Virginia University College of Law's numerical standards are slightly below the national law school average, the school is relatively selective; WVU admits only about one third of those who apply, and very few students turn down a invitation to enroll.

ACADEMICS

Student/faculty ratio	16:1
% female faculty	34
% minority faculty	3
Hours of study per day	4.18

FINANCIAL FACTS

In-state tuition	$3,994
Out-of-state tuition	$10,254
Part-time tuition per credit	NR
Estimated books/expenses/fees	NR
On-campus living expenses	NR
Off-campus living expenses	$23,989
% first-year students receiving aid	75
% all students receiving aid	75
% aid that is merit-based	NR
% all students receiving grants/scholarships	93
% all students receiving loans	75
% all students receiving assistantships	NR
Average award package	$11,800
Average graduation debt	$34,000

ADMISSIONS

# applications received	769
% applicants accepted	38
% acceptees attending	49
Average LSAT	154
Average undergrad GPA	3.28
Application Fee	$45
No early decision program	
Regular application deadline	February 1
Regular notification	rolling
Admission deferment	NR
Gourman Report Rating	3.19

WESTERN NEW ENGLAND COLLEGE 💾

School of Law

Western New England College School of Law presents some attractive features that several of its Boston rivals do not: a peaceful small city location with a low cost of living, the flexibility of both day and evening programs, a close-knit faculty and student body, and a non-competitive atmosphere. Located off the beaten path in the western Massachusetts city of Springfield, roughly three quarters of the school's 800 students come from Massachusetts or nearby Connecticut. WNEC is a moderately priced private school with an evening division that comprises almost 300 part-time students.

Students are overwhelmingly satisfied with the quality of teaching and student/faculty relations at the school. "I find the faculty to be the strongest among all the schools I visited. The faculty is caring, attentive, and willing to share their personal experiences from the law," said a 1L. This support, report current Western New England law students, extends to the student body. The faculty and administration seek to foster a no-nonsense environment that is virtually devoid of the cutthroat competition seen elsewhere. More than one student described WNEC as a "warm and comfortable" place to study law. "As a first year I was surprised at how helpful the second and third-year students were. They helped to provide me with a real sense of community and support," said one student.

WNEC's dedication to the practical aspects of lawyering is evidenced by the fact nearly all the school's full- and part-time faculty have experience practicing law. WNEC's focus on practical legal skills sits well with students, who claim to not want to be inundated with theory. "This institution places an emphasis on practical experience which is essential in today's job market," said a 3L. A new "excellent" law library along with a new up-to-date computer lab also garnered praise from students, although several students cited that the law building is in need of "a serious face lift."

Even though students had all these positive statements to make about Western New England College, a dark cloud is apparently hanging over their school. These students are very concerned—

Victoria J. Dutcher, Associate Director of Admissions
1215 Wilbraham Road, Springfield, MA 01119
Tel: (800) 782-6665   Fax: (413) 796-2067
eMail: lawadmis@wnec.edu
Internet: http://www.law.wnec.edu

bordering on obsessed—about WNEC's ranking and lack of national reputation. Because of its close proximity to Boston, home of six law schools, including the top-ranked Harvard, the school has had to fight an uphill battle to gain recognition. When asked to name the areas in which the school could stand to improve, the responses of students were remarkably consistent. A few constructive criticisms were made concerning a need for more course variety as well as the institution of a joint J.D./ M.B.A. program. Most other negative remarks we heard were far less specific. The frustrations of many were summed up neatly in the assessment from one student who, citing the school's need for "better public relations," added: "We have a great school and receive a quality education to which unfortunately our reputation doesn't do justice. "A rather dubious 1L said: "The rumor is that many students transfer out after their first year because of the school's reputation or lack thereof. The school needs to concentrate on obtaining a national reputation. Although the education is great, it's hard to get your foot in the door if nobody has ever heard of WNEC." While some students reiterated their pride in WNEC, aside from its low national ranking, the prevalence of these concerns should be taken into consideration by prospective students who are looking for a degree from a school whose "name" alone will open doors.

ADMISSIONS

With numerical standards ranking well below the national average for all U.S. law schools, Western New England College School of Law is one of the 20 least selective schools in the Northeast. This could be good news for prospective students who wish to attend law school in New England but have moderate credentials.

ACADEMICS

Student/faculty ratio	26:1
% female faculty	21
% minority faculty	10
Hours of study per day	4.31

FINANCIAL FACTS

Tuition	$14,862
Part-time tuition per credit	NR
Estimated books/expenses/fees	$1,109
On-campus living expenses	NR
Off-campus living expenses	NR
% first-year students receiving aid	84
% all students receiving aid	78
% aid that is merit-based	2
% all students receiving grants/scholarships	6
% all students receiving loans	78
% all students receiving assistantships	NR
Average award package	$3,005
Average graduation debt	$42,000

ADMISSIONS

# applications received	1,681
% applicants accepted	55
% acceptees attending	24
Average LSAT	151
Average undergrad GPA	3.02
Application Fee	$35
No early decision program	
Regular application deadline	NR
Regular notification	rolling
Admission deferment	one year
Gourman Report Rating	**2.68**

WHITTIER COLLEGE 💾
School of Law

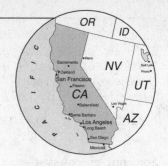

Just over sixty years ago, Whittier College produced its most famous graduate. He would go on to earn a law degree with honors from Duke and to become president of the United States, presiding over an administration that did more to sully the reputation of the legal profession than any ambulance-chaser ever did. It was not until three years after the Watergate scandal broke, however, that Richard Milhouse Nixon's tiny alma mater established a law school of its own. Established in 1975, the Whittier College School of Law is the youngest of California's 16 fully accredited law schools. And while this midsize private institution can claim no such infamous graduates, it can claim to have educated several thousand (law-abiding) lawyers in its Tudor-style facility near downtown L.A. Whittier has not had the time, perhaps, to develop an academic reputation on the level of its many neighboring schools, but its large, well-educated faculty—of whom an admirable percentage are women—and its rising admissions standards spell potential. The law school's curriculum is traditional in scope, and while there is no in-house legal clinic, Whittier does sponsor numerous externship programs. For now, the law school distinguishes itself most for its accessibility. With day and part-time evening programs, a mid-year entry option, and relatively open admissions, Whittier affords many otherwise excluded people the opportunity to earn law degrees. Not surprisingly, the law school draws a group of students who are somewhat older than average (around 29), most of whom come from and stay in the Los Angeles area.

The picture that current students paint of their experience at the law school is decidedly mixed. Most of those we heard from attested to some important strengths, but few failed to temper their praise with some serious criticism. On the positive side, Whittier students are fairly enthusiastic about the law school's faculty and about the quality of the relations between faculty and students. "Our teachers are very caring," went one typical remark. "Because Whittier is small," said another, "we get plenty of one-on-one help from faculty." (Note: Whittier is hardly small in terms of total enrollment, but the size of its part-time division has the effect of making one midsize school feel more like two small ones. As one student put it: "It is not so large as to make you feel

Mary D. Upton, Director of Admissions
5353 West Third Street, Los Angeles, CA 90020
Tel: (213) 938-3621

unnoticed.") Many students echoed this sentiment: "I appreciate the fact that so many of my instructors are women. It makes the atmosphere here that much more comfortable."

On the downside, nearly all of the Whittier students we heard from expressed very serious dissatisfaction with some of the law school's policies and priorities. On the academic front, many said that they find the Whittier curriculum far too narrow, and that they wish it would include "more clinics, workshops and skills courses." But the more serious—even bitter—complaints followed this theme: "Most students feel that the school would rather get rid of them than assist them in passing classes and the bar." Like many young schools, Whittier is actively engaged in trying to establish its reputation. In a tight job market in an economically beleaguered city, such efforts are entirely necessary, but many students regard the measures chosen as draconian. "Whittier accepts as many 1Ls as possible only to drive out a huge number of them before the year is up," reported one student. "This school is concerned with one thing only: increasing its bar passage rate. Whatever they have to do in order to achieve this—well, by god, they'll do it." Indeed, according to data released by the law school itself, anywhere from 10 to 15 percent of Whittier students fall below the minimum grade point average necessary for graduation. Most schools that report this value report anywhere from zero to five percent failures. Given these figures, one takes the calls of Whittier students for a "kinder grading system" more seriously than similar pleas from law students elsewhere.

ADMISSIONS

In terms of the numerical standards to which it holds applicants, the Whittier College School of Law ranks as the least selective of California's sixteen law schools and, indeed, as one of the least selective in the nation. This should come as good news to those prospective students whose numerical credentials might otherwise keep them from pursuing a legal education. It should be noted, however, that Whittier is considerably less charitable to those whose performance falls short once enrolled at the law school.

ACADEMICS

Student/faculty ratio	22:1
% female faculty	38
% minority faculty	29
Hours of study per day	4.52

FINANCIAL FACTS

Tuition	$18,900
Part-time tuition per credit	$630
Estimated books/expenses/fees	NR
On-campus living expenses	NR
Off-campus living expenses	$9,200
% first-year students receiving aid	84
% all students receiving aid	80
% aid that is merit-based	3
% all students receiving grants/scholarships	31
% all students receiving loans	77
% all students receiving assistantships	8
Average award package	$4,300
Average graduation debt	$65,000

ADMISSIONS

# applications received	2,339
% applicants accepted	45
% acceptees attending	23
Average LSAT	151
Average undergrad GPA	2.91
Application Fee	$50
No early decision program	
Regular application deadline	March 15
Regular notification	rolling
Admission deferment	one semester

Gourman Report Rating	**2.53**

WIDENER UNIVERSITY ⊟
School of Law

Delaware has always been a favorite state of trivia-mongers. Any self-respecting purveyor of useless factoids could tell you that this tiny mid-Atlantic state is the home of more U.S. corporations than any other state. But fewer people could tell you that Delaware is home to the largest law school in the country, the Widener University School of Law. Actually, Widener wins on a technicality, since it isn't really one law school. In 1989, this 20-year-old law school opened a branch campus in Harrisburg, Pennsylvania, at which about a third of Widener's more than 2,000 students study. Please note that both the Wilmington and Harrisburg campuses of Widener University have full, independent accreditation from the ABA. In the 1996 edition of *The Best Law Schools*, we mistakenly said that the Harrisburg campus was not yet fully accredited. In fact, it has been accredited since commencing operation in 1989. We were wrong, and we apologize.

The curricula at both campuses are complete; a student at Harrisburg need never see the Delaware campus in order to graduate. Emphasis on practical skills is one of the school's strengths. But the programs differ significantly. Widener has made its main campus, located in suburban Wilmington, the center for its programs in corporate and tax law. The Harrisburg branch emphasizes administrative and public law. Currently, prospective Widener students file a single application, at the top of which they designate their choice of campus. Admissions to both schools are only moderately competitive. About one third of all applicants are accepted, and numerical standards are moderate.

The Pennsylvania students were decidedly more upbeat about their school than those who study at the older branch in Delaware. One Harrisburg student told us that Widener was "the best overall school of 30 I applied to." Students at both campuses admire and respect their professors, for the most part, but the Pennsylvania students enjoy more attention from professors thanks to the faculty's open-door policy. Over and over they made comments such as this 1L's: "I feel I have been fortunate to have extremely intelligent yet accessible professors." "The greatest strength are the profs. They are excellent. They always have time for the students and are more than willing to help. The community is also good. Everyone feels like a giant family.

Barbara Ayars, Associate Director for Admissions
4601 Concord Pike, Wilmington, DE 19803
Tel: (302) 477-2162
eMail: law.admissions@law.widener.edu

Widener University

People really go out of their way for you," said a 2L. Delaware students appreciated the school, too, with a 1L listing the following reasons to attend Widener: "The two reviews on campus, the faculty, ITAP (Intense Trial Advocacy Program), moot court competition, the Widener Law Rugby Team, the Environmental Law Clinic (undefeated in litigation)" and the fact that it's a "young school, [with a] great faculty, great location, solid reputation in Philadelphia region."

Many students however, worry that the school's reputation within and beyond Philadelphia is not strong enough. Consequently, competition and dissatisfaction with the grade deflation common at lower-ranking schools trying to inch their way up are present on both campuses. The faculty's warmth helps to offset this infighting, especially in Pennsylvania, but the lack of community spirit, thanks to a heavy commuter population, and splits between day and evening students in Delaware, plus limited social activities, means the lifestyle can leave something to be desired— unless you are on the rugby team, of course. One 2L summed up quite succinctly what Widener needed to improve on: "Recruiting, better computer systems, more up–to–date buildings (aesthetically pleasing), on campus housing!" Many also called for more practical skills training and legal writing attention. Another gave us his philosophic view of Widener, with all its good and bad qualities. He said it "fits the old cliché that 'it is what you make of it.' I have no doubt one can receive an above–average if not excellent education here if they really strive to."

ADMISSIONS

In terms of its numerical admissions standards, the Widener University School of Law ranks as one of the 50 least-selective law schools in the nation. The numerical credentials of the average Widener student are not all that far below the national average, but few law schools offer applicants with moderate-to-low grades and test scores such a good chance of admission.

ACADEMICS

Student/faculty ratio	23:1
% female faculty	40
% minority faculty	9
Hours of study per day	3.79

FINANCIAL FACTS

Tuition	$15,900
Part-time tuition per credit	NR
Estimated books/expenses/fees	$1,050
On-campus living expenses	NR
Off-campus living expenses	NR
% first-year students receiving aid	100
% all students receiving aid	100
% aid that is merit-based	8
% all students receiving grants/scholarships	7
% all students receiving loans	60
% all students receiving assistantships	NR
Average award package	$9,346
Average graduation debt	$48,000

ADMISSIONS

# applications received	3,137
% applicants accepted	45
% acceptees attending	41
Average LSAT	153
Average undergrad GPA	3.02
Application Fee	$60
No early decision program	
Regular application deadline	May 15
Regular notification	rolling
Admission deferment	one year
Gourman Report Rating	**2.07**

WILLAMETTE UNIVERSITY 💾
College of Law

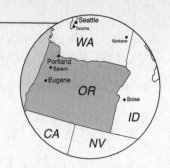

OVERVIEW

Type of school	private
Environment	city
Scholastic calendar	semester
Schedule	Full-time only

STUDENTS

Enrollment of institution	1,713
Enrollment of law school	462
% male/female	57/43
% out-of-state	65
% part-time	NR
% minorities	11
% international (# countries represented)	1 (3)
Average age at entry	26

APPLICANTS ALSO LOOK AT

Lewis and Clark
University of Oregon
Seattle University
University of Washington
Gonzaga University

SURVEY SAYS...

HITS
Great facilities
Studying
Intellectual challenge

MISSES
Students feel poorly prepared
Clinical experience

EMPLOYMENT PROFILE

% grads employed immediately	34
% grads employed within six months	85
Average starting salary	$34,150
% grads employed by field:	
Private practice	59
Business/industry	16
Government	13
Judicial clerkships	11
Public service	1
Military	0

In the 1980s, tens of thousands of southern Californians (and a few others) made a mass exodus to the Pacific Northwest, transforming that region's largest cities, Seattle and Portland, in the process. But the thundering hordes left Salem, the quiet capital of Oregon and home of the Willamette University College of Law, relatively untouched. To be sure, Willamette, like the region's other law schools, has felt the impact of the burgeoning economies of these larger cities: The Pacific Northwest has become a major job market for law school graduates, a market that has absorbed its share of Willamette law grads.

Willamette (locals say wil-LAM-et, not wil-a-MET) University is located literally across the street from most of the offices of the Oregon state government, an arrangement that greatly benefits the students at its law school. The courts and other state offices employ many Willamette graduates full time and many second- and third-year students as school-year and summer interns. Willamette's law school is home to what was one of the nation's first centers for Alternative Dispute Resolution (ADR). The J.D. curriculum allows for formal specialization in this area, which explores alternatives to litigation. Numerical admissions standards at Willamette are moderate, and the overall admissions process is only somewhat selective.

Students at Willamette are nearly unanimous in their praise of both their physical and educational environments. Many students went out of their way to mention their "beautiful" new building, and most agree that the school feels "non-competitive and supportive." "We have a positive, easy-going atmosphere here," reported a 1L. "This really seems to be a 'kinder, gentler' law school—we get called on randomly [in class] but we don't get drilled."

There appears to be a near-total absence of fear and loathing of the law school's strong faculty, who are, by most reports, highly dedicated to their students: "Our teachers are excellent, and always willing to help outside of class." This goodwill stems, in part, from the widely reported "accessibility of professors to first-year students." As for the Willamette curriculum, most students seem content, but see real room for improvement. Students praise

Lawrence Seno, Jr., Director of Admission
900 State Street, Salem, OR 97301
Tel: (503) 370-6282
Internet: http://www.willamette.edu

Willamette University

the school's ADR program, for instance, but complain that it is too restricted, and that the curriculum is lacking in other opportunities for specialization. Many also wished clinical programs were more available. Since we surveyed, however, the school has received a $1 million endowment for its clinical education program. According to the administration, students also have the opportunity to enroll in an externship program with a variety of employers.

Aside from sundry individual complaints ("Dean X needs to wear a belt"; "Anal parking attendants!") the majority of Willamette students seem to be aware of only one shortcoming: a lack of diversity in the student body. The litany of complaints on this matter is impressive. "We have very poor ethnic diversity"; "We need more women in the faculty and more minority students"; "We need better minority recruitment." Indeed, only a small percentage of Willamette's student body is made up of members of historically excluded minority groups. This is one of the lowest figures of any law school on the West Coast. However, according to the administration, "the number of minority students enrolled significantly exceeds the percentage of minorities in the state." However, in general, the few subjects Willamette students had to complain about indicates their overall satisfaction with the school.

ADMISSIONS

The Willamette University College of Law's numerical admissions standard rank well below the national average, and hopeful applicants' prospects are made even brighter by Willamette's overall acceptance rate of 47 percent—one of the most generous in the nation. Those applicants whose numbers equal or exceed Willamette's averages can consider admission virtually certain, and those whose numbers fall only slightly short also face very favorable odds.

ACADEMICS

Student/faculty ratio	24:1
% female faculty	29
% minority faculty	3
Hours of study per day	4.57

FINANCIAL FACTS

Tuition	$16,300
Part-time tuition per credit	NR
Estimated books/expenses/fees	$1,250
On-campus living expenses	NR
Off-campus living expenses	NR
% first-year students receiving aid	78
% all students receiving aid	81
% aid that is merit-based	25
% all students receiving grants/scholarships	22
% all students receiving loans	76
% all students receiving assistantships	NR
Average award package	$6,803
Average graduation debt	NR

ADMISSIONS

# applications received	1,186
% applicants accepted	47
% acceptees attending	25
Average LSAT	156
Average undergrad GPA	3.11
Application Fee	$40
No early decision program	
Regular application deadline	April 1
Regular notification	February-June
Admission deferment	one year
Gourman Report Rating	3.61

WILLIAM AND MARY 🖥
School of Law

The College of William and Mary, established in 1693 by King William III and Queen Mary II of England, is the second oldest in the country. The law school in its current incarnation is a little over 50 years old, but the tradition of legal education at William and Mary dates back much farther, to 1779, when, at the behest of Thomas Jefferson, the university established the first Chair of Law in the newly independent United States. A list of men who studied law at the university in this era reads like an American history textbook; the law chair's first occupant, Declaration of Independence signatory George Wythe, and one of his most notable pupils, the legendary Chief Justice John Marshall, gave William and Mary's law school its full name: The Marshall-Wythe School of Law.

With a student body of about 500, W&M is the smallest of Virginia's three outstanding public law schools, all of them excellent bargains. While numerical standards and recognition at the school are not as high as those at the better-known University of Virginia School of Law in Charlottesville, William and Mary enjoys a strong reputation that extends well beyond the surrounding region, and it attracts a very highly qualified group of applicants.

The school has devised a curriculum that focuses, to a large extent, on practical-skills training, ensuring that the law school graduates a prepared group of students. The Legal Skills Program, a nine-credit, two-year mandatory program, is an innovative approach W&M has taken to help students master lawyering skills and ethical concepts. First-year students enter the program during a week of intensive instruction prior to the start of the semester. Each student then becomes part of a group of about fifteen who comprise a simulated law office. During the program's two-year life, students, representing simulated clients, are introduced to a wide range of skills: interviewing, counseling, negotiating, researching, writing opinion letters and briefs, and arguing cases.

It is no wonder that over 90 percent of current students rated the practical instruction at W&M as excellent. Most of the students we surveyed spoke highly of the school's focus on clinical set-

Faye F. Shealy, Associate Dean
P.O. Box 8795, Williamsburg, VA 23187-8795
Tel: (804) 221-3785   Fax: (804) 221-3261
Internet: gopher://gopher.wm.edu or http://www.wm.edu

William and Mary

tings. "The Legal Skills Program, while it may keep a few people up late trying to finish assignments, is the most practical skill we are learning as 1Ls. It gives a student something concrete and substantive to use analytical and reasoning skills, rather than just being overwhelmed at...the first-semester courses," said a 1L.

Students gave equally strong ratings regarding the quality of teaching at their school. They reported feeling challenged yet supported by faculty and fellow students. This comment from a 2L summed up the general consensus among William and Mary students: "When I tell my friends at other schools that I love law school they often look at me in shock. And it's the quality of the students and the interaction among us that makes this school so great."

The overwhelming complaint we heard from students was that their university needs to expand in curriculum and square footage. When asked how W&M could improve one 3L suggested: "Expand physical size of school building and expand the library." A 1L called for "more course offerings," a common criticism among students. This student, however, spoke for the vast majority of William and Mary students who are happy with their school: "I have heard our school put down because we don't offer more courses, but I'd rather pay state tuition than have Vegetarian Issues and the Law offered as a course."

ADMISSIONS

Eighteen applicants vie annually for each place in William and Mary's Marshall-Wythe School of Law's entering class, making the law school one of the 30 most in-demand in the U.S. If you want to be among the 170 students admitted to William and Mary, you had better be sure your numerical credentials are in shape.

ACADEMICS

Student/faculty ratio	18:1
% female faculty	21
% minority faculty	14
Hours of study per day	3.79

FINANCIAL FACTS

In-state tuition	$6,674
Out-of-state tuition	$17,002
Part-time tuition per credit	NR
Estimated books/expenses/fees	NR
On-campus living expenses	$13,272
Off-campus living expenses	NR
% first-year students receiving aid	90
% all students receiving aid	51
% aid that is merit-based	12
% all students receiving grants/scholarships	30
% all students receiving loans	78
% all students receiving assistantships	10
Average award package	$1,713
Average graduation debt	NR

ADMISSIONS

# applications received	3,057
% applicants accepted	23
% acceptees attending	26
Average LSAT	162
Average undergrad GPA	3.31
Application Fee	$40
No early decision program	
Regular application deadline	March 1
Regular notification	March 31
Admission deferment	one year
Gourman Report Rating	3.45

WILLIAM MITCHELL COLLEGE OF LAW 💾

William Mitchell College of Law traces its roots back more than 100 years. This large private institution evolved from six predecessor schools, the earliest of which was the St. Paul College of Law, founded in 1900, and is named after William Mitchell, an associate justice of the Minnesota Supreme Court. William Mitchell is far and away the state's largest law school, with large entering classes of around 340 students.

The school is best known for its commitment to making law school accessible to all people. As the only law school in the state offering a part-time option—and one of the only law schools in the nation to provide an on-campus daycare for students with children—William Mitchell gives thousands of future lawyers the opportunity to pursue a legal education. The school even offers special late-afternoon courses for added flexibility in addition to day and evening courses.

When asked to discuss their school's strengths, nearly every student surveyed discussed the practical bent of the Mitchell J.D. program. "William Mitchell would be an excellent choice for people who wish to excel in the practical aspects of the legal profession," said one 3L. The school's strong emphasis on practical skills is evident in course offerings, which include an increasing number of "lawyering" classes. William Mitchell also has very extensive clinical programs to help students integrate classroom instruction into practical lawyering early on in their academic careers. Students at William Mitchell praised their chosen school particularly for the most fundamental aspect of their law school experience: their training as lawyers. A 3L praised the school's "hands-on practicum programs and 'real-world' practice and preparation skills." Students also showed appreciation for the school's part-time option, as well as the general "flexibility of the curriculum" that includes over 100 elective course offerings.

While many students praised William Mitchell's curriculum and wide array of courses, a minority of the student body called for more variety of courses offered amid what it claims is a business-oriented curriculum. "[The school] is weak in offering diverse courses from many business-type courses," said a 2L.

Collins Byrd, Assistant Dean for Admissions
875 Summit Avenue, St. Paul, MN 55105
Tel: (612) 290-6329
eMail: dmclellan@wmitchell.edu
Internet: http://www.wmitchell.edu

William Mitchell College of Law

The vast majority of students surveyed rated the quality of teaching as excellent or very good, but we did hear some negative comments, particularly regarding adjunct professors. "The faculty is too unpredictable. [There are] too many inexperienced adjunct faculty, and too much concentration on Minnesota law," said one 3L. When it came to the legal writing program at William Mitchell, students were even more critical of their instruction. "The legal writing course is supposed to be extremely important but some of the adjunct faculty don't have the time to come to class or meet with students," wrote one 2L.

Students did indicate a need for racial, ethnic, and political diversity among the student body and faculty. One student, a 1L, noted: "Most students are from the Midwest. The school would do well to bring in some new blood." Another student, a 2L, was more specific, in calling for "more female and diverse faculty" at the school.

Many students at William Mitchell believe the school's biggest weakness is its lack of a national reputation. William Mitchell students are confident that their school is providing them with a solid, practical education with enough flexibility for many "non-traditional" students.

ADMISSIONS

William Mitchell College of Law is at the bottom third of all U.S. law schools in terms of its numerical standards and selectivity. The prospects of the hopeful William Mitchell applicant are made even brighter by the law school's overall acceptance rate of 53 percent—one of the most generous rates of admission in the nation.

ACADEMICS

Student/faculty ratio	28:1
% female faculty	28
% minority faculty	37
Hours of study per day	3.77

FINANCIAL FACTS

Tuition	$15,330
Part-time tuition per credit	$11,130
Estimated books/expenses/fees	$640
On-campus living expenses	NR
Off-campus living expenses	NR
% first-year students receiving aid	16
% all students receiving aid	NR
% aid that is merit-based	3
% all students receiving grants/scholarships	24
% all students receiving loans	80
% all students receiving assistantships	8
Average award package	$2,874
Average graduation debt	$44,000

ADMISSIONS

# applications received	1,470
% applicants accepted	53
% acceptees attending	42
Average LSAT	152
Average undergrad GPA	3.15
Application Fee	$45
No early decision program	
Regular application deadline	May 1
Regular notification	rolling
Admission deferment	one year
Gourman Report Rating	2.91

UNIVERSITY OF WISCONSIN 💾
Law School

OVERVIEW

Type of school	public
Environment	city
Scholastic calendar	semester
Schedule	Full-time or part-time

STUDENTS

Enrollment of institution	26,207
Enrollment of law school	904
% male/female	56/44
% out-of-state	27
% part-time	7
% minorities	20
% international (# countries represented)	2 (17)
Average age at entry	25

APPLICANTS ALSO LOOK AT

Marquette University
University of Minnesota
George Washington University
U. of California, Berkeley
University of Michigan

SURVEY SAYS...

HITS
Left-leaning politics
Clinical experience
Prestige

MISSES
Facilities not great
Socratic method
Research resources

EMPLOYMENT PROFILE

% grads employed immediately	65
% grads employed within six months	88
Average starting salary	$46,000
% grads employed by field:	
Private practice	63
Business/industry	10
Government	11
Judicial clerkships	4
Military	4

The 125-year-old University of Wisconsin Law School is, simply stated, one of the most highly regarded public law schools in the country. Its long-standing reputation for excellence both derives from and contributes to its parent institution's widely acknowledged status as one of the finest universities in the hemisphere. Some combination of the vast resources of the broader university and the law school's own impressive strengths (e.g., its widely respected faculty) draws one of the most highly qualified groups of law students in the nation to Madison, Wisconsin.

In the eyes of those who run the law school, Wisconsin's success must be understood in terms of the philosophy to which the law school subscribes, an idea they call "Law in Action." As a guiding principle, this phase is meant to convey a recognition on the part of the law school of the social context of the law, or "how the law relates to social change and to society as a whole." The tangible manifestations of this recognition are evident in the breadth of Wisconsin's classroom curriculum and in the size and variety of its clinical programs, which serve the dual purpose of providing law students the opportunity to gain and hone practical lawyering skills while also involving them extensively in the world outside the law school. Wisconsin is certainly not unique in its recognition of the importance of clinical education, but it is notable for its commitment to making participation in such programs possible for more than a small segment of its student body. The school's clinical programs and focus on practical skills garnered high praise from students. "Wisconsin is a hands-on place where students and faculty live and work as professionals," reported one 3L.

Despite the variety of course offerings, students called for a broader range of courses and an increase to the already substantial number of "hands-on" courses offered at UW. "The school is beginning to take a more practical approach but needs to do more. There must be a balance of practical experience with academics. There is still too much of an attempt of the latter," suggested a 3L. Most of the specific criticisms regarding the curriculum focused on Wisconsin's legal writing program. One student, a 2L, made this comment: "Improve the legal writing program! It consumes exorbitant amount of time, but no one really learns the needed

James E. Thomas, Assistant Dean, Dean of Admissions and
Financial Aid
975 Bascom Mall, Madison, WI 53716
Tel: (608) 262-8558

University of Wisconsin

skills." Another student suggested: "If they really want us to write well, offer more instruction and support."

The well-respected faculty figured heavily in Wisconsin students' generally positive assessments of their chosen school. When asked the list the school's strengths, students made comments like "excellent faculty," "faculty that actually knows how to teach," and "professors listen to us!" One student gave us this run-down of Wisconsin's selling points: "Excellent reputation and credentials, especially for the low cost of in-state tuition, nationally-recognized faculty."

The terms most often used to describe the social climate at the law school were "laid- back," "liberal," and "friendly." One student, a 1L, made this observation: "The most surprising—and pleasant—thing about coming to UW law was the amount of beer that is consumed for just about any reason. This helps create a very laid-back atmosphere. Also, in my first semester, three out of four of my professors invited groups of students to their homes for parties or out for pizza and beer." Although certainly not all Wisconsin law students are party animals, this is, for the most part, a non-competitive and relaxed group of students.

The law schools is undergoing massive renovations, which should silence gripes about the buildings we have heard in the past. Although students noted that the new facilities will greatly enhance their school, it is obvious that the work has caused some disruption, as they have been shuffled around the campus to attend classes. "Currently, UW is in the process of a major remodeling of the facility. Although this has been difficult for those of us attending during the construction, once it is completed, the facility will be dramatically improved..." said a 3L.

One cannot help but be impressed by the overall sense of well-being that most Wisconsin students conveyed, as summed up by this 1L: "Wisconsin is the best deal in the country! Great faculty, great students, great environment, great tuition. Now, with the new law library, the package will be complete."

ADMISSIONS

Students admitted to the University of Wisconsin Law School are some of the best and the brightest in the country. Numerical averages of those attending this public law school are very strong, and the admissions process is quite competitive.

ACADEMICS

Student/faculty ratio	20:1
% female faculty	20
% minority faculty	15
Hours of study per day	3.89

FINANCIAL FACTS

In-state tuition	$5,211
Out-of-state tuition	$13,488
Part-time tuition per credit	NR
Estimated books/expenses/fees	NR
On-campus living expenses	NR
Off-campus living expenses	NR
% first-year students receiving aid	NR
% all students receiving aid	42
% aid that is merit-based	10
% all students receiving grants/scholarships	56
% all students receiving loans	77
% all students receiving assistantships	1
Average award package	NR
Average graduation debt	$31,708

ADMISSIONS

# applications received	2,220
% applicants accepted	32
% acceptees attending	39
Average LSAT	158
Average undergrad GPA	3.35
Application Fee	$38
No early decision program	
Regular application deadline	February 1
Regular notification	rolling
Admission deferment	one year
Gourman Report Rating	**4.49**

UNIVERSITY OF WYOMING
College of Law

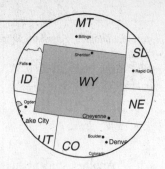

OVERVIEW

Type of school	public
Environment	suburban
Scholastic calendar	semester
Schedule	Full-time only

STUDENTS

Enrollment of institution	7,717
Enrollment of law school	226
% male/female	58/42
% out-of-state	30
% part-time	NR
% minorities	5
% international (# countries represented)	NR (2)
Average age at entry	24

APPLICANTS ALSO LOOK AT

University of Arizona
University of Denver
Arizona State University
Creighton University
University of Houston

SURVEY SAYS...

HITS
Sense of community
Studying
Faculty-student relations

MISSES
Students feel poorly prepared
Not enough courses
Intellectual challenge

EMPLOYMENT PROFILE

% grads employed immediately	40
% grads employed within six months	75
Average starting salary	$33,000
% grads employed by field:	
Private practice	53
Business/industry	8
Government	10
Judicial clerkships	8
Public service	5
Military	7

Until you have been to Wyoming, you have not seen the real face of the American West. The borders of the nation's forty-ninth least populous state encompass some of the world's most spectacular, least spoiled mountain wilderness and some of the nation's best ranch land. Wyoming's economy is dominated by agriculture and natural resources, and it may be the only state in the union that is home to more cowboys than law students. Indeed, the suitably small University of Wyoming School of Law is the state's only law school. If every state were to have only one law school, however, Wyoming's would serve as an ideal model. Situated on the handsome campus of its very well-funded and highly respected parent institution, the UW law school is very small, very inexpensive and very solid. With 16 full-time faculty members and a tiny student body, the law school offers favorable conditions for learning, conditions that are further enhanced by the significant resources of the broader university. Like any good public law school, Wyoming administers a J.D. program that clearly reflects the priorities of its home state. The curriculum is particularly strong, for example, in natural-resources law. Located in Laramie, a university and ranching town of about 35,000 set among the Rocky Mountains, UW is within easy reach of some of America's best spots for hiking, skiing, fishing, and, as the law school's admissions bulletin points out, big-game hunting. These activities are an important part of life in and around the law school, but no more so than is studying, for Wyoming's curriculum is traditional and rigorous. Applications volume at the law school is light, but the overall acceptance rate is kept low. Numerical admissions standards are moderate.

Distinctly immoderate, however, is the enthusiasm most Wyoming law students seem to feel for the quality of life at their chosen school. Though they criticized some important aspects of their program, students here sounded a clear and positive overall theme. In the words of one 3L, "If you want to go to a school where people leave bookmarks in casebooks to help you, where the mountains clear your head, where everybody is nice, and if you don't mind country music, then Wyoming is the place for you." To judge from this and other responses to our survey, the University of Wyoming College of Law succeeds in creating on campus

Debra J. Madsen, Associate Dean
P.O. Box 3035, Laramie, WY 82071-3035
Tel: (307) 766-6416
Internet: http://www.uwyo.edu

University of Wyoming

the kind of "family atmosphere" to which so many other schools merely pay lip service. "The small class size here fosters a great sense of community among the students," wrote one 2L, "and nearly all of them are willing to help one another." "It's a close-knit community based on trust and freedom," added one pleased 1L. "You can leave stuff anywhere in the school and not worry about it being gone when you return." Not surprisingly, most of the students we heard from pointed to the law school's manageable size and favorable student-faculty ratio in explaining their overall comfort and satisfaction. "Both small school size and long, cold winters help build a great community here," explained one 2L before going on to advise that "if you're not prepared for seven months of winter, don't even think about coming here."

Most Wyoming students we heard from tempered their enthusiasm with more substantive criticism. "It's great to be able to get personal attention," said one 2L, "but it would also be great if you could get any book you wanted in the library and access to a working computer." Many others had similar complaints concerning the inevitable limitations of such a tiny school. "Course selection is good in some areas but limited in most," wrote a 3L, "and the small faculty makes the poor teachers really stand out." Indeed, few here raved about the breadth of their curriculum or the overall quality of their instructors. But consider the words of one student who was as critical as any: "I will never regret my decision to come here. Wyoming has everything I want in a school and it is a tremendous value."

ADMISSIONS

In terms of numerical admissions standards, the University of Wyoming School of Law ranks as one of the most selective law schools in the West. This fact is particularly remarkable when one considers that only about 600 people apply annually to this tiny, inexpensive law school. Unhappily for the prospective Wyoming student, however, applicants are not admitted across a relatively broad range of grade point averages and test scores.

ACADEMICS

Student/faculty ratio	15:1
% female faculty	31
% minority faculty	0
Hours of study per day	4.57

FINANCIAL FACTS

In-state tuition	$4,013
Out-of-state tuition	$8,635
Part-time tuition per credit	NR
Estimated books/expenses/fees	NR
On-campus living expenses	$4,274
Off-campus living expenses	$5,850
% first-year students receiving aid	75
% all students receiving aid	75
% aid that is merit-based	NR
% all students receiving grants/scholarships	33
% all students receiving loans	75
% all students receiving assistantships	3
Average award package	$1,200
Average graduation debt	$30,000

ADMISSIONS

# applications received	602
% applicants accepted	36
% acceptees attending	35
Average LSAT	155
Average undergrad GPA	3.30
Application Fee	$35
Priority application deadline	March 1
Priority notification	March 15
Regular application deadline	April 1
Regular notification	May
Admission may be deferred?	no
Gourman Report Rating	2.59

YALE UNIVERSITY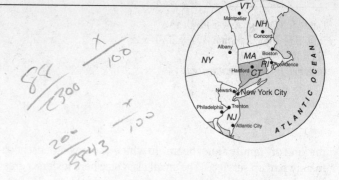
Yale Law School

With two former students sharing the presidential bedroom in the east wing of the White House, the Yale University Law School has earned fairly universal recognition as the unofficial prep school of America's power elite. William Jefferson and Hillary Rodham Clinton may not be entirely representative of the average Yale law grad, but it would be difficult to overestimate the extent of the opportunities available to those who earn their degrees from what is often called the country's finest law school. Yale's reputation is, by anyone's standards, more than well deserved. The law school's research facilities are vast and its curriculum is innovative, flexible, and broad, not only in terms of traditional classroom offerings but also in terms of clinical programs. But without a doubt, Yale's greatest resources are human. No law school faculty overshadows Yale's in terms of scholarly excellence or relative size, and no law school student body tops Yale's in terms of objective or subjective qualifications. One would be hard-pressed to find in any of the country's 176 fully accredited law schools an academic atmosphere that is as demanding yet as free of rancor as Yale's. It is little wonder that admissions selectivity at the law school is as high as it is.

Anyone seriously considering attending Yale should be aware, however, that when people call it the "best"—as so many have—they are not simply calling it a fully realized version of the typical American law school. If your goal is to land the highest-paying job in New York's most prestigious law firm, there are several other schools that might better meet your needs. Yale stands apart from most schools for its unique dedication to serving the law student who does not necessarily intend to follow a typical path. Yale grads are more likely to begin their careers in prestigious judicial clerkships than are students from any other school. Here are two slightly different takes on this matter from two students. "Yale is a little 'zany'—most people here will not end up practicing law. Anyone who wants to be a partner in a law firm is regarded with a little disdain. People here intend to go into diverse fields, which makes the class very interesting"; "The school should cast traditional lawyering in a more favorable light. Despite operating a top-notch clinic, the law faculty sometimes seems to put down traditional law practice. This is a result of the great reverence for academics and research, which is great, but this is also meant to be a legal training-ground."

The telling thing about the comments above is that both came from students who, like most of their classmates, lavished praise on their school for the opportunities it has presented them. As one Yale 2L put it: "A lot goes on here." This world-class understatement neatly captures the feelings of all of the Yale law students we heard from. "The resources available to every student are tremendous," reported one. "You really have the opportunity to do anything." Indeed, with six journals, nearly a dozen clinical programs, and countless student organizations, Yale offers nothing if not options. Just as important, however, in the eyes of Yale students, is the collegial atmosphere that the law school fosters. "The great thing about Yale," went one typical remark from a 1L, "is the low-pressure, friendly, intellectually stimulating environment." "We have very small classes, a great deal of personal contact with professors, and a very close-knit community," wrote another. The closeness of that community derives, at least in part, from the near-total absence of competitiveness among Yale students. By virtue of a grading system that makes ranking impossible, they have little reason to do anything but work together.

When pressed, Yale students will name areas in which their beloved school could stand to improve. In most cases, however, their suggestions would be difficult to follow. And besides, if Yale were to "gut the building" and "move to California," it would have on its hands a group of individuals who were happier, perhaps, than anyone deserves to be.

ADMISSIONS

If you hope to have better than a one in ten chance of gaining admission to what may be the country's finest law school, you had better have an undergraduate GPA above 3.75 from a respected university and an LSAT score at or above 165—the 94th percentile. Even applicants with those kinds of credentials are denied admission 75 percent of the time, and those whose numbers fall more than slightly lower are hoping for a miracle.

ACADEMICS	
Student/faculty ratio	10:1
% female faculty	15
% minority faculty	10
Hours of study per day	3.41

FINANCIAL FACTS	
Tuition	$21,100
Part-time tuition per credit	NR
Estimated books/expenses/fees	$2,240
On-campus living expenses	NR
Off-campus living expenses	NR
% first-year students receiving aid	66
% all students receiving aid	70
% aid that is merit-based	NR
% all students receiving grants/scholarships	40
% all students receiving loans	70
% all students receiving assistantships	NR
Average award package	$8,500
Average graduation debt	$45,000

ADMISSIONS	
# applications received	3,843
% applicants accepted	8
% acceptees attending	59
Average LSAT	171
Average undergrad GPA	3.82
Application Fee	$60
No early decision program	
Regular application deadline	February 15
Regular notification	rolling
Admission deferment	NR
Gourman Report Rating	**4.91**

YESHIVA UNIVERSITY
Benjamin N. Cardozo School of Law

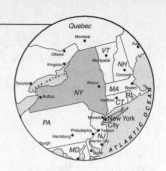

When you think of the classic New York success story, you might picture Ellis Island and the Lower East Side circa 1912, but chances are you don't think of law school and Greenwich Village circa 1976. That, however, is the setting for the story of the Benjamin N. Cardozo School of Law, a success story if ever there was one. In the span of just two decades, Yeshiva University has built an astonishingly successful law school from the ground up, and while the intangible quality "prestige" is generally something that a law school either acquired or lost long before any of us were born, Cardozo enjoys, at the very least, tremendous respect.

To earn this respect, Cardozo has had to impress both applicants and employers, something it has done by assembling a highly accomplished faculty, the indispensable foundation of any good law school. Cardozo's academic strengths are nicely augmented by a heavy emphasis on practical preparation for the practice of law. The law school's own clinical programs are extensive, and external placement opportunities are as numerous and richly varied as one would expect in a city that is home to the country's largest legal community. Cardozo is one of the few law schools in the country that allows students to begin their studies in either September, January, or May. The flexible Accelerated Entry Plan also gives the approximately 90 students who enter in January or May the opportunity to complete their legal education in two and a half years as opposed to the traditional three. These various strengths and the increasing success of Cardozo graduates in finding employment with prestigious firms help explain the rising popularity of this law school, whose admissions standards are quite high. Moreover, thanks to the success of its graduates and to the ongoing efforts of its faculty and administrators, this is a law school still very much on the rise.

Students at Cardozo tell a remarkably consistent story when it comes to the strengths of their chosen school. "We have an excellent faculty," reported one typical student. "They are highly accessible and seem to be genuinely interested in their students' welfare." Others agreed, and many offered ringing endorsements of their program's overall strength. "Our faculty is very

Robert L. Schwartz, Director of Admissions
55 Fifth Avenue, New York, NY 10003
Tel: (212) 790-0274
eMail: lawinfo@yul.yu.edu
Internet: http://www.yu.edu/csl/law

approachable, and the quality of our education is excellent," was the judgment of one 2L. "Cardozo is a great school with great future potential; I would say that in terms of academics, it holds its own with the best." As for relations with their colleagues, most of those we heard from expressed sentiments similar to those of this 1L: "Camaraderie among students is strong, and we tend to help and support and respect one another."

Cardozo students are every bit as quick to answer when asked to name the areas in which their school could stand to improve. Most seem pleased with their general location, for instance, but none could muster any enthusiasm for the law school's physical plant, which several called "absolutely awful." A number of students also expressed dissatisfaction with the homogeneity of the law school's staff and student body. "The law school's great weakness has been its failure to recruit a politically, racially, socially, and economically diverse group of students and faculty," wrote one departing 3L. And though opinion was split on this matter, quite a few students complained about one effect of the law school's Jewish tradition: the closure of its library on Sabbath from Friday afternoon through Saturday. (It should be noted, however, that Cardozo students have library privileges at other area libraries.) Along with isolated but adamant denunciations of the law school's placement office, numerous complaints were heard about what many consider the extreme level of competitiveness among students. Still, employment statistics suggest that these students have less reason to be concerned about the tightening New York job market than do many others, and the overwhelming majority of those we heard from expressed a high degree of fundamental satisfaction with their decision to attend Cardozo.

ADMISSIONS

With more than eight applicants vying annually for each spot in its entering class of about 250, the Benjamin N. Cardozo School of Law is in a position to select its students carefully. Indeed, although Cardozo ranks fourth among Manhattan's five law schools in terms of the numerical standards to which it holds applicants, it ranks among the 70 most selective law schools in the nation. For a law school with such high numerical standards, however, Cardozo has a relatively generous overall acceptance rate.

ACADEMICS	
Student/faculty ratio	21:1
% female faculty	34
% minority faculty	6
Hours of study per day	3.60

FINANCIAL FACTS	
Tuition	$18,100
Part-time tuition per credit	NR
Estimated books/expenses/fees	$1,168
On-campus living expenses	NR
Off-campus living expenses	NR
% first-year students receiving aid	56
% all students receiving aid	NR
% aid that is merit-based	48
% all students receiving grants/scholarships	49
% all students receiving loans	55
% all students receiving assistantships	6
Average award package	$3,636
Average graduation debt	$67,900

ADMISSIONS	
# applications received	2,194
% applicants accepted	48
% acceptees attending	36
Average LSAT	157
Average undergrad GPA	3.34
Application Fee	$60
No early decision program	
Regular application deadline	April 1
Regular notification	rolling
Admission deferment	one year
Gourman Report Rating	3.76

ALPHABETICAL INDEX

STATE INDEX

ABOUT THE AUTHOR

Ian Van Tuyl is a product of California public schools now living as a hunter-gatherer in the lawyer capital of the world, New York City. As a teacher for The Princeton Review, Ian has prepared hundreds of aspiring law students for the LSAT—the Law School Admissions Test. He is intrigued by legal culture and by the overwhelming appeal of law school to the best minds of his generation.

THE PRINCETON REVIEW WORLDWIDE

Each year, thousands of students from countries throughout the world prepare for the TOEFL and for U.S. college and graduate school admissions exams. Whether you plan to prepare for your exams in your home country or the United States, The Princeton Review is committed to your success.

INTERNATIONAL LOCATIONS: If you are using our books outside of the United States and have questions or comments, or want to know if our courses are being offered in your area, be sure to contact The Princeton Review office nearest you:

CANADA (Montreal)	514-499-0870
HONG KONG	852-517-3016
JAPAN (Tokyo)	8133-463-1343
KOREA (Seoul)	822-508-0081
MEXICO (Mexico City)	525-564-9468
PAKISTAN (Lahore)	92-42-571-2315
SAUDI ARABIA	413-584-6849 (a U.S. based number)
SPAIN (Madrid)	341-323-4212
TAIWAN (Taipei)	886-27511293

U.S. STUDY ABROAD: *Review USA* offers international students many advantages and opportunities. In addition to helping you gain acceptance to the U.S. college or university of your choice, *Review USA* will help you acquire the knowledge and orientation you need to succeed once you get there.

Review USA is unique. It includes supplements to your test-preparation courses and a special series of *AmeriCulture* workshops to prepare you for the academic rigors and student life in the United States. Our workshops are designed to familiarize you with the different U.S. expressions, real-life vocabulary, and cultural challenges you will encounter as a study-abroad student. While studying with us, you'll make new friends and have the opportunity to personally visit college and university campuses to determine which school is right for you.

Whether you are planning to take the TOEFL, SAT, GRE, GMAT, LSAT, MCAT, or USMLE exam, The Princeton Review's test preparation courses, expert instructors, and dedicated International Student Advisors can help you achieve your goals.

For additional information about *Review USA*, admissions requirements, class schedules, F-1 visas, I-20 documentation, and course locations, write to:

The Princeton Review • Review USA
2315 Broadway, New York, NY 10024
Fax: 212/874-0775